First published in Great Britain in 2009 by Cherry Red Books (a division of Cherry Red Records Ltd), 3A Long Island House, Warple Way, London, W3 ORG.

ISBN 9781901447415

Design: Russ Bestley at HitsvilleUK.com
Photography: Sarah Dryden

# Independence Days

# Independence Days

## The Story of UK Independent Record Labels

# Independence Days

## Introduction

The status of independence within the music industry is broadly regarded as the autonomous operation of an entity outside the framework of the major labels. The definition of a 'major' has evolved through the last century and beyond; from the early conglomerates such as Victor, Columbia and Edison, to the era discussed in this book (post-1976 to late 80s). At that point EMI, Sony, BMG, PolyGram, WEA and MCA were dominant to the extent that they acquired a secondary title, 'the big six'. Today the major labels have thinned through acquisition and take-over to just four titans; Sony, EMI, Universal and Warner, with much talk of further contraction.

In theory, any label that is not tied to the above institutions can be considered independent. In practice, an independent record label for my purposes is taken as one that does not resort to majors for help with its production, distribution or marketing. However, while a puritanical view is possible, it is not necessarily useful, in that all of the larger independents have at some stage moved in and out of relationships with major record labels. Though this may have produced ideological discomfort, it was often a necessary entanglement, in several instances key to survival.

Some small exposition here in terms of criteria for inclusion. Stiff Records, arguably the most iconic of independents, really only had legitimate claim to that status for a fleeting period; yet this would be a lesser (or perhaps an ever lesser) book were the personalities and artists that Stiff gave us – originally from a wholly independent platform – not included. Beggars would not have survived without a timely cash injection from WEA. Even Rough Trade would employ PolyGram's London Records strike force to help break The Smiths. Mute would eventually pass into EMI's hands, albeit late in the game. So it goes, as someone at Stiff once remarked.

I have focused on the major independents of the period, the stature of several meriting discrete chapters. I have also looked at various tributaries, often piecing them together in an attempt to better demonstrate the interconnections at work. Sometimes this has not been an easy fit, but I quickly abandoned the idea of attempting a chronological narrative overview; some of the stories being sufficiently involved that to zoom in and out would render them impossible to follow.

Of course, there are many labels that could have been included that are not; the weighting of coverage similarly depends on factors including access and resources. Sometimes the rationale was pragmatic rather than theoretical. For example, I have stopped short of profiling Creation Records. Although it would enjoy its headline success in the nineties, Creation's first release was in 1983. Frankly that story has been explored rigorously enough by David Cavanagh in *My Magpie Eyes Are Hungry For The Prize*, whose thoroughgoing nature anyone labouring in this field should remain intimidated by. It was useful to cut off the qualifying period around 1987, when The Smiths signed to EMI, and by which time the emergence of dance music would begin to reshape the perception of independent music.

Similarly, the story of Sarah Records, the *C86* compilation bands, etc, fall outside of my self-moulded remit. *C86* for many heralded the moment, too, when 'independent' morphed into 'indie', a term broadly descriptive of a musical style rather than a technical classification denoting autonomy. And while I make a case for the decade-ish period under consideration as a distinct and artistically meritorious one, I hope I have avoided falling into the trap of gerrymandering this into a seamless and self-contained arc when we all know any artistic culture doesn't work like that. Conversely, I have continued to follow the trajectory of selected independent labels beyond 1987. In most cases, it simply made for a more rounded narrative.

It should also be noted that I have mentioned an earlier independent generation only in passing as part of my opening chapter. There are sound reasons to argue that Island and Virgin are the pre-eminent British independents. Yet as influential as their efforts may have been, these were different beasts entirely from the generation of labels under discussion here; who all sprang directly from the arrival of punk.

A number of potential interviews were derailed by the collapse of Pinnacle distribution in November 2008, towards the end of the project. It hardly seemed fair to pester those dealing with the potential collapse of their business with questions about what they did 30 years ago ("Where were you on the evening of 17 June 1978, Mr Birkett?"). One can only hope for their survival; though the lesson of previous independent distribution bankruptcies is that many will disappear. But I still submit that the interviews provide a reasonable cross section of the most important characters populating the stage in the timeframe concerned.

There is a tension here. While this book argues (usually implicitly though I did get carried away a little in the afterword) against the widespread adoption of the diminutive 'indie' as a prescription for guitar-based post-

# Introduction

punk music promulgated largely by white boys with guitars, that is the focus of much discussed here. Realistically it was not possible to encompass the innovations of independently fashioned reggae, dance music and hip hop (and I am not unaware of the ethnic apartheid hinted at) within the discourse in a satisfactory manner.

Initially, when this project was proposed to me, it was on the basis of a 'celebration' of independent record label culture. And to a certain extent that is what you have. However, the more I became enmeshed in the story, the more I realised the caveats to such unabashed heraldry. Villainy, deceit and gluttony were in ample supply too. In this story there are Fagins, Sykes, Bumbles and Artful Dodgers galore and, by my own crude arithmetic, as many Captain Blighs as Fletcher Christians. At least one Thomas Gradgrind, too, for that matter.

I'd like to think I'm in good company in drawing faintly ambivalent conclusions. "I think there is always the danger of assuming that 'indie' somehow means 'good' or morally correct, neither of which I think are right at all," John Peel would state in an interview with Martin Aston. "There's an awful lot of crap gets issued by indie labels and a lot of the stories I hear from the bands who've got involved with some of the bigger, allegedly indie labels, are as horrifying as those from bands involved with established major record companies. So the idea that it represents an area of superior morality is a non-starter. But the fact is, the best thing that came out of punk was the demystification of the whole process of making records."

The wolf in sheep's clothing battle-cry of 'we're independent' rings hollow on several occasions throughout this book. Amid practice that is often so sharp you could shave with it, the more telling divination, ultimately, is the degree to which these labels were part of the industry of human happiness. One inescapable conclusion is that several independents treated their employees and artists in a wholly disgraceful manner that would never have been countenanced by a major – if not necessarily because of moral scruples, simply for fear of falling foul of employment law suits. It is wrong to entirely divorce some from the Thatcherite creed that ran almost exactly parallel, too. Much as most would publicly shun such an association, these were entrepreneurs in the purest sense. Independent label bosses are separated from that rhetoric solely by motives; and some were not truly separate at all.

Yet it was an extraordinary period of innovation, of chance taking, of opportunities grasped and ruinous mistakes. The story of The Cartel, for example, represents a specific and highly politicised attempt to forge a completely new path for the music industry. That its denouement was ignoble does not detract from the intentions it began with and the very profound impact it had on democratising music making during the eighties.

More than one sage voice within this text will posit that most of the great music of the last 30 years started out, or was inculcated by, independent record labels. It is in no way a hysterical argument.

# Independence Days

# Acknowledgements

This book is dedicated to Joyce Horspool, Ian and Annette Wrench; without whose support, it would never have been completed.

Eternal thanks and gratitude to my partner/life support Dawn Wrench and to my two beautiful boys, Hugh and Laurence. Hoping you grow out of that Arsenal fixation soon. Also, to my ever doting parents. The fools.

I am writing this in the certain knowledge that it will be presented in the best light possible by designer Russ Bestley. I count myself immeasurably fortunate to be able to enlist not only someone who possesses a first-rate 'eye' but also genuine expertise in the subject matter. Bit of a 'Carlsberg' moment, really.

I would like to thank Iain McNay for the original idea.

I am grateful to all those who agreed to interviews; especially those who were so encouraging and sympathetic to my task.

Several journalists were generous with their time, contacts and advice in the preparation of this project. Thanks and hello to all at Next Big Thing. In particular, I am deeply grateful to Marcus Gray for, generously, sharing his research notes on early independent record labels, which proved invaluable. Also, Joel McIver, Kieron Tyler, Ken Hunt, Phil Sutcliffe, Andy Fyfe, Rob Fitzpatrick and Pierre Perrone all selflessly gave me useful information, quotage and leads. Chuck Warner at Hyped2Death graciously clarified my own fumbling efforts at summarising the contrast between American and UK independent infrastructure and distribution.

Others who contributed support, advice, encouragement, occasional nutrition:

Roger Sabin, Josef Loder, Sharon Elliott, Sue Pipe, Gareth Holder, Kate and June Mo-Dette, Mute support staff Sinead and Zoe, Zoe Street-Howe, Gordon Wilkins, Robin Saunders, Jack Thunder at Excess Press, Dizzy Holmes, Rhodri Marsden.

### Notes on Interviews

The vast majority of the interviews contained herein are new. Several of the quotes for the Cherry Red chapter are derived from my research for the *Pillows & Prayers* and *30th anniversary* box sets. In half a dozen instances, quotes are taken from earlier interviews conducted in my so-called career, which may or may not have been published previously, and there are a small number taken from my earlier book, *No More Heroes*. Dead Kennedys material was drawn from the aborted sleevenotes to *Fresh Fruit For Rotting Vegetables*. Also, a couple of interviews were conducted for Cherry Red TV, either by myself, or Iain McNay. So best to 'fess up to that also. I've added a list of interviewees not just as some kind of 'feel the width' gesture, but as a way of acknowledging and thanking all those who took the time out to submit to interviews, answer queries, etc.

## List of Interviewees and Correspondents:

Alan Cowderoy (Stiff)
Alan Hauser (Fresh/Jungle)
Alan Jenkins (Mole Embalming/Cordelia)
Andrew Loog Oldham (Immediate)
Andrew Nicholson (Pathetix/TJM)
Andy Blade (Eater/The Label)
Andy Leighton (Fried Egg)
Andy Ryder (Medium Medium/Cherry Red)
Andy 'Shesk' Thompson (Xntric Noise)
Andy Murray (Stiff)
Anthony Meynell (Hi-Lo)
Barbara Gogan (Passions)
Barry Island (Tights/Cherry Red)
Ben Watson (music critic/academic)
Bid (Monochrome Set/Rough Trade/Cherry Red/el)
Bill Drummond (Zoo/KLF)
Bill Gilliam (Alternative Tentacles/Upright/Workers Playtime)
Bob Last (Fast Product)
Bob McGrather (author/discographer US R&B indies)
Boff (Chumbawamba/Agit Prop)
Brian Sheklian (Grand Theft Audio)
Brian Young (Rudi/Good Vibrations)
Bruce Findlay (Zoom/Virgin)
Cath Carroll (Miaow/solo/Factory/New Hormones)
Cathal Coughlan (Microdisney/Rough Trade/Kitchenware)
Charlie Gillett (Oval/DJ)
Charlie Mason (Xcentric Noise)
Chuck Warner (Messthetics/Hyped2Death)

# List of Interviewees and Correspondents

Daniel Miller (Mute)
Dave Barler (Glass)
Dave Henderson (Dining Out/Illuminated)
Dave Newton (Mighty Lemon Drops/Whaaam!)
Dave Parsons (Sham 69/IRS)
Dave Robinson (Stiff)
David Jaymes (Leyton Buzzards/Small Wonder)
David Marlow (Virgin/Zig Zag Small Labels Catalogue)
David Rome (Drinking Electricity/pop:aural)
Derek Chapman (Backs)
Derek Hammond (Yeah Yeah Noh!/In Tape)
Diamanda Galas (solo/Y Records)
Dick Lucas (Subhumans/Bluurg)
Dick Witts (Passage/Object/Cherry Red)
East Bay Ray (Dead Kennedys/Cherry Red)
Ed Ball (King's Cross/Whaam! etc)
Ed Garrity (Ed Banger/TJM/Rabid)
Ed Mooney (TJM)
Edward Christie (Abstract)
Elizabeth Surles (Starr/Gennett Archive)
Eugene Reynolds (Rezillos/Sensible)
Gareth Main (Bearded Magazine)
Gary Beard (Pwdwr Records/Llygod Ffyrnig)
Gary Marx (Sisters Of Mercy/Merciful Release)
Gem Howard-Kemp (Secret)
Geoff Davies (Probe)
Geoff Travis (Rough Trade)
George Borowski (The Out/Rabid)
George Maddison (Carpettes/Small Wonder)
Graham Bailey (2nd Layer/Cherry Red)
Graham Fellows (Jilted John/Rabid)
Guy Trelford (Northern Ireland punk author)
Helen McCookerybook (Chefs, Attrix, Graduate, author)
Howard Finkel (Cherry Vanilla/IRS)
Iain McNay (Cherry Red)
Iain Shedden (Jolt)
Ian Astbury (Cult/Situation 2)
Ian Ballard (Damaged Goods)
Ivo Watts-Russell (4AD)
Jamie Hill (Revolver)
Jeff Pountain (Again Again/Do It)

## Independence Days

Jeffrey Kruger (Ember)
Jello Biafra (Dead Kennedys/Fast/Cherry Red)
Jeremy Valentine (Cortinas/Step Forward)
Joel McIver (Journalist)
John Brierley (Cargo Studios)
John Broven (author/early US independents)
John Craig (Safari)
John O'Neill (Undertones/Good Vibrations)
John Repsch (author/Joe Meek)
Jon Langford (Mekons/Fast/CNT)
Jonny Brown (Band Of Holy Joy/Rough Trade)
Kate Korus (Mo-Dettes/Rough Trade)
Kathy Freeman (Accelerators/Eric's)
Keith Glass (Rough Trade)
Kevin Hewick (Factory/Cherry Red)
Kevin Hunter (Epileptics/Crass)
Klaus Flouride (Dead Kennedys/Cherry Red)
Linder (Ludus/New Hormones/Factory)
Manic Esso (Lurkers/Beggars Banquet)
Marc Riley (Fall/In Tape)
Mark Brennan (Link/Captain Oi!)
Mark Standley (V2/TJM)
Martin Mills (Beggars Banquet)
Matt Dangerfield (Boys/NEMS/Safari)
Michael Bradley (Undertones/Good Vibrations)
Mick Mada (Probe)
Mick Mercer (Journalist)
Mick Rossi (Slaughter & The Dogs/Rabid/TJM)
Mike Alway (Cherry Red/el)
Mike Heneghan (Rough Trade/Beggars Banquet etc)
Mike Kemp (Spaceward Studios)
Mike Stone (Beggars Banquet/Clay)
Miles Copeland (IRS/Step Forward/Illegal)
Morgan Fisher (Cherry Red)
Nick Dwyer (Molesters/Small Wonder)
Nick Ralph (Midnight)
Nigel Dick (Stiff)
Patrik Fitzgerald (Small Wonder)
Paul Burgess (Ruefrex/Good Vibrations)
Paul Haig (Josef K/Postcard)
Paul McCallum (Puncture/Small Wonder)

# List of Interviewees and Correspondents

Paul Rosen (Irrelevant Wombat)
Penny Rimbaud (Crass)
Pete Frame (author)
Pete Gardiner (Stiff)
Peter Christopherson (Throbbing Gristle/Industrial)
Petula Clark (Polygon)
Poly Styrene (X-Ray Spex)
Richard Berry (No Future)
Richard Boon (New Hormones/Rough Trade/The Catalogue)
Richard Jones (Cherry Red/No Future)
Richard Scott (Rough Trade/The Cartel)
Richard Williams (Passions)
Rick Goldstraw (John Cooper Clarke/Rabid)
Robb Johnson (Irregular)
Robert Lloyd (Nightingales/Cherry Red/Vindaloo)
Robert Worby (Distributors/CNT/Red Rhino)
Robert Wyatt (Rough Trade)
Robin Greatrex (Razor)
Robin Hurley (Red Rhino/Nine Mile)
Roger Armstrong (Chiswick/Ace)
Roger Doughty (Revolver)
Roger Sabin (Lecturer)
Sandy McLean (Fast Forward/53$^{rd}$ & 3rd)
Saul Galpern (Bonaparte/Kamera)
Scotty Parker (Fatal Microbes)
Sean Mayo (Revolver)
Sean O'Neill (Undertones/Good Vibrations)
Seymour Stein (Sire)
Shend (Cravats/Small Wonder/Crass)
Simon Boswell (Illuminated/soundtrack composer)
Simon Edwards (Heartbeat/Riot City)
Simon Morgan (Nine Mile)
Simon Napier-Bell (artist manager, etc)
Spizz (his Spizzness)
Stan Brennan (Soho Records)
Steve Counsel (Puncture/Small Wonder)
Steve Drewett (CNT etc)
Steve McGarry (Rabid/Illustrator)
Steve Melhuish (Napoleon)
Steve Shy (Shy fanzine)
Stuart Moxham (Young Marble Giants/Z Block)

## Independence Days

Stuart Murray (Fast Cars/TJM)
Ted Carroll (Ace/Chiswick)
Terri Hooley (Good Vibrations)
Theo Morgan (Polygon)
Thomas Leer (Cherry Red)
Toby Mamis (Runaways/Cherry Red)
Tom Bailey (Thompson Twins)
Tony Visconti (producer)
Tosh Ryan (Rabid)
Tracey Thorn (Cherry Red)
Trevor Midgeley (Dandelion)
Vini Reilly (Durutti Column/Factory)

**Notes on Release Dates, etc**

All release dates were cross-referenced with Mario Panciera's invaluable, astonishing *45 Revolutions* (Hurdy Gurdy Books).

# Independence Days

# Chapters

# Independence Days

# Chapters

**Chapter Eleven**
Do They Owe Us A Living?
Crass, Southern, The Anarcho Punk Labels and Punk in the 80s

**Chapter Twelve**
Get Rid Of These Things
The Cartel, its labels, and the building of an independent infrastructure

**Chapter Thirteen**
For How Much Longer?
They Also Served

**Post-Script**
Where Do We Go From Here?

# Independence Days

# Chapter One

## Edison... And Light Bulbs

## The Early History of Independent Record Labels

Thomas Edison's first recording of the human voice in 1877 is acknowledged to represent the baby steps of the modern music industry. Pioneered at his Menlo Park research facility, it was the inaugural laboratory of its kind geared to harnessing technological advances for industrial exploitation. It serves as an interesting footnote that the innovation, ascribed to him but the result of collaborative endeavour within that company, derived not from a flash of individual inspiration but as a direct result of profit-motivated industrial research. Nevertheless, the foundation of the music industry as we know it owes much to individuals deriving ways in which to make their creations heard. Wolfgang Amadeus Mozart was among the first to explore the possibilities of marketing his recordings for public consumption, in an effort to avoid indenture to the aristocracy and church. Though Mozart was always in receipt of a steady income through such patronage, his propensity for living beyond his means contributed to the series of 'begging letters' that survive him. Poverty has, seemingly, long held the hand of genius in the story of 'independent music'.

By 1894 Emile Berliner's US Gramophone Company were shipping dedicated musical units, which played a media of hard rubber records, while two years later Frank Seaman created the National Gramophone Company. By the last decade of the 19$^{th}$ century gramophone sales were rising, with the popularity of 'lateral discs' ultimately leading to Edison abandoning his cylinder disc technology in 1913 – the first of the music industry's 'format wars'.

Odeon Records was inaugurated in 1904 in Germany to sell double-sided discs that Zonophone had first produced in South America two years previously. It would later face an ignoble demise when entered into forced administration by the National Socialist Party (its factory was destroyed by the Red Army in Berlin in 1944, though it would survive to release the first Beatles singles in Germany). While HMV put an entire opera over 40 single discs in 1903, it was Odeon who released the first 'album', Tchaikovsky's *Nutcracker Suite*, on four double-sided discs in 1909. Meanwhile Columbia had introduced the more enduring 'Velvet-Tone' shellac disc to reduce surface noise. The first phonograph device to achieve mass popularity came from Victory. Their Victrola upright cabinet design was the subject of mass advertising and rapidly became the first desirable, and commonplace, amplification unit of its type.

# Independence Days

As is readily apparent, the initial innovations of the 'inventor', the creative originator, gave way quickly to companies and institutions with the wherewithal to harness these advances. But the pioneers remained. Not least John Lomax, who in 1908 recorded a black saloon keeper singing 'Home On The Range' in San Antonio, thus providing the inspiration for the Library Of Congress Archive Of The American Folk Song, which would eventually catalogue 10,000 similar 'field' recordings. Irish tenor John McCormack, meanwhile, became the recipient of the first recording contract proper, with Victor Company. In recognition of these developments, ASCAP (American Society of Composers, Authors and Publishers) was founded to enforce America's 1909 Copyright Act.

The Original Dixieland Jass Band from New Orleans' 'Livery Stable Blues' (1917) is widely regarded as the first de facto jazz record. It also heralded the jazz and blues boom, spearheaded by performers such as Ma Rainey and Mamie Smith. The latter's 'Crazy Blues', from 1920, released on the Okeh imprint, is recognised as the first vocal blues recording. Okeh was founded by Otto K E Heinemann in 1916 after he purchased a recording studio and pressing plant in New York. After gravitating to the new lateral-cut phonograph discs, the company pressed in 10-inch and 12-inch denominations, retailing at between 75 cents and $1.25, Okeh enjoyed success with styles including vaudeville skits and popular dance songs, while also servicing Yiddish, Czech and German recordings to America's immigrant communities. But with the success of 'Crazy Blues', the company hired Clarence Williams as director of 'Race' recordings at its New York studios, and also purchased a studio facility in Chicago in order to document the city's vibrant jazz scene, including recordings by King Oliver and Louis Armstrong. In October 1926 Columbia acquired Okeh, one of the first acquisitions of an independent, though it continued to release records using its own marque until 1935. It has been revived periodically ever since, and is currently in the ownership of Sony.

Prior to this, Okeh, alongside other small imprints including Aeolian-Vocalian and Canada's Compo, joined the Gennett Record Company of Indiana in defending a case brought by Victor. Gennett, which has strong claims to be the world's first independent label, was the cradle of much of the jazz boom of the 20s. It was the first clash between the independents and a 'major' label. At this juncture, we can imbue in an industrial heavyweight such as Victor many of the qualities we would later ascribe to a major label, and it was around this time that the term became common currency. Victor, alongside Columbia and Edison, consequently came to be considered the 'three majors' of their day.

## Edison... And Light Bulbs

Victor and Columbia had come to an agreement regarding the 'lateral' recording disc, whereby they could extract licence fees from others seeking to replicate the technology. Starr, Gennett's original holding company, were keen to produce lateral discs and were not minded to pay for the privilege. As jazz historian Duncan Shiedt wrote in 2001, "They were unwilling to go along with the licensing fees demanded by Victor, backed up by their supposed patent and powerful legal threats that had dissuaded previous attempts to avoid payments of fees by other small producers." But the quick settlement that Victor anticipated, after two previous court victories, was not forthcoming. The case fell apart largely due to complications over the validity of various copyrights, including the discovery of an earlier British patent. Starr, an established piano vendor with sound financial resources, had the muscle to withstand a protracted legal dispute. After months in court, it carried the day. In October 1922 the US Supreme Court found in favour of Gennett, holding that Eldridge Johnson's 1897 patent had no application, in the process putting the 'lateral cut recording technology' into the public domain. Victor appealed the decision but failed to have it reversed.

The significance of this is worth digesting. Had Victor won the case, the monopoly on distribution of recorded music – now overwhelmingly undertaken via lateral discs – would have been confirmed and the dominion of the 'major' labels over the next few years would have been absolute. Licence fees backed by a watchful legal team would have ensured that new entrants to the music business would have faced insurmountable hurdles. It would also have narrowed opportunities for dozens of artists, especially in niche markets, where the independents operated most effectively and where there was little or no interest from the majors.

It may have been a highly technical and complex case, but its repercussions were enormous. Shiedt: "[the decision] would not materially affect the well-being of Victor and its ally, Columbia, who were enjoying unparalleled success in an industry not yet threatened by the advent of radio. What it would do was to open up opportunities for a myriad of small companies to enter the recording field, bringing to market new types of product to new audiences. In the process prices were reduced in many different outlets, such as mail order, department stores, and the popular five-and-dime chains. Starr, and its Gennett family of labels, would naturally share in this all-too-brief boom in phonograph record sales ..." From a reported 14 record labels extant at the time of the ruling, soon there were hundreds. From 1920 onwards, Gennett had established its pressing plant to manufacture its own wares and those of other independents, with millions of records released each year covering a diverse array of compositions from symphonies to vaudeville, but also comedy, exercise records and sermons. Among the mainstays of the era were Gennett's King Oliver's Creole Jazz Band, Jelly Roll Morton and Bix Beiderbecke. Gennett would also specialise in hillbilly artists including Gene Autry.

Gennett was establishing a template for independent labels that sign-posted later developments in the industry. Records were tailored for a youth market, often allowing expression to acts who had been passed over by the majors. Its business operated on much tighter margins with limited promotional budgets. Significantly, artists were encouraged to record their own material rather than mimic versions of established hits, and the product line was responsive to regional developments and trends. The key men at the majors included Fred Gaisberg at Victor, and, later, John Hammond at Columbia. Gaisberg encouraged composers and opera stars such as Enrico Caruso and Elgar to make their first recordings. Hammond, one of the most influential men in American music, was a Yale dropout who nurtured the careers of artists from Count Basie to Bob Dylan. These were 'music men' in the classic sense, mavens in their fields with longstanding pedigrees. The staff at Gennett, conversely, would have to halt recording sessions when trains passed, and would record any artist – regardless of race – they felt would provide them with a hit. Elizabeth Surles is project co-ordinator of the Starr-Gennett Foundation. "I believe that Ruby Greenberg, aka Carl Fenton, served as the musical director in Gennett's New York studio at the end of the 1920s. I suspect that the company found talent in several ways: staff at Starr Piano showrooms recommending certain musicians to the recording division, company executives making requests for certain performers and/or styles, musicians requesting recording gigs, and recommendations of other musicians by musicians who recorded for the company. Based on the account provided in an oral history interview the Foundation conducted with a fiddle player who recorded for [subsidiary label] Champion in 1934, the band played an audition before being granted a recording session."

By the mid-20s, Gennett was pressing upwards of three million records annually. Yet the depression hit them hard, and in 1932 it was forced to close its doors (alongside others such as Grey Gull and Emerson) as Victor and Columbia both moved into recording hillbilly and 'race' music, previously Gennett's preserve, and radio's popularity took off. Times were sufficiently hard that even RCA Victor considered closing its record arm while a number of independents merged with the American Record Corporation, which subsequently acquired Brunswick and later Columbia. The first phase of independent record production ended with Gennett's demise.

In the UK the first independent record label of note was not only divorced from the commercial instincts of its early American counterparts, it was diametrically opposed to the tenets of capitalism full stop. Topic Records began life as an outgrowth of The Workers' Music Association, founded in 1936. Around 1939-40 the WMA established a recorded music wing, inaugurated with the Unity Theatre's Paddy Ryan (an alias adopted by the artist for professional reasons since he was a doctor) and his 'The Man Who Put The Water In The Workers' Beer'. It was to run parallel with its Keynote Series booklets such as *Background of the Blues* and *The Singing Englishman – an Introduction to Folksong*.

Only after World War II was Topic cut free from the WMA to lead a life as an independent entity. Ewan MacColl, Paul Robeson and Pete Seeger were prominent early artists, as was Michael Redgrave from the Unity Theatre (his daughter Vanessa later became a Topic recording artist). The catalogue was avowedly political with sundry versions of 'The Internationale', as well as Russian, Irish and English revolutionary material, songs of internationalism and solidarity. Some were perennials such as 'The Peatbog Soldiers'. Others were definitively of their time, such as 'The Soviet Airman's Song' and the Central Song and Music Ensemble of Hungary's Ironworkers' Union (gasp for breath) 'Song of the Tractor Drivers of Deszk'. It would later release work by Woody Guthrie. Topic continues today, as the oldest independent label still extant, with a roster of artists including Eliza Carthy, Martin Carthy, June Tabor and others. BBC radio stalwart John Peel purchased his first Topic release in 1955 and continued to support the label until his death. His protégé, Andy Kershaw, cites it as "the most important record label in Britain". Trevor Midgley, aka recording artist Beau of Peel's Dandelion Records, attests to the label's influence on the DJ. "The first time I went to his mews place just off the Marylebone Road – this would be some time in early '69 – I was nosing along his massive record racks and noticed the number of Topic releases. The reason they jumped out at me was because I was also into Topic (though not as heavily as John!). If I remember rightly, he had a McPeake Family album that was also in my collection and *The Art Of William Kimber*, the great Oxfordshire Morris concertina-man." Midgley doesn't believe Topic directly influenced Dandelion, "but I don't have to look too hard to see parallels between Folkways and Elektra in the States, and Topic and Dandelion in the UK. I think these are comparisons John could live with."

## Independence Days

As Midgley intimates, in many ways an American counterpart to Topic, albeit with a less defined political agenda, Folkways was founded in New York by Moses 'Moe' Asch and Marian Distler in 1948, a successor to the Asch and Asch-Stinson labels. It too remains active today, under the revised appellation Smithsonian Folkways, which gives notice of its historical import to American song development. Folkways' founding principle was to document the entire strata of sound in all incarnations, ranging across ethnic and traditional music to the contemporary, as well as spoken history. It pioneered the concept of world music, as well as left field folk institutions Seeger, Guthrie and Leadbelly. The Smithsonian Institution Center's acquisition of the more than 2,000 recordings made at Asch's behest was completed on the understanding that it would keep all the releases in print for posterity, a commitment it honours to this day.

As demonstrated by the Starr-Gennett case, competition between major labels and smaller entities was a phenomenon that predated the arrival of rock 'n' roll. With the post-war introduction of the long-playing record in 1947, the 'war of the speeds' broke out between Columbia and RCA Victor, with Capitol the first of the majors to support releases in all three formats (78rpm, 45rpm, 33 1/3rpm). A pattern emerged in the business climate of the late 40s and early 50s in which large, monopolistic conglomerates sought to establish and further their dominion by putting the squeeze on smaller counterparts. With the exceptions noted above, the 30s and 40s had been dominated by Decca, RCA-Victor and Columbia. To those three could now be added the growing power of Capital (founded in 1942), Mercury and MGM (both 1946).

But the arrival of rhythm and blues brought with it a clutch of smaller, more responsive labels. They were quick to spot trends and fleet of foot – and sometimes unperturbed by conventional business wisdom – in satisfying demand. In the 30s Beacon, Keynote and Exclusive were founded. The latter, formed by black brothers Otis and Leon Rene in New Orleans, served as a means of distributing songs they had written, before they subsequently founded Class Records. Joe Davis's Beacon had a roster of influential early artists including Savannah Churchill and Una Mae Carlisle. But the real explosion took place from the early 40s onwards. The most notable of these were Herman Lubinsky's Savoy (1942), Ike and Bess Berman's Apollo (1943), Al Green's National (1944) and Ed and Leo Mesner's Aladdin (1945). They were followed in the immediate post-war period by Chess, King, Imperial, Dot, Vee-Jay, Specialty, Excello, Meteor, Red Robin and Sun Records. This growth market coincided with mass migration from southern states to the industrial bastions of the mid west and north east, and a flush of optimism

## Edison... And Light Bulbs

following the end of war among a suddenly reinvigorated civilian nation, awash with demobbed youth. The new independents focused on grass roots forms such as the blues and hillbilly, as the melding of these musical forms began to assemble themselves as the foundation for the coming rock 'n' roll boom. Many of those involved, notably Lubinsky, were equally legendary for their failure to pay a dime in royalties to their artists.

The great American R&B catalogue was established not in boardrooms, but in the bedrooms, kitchens and living rooms of one-man operations run on shoestring budgets. Many are the stories surrounding these 'personality labels'. Notable among the innovators was Syd Nathan's King Records. Nathan, who later added Federal to his empire, set up shop in an abandoned ice house in Cincinnati, and purchased his own pressing plant, enabling him to handle the entire production process in-house, thereby reducing his cost base. A roster that included the Dominoes, Five Royales, Otis Williams and the Five Keys made him a legendary figure on the 50s R&B scene. He would also give Seymour Stein an early break in the music business. Chess, originally Aristocrat, operated out of a Chicago storefront owned by eponymous brothers Leonard and Phil Chess, and documented the thriving local blues scene. So too did Vee-Jay, which was tipped to become the first black-owned 'major' with a roster including Gladys Knight, the Dells and the Impressions, although ultimately it would be Motown who came closest to that achievement.

Most important and emblematic of this young wave of independents was Atlantic, founded by the son of a Turkish ambassador, Ahmet Ertegun, in 1947, alongside Herb Abramson, who had previously served as A&R head for National Records. With the aid of a loan from the family dentist, they rented a small office in Manhattan, with a business desk at one end and a make-do 'recording studio' at the other. With Jerry Wexler sprinkling the studio magic, Atlantic, under Ertegun's stewardship, became one of the world's largest and most revered record labels – and one of the few to treat its artists with a scintilla of respect. Ertegun scouted New Orleans for talent, but, unable to replicate the tonal quality of sessions with Professor Longhair etc, he created the 'Atlantic sound' as a by-product, a luminous mix of blues and jazz with New Orleans mambo, swing from Kansas City and the urbane arrangements favoured by New York.

Routinely garlanded as "the world's greatest independent label", Ertegun's love of black music led to huge success with Ray Charles and myriad others, before branching into jazz and developing the careers of Ornette Coleman,

## Independence Days

John Coltrane, Charles Mingus and others, and later 'white' rock 'n' roll, via Bobby Darin. Ertegun took the decision to sell the label to Warner Brothers in 1967 for $17 million in stock, sacrificing much of its independence in the process. Some of the proceeds saw them found the New York Cosmos soccer team. Throughout, however, Ertegun remained a friend to upstart record companies, helping to finance, among many others, David Geffen's Asylum Records in 1970. Despite his initial love of black R&B, Ertegun also sensed the commercial potential of rock acts like Led Zeppelin, Cream and Crosby Stills & Nash. He also signed the Rolling Stones to a distribution deal, as Atlantic remained probably the only imprint from those glory 40s years to survive the merger-crazed 90s with its identity relatively intact.

During the 50s a profusion of smaller indies like Bruce, Herald, Old Town, Tico and Whirlin' Disc had sprung up to document the melting pot of black and Hispanic sounds on New York streets. They were powered by entrepreneurs such as Bobby Robinson, still active in Harlem to this day, George Golder and Hy Weiss (self-professed payola king of New York and inventor of the "fifty-dollar handshake" to encourage DJs to play his records). Grand, Gotham, Parkway *et al* provided a similar service to the residents of Philadelphia. Many of these were fly-by-night operations, set up by sharp-thinking businessmen with an eye not for the value of the music they released, but for the opportunity of a quick buck.

But as Roger Armstrong of Ace Records points out, there were often more complicated relationships at work beyond the merely exploitative. "The key thing that ran through that – it was mainly white entrepreneurs, with some exceptions, and a lot of Jewish white people running independent record labels. What I boil it down to is this. The Jews and blacks in America were both under-classes. The Jews were white and could get credit. The blacks were black and couldn't get credit. That was the bold truth in those days. You can't run a business unless you get credit. Unless you're born rich. Credit is what you live off. There are other views about Eastern European Jews who got into black music because of the minor chords and minor keys – there was a musical connection. But my old friend Hy Weiss, he ran Old Town Records. He had a lot of success with doo-wop, but he was a blues fan. He made some great blues records. There was some paternalism. And a very close relationship between the artists and the owners; they were really tight. I remember the horrible quote they used when Adam Sweeting wrote about Bo Diddley's death [in *The Guardian*] – 'I was never paid anything'. [The actual quote was sourced to Diddley himself: "I am owed... I've never got paid. A dude with a pencil is worse than a cat with a machine gun."] "That makes Bo look really stupid," Armstrong continues. "Why did he stay with Chess for 12 years if they never paid him anything? Of course they paid him. The interesting thing is not whether he got paid, it's *how* he got paid, and *how much*. Leonard [Chess] once went on record when someone said he didn't pay Bo enough. He said, 'I don't get any money out of his live gigs. He gets his live gigs cos we promoted his records.' Talk about the 360 degree thing mentality [now advanced by the contemporary music industry as a salve to provide income in the download age by taking part of an artist's merchandise and touring money]. It was always there. There was that close but sometimes contentious relationship."

"Hy was a notoriously wild character," Armstrong continues. "Runyonesque isn't in it, and he had every scam in the book going. He told me some of them, and some were brilliant. But every artist I ever met who was on his label said, 'I love that man, he's just fantastic. Never really paid me properly, but I love him!' I remember the Solitaires. The guy was saying, 'Hy, we always thought he wasn't paying us properly. But he was so generous with his information and told us how to function.' And that guy went on to be head of marketing at CBS in black music. He said, 'I learned it all from Hy, if it hadn't been for him, I wouldn't have had my job.' With the American indies, you lived in each other's pocket. That's how tight and close things were. You had an agent to put the band on the road and get the local gigs. Mary Love on Modern Records told us the company used to have a room for their artists with telephones in it. They didn't charge for the telephone, and they could go in there and book their own gigs. And in our early days of being an independent record company, it was very intimate, in that sense, you knew your artists personally, you hung out with them and saw them at clubs. There was a big socialising thing and you had the feeling of all being in the same boat. That closeness maybe doesn't quite exist with majors."

"It is, of course, always a mistake to make sweeping generalisations," notes American R&B independents discographer Bob McGrather. "However, America revolves around the dollar. Making money as a priority is not frowned upon as it is perhaps elsewhere. Someone once asked me when I was interviewing for an advertising position if I wanted to be either rich or famous. It seemed odd to me at the time that these were considered the only options. Oftentimes a producer or artist would get the itch to start a new label and of course enlist partners outside the music business — perhaps the owners of a local beauty parlour or car dealership—the priorities are obvious here and rightly so just as with shareholders in a larger concern. It's not hard to accept that to climb out of the ghetto (or improve one's lot within it) was the prime motivator and to use one's craft to do it was the obvious vehicle. Sports and music being the two most likely as in the early days most everything else was a closed (white) shop."

The ad hoc nature of some of the independents was something Charlie Gillett would experience first hand on his trips to the deep south in the early 70s, licensing tracks for what would become his *Another Saturday Night* compilation. He further endorses the view that equating the music of these times with 'art' leads to some dangerously wrong-headed conclusions. "I doubt if the attitude has ever really changed. The only thing that changed is people like you and me coming in and considering that this music can be cast as art and talked about as art. But it hardly ever has been made with that intention. Maybe Radiohead think that way – but I'm not even sure they do. I'm sure they chuckle at times at what everybody makes of what they do. It's much more instinctive. The reason why people are musicians and become musicians – most musicians are inadequate, it's all they can do, this is what they're good at. It's a bit like footballers. If you could have understood what they were talking about in your history or physics or chemistry lessons, you'd have gone along the track that everybody wanted you to. But you couldn't get your head into that stuff. And the guys running the record labels are pretty similar people most of the time. For a lot of us, it's the only thing we're capable of doing. But a lot of it is doing what you want to do, what you feel is in you. Rather than trying to tailor what you're doing towards what someone says will get played on the radio. There's only a small proportion of all the people in the game, whether running record labels or as musicians, who have any inclination to do that."

Gillett found that few of the record labels he came across resembled anything he might have imagined. "One of the labels, Goldband Records – the guy running it, Eddie Shuler, was a TV repair man, literally. So the label was essentially a hobby. And at an earlier stage we went looking for a guy called JD Miller, a name I was familiar with as a producer of Slim Harpo and one or two quite big names in this blues/Cajun area. We'd been given his address and all we could see was that it was a women's hairdresser's. So we went out on the street and asked people where this address was, and they pointed me back to where I'd been. True enough, you went through the hairdresser's and at the back, there's JD Miller sitting at his desk in the classic kind of back room scene you've seen in so many mafia or gangster movies, like at the back of a restaurant in Brooklyn, or whatever. JD Miller was the sheriff of the town, he managed the local projects, so he had a multiple role in this town of Crowley, Louisiana."

## Edison... And Light Bulbs

Gillett encountered numerous other small label owners on the trip. "We went to a place called Ville Platte, Louisiana, where the guy who ran the label, Swallow – his name was Floyd Soileau, but his label was the bird swallow – to his father's great disappointment, he told us! His was the only one of all those little Louisiana operations that looked like what you might expect to find. The main building was a record shop, or the front half of it, and the back half was a warehouse with stacks and rows of metal frames with records on. Some of which were the stock for the shop, and others were his own records, in multiples of 25 a box. And to the side of that was the studio where he recorded all his records, so that's what felt like a proper record label. And he was just a fantastic man. I'd never be able to express my appreciation of how well he treated us, what a reasonable deal we got – the guy at the back of the hairdresser's said, 'Boys, you can have anything you like – $100 a song.' $100 in 1972 was a lot of money. That would be $1,200 to put an album together, and that was more than we could imagine. Whereas Floyd went $20 a track – that was more like it."

There were undoubtedly good eggs of Floyd's ilk, but the buccaneering 50s was also boom time for a collection of spivs, criminals and hustlers, and ties with mobsters were evident from the outset. These links had been established through the pre-radio dominance of jukeboxes as principal outlets for dispersal and promotion of recorded music. A case in point would be notorious music industry legend Morris Levy, proprietor of Roulette Records (formed in 1956), a man described as an "octopus" by *Variety* magazine in 1957. A perennially shady and intimidating character, thrown out of school for assaulting one of his teachers, he moved from nightclub photography to club and restaurant ownership and thence a record company and publishing. He would build a multi-million pound fortune and become a father figure to CBS head Walter Yetnikoff. Levy continued to deny Mafia links all the way up to his indictment by the FBI for conspiracy to commit extortion in 1988. He died of cancer before serving a single day of his ten-year sentence. But his past enterprises were indeed funded by mob money (rumoured to have come from Tommy Eboli and Vincent 'Chin' Gigante, later head of the Genovese family). He was also brighter and more business-savvy than other early independent operators – swapping the promise of a quick buck for a sustainable income. To this end, he was one of the first to recognise the importance of rights ownership – having started out with staples such as 'The Yellow Rose Of Texas', his Big Seven company went on to hold 30,000 copyrights. He was none too averse to the practice of removing an artist's name from a record label and substituting his own to ensure writer's as well as publishing royalties, nor to settling scores and disputes, either in business or with his artists, with a baseball bat. Present at the meeting at a Broadway Diner with Alan Freed (whom he would manage briefly) when the term 'rock and roll' was first suggested to describe the younger music beginning to filter through, he clearly recognised the ramifications quicker than most.

Tico owner George Goldner could talk with authority about Levy as the 'octopus'. One of the most revered talent spotters in the early R&B boom, he discovered and nurtured artists including Tito Puente – whom Levy enticed away to RCA – and then Frankie Lymon and the Teenagers and the Imperials, among many others. However, the multitude of labels he started – beginning with Tico in 1948 and continuing through Rama, Gee, Red Bird (where he fostered the talents of songwriters Leiber and Stoller, and Andrew Loog Oldham and Seymour Stein first met) and others – was a result of his gambling addiction. When the need for fast cash arose, he would simply sell the labels to Levy to reconcile his debts. Stein knew Leiber and Stoller but principally worked alongside Goldner. "I really worked on the other side of things. But I met Andrew Oldham when he came up to the offices of Red Bird. Jerry Leiber didn't see him. Mike Stoller wasn't around. I chased him out to the elevator and caught him. We were both in our early 20s. They [the Rolling Stones] were not known in America, but I knew who they were. So I said come up and listen to some songs. So I played him a load of songs, and they recorded 'Down Home Girl'."

The R&B independent boom inexorably led to the fusion of white (country or hillbilly) and black (blues, R&B) styles that would birth rock 'n' roll, signified by the arrival of Elvis Presley. And, initially at least, it was independents that nurtured the hybrid. Sun, established by farmer's son Sam Phillips, was one of the few labels borne out of a genuine love of the music it documented. Founded in March 1952, the initial intention was to market 'black' music beyond racial barriers, scoring its first hit with Rufus Thomas's 'Bear Cat' – an answer record to Big Mama Thornton's 'Hound Dog' whose copyright, it was later ruled, the record infringed. Other artists included Junior Parker and Little Milton. But Sun underwent a radical change of direction in 1954 when Phillips first encountered Presley. He recorded him in various styles – ballads, country and R&B – until he stumbled upon the 'Sun Sound'. He would ultimately sell Presley's contract to RCA for $35,000 in 1955 and focus his efforts on turning first Carl Perkins, then Johnny Cash and Jerry Lee Lewis, into superstars. Phillips eventually sold the label to Mercury producer Shelby Singleton in 1969.

The field was open for such businessmen, who could sense profit in documenting what surrounded them, capitalising on local knowledge and contacts. There was also, at a corporate level, a reluctance to embrace either R&B and rock 'n' roll as anything more than a faddish diversion. Rather, they would attempt to 'clone' breakout hits from the indies (Fats Domino, Little Richard etc) with artists like Pat Boone. The initial surge in independent R&B labels in the 40s was thus replicated by the rock 'n' roll boom years, as TV's *American Bandstand* and increasingly radio) came to accept the music as something other than a coarse and ignominious assault on the nation's morals. The independents responded, predictably, much quicker. The first independent regional distributors allowed them to do so, liasing with local radio stations to furnish listeners with the latest sounds. Suddenly, established lines of protocol were smashed as independent labels, promoters and artists found themselves able to have their records heard by audiences hungry for them.

Greg Shaw estimated in his 1982 essay on the music industry for *The History Of Rock* that between 1956 and a decade later, some 150,000 independent records were released, on not less than 500 separate imprints. This 'golden age' was made possible by regional hits reaching a far wider audience. Sun prospered with Jerry Lee Lewis, Carl Perkins *et al*, Specialty with Little Richard, Chess with Chuck Berry and Bo Diddley, Vee-Jay with John Lee Hooker and Jimmy Reed and Imperial with Fats Domino. Dozens of new labels sprang up, including Swan, Bell, Gone, Carlton, Cadence, Big Top etc. The level playing field promised by the R&B boom came to fruition in a tangible and lucrative fashion in the rock 'n' roll years.

The success of the independents was in part an indictment of major label sloth and inefficiency, in particular, its distribution methods, aggravated by America's intimidating geography. The majors opted for branch distribution, shifting records from large industrial units serving huge territories that could contain massive demographic differences. That, to an extent, dictated their A&R policies. As Shaw would write: "The advantage of branch distribution was that a company could deliver hit products anywhere in the country with speed and co-ordination. The disadvantage was that this national scope tended to dictate a concentration on artists with all-round, mainstream appeal. For decades the majors had taken great pains to groom young singers and then transform them into seasoned stars, matching them up with songs, arrangers and orchestras as they saw fit. The A&R men in charge of all this may have been aware that a vital new music was emerging. But their usual response was to wait until a hit song appeared in the 'race music' charts and then dish up whitewashed versions of the same tunes with their own singers."

Armstrong believes that the consequent stratification is vital to any understanding of the way the American music industry operated. "One of the reasons records didn't move outside borders that much in America, apart from the odd crossover, was because someone in Detroit wasn't going to 'get' a Texan record. The proof of the pudding is in the exceptions, like 'She's About A Mover' by the Sir Douglas Quintet in '65. That was a pure Tex-Mex record that was a smash hit. In 1965 you could have bought 2,000 pure Tex-Mex records that weren't smash hits, and that no-one in Detroit bought. I first discovered the blues through the Yardbirds – and then suddenly you find 'Smokestack Lightning' by Howling Wolf on a Pye single – you heard it and it blew your socks off completely. Then you find Muddy Waters and Little Walter, and you think you've discovered the blues. But that was Chicago blues. That wasn't T-Bone Walker and the Texas scene; that wasn't Johnny Guitar Watson on the coast. That wasn't BB King down in Memphis, etc."

Gillett actually encountered the man behind 'She's About A Mover' on his travels. "Whereas JD Miller's office was at the back of the hairdressing saloon, he himself had nothing to do with it, that was just something he owned. But Huey Meaux, the producer in Houston, that was his day to day profession. That's how he made his living. By the time we met him, he wasn't doing that any more, but he had done that for the first 20 years while producing records on the side, until he finally made it big." 'She's About A Mover' boasted a highly unusual pedigree. Legendarily, with the British Invasion in full swing, Meaux had taken a box of Beatles records into his hotel room for study purposes, ingested a large quantity of wine, then decided that the beats resembled old-style Cajun dance songs sufficiently that he might combine both traditions.

"It's a very touch and go game," Gillett continues. "You can have big hit records in America without ever really getting the money back from them. Because the distributors, shamelessly, only pay you back when they want your next record – i.e. when they think your record will be at least as big as the one they've just sold for you. Until then you've got this horrible problem of manufacturing records with the pressing plants demanding to be paid in 30 days – the best deal you can get is 60 days – and you don't get paid by your distributor, at the earliest, until 90 days after the sale. So there's this big gap, and the more successful the record, the greater your problem is. Cos you're having to manufacture thousands of records without getting paid for them. That's why so many of those indies went running to the bigger labels. All those companies down in Louisiana, when they had a hit, they always had to go to a bigger company to carry it to the charts, because they couldn't deal with the problems I just described. If it was a hit in Texas or Louisiana they could manage it, but the minute it went national, they had to go to a bigger company."

Another famous example of which was Phil Phillips' 'Sea Of Love'. Gillett: "That was recorded in the studio of the guy I described, Eddie Shuler, the TV repairman. His neighbour, who ran a little record shop, George Khoury, was the actual producer of 'Sea Of Love'. But Eddie Shuler agreed to record the song in his studio in return for getting the publishing rights to the song. So Phil Phillips brought the song along, George Khoury was going to put it out. He claimed half the songwriting, which is where he added to his income. Shuler published it, and they put this record out – and it was barely taking off locally. Then they went to Mercury and a guy called Shelby Singleton, who was based in Nashville but was originally from Louisiana and had his ear to the ground there, picked up a number of hits from that region that went national on Mercury. That happened a lot in those days. There was an indie scene at one stage, then suddenly it would be on a major, and the majors tended to retain the rights ever after. They could afford to repress, and part of the original definition of a major label in the United States was that you owned your own pressing plants. Except King Records, which had James Brown, was an anomaly, because they owned their pressing plant, so they could be said to be a major, but they were never seen as that, they were an indie really, and their pressings were appalling. So there were a whole bunch of independent pressing plants all around the country, and all kinds of rackets went on in order to get your records pressed here and there. There were, I think, 13 regions, each with their own separate distributors, so if you were an indie label in Los Angeles, you had to place your record with a different distributor all across the country."

The underworld played a key part in financing records and also reaping the rewards of hit singles. The corruption extended beyond the labels to the pressing plants, distributors and numerous DJs, leading to the great 'payola' scandal of May 1960 surrounding DJ Alan Freed. Payola – a contraction of the words pay and Victrola, a throwback to the record playing device – was nothing new to the entertainment industry. It has been rampant in the 20s and 30s in vaudeville and big bands. Indeed, Chairman Oren Harris's House Oversight Subcommittee's inquest into the recording industry was prompted largely by pressure from ASCAP

(American Association of Composers, Authors and Publishers), who considered rock 'n' roll a fad, and the recent denouncement of corruption on rigged quiz shows. The immediacy of the evolving business and its lucrative potential, plus the dispersal of 'shady' money, meant ready temptation for a DJ willing to favour a particular artist or label. In the court case that led to a $2,500 fine for Freed, Dick Clark's association with Jamie Records also came under scrutiny. A total of 25 DJs and programme directors were investigated by the committee, leading directly to the establishment of America's anti-payola statute. Freed, the man who first popularised the term rock 'n' roll, would die a penniless alcoholic. Morris Levy, undoubtedly far further up the payola food chain, escaped any conviction and never appeared at the Congressional hearings.

The case was undoubtedly linked to reservations about the growth of an independent music network that was answerable, if not to nobody, then certainly not to the major labels. Part of ASCAP's motivation was their disapproval of rival organisation BMI (Broadcast Music Incorporated), who principally represented black musicians, and had become more amenable to the artists populating the emergent rock 'n' roll scene. ASCAP believed BMI was using payola to leverage its artists. Many others, however, believe that the organisation's intention was retaliation over loss of market share, while others still contest that institutional racism was a motivating factor.

"One thing I didn't really understand when I was writing *Sound Of The City*," says Gillett, "was the fundamental role of payola of one kind or another, which was what enabled the little labels to get played on radio stations. The paradox being that the bigger labels like RCA and Colombia would not be seen dead in those days paying payola – they had shareholders. So I remember talking to the guy who produced Bill Haley – Milt Gabler – and he said it was incredibly frustrating. Because your records weren't getting played on the stations that should have played them, and would have loved to have played them, because there was no payola. And the other thing was the role of publishing companies in those days. The role of publishing was very critical in America. By the time you get to 1976 in Britain, the role of a publishing company doesn't feel so significant, and I don't think it is. Publishing is more riding on the back of the energy of the record labels. But back in those days, publishers were very active, and were part of the promotion and by implication part of the payola as well, the means by which all that got dealt with. So Alan Freed, his manager was Morris Levy, who ran not only Roulette Records, but Ark Publishing – and Ark Publishing represented all of Chess, and Checker Records, Chuck Berry and Bo Diddley and all those guys. And part of the way those records would get on the radio in New York was through Ark Music having an interest, and making sure those records got played on the right radio shows, etc. Most of the people from that era got away scot-free – Alan Freed himself did do some time, which was always very unfair."

In contrast to the largely enthusiastic if not necessarily altruistic spirit that would define the late 70s UK independent boom, there was a level of cynicism at work beyond payola. Many rock 'n' roll records were produced by house bands and session musicians, some clearly disinterested in their employment. Some of the arrangers and songwriters the labels retained shared their cynicism, resulting in bland 'teenage-fodder'. Partially as a result of these creative frustrations, independent producers came to the fore. Often songwriters themselves, they would recruit musicians and singers to record, then pass the results on to a label to manufacture and distribute, before returning to the studio for their next venture. Music publisher Don Kirshner was one such creature, using writers Carole King and Gerry Goffin to produce recordings licensed to both majors and indies. The team dominated the pop charts of the early 60s. Jerry Leiber and Mike Stoller were veterans of the R&B scene who founded Red Bird Records before selling it on. Kirshner also established his own imprint, Tomorrow, as did his associate Lou Adler, who started Ode. Gamble And Huff wearied of writing bland pop hits for Cameo-Parkway and set up their own operation in Philadelphia, while a short-lived artists' co-operative, AFO, was founded in New Orleans by veteran session musicians. In Memphis, Stax moved from its association with Atlantic to operate in its own right.

It was a fertile period for mavericks, entrepreneurs and square pegs. An illustrative case is that of Phil Spector and his Philles label, founded in 1961. At 21 Spector became America's youngest label head. Already an industry veteran having assisted Leiber and Stoller in New York and produced hits for Ray Peterson and Curtis Lee for Dune Records, Spector grasped the importance of retaining control of his catalogue and the production process. That was all very well while the hits flowed from his Goldstar Studios in LA, beginning with the Crystals and continuing through smashes for Darlene Love and the Ronettes. But after Ike and Tina Turner's 'River Deep, Mountain High' failed to do satisfactory business in the US, Philles closed in 1967. Which was heartening for the distributors who had become used to wielding near total control over the labels they worked with and didn't like Spector's feisty and outspoken style one iota.

## Independence Days

In the process these labels, predominantly working with black singers and artists, committed some of the great American songs to posterity, and were able to assert their claims by dint of talent and personal industry. Others came out of the majors to strike out on their own, notably Berry Gordy Jr, who had piloted Marv Johnson's career at United Artists and started Tamla and Motown, just as R&B gave way to a new generation of soul artists. Alongside Philadelphia International, Motown rose to become the definitive independent of the early 70s, retaining its own masters until its sale to MCA in 1988 for $61 million.

From 1961 to 1971, Motown had 110 Top 10 hits. Key to this was the fact that, unlike some competitors who released singles in a piecemeal fashion, Gordy believed in artist development and a co-ordinated, highly drilled back room operation. In the process he fostered probably the most impressive roster of talent ever to be assembled under the auspices of a single label – from Stevie Wonder and Marvin Gaye to Diana Ross, the Jackson 5, The Temptations and the Supremes. Each was in receipt of fastidious grooming; the maintenance of a dignified image helped make the label appeal to white Americans as well as black. Gordy prized elegance and deportment highly, and refined the manners and speech – even to the extent of elocution lessons – of performers he rescued from backgrounds in impoverished urban projects. They were choreographed and rehearsed relentlessly, and most took part in the Motown Revue tours of the chitlin circuit to hone their performances.

A similar methodology was applied to crafting hits at the label's Hitsville USA recording studio. Every Friday, Gordy would chair quality control meetings, rejecting any recordings that didn't fit the style of the top selling discs that week. The 'Motown Sound' was created around a nucleus of fantastically able musicians known collectively as the Funk Brothers, while the dominant songwriting team was Holland-Dozier-Holland (brothers Brian and Eddie Holland with Lamont Dozier), as well as Norman Whitfield and Barrett Strong. At least until the loss of Holland-Dozier-Holland due to a royalties dispute in 1967, Motown operated in a fashion akin to battery farming, rotating acts in the studio with those on tour, while the studio was open up to 22 hours a day. Visionary and driven, Gordy accepted no compromise in keeping the hits coming, though there have been several who dispute the equanimity of the wealth distribution. Kim Weston, best known for her duets with Gaye, took an action against Gordy in 1994 for non-accounting (her original royalties all having been offset against production costs, she claimed). Teena Marie famously sued Berry over her contract – leading to the Brockert Initiative or 'Teena Marie Law', which acted as a benchmark for limiting the length of recording contracts. Further, she was signed without the use of an attorney, aside from the one appointed to her by the label – the common-law wife of Gordy's brother. Other instances abound, but it's hard to begrudge Gordy his success. Studio musicians were paid relatively good wages for the time ($5 to $10 per session – or until "everything was right") to staff the cramped Studio A they nicknamed the Snakepit. Though $10 was, of course, a long way short of what they could have earned had they retained any of their copyright.

But what of the UK? Here, notable exceptions like Topic apart, there was no such tradition of independent labels. The geography of the British Isles meant that the economics of national distribution were far easier for major labels to navigate, leaving less room for niche outlets. Additionally, the majors had affiliates in America who could farm out American hits to them, giving them an innate advantage. Hence the market dominance of EMI, Decca, CBS, Pye and Phonogram by the 60s.

Formed by Alan Freeman, Polygon was arguably the first documented attempt by a British independent to operate within mainstream popular music. In 1949, armed with a small inheritance, and a promise from a contact in Australia that he could export 'pop' records there, Freeman alighted on the former child film star Petula Clark, who had been performing with the Rank Organisation. Freeman had spotted a gap in the market. EMI and Decca were not prepared to sign Clark as an adult singer, while Freeman could see her potential in that role. He approached her father and business manager, Leslie Clark, who was taken by the idea to the extent that he also invested in what would become Polygon Records.

The first fruits of this liaison arrived with the 1950 cover version of 'Music, Music, Music', which became a major success for Esquire in Australia (whereas in the UK the Teresa Brewer version of the song was a hit in 1950). The first British Polygon releases, meanwhile, were a Louis Prima recording licensed from America, a series of three singles from Clark and future DJ Jimmy Young's 'Too Young', which became the label's first substantial UK hit in the summer of 1951 and sold a quoted 130,000 copies. However, the label wasn't equipped for that success, mirroring the difficulties American independents often faced when scoring a runaway hit. Young would subsequently join Decca and informed the *NME* that the label was unable to press copies fast enough. He further commented: "Basically I wanted to stay with Polygon, partly on sentimental grounds and partly because I had great personal admiration for Alan Freeman, who was running it. However, my advisers felt that I ought to be on a major label with distribution all over the world".

For Petula Clark, speaking in 2007, there are nothing but good memories of Polygon. "I don't think we realised at the time we were making history. Alan was great. I think it was his dad who was financing it. I was a young woman, I didn't know any of the ins and outs of any of this stuff. I just went in and sang. I was only interested in singing. I'm still only interested in singing. Any of the rest of it doesn't really interest me that much. I adored Alan, we had lots of fun together, and it was all on a shoestring. There was nothing glamorous about it at all. He had this funny old car, and he used to go round distributing the records himself, with the records in the back. He would actually physically load the car with records, and I remember the car was scraping the road because there were so many records in the boot and back seat. But he took all that on. Certainly in those days independent really did mean that – you've got to get out there, you don't have the help of the big houses. And of course, getting them pressed too is something else, the whole business is a struggle. If I think about it now, I'm sure it was a struggle for Alan, but he was just spurred on by his own enthusiasm and determination." John Repsch, who interviewed Freeman before his death, casts a slightly different light on Freeman's diligence. "He was in love with Petula. Absolutely."

The main thing Clark can recall, however, is how much fun they were having. "We laughed all the time. He loved music, don't get me wrong, he had a great sense of music. I don't know if he was commercially very savvy, but none of us were really. It was just a joy being in the studio with him. The business was much smaller and the world was very different, so you can't compare it with the record business of today, or even the 60s. It was all very 'artisan'. Having said that, we used huge orchestras. I remember recording with Laurie Johnson [another Polygon artist who collaborated with Clark on songs such as 'How Are Things With You?') in a church, because that was the only place we could get all the musicians in! It was such a huge orchestra and difficult because the acoustics were terrible. But it was because Alan wanted this huge sound." Indeed, several renowned orchestra leaders started out on Polygon, including Johnson, Frank Chacksfield and Ron Goodwin.

Although still succoured by the idea of an entirely independent company, Freeman was aware that Jimmy Young's concerns, or at least those of his advisors, were legitimate. Eventually, this led to talks with Pye about using Polygon as their bridge to the pop market. Negotiations began in 1954 with a view to Freeman being installed as the A&R head of the new venture. Delayed by a bout of illness, the move was finalised in February 1955 when Polygon moved into the offices of Nixa (run by New Zealand-born entrepreneur Hilton Nixon), an earlier Pye acquisition. But the development of (Pye) Nixa meant the end for Polygon, whose final release came in October, after which all the label's assets, masters and artists were transferred to the new label. The catalogue of 78rpm singles, nearly two hundred in total and some 23 by Clark, all produced by Freeman, were deleted. Or, in some cases, accidentally destroyed (towards the end of Polygon, Freeman had exacerbated the confusion by storing releases in garages in pressings of exactly 999 – to avoid VAT charges). As writer Theo Morgan observes, "After the move, the masters were stored in two Nissen huts, one of which Nixa decided was surplus to requirements. So they had it demolished without the contents being removed first. Thus, half the Polygon masters were lost." Which is why subsequent compilations of this material, such as those Morgan has overseen for labels including Redline, have had to be remastered from original 78s. The carelessness with which the music industry has treated some of its prize assets evidently began early.

Oriole was, technically, even older, founded in 1927 by the Levy Company in London as a subsidiary, releasing American masters from Vocalion Records domestically. Though discontinued in 1935 it was revived in 1950 and enjoyed a few major hits including Maureen Evans' 'Like I Do', Nancy Whiskey & Charlie McDevitt's version of 'Freight Train' and Russ Hamilton's 'We Will Make Love', which reached number two. Some of these records even made an impression on a pre-Beatles America, which was highly unusual in the 50s, as Seymour Stein acknowledges. "I always thought it was very strange. There were more hits in America coming from Italy, thanks to the San Remo festival, stuff like 'Volare', and from France, by way of the big French orchestras like Raymond Le Fevre and Paul Mauriat, who had a huge number one with 'Love Is Blue'. Even German records; Bert Kampfert, who later wrote stuff for Sinatra, 'Strangers In The Night'. There was hardly *anything* from the UK except oddball records, like 'He's Got The Whole World In His Hands', by Laurie London, which was a one-hit wonder. Then [in 1957] Russ Hamilton had a big hit – not 'We Will Make Love', but the b-side, 'Rainbow'." In fact, Hamilton always attributed its success to the fact that American pressings had mistakenly swapped the two sides' status. "These were the kinds of records that would break through," Stein continues. "Oriole also had 'Freight Train' by Charlie McDevitt's skiffle group. They had two big hits in America, and the others had none. So Oriole is very important." Oriole also ran the subsidiary label Embassy, producing cut-price covers of chart hits directly for Woolworth's. For a time it also licensed some of the early Motown hits, but was sold to CBS in September 1964 and transformed itself into the conglomerate's English arm.

Aside from Polygon, the most revealing domestic story from the post-war period was Ember Records. Jeffrey Kruger was the owner of legendary fifties jazz club Flamingo in London's Wardour Street, and would work with everyone from Billie Holiday to the Rolling Stones. He founded Ember in 1957 as a direct challenge to the monopoly that existed in record distribution and promotion, largely succeeding by issuing 'budget lines' and targeting non-conventional outlets outside of established record stores, which were sewn up by the majors. The label began as a direct consequence of the 50s independent boom in the US. Kruger, on one of his frequent trips to New York met legendary talent spotter and producer Murray Kaufman, a promoter of the Apollo Theater in Harlem. Inspired by the acts he saw there, Kruger became determined to replicate the success of the American independents. "Albeit a comparatively small fish in a big pond, so far as my contemporaries in the USA were concerned," he states, "but a bigger fish in a smaller pond back home so far as I was concerned."

Ember was envisaged as a joint venture with Al Silver (founder of Herald Records), who had already invoked that name in the US. Kruger's Florida Music Company was to be represented by Silver and Doug Moody in America. Kruger would reciprocate by representing their Angel Music Company throughout Europe. Ember US was already exploiting the breakout of R&B (then still termed 'race' music), enjoying their first hit with Faye Adams' 'Shake A Hand' followed by success with Lightnin' Hopkins. "They had luck running for them and back to back they had at least six consecutive hit artists making the charts," says Kruger, "often with records that were still in rough demo form. But because of the insatiable demand for the new music, records were rushed into the hands of powerful DJs who, to beat the competition, would put them on the air in acetate form." In the end, however, delayed by a government licence necessary to complete transactions in foreign exchange, Kruger met EMI's Len Wood and together they took the decision for Ember UK to sub-licence American chart hits to EMI Parlophone.

Kruger then embarked on establishing the basic networking necessities of an independent label – manufacture, distribution and promotion. "None of the existing British record companies, who each had their own distribution outlets and owned their own record manufacturing plants, would even consider helping us. I felt every door in these vital areas close in my face so

## Edison... And Light Bulbs

I worked backwards through the three basics. I went into what was then a chain of some two dozen record stores owned and operated under the street name Keith Prowse Stores. On Bond Street I met the man in charge, Walter Woyda. He listened to me – in fact he was the first man to give me a dispassionate hearing – and he said he was ready to help and he would order our stock, albeit in small quantities initially. He would see I was paid promptly to help me through my cash flow."

Through Wayda, Kruger linked up with an independent distributor (of radios and televisions) Lugton & Co. Another distributor was found to cover the Midlands, while the north west was covered by NEMS, run by the Epstein family, whose son Brian would shortly shepherd the Beatles to success. That in turn led to Glasgow's Wolfson company, then Ireland's Solomon and Peres – Maurice Soloman having previously helped finance Edward Lewis's efforts to fend off predators at Decca in the late 20s. Soloman's son Mervyn, meanwhile, let Kruger licence country records (via his company Emerald Records), in order to establish an LP line.

Distribution in place, at least theoretically, Kruger set about establishing a manufacturing base. In the end he alighted on a button manufacturing company in Edgware, London, called Orlake. "The same machine that was manufacturing buttons of all sizes was retooled to make vinyl records, and so I had my ability to press records. More importantly, they had storage space to hold some of the stock." The final step was promotion. "I did manage to get an appointment at quite high level at the BBC and was told that they would be prepared to play my records. They were, after all, an impartial body. But the record industry, controlled by the then big boys, EMI, Decca, Philips and Pye, and to a lesser degree by Oriole/Embassy Records, had formed PPL (Phonographic Performance Limited). PPL had an agreement with the BBC. Only members of that trade body could have their records played on the BBC and share in the performance fees – of which I knew nothing at the time – that the BBC paid to the record industry for the right to air their records."

This body, a cartel in all but name, refused Kruger membership. But Kruger wasn't taking the black-balling sitting down. He talked it through with his cousin, lawyer Norman Beech. Beech considered the matter, before informing Kruger that, in his view, the BBC's impartiality would be compromised unless they were able to enter into a similar agreement with Kruger. "It was brilliant. And that's what happened. Ember signed an independent deal with the BBC much to the chagrin of the PPL. I could now get my records played on the air."

## Independence Days

By the mid-60s Ember was beginning to tick along nicely, though Kruger continued to be heavily involved with the Flamingo Club and arranging tours for visiting US jazz stars such as Carmen McRae, who later recorded for Ember. With the crucial support of the BBC, they scored a Top 40 hit with Jan & Kjeld. Other good sellers included Ray Ellington's 'Madison', only their second release, and Michael Cox's 'Angela Jones'. Significantly, the latter was acquired from a fellow independent who lacked the resources that Kruger had built up for Ember.

Ember was able to license US hits, though occasionally Kruger's comparative lack of industrial muscle would show. The Five Royales' original version of 'Dedicated To The One I Love' on King Records was eclipsed by a version from the Shirelles when the song was picked up by a major. He also secured terms to licence 20th Century Fox's music catalogue via Norman Weiser, an association that raised a few eyebrows in the industry. The partnership was inaugurated by the release of 'Little Drummer Boy' by the Harry Simeone Chorale, which reached the Top 40 three times during 1961 and 1962. There were also solid selling album releases from Art Tatum, Glenn Miller, Tommy Dorsey and others under the same arrangement. "All these we issued at a price of 26 shillings (£1.30), that undercut most label's prices. They were, in effect, the first mid-price LPs. Some older material we put out on our Famous Artists series at 9/9d (49p), making them the cheapest albums on the British market – very attractive at a time when a 45 rpm single cost 6/9d (34p)."

According to Kruger, it was bad enough being an upstart independent challenging the monopoly, but his pricing policy was viewed as outright sedition. "Some time later I attended one of the annual trade dinners organised by the Gramophone Record Retailers Association [GRRA] to make an after dinner speech. The room was packed to capacity with all the heads of the major record companies and their distribution arms, the buyers and key executives of all the major and minor record shops and of course the trade press. I decided I might never get a chance to speak before such an august body again so I thought I would aim straight at their jugular. I spoke from the heart and the reaction was forceful. I told them I was in the record business, which no longer was the privileged domain of four or five companies, and was there to stay. There would be more independents coming up fast behind me, and if stores still refused to stock our product, then I and they would find other outlets. If I had to sell records through supermarkets or bookshops or in food stores or photograph stores then I would not hesitate. Records could be, and would be, sold outside of conventional outlets and the stores would only have themselves to blame."

## Edison... And Light Bulbs

The audience was not impressed. "I said what worked in the American market would follow here in the European market and they were visibly shaken. It took five years before I was formally vindicated, on the occasion of Ember's seventh anniversary. In an editorial in the trade magazine *Record Retailer* on 29 September 1966, the editor, also a record store owner, upheld exactly what I'd said at the GRRA Convention. Unless dealers recognised the independents, the day would come when independent product and budget records would be sold against them in bookshops and supermarkets."

A blow came when Weiser had to explain to him that studio politics at 20th Century had led to them assigning a licence for the soundtrack to the company's blockbuster *Cleopatra* to EMI. There were also reversals in obtaining licences from American labels who overestimated the potential of their records in what remained a thriving but niche market. "Betty Chapita of Vee-Jay Records made it quite clear that she thought I was trying to con her and she was interested only in serious money up front. She never made any attempt to speak to anyone who knew the UK market who could corroborate my account of that market. Many fine records were unreleased in Britain at the time, in my view, solely because of her greed."

Similar problems overcame attempts to liase with Herman Lubinsky's Savoy and Don Robey of Duke/Peacock Records. Kruger did, however, fare better with Saul and Jules Bihari's west coast independent umbrella group, comprising Kent, Modern and Crown, leading to a fine catalogue of blues and jazz albums by BB King, Elmore James, Howlin' Wolf *et al*. He was also able to work Syd Nathan's King Records – although their initial meeting had to be convened around Cincinnati's appearance in the baseball world series. "I love America and I love my native England, but I'm afraid that their respective summer games, baseball and cricket, do not hold me in their thrall," notes Kruger. Despite this, he managed to convince an initially sceptical Nathan to allow him to licence a small trickle of records without an advance. Eventually, these resulted in the first UK releases by a young artist Nathan had introduced to him in his studio in 1965, James Brown. Eventually, Nathan gave Kruger access to his album releases, beginning with Billy Ward's Dominoes (featuring Clyde McPhatter and Jackie Wilson). It was the first release on Ember's full-price flagship album range. He also released dozens of rock 'n' roll classics by Jerry Lee Lewis, Carl Perkins, Roy Orbison and others via an agreement with Sam Phillips of Sun Records.

Ember released the Dave Clark Five's debut, 'Chaquita', in June 1962, alongside domestic talents such as Lita Roza, the Dale Sisters, Grant Tracy &

## Independence Days

The Sunsets, Lewis & The Southerners (pre-The Ivy League/Flowerpot Men) and a pre-EMI Matt Monro. Composer John Barry also joined the label in 1963, as a refugee from politicking at EMI. "We were like chalk and cheese," notes Kruger. "I was disciplined and businesslike and watched every penny – at times I had to. John, on the other hand, was a truly talented artist, a man of flair and confidence but not a student of budget control. If he came up with an idea, he wanted to go straight into the studio with a 40-piece orchestra and get on with it." Barry was signed to the label (on a higher than normal royalty) and also became in-house producer. He would provide soundtracks to Bond film *From Russia With Love* and *Zulu*, also bringing the label his proteges, folk singers Chad Stuart and Jeremy Clyde, who eventually found success after being licensed to Pittsburgh's World Artists imprint. Both 'Yesterday's Gone' and 'Summer Song' were substantial American hits.

However, the relationship with Barry hit rocky waters when Kruger queried the escalating recording costs afforded an Annie Ross album, then soured further over Barry's insistence he release any record he liked at any point, even if that stretched Ember's still puny promotional resources. So in the end Barry's contract was handed over to Marty Erlichman, Barbra Streisand's manager. In the meantime, 19-year-old David Jones (later Bowie) signed to Ember's publishing arm Sparta Music, while the record label also helped to turn Swinging Sixties model Twiggy into a recording artist.

The role that Decca's London American operation played in the 50s and 60s is important to note, in so much as, while a major, it helped spread the independent gospel as the primary outlet for rock 'n' roll's first generation. "My sense is that the blueprint for the golden age of UK indie labels came from their US counterparts some three decades beforehand," says John Broven, author of *Record Makers And Breakers: Voices of the Independent Rock 'n' Roll Pioneers*. "There was a similar ethos of giving the public the good music it wanted and not what the major labels decreed. The pioneering US independent companies began springing up throughout the United States in the immediate post-World War II era, when the majors ignored the full impact of emergent rhythm and blues – a stylistic precursor of rock 'n' roll. The names of the leading R&B indie labels resonate with familiarity, especially Atlantic, Chess, Imperial, King, Modern, Specialty and Sun. Other important indie labels such as Cadence, Dot and Liberty were more pop-slanted. In varying degrees, these innovators licensed their masters – hits and non-hits – to London American, part of the Decca Records group, for global distribution during an epic period from 1955 through 1965."

## Edison... And Light Bulbs

"Accordingly," Broven continues, "the fabled London label introduced teens everywhere to a long line of now classic artists, including Chuck Berry, Johnny Cash, Ray Charles, Eddie Cochran, Bo Diddley, Fats Domino, Everly Brothers, Jerry Lee Lewis, Little Richard and Ricky Nelson – and, crucially, to the independent spirit. Only major label signings Elvis Presley, Buddy Holly and Gene Vincent seemed to be missing. Among the eager young record collectors would be impressionable future UK indie artists, shopkeepers and label owners. Just as their US forebears had done, the vibrant UK indie labels injected much-needed life into a moribund musical scene. Then the establishment started to retaliate, in an action replay of the earlier US scenario. It was great while it lasted."

Joe Meek cuts unarguably the most tragi-comic figure in the story of independent UK pop in the late fifties and early sixties. His name has become part of an iconography of 'swinging London' that includes Kenneth Williams and Joe Orton (and also, Brian Epstein). All were gay men in an era, despite the increasingly libertarian climate, that remained almost unremittingly hostile to the notion. His career and life are well documented elsewhere, notably in John Repsch's book *The Legendary Joe Meek*. The lurid tales surrounding his home studio in a flat above 304 Holloway Road continue to enthral as much as the sonic alchemy he produced there. Marshalling household items alongside wholly invented or customised electronic gadgetry for recording sessions that saw musicians perform on stairwells and the bathroom, Meek went to extraordinary lengths to replicate the sounds he heard in his head. Always a notoriously difficult and exacting man, his descent into drug-fuelled paranoia eventually spiralled into murder and suicide, and remains one of the most compelling stories in British post-war history.

Meek was responsible for more than 300 records between 1956 and 1967, among them some of the treasures of our pop culture – notably the science fiction-themed instrumental 'Telstar' and the definitive 'death disc' 'Johnny Remember Me'. Notoriously temperamental and violent, disparaging of the Beatles initially (and much else), Meek's work has latterly been recognised as the output of a kind of *idiot savant*. The fact that he was mentally incapacitated as he faced the final curtain is indisputable. At which point his decline began is open to conjecture. Biographer John Repsch is as well placed as any to comment. "I interviewed about 120 people, and I would always ask each one of them at the end, if I can't find out what made him tick, the story is inadequate. And they would say, 'What made him tick was that he loved his music,' or 'he was so lonely as a person'. And no-one came up with this, but it dawned on me that it was all there in his childhood and upbringing. This desire to overcome his complexes, that he felt inadequate in himself, and he was desperate to prove to the world he was a force to be reckoned with."

Meek grew up in the quiet village of Newent in Gloucestershire, where he was remorselessly teased by his siblings for his theatrical interests and mannerisms, exacerbated by the fact that his mother, who had hoped for a daughter, dressed him in girl's clothing. It inculcated in him a lifelong pursuit for acceptance. "Always he wanted to prove himself," states Repsch. "You have to go back to his childhood, and the fact that he had a tough upbringing in that he was an outsider, and he couldn't bear being teased, and he had a rotten time of it. And he discovered this talent for electronics, and that gave him a way to prove himself as something other than a little wimp that liked wearing girl's dresses, and to prove he had a brain in his head. And the attitude to him in the small village he lived in drove him out. He might well have stayed there had he been accepted. But he went through mental turmoil, and that drove him to London. He thought he would be better accepted there and things would be different. Homosexuality was very frowned upon in those days. It's said in the music business, music is the great leveller. It doesn't matter if you were queer, black, Jewish, two-headed or three-legged, if you could produce good music, you were in, and an equal. But he proved that was not the case at all, as he still had tremendous difficulties. But then he made a rod for his own back, because he was so temperamental. It possibly wasn't always due to that prejudice."

Meek took a job at a radio shop on Edgware Road briefly but then began working at IBC Studios during 1954 as a "glorified projectionist", showing prospective advertisers TV commercials broadcast in America at the dawn of commercial television. Soon he was drawn into the Radio Luxembourg road shows that toured the country, and with whom IBC had a contract to provide technical support. Eventually he became a 'tape monkey', a junior assistant engineer who would make the tea and place microphones. "There was another character there, Allen Stagg, who became the studio manager, and he wasn't an 'inventive' person," says Repsch. "It was all rules and regulations. Allen made life very difficult for Joe. He hated homosexuals."

Meek desperately wanted to become a senior engineer, and would petition Stagg and get nowhere. "So he started asking the producers who came in to put pressure on the office, because he wanted to do big jobs. One of those was Arthur Frewin. Arthur Frewin worked for cheap budget labels, and he was paid for setting up sessions. He said, give the lad a chance. He got nowhere initially, but there was a big studio production, a big orchestral session with Alyn Ainsworth for 'Music For Lonely Lovers'. Arthur was the producer. Joe had never done a senior balance engineer job before – apart from engineering a Big Bill Broonzy blues record – and it was actually Allen Stagg's attempt to undermine and capsize Meek's prospects, because he thought he would fail."

He didn't, and Meek quickly gravitated to becoming producer Denis Preston's favoured engineer. "When Denis discovered Joe, he didn't want Allen any more." On his death in 1979, the *Sunday Times* described Preston as "probably the most important figure to emerge from the British jazz business". Repsch cites Meek's debt to Preston as 'inevitable'. "The fact that they worked together so closely, there's no way Denis couldn't have been an influence on Joe. Norman Granz was the king of recorded jazz in America, and Denis had taken a leaf out of his book. In fact, he said, 'If only I'd had the chance to work with artists of the same calibre, I'd have done even better than Norman Granz.'" That may have sounded a boastful claim, but it was undoubtedly true, at least in terms of sonic fidelity. Granz, the original founder of Verve, was dismissive of 'hi-fi', and instead appended the legend 'Recorded in Muenster Dummel Hi-Fi' to his record labels. This was actually in tribute to two breeds of dogs he owned, and the sound was, usually, dreadful. But certainly Granz served as the model of kindly patrician that Preston came to be to Meek, until the latter fell out with him in yet another fit of pique. The production company he established in 1954, Record Supervision Ltd, enabled him to work with selected artists to produce recordings which were then licensed to major record labels – effectively the path Meek too would follow. This resulted in a long association with Pye Records and recordings by Chris Barber, Acker Bilk and many others, which evolved into a subsequent deal in 1959 with EMI's Columbia label, helping to document the 'trad jazz' boom. But he also dabbled in other fields, including folk, calypso. flamenco guitar, popular song (Roger Whittaker) and was behind many of Donegan's skiffle recordings.

Meek's already fertile persecution complex, meanwhile, was given ample scope to prosper in the stiff, regimented environs of IBC. "He was recording Petula Clark, and they always worked late without overtime, all of the engineers," notes Repsch. "He got back to bed in the early hours, and he was late getting up. So he walks in all smiles, and there's the studio manager at the door, tapping his watch. 'What time do you call this, Mr Meek?' He couldn't cope with that attitude." When Meek told Preston he was leaving, fed up with being 'picked on', not just for his sexuality but also the way he liked to tamper with recording equipment, that gave Preston, who had long harboured the ambition of starting his own recording studio, the nudge to leave IBC too.

"It was on the cards when Joe came to realise how appreciated some of his work was," says Repsch. "It made him ambitious. He wasn't getting the credit due to him, because he was putting the gloss on those records at IBC, but he didn't have his name on the records. Denis Preston did put Joe's name on a lot of jazz records. But Joe was having success with things like 'Lay Down Your Arms' by Anne Shelton, and Frankie Vaughan's 'Green Door', and lots of Lonnie Donegan records. A lot of the pop stuff, the engineers' names weren't mentioned, but Joe thought he was the one making them hits. One of the recordings that Meek made with Denis was Johnny Duncan's 'Last Train to San Fernando', which sold an awful lot of records. With the income from that, they were able to set up Lansdowne, which was being used as a tiny studio by an amateur cellist. And it was just round the corner from where Meek was living. Denis dived in and bought the place, and Joe helped set it up, and became the studio manager. He was there only for about 18 months, but he made his mark there."

By 1960 Meek had founded Triumph Records, using downtime at Lansdowne Road and a flat in Holland Park. Few of his initial releases, with the notable exception of 'Green Jeans', made much impact, though they are recalled today as visionary experiments and early blueprints for 'Telstar'. Triumph, formed with William Barrington-Coup of Saga Films, didn't last long. Meek saw what he believed would be a potential number one hit escape his production of Michael Cox's 'Angela Jones' after the pressing plant he'd found was unable to satisfy demand after the singer appeared on television promoting it. Very quickly Triumph disappeared as Meek assessed he was better served by handing over the masters to those able to get records into the shops. With investment from the colourful Major Banks (to be played by Kevin Spacey in an upcoming film of Meek's life – "I wanted that part!" laughs Repsch, himself an actor), he took up the flat in Holloway Road that would become his stronghold. They jointly formed RGM Sound as a production company. "Without Banks there would have been no 'Telstar'," says Repsch. "He was the one funding it all. Joe was a leper and a pariah in the industry after walking out of Lansdowne. And word gets round. He gave Joe the security. Unfortunately, he could be a little mean too. He was an astute businessman, and he wanted all Joe's money from composing to go straight back into the company. But apart from that, having anyone in authority over him was something that Meek couldn't live with. He thought anyone telling him what to do undermined his ability to be creative." Meek wasn't himself above being presumptuous about financial matters. Money was dispensed often purely on the basis of favouritism. "He wanted the money going into his pockets, but it wasn't re-channelled as it should have. A lot of people sold a lot of records and didn't get remuneration for it."

Meek dismissed all who stood in his way as 'rotten pigs', a term which started out as a collective demarcation for his enemies and increasingly became the basis for a full-blown conspiracy theory. Yet there was evidence to support some of his hostility. White-coated cutting engineers rejected some of his early recordings, believing his distortion techniques would damage speakers. They would be forced to take him seriously after a typically outlandish recording session (some of the musicians involved didn't even meet their colleagues as they were located elsewhere in the three-storey flat) resulted in 'Johnny Remember Me'. Sung by TV star John Leyton and written by Geoff Goddard (aka Anton Hollywood), the single reached the top of the UK charts in July 1961 after Meek licensed it to Top Rank.

The second massive hit from Holloway Road linked straight back to Meek's earlier experiments and, in particular, his fascination with space travel (its subject was the recently launched AT&T communications satellite). 'Telstar' again reached the top of the UK charts, and was the first single by a British 'band' to reach the top of the US charts. This despite initial concern from Decca, who licensed it, that the recording was technically sub-standard. Sadly, Meek would never receive substantive royalties for the record. A court case, not settled until after Meek's death, was launched by French composer Jean Ledrut claiming that it infringed copyright on his soundtrack to the 1960 film *Austerlitz*.

Thereafter, the chaotic world Meek had built began to fall apart. Smitten by blond star Heinz Burt, he dedicated many of his efforts to securing a pop success for him (finally doing so with 'Just Like Eddie'). He was then arrested and fined for importuning at a toilet in Madras Place, resulting in unwelcome press attention on the front page of the *London Evening News* and eventually an escalating number of blackmail threats from alleged former conquests. All of which pushed Meek further into a vicious cycle of pill-popping and bizarre seances where he would consult the spirit of his father, Buddy Holly and Pharaoh Ramesses The Great of Egypt. There was another number one success with the Honeycombs' Have I The Right', but even that brought a further legal stand-off over disputed authorship and a rupture between him and former ally Goddard. "He got worse when the hits stopped coming," Repsch notes. "He felt he was being elbowed out, and then he thought it was due to being caught messing about in lavatories. They [the majors] didn't want to know him any more. They also got fed up with his floods of tears. He'd take a recording that he'd worked very hard on and it would be dismissed, and he'd break down into tears. They'd say, 'Sorry Joe, there's no market for this.' Sometimes he'd get on to Joseph Lockwood, his knight in shining armour, who looked after him because they were similar in a way; he was gay too. But as the hits stopped he became more and more strange. A weird psychic lady would tell him which days to record and which not. And the drugs he was experimenting with made things worse. He was a hypochondriac. All that loud noise, I don't think that's good for you, either. He once said he had to listen to Ted Heath when he was with Denis Preston – he said it was so loud it made his ears bleed. That control room of his was only 10ft by 10ft, full of spinning tape machines as well, which probably made it more like 3ft by 3ft."

Meek had begun routinely bugging his own studio, so convinced was he that the place was awash with spies stealing his ideas and selling them to other record labels. When Phil Spector came to London and asked if he could pass by Holloway Road to show his appreciation, Meek slammed the phone down on him with such force it broke. On 3 February 1967, exactly eight years after the death of Buddy Holly, following an argument with his landlady Mrs Shenton, almost certainly about unpaid back rent, he discharged a shotgun into her back, killing her, and then turned the gun on himself.

The Meek story is as tragic as it is gripping – he would doubtless have been feted had he been able to overcome his neuroses, which Repsch believes could have happened had suitable psychiatric intervention taken place. But for our purposes it is probably the prime example of the way in which an independent producer could overturn the apple cart. Meek paved the way for the likes of Jonathan King (who also recorded unreleased work with Meek) and Mickie Most. "He showed prospective engineers and producers that they could do it," says Repsch. "You didn't need to hire the Royal Albert Hall, or have a studio the size of Abbey Road – you could do it in your own front room." There is sufficient evidence that the establishment did indeed loathe him, though not nearly to the extent his troubled mind presumed. But for a golden period, what is indisputable is that the majors were so dismayed at the way the charts had been overtaken by an 'amateur' that they came to him for hit singles. Meek took enormous delight in the fact that the 'rotten pigs' were emasculated so, if only for a brief but glorious period. As it was, his life mirrored his art rather too closely. "He wouldn't know when to stop," says Repsch. "He would do things that other people were not prepared to do. He would turn the dial that extra turn. And if it wouldn't turn, he'd get his screwdriver out."

By the mid-60s a new generation of labels were evolving. Continuing the producer as independent hitmaker ethos of the likes of Spector and Gamble and Huff in the US and Meek in the UK, came Chicago native Shel Talmy, who had shared a classroom with Spector. Arriving in London to convince Dick Rowe of Decca that the demo tapes he played of the Beach Boys and Lou Rawls were his own work (they were not), Talmy became a freelance at the label. Regardless of the propriety of his appointment in 1962, Talmy soon rewarded his new employers with a hit record, the Bachelors' 'Charmaine'. And, after a couple of years working on stock pop fodder, he became one of the most celebrated producers in rock via his work with first the Kinks and then the Who. By 1965, inspired by Andrew Loog Oldham's Immediate, he decided to take the plunge and form his own record label, Planet. The idea was to work across the board in terms of genre, to make the imprint a mark of quality rather than style, and to this end he set about recruiting R&B singers, crooners, girl groups and strains of the emergent Mod movement.

It didn't quite pan out that way. The label was extant only from December 1965 to December 1966, failing to enjoy commercial success for any of its 22 singles. He was naïve in signing a contract with Philips that was heavily slanted in their favour, and took his eye off the ball while he continued to work on production for major label artists. That said, there is much to admire about (some of) the releases on Planet – notably the Creation's 'Making Time' and 'Painter Man', the group's name subsequently inspiring one of the great UK independent labels of the 80s and 90s. But when Phillips wouldn't renegotiate the contract, Talmy shut it down.

Strike Records, and its subsidiary Go, with releases by Neil Christian, the Deputies, JJ Jackson and a pre-'Kung Fu Fighting' Carl Douglas, added to the 60s pop dynamic over the course of 35 singles. Established in 1965 by Adrian Jacobs and Lionel Segal out of their publishing company, it hinged on the talents of songwriters Miki Dallon and Pierre Tubbs. The latter was the beneficiary of a bespoke studio installed in his parent's Surrey Garden – two pre-cast concrete garages laid end to end with cork and egg boxes for soundproofing. But distribution was one of Strike's great obstacles. Like Ember before them, they used Lugton's, which operated out of a flat above a shop on Tottenham Court Road. Other attempts were made to overcome distribution problems using the services of Max Factor and Smith's Crisps, while releases were supported with airtime on pirate radio stations. But after the initial success of Neil Christian's 'That's Nice', Strike floundered, as Tubbs and Segal moved on to their next business venture. The first Neil Christian knew about its closure in 1967 was when the tour van he was travelling to Germany in was impounded by bailiffs.

In the legal fallout that followed Strike's dissolution, Dallon launched Young Blood Records with his then lawyer Gerry Black. With distribution via EMI and Beacon, it was better facilitated to succeed than its forerunner. And Dallon this time ensured he would spread his net wider, securing deals and licensing arrangements throughout Europe, to facilitate the growth of the label. Launched in August 1969, with an advance from German label Hansa on condition they had an option on any of his recordings, Dallon deliberately targeted records at the French and German markets, tying up a deal with Eddie Barclay in France in addition to Hansa. Famously he was paid in the currency of onyx ashtrays by one Yugoslavian licensee. "I didn't want to be a pop label," Dallon later told Kieron Tyler, "I thought we can be a bit of a rough diamond R&B label, something different to your run-of-the-mill pop." Yet their first UK hit was Don Farden's tribute to George Best, 'Belfast Boy', in February 1970, though by then Dallon had already enjoyed a handful of European hits. '(The Lament Of The Cherokee) Indian Reservation', recorded with Sorrows' singer Don Farden and already an unexpected success in America after it was licensed to independent GNP Crescendo, finally became a major UK hit when released on Young Blood. It was followed by 'In A Broken Dream' by Python Lee Jackson, fronted by Rod Stewart, which charted in 1972 (two years after it was first released). The label persevered with a bizarre mixture of acts, including Apollo 100, who had a major American hit with 'Joy', their reworking of Bach's 'Jesu, Joy Of Man's Desiring', the rock-operatic Julian's Treatment, who enjoyed surprise popularity in Germany and the incomprehensible Dando Shaft. Other oddities, however, like the glam-influenced Damned (titled prior to Sensible *et al* taking the name in the punk years) fell off everyone's radar, though even Bearded Lady stumbled upon a German hit. Despite scoring a novelty chart success with the awful 'Nice One Cyril', Dallon's interest in Young Blood faded and he departed in 1976. The label struggled on for a few years without ever enjoying the same stature.

But the most important, and most arresting UK independent label of the 60s was the aforementioned Andrew Loog Oldham's Immediate enterprise. Oldham, self-confessed 'godfather of hype', was manager of the Rolling Stones and a man upon who you could comfortably weave a narrative that takes in most of the essentials of the 60s music revolution. He founded Immediate in 1965 alongside Tony Calder, with the focus on the British blues boom as well as R&B, though if anything, the label sound-tracked the Sound Of Swinging London. The ethos was to indulge its artists by giving them free reign to make the 'hippest' records they could – artistry without financial impediment – with results that confirmed the genius and the folly of such an approach. With Mick Jagger and Keith Richard serving as producers (and occasionally songwriters), the label's slogan 'Happy To Be A Part Of The Industry Of Human Happiness' did not seem unduly hyperbolic at one point. However, an enterprise untethered by accountants and obeying only its own internal logic, somewhat waylaid by the fleshpot and pharmaceutical attractions of the time, was ultimately destined to consume itself in an implosion of ego and recrimination.

Among the label's roster of stellar acts were PP Arnold, John Mayall, Savoy Brown, the Small Faces, the Nice, Fleetwood Mac, the Groundhogs and Humble Pie, spanning anything from straight blues-rock to folk, psychedelia and prog. The label was behind dozens of touchstone recordings (notably the Nice's eponymous album, the Small Faces' *Ogden's Nut Gone Flake*, PP Arnold's *The First Lady Of Immediate* etc) until the Small Faces left in 1969 as the debts began to mount. The label closed in 1970 due to financial problems, or alleged impropriety. Kenny Jones of the Small Faces, who claims they didn't receive a fraction of the income due to them for their string of hits, states that much of the money the label generated was spirited away by one of the senior accountants to offshore bank accounts.

Questioned about accusations made in pianist Ian McLagan's book, Oldham would concede that after 1970 there were issues about unpaid royalties, caused by his sale of masters to Patrick Meehan and arrangements with Castle/Sanctuary (the subsequent rights holders). However, he insists that monies owed up to 1970 were faithfully accounted, and the black hole that appeared in the Small Faces' finances were due entirely to their own profligacy.

"Independence?" ponders Loog Oldham now. "Independence in those days was a pipe dream. A pretend game. That said, we still pursued it. It was not even pragmatic. You exchanged a producer/artist royalty, which had the overheads of studio, musicians etc, for a larger royalty and a larger overhead. Seemingly some of the annoyance of dealing with a major record company were removed, but some of the restraints, which in hindsight, sometimes had their blessings, went out of the window as well. At the end of the day, I probably achieved us much independence with Decca and The Rolling Stones and Marianne Faithfull as I did with Immediate and the Small Faces; except that when I was right with Decca, they paid the bill. Please do not think that I look back in anger, or rancour, but if, as Woody Allen once said, cocaine was God's way of telling one that one had too much money, then Immediate was God's way of telling me the same. I love the effect Immediate had on the world of music as much as anyone, but know better than anyone the house of cards upon which it was built. I love the fact that, in the UK at least, a lot of the recordings are life-changers and life-givers but the Woody Allen ode remains the truth. By '65 I too stoned to deal with majors. I was banned from the Decca building because my driver cum minder roughed up a doorman who did not whistle me in fast enough for my speedy ego. By '68 I was banned from the EMI building in Manchester Square for putting sleeping pills in the soup of the reps and salesmen at a sales dinner. EMI by now distributed Immediate, having taken over from Philips, who were headed by Leslie Gould, the man who first did a deal with us and let us 'in'. In any event, we paid all the acts and writers' wages, paid the rent on most of their flats, paid their doctor's bills, etc, and their dealers. And when they only sold so many records and people came along whispering sweet nothings and trying to steal them, most of the acts forgot what we had in fact done, and soon the dream was gone. And without the faith and the dream . . ."

In common with other UK independents, Loog Oldham admits to owing "a great debt to America", and, "in particular Jim Lee and Bob Crewe for the independent idea. To Phil Spector I owe a lot, but not structure. Jim Lee wrote, produced and published the Chris Montez record 'Let's Dance' [a # 4US/# 2UK hit released on Monogram Records]. Whilst doing their PR in '62, he was very gracious with his time and sharing and I learnt a lot. He was also the record company. Bob Crewe produced and sold independent masters and he was also generous with lessons about the game."

Crewe is an interesting example of the independent writer-producer ethos in that in some ways he was almost the polar opposite of Joe Meek. A handsome former model and an effortlessly charismatic man, he charmed all he met. Responsible for the lyrics of classic songs such as 'Can't Take My Eyes Off Of You', 'Lady Marmalade', 'The Sun Ain't Gonna Shine Anymore' and 'Walk Like A Man', he would enjoy enormous success with Frankie Valli and the Four Seasons in the 60s. What is most arresting about Crewe in this context, however, is his early years with former bandleader Frank Slay Jr. They were able to place songs with a number of labels, but feared that the inferior nature of the final recordings would damage their reputation. To that end they decided instead to create their own masters, starting labels to market that product.

"But we were all mad and not entitled to be heads of companies," Loog Oldham concedes. "England had a good history of independent producers, way before Immediate or Track. You had the likes of Joe Meek and Robert Stigwood who had velvet entry into Sir Joseph Lockwood at EMI." Please read into that what you will. "Having John Leyton and his looks helped, I'm sure. Then you had Denis Preston and his Lansdowne studio set-up and his success with Chris Barber and Lonnie Donegan. and the often forgotten great couple of harlots; Michael Barclay and Phillip Waddilove, who had a huge house on Gloucester Place, all built upon the questionable longevity of [sixties pop idol] Eden Kane."

David Platz is the other key figure in the development of an independent aesthetic in British popular music, his influence still evident today, long after his death. By the mid-60s his Essex Music was the dominant independent music company in the UK. It held the publishing of The Rolling Stones, The Who and Marc Bolan, and he had a thriving independent production company that would fund producers on individual projects that would then be licensed to majors. This was generally done through the auspices of a raft of production companies such as Straight Ahead, founded in July 1967, by Platz and South American-born but privately educated English producer Denny Cordell. Instead of artists, Straight Ahead used a roster of producers who would cut master recordings at Trident and other studios, their efforts administered by Platz's publishing offices. Cordell would oversee the music side, while Platz hooked up the various projects with interested major labels, notably Decca's Deram and EMI's Regal Zonophone. Major commercial success resulted via hits by The Move, Procol Harum and The Moody Blues. Meanwhile, those session producers that came through the system included Tony Visconti, who started out as Cordell's production assistant, and Gus Dudgeon, who was producing Elton John.

It was the Platz connection that led to Visconti working with Bolan and David Bowie. Both artists were struggling at the time, though Platz managed to revive the latter's ailing progress by using his publishing connections to encourage other artists to cover his material. "Bowie was still signed to Deram when I was asked to produce him," says Visconti. "Deram didn't like our efforts, 'Let Me Sleep Beside You' and 'Karma

Man', which led to him being dropped. Platz knew nothing of Bowie and Feathers [a temporary congregation featuring Hermione Farthingale and John 'Hutch' Huchinson] until I took them into the studio without his approval or knowledge and recorded the 'Ching A Ling' song and the b-side. Platz was very angry with me. I thought he'd love it once he'd heard it, but that was not the case, and I nearly got fired." In the event, the breakthrough that the Platz/Visconti team were looking for came with Bolan's 'Ride A White Swan'. It was eventually released on Fly Records in October 1970, at which time the single (credited to T-Rex) became a number two hit in the UK charts.

There was a nice line of continuity with its indie forerunner Immediate. When Loog Oldham's label sundered, Fly acquired its stock of distinctive lilac labels. Building on his breakthrough, Bolan then piloted T-Rex to huge album success with *Electric Warrior*, which topped the British charts. Fly's success with T-Rex was followed by releases from Joe Cocker, John Williams, Third World War and Vivian Stanshall. However, Fly's brief ascendancy concluded with the release of Georgia Brown's non-charting 'I Scare Myself'. Label manager Malcolm Jones departed, as did Cordell (to form Shelter Records in the US). The label changed name to Cube, and was home to artists including Bolan, Cocker, Budgie and others), with pop chart success for John Kongos, Joan Armatrading, Gordon Giltrap etc. There was also a selection of Pete Cook and Dudley Moore's *Not Only... But Also* TV shows released on *The Clean Tapes*.

Alongside Immediate, the other most notorious 60s independent in the UK was Track Records, founded by Who managers Kit Lambert, once famously described as an 'aristocratic hothead', and Chris Stamp, brother of actor Terence. They were an interesting partnership. Lambert, an Oxford graduate and son of composer Constant Lambert, could hardly have offered more of a contrast to Stamp, son of an east end tug boatman. Their initial problem was in extricating The Who from their contract with Shel Talmy and Brunswick, which went to court. As an interim measure, they had released Who material on Robert Stigwood's Reaction Records, started a year previously. Stigwood, an ex-pat Australian entrepreneur, is inextricably linked with so many other aspects of the music industry's development – he had John Leyton on his books as an actor at the time of his success with Joe Meek, which convinced him there was potential in Meek's model of the independent producer. He would also initially sub-let office space to Lambert and Stamp, who legendarily teased him mercilessly.

Talmy, speaking to Ritchie Unterberger, gave some insight into the way the duo announced themselves to the world. "My problems with The Who were with Kit Lambert, who was out of his fucking mind – I think he was certifiably insane. If he hadn't been in the music business, he would have been locked up. The problem with him was his giant-sized ego plus paranoia. He felt I was usurping his authority because I was producing these [Who] recordings. His partner, Chris Stamp, was hardly ever around. I always got along with Chris, I thought. But Chris never said a word." Track became an outlet for The Who, but also a nursery for the emerging talent of Jimi Hendrix (after Chas Chandler had beaten them to a management contract). Both Track and Reaction were dependent on Polydor Records in the absence of any independent distribution network; part of an experiment in Polydor developing its claim on the emerging 60s pop phenomenon, having previously been best known as an easy listening and orchestral specialist.

Track can lay claim to having released possibly the greatest opening salvo of rock singles – a sequence that ran 'Purple Haze' (Hendrix), 'Pictures Of Lily' (the Who), 'Desdemona' (John's Children) and 'The Wind Cries Mary' (Hendrix) – at the start of 1967. These were accompanied by albums including *Are You Experienced?* And *The Who Sell Out* all in the same year. Though it was impossible to maintain that level of aural splendour, the label continued through the 70s, working with acts such as Crazy World Of Arthur Brown and Thunderclap Newman. However, an inability to diversify away from The Who and Hendrix saw them stall, especially after Hendrix's death and The Who's move to Polydor following *Quadrophenia*. The latter came about when the band discovered gaping holes in the accountancy at the label, with concomitant tax issues. Group members had also become alarmed by Lambert's rapidly advancing alcoholism. It resulted in a writ served in July 1975, which brought the onset of a two-year legal tussle. That left the label with just Golden Earring on its books during that period. Track finally closed in March 1978 – ironically a year after it released the Heartbreakers *L.A.M.F.*, a harbinger of the punk boom, but an album Track effectively signed up for as a last throw of the dice with their creditors circling.

Track made a concerted effort, as best as their sensibilities and finances allowed, to garner a foothold with punk, placing adverts for new bands in *Sniffin' Glue*. As author Marcus Gray would recount, "Lambert played for time by using The Who's name to secure a bank loan of £56,000, but when Leee [Black Childers; Heartbreakers manager] approached Track, time was about to run out. A manic looking Christ Stamp seemed enthusiastic about the idea, seeing it as a last desperate lifeline. The contract that Stamp presented to Leee and business manager Peter Gerber offered a £50,000 advance – coincidentally almost exactly what Lambert had borrowed." Under the guidance of Malcolm McLaren's assistant Nils Stevenson, Siouxsie & The Banshees would record demos for Track, though Stevenson was aware of the situation at Track and quickly circulated the paid-for demos among other labels. When Track finally went phut, Childers arranged to have the offices broken into to secure the master tapes from the hands of the Official Receiver (they were released by Jungle in 1984, in remixed form). Lambert died just three years later. The label has now been revived under the guidance of former Stranglers, Cult and Big Country manager Ian Grant. Stamp, meanwhile, is a psychotherapist specialising in addiction.

The biggest UK independent record label of them all, until it was sold to PolyGram in 1989, was Island Records, originally founded in Jamaica in 1959 by Chris Blackwell and Graeme Goodall. Richard Branson, proprietor of nearest competitor Virgin, has openly acknowledged that Island was the model on which he based his own enterprise. Blackwell, the son of wealthy plantation owning Jamaican parents, named his label in tribute to Alec Waugh's novel *Island In The Sun*. Laurel Aitken's 'Boogie In My Bones' gave him his first hit, topping the Jamaican charts for 11 weeks. His first album release, jazz pianist Lance Heywood's *At The Half Moon Hotel*, was given the catalogue number CB 22 – Blackwell was 22 years old at the time. At this stage, Blackwell maintained, he was only thinking in terms of a handful of releases documenting the Jamaican ska era and not building a global brand.

In May 1962 he moved to London and took out a loan with the specific intention of providing a bridge to the UK for Jamaican artists. Renting a house from Church Of England Commissioners, he piled imported Jamaican records into the back of his Mini Cooper and made daily trips around London record shops. He also supplied sound systems in the bustling ex-pat Afro-Caribbean strongholds of Brixton and Notting Hill. Karlo Kramer at *Esquire* magazine gave him a list of 20 stores specialising in black music to set him on his way. Spooky Tooth (then called Art) and Stevie Winwood's Traffic were the first major white artists to come on board once Blackwell took the decision to diversify the label in 1967, with the assistance of Steve's brother Muff Winwood. He had already had Winwood's Spencer Davis Group on his books, but licensed their hits to Fontana. At the time, he didn't believe he had the wherewithal to take them to market.

By the start of the 70s, Island had become the leading 'prog rock' label, enjoying huge commercial success with King Crimson, Emerson Lake &

Palmer, Free and Jethro Tull, and also, through producer Joe Boyd, the folk rock of Nick Drake and Fairport Convention. John Martyn and Cat Stevens were even more successful. In 1972 Roxy Music were signed, also yielding to solo Bryan Ferry and Brian Eno albums. But it was the breakthrough of defining artist Bob Marley, originally as a member of the Wailers, which returned the label to its Jamaican roots. In the process Island had "a black rock star as big as Jimi Hendrix", according to Blackwell's own rhetoric, promoted in the manner of mainstream white rock acts. Despite warnings that Marley was an untamed ghetto child, Blackwell invested £4,000 to finance the recording of The Wailers' *Catch A Fire*. His sponsorship of Marley broadened the British musical landscape and legitimised a musical idiom Island was uniquely placed to profit from. As well as being the most popular artist on the label's roster, Marley's breakthrough helped highlight a generation of Jamaican acts, many of whom had already recorded for the label in the 60s, but found interest renewed, as well as indigenous UK reggae groups, notably Aswad and Steel Pulse.

While Virgin prospered in the punk years, Island was more hesitant, counting only the Slits among its major discoveries, and even they were signed after protracted inner discussion (though that band's intuitive connection to reggae was, with hindsight, self-evident). Outside reggae, the label's major acts were Grace Jones and Robert Palmer. But as punk's cannons cooled, Blackwell signed U2 in 1980, unarguably the most commercially arable seeding of post-punk guitar rock. By the mid-80s U2's laborious ascent to the self-mythologised position of biggest rock band in the world had begun in earnest. In the meantime, however, Island, wrong-footed by punk, had lost some of its commercial momentum (Marley died in May 1981). Blackwell used the label as collateral to leverage Island Alive, a film distribution company. In fact, U2 were partially responsible for refunding the label. In an astute piece of business, U2 provided Island with a loan, offset by their right to buy back their master recordings and enjoy a much higher royalty rate.

In July 1989 Island was sold to PolyGram for $272 million, ending their era of independence (though by this time definitions of independence had, by popular assent, extended to means of distribution, which Island had long since routed through a succession of majors including Capital, Warners, Atlantic and Phonogram). The deal was overseen by lawyer Allen Grubman, who also handled the $295 million acquisition of publishing house SBK by Thorn-EMI, and EMI's $75 million acquisition of 50% of Chrysalis Records just a couple of months later. It was a period of intense consolidation, triggered by Sony's February 1988 $2bn acquisition of CBS Records at a hugely inflated price. And it wasn't the end of it; in September 1989 Sony also acquired A&M for $460 million and in November 1990 Matsushita bought out MCA.

It's perhaps telling to relate a tale from the board meetings that took place around the time of these transitions. One senior management figure at Island, who wished to remain anonymous, recalls being told that, henceforth, artists would only be paid mechanical royalties if they came after the new-look label with a lawyer. PolyGram, meanwhile, began a major reissue campaign, converting the Island back catalogue to compact disc. The Island Records of the 21$^{st}$ century is little more than a rubber stamp for PolyGram, Blackwell having long since fled, resigning officially in November 1997. Just over a year later, it was part of the Seagram take-over of PolyGram that saw it merged into Universal Music Group, where it currently resides, a meek shadow of its former glory.

Another stain on Island's reputation – and that of U2's – followed the hideous court case against art mavericks Negativland, which occurred while Blackwell was still at the helm. In 1991 Negativland issued its 'U2' record, featuring samples of a recording by America's Top 40 host, Casey Kasem; the band's logo displayed in large type on the packaging. The music was based on parodies of 'I Still Haven't Found What I'm Looking For', with kazoos used to deconstruct the sampled original. Kasem's rant ("These guys are from England and who gives a shit?"), drawn from a fraught rehearsal, was the real motivation behind the collage. In the run-up to the release of *Achtung Baby*, Island's lawyers issued writs against the band for violation of trademark and copyright law. Negativland were forced to settle out of court on the basis that they could not afford to defend the action. Had they done so, the band still believes, they would have established a new precedent for fair use. But this was a case where those with the financial resources rather than the moral high ground dictated events. Negativland maintained (most famously in an interview with *Mondo* magazine where they were able, via a little chicanery, to question U2's guitarist The Edge) that they had been given no opportunity to withdraw the offending release. They also made the perfectly legitimate claim that U2 themselves had glorified indiscriminate copyright infraction by playing a series of clips from satellite TV stations when they set up their Zoo TV tour.

Island pushed for costs, which covered the efforts of an expensive legal team. The fallout meant that SST, one of America's most distinguished independent labels (though not one that has been removed from harsh criticism itself from the artists it has worked with for non-payment of royalties, including several notable court cases), went into a tailspin. The term 'pro bono' has rarely taken on such conceptual duality. Moreover, the incident was testament to the extent to which the Island brand had become an avaricious entity, in thrall to corporate concerns, and incapable of recognising the validity of 'art' outside of the money chain.

And yet, certainly in the 70s, it would be a mistake to underplay the role of Island Records in establishing the foundations for an independent label culture – both in terms of its A&R reputation and its pioneering work in logistics. "Chris Blackwell was the role model for a lot of people," states Richard Scott, then manager of reggae act Third World, and later head of Rough Trade Distribution. "If you think about what they achieved, not only did they have their own distribution, but they did their own manufacturing too; they had their own pressing plant and reps round the country. Island is *much* more important than Virgin. Island did all of Virgin's distribution, and Branson knows nothing about music. Blackwell does. When Third World signed to Island in '75, I spent a lot of time with Chris. I can remember a day we spent talking about whether he should drop Virgin. I spent another day talking to him about whether he should drop Roxy Music! He was using me as a sounding board. But I learnt a lot about the distribution business and how things worked through Chris."

There is no more justifiably loved figure in the evolution of independent music than BBC disc jockey John Peel. Always a fierce but mostly intuitive advocate of the outsider, without his patronage this book would not exist. As an adjunct to his eyrie at the Beeb, he began the Dandelion label in 1969, alongside Clive Selwood, to offer an outlet for artists he liked who lacked any other means of exposure. Yet the part that Selwood played in the development of 'Peel's Dandelion Records' is often overlooked. Trevor Midgley, aka label artist Beau, traces that back to the development of American independent Elektra and its forerunners. "In the mid-60s, Jac Holzman [Elektra's founder] took the key decision to diversify and re-focus the catalogue. In came the Doors, Love, Carly Simon *et al*, and away went Theodore Bikel, Tom Paxton, Phil Ochs and the rest of the troubadours. Jac also launched the highly successful Nonesuch classical label to run alongside Elektra. At just this changeover point, the man who was charged with promoting the new Elektra/Nonesuch identity in Europe was Clive Selwood. When Dandelion was conceived in 1968, I don't think John or Clive were consciously trying to produce an Elektra Mk. II. And of course, in the event, Dandy had neither the artist roster nor the longevity of Elektra.

However, it is interesting that even with its limited number of signings, in its three years Dandelion issued folk, art-rock, old-time rock 'n' roll, hard rock, proto-punk grunge, psych-folk, avant-garde jazz, and classical albums, plus sets in a couple of other genres that even now are tricky to categorise. Without John's inquisitive and restless musical mind, none of this would have come about. But I'm also sure that Clive's years of involvement with Elektra made him the perfect partner for Mr Peel. Extreme diversity within a label might be new in the UK, but it wasn't strange to Clive. In a slightly different way, he'd seen it done before."

Dandelion's name came from one of Peel's pet hamsters (as did the allied publishing business, Biscuit), at the suggestion of his then flatmate Marc Bolan. The label effectively exhibited his personal tastes. As well as attempting to revive Gene Vincent's career, it released material by new artists including Beau, Medicine Head, Bridget St John, Clifford T. Ward, Stack Waddy, Tractor and Kevin Coyne (with his original band, Siren) amongst others.

Medicine Head provided the label with its only hit single, 1971's '(And The) Pictures In The Sky', which reached 22 in the charts (although Beau's '1917 Revolution' had topped the charts in the Lebanon a couple of years previously). While commercial returns were never a motivating factor, a respectable level of sales were required to keep the ship afloat. The label was successively distributed by CBS, Warner Brothers and Polydor, but closed its doors in 1973 when the latter deal ceased. The eventual loss of support from the major labels was, according to Midgley, inevitable. "The Dandelion ethos was at a tangent to the mainline record industry of the time. John's name and reputation were vital when it came to getting CBS, Kinney [for a brief period the holding company for Warners] and Polydor to play ball, but there really was a culture clash which in the end could only have one result. But by the time the plug was finally pulled on Dandelion, foundations had been laid and blueprints established for future independents to take up the baton. As we now know, many did, with a vengeance."

Dandelion released 28 albums and a dozen singles that, collectively, evade easy classification. There's no doubt that Peel was somewhat dismayed by the way some of the artists on the label expected more than he had resources to provide. Speaking to me in 1991, he obliquely referenced this, when I asked if he tended to avoid music that was pompous or the result of overly inflated ego. "Yes, that's right. I always find it quite laughable, really. It doesn't irritate me. There might have been a time when it would have

done, but now it just seems to me to be comic. Nobody's that important.
I suppose it's one of the aspects of the 'rock' industry that I've always
disliked. I've disliked it for lots of reasons, in that in the past it's removed
some very good friends from my orbit. In that they've become 'rock stars',
and they start to live such a bizarre life, through no fault of their own. Most
of them are not particularly bright, and they're surrounded by people
whose jobs depend on telling them how wonderful they are – so that they
lose all touch with reality."

"Whether John was sanguine about things that were going down, I can't
say," admits Midgley. "What I can say is Peely loved to please, and didn't like
aggression or confrontation. If frustrations ever turned into argument, I can't
think he'd have found that agreeable. I personally didn't have an issue [over
promotion], because I knew Dandelion didn't have bottomless coffers. I also
appreciated John's position at the Beeb, and of course I had another career
outside music. I never had reason to discuss lack of promotion with either
John or Clive because, quite honestly, I had enough on balancing the
demands of two careers as it was."

Nowadays Dandelion is remembered as one of the ultimate cult labels but,
as Midgley suggests, it would be a mistake to simply consider it 'Peel's
indulgence'. "To characterise Dandelion [in that way] would be to
misunderstand a basic – and revolutionary – tenet of the label; that of artist
control. In giving control of the recording process to those of us on the label,
John and Clive sowed seeds, the fruits of which others would later reap in
spades. It's no coincidence, for example, that Richard Branson launched
Virgin Records almost as Dandy exited the scene. Richard had that one
tremendous slice of luck when one of his artists – Mike Oldfield – broke very,
very big. If he'd been asked (and I don't know that he ever was!), I'm sure
John would have attributed Branson's success with Mike and *Tubular Bells* to
the promo budget Virgin was able to muster. Not to put too fine a point on it,
Dandelion promoted on a shoestring, and John's privileged position at the
Beeb was only of limited benefit when it came to pushing Dandy and its
artists. Though as I've said at another time and place, 'the simple fact that
John was associated with (Dandelion) gave the label a stamp – not just
credibility, but also the cachet that a lot of people felt about Peel himself. It
was quality stuff Peel would have played on his *'Perfumed Garden.'*"

Midgley remains convinced, too, that the label's legacy should include an
acknowledgement of the soundness of Peel's tastes. "Personally, I always
thought the David Bedford and Lol Coxhill discs were both adventurous and

brave. This was the sort of stuff you mostly picked up on scholarly labels like Deutsche Grammophon; yet here they were, happily sitting alongside the rock offerings of Stack Waddy and Tractor and folkies such as myself and Bridget St John. For me, David's and Lol's releases epitomised the eclectic nature of Dandelion. They still do. All that said, I believe the greatest album to come out of Dandelion on so many levels – the one that will endure – is Kevin Coyne's *Case History*. Quirky, soulful, heartbreakingly honest, I don't think Kevin ever bettered it. That record just couldn't have been made by any of the 'corporates' of the day. Many have said Dandelion was a great A&R resource for other labels. Indeed it was. And some of the music was truly innovative, deserving its place in the discography of the greats. Then there's the spirit. Yes, it should be remembered for that. Dandelion was born out of John's personal ideal, which was a kind of delightful (if naïve) confidence that if you produce something worthwhile, the world will beat a path to your door. But most of all, Dandelion was a trail-blazer. It wasn't recognised as such at the time. But in the light of all that followed, Dandelion's influence is plain. Without Dandy, the great British independent labels of the 70s and 80s would have had a very different look; if, that is, they would have existed at all."

If Midgley makes the case convincingly that Virgin Records was influenced by Dandelion, the contrast between the two labels' founders is acute. It's hard to disassociate the rise of Virgin Records from its founder and relentless publicist Richard Branson, one of Britain's most celebrated wealth-creators. The son of a barrister, and a veteran of *Student Magazine*, he established Virgin Records as a mail order chain, then retail outlet, alongside his second cousin, music buff Simon Draper. Virgin's logo featured naked twins designed by Roger Dean, the centre-hole in the record placed between the crossed legs of the girl. It was a concept built on the casual misogyny of the era, but indicative of the boy's club mentality Virgin embraced. After purchasing the Manor studio complex for £20,000, the label simultaneously released four albums on 25 May 1973 – Gong's *The Flying Teapot*, a compilation of improvised music by friends including Robert Palmer and Elkie Brooks titled *The Manor Live*, Faust's *Faust Tapes* and, most significantly, Mike Oldfield's *Tubular Bells*. The latter would clock up sales of over five million. It established Virgin as a commercial force, even though the notoriously publicity-shy Oldfield proved hard to handle – the sole live appearance he made at the Queen Elizabeth Hall only came about after Branson promised him keys to a brand new Bentley. That early release schedule was an enterprising mix of traditional hippy fare (Gong), Oldfield's extended arias, some messing about in the studio and Krautrock. And instantly there was much about the roster that reflected the 'everything goes' times – Faust once picked up a labourer from the roadside and installed him, on lead pneumatic drill, as an attraction at that evening's show.

Subsequent prominent Virgin artists included Robert Wyatt, Ivor Cutler, jazz saxophonist Lol Coxhill, Kevin Coyne and Henry Cow – significantly, souls cast overboard when the good ship Dandelion hit the rocks. They also signed Captain Beefheart from America, alongside the likes of Link Wray and Yellow Dog. For a time Virgin was the *de facto* home for mavericks, left-field progressives and those who'd arrived too late for the 60s but fully endorsed its creed. But the transformation of Virgin from hippy bastion to the label with by far the most influential cast of punk characters was radical, and affirmation of Branson's ability to shift gears. Of course, they lucked out on the crown princes the Sex Pistols, by dint of having the patience and fearlessness that it took to sign them in the brimstone days of 1977. So it was that, after the chairman of EMI got cold feet, Virgin upturned the jubilee crockery with the release of 'God Save The Queen'. WH Smith left a blank at number two in their chart survey, and insiders are credited with ensuring the record did not overtake Rod Stewart's 'The First Cut Is The Deepest' in the week of the festivities. It was followed by the release of *Never Mind The Bollocks* as the media fires were fanned further by a court case over the linguistic nuances of the title. Yet Virgin also prospered as a home to a clutch of punk/new wave groups beyond the Pistols, including the Ruts, Skids, XTC, Members, Penetration etc, and later Magazine and Lydon's Public Image Limited in the post-punk era. There was no finer catalogue assembled in the period.

Many of the punk set were nevertheless signed to contracts in which royalties were cross-collateralised against dubious recording expenses. XTC, the Ruts and Penetration have all countered that they were badly informed and exploited. There are members of XTC, in particular, who are given to bouts of near psychosis whenever mention of their original contract with Virgin is made. It took a seven-year 'artist strike' to extricate themselves from that deal (though that has similarities with the situation that another punk-era legend, Joe Strummer, found himself in with CBS). It doesn't seem outlandish to speculate that a subliminal mistake was made by many artists in thinking that the new age/new look 'independents', especially the affable hippies at Virgin, had their interests at heart any more than the old school did. "I think that it was definitely the public schoolboy mentality that they shared," notes Poly Styrene, who was briefly signed to the company with X-Ray Spex, "that the artists were the workers and that is just the way it is. You work for peanuts and make the boss rich. But artists on music labels didn't get the same protection as workers, in terms of pensions etc., because they have supposedly entered into a business deal."

Others, like Bruce Findlay, formerly head of Scottish independent label Zoom and manager of Simples Minds, counters that Virgin simply employed the same tactics as everyone else, albeit under hippy camouflage. "Simon Draper is the best A&R guy I've ever worked with. It's like any record label. If they're into you, they're the best label in the world. If they're not, or they fall out with you or go cold on you, they're the worst record label in the world. My experience of Virgin was nothing but pleasure. Virgin were as good to me during the 80s, as Island had been as a retailer in the 60s or 70s. I got very close to Virgin – but then we sold 20 or 30 million albums for them, so of course they liked us!"

As for the cross-collateral approach. "EMI, Warner Bros, they all did that, all record labels," says Findlay. "To be honest, Virgin were a wee bit like that. When I did the deal with Richard Branson, I had two different deals on the table. EMI and Polydor were both after Simple Minds, and I'd managed to split with Arista and we were free. Richard's deal was very good, but not quite as good as the Polydor deal, but I liked them. I said to Richard, 'Your deal's not as good as Polydor's, there are a couple of points I don't like. You say we have to use your studio, I'm not doing it. We're NOT using your studio. Put it this way, Richard, we *might* use your studio, we *might* use the Manor.' Richard was being business-like, he was saying, 'I want to recoup, there's more than one way of recouping. If we're going to spend a fortune on recording, I'd rather our recording studio was making the money. So let's have the best recording studio. If songs are going to get published, let's see if we can get our company to do the publishing.' But all the record companies did that. That expression – cross-collateralisation – until that period, as a manager, I hadn't heard of that before, but I was learning quickly. There's a terrible naivete about bands who say, 'You got us into expensive studios. Why did you not say no?' Why did *you* accept the expensive studio? Why did *you* accept the expensive director to make your videos? Why did *you* accept the expensive photographer? Why did *you* never question the cost?" Presumably because of the naivete Findlay alludes to. "Well, their managers should not be naïve. As bands get more sophisticated and managers became more sophisticated, they got to know better. I'm being defensive of Virgin, because I don't think they were any better or worse. I can tell you horrible stories about independents."

Virgin continued to prosper through the auspices of Phil Collins, Culture

Club and Human League as the eighties dawned, but in 1985, a private placing of 7% of convertible stock with 25 English and Scottish institutions prefaced the company's flotation a year later. This saw all Virgin's musical, retail and property assets become public property, thereby ending any pretence to independence. Over 100,000 private investors applied for shares in a company that now employed in excess of 4,000 people, with an annual turnover of close to £200 million. "In many ways going public was an attractive option," Branson recalled in his autobiography. "It would enable Virgin to raise money which we could invest in new subsidiaries. It would swell our balance sheet and so enable us to enjoy more freedom from the banks and use our expanded capital base to borrow more if we wished. It would enable me to issue shares, which they could easily trade, as incentives to the Virgin staff. It would increase Virgin's profile; and a thought lurking at the back of my mind was that, in due course. It would enable us to use the Virgin shares as currency to make a bid for Thorn-EMI, the largest record label in the country."

While Branson's ambitions to take over EMI never came to fruition, it is remarkable that an independent label founded only just over a decade previously was able to contemplate such a take-over. Moreover, however, Branson's reasoning displays a mind focused on the balance sheet. Music is ranked alongside shop premises and bricks and mortar in these exchanges. And that was surely always the nature of the beast, meaning that, while the company's founding principles were certainly rooted in 'independence', music merely served as a product line with the end goal of being the biggest lion in the jungle. But Branson has never denied his indifference to music. "I'm more cynical than 99 per cent of the people who work for Virgin," he told Paul Rampali of *The Face* in 1984. "Simon [Draper] loves records and his whole involvement is through that. With me it's different. It's not a love of music. I enjoy people, I enjoy working with friends, I like finding out about new things, new areas I know nothing about."

Were labels like Virgin truly independent? For many they were not. As Fredric Dannen would write in *Hit Men*, "For nearly a decade, the notion of the independent label had been largely a myth. By the eighties, a better term for record companies such as Chrysalis, A&M, Island, Virgin and the like would have been 'dependent' labels – dependent on one of the six majors for their distribution and, in a number of cases, manufacturing".

"Island and Virgin were originally independent, depending on your definition," reflects Branson's one-time assistant, David Marlow. "They were privately owned, medium-sized record labels, but very iconic. They ceased to be perceived as independent only because they were successful. I was thinking about Paul Conroy at Stiff Records and people like that, who ended up working for the majors, who were from the small labels ethos, and essentially they were record fans. You could certainly say that of Simon Draper and Chris Blackwell. While some of the acts that Simon signed were commercial and pragmatic, that wasn't always the case. I was always a Henry Cow fan. Who else would have signed them? I suppose they thought they were plugging into the hippy market, but I think Simon was a genuine Henry Cow fan. And his personal tastes extended to ECM Records and all that sort of stuff, which he licensed at one point."

One of the important 'linking' labels to the subsequent late 70s boom was Oval, founded by Gillett in 1972, though it didn't release its first record until two years later. It used Virgin's infrastructure initially, though that "felt different from if you'd been with EMI or Decca or whatever," Gillett states. "Although Virgin were substantial, they themselves at that point were distributed through Island. We were basically piggy-backing on other companies. We put out an album of Louisiana music called *Another Saturday Night* which had a track called 'Promised Land' by Johnny Allen. It got played a lot on Capital and was quite inspirational to people like Nick Lowe, who just loved its rock 'n' roll innocence – it had a bit of accordion in the middle of it which made it sound quite unusual."

The origins of Oval say much about how little anyone knew about the process of starting a record label in the mid-70s. "I was on the radio at that point, just starting to do *Honky Tonk* on Radio London, playing a lot of American music, mostly on independent labels. And a friend of mine asked how do you start an independent label? At the time, it seemed a bit of an unfair question. 'Well, I don't know exactly.' 'Well, if you did start one, what would you put on it?' And at the time there wasn't any British group I was particularly interested in, or British groups that were looking for a home. My instinct immediately went to American music, and although most of it was available in this country, Louisiana music wasn't. We actually went across a lot of America, looking at all sorts of doo-wop labels and different stuff, but when we came home and listened to everything, this definitely stood out as being the best idea, and it hung together as a compilation. It did pick up some interest. Eventually we probably met everyone who bought the album – it did sell 10,000 in the end, but in the early days it sold about 2,000 or 3,000. We ourselves felt it was so good that it was very frustrating never to be able to work out how to sell more. I knew hardly anybody in the industry and I didn't know what to do. There wasn't an independent distributor, or not that I knew of. So it didn't really seem possible just manufacturing a record and putting it out – how the hell were you going to get it into any shops? So having tried one or two labels that I knew, they shrugged their shoulders and said we don't know what to do with it, we got side-tracked by seeing Kilburn & The High Roads and becoming very impressed with them and becoming their managers, and finding a record deal for them."

The Kilburns connection would establish the link to Dave Robinson, Paul Conroy (who booked the band through the Charisma agency) and Stiff. "Of course, the whole thing was, you need an artist to play live to sell records," says Gillett. "I was quite naive in those days and didn't quite appreciate it wasn't enough to put out a good record – you didn't need a campaign exactly, but you definitely needed an artist to work on your behalf, or on behalf of the record they've made. We didn't run across anyone who quite met that brief until Lene Lovich came to us. We were very impressed by her and put together a group, which included her playing saxophone originally, in a band led by Jimmy O'Neill. Eventually we persuaded her to sing and took a demo to Stiff, who had been going for a year or two by then."

Another important link to Stiff came through Gillett's early advocacy of Elvis Costello. "Elvis just posted me a tape that I played on the radio. And I really, really liked it a lot. But I didn't get much feedback from listeners. For Elvis, this was by far the most positive reaction he'd had so far. If we'd had musicians to hand, we'd have got together and made a record with him. But we didn't. So we then ran off to Stiff and they put Nick Lowe and an American band together and put them into Pathway [Studios]. That was what made us think, fuck, we really do need our own set of musicians, so if that happened again, we'd be ready. Jimmy O'Neill was writing terrific songs, but we weren't quite convinced about him as a singer at the time, although he did eventually form the Silencers, after Fingerprintz, who did quite well."

"We had a lot of tapes we'd take to Dave Robinson," Gillett continues, "and he'd turn them down flat, except for Lene. But those tapes we'd then take to A&M, and Derek Reid said, 'Well, I don't know about your tapes, and I definitely don't like that girl singer, but I like you guys, let's do a deal.' So we had a label production deal with A&M for exactly a year, parallel to having Lene at Stiff. At the end of that we just decided we wanted to be a proper indie on our own, and we put out a couple of records. One was a group called Local Heroes SW9, whose guitarist Kevin Armstrong remains one of the greatest talents I've ever known." Oval also worked with Harry Kakoulli, Squeeze's bass player, while running a Monday night residency at the jokingly titled 101 Club in Clapham Junction, which resulted in the submission of demo tapes and eventual releases by Holly & The Italians and the Reluctant Stereotypes. These records were now distributed by Rough Trade and Spartan. "We actually launched the newly, properly independent Oval with an album called *The Honky Tonk Demos*, literally demos sent into my show on BBC London, which I'd done right up till the end of 1978. Most famously, I played the demo of 'Sultans Of Swing' by Dire Straits, and they let me have the original demo for that – which hadn't otherwise come out."

Although Oval's output was limited, thematically it provided a link to the next generation of punk-era independents that is more instructive than any comparison with Island or Virgin Records. Not least because Gillett's diligent first-hand research into the American R&B independents briefly discussed here would prove to have an enormous impact on the foundation of the first true punk-era UK independent, Chiswick Records.

Dansette

## Chapter Two

## Gatecrashers

## Chiswick and Ace Records

Ex-bank teller Ted Carroll first established a Saturday record stall in 1971. Rock On, sited on Golborne Road, off Ladbroke Grove market in West London, sold vintage vinyl from labels such as Top Rank, London and Sue. Its proprietor had picked up a copy of Charlie Gillett's *The Sound Of The City* while in America, using it as a road map to classic early rock 'n' roll and doo-wop records. With the rock 'n' roll revival in full swing in the mid-70s, he found himself able to run a brisk business alongside his management duties with Thin Lizzy, shortly to enjoy huge success with 'Whiskey In The Jar'. Indeed, Lizzy, whom Carroll had first brought to London in 1971, would usually close their sets with 'The Rocker'. It was a eulogy to customers at Carroll's stall ("I love to rock and roll / I get my records from the Rock On stall / Sweet rock and roll / Teddy boy, he's got them all"). Among other notable regular clients of 'The Rocker' were Malcolm McLaren and United Artists' Andrew Lauder, who would buy up old psych records and trade them for imports with Greg Shaw of Bomp! Records in the States. Carroll also imported French editions of singles, which were notable for having picture sleeves, then a rarity in Britain.

One Rock On regular was journalist Richard Williams. "I knew Richard well because he was the editor of *Melody Maker* for a while," remembers Carroll, "then he got head-hunted by Chris Blackwell, and went to work at Island as an A&R guy. It was around that time he was coming into the stall and buying records, doing a bit of lurking like everyone else. He became interested in Thin Lizzy, which I found a bit odd. I believed in them and all, but they didn't seem to be an Island band really. And there was a guy called David Betteridge, Blackwell's partner, he was more or less running Island at that stage because Chris was doing other things. They wanted to sign Thin Lizzy and in the end they didn't because other people at Island thought Thin Lizzy weren't right for them. David took myself and [co-manager of Thin Lizzy] Chris Morrison out for lunch at an Italian restaurant in Notting Hill, to tell us that they'd decided they weren't going to sign Thin Lizzy after this flurry of interest. And this at a stage where we'd been turned down by every record company in town, and we were hanging on for a deal with Decca, who we didn't really want to re-sign with."

Betteridge had an ulterior motive, or at least some sugar for the pill. "He took us out and asked us if we'd be interested in managing any of the Island acts, because we seemed good or honest or whatever, or maybe good management was hard to find. We said maybe. We went down and met a singer-songwriter who did a couple of albums for Island. Nice guy, but we didn't hit it off and we weren't that impressed with his music. That was the end of that. So David went off and started a new label, and later signed Haysi Fantayzee. Chris Morrison remained good friends with him, though they didn't do any business. Just as I quit managing Thin Lizzy and got out of the partnership with Chris Morrison, Dave brought us John Cale. So Chris Morrison and Chris O'Donnell managed John Cale for about two years. That was very hard work! I used to hear wonderful stories. I remember going to the office one day. Soho Market stall was just around the corner from our old office at 55 Dean Street, and they were there for quite a few years. They'd just had a phone call from some irate landlord, who had a small prestige development of half a dozen flats in West London, where John was living with his wife. Anyway John had had some disagreement with Tony Secunda over a proposed management deal or something and Secunda had someone go round to this block of flats and spray-paint in six-feet letters, 'OWN UP, CUNT!' So they had to get someone to go round and clean it off, pronto, to stop John getting kicked out. That was just one little incident of many."

Thereafter Carroll dedicated himself to the world of retail, deciding that the path of rock 'n' roll management really wasn't for him. By the summer of 1974 he had opened up his second premises in Soho Market in Newport Court. He briefly employed Thin Lizzy tour manager Frank Murray to look after the stall, before hiring old friend Roger Armstrong, himself an ex-manager of Horslips, and former social secretary at Belfast's Queen's University.

"I met Ted through Gaye and Terry Woods, after they had left Steeleye Span," Armstrong recalls. "I'd booked the Woods Band while I was social secretary at Queen's from '69 through to '72. We got on really well. They said, 'When you're in London, look us up.' I rang Gaye and Terry from the phone box outside the Kensington, which was one of the big pub rock places. 'You said give you a ring!' Normally people say, well, we're busy at the moment. But instead they said, 'Oh, we'd love to see you, come over!' So I wandered over one day. It was one of those big five or six storey houses in Belsize Avenue, where everyone had a room. There was Frank Murray, who went on to manage The Pogues, there was Gary Moore and Eric Bell. And Ted was there, and he managed Thin Lizzy at the time. Neither Ted nor I can remember if we met, but I think Ted came up when I booked Thin Lizzy in Belfast. And we got on really well. He had this kind of spare sofa bed at the end of his long, thin room, and I slept on this construction he had above the kitchenette. I was slumming around staying on sofas."

At this time, Armstrong had only come to London on vacation. "I was still at college. I was coming to London in those days to book bands. Don't forget, the war had started in Belfast, so that wasn't easy – persuading people to come over. And the reason a lot of people did come over was because we were paying much better money than they were getting in the pubs. We had a good reputation for paying out, and we put a circuit together. Between us we could pay for transport, for the boat over, and their petrol and hotel and money on top. A band like Brinsley Schwarz could come over and spend a weekend and play four gigs in Northern Ireland, and they'd go home with more money in their pocket than if they'd played four pubs in London. So Ted has this room and I kipped on his couch. We just got on really well and got to know each other. Ted was the one that really introduced me to the big record collection thing – as a kid I'd always had records and been a record freak, but I'd never seen anything like Ted's record collection. Ted lived in a record collection, not a room. It was wall to wall. It blew me away totally. So then I left college and moved to Dublin. Thin Lizzy started to take off in Ireland after 'Whiskey In The Jar'. I was working with the Chieftains and I got a sizeable flat in Dublin. I had a spare room at the back of the flat. So to return the favour to Ted, Phil Lynott would stay in my flat in Dublin. Cos his reputation as a womaniser, I assure you, was not a word of a lie, and there was no way an Irish hotel would put up with it in those days."

Eventually, Armstrong moved to London permanently. "I looked after a band called St James's Gate who made a record that never got released. They had a drummer called Bob Siedenberg, who moved on to Supertramp. His brother-in-law was a guitar player, and Ted rang me one day cos he knew Ruan O'Lochlainn, who had been in Bees Make Honey. And I was staying at Ruan and Jackie's place at the time when Ted rang and said, 'Eric's left the band – do you know any guitar players?' 'Yeah, we do, funnily enough, this guy Scott, Bob's brother-in-law, a bit younger, has just come into town and he's a great guitar player.' So Scott auditioned, and they ended up with two guitarists, Brian Robertson and Scott Gorham. So again, there were all these connections with Ted. And we would all go to the same gigs. Eventually my band washed up and I'd had enough trying to be a manager, I wasn't a manager. It wasn't my forte. And that coincided with Ted having had enough of Thin Lizzy. He'd retired from management with the idea that his market stall, that he'd had from '71 in Golborne Road, he was going to just trade records, go to America for three or four weeks at a time and buy records and bring them in. Then a mutual friend of ours, Sylvia, was dealing in clothes at Dingwalls and she found a stall in Soho. I was trying to get a studio gig at that stage as an engineer, I'd have taken a job as a tea boy – I knew I could do it, I just wanted to get in the door. And Ted said to me one day, 'Sylvia's got this stall. She only wants it three days a week, so I'll take it three days a week and turn it into a record stall Monday, Tuesday and Wednesday.' So I said, 'Yeah, I'm not doing anything.' I was still trying to get a gig in a studio." The proposition worked brilliantly. "It was just heaven," says Armstrong. "I'd been stressed cos I had no work and I was living in a squat, things were tough and I was getting pissed off. And it was just great, to go into this place every morning and it was just full of records, what more could you ask?"

The two stalls' catalogue expanded beyond beat, classic rock 'n' roll and psychedelia to encompass imports of a new wave of American bands like the Flamin' Groovies, Iggy And The Stooges and the New York Dolls; groups stripping rock music back to its basics. These records had a fan base in England but no mainstream outlet serving it. Customers included Joe Strummer, Mick Jones, John Peel and Shane MacGowan. "Ted found out that the MC5's *Back in the USA* was available in France," says Armstrong, "and we found someone who could buy it for us and imported it. That was through Marc Zermati. Then we got deletions of the Iggy & The Stooges album. The Stooges are legends now but they didn't sell records in those days. They pressed a lot, but they had lots of leftovers." Even though almost every musician of the 76-79 era claims to have bought a copy? "I could probably tell you who they are, because I was selling them to them!"

"That period of three days a week only lasted a few months," Armstrong continues, "so after that it was really happening. We were the first oldies location in the West End. These guys came in their suits; they would be record collectors that you'd see elsewhere at gigs in jeans. They came in during their lunch hour. The number of people I had to give false receipts to – 'Look darling, I only spent £3 today!' These guys were addicts and we were supplying their addiction in the middle of the West End of London where they worked. But the thing about Rock On was that it wasn't just a collector's shop, we were stocking certain current records as well. We were selling soul records, Dyke & The Blazers, Fatback Band, Kool & The Gang and so on as they came out."

The Rock On hub forged friendships that eventually developed into international alliances. Greg Shaw had been editing garage rock bible *Who*

# Gatecrashers

*Put The Bomp!* since 1969 in San Francisco (there had been a precursor three years earlier, *Mojo Navigator*), before relocating to Los Angeles in 1972. Rock On stocked copies from 1973. Shaw also managed the Flamin' Groovies, whom Lauder would sign to UA after spells with Epic and Karma Sutra. Marc Zermati, meanwhile, ran the Open Market record stall in Paris. The Groovies enjoyed cult popularity throughout France. Via Shaw, Zermati signed the band for two live EPs and a re-release of their 1968 10-inch mini-album *Sneakers* on his label Skydog. These did good business, and although the band failed to take off on UA, they were able to support themselves through heavy touring, much of it in France. Through the auspices of Rock On and his friendship with Zermati (the boyfriend of later Sex shop assistant Chrissie Hynde, who spent time with him in Paris and joined biker band The Frenchies), Malcolm McLaren had followed the New York Dolls from London to Paris in 1973. An axis was thereby formed between Rock On in London, Open in Paris and Bomp! in California, who would release the Groovies' 'You Tore Me Down'. Each component helped cultivate the nameless aesthetic that would eventually take form as punk.

This putative international alliance was based on a swap meet mentality. "Marc and Larry [Debais/Debay] were bringing in a lot of American indie stuff, Ork Records and all that," notes Armstrong. "There was 'Big Black Truck' by Peter Holsapple. Chris Bell [formerly of Big Star] came over with that personally. People would bring us a box of records and we'd buy it off them. Talk about distribution, it didn't exist! Some Americans would come over and bring copies of their record to help fund the trip. Cut-out deletions were huge in those days. Some companies would bring in containers full of records on the way back – a ship would have gone to America to offload stuff, not had enough freight on the way back and they'd put record boxes in there as ballast. Stop the thing from falling over! And these guys would buy these containers of records – 20,000 LPs or whatever you got."

As the stalls grew, they adapted to the musical climate. "We were doing any hip new releases that were coming out," says Armstrong, "stocking those, and then Ted tapped into the fact that Decca kept an awful lot of old stuff in catalogue. Ted couldn't believe it. We had accounts with Decca and EMI. We would buy whole boxes of the first two Them LPs, brand new, this is like '73. '74, and all the Stones EPs, the John Mayall/Paul Butterfield EP, the single with 'Sister Morphine' by Marianne Faithfull and things like 'Caroline' by the Fortunes, which was the Radio Caroline theme tune. We were selling that at over the odds because it was collectable, people really wanted that record, and we simply found out it was still available. Sold loads of that. So in the same shop you could buy 'Caroline' by the Fortunes or *Funhouse* by Iggy and the Stooges. But it was always driven by our tastes. We had all the Beatles 45s and EPs from EMI, which no one else bothered to stock."

Carroll had a natural instinct for sniffing out a good deal, and his time with Thin Lizzy again proved useful. "There was a company called Solomon and Peres," recalls Carroll, "which was a record distribution company. They had a place in Belfast, and a place in Dublin. When the first Thin Lizzy album came out, I went in to see them when we over there on tour, to see how the record was selling and to press the flesh, basically. They weren't that interested. Just by a sheer chance remark I discovered they had loads of old London 45s stashed upstairs – it was kind of a mews place, with a garage on the first floor, and up some stairs were some offices, then more stairs going up. It was one of those old fashioned rickety places that existed in those days. The guy who owned Solomon & Peres was in there – he was Louis Solomon, father of Phil Solomon [who discovered the Bachelors & Them]. He was grouchy, and there was a grouchy woman there too, but I said, 'Would you be interested in getting rid of that stock?' 'Possibly.' I went and had a look. Came down half an hour later. 'Yeah, I'd definitely be interested in buying a thousand or so.' They said – 3p. That was it. I went in there every morning for a week and spent two or three hours before going off to whatever Thin Lizzy gig was happening. And at the end of the week I had about 1,700 or 1,800 45s, many of them the rarest things. I remember getting two boxes of Bo Diddley's 'Say Man', boxes and boxes of Phil Spector produced stuff like the Ronettes and Crystals, including a thing I didn't realise was rare, a single by the Crystals. It had 'Uptown' on one side and 'Little Boy' on the other side, which was never released in England. It was pressed up but withdrawn. And it was really rare and I'd sold them all before I discovered how rare it was!"

There were other unconventional means to acquire stock, as Armstrong remembers. "In those days, they sold records in painters and decorators shops. There would be a rack of LPs. Ted found this guy who was bringing them in and said, 'Look I'll give you more money than you can get off these shops if I can cherry pick.' The guy didn't want to do it. So Ted had a motor scooter. The guy had a fleet of little vans, with these women driving, and they went round the circuit racking these records. And he followed them! Took a load of addresses one day, and went out the next in his car and bought all the great records. Just cleaned them out. They were suddenly racking their places more intensely, and the more intensely they racked them, the more Ted would go round and buy all the good stuff. It was a real hand to mouth thing in those days, but it was great fun, and the market stall really thrived. We had one unit, a lock-up garage-sized unit, then two then three. On a Saturday there were people outside waiting for someone to clear out to get in. It was really rammed. And again, because we stocked it all, on a Saturday afternoon you'd have Jamaican guys buying R&B, you'd have Teddy boys buying rock 'n' roll and the soon to be punks buying garage bands."

During this period, the thought of starting their own label, based loosely on the premise of the 50s R&B American indies, began to take shape. At the end of 1975 they struck on the name Chiswick – a modest nod to their devotion to London Records' output, a 'branch of the tree' allusion. The idea was to release records that would attract collectors, packaged in picture sleeves that they knew had special appeal to that market. "Ted and I started talking about it," says Armstrong, "because we lived in each other's pocket a little bit. He'd be round the market stall each night to cash up, then most nights we'd get something to eat or go to gigs. And we'd talk a lot, Ted and I. It was essentially inspiration from Chess and Modern and Sun and all those kind of labels, independent record guys. The fact that it's called Chiswick is a strange, arcane story that has many versions. It was pretty quick after starting the market stall. What took time was finding a band. Even though we were inspired by the Chess brothers, and Sun and so on, we couldn't go outside our front door and find Elvis Presley or Muddy Waters or Etta James or BB King. Obviously we were doing what they were doing, in the sense that we were recording what was on our doorstep. And that was pub bands in those days. Punk was only vaguely in the air. We wandered round looking for bands. The Feelgoods were big, so that was the sort of band we were looking for."

"I think it was easier in a way to start an American independent label," Carroll reflects, "because there was a heritage there of independent labels. There were quite a few independent labels in England, but they were quite low-level and insignificant compared to the five or six majors. There was a sense that you couldn't do an independent label, it just wasn't a possibility. Charlie Gillett was one of the first people in the 70s to set up an independent label, and I'm not sure if that was an influence or inspiration to us, I imagine it might have been." Gillett isn't entirely sure, either. "When Chiswick started, I never knew whether that was a joke in response to us calling our label after one little district of London – the difference being that we imagined that DJs would say 'this is an oval record' and make a joke of it. So there was a double edge to the name. And Chiswick was just the most unromantic name you could think of to call a record label; it would be typical of an independent frame of mind to think of that. Then Stiff called themselves Stiff – that was another alternative. Oval had a soft, almost feminine feel to it, whereas Stiff was about as blunt as you can get. We never talked to anyone about it, it was our little Oval pigeonhole. We were amused to see these other labels that sprang up whose names seemed to connect to us, without us ever knowing if that was the truth."

"I think Greg Shaw's Bomp! label and the French Skydog label were the two main inspirations for Chiswick," ponders Carroll. "We found that by the time we had Soho we were starting to buy quantities of records that we knew we could sell. So when the guys from Skydog came along to Soho, we bought maybe ten or 15 or 20 copies of things, and very quickly it was up to 25 or more – because we knew we could sell them. With Camden we had a third store in '75 [which became the headquarters for Chiswick], and nobody else was selling this stuff at the time; very, very few, because it hadn't even got into places like Virgin at that stage. So we were really the first people selling that stuff. Rough Trade came along a little while later. After the store, the distribution came quickly afterwards and Geoff Travis saw the opportunity [for distribution]. It was obvious, I suppose, that there was an opportunity. But I was more interested in starting a label, because that had been on the cards since about 1972."

"We found this band called Chrome playing a pub in the Holloway Road," says Armstrong. "They were pretty good. Then this guy, Mike Spenser, came into the record store fresh off the plane from New York. He was playing harmonica and he was looking for bands. We told him where all the clubs were. He ended up joining Chrome, and they changed their name to the Count Bishops. They brought Johnny Guitar in from America. To go back a bit, the first thing we recorded was with Jesse Hector of the Hammersmith Gorillas. He'd done a record for Larry Page, a cover of 'You Really Got Me', and we were selling that. Jesse hung around Ted's market stall in Golborne Road, and that was a whole 'nother hub – mainly the Notting Hill Gate folk. Jesse was hanging around. Davey Robinson had a studio above the Hope And Anchor. We went in there. There was no way in a million years Dave and I were going to make a record with me as producer, the two egos in a room was way out of control. We *kind of* made a record, we spruced it up years later and put it out. It needed post-production work. Which I didn't know much about in those days. But Jesse didn't like the record, and we didn't like how it sounded, so it didn't come out." Carroll picks up the story. "It was all bedroom stuff and Jesse wasn't doing many gigs. When we signed him, I got John Salter, an agent, to get involved as manager, and Paul Charles as an agent, and started to get him gigs. Just as it looked like he was going to take off, we had the front page of *Sounds* and stuff like that, Jesse bottled it and decided it was all too much for him. We hadn't invested huge amounts of money or anything. I respected the fact that the choice was his, we didn't try to browbeat him into doing something he didn't want to do. That's a waste of time."

"Then we recorded Chrome," recalls Armstrong, "with a different bass player, who couldn't even get 'Walking The Dog' right. They did 'Sometimes Good Guys Don't Wear White'. That session didn't work. Finally, Jake Riviera had been working with Clover, and he told Ted about this great studio down the road called Pathway, which they'd been working in. It was where Elvis Costello cut his first record and so too The Damned. Don't forget at this stage Stiff hadn't started, so we were the first in. Pathway became the Sun studio or the Phillips studio of London. It was a very hot August night in '75, and the band just hit a groove. We recorded those 12 numbers with no overdubs, then a week later it was mixed and we'd got the 'Speedball' EP out of it."

Chiswick's investiture was thus marked with the November 1975 release of the 'Speedball' EP, credited to The Count Bishops, an intense 7-inch document of the pub rock generation. Carroll would take his barely roadworthy Peugeot round the shops to foist it on alarmed proprietors. "We'd finally cracked it," reflects Armstrong, "we'd made a record that was more than releasable. It actually sold really well – it was a good start. I think that record stands up and it's one of the records from that era that says, look, Malcolm didn't invent punk over night. 'I invented punk.' No, you didn't, Malcolm! People in the punk bands were going to see bands like The Count Bishops and Feelgoods. Because what they copped from that was the attitude. The attitude was quite tough and heavy, quite punky in approach. The other thing was, they were playing 50s/60s styles of music, but at twice the speed. People used to describe the Bishops first EP as the Rolling Stones played at 45rpm, or even 78rpm! It was totally revved up 60s R&B."

The physical logistics were worked out in piecemeal fashion, utilising various contacts. "The design was done by an old friend called Frank Inzani," confirms Armstrong. "Mike Beale took the photograph. Out of the session, only two images survive, one we used for the poster, which was in focus, and we chose this totally out of focus picture for the cover. Frank designed the little pink logo. Frank was the late lamented [journalist] Giovanni Dadamo's cousin. I don't know how Ted found them, but on Holloway Road was an independent pressing plant called Lyntone. All the Beatles flexidiscs were made at Lyntone." Run by Paul Lynton and his wife Leah, known ubiquitously as 'Mrs Lyntone', the pressing plant became synonymous with cheap flexidisc production, but would later also press huge numbers of important independent releases, including Joy Division's 'An Ideal For Living'. "Mrs Lyntone, oh, she was a laugh!" continues Armstrong. "So Ted went up there and organised the pressing. And the first pressing run, two-thirds of them were warped. We sat by a deck one day and rejected the warped ones. They were warped to the point of unplayability. So we eventually wrestled a flat set of pressings to the ground and sold them."

"When we started Chiswick, the original idea was just to do reissues," adds Carroll, "but then we came across bands like The Count Bishops that we liked. We manufactured 2,500 copies of the Count Bishops EP, which was a huge amount for a totally unknown band on our own label. So I obviously had the confidence that we could sell it – I didn't really think as far as 2,500, but I figured we could sell 1,000 or 1,500 pretty quick. In terms of the economics, it made sense to do 2,500, I can't remember why. Perhaps it made sense in terms of the sleeve manufacturer, but it would have been because 1,000 would have cost maybe 12p or 13p for the physical pressing, and 2,000 would have been a bit less, so by going to 2,500 we would have got a lower price. And the same thing would apply to the label and the sleeves – it was all different manufacturers. There weren't a lot of options. We could see from our experience with Rock On it would be a good idea to have picture sleeves, because that would make the item more collectable and it would be easier to sell. That was definitely the right move. Lyntones were the pressing plant that was nearest to us – maybe we found them in the Yellow Pages. I remember there was a problem. They had the Christmas rush. The record came out at the end of November '75, and Lyntone were unable to deliver the 2,500, which didn't bother me too much, because I didn't actually need the 2,500 there and then – I was doing it for the rate. They delivered 1,500 but we discovered a lot of them were warped – they'd been sleeved up before they were properly set. So we ended up returning 600 or 700 of the first 1,500. They repressed those. She said, 'I can't do it till after Christmas.'"

Mrs Lyntone, however, wasn't the sot of person you could negotiate a discount with, even though Carroll, with his jackdaw eye, did manage to liberate a few sets of the Beatles fan club flexidiscs from the premises with her permission. "We got on very well with her at the end. But herself and her husband were Jewish, and she was tough. She was the businesswoman. She would try to bully you until it got to the stage where you knew her well enough. We gave them a lot of work and brought a lot of work to them because we referred a lot of people to them. So we ended up pressing up the 2,500, but we probably didn't get the rest of them till the end of January. We carried on. As always happens, the initial batch satisfied the initial demand. And we probably found we'd sold them all by the end of March or something, and we ordered some more. I guess we pressed up 10,000 or 11,000 copies of that EP over the years until we eventually deleted it."

The sleeve printer was Delga Press in South London. "We probably found something they'd printed, or it might have been the Yellow Pages or we asked somebody – and that was a lucky thing for them, because they subsequently manufactured for loads of people. Label printing was a separate thing, and we found a company called Hannibal in Leicester, and we worked with them for a long time. Eventually they got taken over by Robert Maxwell, probably for their pension fund! One of the reasons we liked Hannibal was that we used to get 90 days credit, and it helped your cash flow, when you don't have any seed money. We started with money borrowed from the till in the shop, basically."

Distribution was relatively straightforward – or as straightforward as it could be without the assistance of any kind of network. "We pressed it up and vibed people up. Larry [Debais] and Marc [Zermati] probably took 150-200 copies to cart around some Parisian shops. Greg [Shaw] probably took 100-150. There was a lot of wheeling and dealing. He might have been exchanging for *Bomp!* magazines or what have you – it was that pure commerce of just mainly exchanging stuff. There weren't invoices, but delivery notes to keep a record of it. There was a company called Bonaparte, export-import people. They probably took some. I had a few contacts, because I'd already published a book called *The Phil Spector Story*, with Rock On books about a year and a half earlier. There was Pacific Records, a distribution company who'd moved from Shepherd's Bush to Kentish Town. They were owned by an American company called Gemm who were big importers. So they took about 200. And there weren't many chances for airplay, I guess John Peel probably played it, and we got some reviews in the weekly music press, fairly good reviews. That generated interest, and we started getting mail order requests – half a dozen copies from odd shops here and there. There was one in Derby, they ordered ten copies. There was a chain of record shops in Scotland, Bruce's, and they started doing distribution too."

The relationships quickly became reciprocal. "People forget that in the wake of the whole kind of Chiswick thing," notes Carroll, "we started stocking all the other independent labels. Certainly at Camden, through '77 to '79, we sold an incredible amount of punk and indie records. Lightning Records, a one stop distributor in West London, were handling all that stuff, so you'd just go along there and buy five of this, ten of that, whatever. Things started to happen – someone from Buzzcocks rang up and asked how you made a record – we gave them some advice on the telephone, and they put 'Spiral Scratch' together. The guy from the Desperate Bicycles came in to do his record, and we put him in touch with Lyntone and it went from there. Gradually it took off and the next thing, it was burgeoning."

Observing all this was Rock On regular Malcolm McLaren. "Malcolm didn't know much about records," states Armstrong. "Ted would bring in lots of oldies and 45s from America, and sell them to Malcolm. Malcolm would sell them on for 30 bob. Ted had bought them for 10p." McLaren would subsequently offer payback for his musical tutelage by inviting the Rock On Disco to open for the Sex Pistols at early London gigs. Prior to that, however, McLaren nearly derailed their record label by attempting to pinch Bishops' singer Mike Spenser. "Yeah, it was upstairs at Ronnie's," Armstrong recalls. "It must have been before we made 'Speedball', because Lydon had joined the Pistols by the time the record came out. Malcolm was in my ear all night – 'Is this the guy I need for my new band?' 'Fuck off, Malcolm. Stop trying to nick our singer.' I've always said Malcolm was very lucky to get John Lydon instead of Mike Spenser – he got the one was that relatively tame!" However, The Count Bishops story ended prematurely. "The Bishops more or less broke up," recalls Carroll, "and then they dragged themselves together and went off to Holland to do a tour and recorded an album for Pieter Meulenbroeks [Dynamite Records]. He was doing a similar thing to what we were, bringing in Skydog stuff and distributing it in Holland. The time was right to be doing this sort of thing. He put that out, the single 'Train Train', and a few copies came over here. John Peel got a copy and started playing it. We were selling imports, then we licensed it and put it out here, so that became our fifth release on Chiswick."

The other core member of the Chiswick team was Trevor Churchill, a vinyl aficionado who had worked as an EMI management trainee before stints with Bell, Tamla Motown and Polydor. It was his contacts that allowed the label to licence forgotten classics, starting with 'black leather rebel' Vince Taylor's 'Brand New Cadillac', Chiswick's second release in March 1976. Taylor, whose career was brutally curtailed by drug and personal problems, had claims to being rock 'n' roll's very own James Dean, which appealed to most everyone. "Ted knew Trevor because he used to buy records off him," recalls Armstrong, "and Trevor worked behind the counter at Rock On in

## Gatecrashers

Camden on a Saturday afternoon. Trevor was a proper record company guy. He knew how a contract and a royalty statement worked. Ted and I were, well, not fly by nights, but on the company end of things, we didn't have too much of a clue abut the mechanism. And Trevor was off to Polydor in Germany, to be a co-ordinator in Europe, looking after the whole continent. But he was having a farewell party at his flat. Ted and I went to see him in the afternoon and said, 'We're starting a record company, we'd like you to join us.' He said, 'OK, I'll take 10% as an advisor.' We said, 'No, no, we'll give you a third.' The basic theory was that if nothing happened, he'd have a third of nothing. If it did, we'd need a guy like him. We really did. It's always been the secret of our success, in as much as that there's three of us but we all have very different roles in the company. And one of them was someone who from day one knew the mechanisms of the money and the royalties and the contracts. And really understood it, like few people do. There's very few people in the business in this day and age who get it to the level he gets it. So we had a strong team. Ted was always the big personality, the front man. I was always the guy, in the early days, sitting at recording desks for too long making records. Or later on, with the reissue thing, spending months in America digging out tapes and things. I was that form of engine in the thing – and Ted did a lot of that too, but Ted didn't produce records. Ted ran the front end of the company. Trevor was the ultimate backroom boy. But I'd say that he was also better than any of us at spotting a hit. Coming from that end of it, he had impeccable musical taste. He was a pop and rock 'n' roll guy, Trevor. Hated punk. Didn't like that at all. He liked soul music very much, and pop – big Ricky Nelson fan, Dion, the Impressions, all that stuff."

The licence for 'Brand New Cadillac' came with pre-conditions that hint at the way major labels were viewing the emerging independent scene with a measure of suspicion. "I remember once we sold 10,000 copies it reverted to EMI," says Armstrong. "They were really frightened of us getting a hit with something we'd licensed off them." They were absolutely confident of its success, however. "We knew there was an automatic market for that on the teddy boy/rock 'n roll circuit," says Carroll. "In fact, that was the record that really was the inspiration for the label – records like 'Brand New Cadillac' that were in demand but weren't being made available by the majors. Because it was on Chiswick, people who had bought The Count Bishops EP listened to it and liked it and bought it and it crossed over. Apart from the rock 'n' roll circuit, just before we put 'Brand New Cadillac' out, there was another record we wanted to put out, purely coincidentally. But Charly Records secured the rights before we did. It was a record called 'Jungle Rock' by Hank Mizell, and that became a genuine *bona fide* hit record. It created demand for that kind of record. So almost on the heels of that, without realising the significance of the timing, we came along with 'Brand New Cadillac'. We got approached by President Records, which was an independent distribution set-up tied in with a label, run by this character called Eddie Kassner, and they were distributing Charly at that stage. So they were able to give 'Brand New Cadillac' to their reps. I knew who Eddie Kassner was through my experience in the music industry with Thin Lizzy. I knew the Equals, and I knew the history of their relationship with him. And I knew to be careful with the way you dealt with him. So we thought, here's a chance to expand, get more product out, so we did a deal. 'Brand New Cadillac' was taken to the shops by his reps on the heels of 'Jungle Rock' and punters bought it. So we got pretty good sales, we probably sold 4,000 records pretty quickly, which for a second record is pretty phenomenal given that there was no real independent record scene. I had experience of working with bands that were distributed by majors. At that time you were still in a situation where there was a chain of independent shops and not a huge amount of product – so shops generally ordered one of everything that came out. I remember something like the Thin Lizzy EP, their second release and first seven-inch record, probably sold 1,100 or 1,200 copies initially through Decca – who had four distribution depots. They had Glasgow/Edinburgh, Manchester, Birmingham and London. And they shifted 1,200 copies with Thin Lizzy. And we came along and shifted 4,000 copies with 'Brand New Cadillac' real fast. You could see that was quite a shake-up."

'Brand New Cadillac' was later covered on *London Calling* by the Clash – whose singer Joe Strummer would appear on Chiswick's third release, the 101ers 'Keys To Your Heart', in June 1976. But by the time it came out, Strummer had left the band. "Oddly enough, there was a bit of a buzz, but they weren't getting too much press," reckons Armstrong. "They came out of that Notting Hill Gate scene, almost a hippy scene. I saw them – I was meeting a woman I knew at college in a pub in Ladbroke Grove, and there they were in the background. It was the early days with a trumpet player, bit of a shambles, but interesting. Not long later, Ted came into the market stall and said, 'I went to Dingwalls last night, we've got to sign this band, the lead singer's a complete star, he's phenomenal.' Ted and me went to another gig about three days later, and it was like, yep. And with a lot of palaver they recorded with Vic Maille. And they got BBC sessions. I took them into the studio. They weren't keen on that version of 'Keys To Your Heart' coming out. But we were the record company and I was the producer, so we had the final say. I don't regret it, I still think it's the better version."

Regardless, Strummer's defection to The Clash closed that chapter. "I was in the pub one night," recalls Armstrong. "I was meeting someone, and Joe wanders in and there's a tap on the shoulder while I was at the bar. Joe was one of those people who started his sentences in the middle, and then worked his way outwards. And you had to mentally reconstruct what he was saying in the correct order. The first thing he said was, 'Have I done the right thing?' Joe's immediate response to everything, always, was the moral issue up front – then what he'd done, or the practical stuff came later. 'Have I done the right thing? I've left the band!' 'Jeez, thanks Joe, what do you want me to say? We haven't put the record out yet and you've left the band!' He said, 'I've started a band with this guy'. And I saw this skinny guy with long hair standing behind him [Mick Jones]. We were fairly sanguine about it. There's another band around the corner in those days, so I wish you luck. Mick and Joe used to come in and out of our Camden store all the time. We used to get updates on the name. Heartdrops was the first one, then the Outsiders. Lasted five minutes. Then The Clash. Then Bernie [Rhodes] came in one day and invited us up to Rehearsal Rehearsals to see their debut. [Journalists] Caroline Coon and Jon Savage were there, etc. Ted and I arrived, and Bernie had pushed the boat out and bought two bottles of cheap Blue Nun white wine – undrinkable. Ted and I went out and bought a crate of beer and two half-decent bottles of plonk. Dear old Bernie, never knowingly overspent!"

"The 101ers was kind of a precursor of punk," suggests Carroll. "It got to the stage by four or five records in, people were buying everything we put out, and going back and buying the earlier ones. We were selling quite healthily. The 101ers sold quite well, not as well as the other two, but we sold 1,500 or a couple of thousand fairly quickly. Then there was the Gorillas. By that time the label had got a bit of momentum." That despite the fact that most everyone they signed seemed to self-combust or disband immediately thereafter. Carroll considers that. "The thing is, we weren't signing bands to contracts, we were signing one-off deals, so what they did after that didn't really concern us. The idea of a one-off deal was that if they used that as a stepping stone to get signed by a major, with a bit of luck we'd continue to sell copies of the original record – that was my concept. That worked fine until we were a bit further down the line."

The Rock On distributed *Bomp!* magazine had given Mark Perry the idea of launching his own fanzine, exactly a month after the release of the 101ers single. *Sniffin' Glue* quickly proved pivotal to the coming punk revolution. When the young bank clerk asked whether Carroll had any magazines covering the Ramones and UK pub rock, he was asked why he didn't start one himself. When he did, with the first issue appearing in July 1976 (notably featuring a review of the Flamin' Groovies supporting the Ramones at the Roundhouse) Rock On was the first outlet to stock it – taking all 50 of the first copies and even paying Perry an advance. "Yeah, we paid in advance," confirms Armstrong. "He had a girlfriend and her dad had an office, and they were going in at night and using the office photocopier, and they got caught. Suddenly he couldn't use the office photocopier, and he had to pay for his photocopies. So we said OK, we'll take 'x' number of *Sniffin' Glue* and here's the money up front so he could go get it photocopied."

If Skydog had been an influence on the founding of Chiswick Records, Rock On would in turn inspire that label's venture into UK retail. Skydog co-founder Larry Debais established Bizarre Records at 33 Praed Street, W2, in 1976. The store was briefly popular due to its location near Lisson Grove, where so many of punk's prime movers signed on. Others visited from the suburbs while out-of-towners would make the pilgrimage – like Jon Roberts, founder of the first south-west punk band Adrenalin, who would come to track down copies of "Nuggets and 60s garage stuff" before soaking up the atmosphere in McLaren's Sex shop. It also provided shelf space for a limited run of fanzines, following the Rock On! template. Crucially, it was through their patronage of the shop that The Damned ended up being invited to appear at the Mont De Marsan festival in France in August 1976, organised by Debais and Zermati, which led to their signing to Stiff.

The summer of 1976 also saw Chiswick courting The Jam, the besuited Woking boys led by regular Rock On lurker Paul Weller. Rock On organised their fabled 'Let It Be' showcase in nearby Newport Court (which brought damning reviews from Caroline Coon in the *Melody Maker* and from Perry in *Sniffin' Glue*). The shock of the new had dictated that the climate for bands that displayed 'retro' fixations was hostile. That said, the band's maximum R&B aesthetic was perfectly suited to the tastes of Carroll and Armstrong, whose affection for rock's history made them instinctively resistant to any year zero sermons. Nevertheless, The Jam and manager John Weller resisted the three-single deal they offered to sign with Chris Parry and Polydor for a £6,000 advance – a figure Chiswick, who had reportedly offered £500 and the free use of their PA, simply could not compete with. Chiswick were effectively outbid. "It was just a typical indie deal in those days," Armstrong recalls. "We offered what we could afford."

"They were the next band in town," Armstrong continues. "Bernie [Rhodes] had taken the Clash off and Malcolm was never going to sign to an indie, and neither was Bernie. Bernie had courted Chris Parry at Polydor. And Chris thought he was definitely getting The Clash. And Bernie suddenly flipped it into CBS one day." Famously, Parry would burst into tears on receiving the news that Rhodes had reneged on what he took to be a done deal. "It all happened over a period of a couple of days," Armstrong remembers. "John Weller had our contract. He and Paul were coming up to Ted's flat in Camden over the shop. And the day before they were due up, Chris Parry rang John Weller and said they'd got a deal."

"We used to like The Jam," Carroll confirms, "and we went to see them as punters. And also we had Rock On and Paul Weller was always coming in. They did the gig outside the stall when they took the electrical feed from us. They were definitely interested, but by this stage they'd got enough of a profile to attract interest from majors. Chris Parry at Polydor came in for them. At least they got a better deal with Polydor because we were hanging on their coat-tails – they had to offer a decent advance, whereas they'd have got them for nothing if we hadn't been in the picture. I did say it would be a good idea to do a single with us to wind them up a bit more." Armstrong remembers a subsequent meeting. "I was very drunk one night at some gig later, sitting with John Weller. John was really bitching about Polydor, he'd had enough of them. I said, 'John, you're always welcome back – we should have signed you in the first place.' No chance whatsoever! But I would have to say we'd already picked 'In The City' as the first single."

There was also an effort to sign The Damned – Chiswick even paid for their first demos, but missed the boat when Armstrong went on holiday to his parents in Portugal in the summer of 1976 and Stiff nipped in. Instead Chiswick plugged away releasing records by those on the pub rock fraternity, such as the Gorillas and retro rockers Rocky Sharpe & The Razors, as well as France's Little Bob Story. "That was through a guy called Rick Rodgers," Carroll remembers, "who later managed The Specials. He was managing Little Bob Story, a French punk band, so we did them. The first band that approached us was The Radio Stars. They were the first people who came knocking on the door." The latter's 'Dirty Pictures' was the closest to a legitimate punk release (if we overlook the musicians' lengthy musical hinterlands with bands such as Sparks and Jet). "It was a really good power-pop record and we really liked it," says Carroll. "They'd done some demos for Island. And it was basically an Island demo they hadn't got the deal for it, and they went back to Island to get clearance to use the tapes. Island said OK. That was that."

## Independence Days

The Radiators From Space, meanwhile, were an Irish import signed on the advice of Horslips' drummer Eamon Carr. They'd yet to play live, but Carroll was convinced that all available talent of any worth had already been scooped up in England, as he confirmed to *Music Week*. "There are more major record company A&R men than punters in the Roxy Club these days, and the general vibe is, if it moves and has a guitar round its neck – sign it!" Regardless, the resultant 'Television Screen' single was far nearer the real thing (at a time when no-one had truly established what the 'real thing' constituted) and came as compensation, of sorts, for their failure to sign Dublin's Boomtown Rats. "We got some things we didn't do anything with," admits Carroll. "We got a copy of '30 Seconds Over Tokyo' by Pere Ubu. I loved that record, but I thought, we can't sell this – it's too far out and too freaky for us to sell. It's an eternal regret in a way that we never put it out, but it would have taken us in all sorts of different directions. There were a few of those over the years."

Thence came Blackpool's Skrewdriver, a boots and braces punk rock band whose later move to the far right after changes in the line-up was anticipated by neither Armstrong or Carroll. The group's album for Chiswick is the most notable punk era album never to have been legally reissued – evidence of the label founders' aversion to the politics that band's lead singer would later embrace.

"Not on my watch," states Armstrong, asked whether the album will ever see the light of day. "I think, if there was any totally unconscious thing that we did or were part of, was when they did the skinhead thing. It was really an attempt to get them away from punk, and it was an image thing. Let's have a skinhead image, it'll be amazing! And it was quite aggressive. Then when Ian had the skinhead crop, he started hanging out with these Crombie skinheads. I remember the Vortex one night, can't remember the band, the Vortex was the funny club with the steps that was almost like a lecture theatre. People were sitting on sort of bench seats there, and it was really crammed and the aisles were crowded. Ian and two of his twerp skinhead mates were coming up – the record had just come out and we were promoting it – and he was coming up and pushing people out of the way, really nasty. I waited till he came up to me and I said, 'If you want to be on my fucking record label, you don't fucking do that.' 'Oh sorry, Roger, sorry.' He was a bully. That's what those guys are. In a sense, he could have been a football hooligan, he could have taken his aggression anywhere – he took it into fascism and the National Front. That's my view. He was a bully and massively ambitious, and when the ambition wasn't satisfied, he went that route. And it's a shame. I feel really sorry for the other guys in the band, and I feel sorry for me – I think the record should be out. But it's a just a can of worms I'm really not interested in opening. We had the British Movement write a very aggressive, albeit incoherent letter to us, saying they owned the album, on behalf of Ian Stuart. This was before Ian died. It was brilliant – Trevor, who is a very well educated Englishman, and very polite and formal, just sent a completely legal letter back to them – how we retained and owned all and every right under this contract since blah blah blah. And they went away."

The label's roster, like that of Stiff, betrayed the influence of disparate traditions, as well as an attempt to harness some of the energy of punk. Releases by the Rings (featuring former Pink Fairy Twink, who would also record solo for the label), Matchbox, the Stukas, Motörhead and the Jook rubbed shoulders with the first single by Johnny & The Self-Abusers. Featuring the core of the band that would become Simple Minds, they broke up on the day that 'Saints & Sinners' was released, just as had the 101ers. "Something like Johnny & The Self-Abusers," Carroll observes, "was very simple. They brought us the record, I liked it, Roger liked it. We said we'd put it out. They did the artwork. We never met the band, it was all done by someone at Bruce's shop in Scotland. By this stage there was a guy called Dave Hill who used to come into the Soho stall, and he was working at Anchor Records. That was an English subsidiary of ABC, which was run by Ian Ralfini. He was appointed as the guy to find the 'youth trends'. Punk hadn't really started, or was just starting. So he was very interested in the label. Through Dave we went to see Ralfini and arranged a distribution deal with Anchor. And we got out of the deal with President– I think that was just a record by record thing. So we went to Anchor and I remember going to their monthly sales meeting and presenting them with Johnny & the Self-Abusers, and the reps just rolled around the floor laughing. They just loved the name, and they liked the record too. And they went out and sold about 1,800 advance copies just on the name. They were like, 'We've gotta have this!' Two weeks before the record was due, I got a call saying, 'We're not sure about the name, is it too late to change it?' 'Yes, it is, the labels are all printed. What name were you thinking of?' 'Simple Minds.' 'Oh, forget it. Mickey Mouse name! Next!'" The label, too, gave significant early opportunities to some of the finest writers set to emerge over the next two decades. Kirsty MacColl's first vinyl outing came as part of Drug Addix, while her future collaborator Shane MacGowan would also debut on the label as part of the Nipple Erectors. Billy Bragg, too, released his first vinyl on Chiswick as part of Romford punk band Riff Raff.

A healthy but convivial rivalry continued between Stiff and Chiswick in these years. Several artists swapped camps. When Stiff declined to release Motörhead's debut single, Chiswick took the opportunity to put out their album (before losing them to Bronze, again due to financial restrictions and not being able to match the £15,000 offered). "We built from the 101ers and all that," Armstrong elaborates, "and did the Bishops' first album and then did Motörhead's first album. Lemmy had been touting around the Dave Edmunds album that Andrew [Lauder] didn't want to put out. He took it to me at Soho, and I said 'Lemmy, the reason Andrew didn't want to put it out is because it isn't very good.' When it finally came out it was there for all to hear – it *wasn't* very good. So we were going to make a farewell live album at the Marquee with them. Then Ted and I chickened out of that – bit risky, what if they have a bad night? OK, let's do a single instead. They went down to Escape Studios to do 'Motörhead' by Motörhead. Two days later, Ted gets a phone call from Lemmy. Nearly finished the album, Ted, can we go on? Ted shoots down there. And they nearly had. They'd been awake for 72 hours! That's a book in itself."

"Stiff did a record with Motörhead, and didn't want to put it out," says Carroll "They probably had a row with Lemmy. The only reason we did Motörhead was cos the band was breaking up, and Lemmy said we've had enough, we're going to chuck in the towel. He wanted us to put some money in. He said [manager] Doug Smith is putting £100 in, would you be interested in helping us hire the Rolling Stones mobile to record the last gig, and it went from there. The gig was about two weeks later, and I said, OK, it's a lot of money, £300 or something for the day. Why don't we see if we can get another gig at the Marquee in about six weeks' time? We'll have two gigs, and be sure of getting a really good live album out of it. The idea was to do an afternoon gig 'by invite only' for hard-core fans, then a public gig in the evening. We were going to get The Rolling Stones' mobile in, cos they charge the same to hire it for one day, and we'll only have to pay for an extra few reels of tape. Then, to bridge the gap, we decided to do a single, and the single became an album and took on a life of its own."

But soon Motörhead would move on. "Record companies were still wary of Motörhead even though the album had charted," notes Carroll, "and their career was boosted. And they were great live. But the record companies were still afraid of them. Doug Smith was managing them, and he said, 'Look, we need to do another album, and we need ten grand plus recording costs. Can you come up with that?' We just felt at that moment in time, ten grand with probably another 15 grand for recording costs was probably more than we could afford. So they went off to Bronze and had a lot of success there."

Stiff and Chiswick would collaborate to run the Stiff Test/Chiswick Challenge, scouring the country for new talent in late 1977, and also jointly issued a benefit single for MC5 guitarist Wayne Kramer, who had been imprisoned on drug dealing charges. "Both Stiff and us saw the Stiff Test/Chiswick Challenge as an opportunity to steal a bit of limelight from the majors," says Carroll, "anything to garner a bit of publicity. I'd known Dave [Robinson] since about 1964, cos he's from Dublin as well. He'd got involved with the whole Famepushers thing, where they'd tried to hype Brinsley Schwarz [See Stiff Chapter]. Dave was always a devil may care character, with total disrespect for any establishment kind of thinking. And he would bite the hand that fed him. Back in Ireland I played in a band called the Caravells, and I was also in the bank. I had to give up playing in the band because having too many outside activities was frowned upon by the bank. A friend of the Caravells' keyboard player called Kevin Dunn was apprenticed to a well-known Dublin fashion photographer. And a year later he took on a second apprentice, and that was Dave Robinson. Dave took to the camera like a duck to water. There were various Irish showband magazines, and Dave had a deal with them where he would go off and do photographs, and while he was doing it, he would take photos of the band for publicity shots. He'd arrange to have 5,000 postcard handouts done. He was always a wheeler dealer and a very charming sort of guy. Did well with the women and life was never a problem for him. So I knew Dave when he was managing Brinsleys, scuttling round trying to make a living. We were friendly rivals, and whenever we could do anything together to push the independent ball along, we would. The Stiff Test/Chiswick Challenge was one thing, and the Wayne Kramer record to get some money together for him when he came out of jail was another. Dave and Rosemary, when they had the office in Camden, they'd come over to my flat over the shop, and I'd be playing them old records when they were looking for stuff for Tracy Ullman. The good thing about it is that in the initial days of Stiff and Chiswick, people got really involved in the independent thing. They were collecting everything on Stiff, everything on Chiswick, and all the other little labels like Rabid. And suddenly they were having to buy a dozen records every week, without buying anything they really wanted! So then suddenly people started having to be a bit more objective. And suddenly you lost those automatic sales. But at one stage we were selling 3,000 or 4,000 of almost everything we put out."

Most significantly, Chiswick also followed Stiff's lead by signing a distribution deal with EMI in 1978. Again, this came through Churchill's contacts. "We were quite happy with Anchor," says Carroll, "but then ABC in America was bought by MCA, which then became Universal. They closed down the English operation so we had to find someone else. We went to EMI and they signed a licensing deal which guaranteed us an annual advance. We were already doing a lot of licensing to different European people. At that stage we were really focused on building the company and finding talent."

"It was a distribution licence for three years," Armstrong expands, "if we hadn't got the advance we'd have gone bankrupt, we were seriously on the edge. The record shops were a separate business. Ted owned the shops, we didn't. And he owned a third of Chiswick. If the record label had gone under, Ted would still have had the shops, and I would have been back behind the counter or whatever. We were really not in great financial shape at that time. We had an arrangement through Metronome in Germany, Trevor knew them – all those licence deals were through Trevor's contacts because he'd been in the real business in a way that Ted and I hadn't. You got your advance in from your licensing deals, and you tried to get hits and try not to spend too much of the advance." Despite the assistance from EMI however, it had no impact on the label's A&R policy. "Whatever came along and whatever came through the door, bands we saw, friends' recommendations. Our A&R wasn't that clear. Oh, there's a record, we like that."

That hand to mouth existence continued for some time. "We were doing all right," says Armstrong, "keeping our head above water just about. I was probably spending too much money making records by people like Johnny Moped." Croydon's finest were, though hugely amusing, at best a loose fit for punk, led as they were by a kitchen porter with a gruff voice and a harridan wife. "I still stand by that group to this day, fantastic group, but they were never going to have a hit in a million years. And we were advertising them heavily, full page ads in the music press. [Legendary Stiff graphic artist] Barney Bubbles designed it. So we kind of had the punky side going. The second Radiators album we did, after we signed with EMI, was with Tony Visconti. As we came up to the EMI deal in '78, we had Sniff 'n' The Tears 'Driver's Seat' and Rocky Sharpe & The Replays 'Ramalama-ding-dong' in the can. They were both issued with NS catalogue numbers [Chiswick's original catalogue prefix]. We'd done the first Radio Stars record, and actually had to pay quite a lot of money to pick up on the second. Which in retrospect we shouldn't have done. Our fear was that if we went to EMI, who were showing interest, and said, we've just dropped the biggest act we've got... which the Radio Stars were by far at this point."

"By this time I'd arranged an agent for The Radio Stars," says Carroll, "who became their manager, who then tried to take them away to Chrysalis. As far as I was concerned, I wasn't that bothered. There was a contract so we'd have had to work out something, maybe write off the recording costs, and let them walk away. Whatever. Some friends, namely Chris Morrison, my ex-partner in managing Thin Lizzy and Chris O'Donnell, said you can't let them go to Chrysalis. 'You'll never be able to hold on to a band if you let them go.' So in order to stop them going to Chrysalis, we had to do a deal that I wasn't happy with that involved shelling out quite a lot of money. I think the Chris's lent us some of that money and took some equity in the company, that we later bought back from them. But that was the first sign of commercial pressures coming into play." Armstrong still rues that decision. "I remember sharing a bottle of whisky with the EMI rep late one night, and we were smashed as we used to get after hours at EMI, 'Why did you sign us?' He said 'I knew Sniff 'n' the Tears and Rocky Sharpe were hits.' 'What about Radio Stars?' 'Nah. Can't see it.' Shit, we could have let them go and saved a lot of money! All a learning curve."

The Rocky Sharpe connection derived from Carroll's reluctant days as a mobile DJ. "People would come into the shop and say, can you do a disco? I wasn't really into doing that, but I got talked into it. The first one was in a college down in Shepherd's Bush, in Goldhawk Road or somewhere, in 1972. And one of the bands playing was Rocky Sharpe and the Razors, and I think it was their first London gig. They were a New York street hoodlum kind of thing, greased hair and t-shirts and jeans, Sharks versus Jets. They were mostly art students up from Brighton. I remember being taken by them, and saying to Chris Morrison we should sign them up, they'd be great for colleges, but we were concentrating on Thin Lizzy at the time so we didn't." By the time Chiswick released Rocky Sharpe and the Razors' debut EP they'd broken up, with some of the personnel going on to form Darts. Carroll: "A friend of ours who was a fan had recorded some tracks with them and he had a tape, and we did a deal to put that out."

"Sniff 'n' the Tears should have been a hit," laments Armstrong, "internal EMI politics killed that. They had a great set up at EMI. LRD, their Licensed Record Division – Island and Motown went through there and they had a lot of smaller labels. And it had its own sales force. Coming up to Sniff 'n' The Tears, it went into the charts and got *Top Of The Pops*, the whole deal. And suddenly they announced a last-minute reorganisation. GRD, General Record Division, had had two flops in a row – it was Rolling Stones or Queen or Kate Bush, and that was embarrassing when they didn't do as well as they should have. They scrapped the sales force and stole the LRD sales force under the guise of rationalising. The guy that was running the new combined sales force – we were something like 42 in the charts and Ted and I went in and said, 'Look guys, we need one more week on this from your reps. Your guys need to be out there.' We had the picture disc out and everything. 'We just need to hammer this for one more week then fine, it will go or it won't.' 'No, it's fine, it'll be OK.' Number 66 the following week. The guy couldn't face us for days. He used to hide when Ted and I came in!"

Were they, as the above implies, a little more intemperate in their youth? "Yeah, absolutely," admits Armstrong. "I was definitely the more aggressive one. Ted could have his moments getting annoyed. To be honest, in those days, because of the situation in Northern Ireland, shouting at people in a Northern Irish accent could be very threatening to people over here! So there we were at EMI, the Rocky Sharpe thing took off, it got through the change in sales reps, so there we were with one and a half hits. We tried 'I Want Candy' by the Bishops, which got so close, they even got on *Top Of The Pops*. Bow Wow Wow had a hit with it later. We kind of had a phase of that, the Radiators we had three singles off the *Ghost Town* album. One we'd get radio play on but somehow it didn't sell, one we didn't get radio play but the sales looked quite good. We were one of those labels, whether it was because of the records we were making, but we never got that run of hits."

Then, in April 1979, the label was belatedly able to bring The Damned on board. Armstrong had been asked to see a new version of the band (then considered dead in the water) at the Lyceum, long after Stiff had lost interest in their one-time charges. Their Chiswick debut 'Love Story' gave the label a Top 20 hit, thanks to innovative marketing (four picture sleeves, each featuring a different group member). Taking up their option for an album, Armstrong produced *Machine Gun Etiquette*, very much a return to form after they'd stalled on its predecessor, *Music For Pleasure*. "I do think *Machine Gun Etiquette* stands up as a hell of a good record to this day," says Armstrong. "And it's only recently recognised for it. Because The Damned still suffer that hangover from the Anarchy In The UK tour where they allegedly 'broke ranks' and played a gig. The media really hated them for that for years. I remember a breakthrough moment in about '80 or '81, sitting in a pub with Phil [Chevron; Radiators and then Pogues], and there was an *NME* journalist, of all people. They were the ones that detested The Damned and had written all sorts of stuff about them for years. He said, 'Did you produce *Machine Gun Etiquette*?' 'Yeah.' 'That's a fantastic record!' I said, 'I can't believe I'm hearing this from the mouth of an *NME* journalist!' That's the first time that had all changed, and they started to get that sort of reputation. Unlike the other bands, The Damned could actually play. Captain is one of the finest guitar players this country has ever produced."

Armstrong was deflated when follow-up single 'Smash It Up' failed to deliver the chart returns it should have done. "Because of stupid newspaper stories that surfaced, I don't know where they came from. We weren't trying to cause controversy with the band at that point. Some newspaper story appeared saying some punk kids had gone into a party in Ipswich and smashed it up, singing The Damned's 'Smash It Up'. And the BBC dropped us. It would have been a Top 10 record, no two ways about it." However, The Damned's winning streaks were never more than episodic, and after that they once again lost momentum. None of the singles from fourth studio collection *The Black Album*, as excellent as it was, impressed on the charts. Chiswick lost patience at the end of 1980. The Damned were simply costing them too much money.

Some of that fallout has been attributed to the band's penchant for running up damages claims that would have frightened a multinational. Carroll isn't entirely convinced by the self-mythologising. "It's a bit like The Who – it's great publicity. It was never that bad. Sure there was damage, but never that massive. They spent a fair amount of money on recording. At one stage they did owe us a lot of money, but it got recouped fast. With The Damned, that was down to Roger's working relationship with the band breaking down. Not in an awful way, but... The Damned was always very full on, with lots of internal conflict between the Captain and Rat and Dave – whoever was playing bass was almost coincidental. My memory was, after *The Black Album*, which everyone was very pleased with and got very good reviews and was a very good album – it was a question of where do you go next? They went to Doug Smith for management for a while and Doug couldn't handle them, it was just too much of a pain in the arse. Then they got involved with a character that had a recording studio in Denmark Street, where they did that 'Friday the 13th' EP. They were still signed to us at that stage. We ended up buying the tapes for that – it came out on NEMS or something and they went bankrupt. The next thing they got a deal with MCA and managed to blag some money. I think it reached a stage where they were so far in the hole that we really couldn't afford to advance them any more money. We would have done more recording, but that would have involved advancing them more money anyway, and we couldn't afford it. I think they were still under contract, but we had to say thanks but no thanks, and let them out of their contract if they could get another deal. And that's what happened."

Chiswick was holding its own, but struggling to compete with the majors in terms of chart success. There was an obvious reason for that. Unlike Stiff, Chiswick never managed to produce a band that defined the label at a specific time (think Dury, Madness, the Pogues *et al*). There was intermittent success but no one artist who could be relied upon to sell consistently. "Chiswick was never as big in terms of strings of hit singles as Stiff was later," admits Armstrong. "We never had the one big act, though funnily enough we did have the big hit in America, and we did better in Europe than some of the others, Rocky Sharpe did very well in Germany and in Spain. And Sniff 'n' The Tears was a big record all over Europe. And in a certain sense our success was based on that relative failure, because we never washed up with that one big act. Your problem there is twofold. One, there's a lot of money swilling around, but not a lot of it is yours is the reality, and it's hard to keep a grip on that. The other thing about having a huge act is that every act that signs with you expects you to spend a fortune on them. So we had a much more under control scenario. Looking back at some of the things we did, we probably should have tried to get them deals with majors, we should have entrenched ourselves. But because we had licensing deals in Germany or with people around the world, and they were doing well with these acts, you couldn't turn round and say, 'We've sold the act to EMI, sorry about that,' because we'd been advanced by these people. So we were in that situation. In those days it wasn't too bad, we could get hits."

Those hits had dried up by the early 80s though. "EMI dropped us after three years," recalls Armstrong. "We tried to move into the 80s, but the reason we eventually quit really was, again, Ted and I, underneath it all, are rock 'n' roll guys. Records were being hits by men with funny haircuts and strange trousers playing ironing boards – this is not rock 'n' roll. We had a bash at it ourselves, but it was hard work – we had a guy called Jakko Jakowski – fantastic guitar player. And the 'other' Dave Stewart, we did a whole album that only came out in Germany. And the year before Wham!, we had a duo from Hampshire, two nice polite middle class boys, called Two Two. We did an album on them, and three really great singles. The first one was 'Insufficient Data', which was kind of a Hal the computer type deal. But it was a total disco beat, like Wham! did a year later. But the two guys weren't as pretty, our marketing skills were nowhere near up there and ultimately the songs weren't as catchy. We had a group called Albania, very quirky indie-pop type thing, an excellent group again, but the hit wasn't there. And Dave Robinson picked up on them and did records with them. Two Two disappeared, then Dave picked up Jakko as well. We kept Chiswick going. We had distribution through various indie companies for two years, and we had the last hit with Rocky Sharpe and 'Shout Shout'."

The game was up, at least in terms of competing in a changed marketplace with new artists. "Ted and Trevor and I realised, by now it's the early 80s, and you need a video, and to give away a lot of records. It was expensive. In the early days you could float a record for some money, if it was a hit, fine, if it wasn't you didn't lose an awful lot. By the 80s, in order to cover what were going to be losses breaking a band in the UK, you had either to have huge European success or preferably American to get your money back. We were indie again by then. There was no way it was going to happen. The three of us pretty much had a meeting one day and said let's get out while we can. Let's stop pouring money into this stuff. cos we haven't got the money. It's not EMI's money any more, it's ours. We made a deal with this company Metronome where we let them sell through to help to recoup advances, a decent thing to do because they'd been decent to us. I pretty much phoned the bands up, the few we had left, and told them. Some of them got deals, some of them didn't. And we were now an oldies company."

"We said, look, we're making money with the reissues," adds Carroll, "and we're spending it recording these guys and we're not getting any return on it. If there were overseas deals that we were servicing where there were obligations and more money coming in – but it just so happened those deals were coming to an end and there wasn't really anything exciting coming through so they weren't getting renewed. It just made sense. We all agreed. We just couldn't continue. So we basically stopped recording new stuff and concentrated on the old. So Roger went from recording stuff like Two Two and Jakko to helping out on the reissue side. I'd just started Kent Records with Ady Croasdell so I gave that to Roger to work on with Ady. I was also just at the stage of starting Boplicity, a jazz reissue label with Honest John as a consultant – John had record stores in Camden and Portobello Road, a jazz retailer. He acted as a consultant for a year or two with Boplicity, which Roger basically ran. And he was also helping with the Kent and Ace stuff. We just all mucked in together."

While continuing to focus on the company's pure oldies concept at Ace, there were other diversions, the first of which was a venture into the emerging garage scene. In 1981 Carroll was approached by Nick Garrard, a Rock On punter and graphic artist who also produced album artwork for Ace. Garrard was managing one of the new breed of 'psychobilly' bands, The Meteors, who were to be featured in an upcoming short movie *Meteor Madness*, and needed to secure a release for the four tracks they had recorded for the soundtrack. This resulted in the 'Meteor Madness' EP, which quickly became the best seller to date on Ace's Big Beat subsidiary. "Ted sorted out the Meteors deal," says Armstrong. "They sold well. We didn't do the album, we did the singles, and then Nigel [Lewis] split and formed Escalators and Tall Boys. The Stingrays were around, we did some Milkshakes stuff and the Prisoners came in through that Medway connection. In the middle of that we released the cherry on the garage cake *Rockabilly Psychosis*. Which became the record that everyone into that music had to have. That sold enormous amounts. We were the kings of garage at that point, in terms of having most of the decent bands. Then all of a sudden I got the offer of The Cramps. You couldn't turn that one away. To get The Cramps was such a feather in the cap. They came to us from a friend called Steve Pross at Enigma. He was an old mate of mine going way back. He said, 'Look, we're signing The Cramps, you're set up doing Europe, do you want to do Europe?' 'Yes!' *Smell of Female* came out and we became firm friends. And we did a number of records over the years. And that did well."

Big Beat was well positioned to allow them to pick the cream of the garage crop, whereas there were obvious limitations, primarily financial, for Chiswick in the punk years. But, as Armstrong concedes, there was zero possibility of hit records. "You had a healthy enough scene where you could get The Cramps on *The Tube*. Contrary to rumour, *The Tube* used backing tracks mostly, apart from the lead singer. So I went up there and the guy put his hand out for the tape – 'Have you got the tape?' 'What tape?' The look of shock on his face when I told him The Cramps don't do tape, they do live!" Big Beat also helped develop the UK franchise of wild rock 'n' roll that was Billy Childish. Armstrong: "Billy Childish had sent me a copy of the first Milkshakes album. He said, 'Do you want to put this out?'' I wrote back to him and said, 'Well, you seem to have done that! And very well, it sounds great and looks great. But if you want to make another record, we'd be really interested.' Later, someone says Billy paints. So I said Billy, 'Do me a painting.' 'I don't do portraits of people'. 'No, just do me a painting, I'll buy a painting off you.' So he did a self-portrait. And that led me into buying Billy Childish paintings, which I still do. And the boy seems to be finally breaking through on that front. He's starting to be big bucks stuff now. I'm glad to see it, he's worked for it. Billy used to have a very flippant attitude, like all those

Medway guys, they were very offhand. Rough and ready guys. And Tracey Emin just seemed like Billy's girl, a tall girl in miniskirts. She hid her artistic abilities very well, and Billy too. Underneath, a very sophisticated guy."

But the garage boom was a temporary diversion from the company's core activities. Ace was by now a highly regarded reissue imprint, harnessing its three partners' ingrained knowledge of classic American blues and R&B repertoire (and that of consultant Ray Topping). That story took on its own momentum with their exploitation of the neglected catalogue of 40s/50s US independent Modern, founded by the Bihari brothers, whose artists included BB King, Howling Wolf, Elmore James and John Lee Hooker. "We'd always had the reissue thing," says Armstrong. "We did the 10-inch albums originally. That was Ted and Ray Topping, between them. We only put out three or four albums a year of that type, we were mainly running the Chiswick label – the early ones were on Chiswick. Then in 1978, when we went to EMI, they said at the last minute we've got enough old crap of our own – we don't want your old crap."

"We weren't about to dump the blues and rock 'n' roll," says Carroll, "it was selling too well and we needed the money. So, as we had a license with the American label Ace Records, which was based in Jackson, Mississippi, we decided to move all the old stuff off Chiswick and on to a new label, Ace. It was Trevor's suggestion. I called Johnny Vincent, who owned US Ace, and asked him if we could use the name in the UK and he said OK. He never really thought it through. Some years later, when he started to release some new material on his label, he regretted it, as he found that our Ace label was better known than his one."

" Ted and Ray ran the reissues and catalogue," says Armstrong. "Which was always really good, cos that was a very low-risk business to have. It turned money. Back in the days when you could put a 10-inch album out of someone fairly obscure and sell 6,000 copies. It was enormous compared to what you can sell of that stuff nowadays, just because ultimately there was so much less of it around. There was Charly and there was us and a couple of other people that were much lower key. So bit by bit we had built that. We got Ace of Mississippi, we did a deal with Modern Records that we finally bought, we picked up the Glad Music catalogue, which was rockabilly and country with George Jones things. Then we worked with MCA with their Duke and Peacock labels, so we built little catalogue things, just licensing in the early days. That's how we really built the Ace name. I had little to do with that until we left EMI. I stopped producing and hopping into EMI every day. When you run an independent company, you have to be a jack of all trades. You're dealing with the PR people, the pressing people, this, that and the other, and sometimes you're making the record. Suddenly that wasn't happening any more, so I got involved in the catalogue side of things. Then the garage thing came along, so I was distracted by that, I was more involved in that scene than Ted was. And through the 80s Ted and Ray built a fantastic catalogue, and that was where the beginnings of what we do now started – album releases with nice sleevenotes that told you stuff about the music."

Ace became a haven for classic reissues across the rock, soul, blues and blues spectra, growing to encompass labels such as Kent, Cadence and Specialty. "Ted brought Ady Croasdell in to run Kent [its first release was in 1982]. The northern soul thing – what we were doing compiling blues and R&B, we thought we could do with soul. So Ady started Kent with us, and he's run that ever since. But maybe only about a seventh of the records are actually northern soul. The rest are deep soul, more poppy 60s soul, etc." A deal with Fantasy in 1987 also brought a catalogue of vintage jazz recordings from Contemporary, Prestige and Riverside. The label remains by nature acquisitive, to use the singularly inappropriate hard-nosed commercial vernacular. "Modern was a classic example," says Armstrong. "I understand that Charly Records had been offered it, just decided it wasn't for them. Whoever took their decisions obviously thought, there's a bit of BB King, a bit of Ike and Tina Turner – we don't want it. Whereas Ray Topping told Ted that the catalogue is fantastic, we've got to get it. And he was the one who persuaded us. So Ted went and did the deal with the original owners, the Bihari brothers. And Ray was right. Like any of these catalogues, what your reasonably tuned in collector knows about is the top end stuff. Someone like Ray, who had been eating, breathing and sleeping this stuff, knew there were all sorts of things in there, like Pee Wee Crayton, Johnny Guitar Watson, Etta James and so on. So there were great records none of us had actually even heard. Ted was the one who really ran that, and Ted knows records too. In a way it's almost the defining thing between majors and indies. I'm not saying people at major labels have no knowledge. I think their commercial imperative is stronger, and I think they're working in a narrower area."

But it's not just knowledge, according to Armstrong. Good old-fashioned 'taste' is paramount. "Something that always stood Ted and I in really good stead is years working behind a record counter. You'd get a record in, maybe a new release that's under the wire, and it's not going to be a pop hit, or you find 25 copies of a really great old R&B record – you just know. The classic one that had come out a couple of years before and there were deletions around, was Link Wray's 'I'm So Glad, I'm So Proud', on Virgin. Somebody came in from Virgin and offered Ted 600 copies, so he bought them like a shot for 5p each! That was a record that – across the board, people who came in who had bought rock 'n' roll, who bought garage, who bought soul – you dropped the needle on that record and you had a sale. Bang. And that experience, of being at the coal face where people bought records – you could see them come in the shop and play a record and know that they would walk out the door with it. The other thing with us, we may not have had huge hits over the years, but we've put out more records than most people. I don't think I ever had the attention span, funnily enough, to make hit records and break them. It's time-consuming. To work on one thing. To break an act, you've got to have this weird long-term dedication to that act. I don't have that. I like too much music. I've got favourite acts and labels I really like, but I could never see myself spending ten years working with U2, I don't have the attention span!"

Ace also added the GlobeStyle franchise, under the tutelage of Ben Mandelson (who had once recorded for Chiswick with punk era misfits Amazorblades). "I chaired all the meetings for the world music thing," recalls Armstrong. "We were asking what shall we call it. Someone said world beat, someone said world music, we took a vote and world music won. World music was criticised – 'Oh, we don't want to be a world music act.' But it started as a rack in a record shop. That's why Ben and me called the meetings in the first place – we had no presence in record shops, we won't survive without it. That was what I spent much of the later 80s and 90s doing, field trips to Mozambique, Madagascar, Zanzibar. World music is interesting from the point of view of how something developed through independent record companies. One of the reasons I'm not involved in world music any more, and Ace isn't, is that because in a sense it's become more mainstream. In terms of how you have to behave – you have to have the band come in and tour them. Back then in the 80s when we were doing it, Charlie Gillett and Andy Kershaw played your record, and John Peel might if it were Zimbabwean (LAUGHS)."

"We had this thing going with the 3 Mustaphas 3," Armstrong continues, "and they toured heavily. But Ace is not really geared to new acts any more, and to be in the world music business, you're talking about new acts. Which entails a different kind of perseverance. Obviously the *Bob Dylan Theme Time Radio Hour* [the recent CD release accompanying Dylan's radio shows that has garnered huge acclaim] has done very well. But most of these things come out, get their month's shot at it, and they're gone. That's a different world to keeping an act going for a period of time. And if you want to cross over, you have to cross over *from* somewhere. If you're in the world music area, you can cross over. Youssou N'Dour did, Salif Keita did. Poor woman, if she'd lived, Ofra Haza would have – she'd have been much bigger. And in a way world music has grown up, and stuff has been chucked into that pot, things have been spat back into pop from it, Neneh Cherry or whatever. I think it's broadened people's outlook and made them more tolerant to an extent, they're listening to stuff they wouldn't have listened to 20 years ago. Maybe it'll wear itself in time, but world music is a handy tag. And world music developed as a very indie thing – guys would pop a record out, sell a few copies, do well out of it, maybe the band would come in, or would be in through the auspices of a local indigenous group or whatever. It was all very localised, and now it's a very much bigger thing. You've seen something like World Circuit go from being a small company and doing nice touring things and starting a record label to the way things developed around Buena Vista and Ali Farka Touré. That's a little indie business that's grown. OK, the majors are a bit more involved, but it's still a very indie-centred business, world music. It's been nice to see that over the last 20 years. We had a good run at the world music thing, and we put out a lot of seminal records. Ben Mandelson is a brilliant man when it comes to that. He's as good at that as Ray Topping is with blues and R&B in terms of knowing his onions. The world music period came and went, but I'm still to this day quite proud of what we did."

Additionally, the company played a pivotal role, via its Beat Goes Public imprint, in the subsequent Acid Jazz boom. "I don't care what people think about world music and acid jazz at the end of the day," says Armstrong, "they sold records, people made some money, and they were good records. We sold a million records on Acid Jazz. Giles Peterson walked in and said, 'There's an acid house thing that's going round, what if we called ours Acid Jazz?' And again, that's where an indie comes into play. A major would have to have 15 committee meetings before deciding it's too off the wall to do. Whereas I said, yeah, why not. We got someone to design a psychedelic cover. Giles came up with things like 'Psychedelic Sally' and appropriate titles. We stuck it out and it sold 20,000 copies. That's where the indie thing is useful, to be able to move quite fast on your feet and get something moving. In some ways, we're almost more commercial whores than the majors at times. At the time of Acid Jazz, Ady used to do a Friday night at the 100 Club, where he'd play the jazzier side of soul music; organ and Hammond-based stuff. An instrumental version of 'In The Midnight Hour' and stuff like that. I would go down with a friend of mine and dance the night away. After one of those gigs, I said to him, we've got to make a CD of this. Just off the top of my head,

## Gatecrashers

I said why don't we call it Mod Jazz? And now we're up to about volume seven, and people now talk about Mod Jazz as a genre."

As all these tributary interests attest, while Ace is synonymous with specific genres, it hasn't been afraid to test new ground. "People think they know what Ace is about," confirms Armstrong, "but there's so many different threads. Never mind inventing Mod Jazz and New Breed (a development of Northern Soul) and all these things – we did a lot of Cajun reissues for a long time. And then was a strong streak of early country stuff. So to an extent we do respond to the people who are working for us and what they know."

While Chiswick never became a cause célèbre in the music press *ala* Stiff, nor enjoyed the same level of chart success, its Ace outgrowth survives to this day. That longevity is due almost entirely to the accumulated knowledge and expertise of its staff – the sort of dedicated market insight that only comes from a lifetime of devotion. No major label could ever hope to match that time investment for what remains a niche market. Significantly, it took a UK specialist independent label to realise the value in the vaults of the pre-eminent American independents, turning the story full circle. "We get letters from America saying it's a disgrace that American companies don't do this," says Armstrong. "But it's faraway grass and faraway hills. To a large extent what we do now – growing up in the 50s, it was hard to hear this music. You can't imagine what it was like hearing a Little Richard record in the 50s – it could have been from Mars, it was so 'other'. And even soul music, it was brilliant to us, cos it was over 'there'."

"A label like Ace," adds Carroll, "it would be more difficult for us to exist in America. Ace exists because of the European market, and of course that's decreasing as the old collectors drop off the perch. We still manage to sell records, but a lot of the things we do now are more accessible, a lot of the things like the Producers series, the Spector sound-a-likes which sells really well, the Golden Age of Rock 'n' Roll, some of those things. Those support the more obscure releases by lesser-known blues artists and so on. We need the sales we get in America and the European sales and the English sales to make it work. I don't think you'd get the same level of European and English sales if you were based in America. You might get a tiny bit more American sales, but not enough to make the difference. We're kind of number one in a field of one, in that we fall in the middle between say Bear Family Records and Rhino. Rhino have a slightly more commercial spin, and Bear Family are even more obscure and obtuse than us. But what all three of us have in common is that we all produce very high-quality reissues, and we're in the middle, mining a little of the super-specialist area that Bear Family does, and we're appealing also to the sort of people who buy Rhino reissues."

With a glut of 30th anniversaries in the offing around the publication of this book, Ace has long since celebrated its own, intact, and independent. "I'm not one of those people that says we're better than the majors morally or whatever," says Armstrong. "We're different, but why? But in my case, it's the whole idea of dedicating yourself to a big act or two year in and year out. I think people working in the indie world like lots of music. We're maybe more fans, and that fan aspect dominates more than the business side. If you're an independent record company, and you have a desire for power, it's not the place to go. Trevor, our third partner, is the one who is most like someone at a major in a sense. He started at EMI and Polydor and various big record companies. He ended up joining two crazy Irishmen, Ted and me, because he couldn't handle the politics. The politics at majors – a friend of mine went to EMI to set up a world music label and got the job. He came out of the meeting and he was talking to a couple of people. And one of the guys turned to him and said, 'Never forget, in this building there are at least ten people who want your job, and are prepared to do anything to get it.' What a way to come into work in the morning!"

And they've never lost their enthusiasm for turning up a good record. "Well, a few weeks ago the three of us were having a meeting at my house," Armstrong recalls. "Ted was down for some PPL (the music rights organisation) House of Commons thing with his wife. Ted and I ended up at my house for the afternoon, because Trevor had gone off and Ted had time to kill. I thought, I'm not going in to work. So I opened up my record collection. I brought out about four boxes of 45s and set Ted up with a record player. And we just had the best afternoon. The four boxes were random stuff, unfiled, stuff I'd acquired left right and centre. I didn't know if they were good or bad records. Ted just had the nose for it. He was just playing great records, stuff he didn't even know. Only once did he skip a record, and took the needle off, but the whole afternoon he spent doing a crossword and dropping the needle on one good record after another."

# Chapter Three

## So It Goes

## Stiff Records

The year 1976 has become a uniquely mythologised one in British musical culture. It is not that the punk generation was the first to celebrate its youth a quarter century along its timeline, more that, in the new millennium, that same generation enjoys unprecedented levels of media access. While the much discussed tenets of the punk era hold true – a reaction against a stilted music scene, a government in crisis, a peeling back of post-war austerity etc, the crucial enabling event was the piecemeal arrival of a series of labels able to operate outside conventional music industry structures. That is one good reason why the terms 'punk' and 'independent' have become so synonymous. Did punk spawn independent music as we now know it, or vice versa? It is a defining chicken and egg question for any historian of the era.

The historical fudge is, however, appropriate. The stories of the labels and artists who were involved in sowing the seeds of that particular revolution can be individually attributed to either theory of chronological hierarchy – that punk begat the modern concept of independent records or the reverse. Collectively, the evidence is contradictory.

Stiff Records, one of the most colourful stories of this or any musical era, and headed by two of its most abrupt but intriguing characters, was not coincidentally founded in London in 1976 by Dave Robinson and Andrew Jakeman (later to take the name Jake Riviera). The ethos of the label combined self-deprecating and provocative humour, embodied in their defining slogan, "If it ain't Stiff, it ain't worth a fuck", a highly individualistic A&R policy and a can-do work ethic. Another of the label's mottos also proved highly pertinent – "When you kill time, you murder success". It underscored their blunt realism and unabashed concern with the bottom line. Riviera, in particular, cultivated a brusque press image that helpfully intimidated promoters and distributors into paying in full and on time, while many artists were openly in thrall to his domineering persona. And Dave "nor shall my baseball bat sleep by my side" Robinson was no pussycat either.

Stiff was most remarkable, however, in terms of innovation. They were an independent who held major labels in complete disdain, yet exhibited globe-conquering ambition. Certainly their package tours in the late 70s, which featured almost their entire artist roster on a shared platform, were huge logistical exercises that defied the homespun, DIY ethic that grew out of punk. There was none of the timorous hiding behind fringes or aesthetic pretension that characterised some later independent labels, or any shame in hyping records in what was then an otherwise uneven playing field. Their A&R policy, from Nick Lowe to Elvis Costello to Ian Dury, and onwards through Madness and The Pogues, revealed an instinct for discerning creative longevity rather than the pot-shot 45s that so eloquently announce punk's *esprit de corps*.

There was good reason for that. Many Stiff acts had roots in the pub rock scene that immediately presaged punk, and it seems certain that Riviera and Robinson, the latter Riviera's flatmate's boyfriend, would have sustained some foothold or niche in the music industry regardless of the generational upheaval going on around them. But they were smart enough to realise that punk was opening up doors – or forcing entry – quicker and more effectively than they could have managed otherwise.

Both founders had long pedigrees. Robinson had briefly worked for Jimi Hendrix in the 60s, before going on to manage pub rockers Brinsley Schwarz and, intermittently, Ian Dury's first band, Kilburn & The High Roads, as well as Graham Parker. Similarly, Riviera was a former tour manager for Doctor Feelgood and manager of Chilli Willi & The Red Hot Peppers. He had previously been involved in a failed independent label venture, Revelation, which housed the Chilli Willis' debut album *Kings Of The Robot Rhythm* (1972). Robinson too had experienced his share of setbacks – he was behind the famously disastrous 'hype of the century' attempt to launch Brinsley Schwarz by flying a plane-load of journalists, DJs, competition winners and hangers-on to America for a show at the Fillmore East in New York.

It was the Feelgoods' Lee Brilleaux who loaned the duo the initial £400 to establish the label. Or at least, that became the cover story. "We never cashed that!" confirms Robinson. "The cheque was on the wall for years. It was very nice of him to do it. We gave him shares, actually. At some point we gave everyone a few shares in Stiff – not very valuable in the final analysis, but there you are!" In fact, the initial funding for Stiff came from the duo's management activities. "I was a manager and Jake managed the Chilli Willis. I had a management company, so when we decided we might do the label I gave him half of it. And essentially the finance that made the label work was the income from the management company. We were managing Graham Parker at that point and Ian Dury for a while, and obviously eventually Elvis Costello."

## So It Goes

The label was based at 32 Alexander Street, with Blackhill Enterprises, another management concern helmed by Pete Jenner and Andrew King, former Pink Floyd managers, located upstairs (in the mid-60s, the top floor flat had been home to Roger Waters). Robinson had already convinced Blackhill to invest in Ian Dury's publishing, and that eventually led to them taking over Dury's management in February 1976. When the concept of a record label was formalised over a pub conversation between Riviera and Robinson, knowing that Blackhill had some spare floorspace, they decided to site their operation there. Robinson would initially sleep under his desk.

The duo's background in the business proved crucial to Stiff's approach and development. Indeed, the label was named after the industry term for a 'flop', tacitly acknowledging the duo's previous misadventures. The impetus for the label had grown out of their frustration at working with major labels. "It was essentially a situation where we were managers, and had a band called Clover, who were signed to major record labels, Phonogram mainly," Robinson continues. "And the essence was that their marketing was not what Jake and I both thought marketing should be. In those days the groups just went on tour, and you struggled for a bit of tour support possibly, but that was all you got. A quarter page ad in *Sounds* was the extent of their marketing. They didn't have any ideas about how to place the ad and how to make something out of the ad, really, apart from occasionally using a few reviews, if you had them. The great slogan the record industry was run on, and still is, was 'out now'. That was their only way to attract any attention to a record that would obviously have some quality or you wouldn't be putting it out. But they had no slogans, or attitude; they didn't think the public was interested in marketing ideas other than live touring and the odd 'out now'. As a manager you're trying to get some movement forward, and you've got ideas for your artists, but you couldn't get the majors to cough up and take an interest. So we used all those ideas at Stiff." The initial influence for Robinson was Chris Blackwell's Island Records – which would ultimately provide its own horrible irony. "Island was the great model, and I certainly had that in my mind for the record label – a kind of family label that took care of its artists in general, and were able to do quite a lot of the chores of management. Cos a lot of our groups obviously didn't have managers."

Just as importantly, both Robinson and Riviera were aware of a pool of unexposed talent that the majors were effectively ignoring. Robinson: "When I ran the pub thing in 1972, there were an awful lot of bands and musicians – we're speaking pre-computer or digital music – and everyone had to *play*. And I had a predictably close feel for live music. Although I'd made some efforts to get A&R people from major record labels down, and although the pubs were heaving with people, they would just say 'it's a pub thing' and weren't interested. So there was a lot of very good stuff at that time drawing big crowds, with A&R people ignoring it – the majors having decided that theatrical rock and platform shoes were where it was at. So we were diametrically opposed to what was happening musically and stylistically in the major record labels. We were anti-major as a result. We *resented* them. And laughed at them generally."

The first release came from Nick Lowe. His 'So It Goes' has long been considered part of the fabric of the punk story, but in truth is a much more restrained endeavour than its upstart peers, indebted to the artist's long established credentials as a songwriter on the pub rock scene with Brinsley Schwarz. Yet is served as the perfect bridge between the backgrounds of all those involved with Stiff and the new dawn musically. It was accompanied by a mocking press release, advocating sound over technique, and songs of less than three minutes' length and a similar number of chords. The author was Vinyl Mogul, a pseudonym for Riviera. That 'punk' manifesto was also reflected in Lowe's dextrous referencing of the coming era. The song title was derived from Kurt Vonnegut's *Slaughterhouse 5* catch phrase and also used as the title of Tony Wilson's Granada TV music show, which would first screen the Pistols. The b-side, 'Heart Of The City', meanwhile, featured a closing reference to the (pre-Clash) 101ers' 'Keys To Your Heart', freshly released on Chiswick. The recording costs of just £45 were comfortably recouped after sales in excess of 10,000 copies. To that point penniless and dispirited by the music industry, Lowe's days kipping on Riviera's couch were drawing to a close.

The early Stiff discography thereafter ranged from the pub rock of Roogalator, Tyla Gang and Lew Lewis to underground garage rockers The Pink Fairies (who had recently been augmented by ex-Chilli Willis guitarist Martin Stone). Indeed, original plans (ventured in an early press release) were to issue unreleased recordings by prior management concerns Brinsley Schwarz and Chilli Willi. Each of these releases boasted a 'gimmick'. The Pink Fairies (BUY 2) single 'Between The Lines' was the first Stiff release to feature a picture sleeve, while Roogalator's effort played at 33 1/3RPM, with a sleeve that parodied *With The Beatles* (and was withdrawn after complaints from EMI). The Tyla Gang release, led by former Ducks Deluxe guitarist Sean Tyla, was promoted as 'the world's first double b-side single'. If the pub rock connections weren't explicit enough, the follow-up came from Lew Lewis, the former Hot Rods' harmonica player, backed by pseudonymous Feelgood members. A projected concept trio featuring Larry Wallis, Sean Tyla and Dave Edmunds recording themed songs such as 'Food', credited to the Takeaways, was confined to an appearance on the later odds and sods compilation album, *A Bunch Of Stiffs*.

Riviera also made an attempt to licence the Modern Lovers' album from Beserkley, a label he'd been impressed by, but that plan was scuppered where the American label elected to set up its own UK base in Kingston Upon Thames. Stiff also placed an advert inviting new talent to submit demos. The first respondent was Declan MacManus, who turned up for an audition after the release of 'So It Goes' with guitar in hand. In the event, neither Riviera or Robinson were at the office, but they made him their first signing after hearing the demo he left behind (Lowe had never signed an official contract). Similarly, Eric Goulden handed in his demo in person, but was so nervous he got drunk beforehand and bolted from the office after handing it over. Within days he too, under the name Wreckless Eric, joined the fledgling label.

But it was with the release of BUY 6 in October 1976 that Robinson and Riviera's then tiny independent gave the world its first taste of punk on vinyl. The Damned's 'New Rose' beat the Sex Pistols to the punch, providing irrefutable evidence that a new breed of independent could now respond quicker to events than hidebound majors. The Pistols' delay in reaching vinyl, though only a few months, was decisive in this fast-moving timeframe. Despite their unconventional billing and reputation, the Pistols were put through the same 'development' rigour as other EMI artists – different producers were assigned to perfect the sound, discussions were held between management and label as demo tapes were circulated, etc.

The Damned came to Stiff's attention after playing alongside a clutch of their bands at the first Mont de Marsan European Punk Festival and had their effort recorded, cut and in the racks within weeks. They were ably, albeit nonchalantly, assisted by Nick 'Basher' Lowe (nicknamed thus due to his titular ability to 'bash it out') "We were much faster," agrees Robinson. "At the end of the day, we could do everything very, very quickly. And we planned to. We did plan to have the first punk album [a feat Stiff duly achieved with the March 1977 release of *Damned Damned Damned*]. There were a load of punk singles about, but obviously getting the first punk album out was an effort that was worthwhile. There was a huge crowd of people who wanted to buy an album but nobody had made one. So that was a big moment."

## Independence Days

Although the Stiff connection to punk was tenuous, Robinson was quite happy to use the window of opportunity to help the label build up a head of steam. "It pointed the press at us a bit, because we had The Damned and [later] The Adverts. But there were four or five papers at the time, and the amount of weekly news that was required was huge – so any kind of pumped story was of interest to the papers. Any new band you made a bit of a hubbub about, which we planned to each time, would get coverage. Do something unusual, put them in an odd place – we were thinking that punk would be the way to open the door towards music that we considered very good, but was ignored by everyone else. It was a way of getting the focus of the public on it, and of course John Peel – he really liked Stiff, and he played 'So It Goes' – he was a huge part of it."

The immediate successor to 'New Rose' was Richard Hell's 'Another World'. Better known for one of its b-side tracks, 'Blank Generation', it provided a domestic showing for the late 70s New York CBGB's set that many consider punk's true progenitors. Notable for a sleeve featuring a topless Hell and razorblade typography, it was licensed from Terry Ork's independent Ork Records who had also released Television's debut single. This time the gimmick was the numbered pressing – 5,000 copies were seemingly all given the release number '0001', which still bemuses unwary collectors to this day.

Thereafter, Stiff releases reverted to type. Plummet Airlines were a band who established an accommodation between pub rock and punk, while Motorhead offered a similarly perfect hybrid with metal. However, Motorhead's 'White Line Fever' (BUY 9), was pulled from the schedule for reasons aligned to ongoing negotiations with Island for a full distribution deal. Skydog eventually licensed the single for a French release. Stiff's eventual two-year deal with Island was ultimately celebrated by the release of a second Damned single, 'Neat Neat Neat'. Stiff deleted all their previous single releases not just as a mark of respect, but a statement of intent.

"We were very lucky to be able to get some help from United Artists," remembers Robinson, discussing the link to a major that technically saw the label cease to be a true independent. The association had begun when Riviera brought in his old friend Andrew Lauder at United Artists to cope with the demand for 'New Rose'. "To begin with, you couldn't press records. There were very few records made outside the majors' manufacturing factories. And they weren't that pushed about doing other people's records. The whole basis of the majors is that they would be distributors and manufacturers. Because they had factories, they signed up their own groups.

That's how they started. Originally they were manufacturers and distributors. And essentially that's all they were ever fucking good for, in my book. Even to this day, look at the chaos they've caused in the music industry – the fact that people are downloading for nothing and feel that music is free is all down to the attitude of the majors. They've buggered up everybody's game here in the record industry. They're still thrashing around not quite knowing what to do and allowing Apple to run their businesses. They can't last much longer. But they weren't that clever then, either. At the end of the day, manufacturing was hard to come by, so United Artists manufacturing our records through EMI was a boon. Then Island, who were independent, or at least running their own business, came in through EMI."

This was, indeed, revolutionary stuff, and others took note. "All the indie labels started calling us saying, 'How do you do it?' We did a sheet that gave them the in-roads of how to make labels, and what to do and how to get your records made, your 7-inch or whatever. We sent out loads of those. I suppose, to a degree, you'll find that Rough Trade, Beggars Banquet, all those kind of labels, essentially got their start in life from a photocopied sheet from Stiff. We started saying,' We've no time to be dealing with your stupid questions, but here are the details.'"

In fact, despite their accumulated wealth of experience, Stiff's founders were navigating their own voyage of discovery. "We knew nothing about labels. We had been brought up on the idea of signing a band to a major and them becoming Decca Recording artists, etc. It was still in that kind of era. No, we didn't know anything. So when we found we were pressing up a record – we didn't have a huge amount of money but we could press 1,000, which we got rid of quickly. Then we pressed another 1,000 and then another 1,000. Eventually we took the plunge and pressed 5,000. It was all feeling it out. But, between us, Jake and I, I suppose all our efforts in music as long-term managers had been towards this particular end. I started as a photographer, I worked at printing for a while – I had learned a great deal. I had produced quite a few records – nothing very good, but things like Frankie Miller. So when it came to the record label, we found, between Jake and I, we had pretty much all the talents to make it work, from the advertising through to the physical production of the vinyl. And we put it in picture bags because we were keen on artwork – we had Barney Bubbles, don't forget, probably one of the great UK graphic artists. He was working for Stiff. So we had great art. We had a lot of music that was organically produced by the bands themselves, we had Nick Lowe to do it in the studio, and Jake and I were, I think, quite talented promotion men."

Indeed, Bubbles, aka Colin Fulcher, was among the most innovative designers of the punk era – his influence openly acknowledged by the likes of Malcolm Garrett and other scions. A former illustrator for *Oz* and *Friends* magazines, and sleeve designer for underground rockers Hawkwind (he would actually record an album with Hawkwind's Nik Turner in 1982 as the Imperial Pompadours), his friendship with Robinson dated back to the latter's days at the Famepushers' PR agency. He was also an intimate of Riviera, having designed the sleeves for his Revelation releases. Probably his most iconic designs were the mock-Cubist Blockheads' logo and the 1978 redesign of the *NME* masthead that still survives in adulterated form to this day. However, he committed suicide in 1983, and his longstanding refusal to sign his work limited his legacy. "Only a unique man with Barney's immense dignity and talent had both the courage and modesty to do just that," Riviera would later state.

Riviera came up with most of the slogans, though the most memorable, 'If It Ain't Stiff', was coined by Kilburn & The High Roads' drummer George Butler, who was eventually paid a £100 gratuity for his masterstroke. The limited print run of the singles was done with a wary eye on the collector's market – making public their intention to delete everything in the catalogue after release. Bulk orders soon flooded in from retailers. And, as was the case with The Damned's debut album, Stiff weren't above old-fashioned hype – proclaiming the fact that a quantity of the sleeves featured a picture of Eddie And The Hot Rods 'mistakenly' printed on the rear. They were also aware of their own history and that of the band's – the Hot Rods had replaced The Damned at the Nashville after the infamous 100 Club bottling incident, the group being dismissed by the Pistols' John Lydon as "a glossy Eddie & The Hot Rods". "Of course it was a stunt," Scabies later told Will Birch. "Although it was described at the time as a printer's error. But it's safe to blow it now. Jake had worked out how many LPs we needed to sell to recoup the recording costs. That was the quantity that was pressed with the Hot Rods picture on the back; about two or three thousand only. Jake knew that it would appeal to the collector's market. He was totally hip to all that. The marketing was brilliant."

Meanwhile, Stiff's greatest asset had been kept under wraps – principally because it took a little while for everyone to recognise its potential value. MacManus's first recordings for the label had been made with Lowe back in September 1976, but the proposed selections, 'Radio Sweetheart' and 'Mystery Dance', had lost their place in the schedule. So too had 'Whole Wide World' by Eric Goulden (shortly to be renamed Wreckless Eric due to his predisposition for anxiety and alcohol). At one point there was a proposal to release a joint album featuring both. After hearing demo tracks recorded by Costello during studio downtime at a Goulden session, both Robinson and Riviera immediately recognised the potential of the songs. MacManus was thereafter remoulded into the now familiar image – skinny-tied punk rock Buddy Holly complete with horn-rimmed glasses – with Riviera suggesting he adopt the name Elvis. In the event, his first single for the label, 'Less Than Zero' (BUY 11), failed to sell. The same fate befell a follow-up, 'Alison', which led to a revision of plans. Stiff asked Costello to give up his job as a computer programmer at Elizabeth Arden and turn professional. In return they would throw the label's weight behind him and guarantee him a wage – he was married with a young child – and also sponsor a full-time backing band. Costello thereafter became Stiff's 'priority' act.

With the release of music hall comedian Max Wall's version of Kilburn & The High Road's 'England's Glory', two things became readily apparent. First, the label's rising profile could not rescue a commercial flop of that magnitude. Secondly, there was no 'Stiff sound'. Robinson believes that what Nick Lowe, working at the famously budget-conscious Pathway Studios, brought to the table was exactly that he *didn't* stamp his production style on those records. "Essentially the groups at that time would do their own rehearsals," he says. "They'd have written the song, worked it out – they were all live bands, they'd all have played the songs in. And so Nick would, as he well put it – 'bash it down, and tart it up'. And that stops long recording sessions. We were allowing time very much like the Atlantic or early R&B labels in America, where you would come in for a session of three hours, and produce an a-side and two b-sides." That efficient use of time and resources "is the reason I think some of the tracks still sound OK – they were made to a unique kind of ethos. They weren't 'produced' into any kind of stylistic production arena, really." Thereafter Stiff also used the services of a second 'in-house producer' in the shape of Larry Wallis, freed for the task after the collapse of The Pink Fairies. He was set to work on the one-off single, 'One Chord Wonders', produced by Stiff's second legitimate punk act, The Adverts, though bass player Gaye Advert was not best pleased with the scam of using her image alone on the single's cover. The label's unapologetic exploitation of female sexuality would continue well into the 80s.

Despite renegotiating the Island/EMI distribution deal and extending it from two years to three, a third Costello single, '(The Angels Wanna Wear My) Red Shoes', again failed to establish him on release in July 1977. Anxieties were such that when his debut album *My Aim Is True* was finally released, it came with a 'Help Us Hype Elvis' leaflet – the first 1,000 purchasers would be entitled to a second copy of the album to be despatched to a friend. It almost crippled the label financially. That represented only one of myriad attempts to heighten his profile. Costello busked outside the Hilton Hotel in an effort to persuade American CBS executives to attend his performance that evening at Dingwalls. And Riviera took out double-page spreads in *Sounds*, *Melody Maker* and *NME* to promote the album – if each were cut out, they assembled into a giant poster. The album rose to number 14 and Elvis got his American deal through CBS-owned Columbia.

Meanwhile Ian Dury was growing frustrated, as the rest of the pub rock pack seemed to be overtaking him. Indeed, he had produced and drummed on the b-side to Wreckless Eric's 'Whole Wide World', which finally emerged in August. Blackhill had funded the recording of his debut album, but hadn't found a berth for it among the majors, despite protracted negotiations. So Blackhill took the step of suggesting he look downstairs, especially since Stiff now had the muscle of a major distributor. Licenses were signed and his 'Sex & Drugs & Rock 'n' Roll' was released the day after Wreckless Eric's single as BUY 17. *New Boots & Panties* followed at the end of September.

Plans were being hatched for arguably the key moment in establishing Stiff's identity. The *5 Live Stiffs* tour started out on 3 October 1977, just after the release of *New Boots & Panties*, featuring Wreckless Eric, Ian Dury, Nick Lowe, Larry Wallis and Dave Edmunds. Again, it harked back to the American R&B model (the Motown Revue especially), but also to a 1968 tour Robinson worked on with Jimi Hendrix, The Move and Pink Floyd. Over 24 dates, mainly on university and polytechnic campuses, the Stiff bandwagon rolled, each performance concluding with a sozzled choir augmenting the finale of Dury's 'Sex & Drugs And Rock 'n' Roll'. The personnel was flexible. Dury would drum for Wreckless Eric, former Kilburn & The High Roads saxophonist Davey Payne would back both Dury and Wreckless Eric, etc. Kosmo Vinyl served as MC (and the bus driver, Trevor, would naturally become 'Clever Trevor' in honour of the Dury song) while everybody got a flat £50 a week fee. Of course, in later years it has emerged that serious rivalries rippled just below the surface among the label's leading lights, especially concerning the abandonment of the original plan whereby the acts would alternate for headline status. The tour's Olympian levels of debauchery – and the notorious '24-hour Club' of hardcore drinkers – are thought to be the inspiration behind Costello's 'Pump It Up' single. It certainly inspired the memos circulated to all artists telling them to stop charging any additional hotel refreshments beyond breakfast to the record label.

Costello and Ian Dury became natural figureheads for Stiff, but very much in that order. By now, music journalists were describing a more structured, traditional rock format derived from punk as new wave (although the etymology of that term is complicated and weaves in and out of the 'punk' story), and Stiff had the two most inspired and capable songwriters in that firmament. Dury's vaudeville Cockney funk was more playful than Costello's precise, erudite pop, but both were immensely gifted wordsmiths who would reinvigorate the pop charts. Sadly, Costello's potential was only glimpsed at Stiff. Following the end of the Live Stiffs tour, Riviera moved on to form Radar Records with A&R legend Andrew Lauder. In the settlement eked out, he took Costello, Nick Lowe and recent Stiff singings The Yachts with him. Barney Bubbles would continue to work for both labels. The split sprung from a confrontation the two protagonists had on 24 September 1977, at which Riviera was said to have thrown a bunch of empty cider cans through the office window. The incident was later cheekily referenced in Nick Lowe's first hit for Radar, 'I Love The Sound Of Breaking Glass'.

"Essentially it was about 14 months, really," Robinson remembers of the first phase of Stiff. "That's how long it lasted. It seemed an awful lot longer at the time!" It's tempting to assume that this was a natural conclusion for a relationship between two very strong-minded characters who were both natural 'leaders'; that it could only have worked for a set amount of time "There was a bit of opportunism," Robinson states. "I struggled quite a bit and got my foot in the door with CBS to get a record deal in America. The deal we were talking about would have moved us up several notches. But the major interest at the time was Elvis. And Jake saw an opportunity, I think, and wanted to do his own thing."

Although Radar, backed by Warner UK, didn't prosper as many expected, they released close on a century of records, following a similarly wide-ranging A&R brief (though they may have separated, it's fair to state that Robinson and Riviera's musical tastes didn't diverge too greatly). As well as Lowe and Costello, there was power pop from The Yachts, Inmates and Bram Tchaikovsky, French *avant garde* from Metal Urbain, UK psych-pop from the Soft Boys, and a raft of formative American pre-punk reissues, including the Electric Prunes and 13th Floor Elevators. Finally came the experimental post-punk of Bristol's Pop Group – which legendarily tipped Radar over the financial brink. By March 1980, Riviera had set up F-Beat, while the Radar imprint would latterly be used for Jools Holland's solo releases. Later in 1980, in concert with Lauder and Elvis Costello, Demon Records became Riviera's fourth record label in just over three years. Notable early Demon releases include Department S's 'Is Vic There?', their first hit, as well as material by Bananarama, Lamont Dozier, Hoodoo Gurus, Men They Couldn't Hang, That Petrol Emotion and Costello himself. Later the roster was notable for a clutch of US artists such as Thin White Rope, Giant Sand, Dream Syndicate and American Music Club that represented a halfway house between the Paisley Underground movement and the coming age of folk-rooted Americana. Acquired by Crimson Productions, a subsidiary of retail giant and Woolworth's owner Kingfisher, it merged with its Westside Records operation in 1998. It is now known as Demon Music Group, though a repertoire that includes cruise singer Jane McDonald, and the absence of any of its founders, rather distances it from its historical origins.

In the absence of Riviera, Robinson had two general managers to fall back on; former agent and Kursaal Flyers' manager Paul Conroy and Alan Cowderoy, previously a musician with Gracious, and the ex-product manager for Graham Parker at Phonogram. Conroy looked after UK marketing, while Cowderoy concentrated on International Exploitation – expanding Stiff's impressive list of licensees, which at one point topped 36 separate agreements. It was the advances Cowderoy secured for these, as much as the hits that Stiff had, that kept the label profitable – in the process creating the blueprint for many 90s labels. "Jake was still there when I joined," remembers Cowderoy. "I was working at Vertigo Records, and that's how I first met Dave Robinson. He managed Graham Parker and the Rumour, and they were signed to Vertigo. We were creating great marketing campaigns for Graham Parker. And Dave Robinson was bringing in Damned singles and Nick Lowe singles, and saying, 'this is how you need to do it'. We were getting on really well. We came up with creative ideas to market Graham Parker to the extent where he eventually said – 'come over and join me'. I was at the right age. It was worse money, no company car, and no pension. There was no security at all. But I thought, 'this is really exciting,' so I took the plunge. But when I arrived there, Paul Conroy had arrived ahead of me. He was a friend of Jake's, but I didn't really know Jake. Dave and Jake shared an office and they were planning world domination from there. But I don't think they communicated to each other quite as well as they might have done. So when I got there, Paul had set his stall out so that he was looking after the English marketing situation. Which was really what I wanted to do! So I ended up looking after the international situation, doing the licensing deals. Basically what I used to do is generate the income that allowed the label to carry on. Because really and truly, Robbo could spend every penny that was generated in the UK on marketing and being creative, but it was all for nothing unless I managed to get money in from overseas. So fortunately

I managed to coax the French and the Germans and Scandinavians and Japanese and Australians, and get a great network of licensees for Stiff."

Both Cowderoy and Conroy also helped out with A&R, while Cowderoy was additionally in charge of mastering. But the days immediately following Riviera's departure were dark ones. "There was a guy Jake had appointed to be the bookkeeper at Stiff," Robinson recalls. "When I looked at this guy's desk and filing system, I found a lot of invoices that hadn't even been opened. There was a huge amount. At that time, Jake was very keen to run very big ads on pretty much everything. I wasn't against that, but at the same time, when he left, we owed about 150 grand, I think. That was very hard to overcome, because Elvis had gone and Nick had gone, and it was difficult. But we had a few quid in the bank. I started work on Dury. I think Jake, at the time, said that it would just die. I think his idea was that it would be better off me going back to management. That was one of the lines he gave me when he left. Which was guaranteed to make me want to carry on. I thought, fuck it, at the end of the day, if Jake hasn't the bollocks or the bottle to continue, then fine. I don't hold it against him. I wouldn't say we're close friends but we're friendly, and it's all water under the bridge. But at the time it was a bit of a fucking big blow."

Jake's departure was also "a bit of a shock" for Cowderoy. "I have to say I was enjoying the working relationship, sitting in on meetings. And I felt with my major label experience that I had an idea of what may or may not have been successful on radio. And I was trying to help them as best I could with, say, choosing the right Nick Lowe single. Then suddenly one day Dave said Jake was going to leave and he was going to take Nick Lowe and Elvis Costello with him. And that was a shock. That was everything we'd been working towards. We had started to work a little bit on Ian Dury & The Blockheads, and fortunately very quickly they filled the gap. I could have got another job, but I don't remember thinking like that. My overheads were fairly minimal. Dave was a very inspiring person back then. Well, he still is. With hindsight, you can say they weren't communicating as well as they might, even though they were sharing an office. I think they were in their own little worlds, really. Which I suppose is why Jake left. At the point Jake decided to go, I don't remember if that was a shock for Dave at all. I don't remember ever asking him that question. But it was certainly a shock to us, because we had no warning. On the ground floor, the troops didn't have any warning. I think Jake was probably a fairly impulsive person, so it wouldn't surprise me if it all came about over the weekend and was announced to everybody on the Monday."

"Jake had a much higher visibility than Dave," notes Nigel Dick, who had joined the label as a motorcycle messenger. "Jake had done all the interviews whereas Dave was the man behind the curtain – the bad-tempered, Irish, charming, crazy, wily man behind the curtain. He was a brilliant, insightful, difficult man, and I hated and loved him. He was the reason Stiff lasted so long and also the reason the label crashed and burned so brightly. When I joined it seemed every week as if the company was going to implode. There was never any money to pay bills. Soon I reached the conclusion that my £14 a week wasn't enough money to make me lose sleep about whether the company would survive. I figured that was Dave's problem and started sleeping much better."

Dick had come to Stiff as "a rabid music fan with a degree in architecture, who couldn't find a job. I'd spent the summer in Paris sleeping on someone's floor playing my guitar in the subway for dinner money when I saw a *Melody Maker* in the gutter with the announcement of the *Live Stiffs* tour. My immediate thought was, 'What the fuck am I doing in Paris? That's where I need to be!' I cashed in my chips, caught the ferry back to England and got a job as the Stiff motorcycle messenger. The pay was £14 a week and I had to provide my own motorcycle, which cost me £7 a week on the never-never. It was brutal but enormous fun. I'd already bought a number of the Stiff singles and Elvis's album in the months before I went to Paris so I was well into the vibe of Stiff, though my flared jeans and moustache didn't last more than a few days. The company was in huge disarray. Jake left the week I arrived and it was all doom and gloom because Elvis, our only true hope, was leaving with Jake, and the VAT man was after the company for unpaid tax. Luckily Dury's album took off shortly afterwards and the leaking boat managed to continue floating."

Dick's brutal initiation involved "just jumping in and paddling as hard as I could. 'Take this here. Take that there. Now! Faster! Go!' As I said, the company was frankly a mess on an organisational level. I had to take boxes of mail down to the post office every evening and I stunned everybody by saying, 'let's buy a weighing scale and give me a hundred quid so I can buy stamps and we'll do the stamping at the office.' They thought I was some kind of nutcase for suggesting something so organised. Of course, within days I'd lost the weighing scales – one of the roadies was using it for measuring out the drugs! Then I ordered a franking machine and that was the last straw – they pulled me off the bike and parked me next to [Paul] Conroy and promoted me to office boy."

He remembers vividly the chaotic scenes at Stiff, especially when artists were allowed to man the telephones. "When I rang in from the road (this was an era before cell phones and pagers) to ask for my next assignment, Captain [Sensible] would answer the phone and say, "Dick? Fuck off, cunt!" and slam the phone down. This led me to think that maybe he was taking the punk attitude a little far as I was spending half my time working on his career. Dave Vanian was very stand-offish and when I had to drive him somewhere once was mortally offended that I was picking him up in the office Golf and not a limo. He sat gloomily in the back while I debated with myself whether punks should be seen dead in limos."

Larger premises had been acquired further down Alexander Street, with operations shifting from number 32 to number 28 [above John Curd's Straight Music operation, though 32 was retained for merchandising]. But that move had been conceived on the basis of the Robinson/Riviera roster of artists, which had now dwindled in both size and quality. And that wasn't all. The Damned, the label's resident punk rock sensations, were splitting into factions following Brian James's introduction of second guitarist Lu Edmonds. The result would be a poorly received second album *Music For Pleasure*, almost inconceivably produced by Nick Mason of Pink Floyd. Drummer Rat Scabies walked, while the album's sales of 20,000 were less than half of their debut. In critical terms, the Damned were "over". Riviera, it seemed, was the only one capable of keeping the straining chemistry between the band members in place. Robinson lacked the patience.

Crucial respite was derived from the slow-build success of *New Boots & Panties*. Robinson: "Dury's album hadn't really been promoted. Jake was biased towards Elvis quite a bit, I don't think Dury got a fair crack of the whip. He'd sold a few records, but then the album had pretty much stalled, and I thought it had more mileage. So we put the budget that we had left into that, and did a whole series of ads. The major theme was 'give up smoking and give us your money', if I remember correctly. That got going, and then Dury and Chas Jankel produced those great singles, 'What A Waste', 'Reasons To Be Cheerful' and 'Hit Me With Your Rhythm Stick'. So things moved on."

50,000 copies of the album had been sold by the end of the year, boosted by Dury's popularity on the *Live Stiffs* tour [a live document of which would also breach the Top 30]. It would go on to remain in the charts for 90 weeks – an almost unthinkable attainment for an independent label. Those returns, allied to those for 'What A Waste', the label's only significant hit single in the early months of 1978, as well as the overseas licences, effectively bankrolled Stiff through the storm immediately following Riviera's departure.

Pete Frame was another brought in by Robinson on Riviera's departure to handle press – ironically, he'd been one of the journalists to burst Robinson's bubble on the Brinsley Schwarz 'hype' by writing a less than glowing review for *Zig Zag*. "The Fillmore thing was in April '70," Frame recalls, "and you're right, I was critical of the way the band had been launched on a flying carpet of hype. At that time, integrity was all-important, and true underground bands didn't resort to that kind of thing. Most of the journalists on the plane wouldn't have known Brinsley Schwarz from Delmore Schwartz but I had actually seen them at the Country Club some weeks before and knew they were a cool band. I was also the only journalist on the trip who stayed to watch both their sets at the Fillmore. So even though they were unhappy with what I wrote, I think they respected me for it. After all, they knew it was true."

In fact, Brinsley Schwarz would even play a benefit gig for Frame's ailing *Zig Zag* at one point. "I used to hang around with Dave [Robinson] and Nick [Lowe] a bit, after the band split up," Frame continues. "We would bump into each other, here and there. When I was A&R man at Charisma, I would use Dave's studio at the Hope & Anchor to record demos, and Nick played on one or two of them. When punk came along, I knew it was all-change, clean-out time – I'd seen it happen 20 years earlier, with skiffle and the first primitive rock 'n' rollers [documented in Frame's book *The Restless Generation*] and I felt decidedly old and in the way. I always hated old creeps who pretended to be part of something they patently had nothing to do with. So I handed *Zig Zag* over to Kris Needs and went to work for a local building firm, drawing plans for extensions, etc. Stuff I'd been trained to do before I dropped out, man. It was fucking horrible, so in late '77, when Dave phoned and asked if I'd like to be press officer at Stiff, I said yes! What else was I going to say? So I was back in the thick of it, wahooing with Wreckless, Larry, Devo, Jona, etc."

"I always liked and respected Dave," Frame continues. "I still do – even though I haven't seen him since 1989. He had a piece of advice for every occasion – and one I remember particularly was 'never expect someone to give you 100% if you're only prepared to give them 80'. I always kept to that one. He also said that whenever he got a contract, he struck out several clauses as a matter of course – but I've never managed to pull that one off. Anyway, I did OK at Stiff, got tons of good press, even though I wasn't there long. I was never a hustler kind of person and therefore not really suited to

PR, and I went back to scratching for a living. Dave and I were always mates, and I knew Paul Conroy very well too. Great bunch of people, everyone who worked there, everyone on the label."

Another to help fill Riviera's shoes was Andy Murray. "I used to book bands off Paul Conroy, who by 1978 was the general manager. He'd previously been at Charisma agency. So I kept up in touch with him and when I left Leeds Poly in 1975, I came down to London and I was an agent. I decided I was a rotten agent, so I quit my job and went to work for Virgin Retail. I edited *Circuit* magazine for a year, from '77 to '78, and I got a call from Paul in the process, cos I was hyping up Stiff acts. I'd sold the first, Buy 1 ['So It Goes'] at Marble Arch when Jake came in with a little flyer, and said 'pin this up on the wall'. I knew Jake briefly from the *Naughty Rhythms* tour, and Paul Conroy was the agent. So it was all very much that little scene, what came out of pub rock, in essence. I put up displays for Elvis Costello's first album in Virgin Croydon and the display team for Stiff at the time was Paul Conroy's dad Dennis, who was a retired policeman. Anyway, I get a call from Paul one day, saying we've got a tour going by train. Elvis and Nick left to go with Jake to their Radar label. So then you're into the second generation of Stiff, which was just Dave Robinson running it. When I started working there, it was 28 Alexander Street. They were going through a slight expansion, and they added a couple of people to the art department, and Nigel Dick, having been the bike messenger, was then the production co-ordinator. He was getting the records pressed, and they had a new deal with Island. So they were getting much more commercially orientated, shall we say."

The first record that Andy Murray 'worked' was the Akron compilation, a regional sampler that featured the likes of Jane Aire, the Waitresses and The Rubber City Rebels, encased in a 'scratch 'n' sniff sleeve' that supposedly smelt of rubber as a nod to the city's tyre industry. The album concept was inspired by a trip to the US at the end of 1977 by Conroy and Cowderoy, whereupon they first encountered Devo. The latter would enjoy chart success in April 1978 with their deconstruction of '(I Can't Get Me No) Satisfaction', following debut 'Mongoloid'. Despite singing their label's praises with a third single, 'Be Stiff', Virgin nipped in to sign the rights to their debut album. Virgin would also attain the signatures of bright new hopes The Members after they released a one-off single 'Solitary Confinement' for Stiff. But at least Devo led Stiff to the overlooked talent that existed in Akron. Via local svengali Liam Sternberg, they licensed sufficient tracks for a compilation, though plans for individual album releases by the featured artists were either dropped or hastily amended.

For example, an emergency recording session with members of The Rumour was convened to bolster the contents of Rachel Sweet's release with the addition of four cover versions.

The compilation was promoted in typical Stiff fashion. "The first thing Paul Conroy had me do was to call up every airline and ask if they'd sponsor us," remembers Murray, "they'd done a competition to win a trip to Akron. But of course, they hadn't arranged anything. This would have been classic Stiff. They'd made the arrangement, so it was, 'we need a free flight now.' I wasn't able to get one. Everyone said, 'Stiff who? What? Operator? Hello?' We paid for the ticket, if indeed we ever let the person go. We probably forgot all about it."

Murray was specifically delegated the task of organising a follow-up Stiff package tour in July 1978. Sweet, Jona Lewie, Wreckless Eric, Mickey Jupp and Lene Lovich, who had been recruited via a recommendation from Charlie Gillett, the original link to Elvis Costello, comprised the line-up. "She was incredibly charismatic but very resistant to invitations for her to sing," Gillett recalls, "but we prevailed eventually and made a demo of 'I Think We're Alone Now', and took a demo tape of the whole project to Stiff. The only one that Dave liked at all was 'I Think We're Alone Now', which he wanted to immediately put out. Overnight Lene and Les Chappell, her songwriting and life partner, wrote 'Lucky Number' to be the b-side. Dave said, 'Right, let's have an album'. Within a matter of about a week, they wrote most of the album – we put a couple of Jimmy O'Neill songs on the album as well, and one song by Nick Lowe – and they re-recorded 'Lucky Number'. And then Lene went out on that second Stiff tour with Wreckless Eric and Mickey Jupp. This was truly an independent spirit in every meaning of the term. They were conceiving a totally new way – well, it was recreating the R&B package tours that went out in the 50s. Long before even Stax or Motown. In the 50s you'd have a headline act – I saw Frankie Lymon & The Teenagers and The Platters – then a few kind of relatively unknown British acts, and very often a comedian or two. It was a package, all-round entertainment. The greatest thing about those shows was that nobody outstayed their welcome. Everybody did their hits. If they had one or two hits, that's what they did. The band at the top of the bill had five or six songs you knew and they did all of those. And that was the principle behind the Stiff tour, which was parallel to punk – the songs were generally not very long, and it suited every aspect of music at the time to have a 30 or 40 minute set, that was perfect."

## So It Goes

The original intention had been for Devo to headline before their defection to Virgin. Ironically the tour proceeded under the title *Be Stiff*, borrowed from their final Stiff single. Additionally, each member of the tour recorded versions of that track for a promotional 12-inch. Each of the five artists released albums on the same day, 6 October 1978, in three formats (black vinyl, picture disc, coloured vinyl). It was a huge logistical exercise and massive financial commitment. And all five of the albums bombed commercially, at least initially. There was also disquiet between the artists on the tour.

"The idea for the new tour was to travel by specially-chartered train," Murray recalls, "and they needed an organiser – which was me. I joined as the man running the tour, so I had to book the trains through British Rail, have the meetings, and also present it to the trade press. So I did my whole presentation to them, talked it up, then I did all the regional press. I got a train ticket from British Rail so I could go every day. Every morning I'd get up at seven, get on a train with my free ticket, get off at the station wherever the tour was going by. I'd go round the town, speak to the retailers, go back to the station, meet them off the train, and meet them at the soundcheck, which tour manager Kellogs [John Kalinowski] would get them to. I'd whip up a bit of interest, talk to local dealers, give them some free records, see the show, go to bed, get up the next day, do it all over again." This was all Robinson's idea, Nigel Dick recalls. "Then it was all hands to the pump. It was just the idea of survival. Any big plans always got swallowed up by day to day realities."

"I'd see the artists occasionally," Murray recalls, "and they'd say, 'Why are you here?' 'I'm here every day!' But usually we'd never see them because I was off doing business type stuff. But when the tour ended, they wanted somewhere for Rachel Sweet to stay. I said, 'my flatmate's got a spare room,' so Rachel Sweet ended up being my flatmate, with her sister as a sort of chaperone. That was quite entertaining. I have to say that, apart from incessantly playing my copy of *Bat Out Of Hell* and scratching it in the process, they were model flatmates. After the tour ended I officially became the head of press, because we didn't have a press office at the time. Pete Frame had been the previous head of press and I knew him slightly, plus, of course, I was an avid *Zig Zag* reader. So I tried to copy Pete's approach by being iconoclastic and amusing, and trying to do special things. So we did various anarchic photo sessions and quizzes instead of formal press releases, all sorts of bumph"

## Independence Days

Murray worked the aforementioned quintet of releases by Mickey Jupp, Lene Lovich, Rachel Sweet, Jona Lewie and Wreckless Eric's second album. "There would have been a lot of trying to get reviews, plus they almost all had a single. Of course, I knew very little about press apart from having been on the other end of it. I had to teach myself the job, and there was nobody really to learn from. There was me in the basement, and Sonnie Rae, who had worked at Sonet Records. She was our regular plugger, and was far more experienced and far more of a secret weapon than I was, because if she could get something on the radio, on the playlist, you might have some chance of having a hit. Which we did, with Lene Lovich [whose 'Lucky Number' eventually reached number three in the charts after being re-released when its popularity on the *Be Stiff* tour became apparent]. We didn't have very much success at all during the tour radio-wise, apart from Rachel Sweet's 'B.A.B.Y', which was playlisted by Radio 1, which was a source of much aggravation to Dave. But he hadn't really planned it that way. Stiff Mark One wasn't really about having hits – it was about being an American-style indie, like one of those local Louisiana indies that had someone like Professor Longhair on. It was about putting singles out that your majors wouldn't touch. The second part of that was having picture sleeves, which you would only get in France and Holland at that time. But your British standard 'hit' was only ever a 7-inch, never a 12-inch. No picture sleeve, no video, nothing. It just came out, and if you got it on the Radio 1 playlist, it was a big hit. But even then you wouldn't necessarily sell any albums. People didn't relate singles to albums selling until much later, really the early 80s." Robinson, too, didn't make the connection between singles driving album sales that became so prevalent later. "Singles then sold in vast quantities. If you got a big single to go, you might sell more singles in value than you do in albums. After the first year and half, we had worked on a basic audience that bought Stiff stuff, no matter what it was – about 40,000 people. Which was comfortable, but not creasing up the majors. We were in a good, comfortable state, because we were a small record company with a vision."

That said, some mistakes were made. "When we put out our albums," notes Murray, "they all had top-opening sleeves, and some of them didn't even have a list of the tracks on the back. If I'd known what I know now, I'd have said to Dave and Paul – this is madness. So there were various things like that, which the industry taught themselves at the time. Stiff was really artistically orientated in the sense that they weren't ever trying to be cool. The label was actually very uncool in many ways, and would sign people that no-one else wanted. But Stiff was quite guilty of being snobby in one sense. We liked songs over posturing. But we weren't snobby in the modern sense of everybody desperately trying to be cool and looking over their shoulders to see what everyone else thinks. The fact that it was called Stiff in the first place showed that there was a large element of self-mockery as well as iconography."

Finding it hard to break these new artists, at least temporarily, Dury steadied the ship with the label's first number one single, 'Hit Me With Your Rhythm Stick', in January 1979, which sold nearly a million copies in the UK. It established Dury as a major star – at least until the release of his singles-free second album, *Do It Yourself*. There was a licensing deal with Arista for American distribution, but that soured when Kosmo Vinyl, who had moved on to become Dury's press officer, threw Clive Davis out of a dressing room. They did open an outlet in the States, Stiff Inc, though it was largely unsuccessful and quickly became a drain on the UK operation. Of course, the label would maintain its maverick reputation (see the release of 'The Wit And Wisdom Of Ronald Reagan', which sold 30,000 copies despite, or rather because, it contained absolutely no audio) There were also promotional doormats, roadmaps and jigsaws.

"In January 1979 I presented the Be Stiff tour as Marketing Campaign of the year for the Music Week Awards," Murray recalls, "and won – against all major company opposition. The judges were impressed by the strong tour branding, the planning, the merchandising, all the press we got, the different formats, including coloured vinyl and picture discs on every album, etc. But they felt that since we'd only sold 10,000 of each album, it couldn't actually be given the award for 'Best Marketing'. So they invented a new category, 'Top Promotion of the Year', for us specially (they still spelt my name wrong on the award). Paul Conroy made the acceptance speech, for which he, Alan and myself were dressed as undertakers. We were each meant to say a line; 'Thanks for the award / We couldn't have won / If you hadn't lost'. Paul changed it to: 'We won this award because we're the best fucking record company with the best fucking acts,' which shook up the room a bit. Remember, this was all black-tie and very formal."

The internal culture of Stiff at that time reflected the personalities of those involved.. "Paul Conroy can be a big teenager in a lot of ways, which can be one of his strengths," says Murray. "But Dave Robinson was very anti-establishment, and wasn't trying to prove anything so much as wanting to do things his way. And he was very amusing. He was a real Dubliner at a time when to be Irish was really rather denigrated. So Dave was a total outsider having been a roadie for Jimi Hendrix and a photographer, and I didn't appreciate him as much then as I do now. And it's really very sad that the, shall we say, more fairground showman side of his nature has come out subsequently, rather than actually his really aggressive creativity, which was what Stiff was mostly about. Doing different things, not just for the sake of it, but doing different things to make ourselves have success. We were pretty keen to have success on any level. We'd put out a record like 'Toe Knee Black Burn'. It was then, and is now, rubbish, but it came out with as much the thought it might have been a hit as anything else. It wasn't to be nice or horrible to Tony Blackburn. A track came along, and somebody, out of Paul, Alan or Dave, said, 'we can have a hit here'." The last-named oddity, recorded by Binky Baker And The Pit Orchestra, consisted of the DJ's name being repeated, mantra-like, in a broad northern accent by Anne Nightingale's husband. Binky had taken umbrage at Blackburn after an incident at a Mallory Park fun day where Blackburn had chastised him for interrupting his conversation.

The good auspices were cemented later in 1979 when Robinson signed arguably the best English pop band of their generation, Madness. "They were a good band," he recalls, "and I could really see the sense of humour they had. I saw them as London folk music; songwriters who have a social lyric that covers their situation in life, that's the ideal group. But that's pretty much what we signed throughout. We were always looking for that kind of songwriter. We signed songwriters rather than good front people. Obviously, if you look at some of our front people! Chrysalis were keen to sign them, but Chrysalis were very slow." In fact, Madness would release their debut single, 'The Prince', through Chrysalis subsidiary 2-Tone, but didn't commit to them. "Someone told me Chrysalis had seen them eight times," Robinson remembers. "I felt, well, if we're going to sign them, we'd better hurry up! It takes a major about twelve gigs before they sign anyone, so we've only got a few more gigs and they'll get signed. That's the reason I auditioned them at my wedding."

Indeed, the deal was thrashed out following Robinson's nuptials, at the Clarendon Ballrooms in Hammersmith on 17 August 1979; an impressive feat even by his multi-tasking standards. Robinson booked them because, alerted to their popularity in London, he'd not been able to find a date to catch them live. As he would later relate, "I was getting married and I thought that's my chance to see them. Why don't we ask them if they'd play the wedding? And they said they would. They came and played at the wedding and my wife gave me hell afterwards saying you haven't spoken to me all night, you're up there watching the band. They were very good. It was ideal. It was a big record biz kind of party and they were great. I decided there and then that they were likely and signed them up as soon after as I could. Well, in hindsight one shouldn't have done it but I suppose one was in a state of euphoric chaos so it seemed like a good idea. It could have been terrible". There was certainly competition for their signatures. "I actually had Madness for the world," remembers Seymour Stein, "but they performed for Robbo's wedding. And he made such a fuss, that we had to do a split deal, but I think it worked out well for the band, I must say."

"It was a great moment," says Cowderoy. "Madness were all doing the nutty train-dancing around with the guests. Scary but fun! It was an extraordinary thing. Dave was very confident that he was going to get the act, and he developed a relationship with Madness, and they came round and played football with everyone. But they were skinheads, and they had a posse of people who were a little bit scary. But Dave was getting married in a registry office and he decided to get Madness to play at his wedding, and he invited them and they agreed! Everyone was going mad and getting a little bit merry. He continued to woo them after that point. Once you got to know them, they were fine, but I can remember when they played at the Electric Ballroom, and I invited a bunch of foreign journalists over. They didn't speak much English, and the place was full of skinheads and it was very menacing. They'd ask you for 50p, etc. But the journalists didn't know what they were saying. Suddenly I could see a journalist being surrounded by about a dozen skinheads, and they were about to kick seven shades of shit out of him, and little old me had to go in and rescue him! Your heart was in your mouth. It was scary but a lot of fun."

Madness's monumental success meant that the somewhat Machiavellian defection of Dury to Polydor in the summer of 1981 was a much lesser blow than it might otherwise have been. Notable also is the fact that Madness arrived after Stiff had renegotiated their distribution from Island/EMI (then on the point of being bought out by Thorn) to CBS. That new deal was viewed to be the major factor in Madness signing with Stiff, alongside the fact that its roster then still featured their hero, Ian Dury. Indeed, the band's debut album, *One Step Beyond*, rush-released in October within weeks of the contract being signed, featured knowing references to Kilburn & The High Road's 'bus queue' promo photographs, remoulded in their own distinctive style as 'the nutty train' pose. The inner sleeve fan shots, meanwhile, invoked the 'ugly mugshot' ruse piloted as a means for fans to enter the Blockheads '77 Christmas party. The album rose quickly to number two in the charts and Madness were away.

"What was good about it was Dave's confidence he was going to get the band," says Cowderoy. "And once we had them, we had to motivate them. And he was great at that, Dave. He would say, 'Look, there's another Specials single coming out – you've got to step up to the plate.' They were a bunch of lazy bastards and they wanted to do as little work as they possibly could. And he chivvied them brilliantly. As for the distribution, I'm not sure with distribution that our deal was as kind as it might have been. Certainly not as kind as it would have been if there had been independent distributors around then like there are now, that could have taken care of that kind of basic business. They [the majors] didn't go out of their way to help you back then." Nigel Dick: "Obviously you don't sign an artist if you don't expect them to break. So Madness's success was certainly hoped for. The size of their success stunned everyone, though we soon got used to it and did a very good job for them, I think. As a press officer, marshalling their best years, was certainly my proudest achievement."

Despite accelerated levels of success, close bonds between the artists and the label continued to be the norm at Stiff. "There was always a Stiff spirit, but of course everyone wanted a hit," remembers Dick. "However, having worked at and with other labels, I would say that there was more friendship between the acts than any other place I've worked at. Dury was sometimes aloof and at others enormously friendly. He once bought me a huge bunch of flowers! Wreckless was, frankly, a drunk, and I never forgave him for ripping one of my shirts while I was still wearing it. His book [A Dysfunctional Success; published in 2003] was enormously entertaining, but I felt so sad that, to this day, he is convinced everyone wanted to rip him off and sabotage his career. Despite his whining and difficult behaviour we all worked tremendously hard to try to get him some hits. He wrote great songs and he really had something. But in the end the public didn't want to know. If he wants to get angry he should get angry with his public. I made many great friends at Stiff and still keep in contact with many of them (artists included) which I think says a lot about the company and the spirit of the place. The 'mavericks' at Stiff were really no crazier than most of the other artists I've worked with over the years. The difference was we let their personality shine rather than trying to turn them into 'stars'... and if they didn't have something idiosyncratic about them, we invented it!"

Crucial to that sense of camaraderie was the fact that everyone could contribute to the creative 'pot', rather than being delineated purely by a single job function. "Yeah, that was the theory of the whole thing," agrees Robinson. "Everybody was involved. It's my attitude to involve people. And yeah, the staff, all of them went on to do very well. Whatever we learnt, we all learnt it together. People used to come up to me and say, 'What is it you taught these Stiff people? They're just real workers and real grafters, and they all have ideas'. And that's what you'd think the record business was going to be about – you'd think it was going to be an exciting industry and have some razzle dazzle to it – we are in the entertainment, and the illusion business, with some good music. It's much better than a job."

Andy Murray remembers Dave Robinson's favourite moan was about "the English disease", where people would rather spend time and effort on perfecting an excuse rather than get the task at hand completed. "I've never understood it," says Robinson now. "People will trot you out a good excuse. You just say, 'Look, never mind the excuse, why haven't we done the work?' It's an attitude. Nowadays, it's all, 'one can push the worker too hard'. But if the worker works hard, he learns something. That's my belief. Andy Murray and I had a few run-ins on this subject early on." Cowderoy: "I never remember thinking, 'God, I'm really bored, what are we going to do?' It was very full-on and Dave never stopped. Dave's attitude was 'a tired band is a happy band'. And I think he also thought that 'tired workers are happy workers' too."

Of course, there was a downside to that, too. Some felt overworked or under-appreciated, and there was a pattern of casual sackings. But Murray remembers Robinson's aversion to the 'English Disease' as ultimately refreshing. "It's as true today as it was then. It's not necessarily British, but it is a trait of people in business. 'Oh, I couldn't do it.' But that's no good if you're an entrepreneur. If you want something done, you just want it done. But Stiff was very single-minded, put it that way. It suited me very well in terms of the dynamics of the label. It didn't suit me in terms of the way it was communicated. The reason I left was because I never knew what was going on. I was just told – this record's coming out next week, get some press on it. I would say, 'The papers go to press on Thursday, and this is Friday. I keep telling you, you've got to give me the stuff on a Wednesday.' 'Oh, do your best, shut up.' 'I can't do my best because you don't plan anything!' That was my essential frustration. I felt that the marketing people were in charge of stuff and I wasn't. So I got a job in marketing."

In December 1979 the label moved premises again to 9-11 Woodfield Road, just off Harrow Road, above a taxi firm. It had previously been home to Virgin's Front Line reggae imprint. While Madness reinvigorated the label, some of its stars from yesteryear began to fall away, including Mickey Jupp, Lene Lovich (after a last chart hurrah for second album *Flex*) and Wreckless Eric, whose prophetic titling of his third album *Big Smash!*, despite the quality of the contents, backfired. Rachel Sweet, too, had gone by the end of the year, after a second album *Protect The Innocent*, produced by Stiff's new in-house producer Alan Winstanley, alongside Martin Rushent, flopped badly.

The move also coincided with Murray's departure in January 1980. "Felt like a long year and a half! But I felt like I'd worked for the best independent, and I wanted to work for the best major, which was CBS at the time. So I went off to be a product manager at CBS [later working again with Paul Conroy, who became marketing director for Warner UK in 1983 and managing director between 1986 and 1989]. What was interesting was that it was instructive. People would go into Dave and say, 'Well, I don't like this mix'. And Dave would say, 'Well, that's the way it's going to be.' 'Well, I'm just not going to have this! I'm going to...' And you could see it going through their minds – 'I'm going... to speak... to...' And there wasn't anyone to speak to, because Dave owned the label and he got his own way. And in a lot of ways, even though hardly any of the artists overtly liked it, they actually really did appreciate it. When artists dealt with, subsequently, the committees that record labels became, when nothing is ever decided, or worse, the artist could be allowed to entertain their genius in all sorts of expensive ways, absolutely not always successfully."

While gripes were not uncommon, other artists respected Robinson's ability to get things done, accepting the fact, though often in hindsight, that his belligerence may have enhanced their careers. "Well, we had a need to have a high percentage of what we did work at the end of the day," Robinson reflects now. "Somebody has to have a vision. There's no place for committees in a small record company that is constantly reinvesting in the music of that label. You have to have somebody who says yes or no and sticks to it, and that's pretty much me, really." And Robinson's focus on the bottom line was one set by example. His decision to direct many of Stiff's videos was an act born of both parsimony and pragmatism. "Well, the other people would listen to you, and then go and try to make their entrance into Hollywood. On *your* money. Fuck that." The fact that this stoical refusal to throw away money actually resulted in some of the finest and funniest video clips of the decade, most notably with Madness, pinpoints Robinson's dual strengths as a manager and a creative.

"I used to master all the records," recalls Cowderoy. "Once the records were finished in the studio, I would take them to the mastering studio, where we would tweak them to suit Dave. And then I'd bring them back. At that stage you'd be inscribing the little slogans into the run-out grooves. That was one of my tasks. I remember going back to Dave with records and saying, 'I've tweaked this, and I think you're going to like it.' And he'd listen and go, 'No, no, no, I don't like that.' And in the end he got a graphic equaliser in his office. He always liked a lot of top-end, because he thought that would cut through the medium wave, which was the radio transmission medium at the time. And sometimes you'd think it was too much, but radio would add it and it would cut through. He invariably wasn't wrong. And he had a good eye for art. The sleeves were always good. We had a great art department. There was a guy called Chris Morton, who was the first artist there. He designed the first logo and did some of the early sleeves and early compilations. Then Barney became the in-house art guy. And it was very important, that visual style, as much as the audible style – and the sense of humour. They were doing their thing, but at the end of the day, it would have to get past Robbo. And if he didn't approve it, or had a better idea, that was it. You'd try to steer the ship, and Dave was the captain. Occasionally you'd try to sneak up behind him and try to distract him, and turn the rudder whichever way you wanted it to go. But essentially he steered the ship."

New head of press Nigel Dick even found himself playing bass for the *Top Of The Pops* recording of Jona Lewie's 'You'll Always Find Me In The Kitchen At Parties', which reached number 16 in April 1980 (and would later be followed by a much bigger hit, 'Stop The Cavalry'). But the A&R policy remained esoteric. Joe King Carrasco rubbed shoulders with New York splatter-punks the Plasmatics ("*not* very engaging folk," remembers Dick). There was reggae from Desmond Dekker and the Equators alongside medieval-themed folk-punk from Tenpole Tudor. Art lout John Otway and 70s glam leftover Alvin Stardust found themselves unlikely peers of American power poppers Dirty Looks and Any Trouble, whose singer Clive Gregson was deliberately modelled as a replacement for Elvis Costello. "I don't think Stiff had a lot of respect for artistic ... identity," Lene Lovich would later tell Jason Gross, when informed that The Feelies were issued with a dictum to try to repeat the success of her 'Lucky Number'. "They just wanted to be successful." Several of those signings (though not the Plasmatics, whose GLC-aborted gig would hit Robinson in the pocket to the region of £20,000) were part of the 1980 *Son Of Stiff* package tour, the last and least successful of such enterprises.

Everyone, seemingly, was welcome to put forward their A&R suggestions, rather than it being a rigidly discrete department at the label. Nigel Dick remembers Robinson asking his opinion on whether to release Dury's 'Hit Me With Your Rhythm Stick'. "I didn't like it too much, and of course, it went to number one. I also discovered this young metal band from Sheffield who were fucking brilliant and had a single on their own label. I rang their manager who got a lift on the back of a motorcycle from Sheffield down to London to see me and give me a copy of the record. Robbo hated it and told me, somewhat archly, that we needed to sign bands that made money. The band was Def Leppard. 60 million albums later..."

"We all tried to do what we could," recalls Cowderoy. "Dave had a list of people that he said major labels had overlooked. And then the list was added to with people like Wreckless Eric and The Damned. There were people on the list like Larry Wallis, and Ian Dury, and a few other people. Mickey Jupp was on the list, people who had been around a while. Dave was convinced, because they were on the list, they were people we should definitely sign. 'The list' had assumed some sort of magical, mystical property. A few of those that we'd worked with proved successful, so why wouldn't the others? It was almost a religious thing. Paul and I and the others could sit round and say, 'I'm not sure that we're going to be able to sell a Larry Wallis record.' The 'Police Car' single we put out was a great single, but we weren't convinced Larry was somebody that I could sell overseas, and Paul could sell to the Brits. So we had reservations. So we tried to temper Dave's enthusiasm in that way. And if something caught our eye, we'd try to encourage him too."

But the idiosyncratic command structure could cause problems too. Andy Murray: "With Stiff, it was difficult for me personally, because the artists, funnily enough, were a bit snooty. They were used to dealing with Dave. Dave would say, 'We'll do this, and whatever you want, that's fine.' He was very generous to the artists in terms of accommodation or helping them out, or giving them extra money, or listening to them. The artists were a little bit stand-off-ish with me, funnily enough. But with major labels, as I say, they're stand-off-ish with everybody, because they feel it's an 'us and them' situation, which I would reasonably say was not the case at Stiff. They felt that if they were signed to Stiff – bear in mind that, very often they had been rejected by everyone else in the business – they were quite correctly grateful. Notwithstanding that, Dave could be very charming. Paul and Alan were certainly very helpful. If somebody wanted something silly, they would try to get it for them. There was never any talking down to the artists and telling them they shouldn't want something. They might say it wasn't possible, but they might still give it a go. Far more likely, with someone like Lew Lewis, you'd take him in and say, 'Lew, we're launching your album with a harmonica extravaganza at the Hope 'n' Anchor,' and he'd go, 'Fine, good, let's go.' There were positive suggestions about all sorts of things. Then in the 80s it became the era of the big manager, where the big manager would come in and bully the record company."

Murray's replacement would discover similar problems. Nigel Dick: "I was always more into the more jokey and cheeky side of things than Andy. In truth, if you're ever working for Robbo, you will always have to be reactive – he wants things done NOW! Back then, when lead times for some magazines was anything up to six weeks, that was very, very difficult to achieve. Frankly, I didn't much enjoy being a press officer and hated trying to blag articles out of cynical journalists who had seen it all and wanted lots of free drink. I didn't drink."

Dick would also discover the downside of Robinson's perfunctory approach to human resources. "I left for exactly the same reason that everyone left. I was fired! Robbo grew tired of me. I knew it was coming and tried to leave but Robbo asked me to stay. Then one bright and breezy day I was summoned to his chamber and given 15 minutes to get out. After five years of working round the clock and phone calls in the middle of the night, it was all over. Behind his back one of the staff showed me how to fill in the forms to take him to the industrial tribunal for unfair dismissal. Robbo got wind of it pretty quickly and he paid me off." Murray was never fired, however. "Oh, he tried. About three times. But Alan wouldn't let him!"

Nigel Dick: "Then I got a phone call from Lene Lovich to go and work on her current tour in the US and I was off. Everyone on that tour, from the sound guy to the tour manager to the publicist, and even Lene herself, had been fired by Robbo. It was a badge of honour. Six months later, when I was working at Phonogram, I had Robbo on the phone begging for information on something (during my time there I had taken it upon myself to be a sort of archivist – I was always too much of a fan). I found it very difficult because deep down I wanted to help. But I told him that I no longer worked for the company and put the phone down on him. 25 years later, after the release of the Stiff film on the BBC, I sent him an e-mail. I explained that I am still, to this day, enormously hurt by his sudden dismissal, but I am also enormously grateful for five years of amazing times and for everything I learnt there – and I certainly learned a lot."

Towards the end of 1983, Island Records purchased 50% of the label. Robinson was now in charge of both Stiff and Island. He enjoyed immediate and spectacular success with Island, through Frankie Goes To Hollywood and U2, while Bob Marley's *Legend* became one of the all-time sure-fire catalogue sellers under his stewardship. And yet, he now reflects, it was a "mistake". "I didn't want to do it, quite honestly. You look back at things, and you think, what made you make a decision of that nature. I was so happy. Stiff had a new building in Bayham Street [Camden; in September 1982] that I was really happy with. It was a bigger building. It had a recording studio and a big warehouse. So we had everything under our own roof at that time, and I was very happy with the things we were doing. Musically we were good, we had plenty of money in the bank, and we were ahead of the game. We were in a very good position."

"It was around that time when Blackwell called me," Robinson continues. "I think it was November 1983. 'Why don't we work out some deal where he bought some shares in Stiff, and I ran Island as well as Stiff, blah blah.' Quite honestly I turned him down. I thought about it, but, nah, I'm quite happy with the way things are. But he came back, and he's a very charming bloke. And I'd known him for a number of years and I counted him as a close friend, actually. We to'd and fro'd, and Island was the model of the ideal record company in my mind anyway. So it seemed like something could be done. U2 was there. And Blackwell and I came up with a strategy – he wanted to be in the song business, really – so the company was being built up for a sale, and I had a share in Island, as well as them buying half of Stiff. The whole thing was an interesting step up. Nowadays I'd like to think I would have turned him down a second time and that would have been the end of it, but I took it on. What I didn't do was I didn't do any due diligence. Cos Island was a bigger record label than Stiff, on the cards anyway. And it turned out they were totally broke. And I didn't know that. And I didn't think to investigate that, because I wasn't buying into Island, it was just a job with a profit-share."

Robinson soon discovered that he'd have to lend Island £1 million from Stiff's coffers to cover the deal. "At that time I really should have said, 'Look, you've sold me a bit of a pup,' and that's the end of it. But I stayed with it, and they had their most successful year ever. They had Frankie Goes To Hollywood, which I kind of clawed off the floor because it was falling backwards big time [this might be disputed by journalist Paul Morley, who masterminded the project, and marketeer Garry Farrow], and the *Legend* album, which was something I really wanted to do. That was part of the reason I went there, I'm a big Bob Marley fan. And U2. An Irish band whom I originally sent to Island in the first place. There was an opportunity. The thing about Island at the time is, they didn't follow up. They didn't have the

money and they didn't have the attitude. They were kind of like a flaccid
major, and they didn't promote anything. They had a big staff. They had a
lot of potted plants in the place, that I got rid of pretty damned quick. So
that year, we did £56 million. They'd never seen that type of money. They
paid all their debts off. But in order to do that, I had to concentrate on that
label big time. There was a lot of to'ing and fro'ing. It turned out Blackwell
hadn't told me lots of things. America, for example, ran entirely off the UK
label. They didn't make any money. And they didn't pay any royalties to the
UK label. Now, I had a profit-share, so as part of the profit-share, I'm looking
at the financial way the company is set up, and Blackwell and his mother
were all on the American deal, and no money was coming through to
England. Therefore, as a sharer of the profits, I was losing quite a lot of
money, cos there's an awful lot going out to America, and no royalties being
sent to the UK." But was it also a case of someone who had been used to
acting wholly off his own instincts failing to acclimatise to a completely
different culture? "You're right to a degree, I found it to be a bitter pill to
swallow. Blackwell essentially doubled crossed me. At the end of the day,
it's one of those learning curves you can do without."

By the time Madness departed the scene to sign with Virgin, under
something of a cloud, they had scored 18 Top 20 hits as well as six Top Ten
albums. Stiff was left with Tracey Ulman and Kirsty MacColl (who would
soon depart to Polydor) and little else. "Having had a run of singles in the Top
40, there was a time when we weren't notching up the same success rate,"
recalls Cowderoy. "Things didn't get on playlists, things weren't going as
well, and clearly you're not generating the kind of income that you want.
And if the bad times go on too long you get into a bit of a pickle. And at that
point it had been going on longer and longer, and he decided to sell half the
company to Chris Blackwell. I don't think Dave's eye was on the ball at that
point. He was very much focused on maximising the potential there."

Robinson would re-establish full control of Stiff in 1985, piloting its return to
independent status. At which time he signed the last of the 'great' Stiff acts,
The Pogues. "Oh, Shane is phenomenal," he recounts. "There's no doubt that
he was fantastic. But, unfortunately, I led him to Frank Murray to be his
manager, which was really a bad decision. Frank was out of work and I knew
his wife, and he needed something to do. And he did add musically to the
band, I think getting [former Steeleye Span multi-instrumentalist] Terry
Woods in was a very inspired idea. But Frank, generally, I don't think was the
right kind of person. I'd kind of forgotten he was Phil Lynott's tour manager
– and that should have spoken volumes to me. But with Shane being such a

delicate little flower – early on we were kind of controlling his drinking. He wasn't NOT drinking, but he was doing it in a controlled way. We had a grip on it. But as soon as Frank took over, he wanted to get between the record company and the artist, like a true idiot manager. And taking Shane down to the pub was now in some way a managerial duty, and that was really fatal. That was a shame. Although 'Fairytale Of New York' was the height of what we did, perhaps, in the public area, there was incredible music there. Possibly it hasn't been realised just how good he was."

Despite significant success with The Pogues over the next 18 months, and a breakthrough with Furniture's 'Brilliant Mind' that they were unable to capitalise on, the Mint Juleps' 'Girl To The Power Of 6' (BUY 263) closed an illustrious era. Stiff collapsed in 1987 with debts of £1.4 million (less than the headline figure of £3.5 million that was quoted at the time according to Robinson, though others suggest the final figure was indeed close to the larger sum). The label's masters were purchased by ZTT, one of the labels Robinson had helped establish at Island, for approximately £300,000. "It was unfortunate," laments Cowderoy." We tried to make things happen in a different way. But it did survive and we carried on and we had The Pogues. The ship kept sailing but in the end it sank. It ended up in the arms of Trevor Horn and Jill Sinclair. Jill was at ZTT, and obviously Dave had a relationship with them through Island, because ZTT was signed to Island. I wasn't there at the time, but he continued to spend money. And at a certain point of time Jill just said, 'I don't want to spend any more money' and they took over the company and Dave was gone."

Robinson's somewhat weary view on the denouement of Stiff needs to be taken in context. Everyone involved in the stewardship of the label (they even made Robinson joint managing director with Sinclair) wanted it to succeed. One of the final straws for Horn and Sinclair was the sale of Madness's masters back to the band when Stiff couldn't find £70,000 in back royalties it owed to them. To them, this was terrible short-term business. The Pogues catalogue (including masters) was sold to Warners to bail the company out – although that also solved the problem of Robinson's dissolving relationship with Frank Murray - reducing further still its A&R assets. In the end, as the main creditor to Stiff, ZTT pursued a 'hive-down' sale of the company to protect what masters it did still retain. Bailing out Stiff very nearly sank ZTT – which was eventually put back on a firm financial footing with the success of Seal and the Art Of Noise, before it too signed with Warners.

## So It Goes

Stiff was revived in 2006 (without Robinson or Riviera's involvement) with the signing of The Enemy. "We've managed the catalogue for quite a long time," reveals Pete Gardiner. "It was acquired by Trevor Horn and Jill Sinclair at the end of the eighties, because of a tie-up they had with Stiff at the time. We just ran it as a catalogue concern. But at the beginning of 2006, I met someone from the BBC and I pitched the idea of a documentary, just to give us a bit of catalogue profile, to be honest. The BBC ended up producing that documentary [*If It Ain't Stiff*]. As we were doing it, we realised there was still interest and quite a lot of awareness of the brand. So we thought, why don't we do some low-key bits and pieces, in the original manner of the label? We had an A&R guy that worked on the publishing side that went to Warners and came up with this band, The Enemy. So we did the first couple of singles. A lot of the originals on Stiff were one-offs originally. We never had any intention of signing the band to any long-term deal, we're not in that sort of market. We did those two singles, just 1,000 limited editions, and they sold rapidly. Suddenly we had more and more interest and people contacting us. So we just thought, this is a good chance now. And it's something we can manage – it's being run as a relative cottage industry, if you like – we're not heading for the big time with this one, unless something gathers its own momentum."

The documentary proved popular, though not with everyone. Cowderoy: "The real essence of Stiff was never obvious in that TV programme – and that was the humour. We laughed all the time. It was that sense of humour and the trailblazing marketing we did – the visual style. When you look at ads today – there was *Sounds*, *Melody Maker* and *NME* in those days. And we would run ads in a given week in three papers, and each ad for each paper would be completely different. Nowadays you look at ads for Hard-Fi or whatever, and they all look the same. I just didn't think it came across in the documentary the sense of fun we had."

Also, getting everyone to contribute wasn't all that straightforward: "We approached Jake," recalls Gardener, "and apart from the documentary itself, he's never talked about the label. And he was really reluctant to do so. We had a go from here, and then the BBC, and initially he just said 'Fuck off, I don't want to have anything to do with you.' It's a bit like the film *Swingers*. The guy meets a girl in a club, then he phones up and leaves a message. Then he keeps leaving messages until he breaks up without ever having had a date with her. Jake conducted that sort of relationship with us when he kept ringing up telling us to fuck off. In the end he just phoned us himself and agreed to do it."

## Independence Days

Your writer had a similar experience. Not that Riviera has gone to ground completely. Simon Morgan was involved in plans for a reunion of the original Damned in 2006, bridging the Sensible/Scabies divide, to try to get the warring factions to record *Damned Damned Damned 2* with Nick Lowe. Riviera was brought into the equation in an attempt to knock heads together, as only he could. "Apparently, even after an agreement in principle," recalls Morgan, "Dave 'n' Cap were not playing ball. Jake had wanted 2006 to be 'The Year Of The Damned'... but the current Damned were still taking bookings for the UK and Japan for the end of 2006. Dave's email said that he and the Captain had spent the last ten years 'building up momentum' on the back of their most recent work, and that the 'force' was naturally with them. That 'they' were the bigger draw and that some financial dispensation had to be made with regard to this anomaly. Jake's reply accused Vanian of 'suffering from lead singer syndrome', and that if that was the way the two of them felt, then they could both 'go fuck themselves'. Jake signed off: 'May the momentum be with you!'"

Unlike some of its peers and progeny, Stiff did not produce an identifiable sound. It is the spirit of the label, rather than the music (although it produced some of the finest of the era) that endures. Their innovations include, but are not limited to, the packaging of UK single releases, the importance of a good slogan (aped by the advertising industry wholesale), the irreverent pop video, the 'package' tour and high-profile, targeted press campaigns. So, when Carl Dalemo of Razorlight bears the legendary t-shirt 'If It Ain't Stiff...' on the cover of their album, it is a testament to the philosophical principles of ambition and sweat, as well as independence, that marked out Stiff. And singularly doesn't mark out Razorlight or much of today's music scene.

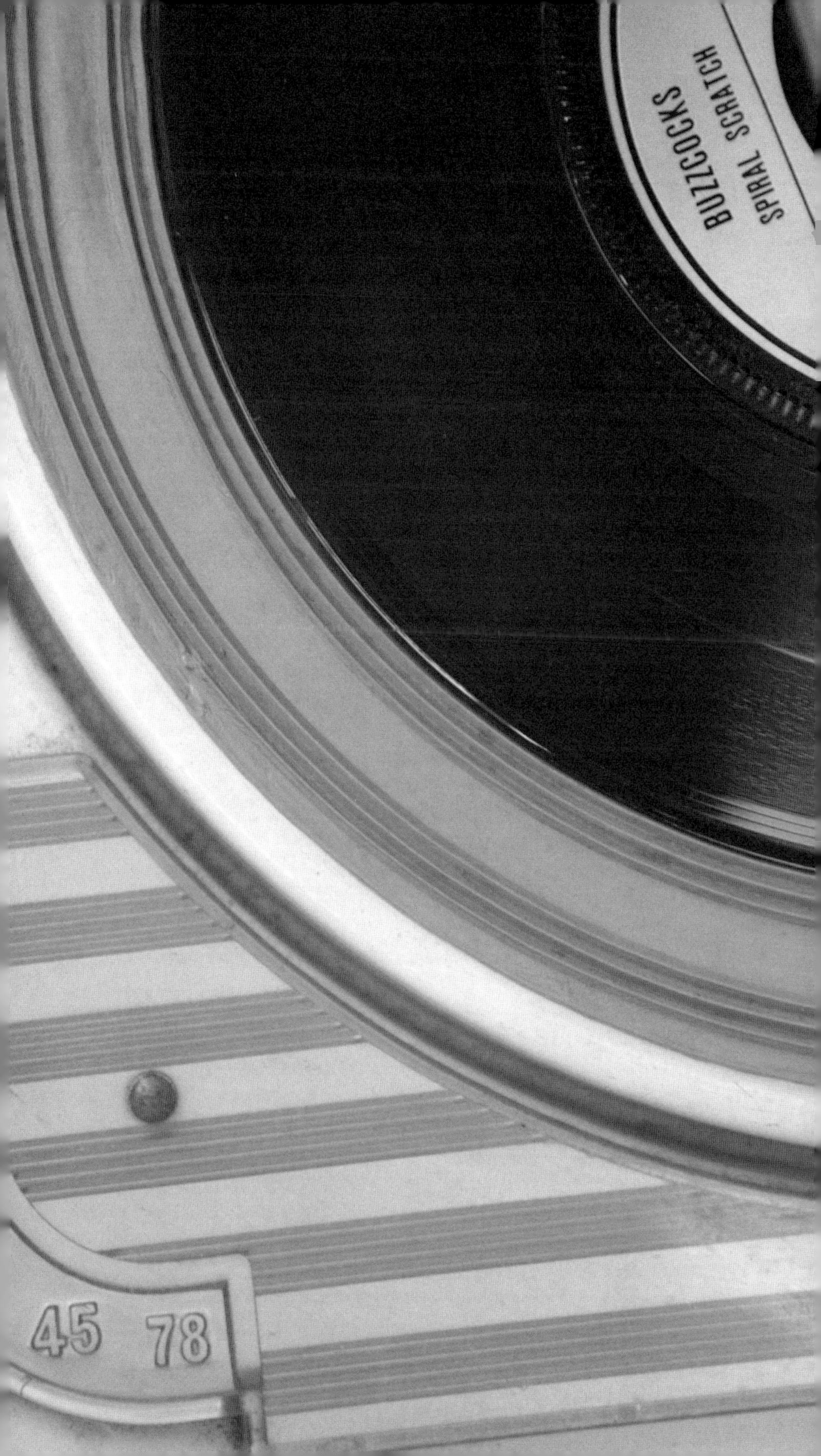
BUZZCOCKS
SPIRAL SCRATCH
45 78

# Chapter Four

## How About Me And You?

## New Hormones, Small Wonder, Step Forward and a Cast of Thousands

Stiff and Chiswick may have been small, but they were comparative monoliths to the likes of New Hormones, formed in Manchester to house Buzzcocks' 'Spiral Scratch' EP, released on 29 January 1977. It was very much a custom label for the enterprise. In fact, apart from *The Secret Public*, a poster collage fanzine that year, a collaboration between artist Linder and writer Jon Savage, there were no further releases on the label until March 1980. New Hormones would eventually be revived to release material from Dislocation Dance, the Diagram Brothers and Ludus, but it has remained synonymous with 'Spiral Scratch' ever since.

Band confidante/manager Richard Boon took the name New Hormones from a magazine singer Howard Devoto had once written. Guitarist Pete Shelley's dad loaned them £250, while friend Sue Cooper donated £100 from her student grant. A further friend, teacher Dave Snowden, was also tapped for funds. Produced by Martin 'Zero' Hannett, the session was recorded ostensibly live at Indigo Studios in December 1976. The Polaroid Instamatic black and white portrait of the group, in front of the Robert Peel statue in Manchester's Piccadilly Gardens, underscored the record's humility and authenticity. It is easy to underestimate how shocking that grainy image seemed in comparison with the garish, over-elaborate artwork of the day (especially since most singles did not have sleeves).

Only the third punk single (after The Damned's 'New Rose' and The Sex Pistols' 'Anarchy In The UK'). 1,000 copies were pressed. They needed to sell 600 to break even. The first pressing sold out within four days. Within six months, 16,000 copies had been sold. A new era of independence had arrived, one arguably more significant than that embarked on by the likes of Stiff and other medium-sized players who were all, to an extent, industry vets of some stripe.

Boon was one of the motivating forces behind much of that early Manchester scene, as Steve Shy (of *Shy Talk* fanzine) recalls. "The fanzine came about from getting mithered off Richard Boon, who did as much for Manchester music in the early days as Tony Wilson did and Pete Shelley. They more or less said you are involved, so now you have to do something." 'Spiral Scratch', similarly, had been put together as an expression of enthusiasm, despite an almost total lack of knowledge of the music industry. "The main motivation, really, was to document this funny little activity," says Boon. "Howard [Devoto] was going to go back to college, so it was just to document it – a souvenir of a small group of people through a short period of time. We had no real knowledge of what we were doing." In fact, the only music industry connection they were able to draw on was Hannett. "Phonogram Custom Pressing made the record," Boon continues, "we find out about that through Martin. He'd produced some funk record for someone at Riverside Studios who used Phonogram Custom Pressing, So we just followed his information – we didn't look about for pressing plants because we didn't know anything about them."

Distribution was similarly rudimentary. "We only talked to people once we'd done 'Spiral Scratch' and it kind of worked," Boon explains, "but we didn't understand how distribution worked. So we talked to Ted Carroll and Roger Armstrong [Chiswick], and probably Dave Robinson at Stiff. Most of our relations were with Rough Trade, but not exclusively. We sold some to Spartan, Pinnacle – almost anyone who phoned up. We probably gave them 500. It just rolled on in a whole series of small pressings to meet demand."

Devoto would indeed leave Buzzcocks immediately following the EP's release, having made it clear to Boon, at least, over the Christmas period that it was his intention to return to his studies (though he has also stated elsewhere that his departure was only marginally connected to academic concerns). ORG 2 (the catalogue number eventually given to Linder and Savage's fanzine) was originally slated to be a Buzzcocks follow-up. "'Spiral Scratch' was a one-off entity, yes," says Boon. "But it worked. Howard had gone and Peter [Shelley] took over vocals and [Steve] Diggle switched to guitar. As it was still selling out of our front room, we were planning another EP, to be called 'Love Bites', which would have had 'Orgasm Addict', 'Oh Shit' and 'Sixteen' on it. We talked about that a lot. But that's when labels started sniffing around us." The band opted to sign with Andrew Lauder and United Artists, partially under pressure from drummer John Maher's father. Maher Snr was concerned his son should not turn down the offer of a job unless he could demonstrate music could offer him a steady income. That was far beyond the reach of the coffers at New Hormones. "John had just left school," Boon adds, "and he could have had a job as an insurance clerk. And his dad was very concerned. So we said, give it a bit of time, and we'll see if we can bring this to fruition. Instead of going straight from school to being a lowly insurance clerk, he signed on for a bit while we talked to the labels who approached us." The most significant other factor in signing to UA being

Lauder himself. "Andrew's really good, and it felt like being on a 'minor major' was more comfortable. We talked to CBS and got a no. Chrysalis said no after coming to a gig. Lots of people just appeared. Also, Andrew was quite convincing."

So New Hormones spent, effectively, two years in hiatus, despite receiving a flood of demo tapes (including Gang Of Four and Cabaret Voltaire) and paying for The Fall's first recording session (later released as 'Bingo Master's Breakout' on Step Forward). It would re-emerge in the 80s (see chapter eight) but the nation-wide DIY revolution it had set in motion with 'Spiral Scratch' was well underway.

Spiral Scratch' vies with The Desperate Bicycles' 'Smokescreen', which came just a couple of months down the line, for the honour of being the most inspirational independent record of them all. Directly influenced by 'Spiral Scratch', and released on the band's own Refill records, its amalgam of garage rock and Syd Barrett-esque pop-psych was similarly a hugely individualistic statement as well as an equally galvanising one. Its compressed, breathless recording did much to augment punk's progression from rock music with an attitude to a deconstruction of rock aesthetics – as evinced by the post-punk period and the restless creativity that fuelled both Mark Perry and Vic Godard. It was also a call to arms. "It was easy, it was cheap, go and do it".

"It was just, 'let's make a record', vocalist Danny Wigley recalled in one of the few interviews the band ever gave, to *Common Knowledge* fanzine in 1979, when asked about signing other bands to Refill. "We didn't even think of it, or think about anything. We never thought we'd sell any copies. We just raked together our holiday money, and just made the record. Everything came afterwards. That was the idea, really. If we'd thought about it, we wouldn't have done it." At a cost of £153, the band pressed 500 copies of the single in April 1977. They could not possibly have imagined the reach it would have, or the fact that it would set in place a template for independent music that would flourish for years after. To wit; blag or borrow the money to press your record, send to John Peel, then sell it via Rough Trade/Small Wonder and mail order. As a means of demystifying the process of recording 'art' it was revelatory. At one point they considered making a film illustrating the entire process; a kind of public information documentary. The rear of the Bicycles' second single, 'The Medium Was Tedium', meanwhile, demanded to know "why you haven't made your single yet". Lots of them did.

## Independence Days

The Television Personalities' '14<sup>th</sup> Floor', for example, was one of the records informed by a brief correspondence with the Bicycles, who were always willing to offer a fee-free consultancy to other aspirants. "We got a leaflet back showing us how," Treacy would recall to John Reed, "and all we needed was £400. So I went to work for a while and saved up the money. I asked Ed [Ball] along to the studio with me to record a few of my songs, and I figured John Peel would play them, as he seemed to air all the other stuff." The single was recorded in Shepherd's Bush in November 1977 in one take at a cost of £17. Plus bus fares.

However, Treacy's plan was knocked off course when he received a letter from the pressing plant informing him they'd hiked their prices. Disappointed, he threw the tapes in a cupboard until, a couple of months later, he decided it was worth the effort of getting at least a couple of white label copies pressed up. The original intention had been to record it as Teen 78, until Treacy was hand-writing the song titles on the labels, and decided to identify the 'line-up' as comprising a bunch of 'television personalities' such as Hughie Green.

The ensuing, and predicted, sponsorship of John Peel led to his parents offering to fund a proper pressing run (Peel had also offered loan capital if he was stuck). But his family's largesse came following the extraction of a compromise – that he would return to work (he would find gainful employment with Led Zeppelin's Swansong imprint). The single was followed in due course by The Television Personalities' 'Where's Bill Grundy?' EP, spearheaded by the inspirationally amateurish 'Part-Time Punks', a song which grooved wryly on the emerging punk phenomenon and its conceits. Released on the King's Road label set up by Treacy and Ball in November 1978 for the purpose, and both child-like and unerringly literal, it was also extremely funny. "By the time I'd written 'Part-Time Punks'," Treacy told *The Face*, "I was more aware of how you could get things done at a lower cost. I got it pressed really cheaply, 1,500 of them, black labels with sleeves that cost tuppence each. Whereas on '14th Floor' about 200 of the early sleeves were hand drawn, and I used to have to take the staples out and then glue them back together. It was a bloody big risk!" Running parallel to the TVPs' releases were singles by Ed Ball's group, 'O' Level (directly referenced in the lyric to 'Part Time Punks'). The line-ups of both groups were identical aside from leadership status. The 'East Sheen' EP (including 'Pseudo Punk' and released on one-off imprint Psycho) was issued just a few weeks later than '14<sup>th</sup> Floor' in May 1978. 'The Malcolm EP', 'O' Level's second release, the lead track a homage (of sorts) to the Sex Pistols' manager, was issued on

## How About Me And You?

King's Road in December, again a few short weeks after the 'Grundy' EP. In the process, what Ball describes as "a casual scene" had begun to coalesce around the King's Road imprint and its progenitors.

The TVPs story would continue (see Chapter 13). Marvellously, however, The Desperate Bicycles have been the one group who have exhibited no inclination whatsoever to revisit or expand upon their agenda. They have been approached many times to re-release their three 7-inch singles, one EP and album (the first to do so was Daniel Miller of Mute), but have shown absolutely no inclination to do so. They have also resisted any invitation to submit to interview, including my own, beyond a polite, but cursory, "I think I speak for the others when I say that our records say it all." And that's doubtless true.

Another group to whom the Bicycles mantra spoke was Scritti Politti, who would acknowledge in print the fact that they gave them the 'incentive' to organise their own release. Just as the Bicycles had done before them, they immortalised the production costs on the cover of 'Skank Bloc Bologna'.

*"Recording: Space Studios @ 19 Victoria Street, Cambridge. £98.00 for 14 hours, master tape included. Mastering: Pye London Studios @ 17 Great Cumberland Place, London W1 – IBC (George) Sound Recording Studios @ 35 Portland Place, London W1. £40.00 for cutting of lacquer from master tape. Pressing: PYE Records (Sales) Ltd. @ Western Road, Mitcham, Surrey. £369.36 for 2,500 copies at 13p, £27.00 for processing (electro plating of lacquer). Labels: E.G. Rubber Stamps, 28 Bridge Street, Hitchin, Herts. £8.00 for rubber stamp on white labels (labels included in cost of pressing.)"*

"Something was happening," notes Richard Boon, "which was encouraging. In terms of the actual tactic of demystifying the process of getting a record out, we'd just written how many tapes and overdubs there were, and The Desperate Bicycles took that further. Then Scritti Politti came out with 'Skank Bloc Bologna', with a foldout sleeve, which detailed how much *everything* cost. It was all part of that process of demystification, which seemed very important."

A little knowledge can be a dangerous thing. Aside from the fact that this was useful data for other prospective entrants to the record industry, its demystifying impact; building on top of 'Spiral Scratch' and 'Smokescreen', was huge. That it's vulgar to talk about money is an oft-cited facet of English life. While a business's assets are, by definition, laid bare for the committed observer at Companies House, what record companies actually 'did' was rarely discussed. Hence the cross-collateral scams, and the industry's lack of disclosure about what real promotion and production costs entailed – and who was picking up the tab. For all but the top earners/sellers, record company-artist relationships came with an implicit subtext that the former should be *grateful* for a recording contract – that it was the 'prize' that denoted success and status, the pot of gold at the end of the rainbow. Hence so many would sign contracts that they would spend the rest of their lives regretting. For a tiny squat band with few resources to box up everything that the record industry was *about* and treat it as an off the peg transaction was an immensely powerful statement.

But then Scritti was a band formed around Green Gartside, a man well versed in Derrida, Gramsci and Marxist theory about the means of production. It's worth pondering here a while, though not so long that the academic quicksand engulfs us, how close these three vital records came to constituting a reaction to the economic determinism of the punk era. Marx and Engels posited that ideology allows the mode of production to reproduce *itself* – therefore when revolutionary force(s) change that mode, the dominant class (not a stretch to see this as the majors in context) will attempt to create a new society to protect their economic order. In the late 70s, the majors' shocked, belated attempts to co-opt the punk generation can be seen as a perfect example of this effect. Resistance to that, and the lionising of independence as a concept, proved viral. Mark Perry's post-Alternative TV group, The Door And The Window would provide a similar 'menu' breakdown of costings to the tune of 'How We Did It' on their 1979 'Subculture' EP. Members of that group, it's further worth acknowledging, were part of the *Common Knowledge* fanzine community from which the earlier Bicycles' quote was taken,

What wasn't reported on 'Skank Bloc Bologna's sleeve was that the necessary finance, £500, had been borrowed from drummer Tom Morley's brother – not that they made any secret of it if you asked. Roger Sabin lectures in cultural studies at Central St Martin's College, and points out that the source of Scritti's initial loan is worth more than a footnote. "No disrespect to Green at all – that record was very important, but I would say that a lot of punks were from quite well-to-do families and their mums would give them a bit of money for guitars and amps, etc. I mention this because my own band had to find other ways to get started – it contained among its number a juvenile thief who managed to purloin a guitar and 'practice amp' from Woolworth's. Later, another member of the band borrowed an additional amp from a kid at school and never gave it back. Thus we began our 'career'. The most expensive thing was a drum kit, so it was essential to be nice to another rich kid at school who happened to have one. I seem to remember he wasn't into punk at all. As for practising, this too cost money. A rehearsal studio was out of the question, so it had to be front rooms. And getting all the gear over to someone's house was a nightmare – you really needed somebody who owned a car, which of course was another big expense. We did our level best to 'live the punk rock dream' and ended up sounding total shit. That was why when we heard The Clash album and how nicely they were playing, and how everything was in tune, etc. we knew that they'd spent a lot of money getting that far. Thus, from our perspective, we felt a bit cheated. Punk was *not* about just getting up and doing it. You had to have a certain amount of cash even to get a little distance. Now I look back on it, I think the economics behind a lot of bands had to do with benefactors, pure and simple – be they creepy managers (Rhodes, McLaren, etc) or mums. I guess it was ever thus in rock and roll, but punk mythology still has it that you could be in a band even if you were a street oik. Rarely true, in my opinion."

Baseline economics are one reason why punk took hold on campus quicker than on (the much mythologised) 'street'. Students (at that time, the overwhelming majority of whom were drawn from Britain's middle classes) were insulated by the old grants system, and the famous lack of academic discipline on arts degrees in the seventies. "Also," continues Sabin, "some bands originated in squats, which were around a lot at a certain point in history, and then cracked down upon by the local authorities. Squat culture meant (a) access to space – a place to practice, even a place to put on gigs; (b) access to like-minded individuals with instruments; (c) access to extra money, because you weren't paying any rent. Again, oftentimes the squat circuit was a bit middle class – and it was quite organised, with newsletters, etc." Certainly those comments characterise Scritti's development and association with squats like 3 Regent's Park Road to a tee. They were originally art students in Leeds who, inspired by seeing the Sex Pistols play the local polytechnic, formed a band then moved to London to enjoy just the lifestyle – and opportunities – that Sabin alludes to.

Music critic Ben Watson also has concerns about too literal a reading of the Scritti mantra. "Scritti Politti notoriously relate to 'Marxist theory', but to a Euro-Communist version, which drops the working class and makes Marxism market-friendly (the sad history of *Marxism Today*). They were the only band I really disliked we put on at Leeds' Rock Against Racism – condescending Notting Hill trendies talking through their noses at us.

# Independence Days

What are 'theories of economic determinism'? Not Marxism, I hope. Labels – major AND minor – put punk under the limbo bar of profit and therefore behaved capitalistically."

Regardless, Buzzcocks and Desperate Bicycles led the charge (Scritti's 'Skank Block Bologna would come later, in the summer of 1978). Advances in cheaper studio technology and production costs enabled these records to be made, but the homespun bedroom indie label could not have prospered without some kind of distribution regime, an umbrella organisation to serve as an outlet for the product. The key players in this development were Rough Trade, Pinnacle and Small Wonder. Rough Trade would become a record label later, but Small Wonder, after Chiswick and Beggars, was the first shop to turn label. Puncture's roustabout punk offering, 'Mucky Pup', came just a month after the release of the Lurkers' 'Free Admission' single on Beggars in September 1977. Rough Trade would not release its first vinyl until the start of the following year (and would eventually distribute Scritti Politti).

It's easy to underestimate the historical contribution made by Small Wonder, operating out of a tiny shop in Walthamstow in East London. Many attest to the fact that, in comparison, Rough Trade was considered 'snooty'. For Simon Morgan, who gravitated to a part-time job at Discovery Records in Sratford Upon Avon, Small Wonder was "the king" of the '77/'78 years. "At school around those times – the first thing we all did on a Wednesday morning was consult the Small Wonder list at the back of *Sounds* to see what we needed to chase down and capture. One person in the class would have a copy of a harder to get title – the rest of us would borrow, tape, barter – and in some cases, even steal – until we owned a copy too. Small Wonder had the biggest lists. They got stuff back to you quickest. They had the stock. Rough Trade only used to list a few items per week. The Small Wonder list just kept growing. And in times of limited picture sleeves, limited vinyl runs and limited patience, haste was important, We also used Recommended Records for the artier stuff, or the hepper cats did. Rough Trade didn't really kick in until '79 (the first time I was inspired to go there was to collect my copy of 'Alternative Ulster' by Stiff Little Fingers). Big Small Wonder records like Crass's *The Feeding Of The 5,000* moved us all on from the basic Patrik Fitzgerald template – we'd never heard anything so real at the time – to suggest a new, truly independent future. Crass were the first group to make me realise that punk had actually happened and that it could make a difference beyond sartorial influence. The shock and awe of the Pistols had been such a brief flame... bright, but, in many ways, hard to take seriously, even then. Obviously, in the midst of all this, we didn't refuse to buy a record if it was on a major. Yeah, DIY records were cooler – but for all the talk of Year Zero etc, it was never as Stalinist as that."

There are two strands to the story of Small Wonder, run by Pete Stennet, permanently resplendent in green bobble hat, and his wife Marion (aka Mari), in 162 Hoe Street, set up with the pay-off Stennet received after being made redundant from a record pressing plant. As Morgan details above, Small Wonder offered mail order to satisfy the rising demand for independent singles, becoming a stopping point for musicians to drop off their wares, and eventually a distribution system. The label span off from those activities quite naturally. Its catalogue of some 28 7-inch singles and half a dozen mini-LPs, LPs and 12-inches was dedicated almost entirely to punk artists – though there was considerable variety among the acts they worked with. Many came to Small Wonder of their own volition. Others were spotted by Stennet's friend, Colin Favor, now a renowned house music DJ. "I used to go around to all the punk clubs acting as a talent scout," he would recall. "That basically is how I got involved in clubs in the first place, because the only way you can get on in London – and I hate to say it – is by who you know." Favor would design much of the artwork for the roster's releases, having trained in design with the company that would eventually become Saatchi & Saatchi.

"I remember Mari was more the brains behind it," recalls Puncture guitarist Paul McCallum of Small Wonder's first single, 'Mucky Pup'. "Pete was more the frontman. I remember him sitting down rolling these huge spliffs and going, 'OK, man, let's talk about business.' Tony [Keen], our keyboard player was going, 'No, I want to be straight!' Our nickname for him used to be Woolly, cos Pete always wore this woolly hat with long hair. It was Colin Favor who introduced me to Pete. I was still at college at the time and doing some silk-screen printing, and Colin was a commercial artist. We used to work in the same studio down in Euston. He was good friends with Pete, who wanted to start up a label. He loved 'Mucky Pup' so much, he decided that was going to be the first release. We had a four-track demo we'd done at the time, and he'd been playing that in the shop, getting good feedback from it." The recording took place at Berry Street Studios, under the tutelage of Pretty Things engineer Bill Farley. "We were into the Kinks," recalls bass player Steve Counsel, "and we read a bunch of interviews with Ray Davies where he said he didn't have reverb on his fretboard. We got it fixed in our heads – NO REVERB. The engineer said, 'You've got to overdub the vocal.' We couldn't get our heads round that. We'd never been in a studio, and stroppy little arses that we were, we had to do it our way. And he was right cos it sounded great. He said to us at the end, 'Don't worry about it, lads. I'll put a reverb on it overnight and you won't recognise it tomorrow.' We were like, 'REVERB!' That was it, big argument in the studio." McCallum: "With all that going on, Pete Stennet was going, 'Oh, man, weird scenes in the goldmine . . .' We freaked him out!" Sadly, neither party were able to capitalise on the single. "'Mucky Pup' got a great review in *Sounds*," recalls Counsel, "and it sold out in a couple of weeks and they were caught with their pants down. They didn't know what to do. And it took them months to get another pressing, by which time the whole thing had fizzled. It was really a shame. You couldn't blame them because they didn't know – it was their first venture, but they didn't have it together. Plus there was the fact that he was chain-smoking dope!" Stennet, for his part, was overjoyed that he'd managed to sneak his logo, which cryptically read 'Fuck off the world', on to the labels.

Punk-poet Patrik Fitzgerald was one of the many customers of Small Wonder turned artist. He pushed a demo tape through the shop's door one Friday evening. "I remember both Colin and Pete Stennet being really excited with that cassette," notes McCallum. "It was a real find." Fitzgerald was so nervous in the studio that 'Safety Pin Stuck In My Heart', the first of three records he'd record for the label, had to be re-recorded. Fitzgerald's open-hearted examination of the punk movement impressed many, including Paul Weller (he toured with The Jam) and Mick Jones of The Clash. But he would leave Small Wonder to join Polydor in 1978 and thereafter quickly lost momentum. "My main problem with the music world was that I didn't have a master plan," he told me in 2005, "and rather like in life, I had no real guidance either (I am certainly not going to say at this point that I have since found God)."

Several other acts also made the leap from Small Wonder to either independents or majors. The Leyton Buzzards switched to Chrysalis after recording '19 And Mad' (and winning the *Sun*-sponsored Band Of Hope And Glory contest). "Pete Stennet was not an easy man," Buzzard David Jaymes recalls, "but I liked him a lot. He could be very encouraging but also very damning. I used to love going into the shop though. A fine and inspired old hippy!" Stennet always objected to the latter description, pointing out that he was an original 60s 'freak' and that the distinction was important to someone who had run with the original 60s counter-culture where 'hippy' was considered a lazy, broad-brush journalistic pigeonhole. Crass took their own path (examined in chapter eleven). However, it is worth noting, as the band indicated in an interview with Mike Stand of *The Face* in 1981, that their relationship with Small Wonder was a learning curve for both parties.

"We were really bombastic. 'Fuck the business people!' We insisted that 'Feeding' went out at £2, which took no account of Pete having a shop, flat and staff to support. It was hard-line and naïve."

Tyne & Wear's Carpettes would become Mike Stone's great white hopes at Beggars Banquet after initially securing a deal with Small Wonder. "Our first contact with Small Wonder was when I answered a small ad in *Sounds* asking for bands for a new record label starting up," recalls George Maddison. "The Carpettes had recently recorded a demo of four of our songs at Impulse Studios in Wallsend so we sent them off, more in hope than expectation. Amazingly quickly we got a reply – they wanted to do a record with us! We had only played two gigs up to this point. I had to then get in contact with Pete Stennet by phone, which wasn't as easy as it sounds as this was decades before mobiles and our house didn't even have a phone. So all negotiations were done via a local call box. Pete wanted us to go down to London and re-record some of the songs on the demo. We travelled down to London in an incredibly slow hire van – ten hours it took – and eventually reached the Small Wonder record shop in Hoe Street. We met Pete, who to us appeared to be more from the 'hippy' generation, a little older than us and totally different to us naive northern lads. We stayed overnight in his flat above the shop where he lived with his wife Mari. I can't remember too much about him apart from two things – he seemed to end each night with a bottle of red wine and start each day with a soak in the bath."

The Carpettes' debut EP did reasonably well, and was played regularly by Peel. "So we decided to chance our arm and ask Pete if he wanted to release a follow up. I think at that time he really only wanted to bring out one-off singles by new bands and it wasn't really in his plans to release any more Carpettes records. However, when he heard our second set of demos, including a song called 'Small Wonder', he couldn't resist." They ventured back down to Hoe Street, but this time had an entirely different experience. "During the first session Pete took a back seat and mainly let us, together with the engineer, record the songs as we wanted, with a similar sound to the demos. This time Pete had a certain sound in mind and took charge. He wanted 'Small Wonder' to be played really fast and with an aggressive sound that demanded a very simple drum beat. Kevin [Heard], our drummer at the time, had a really 'busy' style and found this very difficult, After a lot of takes we were at a standstill. Eventually the problem was solved by Kevin keeping a simple beat and Neil [Thompson], the guitarist, bashing out a bass drum pattern on an old, heavy wooden table that was in the studio. Some tom-tom overdubs completed the sound. At the time we weren't too sure about the way it turned out, but Pete's judgement proved to be correct. After the second single it was clear that Pete and Small Wonder were moving on and that they had released their last Carpettes record. However, we continued to visit the shop after we moved to London. I remember Pete being very complimentary about our first session for the John Peel radio show and he was one of the first to congratulate us when we landed the contract with Beggars Banquet."

The Cockney Rejects were another band to move on to bigger things, via a contract with EMI. The Geggus brothers had taken the bus to Walthamstow from their local Canning Town to deliver their tape. Stennet had already rung up their mum by the time they'd got home. And while it's true that Small Wonder's roster was predominantly punk-based, it's worth noting that the later divisions within the second and third generation waves of punk – anarcho (Crass) versus street punk (Rejects) or plain pop-punk (Carpettes) – were all happily accommodated at Small Wonder.

The release to immediately follow the Rejects' 'Flares 'n' Slippers' came from the anarcho camp, but served as a staging post in the development of a post-punk identity. Scotty Parker was bass player of The Fatal Microbes, part of the Crass/Poison Girls family, whose 'Violence Grows' remains a touchstone recording from the period (having been originally issued as a joint effort, with the Poison Girls, on the latter's Small Wonder-sponsored Xntrix imprint). "A drinking buddy of mine, Dave Parsons, who worked for the probation service, told me of a girl in care at St Charles who was giving the staff there a hard time," Parker recalls, "cos she had a shit load of creativity and no outlet for it. So she was getting destructive to herself as well as others and he asked if we (The Poison Girls) would look at some lyrics she had written and put it to music. Myself with Dan and various Poisons got together one evening and bashed out a quick, uninspiring tune to her words and gave Dave a tape to try to placate his young charge. Within days I had a letter from this young 'un with stinging criticism of our efforts. All that she said was true, the tune was crap, the singing (mine) was even worse and overall she said it was the worst piece of shit she had ever heard." The author was Donna Boylon, aka Honey Bane. "Soon after Dave bowed to intense pressure and after a lot of dealings with the Home Office and the law was able to get a limited release of this bothersome girl to visit the band and speak to us face to face. Enter Honey Bane. She was young, pretty and very tough, but was so full of creative energy it seemed like a tornado had been let loose."

## How About Me And You?

The end result was a hastily recorded session at Spaceward Studios in Cambridge – pressured not just because of recording budgets, but also the limited time they'd managed to negotiate for Donna's 'freedom'. The songs enjoyed excellent reviews in both incarnations. Which actually didn't help at all, as the authorities became concerned at Boylon's extra curricular activities. "There was this cat and mouse game with Donna turning up at Burleigh House. After an hour or so of either pure sweetness and joy or a raging slagging off, she would disappear into the night and we were then treated to a visit from the police or other government heavy, demanding to know where Donna was. This was most unwelcome."

Undoubtedly the group who had the greatest commercial promise, however – and were not coincidentally the furthest away from rote punk – were Robert Smith's Cure. It seemed Stennet was in no doubt about what they represented, either, as Nick Dwyer of Brighton's Molesters, another Small Wonder band, can confirm. "Pete really didn't like me at all. When we first met, he played us the Cure record, which was on the label, and said we could be a bit like them if we tried hard. He then said, 'Nick, some people go far, some people dream of going far' and fixed me with a gimlet stare. He was right about both of us as it happened."

The Cure's origins can be traced to Notre Dame Middle School in Crawley, a Catholic institution with liberal leanings, and later St Wilfrid's Comprehensive. By early 1976 they'd taken the name Malice, deciding, with punk beginning to flower, that they should pursue music rather than go on to university. Robert Smith got his hair cut off after hearing 'White Riot' on the John Peel show. In January 1977 they changed their name to Easy Cure, after one of the first original compositions they'd written. They responded to an advert placed in the music press by German independent label Hansa ("Wanna Be A Recording Star"), and sent off a demo tape. Auditions were subsequently held at Morgan Studios in London in May and they were instantly signed – ostensibly because they looked right (Smith was not, at this stage, the singer). The Hansa deal provided an advance of £1,000, which was used to buy equipment and pay for their first studio sessions at SAV in London on 11 October and 15 November. These resulted in a mixture of originals, notably including 'Killing An Arab', a Smith song based on Albert Camus's *L'Etranger*.

Hansa weren't impressed however, and started advocating alternative cover versions, but the band declined. Eventually they returned to the studio in January 1978. "They made us do things like 'Rebel Rebel'," Smith later opined to *Record Collector*. "We'd learnt standards for when we were playing places like Orpington Town Hall and someone would inevitably say, 'Play something we fucking know, you bastards!'" Hansa was still determined that they should cover rock 'n' roll classics and paired them with producer Trevor Vallis. And it still didn't work out. In March the group officially severed links with Hansa after they refused to release 'Killing An Arab'. Hence its eventual release on Small Wonder, in a one-off deal negotiated by the band's new manager, Chris Parry. After it was greeted with ecstatic reviews, and sales in excess of 15,000 copies, Parry would reissue it in February 1979 on his newly founded Polydor-backed imprint, Fiction.

The Cravats, Redditch's first-generation avant-garde punks, released four of the last half-dozen records on the label. The relationship began when Stennet was the lone enthusiast for their self-financed debut record 'Gordon', as singer Shend recalls. "We made 'Gordon' ourselves [using the auspices of Lyntone pressing plant], and then we sent it out to lots of people. We sent one to Rough Trade, who didn't respond, just a load of people who didn't respond. We probably got a nasty letter from Rough Trade. Pete rang us up and just said, 'this is fantastic, come and visit us'. So we went down to the shop in Walthamstow. He asked, how many have you got left of the single? We'd pressed a thousand, which me mam paid £400 for. We said 500. He said, 'We'll take 'em all of them off you.' They took 500, stamped Small Wonder on them and sold them in the shop. A lot of the stamps didn't come out properly, so it says something like 'Small Wo... then fades. The very first time we met them, you just sat in their upstairs lounge, and they fed you and they were just so into the music. They were the people who had 'Bela Lugosi' and the Cure, so it was really great to join them."

As Dallaway reflected in a 1980 interview for *Sounds*, "Pete's shown great faith in us. He financed the album and everything and we've only got a verbal agreement with him. He knows we'd never write a blatantly commercial song, and he'd never want us to." It did seem, indeed, that in the wayward, confusing, Dada-loving Cravats he'd found the perfect band for Small Wonder (although psychedelic art-punk confrontationalists Punishment Of Luxury probably ran them close). But then it wasn't just Stennet, especially towards the end, as vocalist The Shend recalls. "It certainly was equal, her and him. It was very much a joint team. They just loved the music and were instantly saying, let's sort out an album and do some more singles. There was no messing about, or we'll send you a contract, it was just 'let's do it'. I can't remember signing any contract. We'd hitch-hike down to the shop in Redditch, and Pete would tell us we had to listen to this and that, and we were ransacking his shelves, and he'd give us all this stuff, and we'd hitch-hike back and play all the latest sounds. They had such weird, eclectic singles – things from California that no way could you hear at Rough Trade or anywhere else. I personally would say that their selection of records was better at that time. And it was never 'here's a couple of singles, you owe us a quid'. It was that joy in sharing music. At the time Rough Trade was getting bigger and they were both dead against it – they just said, 'Look, why do we want to be bigger? It's perfect as it is.' They weren't interested in the business side. Obviously they made a living, but it was never a case of let's grow the company and get bigger premises. I seem to remember Mari carried on, on her own. I don't know what happened at the end, because by then we'd moved on to Crass and Glass Records." Penny Rimbaud of Crass agrees. "I think that's right, he didn't want to get bigger. He just didn't want the hassle. Pete was very laid back. I don't think he ever wanted to expand. It was Mari who used to do most of the hard work of getting stuff out."

For all the perceived rivalry, Geoff Travis at Rough Trade has nothing but fond memories of Stennet and Small Wonder. "Lovely Pete. He was great, he was holding down East London. Pete was fantastic. To have long hair in that time was to make a big statement about individuality! He did some great records, Pete, and it was absolutely an important shop." So how did a label that unearthed such a remarkable number of important and adventurous bands stall? Business sense? Perhaps. As intimated above, Stennet never signed artists to long-term deals. Or at least initially: Dick Lucas of The Subhumans remembers being approached by the label in its later stages. "We really liked Small Wonder, but couldn't afford the 'pay no more than' thing, due to overheads. And they had a vast, scary contract, something very alien to us."

Certainly the label's strong output between 1978 and 1979 had slowed to a trickle by 1981. Eventually the shop closed and was relocated as a mail order operation in Sudbury, Suffolk. Pete and Mari divorced and are no longer in contact. Mari no longer wishes to discuss her past, which is her prerogative. Stennet seems to have disappeared off the radar completely. Travis thinks he retired to "grow carrots in the country". Penny Rimbaud of Crass believes he is a wood carver. "He called by [to Dial House] once. He brought some of his carvings along, and they were absolutely beautiful."

Three months before Puncture appeared on Small Wonder, another London-based label released its first single, the Cortinas' 'Fascist Dictator', but the contrast between the two proprietors' backgrounds, and aspirations, could hardly have been starker. Miles Copeland III's father was a former musician, but also one of the founding members of the CIA. He was instrumental in American post-war foreign policy in the Middle East, helping to topple the democratic prime minister of Iran, Mohammed Mossadegh, in 1953, opposing British policy over the Suez Canal crisis and aiding the rise of Saddam Hussein. His offspring, including eldest son Miles, attended the American School while he was stationed in Beirut, before enrolling at Millfield Public School after the family relocated to London.

By the 60s, his head turned by rock 'n' roll, Copeland Jnr had started to become involved with the music business. He went on to produce albums by Wishbone Ash and other 'progressive' acts, and partnered with Dick Jordan in BTM (British Talent Management), a publishing and management concern working in broadly the same genre. Their acts included Renaissance (whom Copeland produced), Climax Blues Band, Caravan and Curved Air – for whom he would locate a drumming berth for his brother, Stewart. His other brother, Ian, also started to work as a booking agent in London. "BTM was a label I did through RCA," says Copeland. "It was their system. We were not really that independent. They gave us the money, it went through their system. We could call ourselves an independent label, but it really wasn't. I signed what I wanted, but they had to approve it."

By 1976 BTM had collapsed. "When I went through huge turmoil, financially or whatever, I stopped the label and stopped everything," recalls Copeland. "BTM had no relevance whatsoever to what I did after that, it was over, finished. End of story, gone." Tipped off by Patti Smith's manager Jane Friedman about London's emerging punk scene, he engaged Nick Jones, BTM's former press officer, to investigate. He'd already befriended Malcolm McLaren, and tried to help the Pistols find venues post-Grundy. It was his suggestion that they secure gigs abroad, leading to their Dutch tour of December 1977. "I was going down to the Roxy regularly," says Copeland. "I had an office at a place called Dryden Chambers. Above me was Malcolm McLaren and the Sex Pistols [The Glitterbest offices]. I would read in the newspaper that they couldn't get a gig. So I'd go upstairs and say, 'I think I can book you.' And Malcolm would say, sure. Then I'd go up there a couple of days later, and I'd booked the Marquee Club and I'd booked some other places. And he'd tell me basically to fuck off. Malcolm had no interest in them doing shows. For as much as he protested, saying no-one would book them, that's *exactly* what he wanted. I kept going up there with bookings, and finally he started yelling at me, saying, 'Don't you get it? I get more publicity saying they can't work, and you're screwing up my whole publicity campaign, get the fuck out of my office!' The Sex Pistols were basically Malcolm McLaren's plaything, and it was a big publicity thing, and he didn't even want anyone to play in the fucking band. And they got rid of the one musician and brought in a nutcase, who was committed to destroying everything in sight. It was a publicity thing, he was having fun with the media and it worked, he was brilliant. But the band used to call me up and thank me for gigs, then they couldn't do them because Malcolm wouldn't let it happen."

Copeland also befriended Mark P, aka Mark Perry, the editor of punk fanzine *Sniffin' Glue*. "I had a girlfriend called Jill Furmanovsky. She was filming some of these gigs, and we'd go see them together. I had very little money at the time because I had gone through lots of changes in my own personal set-up. The punk rockers were all interested in anybody who cared about them, whereas the traditional bands, all they cared about were people who had a lot of money. Cos that's what they needed! (LAUGHS). So I saw The Clash, I saw Generation X, I went to the Roxy every night to see these bands. Basically, I started acting as an agent. I booked Generation X, I booked The Sex Pistols and took them into Europe. I was one of the only people in the business who was paying attention to punk rock. Then I would make the records on the bands that we were booking, because they needed to have records out, so one thing led to another."

"For me, I had to think of something new," Copeland continues, "because I was no longer sitting there with tons of money and major labels backing me. It was now the fact that I could sign a group and make a record for £80, that meant I could be in the game. Where with a major act, you're talking £100,000. The business very much divided at that point, so you could get down and dirty. Because we were a very small operation, it could work. The big companies, it made no sense to them, putting out a record that sold 4,000 copies. When I came into the business in the first place, I was not at the ground floor, I came in mid-stream, with the progressive rock movement. But the beginning of that was three or four or five years before I got to England. With Wishbone Ash, it was already the Floyd, Jethro Tull and the Doors; they were already happening bands. So that world had already matured. I was coming in, in a sense, at the tail-end of it. Whereas the punk rock thing, I was right at the beginning. I was right there, day one. I guess it started six months before I really got interested in it, at least press-wise. But nothing was really happening in terms of real shows or anyone taking it seriously other than the press having fun with it. And that was fun, it's fun to be in at the beginning of a movement."

Brother Stewart was similarly alive to the possibilities thrown up by the emergent punk scene, and quickly put together a trio featuring guitarist Henry Padovani, whom he'd met at The Roxy, and bass player Gordon Sumner, aka Sting, whom he remembered from a Curved Air show in Newcastle. Sting was happy to leave his under-performing jazz band Last Exit, who had refused to move to London with him. The Police were the epitome of craven punk rock opportunism; and everyone in London seemed well appraised of the fact. Stewart Copeland has subsequently talked about riding the bandwagon for all it was worth, and his credibility wasn't helped by the existence of a February 1977 letter to the *Melody Maker* in which he slammed punk and pledged allegiance to Pink Floyd.

After discussions with Miles, Stewart and Sting played a series of shows as backing musicians for American ex-pat Cherry Vanilla (with The Police on the undercard). Vanilla was in the country, as was Wayne County, at the prompting of Miles, as he moved into the London club scene under the auspices of his New Orders agency – arranged through Heartbreakers manager Leee Black Childers. "Cherry was using Miles Copeland as a booking agent and Miles told her to use his brothers band's rhythm section to save money bringing American musicians over to the UK," remembers Howard Finkel of the Cherry Vanilla Band. "Miles put a package tour together where The Police opened the show, then Sting and Stewart backed Cherry. The Police wanted to concentrate on their career and Cherry on hers, so they parted company. Sting and Stewart really liked Louie's (Lepore; Vanilla band guitarist) playing and asked him to leave Cherry and join the Police. Louie being Cherry's boyfriend and musical director, he politely declined. The Police then asked Andy Summers to join, gave Padovani his papers (he was supposedly a great guy but a real basic guitarist and they had bigger fish to fry) and the rest is history."

The Police recorded their first single in February 1977, exactly a month after their first rehearsal in January in Stewart's squatted Mayfair flat. They may have been opportunists, but like Miles, they were quick-moving opportunists. 'Fallout' and 'Nothing Achieving', both songs written by Stewart with assistance on the latter from brother Ian, were recorded at Pathway via a loan of £150 from BTM's Dick Jordan rather than Miles, who was reluctant to put his hand in his own pocket. The label incorporated for the task of releasing the songs, a deliberate attempt to secure a commitment from a major, was Illegal Records.

"Well, look," explains Copeland, "my father was pretty notorious, or at least well known. When Stewart had come up with The Police, I figured, well, if he's going to call it The Police, I should follow suit. Then we called the agency in America FBI, so we had fun with it like that. It was using the establishment as anti-establishment. That's what we were really up to. We would call ourselves something very establishment, but it's always the double-entendre. It's like when your house is being broken into and you're being attacked, boy, you sure want the police there. Other times, they're the pigs, the things you rebel against. So we've always had a double standard, depending on what your predicament happens to be at any given moment. It's the yin and yang of life. The CIA is really there to warn off the dangers to the country, same as MI5. But then they get up to some skulduggery that they shouldn't, or whatever. The other thing, of course, is that it caused notice. I just started my label in America now, and I finally decided after many years of avoiding it, that I would call the label Copeland International Arts – or CIA. And the funny thing is, everyone loves it, just because of that. They think it's amusing. Illegal was a pure independent set-up where I literally got the tapes, went to the factory, got the master made, took that to the factory, got the records pressed, got the labels to the factory, got the sleeves to the factory. If I didn't get the sleeves there in time, I'd bag the records myself, and then I'd drive to the record store myself and sell the records. So that was literally as independent as you get."

His management interests grew to include Squeeze, a Deptford band whom RCA had dropped at the start of 1976 without releasing any material. Though Glenn Tilbrook would reiterate to the NME that Squeeze 'never wanted to be associated with punk', to many it seemed otherwise, and in Copeland's case he thought he'd 'found the Beatles'. Copeland scooped both the band and their unreleased recordings, but his initial plan was to interest a major label. When the search proved fruitless, he scheduled 'Take Me I'm Yours' as a release on BTM in January 1977. But then he reflected that neither the recording nor the imprint were suitable in the current punk climate. When the majors again failed to respond to the mail-out of two separate cassettes, featuring no less than 28 songs, it led to the foundation of Deptford Fun City. The label name masked his involvement in the release and gave it the appearance of being one of the new breed of cottage industry independent singles. The 'Packet Of Three' EP was released in July 1977, the selections drawn from a five-song session produced by John Cale at Pathway a month previously. Cale was an old associate of Copeland, having sought his help in attempting to get the Velvet Underground demo tapes released more than a decade previously (Copeland would also help him book his April '77 tour). Later, Jools Holland would scribble 'I Am A Cunt' in marker pen on the inebriated Cale's forehead after Copeland brought him in to 'punk up' Squeeze's debut album. The EP attracted vociferously supportive reviews, including two single of the week accolades. The success was such that Copeland began to rethink his original plan – of using the singles simply as a platform to secure his charges a berth on a major. Which is exactly what happened when A&M stepped in to sign Squeeze and quickly turned them into chart regulars.

And Copeland's decision not to pursue his already developed relationships with the majors? "Because the music industry at the time had no interest whatsoever in doing what this whole new punk rock thing was," he confirms. "I had talked to the people at PolyGram [Polydor] about doing a label. We talked and talked and nothing really happened. So I decided in the end, I'll just do it myself. And it was an era – you look at Stiff Records and other little things that were coming along. Rough Trade and whatever – all of a sudden, there was a situation where there was a demand for these punk rock records and the majors were not fulfilling it. I figured, you could make a single, you could record a couple of tracks down at Pathway Studios for £80, and go make a record. And put out a single and people would buy the singles. So the fact that the majors weren't in there, and that there was a demand from the street, meant that you could actually get into doing it. You could literally do exactly what you wanted. In the beginning, you could sell almost anything. If you said it was punk rock, it would sell. Then at one point, a lot of people started doing it, and all of a sudden, you'd go out to the record store, and they'd go – who is this act? You'd say, it's the same kind of thing as I did two months ago. They'd go, yeah, but we've had 50 more records come in since then. So finally that bubble burst. Then you had to get back into marketing and building just like any other act. So in the beginning, it was relatively easy. But then it got harder, and you had to get serious."

Before either record was released, Copeland was already planning a third label. At the time The Police single was being recorded, he was in the process of taking over 27 Dryden Chambers in Oxford Street, having previously used the premises intermittently (he'd actually married its previous occupant, Sherry John of Sherry John Artists Ltd, a theatrical agency). From this base he launched Step Forward, installing *Sniffin' Glue* editor Mark Perry as head of A&R. Nick Jones had brought Perry to a meeting in January with Miles. He knew instinctively that his background – both familial and in terms of his involvement with the prog-rock 70s – would do little for the credibility of the project. David Marlow, later Richard Branson's assistant, was offered a desk in Dryden Chambers and witnessed the comings and goings. "Nick Jones was the bloke who did it for Miles. He was the guy who ran a lot of the labels. Miles is a businessman, and he was buying into this. Nick was the guy who really ran the labels. This was a place opposite the 100 Club more or less, set back up an alleyway, a Victorian office building, and Miles Copeland had an office, and he gave me desk space there, as a London base, when I was working for *Zig Zag*."

Relations between Perry and Copeland were cemented as Copeland invested in *Sniffin' Glue* in the form of a series of adverts. Perry, meanwhile, would eventually shift his operations to Dryden Chambers when he noticed that number 28, the office next door, was vacant. By June 1977 he'd left the berth Rough Trade had generously provided them with, and took his team (Steve Mick, Danny Baker and photographer Harry Murlowski) to the third floor of Dryden Chambers. A nominal rent was charged, while an extension lead was run through the window of Copeland's office to supply electricity. Perry would ask Mick to become *Sniffin' Glue*'s editor so he could devote more time to Step Forward and, increasingly, the band he was in the process of forming. The incumbent was sacked after one issue when Perry decided he didn't like the results (or according to Mick, when he attempted to bring his girlfriend Alice into an editorial meeting). Perry was not above using *Sniffin' Glue* as a publicity vehicle for both his own band and several other acts on the Step Forward roster (notably putting Sham 69 on the cover of the final issue, #12, just after they'd signed on the dotted line). The nepotism was rife and in stark contrast to the cavalier attitudes displayed at the most important west coast American fanzine of the day, *Slash*. Editor Claude Bessy, who would ultimately join the Rough Trade team, would delight in slotting any major label advertisements on pages facing editorial cutting those records to ribbons. But, with sales of over 8,000 per issue towards its end, *Sniffin' Glue* was undoubtedly as influential to the development of the fanzine boom as 'Spiral Scratch', 'Smokescreen' *et al* had been to the independent record label explosion.

Step Forward would reflect Perry's tastes but more accurately document those bands in his immediate orbit. Miles had set up a situation where, via his connection to Chris Parry, he could access Polydor's in-house studio with the hope of eventually signing a distribution deal. This solution had the advantage of not costing Miles a penny and leaving Polydor with any liabilities. John Cale came in as in-house producer, following the model of Nick Lowe at Stiff. The label was inaugurated via The Cortinas' 'Fascist Dictator' (though SF2, Chelsea's 'Right To Work', was actually released on 3 June as well). The Models' 'Freeze' followed in July. But Polydor passed when they heard the tapes of Miles' new roster, deeming them 'amateurish'. Thereafter Miles scrapped New Orders to bring all his activities under the umbrella name Faulty Products. All three of those first Step Forward singles had been cut at the Polydor sessions, proving the fiscal wisdom of Miles' initial caution (he had negotiated the right to the masters should Polydor pass).

Another of the acts Miles Copeland worked with in these incestuous times was Perry's debut musical venture, Alternative TV. Copeland immediately became their manager, and sourced a distribution deal with EMI, which enjoyed a similar arrangement with Step Forward. Perry, now famed for his "punk died when the Clash signed to CBS" comment, was understandably self-conscious about his new-found closeness to a major label, but the deal did at least offer free studio time in which to record the band's first demo. He made good use of it, tackling subjects including impotence that he knew the major would never care to release. To quash all doubt, he deliberately inserted swear words into three of the four recordings. Once again, by self-releasing those sessions as the band's first two singles, Copeland had managed to offload his recording costs to a third party. ATV's output, notable for Perry's blunt, highly personal lyrics, was ultimately housed primarily on Deptford Fun City; a now vacant lot after Squeeze's defection to A&M.

Following The Police's debut 'Fall Out' (which had an initial pressing of 2,000 copies but would ultimately sell over 70,000 when the band became superstars), Illegal's second release was Wayne County and the Electric Chairs' self-titled debut EP. But the band would soon depart for Safari when Miles balked at releasing some of their more scandalous material. After an aborted second Police single, recorded with Cale at Pathway, Menace's 'Screwed Up' followed in November 1977. Although Menace would subsequently transfer to Small Wonder, Copeland would later release the 'I Need Nothing' single drawn from the same sessions, and brought guitarist Steve Tannett into his inner circle to help him run Illegal.

Copeland also added distribution to his activities, retaining the name Faulty. His first major project was The Only Ones' 'Lovers Of Today', released on their own Vengeance Records, run by Peter Perret and Zena Kakoulli (sister of Squeeze bass player Harry). Its partial success (Miles advertised it heavily in the final issue of *Sniffin' Glue*) led to the Only Ones signing with CBS. But it seemed Perrett was less than grateful for, or graceful about, Copeland's contribution. See the band's 1979 album *Even Serpents Shine* and the track 'Miles From Nowhere' whose lyric, and lines such as 'cold reaction transcends the myth you built' and particularly 'you always sell to the one who bids the most', can easily be interpreted as referencing Copeland.

Step Forward then secured the services of Sham 69 for 'I Don't Wanna', but they soon passed through to Polydor. "Miles was a no-go area," remembers Sham's Dave Parsons of those times. "We'd hang out in the other bit with Mark Perry and Danny Baker [who had by now joined *Sniffin' Glue*] etc. I do remember we never got paid for anything. One memory I have was when we were at his dad's house (ex-head of the CIA). It was Sham, Miles and his brother Stewart. The next thing we know, his dad bursts in and proceeds to give both Miles and Stewart a huge bollocking. I'm not sure who was more embarrassed – them or us."

Sham had an appeal that far outstripped Chelsea's, who had to some extent become Step Forward's house band, despite never eclipsing the power of their debut single (whose sentiments were roundly misunderstood). The Models simply dispersed while the Cortinas moved on to CBS after a second single, 'Defiant Pose'. "At the time he [Copeland] wasn't popular on the scene," remembers Cortinas' singer Jeremy Valentine, "although he did give a lot of help to McLaren. So his unpopularity made him popular with me. He was basically a businessman who would have made even more money if he hadn't had the silly idea that he could make money out of rock 'n' roll. But he had also lost a lot of money in the early 70s and was a bit down on his uppers when we met him, at The Roxy. But the fact that he was American and his dad ran the CIA was exciting to us. He had enormous energy and drive. Mind you, we thought his brother's band were a bunch of wankers, like trendy teachers. Miles didn't really understand 'the creative process' and liked simple solutions. Usually he was hands-off, but when he interfered it was bit depressing. Mark Perry was and is an angel."

The other important band on the label was Mark E Smith's The Fall, a group whose Can and Beefheart fixations ran contrary to the prevailing influence of the Pistols or Clash. Fiercely intelligent and belligerent, and in perhaps half a dozen ways totally unique, Smith used oral tradition and slang to invent his own dictionary. The Fall's 'Bingo-Master's Breakout' EP was intended originally for New Hormones but cancelled due to financial constraints. When Richard Boon handed over the tapes to Kay Carroll, The Fall's then manager, she sent them south. A fourth track from the sessions, 'Frightened', was dropped from the Step Forward EP, though it would re-emerge in re-recorded form on the group's debut album – the first long player on the label. But even prior to the EP's release, The Fall were artists of some renown, having recorded what would be the first of dozens of Peel sessions for the besotted DJ, and appeared on Tony Wilson's *So It Goes* TV show. Which might have made them ideal candidates for the latter's soon to be founded record label, Factory Records.

Yet it was Danny Baker, prior to joining *Sniffin' Glue* the editor of *Adrenaline* fanzine, who eventually cajoled Copeland into the release. Writing in *Zig Zag* in February 1978, announcing the ultimately cancelled release of the New Hormones EP, Baker ended his eulogy with an entreaty: "What can I say to make you feel enough to emphasise how important this band are to rock music, and me, and hopefully, you?" At one point an arrangement was considered whereby the band were to be produced by Kim Fowley, who also recorded for Illegal, before the band rejected the £2,000 fee he'd demanded. The Fall's stay at Step Forward was brief, but in singles such as 'Rowche Rumble' and 'Fiery Jack', and their first two LPs (*Live At The Witch Trials* and *Dragnet*), it represented the first instalment, and one of the finest, of a formidable career.

"Miles was from the old guard," notes Marc Riley, whose tour of duty with The Fall spanned their entire Step Forward output. "He was a 'player'. If you look at the records Miles put out, I think it's fair to say he wasn't exactly doing it from 'the heart'. It was business. I really don't think anyone who 'got' The Fall and ATV would be particularly enamoured with Chelsea and Menace. I think he knew the business, was ready to go at the right time and, as with The Police, adapted to the changes the Pistols introduced. Mark P was often knocking about, but I never got to know Danny Baker at that time. ATV were one of the best bands around. Strangely they – like The Fall – were very principled. Both bands ended up supporting hippy outfit Here and Now. That's where we met our future 'producer' Grant Showbiz. Miles Copeland drove The Fall van on our first American tour. I liked him. He was sharp. Good sense of humour."

By 1978 Copeland had relocated the Faulty companies to new premises at 41B Blenheim Crescent. But thereafter he would focus on managing The Police and also founding IRS Records (significantly offering Perry a berth for ATV), into which the Faulty labels were folded. Dryden Chambers, once the home of Faulty Products, *Sniffin' Glue* and Glitterbest, was rebuilt and refurbished.

"Look, once The Police started moving, that became such a big deal," says Copeland. "Once we sort of got backing, all of a sudden we had money, because The Police were happening, IRS became a hot indie, and there was a lot less focus on England. The labels morphed into IRS, and then IRS became the label. [A&M] didn't put money into us until later on. What they did was they put the records out. I put the money in. My deal with Jerry Moss was, look, you don't A&R my records, I won't ask for your money. So you put out everything I give you, but you don't listen to the records. When I went in to make the deal originally, he said, 'OK, give me some of the records.' I said, 'No, no, no. You won't know what you're listening to. I'm not asking for your money, I'll pay for the releases, you just distribute it, but you can't listen to any of the records. You have no decision on what comes out. So he said OK. So we signed Buzzcocks and The Stranglers, one after another, just putting stuff out, Wall Of Voodoo, Magazine. We were licensing stuff or signing stuff. I was going to do 'Rock Lobster' with the B-52s, and they had agreed, and I was running around with The Police, and by the time I'd got around to doing it, they had already got into some place else. The B-52's was something I really wanted to do, and I couldn't get A&M interested, they thought they were a college band, and I kept saying, this group's going to be big. I guess the only other act here I wish I had signed, because they did pretty well, was X. But the fucking guitar player [Billy Zoom] decided I was a CIA front! Which is hilarious, of course." In fact, accusations of that ilk had always dogged Miles – including allegations that The Police's far east tours were merely preliminary exercises in information gathering for prospective coups. "He said, 'You're a CIA front.' I said, 'Excuse me? I'm a CIA front? So CIA is funding me? You might want to let them know, cos I could use the cash!' That was always very funny."

Copeland, maligned though he may be, at least has a sense of humour. Having sponsored a band called The Police, set up Illegal Records, and founded a company called IRS, he was clearly having a lot of fun with his reputation. "I was, yeah! The truth is this – we're all tied up to big business in one way or another. If you want to be in the main marketplace, and to have your records sold in Virgin and HMV, and wherever the stores are, there's a structure to get in there. And if you want to play at the Albert Hall, and you want to play at stadiums, in the end, if you want to do that, you're in big business. You can come in and be independent and all this and that. [You might be] really underground and you don't play those places and don't sell your records that way and all that. But once you really are in the game to make money and succeed, inevitably those realities of business come into play."

Though its associated record label would only issue four singles, Bonaparte's shops formed a key part of the pre-Cartel independent network that sprang up from 1977 onwards. "We had half a dozen record stores through the 70s and 80s," says former owner Steve Melhuish, who ran the stores with his brother Guy. "I opened up the first Virgin store in Oxford Street in 1971, and then opened up my own stores in 1973. We were fortunate enough, for the first time it seemed to me, to be at the right place at the right time. We had shops in Croydon [where Kirsty MacColl worked in mail-order], Bromley and Guildford. And we had Siouxsie and the Banshees in the Bromley shop, we had The Damned hanging out in the Croydon shop and we had what was to turn out to be The Jam in the Guildford shop. So we were involved in the punk thing right from the outset. There wasn't really the demand until punk came along. Not only did I find it musically a breath of fresh air, but from a business point of view, it gave us an edge with everybody else. I think I put the first ever advert in the *NME* for punk records. I remember doing it quite clearly – I scratched it out on a piece of rough paper and posted it off. They said they needed it typeset. I said I don't want it typeset, I wanted it to be stuck in just like that. They said it would take up extra column inches. I said I didn't care, and to just put it in as it was. It was called 'Punk At Bonaparte' and I'm pretty sure it was the first mail order advert – either us or Small Wonder. They advertised in the *Melody Maker* and we advertised in the *NME*. From that we had a lot of enquiries from other shops, and from abroad, particularly Paris and New York and LA, so we started to export. I got involved with Geoff Travis at Rough Trade, Tony Wilson at Factory, etc. We were wholesaling – one of the four or five people that were wholesaling punk."

Just like Small Wonder and Beggars Banquet before them, and Rough Trade later, launching their own record label (in November 1977, with Kilburn & The High Roads' 'Best Of' EP) seemed a natural step. "I had a few bands come in wanting to put some stuff out. So we did what everybody else seemed to be doing and what we felt we could do quite well, because we had quite a solid backing from the shops. We had our own demand and our own mail order. So it seemed an obvious step to set up our own label which we did, and use the links we already had. I was very much involved with Stiff Records as well. But when I put out the Kilburns' single, I had no idea that they'd just signed Ian Dury [The Kilburns' now solo singer]. I remember I went up to Stiff one afternoon, as I was wholesaling their product. I used to go up and meet Jake and Dave Robinson. I said I'm going to reissue some Kilburns stuff and they looked at me strangely and wondered what the hell was going on. And they said they'd just signed him. I said, 'That's all right. I don't intend to go on and do anything else.' I'd just been over to Pye Records and said I'd like to licence some stuff, and they didn't really know what I was talking about.

I'm sure I didn't know the legal side myself, but there was a demand for his stuff and it was deleted."

The other singles on the label were new material. The Dyaks' Chris Reeves "used to be my painter and decorator". Tennis Shoes, "the first single to give away a free zoetrope", were "fairly avant-garde; a seven-minute rock opera about a kid who had hippy parents". Those Helicopters were Maidstone Art College refugees whose version of Lennon and McCartney's 'World Without Love' was licensed to the budget MFP punk covers compilation, *We Do 'Em Our Way*. Sales were reasonable. "Ian Dury was never going to be a problem. I think we pressed 5,000 of that, and eventually sold them, which by today's standards is fantastic. I remember we did 1,000 or 2,000 Dyaks, and we did quite a lot of Tennis Shoes. I remember one wholesaler took 1,000 from me, rather enthusiastically, and then got a bit miffed when I wouldn't take them back later on. But yeah, we did a few thousand of each."

"When we did it in 77," Melhuish continues, "we were like a lot of the free spirits, such as Miles Copeland, when he set up his independent labels. This girl who used to be on telephone sales who had been at RCA said to me there's a guy setting up his own label. I rang him up and said, whatever you're releasing, I'll have a hundred of each. He said, 'What do you mean?' I said, I buy a hundred of everything. Anything that was being produced, I was buying. You know, Buzzcocks, Undertones, all those early ones I bought in quantity. That's why we put the singles out. With hindsight, you could look at it as a dry run. That gave me a reality check. It was done pretty much through the shops and our own mail order system, we'd wholesale it with the others like Rough Trade and Small Wonder. So we helped each other out." Thereafter Melhuish concentrated on the shops with the idea that he would eventually start a much bigger label." Saul Galpern, who would later pilot Nude Records in the 90s, came down to Glasgow to work for Bonaparte after answering an ad in the music press, having long used them to feed his own record collecting habit. "They always told you what new albums were coming up, even if you didn't buy it through them," notes Galpern of the distinction between Bonaparte and the other advertisers in the back of the inkies. "But there was an ad there saying they were looking for someone, and I applied for it. I think it was £35 a week – at the time, I would have done it for nothing! They were looking for someone initially just to work in the shop helping out. It was the King's Cross branch [which had subsequently opened]. I was working for the Melhuish brothers on the floor in the shop, and then I moved into the mail order side, and was involved in postage and packing. Then they brought in a guy called Chris

Youle, because they were going to start a new record label called Human Records (see Chapter Thirteen).

Another early entrant was Lightning Records, a distribution arm cum warehouse cum record label stationed in North London that released a host of generally poor punk records, mainly by bandwagon jumpers, alongside disco, novelty cash-ins and, with ultimately much greater success, reggae, often working in tandem with Trojan and Island. It also spawned the 'Old Gold' reissue label concentrating on deleted 'classic' 45s. The partnership included Alan Davison, Keith Yershon and Ray Laren. The latter was the son of Dave Laren, whose Laren For Music company had helped pioneer the UK jukebox industry (his father-in-law Ralph Mandell was also involved in the same business). Laren Jnr founded Lightning alongside Ralph's son Norman to supply the jukebox network.

Davison inaugurated a new independent distribution model after leaving EMI in the summer of 1977. It became successful very quickly, not least because he was able to use Laren's warehouse at 841 Harrow Road on a rent-free basis for the initial six months. Because it carried product from both majors and independents, by 1977 Lightning had worked out that reggae and new wave were selling increasingly well, so took the decision to found their own label. Graham Collins would design the distinctive 'scorched tree' logo that accompanied its releases.

Lightning lucked out on picking up Althea & Donna's 'Up Town Top Ranking'. Produced by Joe Gibbs, another staple of the Lightning catalogue, it employed the 'riddim' from Alton Ellis's 1967 hit, 'I'm Still In Love With You' and was an answer record to Trinity's 'Three Piece Suit'. With initial support from Peel, they became the youngest female duo to score a national number one. With no contract in force to Lightning, Richard Branson stepped in to sign them to Virgin (a dubious choice, as the Jamaican schoolgirls flopped miserably thereafter with the astonishingly awful 'Puppy Dog Song'). The rest of Lightning's catalogue, outside of reggae, was entirely less noteworthy, though Jet Bronx & The Forbidden did count among their ranks a gawky Lloyd Grossman, and the label's initial release by Horrorcomic featured Roger Semon, future Sanctuary Records CEO. By the time the label closed around the summer of 1979 they had diversified into football-related singles in an act of tangible desperation. The label, which was briefly mentioned in a *World In Action* documentary *The Chart Busters* about chart-hyping (jukebox suppliers could exert a lot of influence on the charts by dint of the records they stocked their clients with), was

bought out by US wholesaler Ingram Entertainment Inc. One refugee from
Lightning, Martin Wickham, established the Trump Records chain of stores
in north London. Another, Ross Crighton, was the husband of Rough Trade
shop manager Judith.

Launched in 1977 "out of desperation as the majors were narrow minded", Do
It would become primarily associated with early releases by Adam And The
Ants. The founders were Robin Scott and his then girlfriend and graphic
designer Linda Watham. Max Tregoning provided financial support, while
his brother, Ian, would later collaborate on various label projects. Scott was
an old acquaintance of Malcolm McLaren from Croydon Art College. Indeed,
McLaren and partner Vivienne Westwood had offered him the chance to
become involved in their Chelsea clothes emporium Sex, which Scott
declined in favour of pursuing a musical career. His 'acid-folk' album
released in 1969, *Woman From The Warm Grass*, is highly regarded amongst
cultists and collectors, but the independent label that housed it, Head
Records, stalled almost immediately. After a period as a troubadour in folk
clubs, and widespread travel in Europe and America, he declined a contract
with EMI after winning the 1982 *Search For A Star* national talent contest
when they refused to sign his backing band. Thereafter he produced pub
rock band Roogalator, whose line-up included brother Julian, notably their
Stiff debut 'Cincinnati Fatback'.

Roogalator's *Play It By Ear* album inaugurated Do It after Scott failed to
secure a release for it elsewhere, while Scott himself would also cut the third
single on the label under the pseudonym Cosmic Romance. Otherwise the
label's premier attraction was the Ants, whose debut album *Dirk Wears
White Sox* would be belatedly released in November 1979. By which time
Scott had scored a number two single under the guise of M's 'Pop Muzik',
released through MCA (Do It had hosted his 'Giorgio Moroder meets post-
punk debut, 'Moderne Man', in August 1978). He had by now, however,
handed over the reins. "I brought Adam And The Ants to the label," he told
Jonas Wårstad, "before leaving the business to the Tregoning Brothers, who
were prepared to inherit the hassle. I left to form 'M' in Paris [where he
would work for the Barclay label, settling with partner Brigitte Vinchon, aka
Brigit Novik, who would later record for Stiff]. "Ownership of the label was
not really of much concern to me, it was more a vehicle born out of
frustration when a deal with Virgin for Roogalator went down the pan."

The other stars of Do It's roster arrived were Swiss electro-dance act Yello,
whose 'Bostich' became a major success in 1981 when remixed by Ian
Tregoning. The rest were odd, one-off singings, like Again Again. "I don't

know how we came to Do It," recalls the latter's Jeff Pountain. "I guess they asked us. We'd been talking to a few people, just a blur of ageing hippies or Thatcherite tossers, in my failing memory. Since you're interested, Adam [Ant] used to sit cross-legged on the table in Do It, shouting into the phone, "No toilets, I ain't playin' no more fuckin' toilets!' Which was odd, 'cause he was a quite well spoken geezer. Bit of a 'thesp', as his subsequent incarnations proved. Still, his transfer to CBS paid for our 12-inch." By 1982 Do It had closed its doors. One further Do It release is worthy of mention, however. The Method were formed in Islington and included guitarist Paul de Raymond Leclercq, who had played on the Dangerous Bicycles 'Smokescreen' single – fitting, given that Do It Records took its title explicitly from that band's manifesto.

Two other quasi-indie labels on the London punk scene also deserve mention. Anchor Records was owned by Ian Ralfini with its A&R headed by Dave Hill. Based in Wardour Street, with a distribution agreement with ABC in America, it signed pub rockers Ace (led by singer Paul Carrack, who briefly joined Squeeze) who enjoyed significant success in America with debut single 'How Long'. But when they disbanded Hill joined the A&R throng visiting the Roxy and picked up one of the superior bands he saw there, The Adverts (following their one-off deal with Stiff). Anchor housed two Adverts singles, 'Gary Gilmore's Eyes' and 'Safety In Numbers', both of which saw them appear on *Top Of The Pops*, but shut down shortly thereafter (The Adverts joining CBS subsidiary Bright). Anchor was always a confused and confusing imprint. Its final two releases were a country album by George Hamilton IV and Donna McGhee's disco album, *Make It Last Forever*. In the event, Anchor barely lasted until 1978.

Despite this, Ralfini was a friend of John Fruin, Warners UK managing director, which enabled the spin-off label Hill had formed, Real Records, to find a home. Though it needed the intervention of the omnipresent Seymour Stein. "When I met Dave Hill he was the head of A&R for Anchor Records. At the time, Sire were distributed in America by ABC, the parent of Anchor. Anchor was not a very good company, everyone called it 'Wanker Records'. But Dave was a great A&R guy, and we became friendly. We both tried to sign Billy Idol's band, Generation X. I said, why don't we join forces, then we can offer a world deal? Sire is known here (America) better than ABC. Chrysalis signed them in the end, but we remained friends. Then he called me one day and said I've just been working with an artist, Chrissie Hynde. That name was very familiar to me, I knew it through her writing for the *NME*. I went to see her at the Moonlight in West Hampstead. And I loved her, and I loved the band. Fabulous. Dave and I started Real Records together, and it was half-owned by Sire, and Warner Brothers was involved because I did a deal with John Fruin."

NEMS was the rump of Brian Epstein's North End Music Stores family empire, bought out post-Beatles by Patrick Meehan. It specialised in reissues of Black Sabbath – whom Meehan once managed – and acquired Immediate's late 60s catalogue, as well as a live music agency in London. Around 1977 it began to fancy its chances with new music too, and signed The Boys, one of the new wave's better commercial propositions. "Patrick had an assistant called Ian, who basically did all the work," recalls the band's Matt Dangerfield. "But you were dealing with Patrick Meehan directly. He always had a bodyguard around, a big burly guy. The reason we signed to NEMS – it was pretty early days, at a time when we were playing live, and just about every gig we played, the manager would say, that's the last time you'll darken our doors. All there was to play in those days was the remnants of the pub rock era. We had a gig at Dingwalls as a support one night. I remember the DJ after we'd finished said, 'that's the worst band that's ever played Dingwalls.' The same night there was someone from the *NME* there who gave us a review, and NEMS were there. They told us that night they wanted to sign us. We didn't know anything about them as a record company, but they were a good live agency. We were running out of places to play! So at least NEMS the agency would get us some gigs. So we accepted the deal."

They possessed prior knowledge of what they were getting into. "Cas (keyboard player Casino Steel) knew them before, actually," remembers Dangerfield. "When it was called Worldwide [Artiste Management], it was also the same people, [including] Patrick Meehan. We knew the gangster connection. We didn't care. We were just happy to get the first album deal for any punk band of that era. The trouble was, a few weeks later there were lots of record companies coming to us. We signed a bit too soon. At the time it looked like it would be very difficult for any band to get anything other than a singles deal." Sign in haste, repent at leisure? The Boys had luxurious stretches of time to do so. Any success debut single 'The First Time' might have enjoyed was scuppered when RCA, who distributed NEMS, had to focus all its attention on Elvis reissues following his death. Things became desperate when a third album failed to appear after NEMS refused to pay the studio bills for sessions at Rockfield Studios. In the end, the group embarked on an 18-month 'strike' in order to earn a release from their contract and eventually moved on to Safari. NEMS to all intents and purposes disappeared in 1982 after the release of the UK Subs' *Endangered Species* LP. Nicky Garratt remembers being warned off the label by others, only to discover that the label's *modus operandi* was intact. Halfway through recording sessions, the studio owners grew anxious. After all, the Rockfield story was now common currency due to the Boys' 'strike' story. "Sure enough," remembered Garratt, "the next day a guy in sunglasses and a black suit showed up with a suitcase full of cash." NEMS collapsed shortly thereafter, with most of its back catalogue taken over by Sanctuary.

The Boys' eventual home was Safari, formed early in 1977 and sited in a temporary office in Newman Street, London. Tony Edwards, Deep Purple's original manager, and John Craig were running a management office. "We looked after Whitesnake, Rainbow and Deep Purple," Craig recalls. "We also had two labels, one through EMI, Purple Records, and one through what's now Universal, Oyster. We also had a friend in Germany, Andy [Andreas] Budde, the son of a famous music publisher. We thought, let's start another little label, something a little more frivolous than these big bands, with big sets and big backlines and all that stuff. We thought of it as a pop label. That was 1977, and it was around the time the whole new wave thing started. It naturally progressed that this thing would become a punk label." A meeting with Howard Devoto, at which he revealed 'Spiral Scratch' had sold more than 25,000 copies, helped cement the idea. "We signed Wayne County and the Electric Chairs. They'd had two or three singles out on Illegal. It was all very amorphous in those days. No-one had any contracts or anything like that." With Budde in Germany, Edwards then living in Paris and Craig in London, it was an ambitious attempt to found a tripartite indie. Deals were signed with Teldec in Germany, Vogue in France and Pye in Britain – though it didn't necessarily work out that way. Budde dropped out within a year, though he would still play a part in the developing Safari story by offering a roof over the head of Wayne County when visa restrictions saw him deported to Berlin.

County opened his account for the label with 'Eddie And Sheena', which twisted a boy meets girl narrative into a more topical punk meets rocker tryst. But it was County's expletive-fest 'Fuck Off' released in November 1977 after they'd signed to Safari the previous month (Sweet FA was the band's own label, funded by Safari as an insurance). that really made a dent. Teenagers nation-wide smirked at the lyrics. Elders and betters hyperventilated. When it was subsequently re-released on the 'Blatantly Offenzive' EP, the *Coventry Evening Telegraph* review gave some indication of the reaction. "This is garbage set to music. Did I say music? One track – let's call it Asterisk Off – contains two-dozen four letter words, rattled off at machine gun pace... Shock tactic records like this can only cheapen the cause of rock music..." It was a perfect example of outrage driving sales. "We sold a hell of a lot of 'Fuck Offs'," Craig points out, with barely concealed glee. "Pye, our distributors, wouldn't distribute it. We managed to get independent distribution principally through Lightning."

With Edwards moving back to England and new premises in Manchester Street, under the shadow of EMI central, Safari was definitively in business. Just as Stiff would poke fun at the monolith (whilst being distributed by them) with their slogan "Buy Now While EMI Lasts", Safari bought into the David/Goliath mantra too. "What's the difference between The Titanic and EMI? The Titanic had a good band." To that end they switched from Pye and sought distribution through Spartan, run by Dave Thomas and Tom McDonald. The Boys had talked to Safari during their 'strike' months, and free of their NEMS contract, having been impressed by the label's faith in them, signed immediately. Dangerfield: "I don't think we went to anyone else. What they offered was good, we liked the guys, so we went for it." The connection originally came through Boys' publisher Malcolm Forrester. "The Boys had been to Norway and found a rich Norwegian guy through Casino Steel," Craig remembers. "They made an album in Hell – actually a place in Norway called that. And the album was called *To Hell With The Boys*. As a promotion, we sent out 'Postcards From Hell'."

Safari never did manage to lift The Boys into the Top 20. "It wasn't for want of trying on their behalf," says Dangerfield. "They paid for us to go on the Ramones tour, they hired one of the best pluggers, Alan James, who got us on a Radio 1 playlist. For an independent label, they did a lot." Craig concurs. "We did work very hard for them, and they responded by working equally as hard. We didn't have that magic record, but we did release a considerable number of singles, and we did support tours. One of their successful territories was France, so we supported quite a few tours in France. We never really had a row, which is quite unusual!"

Safari quantifiably had a punk/new wave pedigree through County and The Boys. But the rest of its catalogue was not short of oddities – such as MOR pianist Richard Clayderman or Scots comedian Bill Barclay. Undoubtedly their biggest seller, however, was Toyah, whom they signed in December 1978 after she'd gained notoriety via her appearance in Derek Jarman's *Jubilee* and *Quadrophenia*. After her initial recordings were helmed by Keith Hale and Steve James – son of Sid James – her first major radio success, 'Bird In Flight', was produced by Dangerfield, who became something of an in-house producer for Safari. He also produced Gary Holton's 'Ruby'. "God, I'd almost forgotten that!" states Dangerfield. "It was a version of the country song, 'Ruby, Don't Take Your Love To Town'. But swapping the crazy Asian war for the crazy Irish war. It was a good record, but the BBC banned it outright, for mentioning the Irish war. That was the end of that."

Toyah would go on to huge success, the pinnacle being a number two chart placing, and year-long chart stay, for third studio album *Anthem*. She would stay with the label until her fortunes subsided in 1985. At her peak, the label was profiled in a TV documentary, despite the camera crew being unable to get all the equipment they needed inside the still tiny Safari offices, which also doubled as Toyah's fan club headquarters. Later ventures included Wolverhampton reggae band Weapon Of Peace and South African group Juluku – featuring a young Johnny Clegg. Despite releasing a charting album, the band would suffer from the Musicians Union boycott of South Africa, which had the unfortunate consequence of banning some of apartheid's most vociferous opponents from touring the UK – a situation which Safari eventually overcame after a fierce campaign. Like Stiff, they were unafraid of seizing commercial opportunities as they presented themselves. They scored a Top Five success by releasing a Torvill and Dean version of Ravel's 'Bolero' at the height of their ice stating fame. In one further two-fingered gesture to the majors, they launched Singing Dog Records, which featured a Cocker Spaniel kicking a horned gramophone. The similarity to the famed HMV logo was not lost on EMI, who sued. Safari simply excised the offending gramophone, and then hired a performing dog to service copies of the records to press and radio.

Safari was eventually retired in 1985 as Edwards and Craig devoted more time to the release of stage musicals via First Night Records after they were approached to release a record to accompany Tommy Steele's stage version of *Singing In The Rain*. It was the first of more than 100 titles in their catalogue. It is doubtful if recent purchasers of the soundtrack to Martine McCutcheon's West End *hit My Fair Lady* know they are in the hands of the pair who once terrorised pressing plants with a song called 'Fuck Off' recorded by a potty-mouthed transsexual.

Dave Goodman, the late former Pistols' soundman and another noted bootlegger (though one who drew on his own audio archive) started The Label in late 1976 with friend Caruzo Fuller in an attempt to make some capital out of his unexpected status as 'punk rock producer'. The first band he signed, Eater, were given the sort of run-around you'd expect a bunch of

naive schoolboys to encounter once they'd stepped into the heart of the
beast. "It was an eternal rip-off contract," explains an older and wiser Andy
Blade, their vocalist. Clearly, Goodman was trying to make best use of his
connections – the initial approach having been made under the ruse of him
running the Pistols' new label, Rotten Records. "When I asked Rotten if it
were true that he was setting up a label with Dave," Blade later told *Record
Collector*, "he cackled sarcastically for a very long time in a 'You are fucking
kidding, aren't you?' kind of way. I suddenly felt like a silly 15-year-old.
Which I was."

Eater duly performed the honours for The Label's first release, 'Outside View'.
When Blade queried why 'arranged by Dave Goodman' had appeared as a
credit, he was told "Well, he arranged the studio, didn't he?" The imprint
managed a dozen or so further releases, from bands including The Front and
the Bombers. "They were a bunch of guys that Dave Goodman came across,"
remembers Blade, "basically songwriters who were past their sell by. Dave
wanted them to be an in-house writing team for The Label. We refused their
services! I liked their single though, but they all looked like John Peel (with
the odd razor blade)." But Goodman's most successful wheeze was The Cash
Pussies' '99% Is Shit'; a cash-in the cult of Sid Vicious, using the great punk
intellectual's irony-free attack on the stupidity of the British public as its
intro. Poor sod had hardly been dead a week. Intended as a parody of 'Belsen
Was A Gas' (note the line 'London Town where the Jews all pray'), the
featured musicians included Alex Fergusson, formerly of Alternative TV. The
'executive producers', meanwhile, were none other than Fred and Judy
Vermorel, McLaren's old sparring partners from the Harrow School of Art.

Raw Records provided Cambridge with its first harbour for punk rock.
Founded by Lee Wood, it shared many of the common archetypes of regional
labels; growing out of his record shop on 48 King Street (Cambridge's record
shop hub), Remember Those Oldies. Having experienced working alongside
Wood, a shady character for whom comical levels of ineptitude in almost
every sphere of business and constant insolvency-dodging were a defining
trait, this author can attest to the fact that independent record labels did not
just offer an outlet for the gifted and the visionary. They were also quite
handy if you lacked the discipline to work for anyone apart from yourself,
had immeasurable quantities of personal ego and the moral anchorage of a
twig falling over a waterfall. Wood was also a notorious bootlegger, who
would later tell colourful stories of escaping out of windows in far-flung
record fairs and abandoning his stock there and then when the BPI
inspectors came calling. Since his failed publishing ventures in the early 90s

he has gone to ground; theories abound that he upset so many people during that time, and owed so many people so much money, that he chose it best to exit the business altogether.

Financial problems beset Wood at every turn. It visibly cowed him and made him suspicious of answering the telephone – members of staff would be briefed never to pass over a call to him without a prior, whispered exchange. This could often cause great hilarity. "My only encounter with Lee was at the Falcon," recalls writer Mick Mercer. "I had spoken to him on the phone, and someone pointed him out at a gig. So I walked over simply to say hello. The conversation went something like this: Me: Lee! Mick Mercer... Lee (not looking round): I'll get you your money. Me: (perplexed): I haven't *written* anything for you yet!"

And yet, to give him his due, Wood's passion for music was undeniable, and as capricious as his tastes could be, he was an early mover on the punk scene. An ex-musician himself, he could spin a joyous, uplifting, soft-spoken tale about receiving the latest Who album as a Christmas present as a teenager. Even if such excursions into anecdotage were generally used as diversionary tactics when he was ostensibly being asked about when the promised cheque would be mailed. And the Raw roster, in its own grubby way, contained a smattering of gems. Not least the Users' 'Sick Of You', the first release on the label, and one of the great UK punk singles, which Jello Biafra would later take into the studio in an attempt to get the same production sound for 'California Uber Alles'. Wood was directly inspired by Ted Carroll at Ace Records, and also Stiff. With the advent of punk, he was quick to stock early copies of Mark Perry's *Sniffin' Glue* and also the first Damned single. It was directly through talking with The Users while they were hanging around his shop that he got the idea of starting a record label, and he also helped set up their early gigs.

From there Wood licensed Jesse Hector's Gorillas single, a cover of 'You Really Got Me', originally released on Penny Farthing in 1974. But the label enjoyed its biggest success with the Killjoys, featuring future Dexy's star Kevin Rowland. Their 'Johnny Won't Get To Heaven' single would sell 18,000 copies. That led to a flood of demos and a clutch of punk releases of varying quality. But Raw was never a 'pure' punk play. Wood also indulged his penchant for overlooked 60s greats by reissuing The Creation and Downliners Sect. However, his greatest discovery was an act that effectively bridged the two eras he was enthused by, Robyn Hitchcock's Soft Boys.

He would have his run-ins with the former. But then, it's doubtful Wood ever did put his autograph on a royalty cheque. A straw poll. Ollie Wisdom, the Unwanted. "No, never got paid a penny." Kevin Rowland: "I have never received a penny, not one penny, from Lee Wood's Raw Records". Ozzy Ego, ACME Sewage Company: "Lee came across as a likeable guy, but a lot of bands had problems getting money from him." Between the collapse of Raw and his early 90s magazine publishing follies, Wood also attempted to start a new label – which came unstuck when a two-page *News Of The World* spread accused him of ripping off young bands sending in demo tapes.

Others would defend Wood on the basis of the contribution he actually made. Ted Carroll remembers him almost taking up residence at Rock On. "Lee always had a nose for what might sell. He seemed to have a real brass neck – he was impervious to insults, threats, whatever, he just carried on. At one stage he was driving quite a flash motor and making a lot of money from bootlegging. He was a very shifty guy. He used to come into Rock On and was fascinated by the stall. He was very interested in British 60s stuff, he was collecting that. Then we started Chiswick, and the next thing he started Raw."

Raw is now one of the most favoured labels among collectors of off the beaten track UK punk. That status flatters it a little, but Lee Wood is certainly one of the characters that defined the early independent movement, even if he can hardly be regarded as one of its more agreeable architects. Ian Ballard of Leytonstone's Damaged Goods eventually purchased the Raw masters. "Lee possibly owed me some money at the time. I think, in some ways, he was quite happy that I did it, because I knew him from the Portobello Road, from the record collector days. I think he was quite happy that someone took it who liked it, knew what it was all about, and who was going to do something with it. Also, it probably got him out of a load of trouble with whoever he owed money to from Raw. Maybe it served a few purposes. It wasn't a fortune. I took out a little personal loan to do it. And there are some genius records there. It's a great label, and very eclectic as well – not just punk. Anyway, that's Lee, he's a ducker and diver. Always was. I'd still go out for a beer with him."

A little further down the regional punk ladder, both in terms of chronology and (retrospective) stature, came future EMAP big cheese Dave Henderson's Dining Out Records. It gave the world the first Adicts single, plus The Sinatras, Occult Chemistry (featuring Tilly, later of A Certain Ratio), Normil Hawaiians, Swinging Laurels and Disco Zombies. The latter band featured both Henderson on vocals and future music industry heavyweight Andy Ross, founder of Food Records, on guitar. He, like Henderson, would go on to write for *Sounds* (under the name Andy Hurt). His primary musical influence, Ross would later confess, was "the whole punk rock thing, really".

"I'd started it because my band couldn't get signed and suddenly inherited loads of other people in the same predicament," Henderson would say of Dining Out. He was also responsible for Dead Man's Curve, which had a production and distribution deal with Red Rhino, whose biggest success came with Portion Control – part of the new wave of industrial bands whom Henderson would later champion at Illuminated. "I also had a cassette-only label called Corporate Sounds that released tapes of Funkapolitan, among others. If I still had a copy of that, it would be worth 5p at least."

Ross meanwhile, who ran his first record shop aged 16, set up the South Circular label, while working intermittently as a bookies' manager and tax official. "But then everyone had a record label in 1978," he reasoned. Which was pretty much true. He was also half of the Steppes, a one-off collaboration with Adrian Lillywhite of the Members, who cut 'God's Got Religion (But I've Got A Car)', one of the great DIY punk records. Dining Out later re-released it, with the sides reversed, credited to The 50 Fantastics. "By this time," Henderson recalls, "we lived above Honky Tonk Records in Kentish Town and rehearsed in the label's badly insulated back room alongside 23 Skidoo, DAF, Department S and The Raincoats, among others. It was a glorious shambles that also was home to local bands The Mysterons and author Will Self's The Self Abusers."

Dead Good Records, founded by Martin Patton and Andy Stephenson, held it down for Lincolnshire in the late 70s – not that they were overwhelmed by competition. Its roster featured XS-Energy, Pseudo Existors, Cigarettes and Amber Squad – the latter pair straddling the mod/punk divide, the former labouring under two of the worst names ever conceived even within the punk firmament. But its most successful graduates were B-Movie, who persuaded Patton that his future lay outside of punk (especially after the second XS Energy single 'Use You' stiffed). Patton would follow the band to Some Bizarre, while Stephenson joined distributor Pinnacle.

The outbreak of feverish activity among upstart independents, meanwhile, was documented by the *Zig Zag Small Labels Catalogue*. "I'd been involved in local music scenes in High Wycombe where I grew up and the Oxford area and Aylesbury," recalls David Marlow, "and as a consequence of all that I knew Pete Frame who originated *Zig Zag* magazine. I ended up with a job on the local Oxford music paper which was a means to an end to pay off an overdraft. I then ended up working with the guy who at that point owned *Zig Zag*, Graham Andrews, a printer who had kind of inherited it. By then Kris Needs was the editor. I was taken on as someone who could flog ads, cos I'd done that for the local newspaper. So I was therefore in touch with all the independent record labels, as well as the others, basically to score ads off them, though I was also a consumer. I also got a bit involved in managing the production side of things. I wasn't really involved with the editorial side to much. But at some point, as a fan as well, I was particularly into a lot of the records that Bob Last was putting out with Fast Product. I couldn't tell you exactly when, but I came up with the idea that while everybody was trying to track down these records, it was sometimes particularly difficult. And people could hear stuff on John Peel, but find it difficult to get hold of. Even the Rough Trades of this world were not always finding everything. And I knew the people at Rough Trade obviously. So I decided it would be a good project."

"Really," Marlow concedes, "as well as providing an editorial service to people, it was also an opportunity to sell advertising, which was my primary task – to make *Zig Zag* economically viable. I began to put it together. The primary sources were getting the records themselves, and going to places like Rough Trade, and in particular going to John Peel's house. He was very helpful. John Walters, his producer, was a regular contributor to *Zig Zag* and I was often charged with trying to get copy off him, which meant turning up at Radio One and waiting for him to finish it. So I got to know John Walters, and to a lesser extent John Peel, who also occasionally wrote for *Zig Zag*. A lot of people were sending records in to Peel to play, and that was the other big source of information. On a couple of occasions I would wait for John Peel to finish his programme of an evening, and then I'd drive with him to his house in Suffolk. He'd let me roam the shelves and jot down names, numbers and contact details. Not only from the sleeves, but from the letters that people had sent in to him. So that was an important and unique source of information."

Of course, at the time it would have been almost unthinkable for an independently released single *not* to have been sent to Peel. "Indeed! We put it together and published it. I got it, as I recall, Ray Lowry, the cartoonist for the *NME* and *Zig Zag*, to do a cover. Peel did some editorial preface thing, and that was it. It was well regarded and well liked, and in subsequent years we did three, altogether. I actually left *Zig Zag* and went into the press office at

Virgin Records. Steve Taylor was a journalist that I knew and helped on the last one, as I recall. Latterly, there was more and more of it. The second one was twice the size of the first, etc."

As Paul Rosen noted in his essay looking at the growth of independent labels (almost inevitably titled *It was easy, it was cheap, go and do it!)* the 1978 *Small Labels Catalogue* printed in *Zig Zag* listed 231 independent imprints. "Including both the larger and the smaller ones, the specialist labels catering to specific tastes such as rock 'n' roll and reggae as well as the newer labels inspired by punk. But it was this last category that caused the huge jump to over 800 labels by 1980, although that figure had settled back down to a still high 322 by 1981."

The *Small Labels Catalogue* became the route map and guidebook to thousands of treasures on labels from Brighton's Attrix to Michael Zilkha's ZE. The foundations were being laid for a not so quiet revolution.

The other aspect of the culture of the independent recording industry so often overlooked is that of the handful of recording studios that, between them, were responsible for thousands upon thousands of the releases discussed in this book.

Spaceward Studios, located on Victoria Street, Cambridge, sported a pricing policy that quickly established it, alongside Cargo, as the go-to recording facility outside of London for independent bands – Scritti Politti's 'Skank Bloc Bologna' among its earliest notable efforts. "We were there at the time that punk happened," producer Mike Kemp recalls, "and the fact that we built all our own gear and operated from a rented house in Cambridge kept our costs down. So we could offer 16-track recording below anyone else at a time when that's what everyone needed. Also, we did not exactly like most of the music biz people we met, so that tallied with many the bands' views! Maybe we missed out on the big bucks because of it, but it was fun."

Spaceward started when Kemp and Gary Lucas were still students in 1972. "Gary and I got off to a flying start," Kemp remembers, "as our first recording was a live performance of Hawkwind at the Cambridge Corn Exchange, a notable event in that the legendary Syd Barrett made one of his last ever live appearances. We continued through our student years recording local bands, and when it was time to enter real life, we just had to continue recording. We wanted to offer top quality without costing the arm and leg traditional studios charged at that time. By converting the two basements of the terraced house at 19 Victoria Street we set up a tiny but effective recording and control room. Word got around and we were able to improve our equipment and in 1976 we completed building our own 16-track recorder, allowing us to offer top class facilities just as the punk era was starting."

They were quickly inundated. "There were lots of small record labels, from Raw in Cambridge to Rough Trade in London, and demos and masters for bands from Iron Maiden to Gary Numan and Stiff Little Fingers to Toyah. We worked close to 24 hours a day to make a living on the tight budgets we had, and we loved every minute. It was great to engineer and produce those sessions. Often the bands needed help to get their ideas onto disc. I remember great sessions from The Mekons and Scritti Politti, Gary Numan and local band The Soft Boys with Robyn Hitchcock. I think many bands were surprised by how small the studio was, but the results show that we turned out some great stuff, often to tight time schedules, with mixing running into dawn after a full day of recording."

"I suppose in some ways we were a beacon for the home recording boom of recent decades," Kemp reflects, "where low budgets and limited space are now common. The difference being that then we had to really know our equipment, which, since we built a lot of it, was easy for us. Gary and I stayed clear of the mainstream of the music business. We'd had a few run-ins with record company execs and we sided with many of the bands of the time. We hated that side of things. I suppose if we'd 'bought into' it, we might have got rich on it, but there was nothing like working at the coal face of the punk boom, with so many ideas and kids of all ages making their own music. We were even approached by a local businessman who wanted to buy us out and fund a big recording complex just across the river from the graduate centre in Cambridge with Gary and I running it. But we just hated the idea of becoming mainstream or subservient to the man with the wallet."

In the 80s they moved from Cambridge as their Victoria Street premises, which had always been rented, was sold. Relocating to the Cambridgeshire village of Stretham and purchasing The Old School, they built a bigger desk and 24-track studio, and finally took on more commercial projects. The studio closed in 1988. "Luckily I've been able to keep close to the audio business by inventing novel tools for the recording engineer and musician," says Kemp. "I've also been able to keep my hand in with some recording work, but undoubtedly the fun of working 24 hours non stop definitely fades as time goes by!"

Pathway is another of those institutions that unequivocally deserves celebration. Founded by Mike Finesilver, partially from the royalties he received as co-writer of The Crazy World Of Arthur Brown's 'Fire', it was little short of a shed. A tiny one at that; estimated to be just eight by eight metres. Yet many of the most important records of the independent boom were recorded here, not least a coterie of early Stiff artists (Costello, Damned, Ian Dury, Madness) as well as such notables as The Police and Dire Straits.

Arguably the most significant and prolific studio of all, however, was Rochdale's Cargo, run by John Brierley, whose story overlaps with that of Factory Records. "I was a staff cameraman at Granada," he remembers. "It was a great era for pop music at Granada, and I worked on *Shang-a-Lang* with the Bay City Rollers and *The Marc Bolan Show*. There had been one series of *So it Goes* with Tony Wilson, which was studio bound, with a production crew who I think didn't understand the music. So for the second series Tony persuaded them to record bands live on film. We worked together on the local news programme and we often spoke about recording bands live. He knew about my mobile studio, so when the second series came up, I was called to the seventh floor at Granada. Would I hire my mobile to them? At that time I used to record bands live at pub gigs for around £50 a session. Granada, not knowing my usual rates, asked if I would do a deal. Would £900 per gig be OK? I thought about it for about three seconds and said that would do. I left Granada later that year and the money from those shows helped me set up Cargo Studios in 1977. I have always been into live sound and some of these bands were quite amazing. Recording bands like Buzzcocks, Siouxsie and the Banshees, Elvis Costello, Iggy Pop – they were just so good. I didn't realise initially that this was the start of something new in music. In many cases I found the music too abrasive. But I did appreciate that the punk scene was a rebellion against the established music of that time and fitted into my philosophy."

While Cargo would become synonymous with budget independent labels, Brierley already had some experience of one notable 60s forerunner. "When I was in my late teens I produced some albums for John Peel's Dandelion label with Tractor. A guy called Chris Hewitt became the band's manager and some years later opened a music shop in Rochdale called Tractor Music about the same time I left Granada. He approached me and mentioned the shop he was opening on Drake Street and that he had far too much space and did I want to rent the rear part of the building on Kenion Street from him to set up the studio? I had been on the lookout for premises but it was difficult to find somewhere that didn't have neighbours and at a price I could afford. The building was pretty run down but it had a car park outside thanks to Yorkshire Bank and it was cheap."

Brierley installed a Soundcraft desk, costing him £8,000, JBL speakers, a Ferrograph ¼-inch mastering machine and Cadey 16-track tape recorder. "I made a decision that because I didn't have much money left, instead of spending thousands on sound proofing, I would go for a 'live' studio. I put a carpet down on the floor and cellotex boarding on the walls, which really didn't do much to reduce the sound levels. The control room was fairly conventional apart from two enormous reclining chairs behind the desk and unusually the desk was 90 degrees to the adjoining window and studio. That was deliberate. I really didn't want to have to look through the window all the time at the band or for them to have to look at us in the control room. I found it far less distracting looking at a blank wall when I had to concentrate on mixing."

Studio in place, Brierley waited for the work to roll in. And waited. "By then panic was about to set in, because only a couple of local Rochdale bands had been in. But then The Gang of Four came in from Leeds with this amazing sound and recorded 'Damaged Goods' for Fast Product [recorded June '78, released in October]. There was something immediate and urgent there. That opened the floodgates. Due to the rise of punk, the new bands no longer wanted to spend weeks recording an album, it was almost 'one take and out' and the live sound decision paid off. This is the sound they wanted, like they were on stage. I couldn't cope with the number of bands wanting to come in and so I took on Colin Richardson as a trainee engineer and he proved to be quite brilliant."

Indeed, the list of artists that Cargo would work with over the next few years is almost bewildering. "We were getting bands in like OMD, Joy Division, The Fall, The Chameleons and from Liverpool Echo and the Bunnymen, Teardrop Explodes, Dead or Alive, Pink Military. As most of these records were played on John Peel's show, the fame of the studio spread. We even had some bands who came in just so they could have 'recorded at Cargo Studios Rochdale' on the sleeve, so they would be played on Peel. John used to refer to it as 'the legendary Cargo Studios'. Of course, all these bands were new and these were their early recordings for independent labels, so at that time I had no idea which of these bands would make it big. Unfortunately many subsequently signed up to major labels and their thinking was that you couldn't possibly record a single/album for a major label with a top producer in a 16-track on a back street in Rochdale. It had to be some plush 24-track in

London with some producer the band had never met and then they wondered why the feel and excitement had gone."

Cargo indeed dealt almost exclusively with independent record labels. "They were the only ones who were prepared to take a risk musically," says Brierley. "Record companies like Factory, Fast Product, New Hormones, Rough Trade, Zoo, No Future, Clay, Red Rhino and Cherry Red. Bands were now coming in from all over Britain and France and Germany as well." And Brierley came to know many of the most prominent members of that emerging community. "Tony Wilson spent a lot of his time at the studio with the Factory bands. He once said that his most amazing musical moment was the first time he listened to Joy Division's 'Atmosphere'. Martin Hannett spent a lot of his time in Cargo producing Joy Division, A Certain Ratio, OMD, Nico, Durutti Column, etc. Mike Stone from Clay used to do his own mixing. Another regular was Bob Last from Fast Product. When Bob came in the studio he always altered the loudspeaker settings to his personal setting, an unusual thing to do – took me hours to correct after he'd gone."

Not that Cargo's fame ever made Brierley a rich man. "The rates I charged were too low. I realise that now. I didn't realise until many years later that the bands were actually coming in because of the 'Cargo sound'. Maybe I should have charged more but I thought I was in competition with other studios around Manchester like Smile and Pennine, Revolution, and I didn't want to go back to the early days of no bands coming in. Many of the bands didn't even have an independent label backing them or a great deal of money. It would have been unfair to exclude them or their music because of the price. But if I had charged more then I could have afforded a new desk and new tape machine. Essentially I was trying to make money from the studio and help the bands along the way. It was an awkward balancing act. The rates were around £16 per hour for 16-track and £10 per hour for eight-track. There were many punk bands who managed to record and mix a complete album in a ten-hour session."

Such was Cargo's throughput that eventually Brierley became concerned that the equipment was being worn out due to constant use. "I remember Mark Burgess from the Chameleons, after he had just finished the brilliant *Script of the Bridge* album, saying 'Colin Richardson worked wonders in a dying studio', with reference to the mixing desk getting knackered. That really pissed me off. They were an up and coming group and their record company had come to me with an allotted sum of money to do the album, which is all they could afford. The band actually used about twice that amount on doing the album in endless extra hours. I never charged them extra, just trying to help the band get it finished. If I'd held on to the tape and asked for the amount they had actually used then I doubt the album would ever have come out." It may or may not be coincidental that The Chameleons were one of the few bands Brierley worked with who were allied to a major (Statik Records were distributed through Virgin). "I tried to help most bands financially. In hindsight, business wise, that was probably a mistake."

A combination of factors led to the label's closure. "In 1983 Colin left and all the sessions were then done by me for the last year before I closed the studio. By then the music had changed, it was becoming less exciting and it was starting to bore me. On top of that, I damaged my hearing, albeit not permanently, with listening to those JBL speakers at too high a level. A specialist warned me that if I carried on recording, I would permanently damage my hearing. So that's when I called it a day. Cargo Studios was nothing to look at either inside or out – you certainly wouldn't go 'wow' when you walked in the place. It had a lot of rough edges but the band's felt very much at ease. It was incredibly hard work but it was worth it. I got a great deal of enjoyment out of it as well as a living."

The infrastructure that allowed independent music to thrive is rarely appreciated. The Cartel made the rich diversity of independent music available in nearly every high street. Spaceward, Pathway and Cargo trapped the initial musical ideas on tape. Manufacturers such as Orlake turned tape to vinyl, wrapped in sleeves printed by the likes of Delga Press. The enduring titular myth of DIY music was that you could indeed 'do it yourself'. That's entirely deceptive on one level. In fact, the real story of independent music is to a large extent 'we're all in this together'. Studios, printers, manufacturers and distributors were always part of the equation and no-one in the independent record community, at least prior to the cassette DIY scene, could get by without accessing one or more of their services.

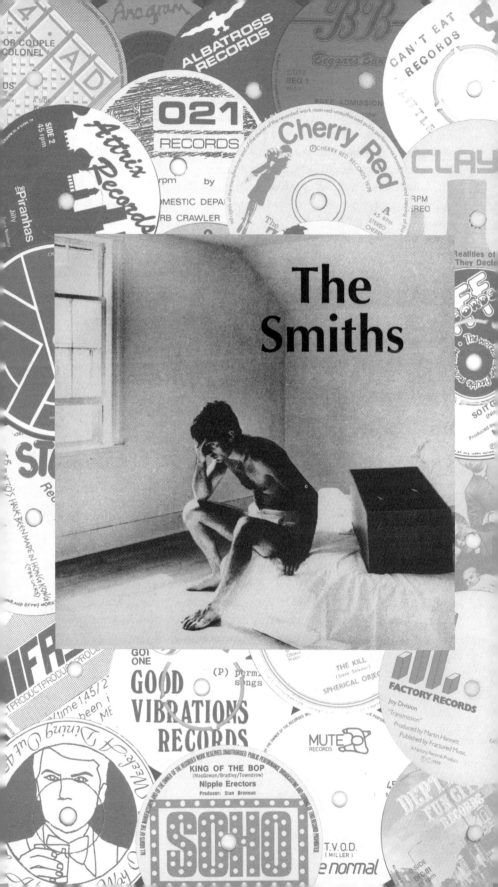

## Chapter Five

## Music Is A Better Noise

## Rough Trade Records

Rough Trade began as a shop founded in 1976 in Kensington Park Road, part of the Portobello district that had been settled by a large post-Windrush West Indian immigrant community. In 1983 it would move to 130 Talbot Road and open a sister branch in Covent Garden. But for its initial heyday – it has had several – 202 Kensington Park, now a toddler's and baby retailer, was the location of London's most iconic record shop, instantly recognisable for its domed arch dominating the front window display and the overhanging wagon wheel that became its logo.

Geoff Travis, the son of a loss adjuster born in 1952 and an eager fan of rock music, had studied photography and English at Churchill College, Cambridge. "I didn't really know what to do when I finished university, to be honest," he explains. "The thing is, I've always loved music, and it had been a massive part of my life growing up in London. I was lucky to grow up in London in that perfect era; The Beatles, Stones, The Kinks, Yardbirds, The Who were releasing their first records, and Stax and Motown – it was exciting times. I've always been a music fanatic from a very early age. Mostly because we had a cousin who came to stay with us from Canada, whose father was a bit of a black sheep in the family and committed some kind of petty crime that we never talked about. And my family very kindly took him in. And he brought with him some fantastic 50s records; Everly Brothers, 'Wake Up Little Susie', 'All You Have To Do Is Dream', Buddy Holly and the Crickets records, McCoys records. They made a very vivid impression on me. Freddy Cannon's 'Palisades Park', which was a fantastic instrumental record. I just remember listening to them over and over again for hours on end. So that was the beginning of my musical obsession."

At this stage, he had no plans for a career in the music industry. Or many plans at all. "I'd been to university and I enjoyed it, I liked reading and studying, so I thought for a while about being an academic." Legendarily, waiting at a bus stop one day, he placed his future in the hands of London Transport, the fulcrum being how long it took the next bus to come. "That is true. I was at teacher training college, waiting for the bus. I really enjoyed the kids, they were fantastic, but I really hated the teachers. They probably hated me, I just didn't like the way they talked about the children; they really talked down to them. It just wasn't really the spirit I wanted to be around. So I did say to myself that. It was like a stupid *Dice Man* moment.

If it didn't come that was it. And the next day I was in Montreal."

There he hooked up with a former drama teacher acquaintance and helped run a health food store. His travels took him through both Chicago and San Francisco, purchasing an album collection from thrift stores *en route*. It was this 'collateral' that convinced him to open his first record shop, initially in Dollis Hill. "Ken Davidson was the person who said, 'Why don't you ship these records back and start the shop?' He was a Dutchman, and he was hanging out with an old school friend of mine, Alan Newman. That was who I went to stay with in San Francisco." But the Dollis Hill venture ended almost before it began. "That was just a false start," Travis confesses, "we didn't really know what we were doing. You could squat in London in those days – nobody had any money, and nobody seemed to care. Especially when you could squat and the living was cheap. So we were squatting there and we found these premises we could rent. We started sanding down the walls and getting ready. Then we started contacting record companies to start up accounts. A man from Polydor came along and said, 'What are you doing?' 'What do you mean? We're opening a shop.' 'OK, good idea, but there's no passing trade.' We said, 'What's passing trade?' You look out on the pavement, and there's three Jamaicans and no-one else. So it dawned on us that maybe it's not the best place to start a shop. It shows how naive we were. But we learned quickly."

They relocated to Kensington Park Road. Part of the attraction was its proximity to Powis Square, where Mick Jagger's arty *Performance* had been filmed. Travis was well versed in the bohemian cultures of New York's Greenwich Village and San Francisco's Haight-Ashbury, and the new enterprise would share similar aspirations. The site, they discovered, was formerly used as a print workshop; a gathering place for 'heads' during the 60s that had fallen to wrack and ruin. Rough Trade would, in turn, add to the premises' legacy of progressive thinking, not to mention financial brinkmanship. The company was founded in the name of Travis and his father, who contributed initial funds of £4,000 and was an intermittent presence in the shop, helping his son with accounts.

While one cornerstone of the shop was Travis's abiding love of music, another was the ideological discourse he had encountered, and embraced, at college. "Absolutely. And from growing up around the counter-culture; *Oz* and *Friends* magazine, Vietnam demonstrations, the Living Theatre at the Roundhouse, the RD Laing era and the beginning of feminism. You had the start of *Spare Rib*, and being informed about women's liberation politics. It was quite a political time when I was at university at Cambridge. There were demonstrations about the Greek Colonels just before I went 'up', as they say. And then when I was there, there were a lot of things going on. It seemed that students were a lot more political in those days, or at least at some tangent to some political party. The Communist Party was very strong, and there were lots of debates. There was the IMG [International Marxist Group], the Workers Revolutionary Party, there was a lot more political debate in the air. I'm more of a loner and not so much of a joiner-in, but I do recognise the need for community. I was also informed by the fact that I was sent to kibbutz when I was a kid, because my family had been involved in setting up kibbutz in Israel. And I spent a happy summer holiday with my uncle in his kibbutz, working on the tractor and the farm. Watching all that – working and eating collectively – that made a big impression. I was very young, and [it was partly] just the excitement of being out of a suburban house! But there was a moment when that was an interesting utopian idea and it worked for a bit, but it's kind of changed and soured as inevitably utopias do. But it was inspiring, really. Also beat culture was important to me. Reading Burroughs and Ferlinghetti and Kerouac and all those things, and the Velvet Underground. And the great American poets like William Carlos Williams, people like Carl Sandburg, the Black Mountain Poets, Robert Lowell and Charles Olson – I really liked all of that. One of the great things about being at university is that you have access to libraries and you can read what you want. I read a lot of American literature. I liked America in the same way that Jean Luc Godard liked America. I liked the plastic facade and the symbols."

His musical interests arose "from just being a typical kid growing up in London with wide musical tastes," he continues, "luckily being exposed to lots of people that had good record collections and good taste. And also going to the Roundhouse in London, that was a big part of my education. They had Implosion there every Sunday. You paid eleven and six and you got there at 3.30 and left at 11.30 at night, and they had the most fantastic acts on. Jeff Dexter was the DJ." The Implosion nights, which began in 1969, hosted bands like The Pink Fairies, Pink Floyd and Kevin Ayers, and were pivotal events in the development of 'freak' culture, a more radical branding of hippydom whose advocates also included Small Wonder's Pete Stennet. "I went to school at the Angel, Islington, and the West End's not that far away," Travis continues. "We'd often go into the West End after school. So I went to The Marquee, with my school satchel, to see The Who. I saw John Mayall, loads of great things and it was just mesmerising. I didn't really ever think I was going to work in music one day. You don't make that connection. When you're just a fan, you don't really think about that, it's just another world. I never had a big plan."

Friend and housemate Vivien Goldman depicted the shop in a *Sounds* article in January 1977 and underscored its thematic link to the American beatnik world. "... lots of green plants in the window; a table-full of mags for the customers to leaf through whilst they drink mugs of tea; nice things on the walls (more a pad than a shop); lots of good sounds and lots of good vibes. Geoff is open, friendly, and a True Fan... It's a traditional California New Wave consumer concept, but since the Alternative Society wheezed into terminal breakdown, nobody's succeeded in reviving that relaxed ambience – in London at any rate. Geoff must feel like ol' Doc Frankenstein when he sees how that simple recipe has blossomed a hole-in-the-wall shop into a nerve centre, Energy Transmission H.Q."

The shop was given the name Rough Trade, Travis enjoying its undertones of illicit vice, though its roots seem to be in either a pulp novel or from Carol Pope's Canadian group of the same name. As he later told *Word* magazine, he had seen the band play in Toronto in 1975. "I didn't think they were any good but I liked the name – and the reference – so I stole it and hoped they wouldn't get anywhere." However, the name did lead to some problems, "mainly some very strange phone calls to the shop about the sort of services we were offering". Clients who were in the market for something even more exotic than American and Jamaican vinyl imports were in for a disappointment.

However, from its opening on 20 February 1976, the shop struggled. Located in a primarily West Indian area due to the affordability of the rents, barely any customers graced the shop in its first few months of existence. "The first few years of the shop were very slow," Travis admits. "There weren't that many customers." Davidson's appearances were almost as sporadic. "[The shop] was his idea, he wanted to be part of this. He opened the shop with me, Ken, but he just got very disaffected very quickly. Because I don't think he had realised that if you have a shop, you have to be there every day, for certain hours. 'I think I'm going to go and play tennis.' 'Fine, see you later, Ken.' As we know, life is unglamorous, and it's 90% work. I think he got disenchanted, Ken, and he had a terrible demise in Amsterdam."

Gradually things improved. Soon, they were able to compete in servicing local and visiting reggae fans, which might have seemed improbable. "You know why I think we did OK?" Travis asks. "Dub Vendor [which opened a secondary outlet in Ladbroke Grove in 1980 as an extension of its original base in Clapham] and Rough Trade would buy our pre-release records from the same source, from a distributor in Harlesden. So it was a matter of getting your hands on the best records. In terms of A&R, it's a fantastic discipline to have to listen to twenty seconds of a pre-release and decide whether you're going to order it. It's a great way of honing your musical knowledge. And of course, being a stupid white boy, there's every likelihood they're going to try to get rid of their worst records, [the ones] that nobody else wants. So you have to be on your game. It's really good fun, and I loved doing that."

Fortunately there were few costly disasters. "Well, I didn't order huge numbers. Certainly, if they weren't the absolute best releases of that week, they wouldn't sell. Richard Scott was working in distribution and mail order, and he had his Jamaican background, because he used to manage Third World." Scott, introduced to Travis by Goldman, was invited on board to extend the shop's acquisition of new reggae releases and also establish a mail order function. "I went to see Geoff one evening in the shop in 1977," Scott recalls. "Yes, Viv introduced us, because she had been the press officer at Island when Third World signed for them."

Scott would subsequently run the distribution arm of Rough Trade – an enterprise which dwarfed the label in terms of personnel and turnover – for over a decade. He also found time to encourage and mentor individual artists, distributing a booklet (based on Scritti Politti's template) advising aspirant musicians how to produce and manufacture their own singles. "Richard had a great collection of reggae records," says Travis. "We were always connoisseurs of good music. That's what it boils down to. And we were pretty secure in our tastes. If we liked it and everybody else said it was crap – what do they know?" he laughs.

"Suddenly it took off and it got really busy," Travis continues. "On Fridays and Saturdays it was really exciting, because it got really jammed. We had these huge reggae speakers and played music very loud, it was really exciting. It was like any other day working in a record shop, the difference being that we were doing distribution in the back yard, making and packing orders. Playing music all day long is the basic staple. Then taking orders and tracking down records. The days went by very fast. And then at night going to a gig." Three or four times a week? Travis smiles. "No, about seven! Most of the time we went to gigs, the Roxy or the Marquee. The other thing was, in the first years of the shop, the pay was so low because there was no money being made, I would DJ at Dingwalls a lot. I would play black music, basically. Except on the Crazy Cavern nights, when I'd play rockabilly. And you had to play really good rockabilly, because you were faced by serious rockabillies. That was fun, and I really enjoyed it, it gave me some living money and an education. Also I used to write reviews for *Record Mirror*. I once got sent to Amsterdam to review The Commodores when they played at an ice rink. They were fantastic. I was a freelancer, and when you went to the *Record Mirror* offices, there were all these review copies in a drawer. And all the ones that nobody else wanted I used to get, and they tended to be the soul ones." Travis has an instinctive distrust of arbitrary stylistic judgements. "And I really liked that! We didn't really sell that many soul records, but I liked the fact that I had knowledge of that area."

More importantly for the shop, a niche was soon established as American imports by artists such as The Seeds started to trickle in. But hadn't Rock On already sewn that market up? "Yeah, but they weren't interested in the same things," states Travis. "Rock On was a fantastic shop, and yes, they would have had the Flaming Groovies. But I think we started to find things like Television, Ork's 'Little Johnny Jewel' single, Blondie's first single 'X-Offender' on Private Stock. That was the fun, tracking these things down and then ordering them. Those were things probably slightly outside Rock On's orbit. Ted and Roger and the boys had a more purist, 50s rocker mentality. You know, Vince Taylor. Of course, we loved all that stuff, but our niche was slightly different. With Pere Ubu, I wrote off to David [Thomas], because it was his label. And those singles were extraordinary. And it was lovely to be able to correspond direct with the artist. That was a new thing. It was exciting. That was part of the do it yourself culture. You can't imagine getting a letter back from Keith Richards, if he can in fact write!"

As Richard Scott points out, such connections also grew naturally from the shop's business. "We'd been dealing with the shop in Cleveland, Discodrome. We'd bought all the early Pere Ubu singles in bulk, the three classic singles. We'd had a relationship with David before that – he was a journalist, Crocus Behemoth, on a Cleveland magazine we used to import, alongside *Slash* from Los Angeles, *Search And Destroy* from San Francisco and others."

More than a retail outlet, Rough Trade became a talking shop, where likeminded individuals – especially those with an interest in the counter-culture and music – could congregate and cogitate as they grazed the racks. There were regular team meetings, and all staff were paid an equal wage regardless of position. Rough Trade was definitively not an entity founded by music industry veterans like Riviera and Robinson at Stiff, though Scott had certainly learned much from Chris Blackwell at Island. In contrast to Stiff's proprietors' back story of tough exchanges with bands and promoters, Rough Trade was formed according to broadly Marxist principles, developed by Travis while a student. It's questionable whether more than a handful of the bands or fanzine writers whose products Rough Trade stocked would have understood the continuum to 60s idealism that the shop represented. This was no year zero concern as dictated by punk's shrill rhetoric, but then so few of the indie start-ups truly were.

Theft at Kensington Road was rife and accounting haphazard. Among the rich mix of patrons were record dealers, attempting to hawk their wares within the shop's chaotic confines, and increasingly a gaggle of aspirant musicians who often ended up on the other side of the counter. They included Ana Da Silva of the Raincoats, a band who, to all intents and purposes, formed readymade from the shop staff. Others included brothers Nikki Sudden and Epic Soundtracks of the Swell Maps and Barbara Gogan of The Passions. "I worked for Rough Trade Records for about a year organising tours for the label's groups," notes Gogan, "up until we got signed to Fiction toward the end of 1979. Rough Trade had never had an iota of interest in The Passions – even to the point of me being told by my boss, Pete Walmsley, that I should 'on no account take advantage of any contacts gained' there. And that I should 'give up playing in that worthless band'. They were a self-righteous bunch for the most part. Not the bands though, they were in the main a pretty decent bunch of people, creative too, and a joy to work with."

As Rough Trade's reputation grew, established acts such as The Ramones and various Sex Pistols and associates also called in, the former playing a memorable one-off gig there, as did Patti Smith. Such in-store performances didn't happen "too often", says Travis. "But if you imagine how many copies of The Ramones album we sold? We were on the radar of the record company. So it was probably their idea to say, do you want the band to visit? Yeah, that sounds great. And Patti we knew because of the 'Piss Factory' single, we got that straight from maybe Lenny [Kaye] himself, so it was exciting that they came to visit us. Talking Heads came as well. What I always say is that when The Ramones came, it was packed. It was a big to-do. And when the Talking Heads came there was nobody there at all." Other regular or casual staff included Jude Crighton, Nigel House, Pete Donne and Shirley O'Loughlin, who later managed The Raincoats. Vivien Goldman and Jon Savage also served behind the counter while establishing themselves as journalists.

## Independence Days

Travis immediately embraced punk when he first heard it, but was at pains not to dismiss the prior musical generation, considered obsolete by more arbitrary and self-conscious taste-makers, who seeded the revolution. Equally, the virtues of the records themselves, rather than the hipness of their creators, was his paramount consideration. "I loved the [new] records. 'Keys To Your Heart' by the 101ers was a fantastic record. The Damned's first single was fantastic. Everyone derides the Damned. But they made some wonderful records. They were brilliant in those days. Of course they were uncool, in terms of the gradations of what was acceptable to the musical hierarchy. But they were terrific. The other thing is pub rock. I loved Brinsley Schwarz and Kilburn and the High Roads. I saw them a few times and they were really fantastic. Ducks Deluxe really were good to go and see. The Tyla Gang, and obviously Doctor Feelgood were fantastic. It was a great time for music in London, pre-punk. And then punk happened and it was *really* exciting. The Nashville changed from being Elvis Costello, Brinsley Shwarz and Eggs Over Easy and those American bands, I liked all those bands unashamedly. I loved The Band, and I love The Grateful Dead. I always will. I'm not ashamed to say it. It's great music. There's not much better. But I can't see why you can't like that and also love 'Anarchy In The UK'."

As the first handful of independent releases turned to an avalanche, Rough Trade found itself at the heart of the careering snowball. The shop proved crucial to the fortunes of the likes of Stiff and Chiswick in the days before they were able to secure distribution from majors. While such releases began to take up more shelf space, and the shop clientele underwent a subtle shift, Travis also kept his ear to the ground for emerging opportunities. One arose when The Sex Pistols' aforementioned 'Anarchy In The UK' became briefly unavailable despite the band's notoriety. Rough Trade satisfied that demand by importing the Barclay edition from France, with Malcolm McLaren and Glitterbest's approval. "I knew that Malcolm had done a deal in France that excluded the rest of the world," Travis confirms. "The rest was common sense."

There was plenty of product, legitimate or otherwise, to service. When *Zig Zag* magazine published its *Small Labels Catalogue* in 1978 it featured 231 entries. When it did so again two years later, there were over 800 labels listed. Rough Trade, following Richard Scott's arrival, had long since acted as a portal for this new breed of labels, supplying other shops and outlets from 1977 onwards.

Of course, the two most luminous examples of the DIY boom were Buzzcocks' 'Spiral Scratch' EP and the Desperate Bicycles singles. Both parties were visitors to the shop. "They just came in and were really lovely people," Travis remembers of the Bicycles. "A little blue bag with their record in, 'this is our record, would you like to stock it?' Love to, really interesting. Not the world's greatest record, but what an artefact – and it has a lot of charm." He was knocked out, however, by 'Spiral Scratch'. "Absolutely thrilling. Immediately. I think we said to Richard [Boon], we'll take 250. They only pressed 1,000, so it virtually sold out, which was fantastic."

The economics of releasing a single from a standing start became tenable almost overnight. Rough Trade would customarily stock between 300 and 500 copies of your self-released 7-inch single – nearly recouping the initial outlay in one fell swoop. For that reason, Rough Trade could count on flocks of impish young bands from all over the UK descending on them, usually on an away day ticket that would also stretch to a visit to Small Wonder. The third leg of any aspirant DIY band's illustrious voyage would often be an attempt to sneak past BBC security in order to hand deliver a copy of their precious cargo to John Peel. Who would, seemingly more often than not, play it. And that direct route from creator to audience, unfiltered by the raft of considerations and compromises that to an extent *was* the music industry, was completely extraordinary too. The link between the Rough Trade generation of bands and Peel has been made frequently. Partly, to an extent, because they shared an ethos. Peel championed the underdog, and made it his business to support those in most need of his patronage (sometimes, one senses, at the expense of critical judgement about merit). There were other similarities, too. Neither Peel, who always maintained that he was able to exist happily on his BBC salary, the odd voiceover for adverts aside, nor Travis, were money-orientated. Similarly, although playful at the notion of their 'celebrity', they were by and large not interested in inflicting their egos on others. Contrast that with the loudhailer personalities running the majors across the Atlantic, where CBS's Walter Yetnikoff, David Geffen *et al* indulged themselves in endless turf wars. Or in the UK, Richard Branson's use of his record empire as leverage for a quasi-Boy's Own adventurer lifestyle.

I wondered whether Travis actually bought some of the more dreadful singles out of sympathy? "Honestly, the standard was good," he states. "There weren't that many awful records. The awful ones were things like Skrewdriver, which we didn't want to stock. When you get someone like The Rezillos coming down from Edinburgh with their first singles, and asking us to stock their records – it wasn't like us being benevolent and acting like we really cared, it was mostly really good stuff. It didn't happen every day that someone came in. There were lots of visits. The Bluebells arrived exhausted, virtually sleeping on the floor of the shop. It was exciting. But it was such a fantastic thing to have distribution and the shop, in terms of being an A&R source. I don't think you could ever again be in such a powerful position in terms of the market, it's something I miss really. It gave us such a huge advantage over everyone else. Being the first port of call. Johnny Marr [of The Smiths] came to us to give us 'Hand In Glove', and if we didn't have the shop, it would have made it much more difficult for them to find their way to us. It was deliberate, that access and open house [policy]. And even now we're on the street, you don't have to take an elevator and get through four security people, that's not us really. You never know what might happen, some determined person might walk up and be the new Prince."

Between the trickle and the flood of independent releases, Travis found that "If you had something good, you could really sell a lot of records quickly. There was initially a sense of anticipation and excitement in the early days. Because there weren't so many records, a remarkable number of records were sold that weren't actually that good. But you were kind of caught up in this wave of wanting to hear everything. I don't want to be unkind, but things like Chelsea's 'Right To Work', and things that obviously weren't in the same league as 'Spiral Scratch'. But it was interesting, there was a moment, I don't know how long it lasted, when everyone wanted to hear everything and have everything."

The shop also became a focus for related activities, selling fanzines and periodicals following Rock On's example. The reading stock included Adrian Thrills' *48 Thrills*, Jon Savage's *London's Outrage*, Scotland's *Ripped And Torn* and Shane MacGowan's one-off *Bondage*, as well as the better established *Sniffin' Glue*. From its sixth edition onwards, until it moved to Miles Copeland's Dryden Chambers base, Rough Trade provided the latter with 'office space'. *'Glue* photographer Harry Murlowski had negotiated a deal with Stuart Joseph, another in a long line of Rough Trade 'staff', to use the back store room as its editorial base.

Rough Trade eventually moved from simply being a vendor of records to playing the pivotal role in bringing them into existence. Yet it happened largely without forethought. "It wasn't in our minds," insists Travis. "It wasn't like, OK, we'll do this distribution thing and see how it goes. Honestly, we were so busy every day. Packing boxes, selling records, having fun, playing music really loud, meeting loads of people, just really fantastic to be alive. It wasn't like I was hatching a master plan." In fact, it was Richard Scott who was behind the 'first' Rough Trade vinyl release. "The first record actually put out by Rough Trade was Tappa Zukie's *Man Ah Warrior* on the Mer label, through Lenny Kaye and Patti Smith." he states. "I put that one out." However, the first record to be given a Rough Trade catalogue number would come from French proto-punks Metal Urbain.

Formed in Paris in 1977 in response to what was happening in London, Metal Urbain married elements of Krautrock and primal Stooges with screamed vocals and overdriven, effects-heavy guitar, plus Eric Debris's synthesized percussion. 'Paris Maquis' sounded unlike anything else ever released at that time or arguably since. "Peel started playing the first Metal Urbain single, 'Lady Coca-Cola' and 'Panic'," remembers Travis, "and we really liked it. So we tracked them down and bought some copies. We ordered about fifty, sold them, and then ordered another hundred. Then they came over and came into the shop. 'Hello, we're Metal Urbain.' 'Nice to meet you, we love your record.' They said, 'Listen, we've recorded two tracks, we don't know what to do, could you help?' 'You know what, we probably can help.' So as they say, necessity is the mother of invention." How much had he learned about the mechanics of releasing a record? "I think I was already learning about it. It was kind of in the air. And the fact that Chiswick had done it and that Stiff were doing it was a factor. They're doing it, we know them, they're just human beings, why can't we do it? It definitely gave us confidence." Metal Urbain would never appear on Rough Trade again, however, after a staff meeting at the label blanked their choice of pornographic cover for a follow-up single.

Rough Trade issued exactly twelve singles through the course of 1978. Following the distribution model, artists were allowed a 50-50 profit split, after manufacture, distribution and promotion had taken place. Importantly, artists would, in general terms, retain the rights to their masters rather than the label owning them in posterity. This was not only a revolution in terms of a standard music industry contract, but also rare in terms of the way most of the larger independents operated. "I drafted the 50-50 contract," says Richard Scott. "It's actually just two sentences, and I still think it holds together."

Travis was very aware of the history of independent music from his travels in America. "I knew that really, every great label was at one time independent. Pretty much so. I also knew the flip of that. Actually, independent labels have got a pretty bad reputation in terms of having mavericks who didn't pay their royalties and treated their artists with disdain. All those kinds of things. So we were trying to take the best of what independents did without the bad parts." It was an immediately successful template for both parties. Bands were allowed to release material at their own pace rather than under the auspices of a major label with a schedule. It succeeded, initially, because the market for independent singles was at an all-time high – with sales of over 10,000 commonplace for the more successful releases.

The immediate follow-up to Metal Urbain saw Richard Scott turn to his beloved reggae via Augustus Pablo (offered to them when his friend walked in off the street with a tape that was taken straight to a cutting room), preceding the Burroughs' inspired experimental cut-ups of Sheffield's Cabaret Voltaire. The most conventional punk band ever to settle on Rough Trade's roster, Belfast's Stiff Little Fingers, saw huge success with both the self-released 'Alternative Ulster' and 'Suspect Device', as they were embraced – with hindsight perhaps naively – as the authentic soundtrack to the UK's fraught ongoing relationship with the province. The Monochrome Set could hardly have provided much more in the way of contrast to Jake Burns' impassioned growl, with singer Bid's perverse, arch lyricism gliding nonchalantly over hook-laden, 60s-infused art rock, one eyebrow seemingly permanently raised.

Vic Godard's Subway Sect were veterans of the first wave of punk. Their lack of careerism (the title of their definitive single 'Ambition', containing the world-weary lines 'I hope no-one notices the sleep on me', was marvellously disingenuous) and suspicion of the invitation to be beholden to a musical straitjacket made them perfect candidates for Rough Trade. Others in that first batch of 7-inch singles included the pioneering (and then defunct) Cleveland hell-raisers the Electric Eels, Swiss art-punks Kleenex and Swell Maps – whose debut single on their own label from December 1977 was eventually re-housed in Rough Trade attire. File Under Pop featured Simon Leonard dicing field recordings taken from Heathrow Airport. Rough Trade's first dozen releases, ultimately, could hardly be said to have any defining characteristic beyond the budgetary constraints their productions revealed.

The hand in glove marriage of shop and label, as Travis intimates, worked perfectly to this juncture. The retail side benefited from the renown the label afforded it, though knuckles were firmly rapped by industry watchdogs over bootleg sales. "The record company was upstairs from the store," remembers Barbara Gogan, "and I remember for a couple of days there was this car sat across the street with two men sitting in it. We were joking about how it was probably spies from major labels listening in to our conversations. Turns out, that wasn't far from the truth. One evening, after the record company employees had left for the day, the store got raided by these music business cops (BMR, or BMRB in those days). They busted Travis and co for bootlegging, and the men had actually been listening to conversations within the office with this highly sensitive microphone trained on us from inside the car." Richard Scott also recalls a minor incident over pre-release Stranglers' records. "We had real problems with them. The Stranglers management had given us promos to sell prior to release; kind of for kudos. That was another very common practice then. But there were problems when it came to light."

In 1979 Rough Trade was featured on *The South Bank Show*, presented by Melvyn Bragg and narrated by Simon Frith. Footage included The Raincoats recording 'Fairytale In A Supermarket' in Spaceward's cramped studio. Mayo Thompson was at the controls. A Texan born in 1944, he would make a crucial impact on the Rough Trade 'sound' by, to an extent, not shaping, perfecting or normalising such musicians (the trebly guitar sound on 'Fairytale', it has to be said, remains bracing at even two decades' distance). A former studio assistant to Robert Rauschenberg at the Art & Language collective in America and a founder member of Red Crayola, he came to the UK and fell in with Jake Riviera's Radar Records. Radar released a single, 'Wives In Orbit', in 1978, as well as reissuing two of the band's LPs. After reading about Rough Trade in the *NME* he made a pilgrimage there to try to offload surplus copies of *Corrected Slogans* (a collaboration with the Art & Language collective originally issued in 1976). Travis took twenty-five and a bond was formed – Thompson's counter-cultural credentials and instincts providing a perfect foil.

Their initial joint production was of the Monochrome Set's debut single, though it was not all that it could be, according to the band's main songwriter, Bid. For a start, 'He's Frank' was listed as the a-side on the label, while the sleeve gave 'Alphaville' that status. "'Alphaville' was meant to be the b-side," admits Bid. "They just cocked it up." Travis's co-production credit was, at this stage "like an Andy Warhol thing," thinks Bid. "I hated that single. I really hated the production. It was pretty much the way we were playing, but I didn't like Mayo's arrangement of it. A very nice bloke, but not easy to work with." Thompson would later invoke a new incarnation of Red Krayola featuring a Rough Trade house band – including Gina Birch of the Raincoats, Lora Logic of Essential Logic and shop worker Epic Soundtracks.

Rough Trade were "completely incompetent but huge fun," Bid continues. "Everyone was really nice, apart from one person. [Memories were] the traffic of bands between New York and London. The incredible help you got from Rough Trade when you were playing live. The amount of work they used to put into it – and yet it was incredibly inefficient. It was like a whole bunch of students working on something and nobody knew what they were doing. And the 50-50 contracts they signed with bands that lost them an enormous amount of money [an assertion that Richard Scott disputes]. It was just great, but you had the feeling that this was a launching pad only, sadly. And Geoff may well deny this, but I remember it wasn't certain that they could afford to pay for us to record an album." Travis concedes that this may well have been the case.

Mayo Thompson's second major production for Rough Trade was entirely more successful. He was at the helm of Stiff Little Fingers' debut album *Inflammable Material*, the jewel in the crown of orthodox punk's second wave. A Clash-inspired punk band with more than a hint of classic old time rock 'n' roll if you scratched the surface, SLF ended up on Rough Trade when they were first courted, then spurned, by Island Records, via the direct intervention of Chris Blackwell. Following the success of 'Suspect Device', their debut, they'd given up their jobs and moved to England in the expectation of a deal, and recorded demos in London with Ed Hollis of the Hot Rods. In crisis, it would be to Rough Trade SLF turned, penning a song of the same name on the album, chiding Island for their negligence. "We're gonna do it our way," ran Jake Burns' lyric, "We're gonna make it on our own/Because we've found people to trust/People who put music first". There's no more acute, or at least literal, example of an artist drawing comparisons between the old and new orders. *Inflammable Material* would reach number 14 in the UK album charts in 1979. On the day of release a fleet of three taxis pulled up outside Rough Trade, from the *NME*, *Sounds* and *Melody Maker* respectively, to buy the record – Rough Trade simply didn't believe in the concept of 'promo' copies.

Both The Monochrome and Stiff Little Fingers were ultimately lured away to major deals – The Monochrome Set to Virgin subsidiary DinDisc, Stiff Little Fingers to Chrysalis. "Dave Fudger was a friend," Bid explains, "a journalist at the time, and he was the A&R man at Virgin. I think we may well have ended up recording an album for Rough Trade, but I do think it was inevitable that we would have left at some point." This would prove a recurring situation not only for Rough Trade but for several independents, as bands chose to 'graduate' by signing with previously mistrusted majors.

In most cases, of course, it ended in disaster. In Rough Trade's case, what 'their' bands did beyond agreed projects was up to them. Indeed, some, such as Seymour Stein, openly acknowledge that Rough Trade were "like an A&R team working for me in the UK. They were so brilliant. They still are, they're still the same kind of fans that they were back then."

Travis views the departures quite differently. "The Monochrome Set were great in those days. The credo in those days was, we don't make a Rough Trade record unless we love them. It doesn't come out. If we'd have made it, and we didn't like them, it wouldn't come out. Those three singles are excellent." Did the departures hurt? "Not The Monochrome Set," he says. "To be really honest, I don't know how much we believed in them. Maybe we thought we'd got the best of them. It wasn't an emotional upset when they left. It *was* with Stiff Little Fingers, because that seemed stupid." Richard Scott is able to throw some light on their departure. "I still remember that meeting. They asked to meet us, and Jake Burns is a nice man, but what they wanted was for us to put a series of ads in the music press. And we said if we did that, it would destroy their market. But we were right, I think. That was what the argument was about."

Even so, Travis concedes that at that time, things were still conducted on a project by project, if not day by day, basis. "You know what? It took us quite a long time to think about the future. We weren't at all concerned about, or worrying about, when the Subway Sect album was coming. Perhaps we just weren't being ambitious enough. We should have said to Augustus Pablo, this is great, why don't we do an album? Maybe he would have said yes. [Richard Scott contends that the Pablo trail went cold when his 'fixer' returned to New York and died] But we weren't thinking like that. We were just living in the frenzy of each day. It was so busy. We weren't thinking ahead at all – thinking about building an empire, or thinking about building a catalogue. We didn't have any knowledge of that kind of thing. We were very much living in the moment. We weren't thinking about the future at all, or missed opportunities. We were thinking – it's really exciting to do this *now*. We didn't even think about tomorrow. With the Buzzcocks EP, it didn't occur to me. Perhaps it should have done. We probably should have gone up to Richard [Boon] and said, 'Know what, we can probably raise ten grand, let's do an album with Buzzcocks', and that would have done it. I suppose it wasn't really until Rob Gretton said to Tony Wilson, 'No, let's not sign to EMI, let's make this Joy Division album ourselves.' That was an amazing moment that sparked the possibility of carrying on and going forward and being more – not more serious – but responsible for a band's life than just doing a record. Those were the important moments. And obviously doing our first album was part of that, with Stiff Little Fingers. I find it quite hard to think about the future even now."

The themes on Rough Trade's 1979 output and beyond shared several concepts. Many were concerned with the politics of the personal, particularly compromise. 'We Are All Prostitutes' by The Pop Group, which *Melody Maker*'s Chris Bohn accurately described as 'intense and disturbing', was one example. 'Nobody's Scared' by Subway Sect used specifically the same angst-driven vernacular in an altogether different musical setting. Body space and physical geography were frequently referenced (The Delta Five's deceptively clever 'Mind Your Own Business' and Kleenex's 'You'). It was as if the tenets of political struggle were a 'given'. As though the dialogue had moved on. Beyond Stiff Little Fingers, slogans were disavowed at Rough Trade as simplistic and inflexible. The hinterland of the independent boom comprised a husk of punk bands who stayed welded to both a sonic (speeded up R&B) and philosophical (statements about immediate desires and impulses alongside blanket denunciations of authority) template. Others would suggest, though it's possible to consider their arguments wishful thinking, that the bands under discussion were core to punk, and a hiving off of the more progressive elements within the movement into something separate unfairly ignores the historical connections at play. There's also the small point that bands who attempted to make the most progressive, intelligent and searching music didn't necessarily make the best records.

Subway Sect are a prime example of the creative confusion. They would not have existed without punk, and their appearance on the White Riot tour was, for some, arguably more transforming than that of The Clash. Certainly Vic Godard became a figurehead to bands such as Orange Juice, Josef K and The Fire Engines, as well as the soon to emerge Cherry Red roster almost *en masse*. While Godard has stated he felt 'out of step' with punk, he would extend that to being out of step with 'everything'. His statement, 'We oppose all rock 'n' roll' (as expressed on the rear cover of 'Ambition'), would become a credo for many who followed in his wake. But denying the connection is tantamount to disowning one's parents. They may embarrass you, but you remain the fruit of their loins. 'We Oppose All Rock 'n' Roll' was actually a complete song written in 1976 at the height of punk, though never released at the time due to manager Bernie Rhodes' self-serving, erratic behaviour. As Pete Silverton wrote in his review for *Sounds*, the statement offered "a plain lack of gratitude. Their mothers should have taught them better manners." He still made 'Ambition' his single of the week, though.

Or perhaps we can alight on The Fall and Mark E Smith's spoken observation on the title-track to *Live At The Witch Trials*, before they moved from Step Forward to Rough Trade, that "I still believe in the R 'n' R dream". A statement he would partially qualify in an interview with Tony Fletcher. "It's ambiguous. But I do, in a lot of ways. Like, people say The Fall aren't rock 'n' roll, you know. My attitude is that we are rock 'n' roll and no other fucker is." "Everything that makes a mark as a movement tries to have a break with the past," Travis notes. "Sometimes it's artificial and sometimes there's a validity to it. As an artist, you sometimes have to draw a line in the sand, and say – 'We oppose that. That's rubbish.' And that's just the history of art. You reject the past to make something new. But of course you can't really reject the past, because it's always got its claws in you."

Cabaret Voltaire's 'Nag Nag Nag' was trashed by Danny Baker in the *NME* for being 'as flat as a witch's tit', which is one way of analysing its attempt to quash harmony and conventional song structure. It was nevertheless part of a looming electronic scene alongside various Mute projects. The influences here were James Brown and Can, Stockhausen and Eno. Alongside 23 Skidoo and Clock DVA on Fetish and Throbbing Gristle at Industrial, the cumulative effect was a wave of ferociously intelligent, subversive artists punch-drunk with the possibilities offered by increasingly cheap technology. While some took punk's clean slate as an opportunity to open up a new channel for 'classic', 60s-inspired songwriting (Mike Alway at Cherry Red, and later Alan McGee at Creation) these were a cadre of groups who wanted to phase-jump to a new universe of sonic possibility altogether. Which is why comments such as those by Baker and Silverton are so interesting – both were punk era writers who shared an affection for the roots and the legacy of rock 'n' roll – seeing its best instincts and practice as *salvageable*. There is some substance, then, in shifting the common perception of 'year zero' to 1978 or 1979 and the dawn of post-punk rather than the established reading of 1976.

The Cabs, Clocks and Gristles of this world were, in turn, antecedents both to the industrial genre and the rise of dance music in the late 80s and beyond. Probably the most critically revered independent dance label of the 90s was Warp, formed in Sheffield, and steeped in the cultural capital of that city. Fittingly, it would release work by Richard H Kirk of Cabaret Voltaire. The Industrial label bequeathed its name to an entire music genre, one that continues to thrive in Europe. With a side-serving of angsty self-reverence, Nine Inch Nails would make elements of that sound palatable to Stateside rock fans (though a possibly more accurate comparison would be to Al Jourgenson's Ministry).

But rather than be defined by a musical genre, which to a certain extent Mute was, at least momentarily, Rough Trade signed whatever appealed to the tastes of Travis and other Rough Trade insiders. Hence amid the shock of the new came reissues of material by the Television Personalities and Prefects, as well as Scottish kindergarten punks The Prats. The latter were veterans of Fast Product's *Earcom* sampler series, while the now defunct Prefects, who had also appeared on the *White Riot* tour, only agreed to their retrospective single on the promise Travis would release something by Rob Lloyd's new band, The Nightingales. The Television Personalities' 'Where's Bill Grundy Now' EP had originally been housed on their own King's Road imprint in 1978 – an enterprise predictably indebted to The Desperate Bicycles and Scritti Politti (see chapter four). Scritti themselves eventually found a natural berth at Rough Trade. Their records are lynchpins in the development of a post-punk aesthetic, explored in depth in Simon Reynolds' *Rip It Up*, where vocalist Green observes that "We were anti-rock, it was too strong, too sure, too solid; a sound. We wanted music that *wasn't*, because *we* weren't strong, sure or solid.' If the previously mooted crossover that existed between the 'punk' and 'independent' mentality had great and obvious commonality, that was equally true when the former genre acquired its historical prefix.

This marriage of the old and new was indicative of a commonplace attitude across the independent landscape. At this stage the reissue industry was nowhere near as mature as it would become a decade or so later with the advent of the compact disc boom and specialist reissue labels. Records, once released, were conventionally deleted. That offered the gap in the market that stalls such as Rock On and Beggars Banquet fed. But it also meant that, particularly as the majors generally ignored anything that didn't yield much greater potential margins, there were opportunities for 'retrospective A&R'. Geoff Travis recognised this just as Chiswick had done before him. As an extension of that, Travis would work with artists of distinction who had disappeared off the radar. The most obvious example being Robert Wyatt, formerly of Soft Machine, who came to Travis's attention via Vivien Goldman and Brian Eno.

Wyatt's recordings betrayed an idealism much in sympathy with Travis's own, though his output was more in keeping with the traditions of fifties folk-protest songs from Topic Records' heyday. His debut for Rough Trade, 'Arauco', a cover of Chilean political activist Violetta Parra's song, was sandwiched by releases from The Swell Maps and Cabaret Voltaire in a perfect encapsulation of Rough Trade's refusal to be limited by genre or generation. Wyatt would later provide Rough Trade with one of its most enduring singles, when Elvis Costello and Clive Langer specifically wrote 'Shipbuilding' for him, as a lament for the Falklands War in 1982. At Wyatt's insistence it was released on Rough Trade (it was originally envisioned to be the first single on a new label founded by Costello) out of loyalty to Travis.

Wyatt is not any less fond of Travis to this day. "The first few records I was on in the 60s were recorded for a massive US label called CBS, which became Sony," he states. "I found that really unsatisfactory. There's no-one really there, it's just accountants and lawyers. When you're trying to check up on stuff, it's just an anonymous corporation. They may have been a small bunch of enthusiasts when they started out, but they became a big, bland institution. It was cold, you couldn't feel that warm, beating human heart there." Later, he'd seen the false dawn of the first wave of 60s independents. "Virgin made a few innovations. For example, Richard Branson grew his hair – that was a new one! He looked like one of the lads. They made LPs by people who wouldn't necessarily make singles, like Henry Cow, Mike Oldfield and me, really. They realised there was a gap there. Before it had been the case that you had to have a hit single before any record company would finance an LP. And they said no, you don't need to. They looked on the continent to see how many groups were popular just as live acts, didn't have hit singles and weren't really pop groups anyway. They had the bright idea of altering that. But in terms of the way the contract was worded and the economics of it, I have to tell you, it was absolutely straight-forward, old fashioned – 'We take the lot, and we give you the crumbs'. So the first indie label that I think deserved the name in terms of an ideological shift was Rough Trade, and the lovely, wonderful Geoff Travis. What a great man. Just a lovely bloke. As ramshackle as it was, it came from musical theatre rather than business school, but it was worth it for the heart and enthusiasm. Not just that, but the real intention to do things that were worth doing, and to risk making mistakes. And I think it's great that Geoff's still like that, picking up Anthony And The Johnsons and stuff, the unusual projects he takes on. That was my first realisation that the record industry doesn't have to be this massive, anonymous, untouchable behemoth."

"You know," Travis continues, animatedly, "that whole idea of making money and being 'successful' just never entered the equation, perhaps naively. It just wasn't part of it. It was more about having fun, and creating an opportunity, and creating a structure, which was hard, hard work, to allow these musicians and artists to realise their dreams – that was the all-important thing. It wasn't even really about Rough Trade. It wasn't about us. Always as a label, it might seem strange, but we've tried to keep a low profile. It's really about our artists. I'd much rather you talked to our artists. We always say that. We decline a million interviews – though it seems to be the time for it now!" He's referring to the fact that, as well as the recent publication of a history of Rough Trade, at least one more is underway. "I do think that we're just humble servants to our artists. I don't mean that in a facetious way. We feel lucky to be working with some of the best working artists on the planet. We feel lucky to be involved with that. Because we have quite a high standard of taste, that's what it really comes down to, and as I said before, we're not insecure about that. But it's quite hard to have your own original reaction to something, because there's such powerful peer group pressure. And you think you should like something, because everyone likes something, or people you respect like something. So it's quite difficult to create that state of innocence, when you actually respond to something unmediated. Maybe you never did, but when you're 16, and you get a new record home and you play it hundreds of times, you know if it's really reaching you. It gets harder and harder to find space to do that, but it's really important, I think. It's the only thing that matters, when you're making a judgement. You're lucky you can still recreate that thrill of listening to music. I'm sure you get that. That's why I love music, really. And you want other people to share the things you love. People have a different relationship. It's a difference in degrees. Some people are passionate, some less so."

Stiff Little Fingers' departure had, however, persuaded Rough Trade to take themselves more seriously in business terms. In March 1979, Scott Piering, previously PR for Island in the US, joined the label at Richard Scott's suggestion, handling promotion as it continued to expand. Prior to this, Rough Trade had considered the process of sending out advance copies of records to journalists unseemly, though they were, of course, welcome to come into the shop to check things out. Piering started producing mail-outs and booklets with information on new releases. These grew into first *Masterbag* and then *The Catalogue*.

"The whole point was that, with Rough Trade, any information we had we would freely give to you," says Travis. "Demystification was important. And that's where the politics came in, really – the sharing of knowledge. And the encouragement of anyone trying to make any kind of artistic endeavour, or entrepreneurial endeavour, to try to make their own way and do things on their own without getting permission – all those things were very important and very empowering." Of course, the rise of the independents happened only slightly prior to the advent of the Thatcherite yuppie archetype. "Horrifying to be aligned to that, but yes, you're right," Travis concedes, "there was a kind of weird, strange unconscious collusion in that ethic, if you can do something, do it yourself. But obviously what we were doing as an independent label was in opposition to the establishment. We weren't trying to be a major label, we were trying to buoy people not having to engage with that system." He lists, almost inevitably, the Clash signing to CBS as the perfect example of how not to do it.

Piering was crucial to so many of the Rough Trade acts but also the entire independent genre, fighting stiff resistance to get 'indie' records played on daytime radio against the stonewalling of dismissive BBC DJs and producers. "Without [Piering]," wrote Bill Drummond and Jimmy Cauty in *The Manual (How To Have A Number One The Easy Way)*, about the KLF's exponential success, "this book would have to be retitled *How To Get To Number 47 – With A Certain Amount Of Difficulty*." Whether or not we wish to quantify the music industry's current infatuation with 'indie landfill' as a good or bad thing, the transition in listening expectations had much to do with Piering's inch by inch diplomacy. Ably assisted, as he was, by the efforts of Shirley O'Loughlin, who had the task of delivering new product to both John Peel and the music press.

One of Peel's most beloved institutions was The Fall. Moving on from Step Forward, they released three albums for Rough Trade over two spells, bouncing back to Rough Trade after a brief interlude with Kamera Records. It was a highly productive relationship, though Smith would complain to the press about stipulations being placed on his lyrics – notably 'Slags', which, in his defence, he has always used as a non-gender specific term. He would maintain that Travis and Rough Trade's functions should not intrude on his own – later growling in an interview with David Cavanagh for *Volume* magazine that Travis should "just sell the fucking record, you fucking hippy". Yet those remarks, made in 1992, came ten years after the fact. "I remember Mark E Smith hated it when anyone had anything to say about anything he had done," recalls Travis, clearly amused. "'No-one has a right to say anything to me about music.' That was hilarious, it really irked him. Mark would say, 'I worked in an office, I know what you have to do. Why are these people not here yet?' But I personally actually don't like people running late, I think you do have to fulfil your responsibilities."

There were problems emerging, meanwhile, in the company's separation between its label activities and its role as a distributor. Travis was primarily concerned with the A&R of the label, Richard Scott with distribution. They had built a second outdoor shed to serve as warehouse space, but that was quickly to prove insufficient, as the offices upstairs were colonised – often as living quarters. Rough Trade had become a rabbit warren wherein the pursuit of work, pleasure and sleep were confused and often overlapped.

Eventually the two discrete functions that Rough Trade had evolved were separated into difference premises. The label and distribution arm took a lease on 137 Blenheim Crescent, a ten-minute walk away. The two-storey detached house quickly became a drop-in centre for the waifs and strays of the music business, including sympathetic record company workers, journalists and a menagerie of artists. Many periodically slept there, while the building also sheltered equipment and a 'free' restaurant (though the food was intended for the consumption of the workers, it was often diverted to hungry visitors). In essence, Blenheim Crescent was the nearest the English music industry came, short of Crass's Dial House, to a thriving co-operative in the spirit of Robert Owen or William King, with vinyl the economic engine rather than cotton or vegetables. Though it should also be noted that Travis's and Scott's own work ethics ill-fitted the stereotype, philosophically, Travis endorses the comparison. "No, I don't mind being called a co-op," says Travis. "We were in Dave Marsh's book as 'the only co-op in rock 'n' roll'. I'm quite proud of that."

And then there were the meetings. These have been much mythologised as either key to Rough Trade's ideological identity or a deep irritant, depending on whom you ask. But the committee structure of the enterprise prevailed. Fanzines that they might distribute were read from cover to cover (at least, in principle) and would be discarded in the event of the discovery of any sexist or racist content. That happened with records as well, meaning a number of bands would naturally take advantage of the situation by pushing the buttons of what were perceived to be the new purists on the block. Rough Trade would not, for example, sell Stranglers records due to Jean-Jacques Burnel having assaulted critic Jon Savage (strangely, Pete Stennet of Small Wonder would similarly discourage his clientele from purchasing records by the same group – though simply because he disliked them). Early punk band Raped's 'Pretty Paedophiles' single was not stocked, causing them to change their name to Cuddly Toys, setting a precedent revisited when Steve Albini's post-Big Black project Rapeman was turned away.

For Travis, though, there is little substance (or perhaps fibre) to the 'brown rice' myth of Rough Trade – a dismissive judgement that was based partially on punk's aversion to any semblance of 'hippy' affectations. The perception was certainly abroad that sandal-wearing, middle-class drop-outs munching on health foods spent interminable hours discussing how their efforts split or enforced hegemony. Or the infamous dish-washing rota. The fact that Rough Trade did, indeed, release records that discussed 'hegemony' (for which, predictably, we have Scritti Politti to thank) didn't help. The assumption is largely a nonsense, though, given that most of those who worked for Rough Trade repeatedly point out the long hours this entailed. Travis is clearly weary of it. "We worked all the time. My lecturer at university in philosophy said that a meeting or a lecture should not last more than 20 minutes, because no human being has an attention span operating fully beyond that, and that struck me as very true. I hate meetings. Sometimes they're very necessary. But I'd much rather be actively doing something than having a meeting. That's a complete myth, I think. That's kind of a lazy depiction of – that's what a co-op is. We *were* a co-op, but it's kind of a *Daily Mail* version of what a co-op is. Lots of people sitting around and doing nothing. There was no time to sit around. It might have been better to sit around a bit more!"

Describing those meetings, Richard Scott recalls that, almost despite themselves, a hierarchy emerged. "People who had been there longer held more sway; Geoff was never particularly keen on his line being voted down! Geoff is very eloquent. Broadly we'd talk about the line that Geoff and I had decided on. I think that's fair. Everything was talked through, decisions were written down. The race was always to get out to get a gig that evening. There was a good saying in the early days – if there are more than six other people at the gig, you're at the wrong gig. So there was that quest – to find things that people had never seen before."

Blenheim Crescent became a magnet for displaced souls, notably Kick (Claude Bessy) of LA's *Slash* magazine, who had fled America following Reagan's election victory. Having once started the first American reggae fanzine, *Angeleno Dread* in LA, he fitted perfectly with Rough Trade's spirit and heritage. At almost the same time Rough Trade opened its first US office, in Grant Street, San Francisco in 1980, and also set up a German label and distribution operation.

Under Allan Sturdy's supervision, later joined by Steve Montgomery, Sue Johnson and Pete Walmsley, Rough Trade's San Francisco operation was originally just a shop and distribution headquarters. Later, in the mid-80s it began to make its own signings (relocating to New York in 1989, after Robin

Hurley had taken over in 1987). Prior to the alt-rock boom that hallmarked the catalogues of 4AD and Blast First in the late 80s, Rough Trade America provided a conduit for the Paisley Underground revival and acts such as The Rain Parade and Dream Syndicate. They also signed post-hardcore band Soul Asylum prior to their less appealing MTV/grunge incarnation, and art-pop mavericks such as Beat Happening and Camper Van Beethoven. There was also, over a sustained period, attempts to sign a quality hip hop artist, but both Run-DMC and De La Soul escaped their grasp (as had Prince, incidentally, much earlier). "They also got a demo tape from REM, which was really poor, apparently," notes Richard Scott.

The new premises in West London, meanwhile, allowed Rough Trade to expand. Anne Clarke set up Rough Trade Music (which would be taken on by Cathi Gibson from 1981) to handle publishing and copyrights, and alongside Sue Johnson helped set up tours for Rough Trade's expanding roster of bands. Resources were minimal, but generously shared, as Richard Williams of The Passions, notes. "We occasionally used to use the Rough Trade van to get to gigs and I remember coming down the M1 looking straight down onto the tyre and the tarmac through a huge rusty hole in the front wheel arch." One of the first joint touring ventures featured Kleenex, The Raincoats (managed by O'Loughlin) and Spizz Energi. Hilariously, the latter band was recruited at short notice when Cabaret Voltaire's girlfriends became unhappy at the prospect of their menfolk spending several weeks in a van with two female groups.

It's worth dwelling on the number of women who were involved at Rough Trade, either on the shop floor or as artists. Many of the 70s indie record labels were powered by the male record collector dynamic, long before *High Fidelity* underscored the geek gene as being seemingly wholly male. "Feminism was just part of my growing up, and a natural thing for me," suggests Travis. But when pressed, he will also differentiate between his own persona and that of the collector caricature. "I'm not really like that. I don't know where my records are. Which is not a good first step for a record collector. They're scattered, I couldn't necessarily lay my hands on certain records. I'm not your classic anorak record collector. I don't have that mentality. I buy records every week to keep up to date. I'd love to have some old records, but I'd never pay over the odds to own something. My job is all about listening to new things. If I get a free moment I enjoy listening to old music that I love. But I don't collect anything. I could have – I should have kept an archive. But I haven't really got any of my original Sex Pistols records, for instance. It would have been wise to collect them. Everyone says

Mick Jones has a garage of amazing artefacts, which is quite a wise thing to do, but I don't – I don't have a garage! And I wouldn't ever keep bad records."

The balance of staffing made the environs of the shop, and partially as a result the label, more open to women. "Yes, Rough Trade encouraged women," confirms Kate Korus of the Mo-Dettes. "I would even suspect that Geoff was one of those male women's libbers (among whom I have several friends – Strummer was one too). We went to them because [manager] Bob Black knew him and they were flexible in their deals, willing to give us distribution without hogging all the credit or giving orders. They did put a lot of women on their books as I recall. I have to confess that we considered them very old-fashioned 'up-the-rebels' hippies at the time. We tried to distance ourselves from their 'worthy', serious image. We were all about injecting some humour and fun back into the business, at least our little corner of it, and getting away from preaching and politics. Rough Trade was all about pushing the envelope socially, often with very sombre results. With hindsight, and even at the time, it was great that they stood up for all us otherwise outsiders. 'White Mice' was our most successful record partly because they let us get on with it and despite our silly contempt didn't meddle with us the way 'real' record companies would (and did)." As Richard Scott points out, "The best days at Rough Trade were when it was largely women – the final days at Kensington Park Road, where there were seven women and five men. On the wholesale side, there were three women and me. And those were the best times."

The aforementioned Spizz had, in his own inimitable way and under innumerable guises, become one of Rough Trade's bedrock artists. Engaging and boundless of energy, a veritable post-punk Tigger, he amused most everyone under the billing Spizzenergi with two Rough Trade singles, 'Soldier Soldier' and 'Where's Captain Kirk?'. "Back in 1979, after rehearsals, me and Jim [Solar; bass] would have a few beers and we had been running through one of Mark [Coalfield's] tunes which had a very obscure lyric, except for the line 'Oh, but it's true – you are a nobody's who'. So on the bus home this metamorphosed into the first two verses and choruses. I had no pen or paper, so for the entire journey I repeated those in my head until I walked in the house, wrote them down, and within a few minutes the third verse came to me. Next rehearsal, I said I had written some new words. We went through it and we thought it was so funny we played it over and over. That's when I added the *Star Trek* theme tune because Jim had a Wem Copycat echo unit. We knew then that this was more catchy than 'Soldier Soldier'." 'Kirk' topped the first published Independent Chart in 1980 and didn't budge for seven weeks. For a brief period, said chart was almost colonised by Spizz (who had five separate chart entries for his Rough Trade output under three separate names at one point). But thereafter, under his latest nom de plume, Athletico Spizz '80, he took A&M's shilling.

The relocation meanwhile hadn't, on its own account, ended ongoing frictions. Travis remained primarily concerned with A&R. Richard Scott was building the group's distribution network and wanted more professionalism. Travis's perspective remained the long-term development of artists, while those working in distribution were plugged into a network that demanded more responsive and time-sensitive decision making. It didn't help, either, that there the dividing lines were sometimes fudged. Travis would sign labels to Rough Trade (notably Postcard) rather than to the distribution arm. "I was away when he did it," notes Scott, "and I was really pissed off when I got back. Postcard would have been a really good regional example. I thought it would have been much more interesting if we'd tried to keep it in Glasgow. I didn't understand, until I twigged that Geoff saw stars there – especially Roddy Frame [of Aztec Camera]."

The situation became far more critical in 1982, when distributor Pinnacle went bankrupt (though it was re-financed three months later). Dozens of labels were affected and many went under. Rough Trade found themselves inundated with new work when they were already stretched. Scott's solution to this was to set up the Cartel (see chapter Twelve). Travis was advised by his accountants to close the shop (and thereby keep the label afloat). But his long-term staff, Nigel House, Pete Donne and Jude Crighton, managed to avert looming redundancy by offering to buy out the shop, to the value of the stock. They did so and the doors – which at one point famously conveyed a note to the public asking them to keep faith – stayed open. Another hurdle was overcome when the shop's Kensington Park landlords decided not to renew the shop's lease, leading to the move to Talbot Road in July 1983.

Richard Powell came aboard after working for the GLC helping companies refinance and reorganise. "He had an MBA, and the main company he'd been working for was a telescope company, and he'd done a good job helping them rebuild," Scott notes. He and Will Keene, who had joined Rough Trade as an accountant after becoming disillusioned with Virgin Records and Richard Branson, made the appointment. Published character portrayals of Powell as a kind of Thatcherite bootboy are, according to Scott, far from the mark. "He used to joke about being a Stalinist," Scott notes, "where we were a bunch of Trotskyists."

Powell instigated root and branch reforms, redressing what Green Gartside famously ridiculed as Rough Trade's "tyranny of structurelessness". Rough Trade would ultimately become a Workers Trust (The Tim Niblett Trust, named in memory of the Cartel's Nine Mile employee, who had died in a car crash). Out went the equal pay structure (£8,000 per annum for everyone, regardless of responsibilities) and in came, initially, a six-monthly profit share. 85% of the shares were given to employees; the remaining 15% split three ways between Scott, Travis and Travis's father. There was also a committee structure set in place. "What was going on inside the company was that we were trying to split it into separate companies," says Scott. "The sales of the record company at that time were so poor that we couldn't."

Certainly the dismantling of parity in terms of the all-for-one pay scheme caused some upset. "By that stage though," reasons Scott, "the scale of the operation had reached a point where meetings weren't four or five people sitting around the big table at the back of Kensington Park Road – it just all got more complicated. We had to move to a more structured and organised basis, it was the only way to go. The wage differential was a source of *endless* discussion, but in the end it was accepted." As he further points out, in the early days, he'd proposed that the equal pay scheme was extended to artists, so that any revenue earned after costs and the 50-50 split would go back into the communal pot. "That didn't go down very well!" he concedes.

Conventional business concepts such as upward reporting were established. Powell talked about 'The Model' (the means of conveying information up, down and sideways within a business) and introduced the American concept of 'The Critical Path'. The Critical Path turned out to be a project management technique invented in the 50s for the effective deployment and arming of nuclear submarines. Rough Trade's cherished counter-culture ethics had just slammed up against new age shite-speak mingled with clinical business logic. Rough Trade employees, to a man and woman, took the piss out of it remorselessly.

Or at least, that's how Powell has been represented. Yet Scott maintains that "The critical path thing was just a joke! It was never meant seriously at all. But I guess if people read about it, and take it literally... Richard Powell is a seriously misunderstood and misrepresented character in this story". To that end, Scott forwarded the following quote from Richard Buckminster Fuller 'explaining' the critical path model. "Conventional critical-path conceptioning is linear and self-under-informative. Only spherically expanding and contracting, spinning, polarly involuting and evolving orbital-system feedbacks are both comprehensively and incisively informative. Spherical-orbital critical-feedback circuits are pulsative, tidal, importing and exporting. Critical-path elements are not overlapping linear modules in a plane; they are systematically interspiraling complexes of omni-interrelevant regenerative feedback circuits."

"There," notes Richard Scott, "I think that describes what was going on pretty well."

Travis found developments unappealing. The antagonism between he and Richard Scott grew. Increasingly, the distribution arm of Rough Trade was starting to prove more profitable than the label. With huge hits from dance imprints Big Life (Yazz, Coldcut) and Rhythm King (S'Express and Bomb The Bass) as well as Mute (Depeche Mode, Yazoo and Erasure), Rough Trade Distribution (RTD) was now a serious business. Travis took this opportunity to reassess and play his part in making the label's prospects stronger too. To that end he decided to break with the company's legacy by trying to find an artist of potential longevity who would be tied in with the company's fortunes going forward. Had Mark E Smith not proved so implacably truculent, The Fall might have fit the bill. But then, when did they ever fit any bill.

The two likeliest candidates for a breakthrough success were Scritti Politti, who had recently adopted a post-modern contemporary soul sheen that was more appealing to the readership of *Smash Hits* rather than *Marxism Now*, and Aztec Camera, who'd thrown in their lot with Rough Trade following their move from Postcard. So desperate was Travis to have a hit with Scritti that meetings were held at Blenheim Crescent prior to the band's August 1982 appearance on *Top Of The Pops* about whether it was a good idea to buy Green Gartside a new jacket for the occasion. When Scritti moved on to Virgin, Travis was right to be concerned that the vultures might be circling for Aztec Camera, too. To that end Independent Distribution Services, or IDS, to all intents and purposes a Rough Trade Distribution competitor, and a company lacking any of Travis's egalitarian principles, was hired to try to get a decent chart return for 'Oblivious'. It should have worked – it is doubtful if Rough Trade has ever released a more commercially 'ripe' single. But it stalled at number 47 and almost inevitably, the Aztecs moved on to WEA. Questioned on the switch by *Alternatives To Valium* fanzine, Roddy Frame was succinct. "Well, they can't put records in the charts. They can't do much abroad. The one good thing about them was Geoff Travis, he's one of the best people in the music business. Apart from that they haven't really got much going for them. I don't see what they've got at Rough Trade that I haven't got now at WEA."

This unhappy pattern changed – at least for a while – when Andy Rourke and Johnny Marr personally dropped by to hand over a copy of a demo featuring The Smiths' 'Hand In Glove' on the advice of Richard Boon. "Initially I recommended they go to Simon Edwards in distribution." Boon recalls, "By then, Rough Trade were doing M+D deals, so they would do the manufacturing and distribution. I was just sharing the little bits of knowledge I'd acquired. That was part of the operating principle. So they went down to see Simon, who referred them to Geoff." It was the second trip by the deposition, and they had to wait until a busy Travis could free himself from other responsibilities. But by now he'd seen the band play at the Rock Garden and grasped their potential. On the Monday following that meeting he rang Marr to inform him he'd like to press the recording up as a single and offered them a one-off deal. "It was just thought that the label's resources might be better equipped to handle them rather than just doing manufacture and distribution," adds Boon. Though not immediately a hit single, 'Hand In Glove' helped make The Smiths highly newsworthy, especially when their leader's ability to generate contentious press copy emerged, and the majors were quick to volunteer more lucrative deals.

"I suppose it wasn't until the Smiths," says Travis, "that I realised, OK, this group is so good, it would be stupid to do one record. But my lessons had been taught – the two acts that taught me to think more about the future were Aztec Camera and Scritti Politti. Both of whom, I think it's fair to say, we got on fantastically well with. We had a brilliant relationship and had a great time making records with them. It was working. When Roddy [Frame] said, 'I've got an offer to do this, I think I'm going to go,' we said, 'Yeah, I think you should do it, because we haven't really got the resources to do it properly.' Green? The same thing. Green would tell you that Rough Trade was going down a musical path that he felt alienated from. Because he had 'discovered' black music – which I find hilarious. I knew a lot more about black music than he does, even now. But I love Green, and of course we're working together now, which I'm really pleased about. Also, he wanted to have a pop project, and that meant expensive production, expensive videos, etc, and we couldn't afford that. I didn't want to be in the position where a lack of finance meant that we would be holding someone back. But then when I saw what they went on to do, I realised probably we *could* have done that. And it wasn't always the fact that when people left they were meteorically successful. I think The Smiths was the first one where I realised it would be pretty foolish not to try to make this more successful. Also, we set up this structure with The Smiths where I felt there weren't any gaps in what we were doing. We employed London's sales team to help up have a better chart placing – not cheating or doing anything illegal – but competing on the same terms as everybody else. We were really professional. I felt really confident. We had a great plugger, we had the complete package."

"I ran the strike force for London Records," recalls Mike Heneghan, "which at the time was like an underground part of PolyGram. Roger Ames introduced us to Geoff. Roger had a lot of foresight – London at that time had quite a lot of the culture that the independents had – it was in a lot of ways more like an independent than a major. They were in the basement of the building. They were the underdogs, they didn't have big budgets. Even though it was inside a major, they had a bit of an ethos. And I think what Roger saw was that there was a lot of talent in the independent world, and there must have been some way that they could work together. And so Roger introduced me to Geoff and we started talking. We started helping them. The first record we worked on was The Smiths. Geoff and a lot of other independent label heads wanted the best for the bands. They didn't want to be falling down anywhere, such that a band would have been better off on a major. At that point, the chart was very influential, and a lot of major media was driven by the chart, getting on TV was driven by the chart. An independent label could build up a strong fan base, and if they wanted to expand it, they needed to have a chart presence. In order to do that, they needed to have some structure in the organisation of the planning around the band's availability to do the promotion, some planning around stock control. And, at the beginning, some of those elements at some labels were a bit unstructured. I'd go to Rough Trade and they'd send someone to the back room. 'How many boxes of that 12-inch have we got left?' And they'd send someone through and count them. It was helping with some of the organisation and planning." The hiring of a 'major label' plugger caused some furrowed brows within Rough Trade, and played no small part in the formation of trade body Umbrella [see chapter 12].

The Smiths signed with Rough Trade in July 1983, telling the press the decision "represents a conscious decision of preference" against the majors, one of whom had reportedly offered a six-figure cash advance. Later, Morrissey would confirm the reasons for their choice in interviews with his rapidly gathering press entourage. He told Dave McCullough of *Sounds* "what we want to achieve CAN be achieved on Rough Trade" and Frank Worrall of *Melody Maker* that "In the world of indies, Rough Trade are a major. We like Rough Trade and the people and they like us – that has to be the most important thing. And if people want to buy the records, Rough Trade will supply them." He elaborated on that prosaic description of their relationship in *Deadbeat* fanzine, back in the days when he still answered fanzine postal interviews: "We will stay with Rough Trade as long as things work. My overall loyalty is to myself, to The Smiths, and I protect Smith-interests regardless of cost or consequence."

But if The Smiths marked a new dawn for Rough Trade Records commercially, it also deepened the fissures that had opened up within the company. From this point Richard Scott's views become progressively more jaundiced. "Rough Trade, if it had been a better label, then things might have turned out differently. In the end it tried to emulate bits of Factory and 4AD and never quite succeeded. I think that there is an imbalance in people's view about what happened at Rough Trade. If you talk to people at Rough Trade, there is a strong view that Geoff used people. And that the Marxist backbone disappeared quite quickly when Geoff tried to move the label into central ground, with first Scritti Politti then The Smiths. Then the politics all became slightly confused. There were a lot of people doing a lot of things [at Rough Trade; which by 1982 had expanded from eight to 40 staff covering a booking agency, distribution, licensing and promotion] and I slightly resent the fact that Geoff puts himself forward as being the sole mover. There were an awful lot of people there. My only interest in trying to put the record straight is to try to recognise that fact. I have the view that Geoff built his position on the back of an awful lot of people."

The Smiths stumbled over their first album (the initial tracks recorded with Troy Tate, formerly of Teardrop Explodes, were considered too rudimentary and were ditched in favour of new sessions with John Porter, who had produced their Kid Jensen session). But their breakthrough was not long delayed. Travis, meanwhile, helped them broker a deal in the US with Seymour Stein at Sire Records.

Boon, who had been the link to Rough Trade initially, had by now arrived there to work as production manager. "The guy tied in with production was Bob Scotland, who was going to college to do botany." Boon recalls. "He's an academic now. I'd sent Geoff some Dislocation Dance demos, cos I couldn't do anything with them. Several months later, he got back to me, and said could he meet them? So they went to meet Geoff, and while they had their meeting, I hung out using the phones upstairs in the booking office. Afterwards Geoff came up and said, 'I think we're going to do something.'

I said, 'Why did it take you so long? He went, 'Oh, my office is chaos, blah blah, I could do with some help.' 'Well, I might be interested.' He was about to go to America for a couple of months. He asked if I would be interested in covering his office. I said yes. Only he didn't go in the end, and Bob was going to leave, so I moved sideways into production – organising the pressings, artwork, sleeves, labels. Juggling everything around and hoping they all arrived at the same time. It was fine for small things like Robert Wyatt, you knew what the market was. It was easy to deal with. When The Smiths began to chart it was completely a different thing – very stressful, in fact. Also, my future wife was in London, and we were getting very tired of this alternate weekend relationship commuting between Manchester and London. So it worked for me."

The success of The Smiths, alongside other Rough Trade distributed companies, forced another move, this time to Collier Street near King's Cross, some distance from the group's historical homeland. But Travis sensed ill omens in the giddy expansion plans. "When we moved to King's Cross, distribution was downstairs, we were on the floor upstairs. The tension and split between label and distribution came when lots of people came in to be middle managers and upper managers, and they hadn't been a part of any of those first few years. I just think they had a bad attitude. It got worse and worse, and I think there were a couple of individuals who poisoned it all and just were either jealous of the record company or didn't treat the record company with respect, or just thought we were being irresponsible, and that ruined it all."

"Richard Powell was brought in to tighten things up and bring some backbone into it, which he did," says Scott. Certainly, judged by conventional business logic, he was eminently successful in 'growing the business'. "And if the relationships at the top of the company had been maintained, he would have given the Cartel a structure where it could have competed very healthily," Scott continues. "When I last spoke to Geoff, we shared the view that once Rough Trade had grown beyond twelve people, all the original attitudes fell apart by default – it can't work. Political theories about middle management don't really apply. If you've got 40, 50 or 60 people working for you, you need people as go-betweens. There had to be some sort of structure. I contend that criticism of Richard for doing that is seriously misplaced. It would have worked if the 'old hands' hadn't stopped talking to each other. Geoff just became extremely difficult to deal with. He had an arrogance and a way with words that made him harder and harder to deal with. When it gets into that situation, people just become more extreme. Once you've started something, it becomes incredibly difficult to change the structure. The structure that we started out with wasn't capable of dealing with the scale of what it became."

Travis wasn't the only one who was unhappy. Often cited as one reason for The Fall's departure was Mark E Smith's growing displeasure at the attention lavished on a competing Mancunian band. Clearly one brusque, petulant Mancunian polymath is enough for any label at a time, though Travis maintains good relations with both to this day. "Morrissey, as we know, moans about everything," Travis recalls. "He was always – 'we were never on the radio'. They *were* on the radio. We actually won an award one year for best marketing campaign. It was very important that we did that properly. The Smiths obviously took Rough Trade to lots of new places, but we also took them there. I think it was a good relationship. Mark and I get on fine, too, I've got a great deal of respect for him. He's actually been very restrained in the things he's said about us. I think he knows we made a lot of good records together. Also, I produced *Grotesque* on my own, and that brings you close, when you do real work with someone." (The latter album recently topped a *Mojo* interactive poll on Rough Trade's greatest releases; The Smiths and Young Marble Giants filling out the podium)

Other highlights of Rough Trade's contemporaneous roster included The Go-Betweens, featuring Queensland songwriters Grant McLennan and Robert Forster. But they served as an example of how, even at the nation's most highly respected indie, relations were not always cordial. So suggests the man who first nurtured them, Keith Glass, who was also responsible for bringing The Birthday Party to the UK. "A small advance for the first album went totally to the band, to get to the UK, and then no statements – no money. Had me thinking it had sold really poorly. I later found Rough Trade contracted with the band for a second album, protecting the deal by holding on to any further royalties from the first. And, of course, the snivelling shits went along with it. So in effect I paid for some of the production of album number two without sharing in rights or receiving any further payment for my considerable investment. To compound the problem, Rough Trade then sold many copies of the first Go-Betweens album back to another Aussie label. For a supposed co-op company, Rough Trade lived up to their name. Geoff Travis may be exonerated being the artistic director and above such dealings, but Pete Walmsley is in the Dick Cheney category as far as I am concerned."

But while disputes – real or imagined – are inevitable in a franchise the size that Rough Trade had become, they are relatively rare. Asked to remember his time at Rough Trade, The Band Of Holy Joy's Johny Brown, usually such an effervescent observer, is stuck for words. "I love Geoff – ultimate admiration for him. He was immense towards – with – The Band Of Holy Joy. He's tireless, and still very much on the button. Sorry, I've nothing more perceptive to say – I'm unashamedly partisan." Several other artists provided similar testimony. Others, notably within the distribution network and the Cartel, have a different take. Notably that he was invariably artist-focused at the expense of some of his colleagues.

If Travis's shifting of Rough Trade's agenda to promote The Smiths to the mainstream caused ripples, his next move was more contentious still. In 1983 Travis was approached by Mike Alway, head of A&R at Cherry Red Records. Alway's relationship with the label's founder Iain McNay had begun to strain. "[Mike] came to see me one day," Travis recalls. "He said, 'Iain's driving me mad, he's not giving me any money, and I hate it. He's not appreciating me.' I said, 'What's the problem? What can I do to help, Mike?' He said, 'I want to start a label.' 'That sounds exciting. What do you want to do? I like what you do, let's do it, we're friends.' He said, 'OK, let's go to a major and start a label.' I was completely astounded, because I thought he meant starting an independent label. But then I thought, well, this is Mike's thing really, so if he wants to do that, we'll do that. So we went to see Rob Dickins, and five minutes later we had a label of our own."

Travis's connection to Dickins was well established. Back when he and Richard Scott had first mooted the idea of starting a publishing company, they'd consulted Dickins, then managing director of Warner Music Brothers Publishing House, for advice. Travis and Dickins had much in common – both huge Tim Buckley fans, Dickins was of a similar age, and had studied politics and sociology at university. Later, Travis had considered Dickins a safe pair of hands when he reluctantly let Aztec Camera go. By 1983 Dickins had become the head of WEA in the UK aged only 32. He made his intention to revive the flagging British arm of the major clear, and part of his strategy would be to 'get Travis'. He did so, but not before Travis had cautiously studied his options in relation to other potential suitors, including A&M, London and MCA. In the final analysis, Dickins was prepared to go a little bit further – in terms of the bottom line – to secure the deal.

Travis introduced the increasingly frustrated Alway to Dickins, who liked the idea of the label. The third party to be involved, at Alway's insistence, was Michel Duval of Belgium's Les Disques Du Crépuscule. Not least because Alway was desperate to commission Crépuscule art director Benoît

Hennebert. The principals were christened 'The Gang Of Three' in the *NME*. Titled Blanco y Negro, the label enjoyed immediate success with Everything But The Girl's *Eden*, poached from Cherry Red. A glorious future awaited. But for Alway at least, his dream grew weeds very quickly. The outcome of all this is discussed elsewhere (Chapter Ten), but for Travis's purposes, it had the effect of alienating him from his own company. Former friends judged this an embrace too close with the enemy, and the perceived concomitant rewards offered were the subject of envy. "When I found out what Geoff asked to be paid when he started Blanco," says Scott, "I was profoundly shocked. I could not believe I'd been so naive. It caused huge ructions at Rough Trade, because up till that point nobody had been allowed to do anything outside."

Blanco was undeniably a step down from the lofty idealism of old. But as Travis counters, "My attitude was it kept me sane and alive in a period when I might well have gone under." Additionally, both Scritti Politti and Aztec Camera had told him that, had the option of a Blanco y Negro style interface been available, they wouldn't have signed to their respective majors directly.

Blanco, in theory, had plenty to recommend it. It would prevent any talent drain of artists who had achieved as much as they thought they could with an independent. It would also mean Rough Trade not having to bet the farm on a single act, while allowing Travis the opportunity to work alongside artists as they grew. Conversely, the concession that artists 'needed' to graduate to a major label was in many ways insidious, and could equally be said to have helped double-glaze the indie-major 'glass ceiling' – an implicit abandonment of the 'anything is possible' DIY dream. Mute had already proved (Yazoo's *You And Me Both* sat atop the UK album charts as the Blanco plan formulated) that they could facilitate mainstream pop hits while maintaining a relationship with its artists. Yet Mute, via Daniel Miller, was an auteur label, Rough Trade a collective. To a large extent Travis's decision was predicated on the fact that Blanco would allow him to develop repertoire in a well-resourced environment where his decisions were not subject to committee.

"We sold millions of records with Everything But The Girl and Catatonia and Jesus & Mary Chain," Travis says now of Blanco, which lasted for more than two decades. "It was a very successful label for Warners. Honestly, in terms of a label attached to a major, it was a big, big success. It was renewed about five times. You don't get that unless you're being successful." Travis's other subsequent flirtations with the majors, sometimes overlooked in comparison to Blanco, include the short-lived mid-80s Chrysalis subsidiaries Big Star (run with Pete Lawton) and Blue Guitar (with Mayo Thompson).

One band who ended up on Rough Trade's books as a result of the Blanco situation were Microdisney, whose gentle tuneage contrasted starkly with singer Cathal Coughlan's caustic lyrics. They had come to the label through Garreth Ryan and also, more circuitously, Alway. "I first met Garreth in Dublin in 1981 or thereabouts," notes Coughlan. "His then-intimidating appearance belied a refined and generous disposition, but did accurately indicate that here was someone who had no truck with any kind of orthodoxy in musical culture." Ryan was one of so many lost souls who washed up at Rough Trade, in this case, staffing the distribution department. "Myself and Sean [O'Hagan] kept plugging away with various versions of Microdisney in Cork. Sean and Dave [Clifford; *Vox* magazine] used to take periodic trips to London, and would usually see Garreth, so when he decided to start Kabuki [Ryan's own Rough Trade-distributed label], he asked us for a record, which we were more than happy to provide." Both their singles became John Peel favourites, leading to their relocation to London in the middle of a July 1983 heat wave. "The idea at that time was that we'd either sign to Cherry Red or to Blanco y Negro. Mike Alway had become interested in working with us, after our hassling him postally for several years."

Microdisney recorded an album for Blanco "very fast, but under circumstances which were probably a bit too expansive for our capabilities and for the songs. Their parent company, Warners, didn't want it. The to-ing and fro-ing took ten months or so. Somewhere in there, Geoff Travis said that if it couldn't be released on Blanco, Rough Trade would do it. We took him up on this when things got impossible. The whole process was a bit of a mess. Rough Trade had to buy the first album from Blanco, or be in debt for it, not sure which. I don't recall getting any cash advances at that time, maybe a few hundred quid for some equipment, but we signed a small publishing deal which at least kept real starvation away, after the first horrible half-year was over. Still wasn't the penurious but fertile bohemia of popular perception, however, for us. When you're skint, you can think about money way too much."

"Rough Trade was still in Blenheim Crescent as the first album was set to come out," Coughlan continues. "The move to Collier St happened just as it was released. Blenheim Crescent was obviously far more colourful, in good and bad ways – the decayed grandeur of the building, the crazy people wandering off the Grove, and the many welcoming and interesting people who worked there. Sean and I did a few stints there packing Smiths 12-inches for Richard Boon, whom I revered as 'the New Hormones man' and quite a major wit, and whose job appeared to consist of managing the fallout from the whims of the fellow Mancunian whom he called 'Sod-Misery'. And we could console ourselves that we were, after all, on the same label as Robert Wyatt."

Frustrations, though, were growing. "A longer-term deal was mooted, but the fact that Geoff had merely inherited us made everything feel rather tenuous and second-hand. Most of our support at Rough Trade came from the warehouse floor, we thought. If you add too much alcohol and speed to this mix, it gets tediously combustible. We didn't keep the best of company. We still kept appearing on Peel, got a rhythm section and played shows. My various dysfunctions, my greeds, grudges and anaesthetics, didn't help anything. I was verbally unpleasant to a few people who had tried to help us. Eventually we began speaking to Geoff directly again, and figured out how to make *The Clock Comes Down The Stairs*. Flawed as it is, that was our coherent statement, and not many labels could have let us do it, given its gaucheness in the context of those times. In many ways, it seems stupid that we left Rough Trade after the album, but we had such debts and tax problems that we were really too scared to contemplate anything else. You can't argue with the kind of freedom we were given at Rough Trade, as we subsequently learned at the other end of Ladbroke Grove [when they moved on to Virgin]."

The Smiths were also displaying growing pains. By the advent of sessions for *The Queen Is Dead* at the end of 1985, there was little short of open warfare between the band members, while Morrissey's sniping at his label had become an almost obligatory act in any dealings with the press. EMI, Virgin and Warners made themselves known as potential suitors. In the event, Travis was forced to serve an injunction on them to prevent them recording for another label. As stalemate ensued, bass player Andy Rourke was temporarily suspended from the band due to his growing heroin addiction. Johnny Marr went so far as to try to burgle the master tapes from Jacobs Studios. And when *The Queen Is Dead* finally emerged, it contained the caustic 'Frankly Mr Shankly', in which Morrissey lampooned Travis and made his 'want away' feelings clear. "I want to leave, you will not miss me, I want to go down in musical history'. It also savagely disparaged Travis's 'bloody awful poetry' following a note he had the temerity to send the Moz in verse form.

The misery ended, if stockpiled grievances against the music industry ever could truly evaporate for Morrissey, when Smiths manager Matthew Sztumpf engineered a way out of the deal in July 1986. Had he not been able to do so, we can only imagine the venomous Smiths songs in which Travis might have been immortalised subsequently. The split was roundly greeted with dismay, coming in the same month that Stiff was forced to declare bankruptcy. "Though Rough Trade have been expecting to lose The Smiths for some time," ran a *Sounds* editorial, "it will still come as a body blow on the indie scene, as it would seem to confirm that the indies cannot compete with major labels once a band passes a certain level of success."

In the event a new contract was negotiated in which The Smiths would deliver one further album to Rough Trade before departing for EMI. The band recorded *Strangeways Here We Come* in Bath, wrapping the sessions in April 1987. Marr announced his intention to quit the following month, and the news was made official in August. After a superhuman tug of war, EMI had been sold a pup. Quizzed by Richard Boon in a post-break-up interview for *The Catalogue* in 1988, specifically about the symbolic break from independent to major, Morrissey was both taciturn and evasive. "Richard, I believe Rough Trade Japan is a lift in a small building. Is this true? Walk into any Japanese restaurant and you'll find whale penis on the menu. They call it Takeri. And you wonder why The Smiths never went to Japan! The last situation I expected to find myself in was... a solo artist on HMV!" But then times change. A recent advert for Morrissey's *Years Of Refusal* album announced: "CD, vinyl, download, strictly limited edition deluxe CD, DVD, limited edition features exclusive filmed interview ..." Eyebrow raised, one fires up 'Paint A Vulgar Picture' on I-Tunes and sighs.

Where did The Smiths' departure leave Rough Trade? Easterhouse [whose Ivor Perry had temporarily replaced Marr in Morrissey's frantic attempts to keep the Smiths afloat] were probably the most avowedly political band to record for any label in the 80s, such was the intensity of their disgust at recent developments in the Labour movement. The Woodentops were briefly a compulsive live act. But no-one on the roster would have a similar impact; at least not for a decade or so.

In 1987 Travis was joined at the head of Rough Trade Records by Jeanette Lee. Formerly an adjunct member of John Lydon's Public Image Limited, though never a musician, Lee had strong working class roots and was a seasoned veteran of the punk wars, alongside her then boyfriend Don Letts. Later she would marry Gareth Sager of The Pop Group, meaning she was well acquainted with the counter culture cologne that permeated Rough Trade. The invitation to join Travis had come, with absolutely no prior warning, through mutual friend Roger Trilling, while Lee was pregnant with her first child. She declined and concentrated on motherhood, until they met again at a friend's birthday party and Travis repeated his offer. Eventually it was accepted, leading to a 50-50 split in the label's ownership and A&R function that has continued successfully for over 20 years. It was immediately cemented by the successful signing of The Sundays. It should have proved another boom period for Rough Trade; but developments elsewhere precluded that when Rough Trade distribution collapsed in 1991 [see chapter 12].

Travis was devastated. Keen to do all he could to repay what he considered friends rather than business acquaintances, Travis threw the Rough Trade label into the pot. As a now separate business, he was under no compunction to do so. "In a way, I was very generous by saying, OK, I've moved to the label now, and now I'm on the board, and you do distribution, I won't interfere. And I don't expect to be interfered with. And I also invested loads of my own money in doing projects. The thing is, we were making money. We always made money. Right up until the point where the whole thing collapsed, we had the Sundays in the Top Ten, Carter [USM] in the Top Ten. We were selling records. It was a terrible, horrible two years for me, where all these characters that caused the demise of Rough Trade just ran away and disappeared. And I picked up the pieces. Fortunately people like Daniel [Miller] and the rest of the independent world were just absolutely incredible in rallying round and doing all they could to help. That's something I'll always be grateful for. On the other hand, I lost the catalogue of my label, and was left with absolutely nothing." He pauses before concluding with a thoughtful, but no doubt painfully accurate summary, "Which was a bit of a shame!" At least one artist he worked with recalls that Travis retrieved his masters and handed them over directly for fear the tapes would be unfairly treated as collateral. But he couldn't do that for everyone. He was one man, albeit with some sympathetic allies, and he was forced to endure the slow death of everything he had built in front of his eyes.

He and Jeanette Lee would soon resurrect the imprint, and continued to release music by artists including Tom Verlaine, Robert Wyatt, Ultramarine and Shelleyan Orphan. One Little Indian acquired the label and invited Travis and Lee to run it in 1993, but the relationship never gelled. The same could be said for a further incarnation of the label, Trade 2, through Island Records, which lasted just two years, working principally with Ashley Wales'

Spring Heel Jack project and Tiger. "It didn't work out," Travis concludes, "and they were just kind of interim things, whilst we were trying to get our focus back." In the meantime, however, Travis and Lee had formed their own management company, clients including Pulp, Spiritualized and Bernard Butler. In 1999 they were able to buy back the Rough Trade name from One Little Indian, who had allowed the label to fall into a state of neglect under their watch.

Almost immediately, as though the very act of reclaiming its birthright was of itself rejuvenating, Travis's A&R sensibilities proved themselves to be in rude health. With financial assistance from Sanctuary, they were able to sign New Yorkers The Strokes and saw them feted by the UK press as spearheads of the 'new garage threat'. Within a further six months the home-grown rock 'n' roll scandal-engine (though it also possessed, admittedly, a stellar songwriting base) that was The Libertines had also committed to Rough Trade.

The label has grown in strength ever since, with a roster now encompassing Arcade Fire, Sufjan Stevens, Belle & Sebastian, British Sea Power and Anthony & The Johnsons. There was one further twist in the tale when Sanctuary itself collapsed. It probably came as a relief. There were awful similarities to Rough Trade Distribution in the way Sanctuary had rapidly expanded and, on the hyperbole of 'market prospects' as a fully floated company, had bitten off way more than it could chew. Sanctuary's slow, inevitable decline had begun in 2000. Travis and Lee, working extremely successfully by anyone's standards, were dragged down by the uncertainty. "We need a white knight to ride in and rescue us," Travis would tell Dave Sinclair of *The Independent* in September 2006. It would take just ten months for one to gallop into view.

Since July 2007 the label has become a joint venture with old friends Beggars Banquet. It's proved a natural fit – the mutual respect in which Martin Mills and Geoff Travis hold each other is self-evident – allowing Rough Trade to become as stable as it has been for at least two decades. "Martin has really rescued Rough Trade," says Travis. "I think we'd have always been doing our thing. But certainly we needed a partner. And it's great to finally find one who understands what we do. He's a very important part of what we do now. Rough Trade is me and Jeanette. But he's become the third part of that partnership. And Martin is more business orientated than I am, because that's his responsibility – but he loves music. But he's not in the least interfering. He says if you believe in it, then that's all I need to know. It's a bit like Arsene Wenger – my chairman believes in me! It's nice to have that! We've proved we know what we're doing. The interesting thing is, it doesn't matter what you've done, it's always what you do next. That old cliché is really true."

Travis's enthusiasm for what he is engaged in right now suggests he is enjoying himself as much as he was prior to the first of the ructions that hit Rough Trade in 1982. He remains, while graciously tolerant of discussing his past, fixated on the future. He is not shy of expressing that forward-facing mantra in words. As I am about to leave his Golborne Road premises, immediately handshakes are completed, he has logged back on to his computer. Gladly, at least behind the scenes, this is not an age-defined industry. "I don't think so, not unless you go deaf," he says. "Or they won't let you in the gig any more because you're liable to pee on the floor from infirmity."

## Chapter Six

## Echoes In A Shallow Bay

## Beggars Banquet and 4AD Records

The origins of Beggars Banquet can be traced to the late 60s mobile disco scene, when Martin Mills was running Giant Elf with a friend, before merging it with a competitor. "Giant Elf was a disastrous name for a mobile disco that my then partner and I started off," admits Mills. "It was fun going around and playing at parties and so on. But it was a very unfortunate name. And some friends who were running a similar mobile disco to ours in Oxford called Beggars Banquet [from the 1968 Rolling Stones album] wanted a London base. So we kind of merged and adopted their name – because it was a lot better than our name! It was just fun. It was being involved with music at a time when I was doing work that was nothing involved with music."

At the time Mills, a graduate in Philosophy, Politics and Economics from Oriel College in Oxford, was working at the Office of Population, Census and Surveys. His vigil was on reforms to abortion law. "For a long time [music] was just a hobby. When I left university I wrote to every record company asking if I could sweep the floor – and no-one answered. So I would have loved to have been involved in music, and doing a mobile disco was a way of doing something that made a bit of money and was fun."

Eventually, he joined the staff of the Shepherd's Bush branch of Record & Tape Exchange. "My work on the Abortion Law had finished. I wrote a government white paper, basically. I was one of the people behind the scenes. So I asked myself what I wanted to do, and I thought, let's get a job at the Record & Tape Exchange; that sounds like fun. They paid a lot of money for four days a week." He had the musical knowledge, but found them also very 'picky' about the 'the kind of degree you had'. "And you used to have a chronometer so that you could time yourself to the split second in terms of pricing up second hand records. You needed a broad musical knowledge, but then they didn't price according to what the record was – they priced only on quantity and condition. Every two weeks, you marked the price down, so the price dropped automatically."

By 1974, together with partner Nick Austin, he'd set up his own record store, retaining the disco's name, expanding on the R&T Exchange model. "The idea was to offer people a choice of new records versus second hand records at different prices. It was a great idea." The first branch was opened at 8

Hogarth Road in Earl's Court. "We had six stores at one point, over a period of about five years. It was funded by the success of the first one. The first three were Earl's Court, Fulham and Ealing."

By 1975 they'd begun promoting 'off the wall' concerts. Initially they managed a major coup by hosting Tangerine Dream at the Royal Albert Hall, followed by acts such as The Crusaders, Southside Johnny and Dory Previn – facilitating, they felt, a market that was being otherwise ignored on the London scene. "They had huge audiences out there that no-one was catering for," says Mills. "It sounds incredibly middle of the road now looking back – but it wasn't then. They were quite left field artists then." Mike Stone, meanwhile, had now joined the Beggars retail team. "I remember the Southside Johnny & The Astbury Dukes gig," he recalls. "Ronnie Spector actually appeared on stage, doing 'Be My Baby' with the Dukes. That was great. The Crusaders was also a bit of a coup – it upset a few promoters, because we weren't known for that – and they couldn't understand where we came from to get a band like that. I also remember the Tangerine Dream show at the Royal Albert Hall, and carrying these massive computer things in from Artic lorries, and they did this extended improvisation on the night. We got a pretty big house for that."

Stone had joined the group after moving down to London from Leeds aged 16. "I bluffed my way into the whole business. I remember sleeping under Cleopatra's Needle on the first night with my mate; we couldn't find anywhere to live. I was born in Folkestone and my father was in the army, and we traveled a lot, typical army kid. Didn't settle down, so the education suffered. I moved to London and worked for the *Evening Standard* doing copy chasing in the adverts department. Eventually I thought, this isn't for me – I looked at the people in the office and didn't want to end up with a gold watch after 40 years. I was always interested in music so I started working as a DJ with a mobile disco. When I left the *Evening Standard*, the manager thought I was mad. I did all kinds of things, I had a transit van and a company called Quick Van. The first day I got the van, I got it taxed at the Embankment, and coming out I smashed it straight into the railings. The whole front wing concertina'd. That was before our first job! I had to pay for the railing too! So I got into DJing and we did quite well at weddings and pubs, like the Chelsea Drugstore down the King's Road. I did odd jobs in supermarkets, you name it. Then I was living in Hogarth Road in Earl's Court. Walking down the road, I saw these people building a shop. It looked like it was going to be a record shop. I just walked in and said, 'Do you need any staff?' Martin was there, and he asked me what I did. I said I DJ, and I know a bit about music. He said he could do with someone who knew about disco music. And that's how I wangled my way in. I think I was actually the second person that Beggars employed, after their friend Steve Webbon. I started work at Earl's Court. Then I went over to Fulham, to North End Road, with Steve. He managed that shop. He then left that shop and I ended up managing it. We opened up a rehearsal room there, and that's how it all started."

Punk's arrival was signaled to Beggars by the changing record-buying habits of their customers, so they started stocking more punk releases and promoting punk gigs. Specifically, their once album-orientated market disappeared as a younger demographic renewed interest in the 45rpm single. Beggars responded, Mills noting this period as both "a sea change" and "incredibly exciting". "At that time, we didn't even stock singles. Singles were Mud and Sweet, and stuff like that. And then probably around '76, the Bizarre [aka Marc Zermati's Skydog enterprise] van started calling on us. So we suddenly started stocking The Ramones and the first Talking Heads single, probably. And then Nick Lowe came out on Stiff. We started to apply that to our concert promoting. At the time we were promoting in places like the Albert Hall – when punk happened no-one wanted to go to those venues any more – it was completely antithetic to everything that was happening. So the fact that we were stocking the Nick Lowe and Damned singles meant we started looking at promoting shows. We did one with the Damned, Graham Parker – punk in the broader sense! We were asked if we could do a John Cale show as well. But what we were doing didn't really work at a club level, it only worked on a theatre level – and theatres were just not what you did any more."

The record label was founded principally at the nagging instigation of Stone. The Lurkers had been rehearsing in the Fulham shop's basement, alongside other aspirants such as Generation X, the original Ultravox!, Dave Edmunds, Graham Parker, Nick Lowe and others. "That was the only shop with a basement," adds Mills, "well, there was a basement in Earl's Court, but we had a quadraphonic record centre in there for a while. No, it was all credit to Mike Stone. He convinced us to use the basement as a rehearsal room. He got involved with The Lurkers, and then he got us involved."

Stone remembers "Ultravox! going down there with that big board with pegs in it. I asked what it was – it really was like a prehistoric synth. It was around the period that they brought out *Systems Of Romance*, which was the album that really influenced Gary Numan. News about the rehearsal rooms got out by word of mouth, and these people used to turn up. I remember Graham Parker rehearsing down there before a show, and he came up and asked me for a copy of 'Hold Back The Night' by the Trammps, and they ended up covering that."

His initial reaction to The Lurkers was lukewarm. "They turned up one day and I listened to it from outside the door. You couldn't avoid it really! People were playing while we worked upstairs. I thought, what a bloody racket. I was brought up on early funk, Motown, The Who, Hendrix, Free. Going right back to Buddy Holly. So listening to The Lurkers – complete and utter racket. But the one thing I liked was the freshness and the energy. I thought, this is all right, actually. I just got talking to them. [Guitarist] Pete Stride was there. I asked him, 'How are you getting on? How do you get gigs?' He went, 'Well, we could do with a manager, really.' I said, 'Can't you find one?' He turned round and pointed at me and said, 'Why don't you manage us?' I went, 'What? Oh, OK. I'll have a go, I'll ring round and get a few gigs.' That's how the collaboration with The Lurkers started, and also the beginning of Beggars Banquet."

Lurkers drummer Manic Esso has a forthright view on where any credit should go: "Beggars owned a few shops and did the student record exchange thing. Having the rehearsal room downstairs at the Fulham shop brought them into contact with people wanting to play live music, but the owners Nick and Martin had no plans to get involved in any way to manage anybody, let alone start a record label. That whole thing was brought about by Mick Stone. He had his ear to the ground and knew what was going on. Remember, Mick was an old mod, having a love for fast three-minute songs, i.e. The Who etc, and the feel that goes with it, whilst Nick and Martin were from the boring brigade."

The gestation of the record label took some time. "I had gone on about starting a record label quite a bit with Martin and Nick," Stone remembers. "And funnily enough, they did have this strange thing they were going to do – an album of music that featured on adverts. It never happened, possibly thank God! I even remember the artwork they drew up, and I'm sure it was a Campbell's soup tin. They didn't take it any further. In the meantime I'm at North End Road, and all this independent record thing is taking off, and anything in a picture sleeve sold. It was all the indies that were doing that. I really loved those bands, coming out the woodwork. So I said to Martin, why don't we do an independent label? So it wasn't a great innovative idea. I just picked up on something and said, why don't we do it? I talked about it till I was blue in the face. Eventually Nick came down with me to see The Lurkers at the Roxy. And they put on a pretty reasonable performance, and that was it." Prior to this, Stone had also tried to get Decca to sign the Stranglers after he'd seen them at the Nashville Rooms. "In my naivete, here I am – a record shop assistant trying to get a major label interested in a punk band!"

Mills and Austin tried to get The Lurkers a record deal, though Stone had no part in that. They got nowhere – giving the lie to the oft-repeated observation that the majors were signing anything that moved in the period. "By the time we started managing them," explains Mills, "every major label – they weren't even called majors in those days, just labels, because there weren't any independents – every label already had a punk band. And most of them had one as an insurance policy, just in case. Virgin was a bit different. The Clash were at Columbia, The Jam at Polydor. And by the time we came round with The Lurkers, everyone already had one. We tried everyone!"

Instead, they bowed to Stone's overtures and elected to proceed themselves. Released in August 1977, the 'Free Admission' single paired 'Shadow' with 'Love Story'. It was a short, sharp coda to the ongoing punk revolution, slated by Charles Shaar Murray in the *NME* while *Sounds* dismissed it as being 'pretty vacant'. On the upside, *Record Mirror* made it single of the week, while *Chainsaw* fanzine observed that it made "the Ramones sound as complicated as Yes." In keeping with the sly rhetoric of catalogue numbers fashioned before them by Stiff's BUY prefixes, it was released as BEG 1. It came out almost exactly a year after Nick Lowe's Stiff debut. Initially, distribution was handled by the distinctly 'old school' President. Had Stiff set the template? "I've never really thought of it as following their example," thinks Mills. "In retrospect, it looks like that, and it was definitely us, Stiff and Chiswick at around the same time or a few months apart. I guess we probably all saw the same opportunities at the same time. But I guess Stiff were leaders of the market at that point. And they did it with tons of style and character. But they weren't particularly punk. But then, we weren't particularly punk either."

A second Lurkers single, 'Freak Show', followed in November, by which time they'd also assembled a compilation LP highlighting the recent independent labels boom. *Streets* (BEGA 1) contained licensed material including The Members and a large Mancunian contingent comprising Slaughter And the Dogs, The Drones and John Cooper Clarke. It was followed by The Lurkers' debut album *Fulham Fallout*, which reached the Top 60, sandwiched between two Top 50 singles ('Ain't Got A Clue' and 'I Don't Need To Tell Her').

The label was thus initially a broadly successful venture, but Beggars were unable to follow up with another breakthrough act as The Lurkers began their commercial slide. None of their other signings, including The Doll and Johnny G, were able to capitalise. "The bands I was responsible for were The Lurkers, Merton Parkas and the Carpettes," says Stone, "who were fantastic, but they just didn't do it. Image? Time? Name? The latter possibly. But what Beggars Banquet needed was turnover." Breathing space came from an unlikely source. Ivor Biggun's 'The Winker's Song', a joyful ode to onanism, caught the imagination of the pubescent playground. "Yeah, that made us a ton of money," laughs Mills, "thank you Ivor! That record sold a ton."

A more viable act was finally discovered after Tubeway Army's Paul Gardiner came into Beggars' Ealing branch to dispose of a few unwanted albums, and used the opportunity to pass on a demo of a song called 'That's Too Bad'. Mike Stone witnessed a subsequent meeting with the band's *de facto* leader: "I remember Gary Webb walking into Earl's Court when I was there. Nick invited him downstairs, and by the time he'd walked back upstairs, he'd signed him."

A remixed version of 'That's Too Bad' became Tubeway Army's debut single on 17 February 1978. Webb (or 'Valerian' on the sleeve, before later adopting the billing Gary Numan) had for some time been a slightly uncomfortable presence on the periphery of the punk scene. He'd started out with Vortex regulars Mean Street, but his interest was much more in electronics and Bowie than three-chord bluster. Yet while he was a clear talent, initial success for Tubeway Army was fleeting, 'That's Too Bad' earned coruscating reviews across the board ("Turkey" noted *Sounds*, "Feeble" said the *NME*, "Mundane" stated *Record Mirror*, "sub-Bowie" judged *Melody Maker*). One can easily see where Numan's terse relationship with journalists, famously recounted on a later Beggars single 'I Die, You Die', began.

"Ivor Biggun's single was paying the bills, to be honest," admits Mills, "while we were investing in The Doll. We definitely thought Gary was a huge talent – but I think Gary always felt that we thought The Doll was more commercial than he was – and I guess initially he was probably right. Gary's potential unveiled itself more gradually." In truth, Beggars was suffering and near bankruptcy. A distribution deal with Island fell through when that company fell into difficulties and had to negotiate a bailout with EMI, leaving Beggars with no room at the inn. Eventually WEA stepped in with a cheque for £100,000 that helped keep both the label and the shops afloat. The cash infusion allowed them to pay off a growing army of creditors, with no 'breakthrough' on the horizon. "I'm not sure we even knew what the concept of breaking through meant, to be honest," says Mills. "It was very much one foot after another. I think The Doll was what we perceived at that point as our next one that would sell."

How near to closure did Beggars get? "We were pretty much on our knees," Mills admits. "We were funding it all out of the cash from the shops, and there came a point where we were bouncing salary cheques, so it was pretty tense. The credit for the Warners deal is due to a guy called John Cooper, who was introduced to us as a consultant by our accountants, who used to run Arista of all places, and he was well connected. And he got us in to see Dave Dee at Warners. And thanks, I think, to Mike Heap, who was the sales and marketing guy at Warners, they decided to invest in us. It kind of fitted there with what they were trying to do at that time – they had a load of licensed labels, and they were active in acquisitions. And we were one of many labels they were working with." Nevertheless, £100,000 was a fairly substantial investment in an unproven company, especially as they weren't taking any stake in the company itself – just a one-year advance on licensing. "No, we couldn't believe it!" laughs Mills. "I can't remember if we had a party afterwards – we should have!"

"They were really struggling," remembers Stone. "They didn't tell me everything, but rumours go around the staff. I think it put the shits more up Martin and Nick than us though, to be honest. But they started to do quite well with Gary and things started to happen. I left Beggars Banquet and the week I moved to Stoke-On-Trent, Gary Numan went to number one! I'd met a girl from there – it changes your thoughts! We were both a bit fed up of London, so we moved up there with the intention of starting a record shop."

The transformation of Beggars' fortunes was completed by the runaway success of Tubeway Army's 'Are Friends Electric?' in May 1979, one of the unlikeliest hit records ever – over five minutes in length, featuring no recognisable tune as such, and spoken lyrics. Themed ostensibly on Philip K Dick's *Do Androids Dream Of Electric Sheep* (later the inspiration for the film *Blade Runner*), some of the lines were inspired by Webb's friendship with Beggars staff member Su Wathan (later said to have also inspired the bitter 'I'm An Agent' on *Telekon*). "She was a close friend of Gary's," says Mills. "No-one ever knew what the lyrics meant in 'Are Friends Electric?' But there was that line, 'About little deals and issues and things that I just don't understand.' And the 'issues' was actually 'SU's – that referred to Su."

The single rose to number one, followed there by an accompanying album, *Replicas*. Numan's subsequent solo album, *The Pleasure Principle*, also topped the album charts. In 1979 alone Numan gave Beggars an unprecedented two number one albums and two number one singles. It was a dramatic upswing in Numan's fortunes – Tubeway Army's original self-titled August 1978 album and a trio of singles had all flopped. Warners' money had allowed Beggars the luxury to afford Numan a decent budget to record *Replicas* at the 16-track Gooseberry Studios in Soho. "We'd done the Warners deal in November 1978," remembers Mills, "so there would have been more money. By more money, we're talking about six grand rather than three." Could that not have made a difference, though, to an artist who was feverishly obsessed with new technology and harnessing the latest production methods? "Well," Mills continues, "when Gary bought his first synth, a Moog, we had to buy it on hire purchase. When he'd exhausted that after a few minutes, he wanted the latest one, and it was the same thing again. So for a long time we had these odd little £25 monthly payments going through. At the end of the first year, Tubeway Army had pretty much recouped that advance on their own by having enormous success. And by the end of '79, we had three Gary Numan albums, including Tubeway Army, in the Top 20. Three new albums, not catalogue!"

In the end, Warners too recouped on what might initially have seemed an unduly generous offer. "Oh, yeah!" says Mills. "It was a great deal for them. They gambled and they gambled well." Numan's chart success continued with top ten singles in 'Complex' (November 1979), 'We Are Glass' (May 1980) and 'I Die, You Die' (August 1980), preceding a third successive number one album, *Telekon*, in September 1980. Thereafter the hits faded away, though Numan always kept a dedicated fanbase. In any case, the aforementioned releases had netted him a personal fortune estimated at just under £5 million.

Numan's breakthrough utterly eclipsed the rest of an under-performing roster. Ivo Watts-Russell was by now overseeing the whole retail operation, which amounted to five shops, and was based upstairs at the Beggars offices in Hogarth Road. Peter Kent ran the shop downstairs. "I was born on a farm in the country in Northamptonshire," says Watts-Russell. "To paraphrase John Lennon, the first thing that made sense to me was rock 'n' roll. Jimi Hendrix, literally, on *Top Of The Pops*, changed my life. I was 12 years old, and I didn't really know what it was, but I knew it was exciting. And then John Peel effectively became my professor. And then getting away from there as fast as possible to get down to London to be near music, getting a job in a record shop. I just wanted to be around music. If you've ever worked in a record shop – after a year or so, you have to be interested, and you have to explore. Within six months of moving to London, I was lucky enough to work at the Musicland shop in Ealing where the manager, Mike Smith, exposed me to things like Terry Riley, John Cale's *Paris 1919*, the Pure Prairie League records, which to me are still the only true country rock records. I was getting excited by pedal steel guitar! And Gram Parsons and Emmylou Harris – absolutely, in love with that voice – shivers down the spine." Mike Stone remembers Ivo's advocacy of classic 60s west-coast rock and country. "He had a vast knowledge of all those bands; the Byrds, Tim Buckley, Emmylou Harris, Flying Burrito Brothers, that was definitely his bag. That seemed to be all he'd play on the stereo at Beggars."

"So, hungry and enthusiastic and interested in music," Watts-Russell continues, "one starts to explore. So when the thing called punk came along, in terms of me needing to have the table swept clean, and a different attitude – I wasn't looking for music. There was plenty of music around, and plenty of obscure music to find. And what really inspired me far more than punk itself was 'Little Johnny Jewel' on Ork and Pere Ubu. Those were the first signs of – what is this? Really, punk in England was gobbled up by the majors. Extraordinarily so. Ninety-nine per cent of it was just taken by the majors, because there weren't labels and a system to deal with it independently. And it was the onslaught of music that was inspired by the attitude of punk and the journalism and the change of fashion of the time – a system to take care of that HAD to be created. It obviously had to be created outside of the mainstream major record companies, because they were completely clueless. I think it's fantastic when something is generated out of necessity. People talk about reggae having to be played at the punk clubs because there wasn't any punk music. What else was considered outlaw music? You can't get much more interesting and inspiring and fucked up than good dub singles. Much in the same way, the music just kept on coming, and studios cropped up everywhere where people could make records cheaply. Therefore an outlet was needed."

Between them, Watts-Russell and Kent became Beggars' unofficial A&R antennae. They were the first point of contact with bands shopping demos to the store, and would make recommendations to Mills and Austin. After they became enthused by a cassette handed in by a band called Modern English, it was suggested that they take the concept further and they were offered the money to start their own label.

"I'd left and gone to America for three months," remembers Watts-Russell, "and I came back to England and they gave me my job back. But Mike Stone had a rehearsal room at the shop at North End Road, and these people were making a noise in the basement that he enjoyed, and so I guess he took them to Martin and Nick and that's how the label started. Yeah, it was a similar thing, at Earl's Court, this little shop, quadraphonic department in the basement, and upstairs there were a couple of little rooms, which became known as the record company. Myself and Peter would be the people standing behind the counter in the shop when people came in to deliver a tape inspired by – I dunno, Ivor Biggun? Or Tubeway Army, to be kind! People were inspired by that. So what do you do? You're standing behind a counter, someone offers you a tape. You listen to it. The one I remember most clearly was Modern English. Their first batch of demos were excellent. I remember both me and Peter saying to Martin and Nick – I threatened to walk out the door if Nick signed another Ivor Biggun! He's a lovely man, that Ivor B. Really nice person and music fan who would always be in all the Beggars shops, hunting for obscure 7-inch singles. But his music was truly silly and a lot of BB releases were, frankly, embarrassing. Perhaps that served as inspiration for Peter and I to do something quite different."

"One of the reasons we started 4AD and one of the reasons we struggled to find an identity," says Mills, "is that Gary's success was so enormous, that it kind of swung the other way. Gary Numan and Beggars Banquet were seen as being completely interchangeable. Gary's later albums we felt less attached to than the first ones, and we wanted to do our own musical things. So it was a struggle for Beggars Banquet to emerge from Gary Numan's shadow, not withstanding the fact that, had it not been for Gary, we wouldn't be in business today."

"I think at that point we probably were struggling for an identity," he continues. "That's partly because my partner and myself had different musical tastes. Nick's were more commercial than mine, he was very much the Merton Parkas guy, and I was very much the Gary Numan guy. Gary never got on with Nick. So there was quite a split. We were perceived as a label that started in punk, but we were a rag bag of styles initially." That's a criticism that could also be levelled at Stiff's roster. "Stiff kind of imposed their label identity on their artists, though, which we never did," says Mills. "And I suppose since then the ethos of the label is that it would be determined by the identity of the artists, and that has grown in a much more organic way over the years. At the outset it was always a bit of an odd connection. And it probably wasn't until Bauhaus transferred from 4AD, and then we had the likes of Birthday Party on 4AD and Southern Death Cult and so on – that [an identity for] Beggars Banquet started emerging. And it took five years, really, for that to emerge."

Ambitiously, Watts-Russell and Kent decided to release four records simultaneously to inaugurate their new 'feeder' label. "I was inspired by Factory definitely," says Watts-Russell. "I was inspired by the fact that if something from 1977 onwards came out on an independent label; it deserved to be listened to. It could be on Fresh or a label that only did one single – to hear Glaxo Babies, to hear Family Fodder or Modern Eon before they were China Crisis – it was all so exciting. I'd started a conversation with Martin Atkins [ex-Public Image]. I'd actually started the idea of doing something myself [with Atkins' Brian Brain project]. But I didn't have any money or even knew how to do it – but I was talking to Martin and his producer John Madden about putting out a single. Maybe Martin and Nick got wind of it? I don't know. But around that time they came to me and Peter and said, you keep telling us to sign these things, why don't you do it and start a label. And we had a budget of £2,000 to begin with. And without even really talking about it, me and Peter really wanted to make an impression. So we started with the four singles." The initial proviso was that any success they had would see the artists transfer to the 'big brother' imprint. Kent came up with the name Axis Records.

It was a troubled birth – the records came back from the printers in shoddy form, with the covers compromised and the vinyl suffering noticeably poor pressing quality. On top of which the press release they sent to the trade publication *Music Week* announcing the investiture of Axis was met with a phone call from an established label of the same name. A hasty deal was struck whereby they could sell off the remaining stock they'd had pressed, on the understanding that they then rename the company. Short of time, they chose 4AD – inspired by a promotional flyer for the original Axis label where the designer had added the legend '1980 – Forward'. "I think we must have been inspired by Factory," ponders Watts –Russell. "I mean, the mere fact that we called the label Axis. Thank God there was another label with that name. We didn't know what we were doing at all, but thank goodness that got changed."

The four Axis singles hardly flatter the label's legacy. Only Northampton art rockers Bauhaus's 'Dark Entries' [who had gravitated to the label from Small Wonder] would have a significant impact. The Fast Set's 'Junction One' was the work of David Knight, a later collaborator with The Shock Headed Peters,

Danielle Dax and Cherry Red's Five Or Six. But neither their effort nor the Bearz' 'She's My Girl' (whose David Lord would later work with Tori Amos), nor Shox's 'No Turning Back' (whose Jacqui Brookes would re-emerge, briefly, on Beggars as a solo artist), excited much interest. "Pretty clueless, really!" admits Watts-Russell. "It was like, we're going to start a label, he's pretty good, I like his ideas, someone's got some studio time we can use for nothing, and he's going to do a T-Rex cover – that sounds good! The first singles we had pressed up, and at least for a year after that, you'd stick em in the back of your car, drive to the Rough Trade shop, they'd have a listen and say, we'll take 200 of this, 200 of that – and they'd write you a cheque! That was so important. Their ability to pay cash up front enabled the individual, person, or label or artist, to get an income to be able to consider funding the next release."

As 4AD established itself during 1980, there would be two further singles and also debut album *In The Flat Field* before Bauhaus transferred to the main Beggars imprint. In the interim there were singles by the likes of Rema Rema, In Camera, Bruce Gilbert and Graham Lewis of Wire and, belatedly, Modern English. "No offence intended towards Bauhaus at all – they were probably solely responsible for our solvency in that first year," says Watts-Russell. "But in some ways, I always think 4AD started with the Rema Rema EP. It was the first record to appear on that label – though we repressed 'Dark Entries' on 4AD. Pre, the Charisma label, had paid for the EP but weren't going to put it out, because one song contained the line 'And you fuck just like Jesus Christ'. And ironically we didn't put that track on the EP because Rema Rema didn't want it included. But when I heard those songs and met them, that's when I realised this was real and serious. I felt it was as good as anything that was coming out at the time. Those people, those individuals, they were extraordinary. Mark Cox is still my closest friend. To this day they're exactly the same – that true attitude that came from punk." They also shared his convictions about quality and value. "I responded more to the attitude of – a single is two good songs, an album is ten or 14 good songs – it's not a-sides and b-sides and flogging albums made up of three singles and some bad tracks. That was a no-brainer. I love and respect music, and respect those that respect their public. Those principles from the early days are still ideals I hold today."

Rema Rema had split up by the time they contacted Watts-Russell. "That's a fairly important thing. Nick and Martin had said, 'Here we are, start a label', and they presented us with contracts that they'd used to sign artists to Beggars. I was sitting with Nick for the first time, watching him negotiate a lifelong publishing deal with these writers – Rema Rema – who were a group that were never going to write again. It was a stuck in the mill thing: this is the contract we use, we'll make it work for them. It was seeing that, and seeing Peter's enthusiasm and ambition, seeing how rapidly that grew. And also starting to realise one could work with something of the calibre of that EP. There was no way I wanted it to be a stepping stone to Beggars Banquet, which was part of Warners as far as I was concerned. I love Martin – don't ever, ever let anything come across other than my love and respect and gratitude towards that man – but that sowed the seeds for what happened."

The label's early roster remained slightly lopsided, however. "Modern English was something both Peter and I had liked," explains Watts-Russell. "In Camera was Peter more than I. Graham and Bruce, that thing was both of us, maybe more me, because I developed a relationship with them. The The was totally me. The *Presage(s)* thing was a compilation that was bits and pieces of all of us. The fact that [novelty track] 'Hunk Of A Punk' was on there shows a huge separation between me and Peter. Pete thought it was funny, I just thought it was fucking stupid. The Birthday Party was me. Mass was three members of Rema Rema, that was natural for both of us, because we'd become very fond of them as people. Dance Chapter was both of us. I clearly remember being upstairs, a day after Ian Curtis had died, or very close to that day. I was upstairs and Peter buzzed up. 'You know how we were talking about how someone was going to walk in and fill Joy Division's shoes?' 'Yeah.' 'I think they've just walked in!' Lovely as they were, I don't think that was the case!"

Modern English's second single, 'Gathering Dust', helped secure 4AD's legacy by introducing graphic designer Vaughan Oliver, whose work became – almost in symbiosis with the music – the aesthetic identity of the label. Especially so after he teamed up with photographer and old school friend from Ferryhill, County Durham, Nigel Grierson for Modern English's *Mesh & Lace* album – the official debut of the famed 23 Envelope design team. Thereafter 4AD sleeves became, with little exaggeration, fine art, using the LP sleeve as canvas – working in sympathy with each artist to the extent that their creations often added an extra layer of meaning and wonder to the music itself. And often, it has to be said, revealing an innate ability to turn the everyday and the unremarkable into something unseemly and subversive. As Kim Deal of the Breeders would later point out when confronted with projected cover art that included Vaughan's own body parts, "That man is a pervert".

The meeting with Oliver was, according to Watts-Russell, sheer serendipity. "A friend of Peter's, Alan McDonald, was a graphic designer, and I think he worked with The Associates later on. Alan said, 'Oh, I'm too busy, work with my friend Mark Robinson. So Mark had designed the original blue 4AD logo, and had done a flyer that the 4AD name cropped up from. A play on words. And he'd done Modern English's 'Swans On Glass', and a few months down the line we had another Modern English single. Mark was going to America and couldn't do it – he said 'I've got a friend called Vaughan. Get in touch with him.' I called him up, and Vaughan came in that evening after work to see me. Modern English had been using a Diane Arbus photograph, of a naked man and woman, sitting on a sofa with a seal between them. They'd replaced the seal with a television, with the broken screen saying Modern English on it. They wanted to use that image somehow. Vaughan came in and ridiculously, he had in his portfolio a variation on the theme of that very same image – just using silhouettes. What was the chance of that? That's how I met him. He did that sleeve and slowly over the next year or two of getting him a bit more involved with things, and also getting to know him – many a Monday night at the Venue where we got to put on anything we wanted pretty much once a month – Vaughan was always in my ear about logo, label identity, trust, brand name – hammering away at me. At the time I didn't have the confidence myself to feel it was right to foist that on every artist we worked with – but having an appreciation of Vaughan's talents, and growing with everything I did, that became more appropriate. He was my first employee and came to work with me in 1983."

The The also recorded their first record for 4AD, though the label's next substantial breakthrough came with Australian imports the Birthday Party's 'The Friend Catcher'. "I'd gone to see the Lines opening for DAF up at the Moonlight," Watts-Russell remembers. "DAF were on Mute. I got there earlier and there was this group playing. I seemed to be the only person who liked them, and I really, really liked them, I loved the Farfisa organ that Mick Harvey was playing. I was asking round, and someone said Daniel [Miller; Mute head] told them to come down and play. I called Daniel the next day and he gave me a phone number, I called up and I started to be very enthusiastic in a very naive way. I said I particularly liked the keyboard playing, And it was Mick I was talking to, which I didn't realise. He said, 'We're playing tomorrow night at the Rock Garden, why don't you come along?' I went along and they were really, really good. I went into that little cubby-hole at the back of the Rock Garden that's a dressing room, said I thought you were fantastic and that my favourite song was 'The Friend Catcher'. Mick said, 'Oh, we've recorded that, do you want to put it out?' It was as simple as that. Peel had already been playing 'Mr Clarinet' and 'Happy Birthday', which they'd released themselves, and I later re-released. He'd probably given them a couple of sessions, certainly one, by then." Wasn't he amazed that Mute didn't pick the band up? "Not really, because it felt like I was the only person who enjoyed them that night at the Moonlight."

But by the end of 1980, with 19 releases under their belts, Kent and Watts-Russell parted company, with Kent given his own Beggars-backed imprint, Situation 2. From now on, 4AD would stand as a separate and unique entity, Bauhaus being the sole artists to have made the planned transition to Beggars. "I'm not really quite sure why Ivo and Peter Kent parted company," says Mills, "probably because Ivo became very much the dominant character within 4AD, and Peter wanted to do his own thing. When he started Situation 2, again, it was much less musically focused. It had a Ministry single on it, and The Associates were obviously a key band. But it was relatively fragmented. So Peter went off and ran that for a few years."

Kent was also keen to maintain a link with Bauhaus. "Yes, absolutely," notes Watts-Russell. "Maybe it reflected on his character that he didn't just become their manager – he started Situation 2, and one of the first things that was agreed was this series of Associates singles – which was fucking fantastic. It was a coup to get them. The music was brilliant. Then he did actually make that step to becoming a manager. But with 4AD by 1981 – yeah, OK, it's my label now!"

There was a further important parting of the ways. By 1982, Mills had taken over primary stewardship of Beggars Banquet Group, a situation that continues to this day. "Nick and I didn't finally split up till 1989," says Mills, "though we drifted apart for a number of years before then. Nick married Claire Hamill the folk singer, and through her got to meet lots of jazz musicians like Dick Morrissey and Jim Mullen, and got very absorbed in jazz and new age. And that was so at odds with what the rest of the company was that we actually genuinely had musical differences, as a record label rather than as a band. And so we reached an agreement whereby he took some of the company and went his own way and I took the rest and went our way. That was probably the only solution to what had become a very divergent business. And probably an inevitable culmination of what had been growing differences." But the divorce wasn't without acrimony. "They were going in different directions and they fell out," notes Mike Stone. "There was a court case and that was a shame."

## Independence Days

As far as Mills was concerned, Situation 2 handily allowed the company to get into the independent charts, given that Beggars was distributed by Warners. The decision was taken to use Rough Trade and Pinnacle. "The independent chart didn't matter to a Gary Numan, but it did matter to a Bauhaus," he reflects. Situation 2's first release, and initial focus, was on The Associates, but they would eventually transfer to Warners in a kind of reciprocal arrangement as repayment of the major's investment. "The Associates had always had extra funding from Warners," notes Mills, "because it was an expensive deal for us, very expensive. So from the outset they always had more control over The Associates than they did over the other artists they distributed – and The Associates were a very needy band, and more and more needed to get brought in. It got to a point where Warners weren't prepared to do it with us in the middle, and we were also feeling somewhat divorced from the process, as we felt like an unnecessary step in the middle by that point. Which was frustrating, because we loved The Associates and I thought the music they made was absolute genius. But there were three people in the bed and it was one too many. By that point, what we were doing and what Warners wanted from us had diverged to a point whereby, as with every independent-major label association, you want them to believe in everything as much as you do, and of course they can't. So those frustrations were building up and what needed to be done with The Associates provided a natural opportunity for the rest of the situation to resolve itself. So our licence deal became a distribution deal. So we were funding ourselves and making our own decisions and investments, rather than trying to persuade them. If you were a retailer, you wouldn't have noticed any difference – you'd have been ordering the same records from the same distributor. But behind the scenes it was very different because we were not relying on anyone else's money, we were using our own."

Although they would shortly transfer to the main Beggars imprint, initially Beggars' biggest selling rock band of the 90s, The Cult, had started out on Situation 2, under the lengthier name Southern Death Cult." The biggest dream we could have in our whole lives at that time was for that magic 7-inch vinyl," remembers singer Ian Astbury. "I remember we were so desperate to get it so incredibly right. We were pretty unaccomplished as musicians, it was all adrenaline and earnestness. First of all Martin Mills from Beggars Banquet was introduced to us by a guy called Pete McCarthy, a rogue A&R guy. There was quite a few of them running around London at the time. He came and saw us live. And by this time our live reputation had exploded. We were opening for Bauhaus, for Theatre Of Hate, the Futurama festival blah blah. So Martin Mills signed us. Initially we thought we were getting a great deal, but he put us on Situation 2 because he didn't want us to be on the main label. We were pretty unaccomplished so he wanted to try us out on Situation 2. Well, we didn't actually sign, it was like word of mouth, a gentleman's agreement. I don't think we actually physically signed a contract as Southern Death Cult. I'm pretty sure it was a handshake. So we did that and we recorded with Mike Hedges, who was huge at the time because of the Banshees. So that was a big deal. 'Fatman' and 'Moya', we felt were our two best songs, so we made it a double a-side. Buzz [Burrows; guitarist] and I did the cover, knocked it up, Xeroxed art, Buzz did an illustration, I did a Xerox graphic. My girlfriend at the time helped me with the logo, which was hand-drawn. Name out of a book. It was totally punk rock, A-B-C 1-2-3, like the fanzines, *Sniffin' Glue*, here's three chords, form a band [a phrase actually taken from an early Stranglers fanzine but widely attributed to *Sniffin' Glue* thereafter], that's what we did."

Situation 2's identity eventually became synonymous with other bands that, like Southern Death Cult, followed in the wake of the Birthday Party and Bauhaus; Gene Loves Jezebel, Fields Of The Nephilim, The Bolshoi, Red Lorry Yellow Lorry etc. Essentially, in fact, nearly all of the first rank 'Goth' bands with the exception of the Sisters Of Mercy, though practically all of them resented that description. With punk, many of the start-up labels ended up road-sweeping the leftovers. This was the first time that Beggars had been able to establish itself at the forefront of something. "I suppose it was," says Mills, "and I suppose you're right. With punk, the majors all had one or two of the great ones, there weren't any independent labels that had a whole bunch of great punk bands, so you're right, we did have all the important Goth artists probably other than the Sisters. And I suppose that did give us a certain presence and a certain position, and a certain identity."

For Britain's premier writer on the Goth movement, Mick Mercer, that is certainly true. But note how for him at least, the Beggars canon could be seen as an inter-linked, cohesive body of work despite the stratification of different labels. "The 1980s was the greatest decade for independent music the UK has enjoyed, as the graph of creative attainment showed a devastatingly steep incline after punk. Inner machinations are always irrelevant to the fan and so Beggars, 4AD and Situation 2 should be seen as one entity, as they stood for the same thing, and shared similar levels of quality. They were, to be technical for a moment, less wanky than Factory, with no sign of their self-indulgence, or any desire to be seen as cool, and they were always considerably more adventurous than the comparatively cozy Creation would turn out to be in the 90s. Beggars and their wily brother and sister labels were simply the best labels we have ever had in this country, with a striking instinct for powerful and oddly vivacious music, and artwork that left an equally strong impression. I have no idea what they have on their roster nowadays, but their achievements through the 80s are undeniable. Look at their back catalogue and there's an astonishing lack of dross."

Elsewhere, the Beggars imprint itself also began to evolve. There was the signing of Brit-funk group Freeez, rock-pop thoroughbreds the Icicle Works and The Fall, during one of their intermittent periods of brilliance. "It was all different but compatible," thinks Mills, slightly disputing Mercer's logic. "So the labels at that point were all beginning to really acquire an identity – Beggars Banquet and 4AD and so on – which had not been evident early on."

4AD's roster had grown slowly but, aided by the striking designs of 23 Envelope, the label began to build a totemic identity in independent music. Some fell by the wayside – The Past Seven Days and My Captains – yet critics and John Peel in particular was staggered by the Birthday Party's ferocious 'Release The Bats' and their debut album proper, *Prayers On Fire* in 1981; birthing ground for a contemporary, and demonic, blues. Matt Johnson of The The (who had moved to Some Bizzare from 4AD) also cut an album for 4AD – Ivo's first co-production credit resulted – and there were solo excursions by members of Bauhaus and Wire's Colin Newman. In 1982 The Birthday Party released a second and final album for the label, *Junkyard*, in the same year that Modern English's *After The Snow* saw them enjoy a huge American radio hit when Sire licensed 'I Melt With You'.

A trio comprising Elizabeth Fraser, Robin Guthrie and Will Heggie, the Cocteau Twins had handed a demo to Watts-Russell after following the Birthday Party tour to London. "I can recall the moment when that tape was literally popped into my hands," he remembers. "All the 4AD stuff was stored on the floor in the basement of Hogarth road, the quadraphonic department, so I was there packing boxes for deliveries or distribution. I remember running up the stairs that were in the middle of the shop. And this person was standing at the counter. Whoever was behind the counter said, 'That's Ivo', and Robin put the tape in my hands. He said very little, or what he did say I perhaps didn't hear, because he was very quiet and talked in a very broad accent. The first time I heard that tape I remember very clearly. I'd been to Cambridge to see Dance Chapter in the studio at Spaceward, and it was really going badly. I was driving home and stopped off to see Danielle Dax, who was living out in Milton Keynes. I was driving back to London to see Bauhaus playing or something at the Rock Garden. When I left Danielle, I stuck the tape in and I heard the infamous Cocteau Twins. You could hear there was a voice on there, but you could not tell remotely the calibre of the voice. I later invited them down to record a couple of songs at Blackwing. When Liz started to sing, when I heard that voice properly for the first time, I realised that I was in the presence of something quite special. In some ways, the demos they recorded were incredibly familiar, suggestive of the Banshees, and in some ways [debut album] *Garlands* hints at that, but it was even more so before then."

So enthralled was he by Fraser's vocals that he immediately asked them to record a debut album, and later offered to bin 4AD to look after them as his sole focus. "Yes, it was absolute awe. Probably in 1983, after Will had left, I said I would stop the label and just manage them. Thank God, they never answered. Which was typical as well. I was perfectly serious about that. Yeah, the idea of perhaps just focusing on one thing with every ounce of my being, or enthusiasm, was quite appealing. Yeah, their music just meant everything." They were invited to join The Birthday Party on tour while John Peel gave them his immediate and ecstatic endorsement. They also had Watts-Russell's emphatic support too. "That's where any allegations of perceived arrogance that were hurled in my direction came from," he ponders. "Much as I said that Rema Rema was as good as anything that was being released and it was something I would buy and be excited about, when it came to the Cocteau Twins, I didn't care one iota what anyone else thought about them. They were just so musically important to me. Not a lot of people have had that experience. But to be in the room when Liz was singing – not to take anything from Robin or Will – but that instrument, that weapon that she has – for me, it was like a living Tim Buckley."

The Cocteau Twins arrived with their own entourage. "Gordon Sharp of Freeze/Cindytalk was one of them," remembers Watts-Russell. "The other two, Colin Wallace and Scott Roger, had two of the most bizarre haircuts you've seen in your life, crimped Flock Of Seagulls things, on two shy and severely depressed individuals. Colin ended up working with me and beyond that with Geoff at Rough Trade and now works with Alan McGee and manages Liz Fraser. Scott Roger manages Bjork and Arcade Fire. The latest thing I heard is that he was tour managing Paul McCartney. These grubby little individuals who came along with the even grubbier Cocteau Twins – Liz with her necklace of Kentucky Fried Chicken bones!" And of course, the Sex Pistols tattoo. "I believe it's Sid on one arm and Siouxsie on the other – I think there was some mis-spelling involved too!"

Watts-Russell was finally able to relinquish his commitments to Beggars' retail outlets. "I was running all of the Beggars shops. Here's an interesting thing, and an illustration of my personality. I remember the day I was over in the Kingston shop they'd recently opened, and Nick Austin came over and said, 'You know, Martin and I have decided that it would be best if you just focused on the label and stopped doing this.' That was actually the first time – I'm a fucking fruitcake! – that I can truly remember being happy. I couldn't handle it, I was so happy! I'm a naturally depressive character, or used to be. I just remember driving back to Earl's Court from Kingston being so happy."

In 1983 the whole operation relocated to Beggars' new offices in Alma Road, Wandsworth. Watts-Russell hired Vaughan Oliver full time, followed shortly after by Deborah Edgely. "The three of us shared a room separate from the Beggars offices, but we had shared warehouse space underneath. We also shared an accounts department and had access to the same legal team as Beggars. Vaughan was employed by me to jump in and get involved – but it didn't really work out that way. He focused on the design element rather than humping boxes!" Oliver's designs, as stylistically individual as they remained, were now growing organically from the music. "He would always argue that," says Watts-Russell, "and describe a process. I remember seeing him give a lecture in Japan with the Cocteau Twins – he would talk about how listening to demos would inspire an idea that he'd present to the group and refine and change. To an outsider, would it have appeared like that? Possibly not. But that was absolutely the process. To have the thing start to grow to being myself and Vaughan and Deborah – wonderful really! To go see a record company and be presented with us three! Thinking about it now – just three people. I was the oldest. It was clear that there was passion and drive there. There wasn't experience. There weren't connections. We're all very shy people. Vaughan can take a drink or two and come out of himself. Deborah was probably the most natural and gregarious. And it suited us well when she flipped into the role of doing press for the label."

The Birthday Party, meanwhile, decamped amicably to Mute (Nick Cave quickly going solo soon thereafter) when the infant 4AD worked out it couldn't underwrite the group's efforts much further, following an expensive trip to Berlin. "It was financial reasons," admits Watts-Russell. "They wanted to be in Berlin full time. I'd paid for them to be there for a brief period of time to do the 'Bad Seed' EP. But they really wanted to be there. If you know anything about certain members of the Birthday Party – it kind of gets difficult. Though I remained friends with Mick [Harvey] for a long time. It was very natural for them to go over there [Mute] and absolutely right.

Nick has gone on to make some of the most beautiful music. But yes, it was financial. I can remember the conversation where that was expressed, and everything was fine. It was just dead right. I don't know that the kind of savagery that was becoming Birthday Party performances was something that I really thought could be sustained creatively." Of course, it's easy seeing the 'asset' that Cave would become with hindsight, but at the time, it certainly didn't seem a given, in light of his more self-destructive energies. "What a wonderfully creative person," states Watts-Russell. "But, in the space of a year, I remember sitting on the steps outside of the Rock Garden talking quietly with Nick. Flash forward a year to him being passed out on a couch post-gig where he'd kicked someone in the face – it was a different thing. And the appropriate steps were taken, and he found an ideal permanent home."

But 1983 was very much the year of the Cocteau Twins, who lost bass player Will Heggie – ultimately replaced by Simon Raymonde – but released the 'Peppermint Pig' and 'Sunburst And Snowblind' EPs and the *Head Over Heels* album. It saw them emerge from a period in which influences were generally worn on sleeves to one in which they set out their own baroque pop agenda; a netherworld of enveloping sonic textures which were emotionally resonant while being lyrically impenetrable and playfully opaque. They supported Orchestral Manoeuvres In The Dark on a 50-date tour (though they would never be nearly as compelling a live band as they were in the studio) and made light of their perceived status as classicists by claiming, with some accuracy, to be beer monsters in the press. Peel was so impressed by the album that he played both sides in their entirety over successive nights.

Others to release material that year included X-Mal Deutschland (who would subsequently sign to Phonogram), the willfully obtuse Wolfgang Press, featuring Mark Cox and Michael Allen who had previously recorded for the label as part of Rema Rema and Mass, and Colourbox. The latter would begin to integrate hip hop references into their music, and later expanded that when Watts-Russell lent Martyn Young a bunch of his favourite reggae records – notably toaster U-Roy's 'Say You'. The signing of Colourbox, masters of a very idiosyncratic avant pop-reggae groove, in the same year as the Cocteau Twins, gave the lie to the common perception of 4AD as a label dedicated to the 'dark and doomy'. Indeed, Young confessed that he would 'never have sent a tape to them' given their reputation, had a mutual friend not intervened.

For Watts-Russell, the label's growth can best be gauged by tracing the evolving line-ups of the residency they took at The Venue. "We had this residency for a long time. The promoter John Reed gave us the first Monday of each month – unlimited guest list – just pack the place out. So 1981 or 1982, in those two years, it would have started with the Birthday Party supporting Modern English, then the Cocteau Twins supporting the Birthday Party, then Xmal Deutschland supporting the Cocteau Twins. But I guess the success ground to a halt when the Wolfgang Press opened for Xmal Deutschland! You could see new highlights each year. Bauhaus the first year, the Birthday Party in the second year, Cocteau Twins in the third. Is it fair to say This Mortal Coil in the fourth year? One could. Or one could say Xmal Deutschland, which at the time was quite a big deal. Then it was Dead Can Dance and then Xymox. So there was always something new released through the label that felt worthwhile, different, inspirational, and I guess people responded, collectively adding to the label's reputation. And beyond 1983, visually as well, there was a consistency. I became the biggest champion of the Vaughan Oliver mantra of all. You see a 4AD logo on it, you'll trust it, and you'll think it's worth listening to."

Appreciation for the efforts 4AD put into packaging was widespread, establishing a marque of quality that matched, and some would say surpassed, Peter Saville's designs for Factory. "Somehow to me," notes Watts-Russell, "it didn't seem something that your average record buying person would know as a fact, but they would instinctively feel it when they held the record in their hands. We would spend more, the weight of the board was heavier, we would print on special boards." Budgets, apparently, were never much of a concern. "Frighteningly, I've never really budgeted. The one time I remember was the mid to late 80s. Overall accountant Nigel Bolt would come around with pad and paper and say, 'OK, we need to do some cash flow projections, let's go through what you're putting out this year.' A classic example was a couple of months before 'Pump Up The Volume' came out and we said, 'that might do 10,000?' That was as close to budgeting as we came and look at how completely inaccurate it was! It was just going OK. The overheads weren't really that huge. There were really three of us doing everything. Vaughan might not have been down there packing boxes, but Deborah and I were. Deborah and I did everything physical. Then somewhere in there, around maybe 1984, God bless him, the late Rob Deacon, the smiling postman, came to work at 4AD part time. In exchange for helping out in the warehouse, and getting paid, he could learn the ropes, or some of the ropes or have access to photocopiers and so forth. And then he went on to start *Volume* magazine."

The concept of This Mortal Coil evolved after Watts-Russell failed to persuade Modern English to re-record '16 Days' and 'Gathering Dust'. Instead, he asked Gordon Sharp of Cindytalk and Liz Fraser to contribute as vocalists alongside Modern English's Mick Conroy and Gary McDowell. It would be issued as the first a-side credited to This Mortal Coil, backed by a version of Tim Buckley's 'Song To The Siren'. One of Ivo's favourite songs, it again featured Fraser, the finished version retaining the Robin Guthrie guitar part he'd laid down as a guide on the demo; producing a stunningly evocative piece of work. 4AD's roster would frequently interact and record with each other, but this was arguably the most enduring, instantly brilliant collaboration. "The story there," expands Watts-Russell, "it was the Ritz in New York, Modern English encoring at a headlining gig, doing really well. They ran the encore of '16 Days' into 'Gathering Dust'. Really exciting, the place was jumping. 'Why don't you re-record those two songs for an EP? They said, 'Fuck off, why do that? Why would we want to go backwards?' So I thought I'd have a go. My first experience of expressing an idea to an engineer and actually hearing it happen had been with Modern English during the recording of 'Gathering Dust'. It was incredibly exciting for someone, a non-musician who had spent years listening to the detail of music, to suddenly be part of the creative process. That's how I slipped into the role of producer. But I never felt comfortable with that role. I didn't have the right, or technical savvy, to impose my ideas onto someone else's work. With the Cocteau Twins, though, I think my input on *Garlands* probably helped Robin become determined to produce himself!"

"That's what This Mortal Coil became to me," he continues, "my own project. This Mortal Coil was created because I could, I suppose. No-one would have paid me to do that. It was only because I owned the company that I got away with it. Also, I created the situation where I could be most confident, because I wasn't mixing in front of five people and arguing about levels, EQ etc. To this day quite a lot of contributors to This Mortal Coil have never met each other. Yes, it became an escape for me, it was wonderful to get out the office and go over to Blackwing and work there till midnight. John Fryer was a delight to work with and seemed undaunted by my lack of technical ability or jargon. It was a real escape from the business side of things, and also lucky and exciting to have a creative outlet."

Cocteau Twins enjoyed further sustained success through 1984, despite turning down the opportunity to make a *Top Of The Pops* appearance for 'Pearly Dewdrops' Drops'. "Elizabeth fits into a similar thing with Kristin [Hersh]" notes Watts-Russell. "It might be something as simple as their irises. You look into their eyes, both Elizabeth and Kristin, and you see this terror there – you want to protect them, you want to keep the big bad music business at bay. And in some ways that probably proved to be inappropriate. But there's nothing on earth that would entice me as an individual at any point in my existence to appear on *Top Of The Pops* should I ever be given the opportunity. There's nothing on earth that would persuade me to do inappropriate tour supports, or probably even press. I was totally sympathetic and supportive in helping them avoid the apparent agony they experienced when trying to do anything other than make records. Perhaps that was a mistake. Certainly later in life, all sorts of water under the bridge by then, but the dissatisfaction and anger that would come from Robin in particular about us as a record company – he started to treat us as a record company. It made me wonder if he would have been happier had we behaved like bullying 'you've got to do this, or that' – I don't even know how to behave like that. How on earth could you possibly have a working relationship with creative people, musicians and artists that you like, if you're saying you've got to do this, or else? We were supposed to be an alternative to the bullying majors. And doing things differently, and doing it together. Maybe briefly somewhere in there, there was a six-month period of this really inspiring happy family at 4AD, where all the bands got on, and helped each other out and hung out together, with Vaughan and Nigel Grierson too at 23 Envelope. It was briefly a really fantastic place to be part of, at a fantastic time. People talk about Paris in the 20s, or Hollywood in the 30s. I think London in the late 70s to the mid-80s was just overflowing with original ideas and creativity, and I think we were lucky to be part of it."

The third Cocteaus' album *Treasure* (1984) even featured a tribute to their record label head in lead track 'Ivo' (though Fraser actually sings 'Peep-Bo' on the recording, its original title – the band subsequently decided each track would be given a 'first name'). Meanwhile they moved to set up their own 16-track studio in an apartment rented by William Orbit, whom they'd met through Colourbox. 4AD also signed Dead Can Dance, a barely quantifiable unit who would build a rich catalogue of challenging music (critics struggled for appropriate terminology, but "ethno-Goth" probably came closest) around Lisa Gerrard's soprano and Brendan Perry's baritone, featuring chants, madrigals and Eastern influences.

The first This Mortal Coil album featured an impressive cast list including Alex Chilton, Howard Devoto and Roy Harper, in addition to much of the label's roster. The most obvious song to deliver on the exquisite premise that was 'Song To The Siren' was the second single to be taken from it, 'Kangaroo', featuring Gordon Sharp covering Big Star's lost classic. Sharp actually appeared on two other songs on the album, 'Fond Affections' (originally a Rema Rema song) and 'A Single Wish', which he wrote with Simon Raymonde of the Cocteau Twins and Stephen Young of Colourbox. As he reflects, this was typical of an atmosphere surrounding 4AD artists where allegiances were quickly and amicably forged. It led to the apocryphal story that he was invited to join the Cocteau Twins. "Possibly one of my own, naive, making! Around the time I was recording the 1983 John Peel session with them and singing at the occasional gig, Ivo spoke to me about the possibility of joining up with the Cocteaus. He was musing over the possibility of adding new instrumentation, developing new ideas with their sound. He suggested that the combination of our voices (Eizabeth's and mine) might be a unique way for them to further that sound. I'm fairly sure he had not discussed this with any of the band and I'm even more convinced they would not have been interested in the idea. They quickly showed they had enough in their armoury to develop their sound without me. Anyway, I quickly passed over the subject with Ivo. Cindytalk was gearing up to record its first album *Camouflage Heart* and that was my main concern. Incidentally, one of Ivo's early ideas for This Mortal Coil was to use some of the tracks I was recording for Cindytalk (along with tracks by Dead Can Dance and Cocteau Twins). I declined this offer as well, because I was following my own path."

Ivo began work on a second This Mortal Coil album shortly thereafter. Eventually titled *Filigree & Shadow* (from the song by 60s band Fever Tree), it was again produced alongside John Fryer, who would become synonymous with the label through the mid and late 80s after earlier work with Mute artists including Depeche Mode and Yazoo. On this occasion Watts-Russell again used 4AD musicians, including Simon Raymonde and members of Dif Juz, Dead Can Dance, Colourbox and The Wolfgang Press, on a double album of songs featuring a number of cover versions; Buckley again, Quicksilver Messenger Service, Gene Clark, Van Morrison, Talking Heads, Judy Collins. The vocalists were mainly drawn from outside the 4AD inner circle, and included Rutkowski sisters Deirdre and Louise and Breathless vocalist Dominic Appleton. Ivo's core influence, again though, remained the classic west coast songwriting of the 60s. "This Mortal Coil would often be referred to as a 4AD house band," notes Watts-Russell. "Yes, the first record did have people who were close to hand, and most of them were connected or on 4AD to a certain extent, but I consciously moved away from that. There were less people on *Filigree and Shadow*, and by the time it came to *Blood*, there was no-one on there from 4AD – even Heidi Berry wasn't on 4AD at the time."

This Mortal Coil's spirit of shared adventure and collaboration was very much key to 4AD in the 80s. There were numerous collaborations. Elizabeth Fraser would work with The Wolfgang Press (on *Standing Up Straight*), for example, a band which featured former members of Mass and Rema Rema. Robin Guthrie would produce the same band. "It was a natural consequence," notes Watts-Russell of these overlapping projects. "The engineering part would be engineering them towards Vaughan in terms of Vaughan and Nigel doing their sleeves, or saying we've got a really good relationship with Blackwing, or later Palladium and prior to that Spaceward. No, once people were 'in the door' of 4AD they would meet each other and be interested in each other's music."

This also prompted healthy competition, with some amusing results. "I would personally put my hand up and say really, the master of all this was Trevor Horn," he notes. "His ability, as a producer, to present complex treatments and reverbs, conflicting treatments of drums or whatever, but still to have the clarity and power there, was absolute genius. Brendan and Robin and John Fryer and Martyn Young would never entertain the idea it was Trevor Horn as much as it was Martin Hannett or whatever who inspired it. But I think there was something of a reverb war going on with my approach with This Mortal Coil and the Cocteau Twins with *Head Over Heels* and Dead Can Dance with *Within The Realm Of A Dying Sun*. The first time I ever met Brian Eno, I was quaking in my boots, I invited him to meet Robin and Liz with a view to producing their next record, which would have been *Treasure*. Brian Eno came to my flat in Acton with this other guy who didn't say much, just sat on the floor. Brian said, 'I don't know what I can bring to your next record, because you had far more courage in the making of *Head Over Heels*, when it comes to reverb, than I would ever have done. You just took it so far, it's fantastic.' He was almost in awe of what they'd done. But then he pointed to the little chap in the corner and said, 'But you might want to work with him, he's an engineer.' That was Daniel Lanois."

The Cocteau Twins' experimental instincts took hold in 1986 in the form of the acoustic *Victorialand*. Shorn of Raymonde's bass, the frequency necessitated that the album be released as a 45rpm 12-inch. A subsequent collaboration with jazz pianist Harold Budd led to an album, *The Moon And The Melodies*, released under the billing Budd-Fraser-Guthrie-Raymonde – a seemingly natural exchange in which Budd lends ambient texture to the familiar but still radiant Cocteaus' song cycles.

That same year Watts-Russell was played an unlabelled tape by Peter Murphy while working on his solo album *Should The World Fail To Fall Apart*, his first non-4AD production. He determinedly tracked the source down, thrown by the purity and swell of these ostensibly choral sessions. The recordings were duly licensed from field recordist Marcel Cellier and released on 4AD as *Le Mystère Des Voix Bulgares*. Somehow, the recording fitted perfectly with the label's ethos and identity – an emerging element of which was that of the primacy of the voice, often solely as an instrument rather than lyrical medium. "Still to this day," Watts-Russell reflects, "Tim Buckley is the most beautiful sound I've ever heard in my life, his voice and what he did with it. Somehow, with Elizabeth and Lisa Gerrard and Gordon Sharp of Cindytalk and the Bulgarian Choir, my God, I was working with, for me, the most beautiful, stunning voices on the planet." 4AD consumers were almost wholly trusting in their embrace of such unlikely detours, growing their tastes alongside the label's founder. On a less high-brow note, Colourbox's 'The Official Colourbox World Cup Theme' had a good run for selection as the year's World Cup theme.

That image and identity shifted again when Watts-Russell first heard a demo tape of a Rhode Island quartet led by step-sisters Kristin Hersh and Tanya Donnelly. Throwing Muses were the label's first American signing, and Hersh narrated a fascinating story about Ivo's initial reluctance to sign them to Gareth Grundy: "Ivo, who is the only record executive I've ever heard of who actually listens to demos – and still does – called us." Initially, Hersh had to work out which of bass player Lesley Langston's boyfriends this might be, and what lie she therefore had to tell. "He said he liked the demo, but he didn't sign American bands. I'm like, 'yeah, well, whatever. Bye, Ivo.' Then he called back a few weeks later and said, 'It's still a good demo, but I still don't sign American bands.' I was like, 'Who is this weirdo?' So finally he called again and said, 'OK, I'll sign an American band, but JUST for one record.'"

"I read about those phone conversations," says Watts-Russell. "I have no recollection of them! My recollection is only of talking to their manager Ken Goes. Certainly my first response was to Ken. But what she describes, yes, that had been the pattern for quite a few years. I still, to this day, enjoy, if I can, expressing to someone how much pleasure their creativity gives me. 99.9% of everything I ever signed was from demo tapes. People always told me that was highly unusual. In 1986 I was at the New Music Seminar in New York. There was a hurricane coming in. I was staring out of my window looking down on the Marriott Hotel, thinking I would, actually, be prepared to sacrifice myself, because the hurricane would take out about 80% of the

English and American music industry – which wouldn't have been a bad thing, even in 1986. I remember some arsehole at the opening ceremony addressing Joe Public, the people who had spent $150 signing up to this thing, where they might have the chance of meeting the world's music industry under one roof. The keynote speaker said, 'Don't be so tasteless or tacky as to hand out demo tapes to A&R people.' Why else would they want to be at this thing? I can't believe that people don't accept unsolicited demo tapes. If I got a tape from somebody and if I liked it, I would call them and say so. I would say I liked your tape, but I'm not looking to sign anyone. I wasn't really looking to sign too many things, I actually liked working with a smaller group of artists."

"It was a similar thing with answering the phone," he continues. "There were lines flashing that were specifically for 4AD, and I thought anyone, including myself, should pick up, rather than waiting for it to go through reception. People would be very surprised to have me saying 'Hello, 4AD.' But that's part of the enjoyment, and being hands on and being aware of every stage and every aspect was absolutely critical to independent labels at that point of time. That's why the whole thing was required and generated in the first place, because the industry had become bland and complacent and arrogant. I'm no socialist, but to an extent it was doing it for the people, and doing it an alternative way to the way that was owned by half a dozen companies."

4AD's biggest, and most debilitating success, came about when AR Kane, the duo of Alex Ayuli and Rudi Tambala, gravitated to the label from One Little Indian. In the process of completing their 'Lolita' EP, produced by Robin Guthrie, they considered a collaboration with Adrian Sherwood. Watts-Russell suggested Colourbox instead. 'Pump Up The Volume', credited to M/A/R/R/S (an acronym devised using the first names of the participants), was the result. Despite legal action by the Stock, Aitken & Waterman production team, the single went to number one. It had initially been circulated around clubs as a blank, white label 12-inch (the 7-inch version was edited down and featured a number of new samples). In the process, it became a milestone in the development of both house culture and sampling. There had been precedents, notably by Coldcut, but this was Britain's first domestic house music hit of major size. It also became one of the strangest stories in the history of popular music – few artists have ever reached such dizzying heights without ever issuing a follow-up, as divisions between the artists emerged. Colourbox did attempt to carry the name M/A/R/R/S forward, but backtracked when A R Kane demanded £100,000 for permission to do so.

"It was a frustrating project," states Mills. "Well, it was a mixed-emotion project. Because not only did you have the two components of M/A/R/R/S not getting on well together – the Colourbox camp and the AR Kane camp. We had a lawsuit going on with Pete Waterman about his sample. And, in fact, it destroyed Ivo's enthusiasm for being involved in the business of music. The disagreements that ensued from the success of that record just drove him out. And it was a shame. It was a classic example of 'where there's a hit, there's a writ'. But it was a complex record legally in most ways, apart from the fact that 4AD owned the rights to the recording. But it was a groundbreaking record. I think it was the first Cartel-distributed number one single. And their first number one album had been the Yaz album [*You And Me Both*], so it kind of validated the reach of independent distribution in the UK as being competitive with the majors, which was really important I think, in retrospect."

Is Mills right to characterise this moment as the time when Watts-Russell's interest in the music business took a sharp downturn? "(LAUGHS) He's spot on! Up until that point, metaphorically speaking, just like in the cowboy movies, I was the guy in the white hat. I was the good guy. I worked really fucking hard, I was really fair, I loved music and was supportive of it, and people seemed to like me because of that. God, how insecure can you get! But because of the falling out over the M/A/R/R/S record, friends, people I'd known for quite some time, whenever money is involved – God, the rulebook is out of the window! Yeah, absolutely falling out. All I tried to do was remain unmoved. I just stuck with the original idea. The original idea was that AR Kane had come to 4AD from One Little Indian and wanted to make a record. They'd liked Derek [Birkett], but Derek's idea was that they maybe work with Adrian Sherwood. But Derek wasn't committing to anything with them. So they came to me. I said, 'Everyone works with Adrian Sherwood. Why not work with Martyn Young? He's better.' That was the seed of the idea."

In the end, however, producer John Fryer couldn't get the two parties to gel in the studio and both recorded tracks ostensibly separately. "The reality is that 'Pump Up The Volume' had that errrrrr-eerrrrrr bit [a guitar overdub], that was AR Kane," notes Watts-Russell. "And the only thing that was Colourbox on 'Anitina' was the drum programming by Stephen Young. So they were two very split sides. But at the time it seemed like we'd never, ever get Martyn back in the studio. He'd dried up. Colourbox kind of realised this was going to be quite successful, and they wanted to get rid of 'Anitina' on the b-side, because they didn't see why they should give up any money to these people. My attitude was, that's really unfair having agreed to do this. If it hadn't been AR Kane being the catalyst for the project, this thing wouldn't have happened anyway. So no, we're going to stick to it. In hindsight, I wish I had sided with Colourbox. We might never have got a b-side, but the whole experience would have been less traumatic. It was a bad year. My father died, my cat died. We got sued by those awful people!" He is referring, of course, to Pete Waterman's lawsuit. "I remember sitting with a barrister in cloisters discussing this case. (ADOPTS POSH VOICE): 'In *Smash Hits*, Martyn claims 'we bunjed' 'Roadblock' all over it. What does he mean, 'bunjed'?' '*Bunged*, your honour, we *bunged* 'Roadblock' all over it!' Martyn, the idiot, had admitted it in print."

The sample as such was merely seven seconds of an anonymous voice saying 'hey!' and could never have been considered plagiarism in the standard literary sense. Others pointed out that at the same time Waterman was claiming 'wholesale theft', his artist Rick Astley's 'Never Gonna Give You Up', locked in competition with 'Pump Up The Volume' at the top of the charts, employed the bass line from Colonel Abrams' hit 'Trapped'. "It was all too much," sighs Watts-Russell. "The record was flying. I never had it in stock. I literally touched every box that came through our building, because I could never keep it in there – it always had to go directly to other places to be distributed. It was just flying out and somehow, after an injunction and losing the 'important' weekend sales, it still got to number one the following week. That was the closest I got then, from just work alone, to having a nervous breakdown. It was horrible. I never allowed myself to get as close to the artists I worked with ever again."

Didn't that strip away some of the joy of running the label? "Yes. Equally at that time Robin Guthrie was being – not himself. And being incredibly rude and critical, and plain outright nasty, especially to Deborah. It took a couple of more years before it got directed at me. But you started that game of treading on eggshells around Robin because you didn't want to upset him. I remember being out with the Pixies somewhere, and someone pointing out that Robin and Charles [aka Black Francis] were in a corner – OH NO! Robin's going to poison Charles against us! Whether he did or didn't I don't know."

Some would have taken a number one single as validation. "I don't need a chart position to tell me that the record is good or beautiful," Watts-Russell counters, "and that we should have put it out – almost the opposite. I'm really proud we had the first Rough Trade distributed number one single ever, great. What was interesting was that the people in the office came alive, their eyes were sparkling from this success. [It meant something] to their contemporaries and peers at other labels and the press, and people they hung out with. It sounds naive, but it was an eye-opener to me. Everyone had been wonderfully supportive of my music taste or direction or ideas, but it was interesting to see that there was something else that would make them feel even happier. And that was the start of chart position expectation with every fucking release."

In what might have been taken as a portent, or perhaps metaphor, for the trouble that success would bring, Richard Scott at Rough Trade remembers the celebrations for that first number one single. "We had a party in the pub next to 4AD," he recalls. "We'd ordered the biggest bottle of champagne we could find – from Harrods in the end, I think. It was three or four feet high. But we couldn't get it open! We had to attack it with a Swiss army knife to get the cork out."

Throwing Muses' debut album, meanwhile, produced by Gil Norton of *Ocean Rain* fame, was immediately critically revered. "Chris Bigg, the first sleeve he got to do alone with 4AD, without Vaughan, was the Throwing Muses record," says Watts-Russell. "I can't remember if there were five or seven special colours [beyond the conventional Pantone matching range], and everyone was a 'special' colour on that sleeve. If you get one 'special colour' on a sleeve, it would be more than a major label would pay, going for five would be extraordinary." In the end, in a rare act of fiscal prudence, the outlandish design was ditched. But it had little effect on the record's reception. "When the first Throwing Muses album came out, it was received really well. They were brilliant. That original four-piece – some of the best times I've had in my life in a live music situation. Just simply to watch Leslie Langston, and to watch Dave Narcizo, not taking away from Kristin and Tanya, but Leslie and David were quite extraordinary considering their years. So there was a hell of a lot of interest. Dear old Seymour Stein from Sire came along. I signed them for that one album, and for the world I felt, how on earth can I represent, long-term and internationally, a band that isn't even in the same country as we were? I didn't think that was right for them. So Seymour signed the band worldwide excluding the UK. And that led to my visit to America to meet Ken (Goes) and the group themselves to persuade them not to sign with Sire for the rest of the world – sign with Sire for America, that would make sense. But not for the rest of the world. Warner Brothers [Sire's owners], a group like that, was going to be a disaster. So I pleaded with them not to do it. And that visit was when I was handed a Pixies tape."

Though initially sceptical about whether or not the Pixies' punk-derived ferocity would sit well with the roster he'd built up, after playing their demos several times on a Walkman in New York, he was persuaded to sign them by the enthusiasm of Deborah Edgely. His initial reluctance came because he thought it might be 'too rock 'n' roll'. "That is true," he admits. "Quite a lot of my experiences of listening to the Pixies ended up for one reason or another being on a Walkman. I remember being in New York, striding around – not my favourite place on the planet – listening to that infamous purple tape, and having a thoroughly good time with it. This was 1987. And at that point in time I think I really felt that 4AD could be something that was really nothing to do with rock 'n' roll any more. I really liked *Le Mystère Des Voix Bulgares*, This Mortal Coil, Cocteau Twins, Dead Can Dance – things that were vocal-based and non-quantifiable apart from, maybe, the 4AD adjective itself. Otherworldly voices singing in non-language, or at least non-English, combined with an infatuation with reverb that we all had. Yeah, that generated one thing, which I still find very attractive. I was thoroughly enjoying The Pixies, but I thought it was a bit rock 'n' roll for what I want 4AD to be. And I may well have said something like that to Deborah. And she definitely turned round to me and said, 'Don't be so bloody stupid, they're brilliant, let's do it.'"

By signing The Pixies 4AD confirmed its position as the lightning rod of the soon to be huge American alt-rock boom when seven songs from that original demo became part of the *Come On Pilgrim* mini-album, which instantaneously won over both the press and John Peel. "The only time I noticed something happening really, really fast, in my entire time of being involved in the business of music, was The Pixies. That exploded from nowhere." But it was never a conscious plan to be at the forefront of anything. "Ultimately I responded to the music. I can still see cassettes that came through that demo route." Among those he was offered were both Sonic Youth and The Swans. "But again, having just signed Throwing Muses, I probably wasn't in a hurry to sign anyone of ANY nationality. I definitely remember being handed the Pixies tape by Ken Goes. He'd only heard it the night before and he'd passed it on to me. Dave Narcizo is responsible for giving it to Ken. I don't know if Ken specifically said, 'Well, if you're interested, I think I'll manage them.' I didn't feel like we were at the vanguard of something American any more than I'd felt at the forefront of any kind of movement, other than what I perhaps considered in terms of NOT signing. In terms of not signing the Pixies – I perhaps consciously thought I wanted to shape the label perhaps for the first time. The next artist that I signed, yet again – bugger, he might well have been living in England at the time, but he was American – Kurt Ralske, Ultra Vivid Scene. And I think the very next thing we signed was Warren Defever of His Name Is Alive. Yes, there was a whole string of American artists that we worked with next."

When Throwing Muses, supporting their second album *House Tornado*, joined The Pixies to promote their *Surfer Rosa* LP on tour in 1988, 4AD was widely seen to have entirely reinvented itself. Despite a routinely favourable press disposition to them, some 4AD artists had been irritated by the representation of their work in the media – a select range of adjectives had become a choking cliché. There was little that was 'ethereal' or 'celestial' (or even, to use the less complimentary *lingua franca*, 'Victorian nightie music') about either The Pixies' molten art-rock or Kristin Hersh's anguished introspection.

"The Pixies-Throwing Muses tour," says Watts-Russell, "I like to remind everybody that, as fantastic and totally exciting as it was, and the Pixies were just mental, but every single night of the shows that I saw, the Muses rose to the occasion. Saying they blew the Pixies off stage would be a slight exaggeration. But in Europe, we had licensees, Virgin in France who were fantastic, Play It Again Sam in Benelux and Rough Trade in Germany – these were good, individually selected licensees, and good people. And they did a damn good job on promoting the fact that The Pixies had their first full-length album out. With Warner Brothers, all I remember is getting a phone call from someone tour managing in Europe – and Throwing Muses going to Warners for a bunch of interviews. Drummer David Narcizo wasn't in the room, and the person in charge asked when the lead singer was going to arrive. So the person who was handling Throwing Muses in Europe didn't know anything about the group. It wasn't a disaster, but it was very difficult for them. They were switched – the Muses opened for The Pixies in Europe. I had to call Seymour Stein and plead with him to do something about the situation. I had the strongest words I ever had with him saying you've got to do something for this band – this is a band you represent in these countries, I don't – and they're going through shit."

His response? "Oh, he probably cracked a joke. Seymour's a very funny man. But I'm not going to be critical of him, he signed all sorts of things. There are many, many people who have nothing but gratitude and praise for what Seymour did for them on an international basis. But you can imagine at 4AD, the individuals that we were, and totally passionate and totally in love with these little children, really, Throwing Muses. Me and Deborah and whoever, Oh, God, we know what's going to happen, if they sign to Warners in Europe, it'll be a fucking disaster. And of course it turned out to be very disappointing."

The other label to highlight the talents of a crop of emerging American bands [not least the aforementioned Sonic Youth] was Blast First [see Chapter Seven], helmed by Paul Smith. Smith was not averse to the occasional bitchy comment about 4AD in the press. "It probably speaks more about differences of personality," notes Watts-Russell. "Whenever I saw Paul Smith face to face, he was interesting, polite and funny. I do have a memory of him saying not unduly kind things about 4AD in the press. There are some people who enjoy drawing attention to themselves by saying outrageous things, and there are people who have nervous breakdowns and drug addictions in public and thrive on it, and there are others who don't pursue that. I always felt that 4AD was an esoteric soapbox for the shy person – we stood up for the shy person – the musicians and everyone behind the label were pretty introverted individuals, who didn't really like the spotlight on them."

The Cocteau Twins, having taken four years between albums, issued *Blue Bell Knoll*, which was licensed to Capitol in America. Dead Can Dance continued to release material that surprised and delighted in the Eastern-influenced *The Serpent's Egg*. But 1989's two key releases for the label were the Muses' most commercial effort thus far, *Hunkpapa*, and The Pixies' *Doolittle*. Both were extraordinary, though it was the latter that captured the imagination and propelled The Pixies to iconic status. On a domestic front, Ivo also added The Pale Saints and Lush to the roster. "That was the first and last time that I was specifically and consciously looking to sign anything. And as it happened, two tapes that came out of the same demo box, Pale Saints and Lush, were actually playing the same night at the Falcon. And we all went along. And I think everybody thought I was mad. Miki (Berenyi] and Emma [Anderson] weren't the most tuneful of singers at the beginning. Pale Saints probably hadn't played many gigs. These weren't two professional outfits. But with Lush it was 'Ethereal', and with Pale Saints 'Sight Of You'. Both of those songs I thought were really, really good."

The Cocteau Twins released what would be their final album for 4AD in 1990, *Heaven Or Las Vegas* – described by Watts-Russell at the time as the finest recording he had ever been involved with, a statement he stands by still. The band was by now widely heralded as the starting point, alongside My Bloody Valentine, for a whole subculture in music, which the UK press dubbed 'shoegazing' and the Americans translated as 'dream pop'. Few bands can realistically claim to have been the engine of discrete musical movements but both the Cocteaus and Pixies – whose start-stop dynamics were to be cited as a key influence by everyone from Nirvana to Radiohead – had reason so to do.

Watts-Russell's partisan endorsement of *Heaven Or Las Vegas* wasn't enough, however, to stop the Cocteaus moving on to a major label. The split was less than amicable. "I think we'd felt somewhat constricted by them for the last few albums in fact," Robin Guthrie would tell Andy O'Reilly. "And I decided that their strong point is really in discovering talent and then working with bands in the early stages, giving them guidance. I really felt that we'd outgrown one another. It had stopped being a priority for them that we should be successful. It was just – 'Oh, another Cocteaus LP, let's put it out, it'll sell loads.' And I really missed the enthusiasm." Of course, they would soon discover that any perceived absence of enthusiasm at their old label did not amount to the cold indifference that a cyclical old school major label can foist on its artists. But it was actually Watts-Russell who called time on the relationship: "Years later we patched things up and became friends again, and I remember Robin standing in front of me and saying it was the biggest mistake he ever made. By then he and Simon had started Bella Union and were getting a taste of what it was like on the other side of the table."

By 1990, Beggars was in a position to jostle at the front of the queue when new talent appeared. The Charlatans became a serious coup for the label (after a nursery period on Situation 2), as the band, on the back of their independent single 'Indian Rope', were being courted by a series of major label A&R departments. The deal was clinched, according to manager Steve Harrison in conversation with John Robb, due to Mills trekking up to Manchester back in January 1990 to see them play at the Boardwalk "It was totally horrendous weather that night and it was still packed. I remember that most of the A&R people that were going to come up and check the band out couldn't make it because of the weather. About the only one who managed to come was Martin Mills of Beggars Banquet." Mills: "It was funny – it was an incredible storm. Roger Trust [A&R head at Beggars Banquet] and myself, we were looking at the weather forecast. It said, 'On no account venture out – go home, lock your doors, bolt your windows. Don't even think about going on a motorway.' And we just looked at each other and said, 'We've got to go, haven't we?'" So, was that instinct or hunch? Mills answer is succinct and highly illustrative. "To be honest, it was as much honouring a commitment as anything else – because we said we would."

Over at 4AD, 1991 brought the Pixies' *Trompe Le Monde* and the final Muses album to feature Tanya Donnelly, *The Real Ramona*. The fact that the former was also the Pixies' swansong didn't emerge until Black Francis revealed the fact in an interview with Mark Goodier, without having made his intentions clear either to his fellow band members or 4AD. Watts-Russell has a rather different take on events. "The announcement was a surprise but its content was not. I remember a meeting several weeks before with Bob Krasnow, head of Elektra at the time, where he was insisting that I renegotiate with the band to get more albums. We had licensed Pixies to Elektra and had another two albums under our existing contract. Krasnow was insinuating that if I didn't renegotiate for at least another three albums, then he would go directly to the band and cut 4AD out of the deal. At that time I already knew there would never be another Pixies record but had agreed not to let the world at large know. I still think they stopped at the right time. There aren't many bands that have released five albums as strong as the Pixies catalogue."

Although Black Francis complained to the press of 'record company pressure' contributing to the demise of the band, he grudgingly accepted that he remained under contract to them and would release two solo records for 4AD (as Frank Black) thereafter. "As I say, it [the Pixies' demise] was not something I was unhappy about," notes Watts-Russell. "I don't think there could possibly have been another Pixies record, it just wouldn't happen. What I truly am disappointed about is becoming the brunt of a less pleasant side of Charles. I'd seen it and experienced it [used] against other people, but I'd never had it directed at me. The idea of working with artists without a mutual respect for each other just seems like a sham. I think both he and Ken felt if they were unpleasant enough to me I'd let them go – because that's exactly what had just happened with the Cocteau Twins. And that's what happened with Frank Black. With one more album owed I chose not to take up that particular option. They already had Rick Rubin and American [Records] waiting in the wings so it worked out fine. I want it to be clear that ultimately, especially with the Cocteau Twins, I'm disappointed with myself that somehow I didn't manage to fix it – I'll use that expression. And equally I'm disappointed that I and or the company was no longer considered appropriate for Charles. But that's purely on a personal level. We were lucky to have released both artists' best work."

Situation 2, meanwhile, released its last record in 1992, with many of the artists absorbed back into the Beggars fold. "We simply decided that we wanted to be Beggars Banquet," Mills would tell Martin Aston the following year. "Situation 2 was always perceived as Beggars anyway, we should be what we are, so we've just changed the identity."

That same year, Lush released *Spooky* and the Throwing Muses' *Red Heaven* for 4AD, while 1993 brought Belly's *Star*, the Red House Painters' self-titled debut and the Breeders' *Last Splash*. Watts-Russell remains a staunch advocate of these releases, though tellingly contemporaneously noted of the Red House Painters' debut that "I don't think it's going to sell very well." In an interview with Gareth Grundy he confirmed that, despite huge critical success, financial pressures and considerations had been exacerbated rather than minimised. "Fuck no, because what happens then is that everyone gets involved with management and lawyers. The kind of funding that people need up front has multiplied by twenty or thirty times. It's absurd. You get a situation where a band will sell millions and millions, and the industry rushes like a magnet towards that type of music, without discrimination, without any kind of understanding." He also revealed his increasing boredom with the way that the Pixies' influence, in particular, had resulted in the grunge era of "guitar-fronted American groups where you can't hear the words". While tangentially amusing that this remark should come from the head of the one label in the history of recorded song most associated with inaudible lyrics, he had a point.

Watts-Russell had signed a deal with Warner Brothers in 1992 to distribute 4AD in America, but it quickly became evident that he was unhappy with the compromises and intrusion that entailed. "It became a struggle pretty much as soon as I moved to America. The reality of what we'd done, this licensing of the whole label to Warners, other than what we'd licensed elsewhere. I spent most of the time from '92 to '94 going backwards and forwards. I don't do well with jet lag – I never have. I was spending a month in LA and a month in England, and I didn't feel I was functioning well in either place. I'm afraid that reality of – the deal is done with an American label, now what? I thought they were going to bring something to it as well! They didn't. They just looked to us to bring appropriate things to stuff into their machine. And we're the wrong label for that, and I'm the wrong person. It stopped being fun. It took me a long time to admit it wasn't fun anymore. Colin Wallace came with the Cocteaus, and ended up working at 4AD in the warehouse. He was everybody's friend, and Colin had suggested Steve Albini to me as an idea to produce *Surfer Rosa*. So when I went to America, he was put in the position of doing what I call negative A&R. All I wanted him to do was vet tapes, and forward them to me in America or keep in a box for me the better things. So from probably '93 onwards, that's how things were listened to. How frustrating is that, to get excited about something and then get it turned down the whole time by me? And also feeding this Warner Brothers machine, and also keeping the company afloat. Much as there was assistance financially from Warners, you end up spending it so quickly. They want videos and all this other bollocks, which we didn't really do to the extent that was expected of us in that system. It became shaky."

"My day to day worries and concerns or involvement," he continues, "were more to do with the stability of the thing, and how we were fitting into Warner Brothers. 4AD was a company where, for better or worse, the decisions were all taken by me. When you do things by committee, it's difficult. So for all those reasons I was unhappy, and I really wasn't doing a good job. We had Robin Hurley running the company in LA, and Simon Harper, whom I wished was running the company in England, but would never take on the responsibility. He was head of international. I fell in love with him when he worked at Rough Trade. Dealing with M/A/R/R/S, we both had nervous breakdowns on that! Robin Hurley came from Nine Mile, part of the Cartel. Then Robin went to San Francisco to set up Rough Trade there, the shop and the label and distribution. When they moved to New York, 4AD's first office was a shared space with Rough Trade."

Hurley had first come into Ivo's orbit while at Nine Mile. "I'd pick up the phone and order boxes of *Treasure* or *Head Over Heels*," he recalls, "and Ivo would often pick up the phone and take the order. I got to know Ivo because he'd attend some of the bigger Cartel meetings. When I moved to Rough Trade America I got to know him even better, because he *hated* American major labels. And he really wanted Rough Trade America to grow and thrive so he could deal with people he enjoyed dealing with, knowing it was in good hands. There was a guy called Steve Connell who worked at Rough Trade America, who alerted me to The Pixies, and said, 'You know Ivo, you should talk to him about this.' So we did the first two Pixies records, then the Breeders record, then a couple of other 4AD records like Ultra Vivid Scene and the Wolfgang Press. Through that relationship I grew to know Ivo very well. He was completely privy to Rough Trade's problems, and he said, if it does all go under, I'd like you to come and work for 4AD. I couldn't believe my luck, to be honest. I'd moved my whole life to New York, and I was thinking – what the hell am I going to do?"

"We became really good friends, still are," Watts-Russell continues. "I invited him to head the label in advance of doing a deal. Sherri Hood was running 4AD in New York. Those were the best times for the label in America, when we didn't have proper distribution or representation. What she did with college radio etc was the absolute peak. To this day I feel I did wrong by her as a person by bringing in Robin to in theory work side by side. We all knew their personalities well enough to know that probably wasn't going to work. And she chose to leave. She managed Cranes, Ultra Vivid Scene and Stereolab, so she probably made the better choice. Robin was much better suited to dealing with a company like Warner Bros and did a fantastic job of protecting me from them! Robin now works at Rhino, alongside Warners, so his time at Warners served him well for the future. That would never have happened with Sherri, she despised major labels, bless her. Sherri, if you read this, I am so sorry. I never told her how grateful I was for the way she represented the label over there for a couple of years. She was brilliant."

Watts-Russell's own enthusiasm was nose-diving. "The last idea I'm truly proud of was to take over the ICA for the 13 Year Itch". A series of concerts over five nights at the London venue in 1993, it featured live performances from the label's roster. "13 Year Itch – does that not make anyone think? On the t-shirt it had 'shuffle' – i.e. 'shuffle off this mortal coil', in brackets. I thought it was clear as daylight in 1993 that I was really losing it, but no-one was reading the signs. It was a changed beast, all of my own making, I didn't have to do the label deal in America or move out there. I fell bonkers in love and got married, but we could have moved back to England. I was lost. I got lost! It was a big lesson – but it felt obvious to me how and why things were done at 4AD for the first 13 or 14 years, and people around me had seen a lot of those years – but I have learned that I expect people to read my mind. In the past, I've not been very good at truly saying what my thoughts were, and I assumed that people got it. For better or worse, for a label like this to function successfully with the kind of individual direction it had for its earliest years – it's virtually impossible to change that and expect it to function satisfactorily."

He concedes that he made 'poor choices'. He needed someone to steady the ship back in England. "I chose two wonderful people, but two poor choices in terms of taking on those jobs. Simon [Harper] wouldn't do it, he wouldn't take it on – so we hired someone who didn't work out, followed by someone else who didn't work out." Being absent from the UK operation didn't help. "Oh yeah. I think there were even, perhaps, factions growing up – 'We're doing this for fucking America,' perhaps. I'm not sure. It got to a point where I wasn't going back. I wasn't going anywhere. I wasn't even going into the American offices. People had to make decisions because I wasn't making them. Then being the kind of person I am or was, I wasn't happy with those decisions. It was terrible. This thing was collapsing, and to get to the point of perhaps getting it back, there was a realisation that moving back to England would be required, and that wasn't even on my radar at that point."

There were still good 4AD records to come [Watts-Russell particularly enthuses about Red House Painters, Mojave 3, His Name Is Alive and Heidi Berry], but not everybody was taking the label's stamp of quality on face value, after under-performing records by the likes of Scheer, Tarnation, Liquorice, Air Miami and the Amps, etc. There was some chart action in 1996 for Lush, with their uncharacteristic 'Ladykiller'. The band reported that Watts-Russell laughed his head off in the studio the first time he heard it. "You always have to put it in context with what was going on at the time," he says. "Tim Carr was the A&R person at Warner Brothers who had already licensed Lush, so that was top of his list of things he really liked and thought could be successful. Tim's a nice man. But there was definitely [a feeling of] – 'Christ, something needs to sell and break through'. Britpop was happening then. Irony of ironies – the first band that ever agreed to go on *Top Of The Pops* was Lush [for follow-up, 'Single Girl'], and I wasn't even in the country. Knowing Miki [Berenyi; co-vocalist] and who she was singing about – maybe it made it funny. Maybe it did make me laugh. But if I was talking about Lush, I'd be talking 'Ethereal' and 'Desire Lines' in particular... I'll stand in defence of Lush any day of the week. I think by then there was something much bigger that was so horrifically distasteful to me, but yet we were participating in it. The whole formatting idea to try to achieve a chart position is so disrespectful of the public and the antithesis of what I believed in. Ambitious artists and, especially, managers, were a relatively new and not particularly enjoyable part of day to day life."

Eventually Watts-Russell offered to sell the label back to Beggars in 1999. "Martin and I always had a buy or sell option. If either one of us wanted out, we contractually had to offer it to the other one first. Between '94 and '98, when the seeds were sown for my departure, whenever I was thinking about it, what always sprung to mind was that I was a caretaker of copyrights. I felt guilty. I couldn't let stuff go. Then one had to be honest with oneself." He is understandably reticent about revealing much beyond that. "I choose not to take that path. For most of the people working at 4AD I did compose, in 1994, a fax explaining what I was going through. Most of the people working there had a vague idea for the reason behind my disappearance. A lot of the musicians don't. I've never had anybody call me up about it. I always assumed everybody knew enough to let me off the hook for dumping them." He reconsiders. "Hang on, that isn't really true. Simon Harper was still there,

Robin Hurley and Chris Staley were still there, and Deborah, although we'd split up, was there before she went to Island. There were still some fabulous people regardless of my lack of involvement. It did mean a couple of signings that I should never have approved. There's no excuse for Cuba!"

It's evident Watts-Russell's complete enthusiasm for music hasn't deserted him (during the course of our conversations, he made me copies of some albums he thought I should listen to – which were only tangentially linked to 4AD). And he's clear on the impact of this period in music. "It's as real as someone being inspired by history or archeology or something at an early stage, and they go off to pursue that inspiration and end up being authors, lecturers or whatever on the subject. The tuning into Luxembourg or John Peel at Radio 1 later, that thing of the light bulb going off for all of us would have been the mid to late-60s in music, is something that changed our lives forever. And we simply ended up making use of that at a point in time where the stars were all aligned for an explosion of creativity and originality and a clean slate." 4AD continues to this day, signing new artists including Bon Iver, TV On The Radio and Blonde Redhead. But Watts-Russell is no longer involved. "People like Martin and Geoff Travis and Daniel Miller I have extraordinary admiration for," he states. "They managed somehow to translate their passion and enthusiasm into 'enjoying' running a business. And it's a talent that I lack. I managed to run a business, but I ended up hating it. I moved to America and fell in love, then found a piece of land in the middle of nowhere and ended up building a house."

In the late 80s, before 4AD had its unexpected success with 'Pump Up The Volume', Beggars expanded again in order to carve out a slice of the dance market. Citybeat Records was inaugurated in 1986 under the auspices of Tim Palmer (who ran Groove Records in London's Greek Street with brother Chris). "It's weird how the first great British house record ended up on 4AD," says Mills, remembering 'Pump Up The Volume'. "We'd never have planned it. But you're right, we were getting involved in Citybeat, because that period in the 80s reflected the period in the 70s. The DIY ethos of punk was also there in house music. Although the music sounded very dissimilar, the spirit was very similar."

Although Citybeat had some success (with the likes of Rob Base and DJ EZ-Rock, and in particular by licensing the dance smash 'Doop') it more significantly provided the foundations for the XL imprint in 1989. XL, with Tim Palmer as MD running the label alongside the reclusive Richard Russell and Nick Halkes as head of A&R, enjoyed huge success with a roster that included The Prodigy (who achieved a number one in 27 countries and sold seven million records with *Fat Of The Land*). "The bizarre thing about XL," suggests Mills, "is that initially it was started as a company releasing underground 12-inch dance singles that were chart-ineligible. It was meant to be the uncommercial arm of Citybeat."

By 1993 Halkes had left to run EMI's commercial dance subsidiary Positiva, and then his own independent dance label, Incentive. Palmer also exited in 1994, retiring from the music business, leaving Russell in sole stewardship. He moved to broaden the musical catalogue from that point. Mills watched the personnel come and go, and at least partially helped steer the ship. "Much more so than at 4AD," he says, "because 4AD was a free-standing operation until Ivo and I parted company, and Ivo decided to get out of the business. XL were always plugged into Beggars for everything except A&R, and for a small period of time press. Citybeat was always much more plugged into Beggars than 4AD." That extended to hiring and firing. "Yes," admits Mills. "But a lot of it is driven just by people wanting to do different things with their lives. We took over the rest of 4AD because Ivo wanted to retire from the business. We took over the rest of Citybeat because Tim wanted to go and live on a beach in Goa."

For a while 4AD's success and standing was such that Beggars itself took a step back from the limelight. That same situation has developed in the noughties with the phenomenal hit rate of XL, via the White Stripes. Basement Jaxx, Vampire Weekend, the Horrors, the Raconteurs, Dizzeee Rascal and the more recent adventures of Radiohead – in essence, the strongest stable of contemporary artists in the UK alongside Domino Records. The pattern appears to be, throughout Beggars as a group's history, that some labels come to the fore as others recede into the background – but Mills seems quite comfortable with that. "I have to say that it's the secret of our success. As an individual independent label run by an individual – you can't be 'on it' year after year after year. You just can't do it. Nobody can, and nobody ever has. You just don't have the energy to hold your breath for that long. I think that having a stable of independent labels that ebbs and flows has been the secret of our success."

The Radiohead snatch is hugely significant, in that it indicates the near 180-degree turn in the music industry. The Oxford quintet's early, unapologetic decision to throw their lot in with the UK's most famous major label attracted no little conjecture (admittedly mostly retrospectively, when they actually started selling records), as too did their decision to give away 'for donation' their most recent studio album, *In Rainbows*. Given their privileged position, the decision to sign to an independent marked some sort of tacit admission that a stable, well-run independent like Beggars/XL could provide every advantage, and few of the disadvantages, of a major label in 2008.

Beggars, meanwhile, continues to enjoy success in its own right with Biffy Clyro, The National and Tindersticks. It now has offices in most major territories, including Japan, America, France and Germany, as well as joint-venture outlets in Australia and Spain. Mills: "Those territorial operations allowed us to move from licence deals, where we were in effect sub-contracting our responsibilities, to distribution deals, where we had our own people who really understood how best to represent our music. With us making our own investments and taking our own risks, and operating as a global business." There have also been a number of acquisitions. Notable examples have included Too Pure, originally formed in 1990 by Richard Roberts and Paul Cox, and the launching pad for PJ Harvey and Stereolab. There was also an association with Wiiija Records, formed by Gary Walker of Rough Trade Records in 1988, and acquired by Beggars eight years later, whose most notable successes were the launch of riot grrrl act Huggy Bear, Cornershop and Therapy? A 50% share in Matador, one of the most respected independents in America, was agreed in 2002. As well as the Momentum Music Publishing Company, Beggars has also formed an alliance with the internet site Playlouder for more effective distribution of digital content, as well as being one of the key contributors to the success of e-music (licensing whole catalogue content). It was one of the true visionary labels in this area, having digitised said catalogue well before the turn of the century.

The 50% deal with Matador, according to Mills, is among the company's most important ones. "Our relationship was crucial for us in terms of growing as a company in America. At the time we got into bed with them, we had eight people in America and they had 30, so they were much the bigger company in terms of size. But we've settled down to pretty much the same, it's 60-40 or 40-60 Beggars/Matador, in terms of our American business. And the input of Matador Music around the world has been good for the group in America, because the partnership has been critical in establishing ourselves as a local company."

Not every tie-up has panned out as well. "We never really got on top of the Mo Wax situation," laments Mills. "James Lavelle is a tremendous person in many ways, but we never really succeeded as business partners. We made some really good records and lost a fortune. That's life!" There was also a small investment in Badly Drawn Boy's label Twisted Nerve. "That was a very silent investment, and closely allied to having Damon as a recording artist. One of the things that we can do here is just give people a leg up and see if it works for both of us."

The concept behind the acquisitions is simple – that Beggars can provide central office functions – marketing, stock control, and both physical and digital sales – while the label itself retains a free hand to concentrate on A&R development. "There's no point in interfering with the A&R," states Mills. "Clearly I and other people here are closely involved in the deals, and in the terms in which we sign people and the terms in which we work with them. But it would be fairly pointless for me to get involved with businesses who are great with music and musicians and then try to tell them what to do – there is absolutely no point in me doing that. So I see myself as a sounding board and facilitator more than anything else." Does that involve treading carefully with 'passionate' music fans – i.e., is Mills in a position where he has to say, that's too much for that artist, you can't do that? "Absolutely! Well, the first part, not the second! I would definitely say that's too much for that artist, but I would never say, 'you can't do that!' With all my partners, we always arrive at a consensus of what's a reasonable position." In terms of his expectations, too, he has a similar mantra to one or two other independent label heads featured in this book. He doesn't expect anyone to turn a loss, but he doesn't necessarily enter into a relationship with an expectation of profit.

However, his most noteworthy acquisition, and the most historically piquant, was the July 2007 decision to purchase the remaining 49% of Rough Trade Records from the ailing would-be giant Sanctuary Records. The price tag was £800,000. Geoff Travis would confirm in press releases the "full circle" nature of this deal, given that he once sold Lurkers singles in his shop in Golborne Road (not that he actually admitted to liking them). The move was widely welcomed by those in the independent music community as a means of Rough Trade (which had enjoyed sustained recent success with the likes of The Libertines) reacquiring its independent status. "We share a culture that is about our artists and their work," Travis stated. "To continue to be a wholly independent label, with the support of the Beggars Group, is the best of all possible worlds to our way of thinking."

"We're equal partners with Geoff and Jeanette [Lee]," says Mills. "They still run it and manage it. It's odd with Geoff, we've been in the same game for 25 or 30 years, but it took until Christmas before last [2006] for it to become evident to me that the Sanctuary ship was sinking. To pick up the phone to him and say, 'Should we talk about getting involved?' And it just naturally emerged from that. I think there's a lot of respect between us and so far, so very good. We had an awful lot to fix, and I think we've fixed that, and now we have to fix the future."

But even a well-run company like Beggars is not immune to the new economics of the download generation. In April 2008 it was announced that both Beggars and Too Pure would fold as part of a restructuring, though several acts including The National, Stereolab and others would be transferred to 4AD in an effort to pool resources. Although there was a little hysteria in some elements of the press, this seemed in essence to be just another of the periodic occasions when Mills shuffles his pack.

Mills continues to fight for the rights of independents; having served on the BPI Council from 1987 through to 2000, he was instrumental in setting up the Association of Independent Music (AIM) in 1999 and IMPALA in 2000, as well as the Worldwide Independent Network. He is especially well informed on both technological developments and their impact on the infrastructure of the music industry. Recently quizzed on the downgrading of music's proprietary value, he made reference to the concept of branding as being little more than "an updating of the Florentine patronage model". He has similarly made poignant entreaties on the need for global licensing and the folly of the majors pursuing a DRM model (also licensing the original Napster, at a time when the major labels were completely spooked by its development).

"I go back to the ladder analogy," Mills says of his various positions of advocacy for independent music in the UK. "I'm not sure if I helped build the ladder to climb up, but I do want to preserve every rung on the ladder for future people to climb up. And I think we've succeeded in creating through AIM a community for the independents here, which simply didn't exist before. I think that's been incredibly healthy. The independent sector has been through its ups and downs since AIM started, but it would have been miles worse off without AIM, and similarly around the world. I think it's created a community of interest and a collective strength for independence."

It's an important voice in an age of increasing acquisition and consolidation among the majors. And they do genuinely affect 'big' policy. "We really do. We have at least as strong a voice with governments around the world as the mainstream music industry does. And it's clearly received as a very differentiated voice, and people like speaking to us because we're all entrepreneurs, we run our own businesses. And I find it very satisfying the way people are prepared to put time into IMPALA for nothing, for the greater good. I mean, I'm sure there are intangible benefits that emerge – if you put time in, you get something out, I'm not sure what. It does help to form relationships. If you look at the classic MTV-VPL-AIM face-off of five years ago, that deal wouldn't have happened if the independents hadn't been collectively organised. And because it's happened, those of us who have videos played on MTV get paid a decent amount of money for it. And that wouldn't have been the case had we not done that."

In straitened circumstances for the music industry, every such revenue stream is important. "It's crucial, yes. And we are actively engaged through those bodies and through Merlin in trying to make sure that independents have access to those revenue streams in the same way as a major. That's, I guess, a bit of a crusade – that there should be alternative ways of doing it. If you look at how most great music in the world has started and emerged, it's not been with the majors."

# Chapter Seven

## Behind The Wheel

## Mute Records, Industrial, and the New Electronica

Of all the storied independents of the late 70s, one of the most arresting tales is that of Mute Records, and the birth of a distinguished, distinctive and hugely influential record label that had absolutely no intention of being anything of the sort at its outset. Daniel Miller was a film student with a particular interest in silent cinema when he embarked on his accidental career. It was that background that gave him the idea of choosing Mute from a list of some 50 potential names he'd juggled with – that fact alone giving notice of his thoroughgoing, meticulous nature. Initially, all he had in mind was the release of just one single. Credited to The Normal, 'T.V.O.D.' and 'Warm Leatherette' (the latter, inspired by JG Ballard's *Crash* novel, was later covered by Grace Jones) was as starkly impressive, and genuinely left field, as anything released in the 'mushroom' year for independents of 1978. Its execution was as singular as its evolution. Unlike other totemic independent releases like The Undertones 'Teenage Kicks' and Buzzcocks' 'Spiral Scratch', its raw, percussive electronica and macabre lyrics spoke to the future rather than the present – in which the guitar, the dominant strain of outsider pop, was conspicuously absent.

"I think it was quite a few different things coming together at once," says Miller now, almost exactly 30 years since the single's release. "I'd been in bands when I was a kid, and even into my early 20s at college and afterwards. There was a lot of stuff I wanted to play and wanted to get involved in, that I couldn't really do, like electronic music. I went to art school [Guildford School of Art] to study film and we had a film studio with a few tape recorders, and we did tape loops and worked with oscillators and things like that. It was great to do and I wanted to take it further, but it was difficult at the time because synthesizers were too expensive. But a few things came together at once. Punk happened, and possibilities seemed to open up for anyone to try anything they wanted to do. The first wave of cheap, second-hand Japanese synthesizers came along in the mid-70s, with people like Korg and Roland."

The one Miller settled on was the slightly more expensive 700S model. "The 700S has a bit more on it, that's all. But I wouldn't have been able to make the record with the 700. They looked the same – they're both tiny synths designed to go on top of a keyboard so people can play a few weird effects and lead lines. It wasn't meant to be a standalone music-making machine or instrument, which is what it was for me. Very simple, but very effective. I'd started to read about these people like the Desperate Bicycles who had put out their own record, and I was getting very excited about the whole thing. I was 24 or 25, and had worked and travelled after college." In fact, he had been employed variously as a mini-cab driver in London and as a DJ in a European ski resort on his adventures. "I always had ways of earning money from my film-editing experience. So I said, fuck it, I'm going to get another film-editing job – which I didn't really want to do – just to earn as much money as I could to buy a synth."

Miller recalls his starting costs equating to roughly £200 for the second-hand Korg, and between £200 and £300 for a TEAC 2340 tape recorder. "That was quite a lot of money at the time. But I was working at ATV as a freelance assistant film editor, and there was always voluntary overtime to do. So I did as much overtime as I could, at double time – thanks to the ACTT film union at the time."

Despite it remaining his primary source of income, he had realised that film could never be his chosen medium. "Music was my first love, always. I like them both. But I knew I had to be, ultimately, the auteur. I learned a lot, but I knew that I didn't have the personality to make it in the film industry as a director or a producer. There were very few opportunities anyway. Nowadays there's an entry through pop videos, but there wasn't even that in my day. I was working in commercials, which was interesting and educational, but I knew I'd never be satisfied doing that. I knew a lot of people in the film industry at that point, and I could see the kind of people who were successful. I didn't feel I was one of those people. I don't think, really deep down, I have the passion, but I did have the passion for music. I fell in love with pop music when I was zero. So I got to this point, and I thought, fuck it, I'm going to put out a record, buy a synthesizer and a tape machine. I think in the back of my mind, I thought I'd get those, and whatever happens, I'll have a lot of fun with it. And if I think it's any good, I'll put a record out. Nobody will buy it, nobody will be interested, but I just want the experience of doing it, then I can get along with my life! Basically that's what I did."

There was a hitch, though. "People seemed to like it! That hadn't figured in my plans at all. I'd pressed the minimum, which I think was 500 at the time. But once I'd decided to do it, I phoned up a few people like Rough Trade and Pete Stennet at Small Wonder. I didn't know them at the time, but they'd just started putting their own records out. I phoned up Pete and said, 'I want to put a record out – how many do you think I should press?' No-one knew fuck all. I didn't know, and he didn't know. But he gave me an address of a sleeve printer and label maker. Everyone was in it and enjoying it, and there was no territorial sense. Then I spoke to someone at Rough Trade. I said, 'I want to press 500. 'Ah, we're only interested in records that sell more than 10,000,' weirdly enough. I said, 'OK, fine, whatever.'"

That was, in the circumstances, an odd answer. "Yeah! I know who I got, and I got an odd person at the wrong time, and I spoke to them about it afterwards. And I got to know everybody at Rough Trade very well and we became friends, so it was fine. They'd just put out their first Metal Urbain single, which was RT001. I decided to go ahead and do it. I went to the pressing plan in Dagenham that everybody used at the time, Orlake. Delga was the company that did the sleeves. If you look at a lot of old punk 7-inches, it's always got Delga on the sleeve. And Peter Gray printers did the labels. They are important, those names. I walked in off the street. These were old fashioned companies, been around forever. I didn't know what the fuck I was talking about, and they were really friendly and really helpful. All of them: the pressing plant, the sleeve maker, the label maker. I was just some bloke making 500 copies – it was nothing for them. A small hit in those days sold 150,000 singles. And they were all really helpful to me, and not just to me but to other people, and I don't think they ever get any credit."

That was the manufacturing taken care of. The next stage was distribution. "I went to Orlake in East London to pick up the test pressing, and I thought I'd pop into Small Wonder as it was on the way home. I saw Pete and introduced myself. He said he vaguely remembered talking to me. 'Here's the single, what do you think?' Because I thought I'd take it round to shops, to see if they'd take it. I didn't understand the concept of distribution. I knew nothing about the record industry. He said, 'Yeah, it sounds pretty good. It's all right. I wouldn't have done it that way, but it's not bad. I'll take a box.' Twenty-five! Fucking hell. That's brilliant! Somebody in a record shop listening to my record? I can't believe it. It was unbelievably exciting. I can remember every moment of it. Then I went to Lightning Records, and they didn't seem that interested in seeing me. So I thought, I was near Rough Trade, and I'd never been to the shop before. During the period I was buying all those 7-inches, I was working in Boreham Wood at ATV, and there was a little shop there. He used to go to Rough Trade once a week. I would put my order in, and he'd get me the records. I was working so I never had the time to go. So I went to Rough Trade, which was like the centre of the whole world of coolness. And I was very intimidated – not by them, but my perception of it. And I walked in the door with my single, and Judith [Crighton], who is still there, said go through the back and see Geoff [Travis]. And Geoff and Richard Scott were there. They were dealing with some export customer or something. They asked me to hang on a second. I was just standing there with all these records in this tiny little room. Then we went to the shop and played the record in front of all these cool people."

It sounds like the definition of terror. "It was and it wasn't. It was because I was nervous. But my expectations were so low. I wasn't thinking this is the make or break of my career, but in terms of putting it out there in public? I made the record in 24 hours because I had to hire one piece of equipment, which I could only just afford. So by the time I'd finished I didn't really know what I was doing, it was a solid 24-hour recording session at home. And they liked it. They said, 'How many do you want to press?' I said, 'I was thinking of 500'. 'I think you should do 2,000, we could easily do 2,000 of this.' I think they gave me a bit of money [they advanced him £300] to help me get those pressed, and off it went. And it got amazing reviews."

Indeed one review, by Jane Suck for *Sounds*, which ran in their 8th April edition, described it as 'single of the century'. *Record Mirror* made it joint single of the week a month later, by which time it had actually been officially released. "Jane Suck had got hold of a test pressing from Rough Trade," Miller recalls. "And I got this message, a telegram or something – I'd gone away to visit friends. It said 'single of the century'. I couldn't believe it. And that's how it was in those days. I was just some bloke in off the street who'd made an electronic record. And there weren't really electronic records around at the time. Obviously there was Kraftwerk and those kind of things, but the post-punk electronic scene, Throbbing Gristle, and those things? I was aware of them. I was aware of The Residents, and early Devo. But I hadn't really heard any of it. In a way I didn't want to listen to it. I had a very clear idea of what I wanted to do, and I didn't want to be influenced either way by hearing someone else. I wanted to be pure. Obviously I was a massive Kraftwerk fan, but also The Ramones. I was actually listening more to The Ramones when I made my record, rather than to other electronic records. I wanted to make a punk rock electronic record, or an electronic record in the spirit of the time, something that wasn't rooted in the hippy era. And I wanted to make a bit of a statement – I was a big believer in electronic music as being the next thing. And the fact that it [electronic music] was more of a punk rock music than..." Anything with guitars could ever be? "Exactly. It wasn't really that revolutionary, and you had to learn three chords. Which you certainly didn't have to do with a synthesizer, you just had to play one note and make a noise. That seemed a much better option to me."

Miller put an address on the rear of the sleeve, his mother's house in Decoy Avenue, Golders Green, where he'd recorded the songs and was staying after returning from travelling. He still doesn't know why. "I thought that's what you do. I don't know why I did it, but I did it." It's worth considering how Miller's 'it's what you did' insouciance contrasted with the explicit political convictions behind Scritti Politti's debut, a band with whom Miller would later share a stage. But the effect was similar. "I immediately got demos. I got a Clock DVA tape very early on. But I didn't want to be a record company at that point. I just wanted to put a record out, see what it felt like. I wanted to experience the feeling of putting a record out."

Mute might have ended there, had it not been for Miller meeting some of the other early electronic adventurers – fellow bedroom mavericks emboldened by the affordability of synthesizers. One-time collaborators Robert Rental ('Paralysis') and Thomas Leer ('Private Plane') also released pioneering electronic-based solo singles for similarly home-grown labels in 1978. "I met up with Robert Rental at a Throbbing Gristle gig," recalls Miller, "the famous one at the London Film Makers' Co-Op [July 1978] that ended in violence. We were talking to the band – I'd vaguely met Throbbing Gristle at that point through Rough Trade. Then Robert came along. And separately, there was a gig promotion company called Final Solution [partly founded by Colin Favor of Small Wonder]. They were very much the post-punk people. They put on Joy Division etc. And they wanted to put on a gig of the new electronic bands. They asked me if I'd play, and asked Robert if he'd play. Neither one of us really wanted to do it on our own, so we decided to do it together. I'd done a few gigs, we didn't do that many – it wasn't that I didn't want to appear in public, because I kind of wanted to experience that as well. It was more that I didn't know how I would do it on my own. That ended up with us doing the Rough Trade tour, with Stiff Little Fingers and Essential Logic."

Said tour was chastening, as the duo played to non-plussed die-hard SLF fans every evening as they criss-crossed the UK together on a 30-date winter tour. There were further adventures on the continent, too. "There was a venue in Paris called the Gibus Club, and they used to bring punk bands over, The Slits and The Damned etc. You basically played three nights, they put you up in an awful hotel, and they fed you – a bit. We had a laugh. We did that, and got so drunk that on the last night we had a massive fight on stage. Had to be broken up by a guy called Simon Leonard who was in various bands later on Mute, like I Start Counting and Fortran 5. He came to the gig and ended up having to run up on stage and separate us. So I wasn't really running a record company, I was leading the rock 'n' roll lifestyle! There were things I wanted to experience, so I did. I was also helping Rough Trade out a little bit, doing a bit of promotion and stuff like that."

The idea of the label still hadn't formulated, but the success of 'T.V.O.D.' ensured he was at least able to stop work as a film editor. "At that point the record was selling enough, and I was having to keep track of getting it pressed, and there were a few interviews coming in and it started to get played in America, which was very weird." Sire president Seymour Stein, who would become a long-term ally, was the connection here. He quickly licensed the single for America. "I saw him [Miller] at Rough Trade, I used to hang out there a lot," Stein recalls. "I said, 'I'm Seymour Stein.' He said, 'I'm Daniel Miller, this is the first record I've put out. And it's The Normal.' I loved both sides of it, and I said I think this could really do something, and he licensed it with me. Then later on he got involved with Rob Buckle, an old friend of mine from Sonnet Records, and I picked up [Miller's second record] Silicon Teens."

"I started to get these college radio playlist reports through with my record on it," recalls Miller, visibly still bemused at the memory." I did an interview with Rodney Bingenheimer [famous American KROQ DJ]. He called me on the phone and I couldn't quite believe that. I came to a point where I thought, I've got to decide what to do next. I didn't feel like doing another record. But I had a Silicon Teens record, half of which I'd done before anyway. It was never meant to be a record, it was just experimenting with Chuck Berry songs." The Silicon Teens project is recalled as "The Archies meet Kraftwerk" by Dave Henderson in the *Mute Audio Documents* box set, a description this author can't improve on. "Then I met Fad Gadget through Edwin Pouncey [*NME* cartoonist Savage Pencil], because they shared a flat. I think that Edwin's goal was to get Frank a record deal so he could afford to live somewhere else! But they were very close friends. That was the first thing that I heard where I thought it was something I could really get into. And I met Frank [Tovey; aka Fad Gadget] and we got on like a house on fire, and we had really similar ideas. So I just said, 'Why don't we record a single?'"

That effectively marked the start of Mute Records as a going concern. Miller retained the name because "it had been difficult enough making a decision in the first place! Even though we'd put just one single out, by that time it had a little bit of a reputation. So we did the single together, a hand-shake deal, 50-50 profit-share, no commitment to further product, etc. It was a really casual thing. And that was a song called 'Back To Nature', which was a great single. I had the Silicon Teens thing, but I didn't want to put that out as the second thing on Mute. So we did Frank's single and then I did the Silicon Teens' 'Memphis Tennessee' single. And again that took it to another level. That got picked up on Radio One, mainly through John Peel, who played it an awful lot. I remember him playing it twice in one show. That was it. You should just retire when that happens – when John Peel plays your single twice in one show. And then it all got weird. Major record labels like this [he is speaking from EMI's offices in West London] started to ring up and say, 'Are you interested in signing?' I went to see all these people, though I had no intention of doing anything. Coincidentally they're people you end up working with 30 years later. Like Chris Briggs, famous A&R man, he works here now – he signed Wire and Gang Of Four to EMI, and Roger Ames. All these people were trying to nick my bands!"

But of course, to a large degree, Miller *was* the bands. "Exactly. There was interest in Frank, but that was slightly different, because that was his life and career and I couldn't make those decisions for him. We went together to see CBS, Muff Winwood was really interested in it. It was great in a way, but we were enjoying doing it on our own, and we wanted to keep it so that it wasn't driven by commercial considerations. We were doing it for fun. We were learning a hell of a lot. I knew nothing about the music industry. Nothing. Zero. And I still like to think I don't know as much as I should know, which is a good thing. People say to me, 'Daniel, you should be thinking out of the box.'" Miller can't resist paraphrasing the famous *Monty Python* sketch. "In my day, we couldn't afford a box to think out of – box were a luxury!"

By the time Miller had committed to the Fad Gadget record, almost a year had elapsed. "Yeah, there was about a year, I guess, between 001 and 002. Then there was a flurry of releases. Then I was off and running in the sense that, mentally, I'd made that leap, that I was happy to be a label." If the Fad Gadget arrangement hadn't worked out as well as it did, that might not have happened. "I think if it hadn't been good fun I wouldn't have gone on with it. I don't know about success. It was more about it being good fun at that point. Nobody was making any money, and the goal was to learn and to enjoy the experience of putting out a record, and just make enough money to get the next record pressed."

The Fad Gadget and Silicon Teens releases were further important staging posts in the development of an indigenous post-punk electronic genre. Miller has remained adamant down the years that this was not just predictable, but a 'historic inevitability'. "I knew it was going to happen. And the Silicon Teens *was* a concept – it was a total lie obviously, but it was billed as the world's first all-electronic teenage pop band." There was also a little mischief to be made by hiding the group's identity, leading to an irate exchange with an *NME* journalist demanding that Miller 'own up'. But there was also a serious edge. "I knew that at some point, and it came very quickly actually, you'd get a generation of kids that had a choice when they decided they wanted to make music. They wouldn't just automatically buy guitar, bass and drums, they could choose to buy a synth. And that, conceptually, is what the Silicon Teens was." Was it that the technology was so enabling, it had to be the next step? "Yeah. And it was exciting, because I loved electronic music. I was 26 or 27 by that time. I'd been listening to four guys with guitars, bass and drums for 18 years or something. And I loved all that shit. But by 1977/78 it was enough. And pub rock killed that – I didn't listen to English or American music for about five years, because it was shit as far as I was concerned. I only listened to German music. Not because 'it's got to be German', but because that was where the only interesting music was coming out, with a couple of notable exceptions. And I was bored with it, I thought this has got to move on. Between 1963 and 1977, it's not that long, there had been incredible changes in music. But then it felt like it had stopped and hit a brick wall. And nothing much was happening. I had enough passion about music to think, let's push it forward, let's get to the next bit."

Miller recognises the importance of records like PiL's 'Public Image' and other harbingers of the post-punk dialectic, but insists "that was a bit later [than the immediate punk explosion]. By the end of 1978 when my single came out there was tons of interesting music out there. All that stuff started to come in. Throbbing Gristle made their first single, Cabaret Voltaire made their first single, Human League, OMD, plus all those other guys – Gerry & The Holograms. Brilliant. Who *is* Gerry? Who *are* the Holograms? Who knows! They made one fucking great single. And bands like Tuxedomoon came over. Joy Division was slightly different, and even though it wasn't electronic, it was coming from a similar place. It was all getting very exciting. And it was a historic inevitability. That's not even in retrospect, at the time it felt like that. It's not just looking back and going, 'Ah, I can see now why that happened.' It actually felt like it was happening at the time. I'd talk to people like Robert Rental, people I was hanging around with like the guys from Wire, whom I became really friendly with early on and loved. They were a great example of a band who didn't sound like they looked – they didn't sound like the instruments they were playing. We would just hang out and talk about it in the pub, just on a very casual basis. And it was very much – this is what's going to be happening."

Those changes were reflected by the content of fanzines like Sheffield's *NMX*, which was loosely associated with the university's Now Society and its attendant manifestos, as well as Stevo of Some Bizzare's Futurist chart in *Sounds* and the work of Throbbing Gristle's Industrial Records. A network was building. For example, by April 1979 Throbbing Gristle would be hosted by NowSoc, and there was also a crossover with the emergent tape-trading scene. *NMX* would sell live tapes of NowSoc performances featuring editor Martin Russian's band They Must Be Russians, alongside the Extras, 2,3 and Cabaret Voltaire, for the bargain price of £1.50. "But none of these people were new romantics, that happened a bit later," Miller is immediately at pains to point out. "And yes, there were loads of manifestos about." Historically, early 1981 was the breakthrough year for the new romantics, but that was a movement orchestrated almost exclusively by major labels, which can legitimately be seen as a retrenchment following the unruly mess created by punk and post-punk.

It is not hysterical to locate the fulcrum of the emergent electronic movement as the South Yorkshire city of Sheffield. Certainly many of the most influential post-punk, but equally importantly, post-guitar records, emerged from there (Cabaret Voltaire, Human League, Vice Versa, etc). It has been said that 'there were no punk bands at all' in Sheffield, the city which, by dint of the location of so many synth/keyboard-driven artists, became the perceived base of a type of ostensibly serious electronic music. The quote itself comes from no less an authority than Phil Oakey of The Human League (whose polemical stance was such that, before he joined the band, they had a song entitled 'Destroy All Guitars'). But that statement, accepted as truth without query, ignores the input of bands like the Stunt Kites, the Negatives and, to a lesser extent, the Extras. Missing the point that post-punk was generally fashioned *in sympathy with* as well as in reaction to punk is a mistake. Miller, like McGee (Creation), Alway (Cherry Red), Mills and Watts-Russell (Beggars/4AD) and even Carroll and Armstrong (Chiswick/Ace), all recognise punk as the enabling force that spurred them to pursue their own musical vocations. In fact, if any of the new breed of independent labels had true claim to antecedence of that crucial moment, it was Throbbing Gristle's Industrial label.

Established in 1976 by Throbbing Gristle, Industrial housed the explicitly 'non-entertainment' sonic experiments of band members Genesis P-Orridge, Cosey Fanni Tutti, Chris Carter and Peter Christopherson. The intention was to provide a platform for the openly confrontational works of Throbbing Gristle, who specialised in acts designed to inflate the moral hubris of mainstream media, although they claimed not to seek shock value *per se*, but were 'interested in those things personally'. "We wanted to re-invest rock music with content, motivation and risk," they would write in the sleevenotes to *TG CD 1*. "Our records were documents of attitudes and experiences and observations by us and other determinedly individual outsiders. Fashion was an enemy, style irrelevant... We wanted to also investigate music as a Business phenomenon and propose models for entirely new and innovative modes of commercial operation."

Variation in accepted methods of 'operation' also extended to the group's musical vocabulary. Industrial Records were among the subjects addressed by Robert Worby in his essay, *Cacophony*, "The punk sound was constructed with loud, noisy guitars, industrial music maintained the noise but used an extended instrumental palette. The tape recorder became a commonplace musical instrument rather than a documentary tool and musicians were credited as playing 'tapes'... Throbbing Gristle and Industrial Records were extremely influential in the creative climate that flourished during the punk era and beyond. The enthusiasm for sonic exploration and experimentation, within an ethos that said 'anyone can do it', encouraged many young pop musicians to question notions of conventional musical structure – melody, harmony, rhythm – and search for other structures, other ways of putting sounds together."

"In my view," notes Christopherson, aka Sleazy, "Industrial Records was set up as a kind of ironic comment on the music industry, rather than being part of it. Especially as it was started in 1975/1976, the days of The Sweet, Abba, prog rock etc, before indie or punk had even been thought of or named (in the UK at least). I think the first Throbbing Gristle album was already out when I took the first photos of the Sex Pistols, even before they played their first gig – or certainly before they were signed. Throbbing Gristle always were proud to be outsiders who did things simply for the fun (and artistic purity) of it, rather than as a business or to make money. This usually incurred the wrath of audiences and the incomprehension of actual industry folk – we were so far 'out of the box' that there WAS nothing to compare us to. There was no pigeonhole that suited or applied to Throbbing Gristle. Obviously the industrial genre was only established because record shops didn't know where to rack our records."

Rather than being influenced by any forerunning independent labels, Industrial actually benefited from Christopherson's association with majors. "I was working for mainstream labels, designing and shooting album covers with design group Hipgnosis, famous for its work with Pink Floyd, Led Zeppelin, Genesis etc, at that time. So I had some inside knowledge of the industry, printing plants etc. The staff all wore suits and ties, and had to be caught before their extended lunches to obtain any decision, because after lunch they were all too drunk to decide anything. Ironically it was the money I was making from that, that financed the start of Industrial Records."

"In the beginning we all felt a 'corporate style or voice' was totally appropriate for our highly non-corporate approach to life and music," Christopherson states. "During the life of the first incarnation of Throbbing Gristle, that largely remained intact, and held good, so strong was our bond and shared understanding of Throbbing Gristle's method and philosophy. At that time Genesis and Cosey lived together in Hackney in East London, so their house became a kind of hub for the Industrial cottage industry. Cosey had the most aptitude for paperwork and accounts, whilst also following her alternate persona as a self-aware erotic dancer. Genesis took care of the day to day operations, duplication of cassettes etc, as well as keeping track in some way of 'the bigger picture', writing to interesting and useful people, making tea and being generally the most outgoing of the four of us. Chris and I, though we led lives less solely concentrated on Throbbing Gristle, went to the house as often as we could, usually several times a week or more. It was rare that any significant decision about the band was made without the input of all four members and it was always democratic. Where there was a specific affinity – such as mine for design and graphics or Chris's for technical things and manufacture of specialist electronics, we certainly made use of it."

Other artists on the label included Clock DVA (specialists themselves in media inversion), the Leather Nun (glorying in sexual perversion and display) and Monte Cazazza (an artist whose entire output was dedicated to a thorough exploration of the geography of 'outrage'). There were also collaborations with beat author William Burroughs and Derek Jarman (via Elisabeth Welch, whose 'Stormy Weather' appeared on the soundtrack to *The Tempest*). It was Cazazza who gave them the slogan 'industrial music for industrial people', though the more telling alternative was 'Music From The Death Factory'. The packaging of these releases explored similar themes – why is society so irked by graphic projections of sexuality or violence, when it accepts a deluge of tacitly similar and often deliberately titillating examples of the same in newspapers, magazines and video/TV? A prime example was Industrial's own logo, a monochrome photograph of the Tate

Modern art museum which many were convinced was the chimney at the Auschwitz concentration camp. The group relished indulging in such games of duality; the idyllic, chocolate box cover of their *20 Jazz Funk Greats* album saw them pictured on Beachy Head, the noted suicide black spot.

Distributed by Rough Trade from the summer of 1977 onwards, Industrial's collective releases had great impact, many selling out quickly. But the label was abandoned when Throbbing Gristle disbanded in 1981. Thereafter the catalogue lay dormant aside from reissues on Mute, although it has been revived in recent years. "It was important to us not to become pigeonholed," Christopherson continues. "We were horrified when some other artists who did not seem to be doing the same thing as Throbbing Gristle at all became classified as 'industrial'. Irony, humour, a low threshold of boredom with what we had done before, and the confounding of audiences' prior expectations were cornerstones of what we did, so when we felt people were already expecting, and would be unfazed by, whatever unexpected thing we might do, we stopped."

"Both Mute and Some Bizzare were the products of easier times, even though only a few short years later," he continues, "when 'do-it-yourself' had become fashionable and desirable. And even then they only embraced Throbbing Gristle (and its offshoots) when they were proven to be selling as much as many small bands on major labels, but without any promotional business machinery, middle management, press office, A&R etc. Whereas they were trying (boldly) to do the traditional thing in a new way, Industrial was not. Industrial was not on the same page, or possibly even in the same book!" Given that the venture was so determinedly non-commercial, was it a surprise when Industrial's records sold in the quantities they did? "Perhaps naively, no," he reflects. "I was not surprised. I felt we were doing something so much more potent and important than the latest Mud or Sweet single, that it stood to reason that people would be interested – not everyone to be sure, but enough to make it a viable concern. Since commercial success was not our goal, only honesty mattered. We did what interested us most acutely, and consequently that power, that concentration, was committed to vinyl, and to every part of the way we ran the business. If it felt that potent to us, how could it not to others, and even if it turned out we were the only people in the world that were interested, what did that matter? Although the personal agendas of the four members of Throbbing Gristle may have changed over the years, I hope the principles of making sound purely for our own enjoyment, without the slightest regard for the prevailing trends or business sense, that we started back then, remain with Industrial today."

Fetish Records is also of note here, another London-based imprint whose catalogue featured The Bongos, Snatch, Throbbing Gristle, 23 Skidoo, the Bush Tetras, 8 Eyed Spy and Clock DVA. In essence, a meeting point between New York's No Wave troublemakers and the harder/more challenging end of the UK's electronica/industrial spectrum. Formed by Throbbing Gristle fan Rob Pearce in 1979, it garnered significant press and almost had a hit single in the form of 23 Skidoo's 'Seven Songs'. The most distinctive aspect of Fetish's output was Neville Brody's 'human decay' designs, typically hand-crafted and then re-photographed, offsetting the disturbing subject matter with contrastingly vibrant colour schemes. After being sacked from Stiff's art department, Brody was able to enjoy total freedom of expression at Fetish, before subsequently becoming *The Face*'s art director in its glory years. Indeed, such was the label's focus on style that in the summer of 1982 Fetish launched a line of t-shirts, featuring designs by Malcolm Garrett, *NME* illustrator Ian Wright and Brody himself. However, at the same time Pearce would retire from the label, announcing that it would be taken over by ex-Beggars employee Steve Marshall. But the imprint had fizzled and stalled by 1983. Pearce, who went into management, was murdered in Mexico in 1987.

The aforementioned Some Bizzare, at the other end of the scale, was employing electronica to tackle the charts with the seedy, *Cabaret*-informed Soft Cell. Founder Stevo had played a role in Mute's history but is worthy of note in his own right. While Stevo had no problem affiliating Some Bizzare to whichever of the majors flashed the most ample cheque, his modus operandi was quantifiably 'independent'; and his self-billing as a 'music industry anarchist' was little short of exaggeration. However, his tastes were easily differentiated from the more orthodox, worthy dialogue of the punk-influenced 'anarchist' bands, focusing instead on a series of artists who were, almost, as flamboyant as he was.

Having left school in East London aged 16, unable to read or write, Stevo (Steve Pearce) took a training placement with Phonogram and started working as a mobile DJ, notably at the Chelsea Drugstore on King's Road and subsequently The Clarendon. He was almost certainly the first mobile DJ to play records by Throbbing Gristle, and would legendarily dance nude while mixing samples of Mickey Mouse over Cabaret Voltaire records. The Clarendon nights led to him being invited to submit a 'futurist' chart to *Sounds*. This, in turn, led to a Some Bizzare compilation album, featuring artists who 'broke down barriers'. It was intended to highlight the talents of a raft of bands who had posted demo tapes, which he thereafter licensed to majors. That policy of recording an artist then negotiating a deal with companies such as Virgin or Phonogram for the masters, thereby accessing their distribution muscle and mitigating costs, made him, effectively, the Joe Meek of the 80s.

Yet Stevo could have taught Meek a thing or two about misbehaviour. Tales of his interaction with major label bigwigs are legion – often contemporaneously recalled in the then still entertaining *Smash Hits* pop glossy, which flourished during the new romantic boom. He insisted on a weekly delivery of sweets as part of a deal with Phonogram, signed Test Department sat astride a rocking horse named Horace, and concluded a further deal with Soft Cell via an emissary – a teddy bear dressed as Robin Hood. Stevo was only 17 when he signed off on a management contract with the latter. He delighted in keeping CBS's Maurice Oberstein waiting for a meeting, hopping tube trains and insisting he follow him – a stark contrast to The Clash's cap-doffing genuflection to the same mogul. Indeed, in playing the role of maverick for both fun and advantage, Stevo's penchant for mind games scared the music industry to an extent that rivalled the more prosaic rebellious gambits of many of the punk generation. Specifically, after delivering The The's *Soul Mining* album to Phonogram, ostensibly his paymasters, he then sold it on to both Warners and finally CBS – a move of consummate arrogance that outdid McLaren and the Pistols at a stroke.

Another charm offensive – to get Psychic TV a deal – saw him send out brass phalluses to record company executives with the legend 'Psychic TV: Fuck The Record Industry', engraved underneath. And his playful spite wasn't just directed at the music industry's upper echelons. He famously 'installed' a chapel and confession box as part of his offices in Mayfair where those handing in demo tapes would be inducted – though other sources suggest this was one of many apocryphal stories he was happy to circulate. His relationship with his own artists, meanwhile, similarly stoked controversy. His fall-outs with Marc Almond were widely chronicled, and he was publicly criticised by both Genesis P. Orridge and Einsturzende Neubaten. Coil (formed by Christopherson with Throbbing Gristle 'fan boy' and lover Geoff Rushton, aka John Balance), went to the trouble of subtitling one of their releases: 'Steve, Pay Us What You Owe Us'.

When asked in 1990 by Ian Gittins if he shared any affinity with the likes of 4AD, Factory or Mute, Stevo's response might have been easily guessed. "Yeah, but I think I'm better than all three of them, musically speaking... I look at Some Bizzare like this – a sculptor with mallet and chisel, or an artist in a recording studio, or a painter with a canvas, that's the outlet for their frustration. They all have an outlet for their creativity. Some Bizzare is my outlet, and the way I sign people up is very particular. I'm playing chess, and I'm going to win."

Stevo's link to Miller initially come through Depeche Mode, though via long-term collaborator Jim Thirlwell [an Australian ex-pat raised in Brooklyn whose artistic *nom de plume* was Foetus] he also brought subsequent Mute mainstays Einsturzende Neubaten to British ears. Depeche were unsure whether committing a track to Stevo's proposed 'futurist' compilation would be in their long-term interests. It was during these negotiations that Stevo first suggested they approach Mute (in the end their track 'Photographic', produced by Miller, did indeed emerge on the Some Bizzare compilation). Ultimately, though, he would pass on offering Depeche Mode a management contract, as he had Soft Cell and The The, telling Simon Reynolds in *Rip It Up* that they were 'too commercial and poppy' for his tastes. Yet that was certainly part of Depeche Mode's appeal to Miller.

Thirlwell, meanwhile, also had his own label, Self Immolation, for his various exploits as Foetus (later serving as a 'vanity' stamp on his Some Bizzare releases). In a *Magnet* interview with Matt Johnson, Thirlwell remembered how the imprint grew out of his job in retail at Virgin – and how easy it was to benefit both in terms of finances and resources from the indie label surge. "I worked behind the singles counter for a couple of years. After that, I moved on to the warehouse, where I was buying all the independent 7-inches and 12-inches for the entire chain. So it was like, 'Ooh, looks like we're sold out of Foetus records. I guess I'll have to order some more. I was just giving them away. I was buying them from myself. I was working at Virgin and doing Foetus concurrently. The way Foetus came about was when my lung collapsed. I had glandular fever. I was squatting at the time. I was out of commission for two months, collecting unemployment from Virgin. I couldn't get out of bed, so I put all that money towards the studio, and that financed my first Foetus record. That was in 1980."

It took some time for Mute to shift its focus from singles to albums. The process began with the release of DAF's (Deutsch-Amerikanische Freundschaft)'s *Ein Produkt Der* debut. "Frank's single came out around September '79," says Miller, "so roughly a year later the albums came in fairly quick succession – DAF, Frank and then the Silicon Teens albums all came out pretty close together. All the singles were selling well – the Silicon Teens in particular. So I'd made enough money off them. The DAF album took three days to record. We'd started to get a really good relationship with

Eric Radcliffe at Blackwing Studios. Any recordings we weren't doing at home we were doing there, because it was cheap and he was great to work with. And none of us knew what we were doing. Frank recorded his album there, probably in about ten days. It was tight – it was always tight. But there were moments earlier on in the process when it had been more difficult. When I started to work with DAF, and they were sleeping on the floor, I really had no money at that point. Difficult times. When the singles started coming out, there was enough cash flow to do the stuff I needed to do, *just*. Now, you wait for six months after you finish an album to put it out; in those days you just put it out as soon as you could. You did everything as quickly as possible. We were spending virtually nothing on marketing or promotion or those sorts of things. But in those days you could sell enough singles to just about keep going."

In fact, the reason Miller was unable to initially sign The Birthday Party – who would move to 4AD instead – was due entirely to those stretched finances – and a floor full of Germans. "I was broke. It wasn't that I couldn't sign them, because nobody was getting advances anyway. The point is that I had DAF – five German guys sleeping on my floor, and no money. When I first met The Birthday Party. they'd come recommended to me by their label in Australia, a guy called Keith Glass. How he would recommend Mute, a record label that had only put out a few singles, I have no idea (Glass himself can only recall dealing directly with 4AD). And I loved the album. But that's five Australians and five Germans – I don't know how I'm going to deal with this. I was pretty stressed out at the time. So I might have phoned Ivo and said, check it out. There was definitely that kind of a dialogue going on between us. It would never happen today, even between independent labels. If you heard something and thought, this is really a Factory or a Rough Trade record, you'd ring up Tony Wilson or Geoff Travis and say, 'Check this out, it might be up your street.' You weren't keeping things to yourself."

The reason The Birthday Party would eventually bounce back to Miller's custody had much to do with the label's ability to market Depeche Mode, who quickly validated his conviction that a new era in music was imminent. In many ways they also built on the premise Miller had explored with the Silicon Teens. "I thought, fucking hell – they weren't like the Silicon Teens, but this thing was inevitably going to happen. And it happened and there they were – kids aged 17 and 18 on stage, each with a cheap synthesizer, the only synthesizers they could afford, on beer crates, playing along to a little drum machine. And Dave Gahan with one light pointing up to his face to make him look Gothy. In a pub, with great pop songs."

## Behind The Wheel

As Tom Bailey of the Thompson Twins confirms, the choice of instrument was as pragmatic as Miller has always maintained. "It's one of those things that nobody talks about – in those days, a guitar was £100, and a synthesizer was £3,000. So guess which one you bought to get on stage?" Miller's dream of a gathering army of young men (and admittedly, most such musicians were indeed male) marching forward into history's lens with Korgs and Roland synths slung under their arms was not unique to him. But his committed sponsorship of the band who would 'break' electronic instrumentation within a conventional pop music context probably was. The Human League would admittedly reposition themselves at around the same time and commit to a similar aesthetic, and it's important to remember Numan's contribution in this sphere. But his Tubeway Army records and beyond were never rooted in conventional melody and song structure at this stage. Those records were instinctively alien to the pop discourse, no matter how well they sold. Depeche Mode were, to all intents and purposes, about 'pure' pop records; a shift in form rather than substance.

Though he didn't recall it at the time, Miller had met Depeche Mode briefly at Rough Trade. "Oh, God! I was doing Fad Gadget's album, *Fireside Favourites*. I remember the sleeves had come back to Rough Trade that day and there was some error or something, and I was really fucked off and angry. And the late Scott Piering, who was a very important radio promotion person from that era and right through the next 20 years, was working at Rough Trade. He said, 'Daniel, you might like these guys, come and have a listen.' And I just saw these four spotty new romantics, and I thought, 'I can't handle this now, I've got to sort out my sleeves.' And they remembered that very clearly. I didn't. Even when I saw them play. I didn't connect them as being the people who had been in Rough Trade at that time." Miller's trusted associate Seymour Stein was equally enthused by a Depeche Mode live performance, this time in their native Essex. "I got up early one morning and was reading the *NME* – 'Daniel Miller has a real band, and they're playing such and such a day.' This is Daniel Miller's band? They've got to be fantastic. So I flew right over and I signed them right there on the spot."

Depeche Mode broke through to the Top 20 in June 1981 with 'New Life', followed by a Top 10 single in 'Just Can't Get Enough' and a Top 10 album, *Speak & Spell*. It was satisfying for Miller, who had been repeatedly told – the message relayed in whispers to the band – that it would be impossible for them to enjoy chart success on such a small label. At the exact moment of his vindication, Depeche Mode's principal songwriter, Vince Clarke, made the decision to leave. "I think a lot of people thought when Vince left

Depeche, it was the end of the group," says Miller now. "On paper it was. He was the main songwriter, he was the driving force behind the band. It was his sound. And he was the guy who was the most ambitious. So on paper, yeah, the end of Depeche Mode. But by the time he'd left, they'd all become much more ambitious. They saw the possibilities. I don't think they'd have got there without him, because he was the really pushy one. But once things got going, they're all smart guys – they were just a bit cautious before. They all had jobs and he didn't have a job. That was the thing. In the end, he needed the job."

Rather than seeing his best-selling act disappear, Miller found himself with two major chart acts when Clarke went on to form Yazoo with Alison 'Alf' Moyet. *Upstairs At Eric's*, their debut album, stormed the charts, despite the humble origins its title reflected. "I remember that we had to build a studio in my house in about ten days," the eponymous Eric Radcliffe would subsequently recall, "to complete the recording of *Upstairs At Eric's* because Blackwing Studios was fully booked. My mother provided us all with her famous 'egg and chips' and also appeared on the record. Wonderful days!"

"It was insane," Miller confirms. "Vince left at the end of '81, and by the spring of '82 we had the Yazoo album selling 600,000 copies in the first week or something." However, Miller is honest enough to concede he didn't see that coming. "I wasn't sure. I only heard [the single] 'Only You' at first, and I wasn't sure about it. It was confusing to me. I got it in one sense very quickly, but my enthusiasm for it – shall we say it developed over time? It wasn't immediate, and I think Vince was quite downhearted by that. He said that, which is fair enough. But then I met Alison and heard her – and we'd decided to put the single out anyway. By that time I had a little team of people, not actually working for Mute, but a freelance radio promotions guy, another guy doing press, and they said, 'You've got to put this out, it's brilliant.'"

The second Yazz long-player, *You And Me Both*, became the first number one album distributed by Rough Trade. A fact that, tellingly, Miller has no recall of. "I know we didn't have a number one single till 1992 or something. We had loads of hits and number twos, but 'Abbaesque' [by subsequent Vince Clarke vehicle Erasure] was the first number one. I had a vague recollection the album went to number two... Rough Trade had already done well with the Stiff Little Fingers album, and they'd done very well with *Unknown Pleasures*. They were building up to it. It was there to be done." With Erasure proving hugely popular throughout Europe, and Depeche Mode being one of the few UK acts of the last 20 years to enjoy sustained success in America, Mute would achieve financial stability at exactly the time when several other notable independents such as Factory were beginning to struggle.

That unique situation – Mute having two highly successful acts at the same time – and therefore not undergoing the destabilising impact of having one 'star' name on the roster, helped shape not only the label, but Miller's role within it. "Yes, partly because I took the responsibility in making sure those artists and projects worked at the level everyone was expecting them to, not just in terms of marketing and international sales, but also in terms of the records themselves. In those early days, we're talking about the early 80s, especially with Depeche, I was still very much in the studio with them as well, three or four months each year, and they were making albums every year. And obviously I was overseeing Yazoo and then Erasure. Erasure came along when I was finishing my stint with Depeche – I did five albums with them between 1981 and 1985/86, and that's just when Erasure started to take off. But yes, I hardly signed anybody in that period. I started to work with Nick Cave, but virtually nothing else really in that period between '81 and '85, those four years, I can't think if I signed anyone in that time. Which was weird. But I was just so deep in what I was doing, and it was still a very small company and I was doing all the A&R. I wasn't really at a moment when I wanted to hand that off to anyone, so it was kind of down to me. I wasn't complaining – I enjoyed it. I was in the studio most of the time, and the rest of the time, I was trying to get those records finished, marketed and sold. I felt a huge amount of responsibility. Those artists put their trust, and their careers, in my hands. They didn't have to. They had plenty of other options. So I felt very responsible that I did the very best I could do for them. It was making sure they developed as artists and made good and interesting records. And then we ended up having hits, and meeting the expectations we all had for it – they were basically pop bands and we wanted to make sure they sold as many records around the world as possible, and developed their careers."

The emergence of both Depeche and Erasure did indeed enable the label to put their energies into the long-gestated relationship with The Birthday Party. "I'd kept in touch, because by that time they were living in London," says Miller. "I saw them at gigs and stuff, especially Mick Harvey and Phil Calvert, the drummer at the time. Chris Carr, the publicist, was doing some stuff for Mute, and he was also sort of managing The Birthday Party. His wife was an Australian and knew them from the old days, and somehow they landed on his doorstep instead of my doorstep to crash. Initially they came to me about publishing. I didn't have a publishing company, so I started one, 'cos I wanted to work with the guys – I always loved them. So, yeah, let's do the publishing thing together. Then soon after that, Chris was a bit concerned because 4AD needed a bit of money to make the next record. And by that time I'd had some hits. So I said, well, if it's OK with Ivo, I'd love to. I don't even know if Ivo and I discussed it. It just happened and it was very natural. And then of course they split up almost immediately! We only got an EP out of them. Then I got another two and a half or three bands out of the split!"

Despite such capacity for implosion, Miller was willing to keep the faith. "The individuals in the band were all really talented. And Nick was the writer of the lyrics and the singer, so his talents were more obvious in a way. But it wasn't *his* band, it was *their* band. It was him, Mick and Roland, and Tracy. Mick Harvey, then as now, manages them, effectively. He was the only one who was in any state to do anything that made sense. He doesn't get enough credit either. He kept a level head. For a lot of things, that's still the case."

There were other parallels with 4AD. Shortly after Ivo Watts-Russell chanced upon Throwing Muses, Mute's Blast First subsidiary, run by Paul Smith, was inaugurated with the release of Sonic Youth's *Bad Moon Rising*. Smith had previously run the Doublevision label from the back bedroom of his house in Nottingham, in association with Richard H Kirk and Stephen Mallinder of Cabaret Voltaire. After a disillusioning spell working in music retail and managing acts in Yorkshire and the Midlands. he and friend John Moon started a music video project at the Midland Group Arts Centre, presented on a bank of ten second-hand televisions. Among those he collaborated with were Cabaret Voltaire. "Cabaret Voltaire released *Red Mecca* and did an interview with the *NME*," he told Mute's Documentary Evidence website in 2005, "talking about their interest in funding a pirate radio station. As this was at the height of Thatcher's powers I was doubtful such a notion would last for any length of time and knowing the Cabs' interest in film and video, I re-contacted them about the possibility of starting an independent music video label. This, with Cabaret Voltaire's sole funding, and their considerable effort in making their own 90-minute programme, became Doublevision DV1."

*Doublevision Presents Cabaret Voltaire* was released in 1982, initially as a standalone project, and as such was the first independent music video release. It went on to showcase material by Throbbing Gristle, Chris & Cosey, 23 Skidoo, The Residents and filmmaker Derek Jarman and the *TV Wipeout* compilation, available free in exchange for a blank VHS. Vinyl followed, ultimately including various Kirk and Cabaret Voltaire related projects, plus Clock DVA, The Residents, Chakk and The Hafler Trio. These were initially marketed as 'soundtracks', as that was the only way to get the label's video output reviewed in the press. The founding of Blast First rose directly from this; Smith had intended to offer a deal to Lydia Lunch, then domiciled in South London, to record her *50 One Page Plays*, written with Nick Cave. When that fell through he offered her a deal for her *In Limbo* mini-album, in exchange for a ticket back to New York. It was Lynch who would tell Thurston Moore of Sonic Youth about Smith, who in turn supplied him with a cassette of an early version of *Bad Moon Rising*. Kirk wasn't interested in releasing 'American rock 'n' roll' on Doublevision, so Smith endeavoured to find a different outlet. Eventually he persuaded Pete Walmsley, as head of Rough Trade International, to provide finance to press it.

By this time, Smith had taken *Bad Moon Rising* to "everyone I knew", precipitating the founding of Blast First when his entreaties were spurned; the name taken from Wyndham Lewis's poetic 'manifestos' as part of the Vorticist art movement. Smith envisaged a label run along the lines of Harvest, and would sign a series of bands, including Dinosaur Jr, the Butthole Surfers and Steve Albini's Big Black, ostensibly rooted in punk, that helped define the alt-rock generation (as risible as that term sounded then and now). "After we'd finished [Depeche Mode's fifth studio album] *Black Celebration*, at the end of '85," Miller remembers, "I felt it was getting quite tough keeping the label running and everything else, because Erasure were starting to go. It became quite difficult to do all the roles. Plus I'd done five albums with the band, and it was enough – we needed fresh blood and fresh input. I came out of my Depeche world, in a way. I started to think, fuck, I haven't signed anyone for five years, I'd love to know what's going on. I'd heard a couple of tracks, one by a band called Big Stick, and another by a band called Head Of David, both on John Peel." Both had been Smith's immediate post-Sonic Youth signings.

Head Of David, indeed much beloved of Peel, were harbingers of the UK post-hardcore scene, having grown out of his long-time favourites Napalm Death. "My best night ever was when I went to see Nana Mouskouri and The Head Of David on the same night," he told this writer in 1991. "Not on the same bill! The venues were about a couple of hundred yards apart. I actually got a headache in the Nana Mouskouri thing because I hate perfume. I hate artificial smells like that and I was sitting in an absolute cloud of cheap perfume, which to me is worse than being in a room full of cigarette smoke.

As I say I got a blinding headache. I tried to persuade the three women sitting in front of me to come to the Head Of David gig afterwards because I'd like to get their opinion. They all shuffled away without a word, but it would have been interesting, because obviously they would have thought they'd arrived at the gates of hell, really." Big Stick's 'Drag Racing' EP, an unlikely update on the lost tradition of hot rod-themed repertoire by Jan & Dean and the Beach Boys, was among Peel's favourite records of all time, occupying a berth in his fabled time capsule box of treasured vinyl.

"I thought they were both [Head of David and Big Stick] amazing," Miller continues, "and I phoned up Rough Trade and asked who put them out. They said it was Paul Smith. I'd vaguely known Paul before, because he'd done stuff for Cabaret Voltaire. I met him and said, 'These are fantastic records, what are your plans?' He said, 'I really want to put these albums out by these guys, and I'm also trying to work with Sonic Youth, and I just don't have the resources.' So I said, 'Why don't we go into partnership and do it together?' And he said yes. It was an area of music I loved, but I wasn't as close to it in terms of my understanding as I was with electronic music. Obviously Paul was very deep into that thing, so it seemed a good way of moving forward."

Mute also inaugurated its own dance imprint. "A very similar thing happened with Rhythm King at almost the exact same time," says Miller. "I'd come out of the studio and really wanted to do stuff. And I knew James Horrocks very well. He was one of the partners of Rhythm King – he used to work in the same building as me. He worked for Cherry Red, which was upstairs from Mute at the time in Kensington Garden Square. I just bumped into him on the stairs, and he was carrying a bunch of records. 'Where are you off to?' 'We're thinking of starting a label with Polydor or something.' I said, 'What sort of label?' 'It's all this new house music coming out of Chicago.' I said, 'Why don't we have a chat about it? I'd love to work with you.' He introduced me to his partner [Martin Heath] and I just said, 'OK, let's go.' So we formed Rhythm King, and both those labels, in different ways, had a lot of success early on."

The basis of both deals was a 50-50 partnership where Blast First and Rhythm King brought in the acts, Mute funded the venture and they jointly handled the marketing. Miller: "Rhythm King was more needy just because they were working in a very fast way, and it was a scene that was just exploding and they were right in the middle of it. And they were releasing a lot of singles and there was a lot to do. They always wanted to do so many things and I had to hold them back a bit, because we didn't have the capacity to do that many things. Paul, I wouldn't say he was more experienced, but he had more of an overview. And most of Paul's bands were based in America and he spent quite a lot of time over there with them. But they both took up a lot of time, not so much necessarily from me, but certainly from everyone else in the company, from a marketing, promotion and distribution point of view."

Rhythm King and Blast First both started in 1986. "At that time we moved from Kensington Garden Square, which was a very small office, to 429 Harrow Road, where we were for some 20 years. Which was much, much bigger, and we re-housed Rhythm King and Blast First within that building. We also built two studios in there, and later had a warehouse. It was quite an ambitious thing. We took on a lot of space, more than we really needed. But it was very cheap at the time, in a rough area, and it wasn't a particularly good quality building, so we just got it cheap and made it our own." Rhythm King enjoyed spectacular success from 1988 onwards, when they hit number one with S-Express's 'Theme From S-Express' and a roster that included Baby Ford, Bomb The Bass and Betty Boo, as well as the 'rave' subsidiary Outer Rhythm which launched the career of Leftfield (and also Moby). But thereafter the label moved to Epic. Miller: "James and Martin parted company, and James left Rhythm King after a couple of years. Martin and I decided to call it a day – we were going in slightly different directions, really. He wanted it to be a pure pop label and I wasn't really interested in that. He was very ambitious, so I just said, why don't we call it a day."

Blast First faced its own problems, especially after the opening of a US office backfired and Geffen came along to scoop up Sonic Youth. The latter told Smith in a meeting at his apartment in New York that his services – which effectively extended to that of manager as well as UK record label head – were no longer required. Smith cited tensions with, in particular, Kim Gordon. The band countered that the decision was a long time coming and Smith hadn't been taking numerous hints. Talking to Alec Foege for his book *Confusion Is Next*, Smith reflected that "When the bottom line came down to it in terms of the major label thing, Kim had two things to say about it. One, I could never truly understand because I wasn't American; and two, she felt that they were looking to get in with a major label and they wanted to have people around them who would reduce the friction. Whereas I was far more of the attitude that the major labels were there to 'use'."

Unfortunately, that was only the beginning of Smith's problems. Big Black walked over a 'bootleg' of *Sound Of Impact* that allegedly (according to Smith) originated from within the company. And the Butthole Surfers have fallen out with every label they have ever worked with. While Smith was dismayed, others considered the repercussions of the bands' growth highly predictable. Their immediate forerunners had all taken similar options. The Replacements signed with Sire in 1985, while Husker Du also joined the Warners network a year later and R.E.M. had abandoned IRS for Warners in 1988. The precedents for successful American bands staying faithful to independents were even scarcer than for those in the UK.

In a terse interview with former employee Liz Naylor for *The Catalogue* in October 1989, its cover adorned with a memorial tombstone, Smith lamented the label's decline. "We're kept afloat by the wonderful chimings of Erasure and Depeche Mode". He was nothing if not open about the scale of problems, which amounted to, according to one report, falling £240,000 into the red (information he himself volunteered). "Labels like Blast First are not likely to make money," he stated. "That's why the whole Sonic Youth situation has become so crucial; if you invest that kind of time and effort in a band, money is the pay-off – if you don't get the pay-off then who's to say. In the end it's a frail existence." Smith's confrontational nature had earned him enemies in the press. Yet there was something disarming about his honesty. In this case, it manifested itself in open recognition of the infrequently aired suggestion that many independent labels were actually run by Thatcher's children, entrepreneurs a little less distinct from the armies of Burton-suited yuppies than many, including they themselves, might like to think.

Miller, too, was disappointed with Blast First's retreat. "Yes, I was. The thing is that I think for a lot of the bands that were on Blast First – Butthole Surfers, Dinosaur Jnr, Big Black – Sonic Youth were a bit of a beacon for them. They were a bit older, I guess. I think that benefited us, definitely. Sonic Youth were the first of those American bands we worked with, and when those other bands came along, I think it was helpful that Sonic Youth were with us. I think it got to a point when Sonic Youth decided they needed to go to a bigger label in America, and that label, Geffen, weren't prepared to do a split deal with us for the rest of the world. Big Black never went to a major but they kind of broke up, and Dinosaur Jnr went to Warners and the Buttholes went to EMI. Blast First didn't stop there, it continued, but it was quite traumatic for Paul, I think, that it all happened so quickly. So the first phase of Blast First, unfortunately, ended there, and then nothing much happened for a while after that. But Paul's still around, and in the end he found The Liars, who we're still working with, and Suicide and things like that. So Blast First continued, but Paul went into semi-retirement for a while."

Mute, meanwhile, did indeed continue to prosper on the back of the
'wonderful chimings' of Depeche Mode and Erasure. In 1986 Miller had
recruited Mike Heneghan of Platinum Promotions to help orchestrate the
label's greater profile. "I started working with Daniel on Depeche Mode's
'A Question Of Time'," Heneghan recalls. "I worked with all sorts of
independent companies, as well as majors. But a lot was with Daniel at
Mute, Tony Wilson at Factory, Geoff Travis at Rough Trade, Derek Birkett at
One Little Indian, Bill Drummond at KLF, a little bit with Martin Mills at
Beggars Banquet, Martin Heath at Rhythm King through Daniel." Heneghan
had originally been part of the London Records strike force team brought in
by Travis to help with The Smiths before going independent himself. "Most
weeks I'd be at the independent labels' marketing and planning meetings,
strategising their campaigns. And I did a lot of work with major labels. So it
was quite a good vantage point to see what everybody was doing. Part of it at
the beginning was taking some of the learning from the major record labels,
and giving some of that learning to the independent community."

Much of that 'learning' was, essentially, knowing how to plan things. "You'd
say, here's what's happening," says Heneghan, "and I'd talk them through
week by week what would happen with releasing a record. And I'd work
closely with the plugger. Scott Piering, in terms of planning when he would
get the video shown, when it was on TV and radio. We'd plan all that
together. Then we'd get some logic into the structure of the whole thing.
Scott and Neil Ferris, who did a lot of stuff with indie companies, and
Depeche and Erasure, were brilliant. Neil would just come and say, 'we'll go
to radio here, get record of the week here, get a playlist here.' It was more
planning and clear communication. I think the contribution in structuring it
was a small part. The big part was individuals who were working great
music with a lot of energy and still had a great post-punk DIY ethic to the
whole thing. All we were doing was really to harness that and put it into
some kind of structure so they could get the best out of that. Just making
sure the records were manufactured and were in the right shops at the right
time. Trying to get a bit of cohesion between promotional elements like
radio, TV, live and club stuff."

Heneghan also saw first-hand the difference in philosophy of a Mute or
Rough Trade as opposed to the major labels. "In most of those visionary
independent companies, oftentimes it was just one person, and that person
is really obsessed with something," he notes. "And they've got a really clear
vision for that obsession, and they find likeminded people in bands, and the
relationship is different – by the nature of them being obsessive, they want

the best for the bands and artists they're working with. So they become competitive *as a result* of their obsession. In a major record company the set up is completely different. Because of the structures of the organisation at a major, which is much bigger, somewhere along the line there has to be an interest in the share price. If not, then there's a bigger company providing the funding, and the dynamic is different. And the competitiveness is more being driven by market share. With independent companies, the competitiveness was driven by the obsession of the vision."

He also observes that the model was more one of partnership rather than business. "If you take Daniel for example, a lot of the things he did right at the beginning, the whole industry's coming round to thinking more in those terms now. With Nick Cave and the Bad Seeds, it was a 50-50 split and no contract. And there's still no contract – it's been like that for more than 20 years. With Nick Cave & the Bad Seeds, they don't have a manager as such. Rachel Willis, who used to work at Mute, runs their office and takes care of organisation and works with founder member Mick Harvey to take care of the business decisions. The relationship between the label and musicians is much closer, it isn't being filtered through management. And often the labels would do part of the job a manager would do. It's very different from a structured organisation inside a major. Often if they're on tour, you'll find the visionary behind the label is out with the bands on a lot of dates. Daniel is very much like that."

In many ways, Mute served as an interesting paradox – the first independent label in the UK to prosper with ostensibly 'straight' (although that description is fantastically misleading on many a level) pop music – the preserve of the majors since time immemorial. It is probably Miller's greatest quantifiable achievement – but one that could only, seemingly, be realised by being essentially disregarding of such trappings.

There were also significant records released by Nitzer Ebb, Laibach and Einsturzende Neubaten, as well as the establishment of Novamute Records in 1992 as a channel for experimental electronic music and The Grey Area for reissues. They were, in further demonstration of the forward-thinking nature of Miller, also the first UK record label to establish an internet presence.

Novamute was borne out of a wish to build on the Rhythm King experiment and maintain an interest in "that underground dance music area," notes Miller. "There were quite a few people at Mute who were very into that scene. I was getting very excited by techno, especially the stuff coming out of Germany in the late 80s. It was just very exciting. So we decided to start Novamute, and that was all done internally by people at Mute." The Grey Area grew out of an approach made to the label by Throbbing Gristle. "They had given up Industrial Records basically, and licensed their catalogue to a company called Fetish Records. I can't quite remember why that deal ended, but we were quite friendly with them, and they asked us if we wanted to licence the catalogue and we said yes. And that was really our first reissue project. We started to think, this isn't a bad thing, if anything comes up that's interesting, we should go for it. It wasn't a standalone label, it was part of Mute, and it didn't have to sustain an overhead or anything, so we could just pick and choose as things came along. The Cabaret Voltaire catalogue became available and they licensed it to us. And then of course the Can catalogue, which was a big thing for Mute and me personally. Throbbing Gristle and Cabs were ultimately my generation. Whereas Can were the generation before, and were a huge influence on me. And that was an incredible opportunity and huge honour for me."

Like so many, Mute's ascent had been dealt a huge blow by the Rough Trade Distribution crisis of 1991. There was also a comparatively fallow period in the mid-90s. "It was not a good time," admits Miller. "Obviously we had Depeche Mode going strong and doing well in Europe, and Erasure were going strong and so was Nick Cave. It was a tough time because of Britpop, basically. I didn't really like Britpop, and I wasn't really interested in signing Britpop bands. We did have the Inspiral Carpets, who were kind of a precursor to Britpop, but there was something about them that was different." The signing of the Inspirals, then the subject of intense press interest, seemed at odds with the Mute dynamic. Especially when the press trumpeted the apparent size of the deal. "It was a very competitive deal, actually," says Miller, "and a lot of other people were after it. But it wasn't that expensive. Most of the press around that time was about how many t-shirts they sold, the 'Cool As Fuck' t-shirts. In the end, they kind of fell apart. One of the interesting things about them was the fact that there was quite a big age range in the band, and musical experience and taste. The drummer was 17, and Clint the keyboard player was already in his early 30s. That's one of the reasons I thought it worked, but it was also one of the reasons I think it fell apart. It was quite a natural parting of the ways."

If the Inspiral Carpets never delivered the hits some had forecast, Miller had other problems. "At that time, the whole media was dominated by Britpop and fucking Tony Blair, and it seemed like a terrible time to me. And some of our artists like Moby were struggling in the UK. And I wasn't inspired to sign stuff. Because I didn't hear much that I liked, and if we did sign stuff, what the fuck could we do with it? To side-track slightly, one thing we did at the time was licence The Prodigy for America. That ended up being huge for us over there, and kept us going for a bit. But it got to a point where we were in financial difficulty. It wasn't terminal, but it was very unhealthy. And I was in a position where I was going to have to do a deal with somebody for something, like a worldwide distribution deal, so I could raise some money. I had a lot of friends in the industry who were in a position to be helpful, which they were. Like the Play It Again Sam people, who were our licensees in Benelux. They'd just sold their company, got a lot of money, and were interested in doing something with Mute. But I wasn't feeling very comfortable with it. I'd always done things on my own terms, really. I'd been very lucky to be able to do that, but nevertheless that's the way it was. I just felt while everybody was being helpful and very respectful, it felt like going cap in hand, and I didn't really like that."

While Miller considered these options, the label's luck changed. "Just as things got to their worst moment, the Moby album *Play* broke, a year after being out." Indeed, *Play* became the 'coffee table album' of 2000, and would sell, internationally, over nine million copies. "That changed everything. People's perception of Mute, especially in the UK, was – 'Oh, Mute's over, basically. Hasn't done anything interesting for a few years.' There were a few articles that weren't very pleasant. And then Moby broke massively and became our biggest album ever. That paid off a lot of the things we needed to pay for, and I thought, this is my moment to sell the company on my own terms, from a position of strength. So I talked to Play It Again Sam and Virgin France, who had been our licensees since the early 80s. I had a very good relationship with the people there. Emmanuel De Buretel, who had run Virgin France, had become the head of continental Europe for EMI. I'd known him since the beginning. I got very close to a deal with Play It Again Sam, but in the end, I did it with him. He was in a good position to do it, he completely understood Mute. Though he was at a major, he knew how Mute operated, he knew where the skeletons were buried, how the financial dynamics worked. I thought, I'm in a really strong position, my luck has played out, and if I can get the kind of control I want? I made a list of things that I thought were deal-breakers essentially, in terms of control and autonomy, and they agreed to all of them. It wasn't quite as simple as that, but basically they agreed to everything, and I thought OK, this sounds like a good way forward for everybody. It stabilises things. I've got creative freedom, obviously I have to work within budgets like you always do, but basically we were our own label still. Obviously we ended up going through all the EMI territories, which was fine."

On 10 May 2002, EMI acquired Mute. Miller became executive chairman. "I was trying to secure the future. The artists were all very cool about it. Everyone was amazing and really supportive. I was very nervous at the time about how the artists and staff would respond. But I think they all felt I'd made the decision based on the right criteria. I didn't really have any backlash about it, which was amazing, and a great credit to them. Obviously, that situation has changed a lot, because the industry has changed a lot. But we still have the autonomy we need creatively, and although it's been a very rough two years to be honest, the air is clearing now, and the new people at EMI are very supportive of Mute. And fingers crossed, I feel fairly confident about the future." Mike Heneghan, having moved on from Platinum Promotions through 3mv to becoming the general manger of Go! Discs, became the group's new managing director. "Daniel and I had kept in touch and been friends, and always said we'd try to work together. It was a good thing for both of us. I loved him and respected him, and respected what he'd done for the label. I understood a lot about the DNA of the company and the people – a lot of it is Daniel's taste in music that is very particular, something that connects all of the bands, but is very different."

Eventually, in 2006, Mute relocated to EMI's offices. "We were still in Harrow Road until about a year and a half ago, and then sadly the lease on that building ran out. They basically knocked it down. It was worth a lot of money then, the land, not the building, so they sold it and it's been converted to flats and offices or whatever. We planned on having our own office after that. But EMI, how do I put it politely? They had restructured so drastically, they said in the current climate we don't think we can justify having an external office when we have so much space in our own building. And I said, OK, fine. I wasn't over the moon about it, but in the end it's not about the office you work in, as long as it works as an office, it's about the records you make. And that was still the priority. So we moved in and it's been fine. A bit posh for us!"

Surveying Mute's catalogue now, it occurs that one of its strengths is that it didn't, like others, over-commit. There is no obvious occasion when Miller used his leverage to scoop up a clutch of similar, or perhaps even complementary artists. Depeche Mode and Erasure soundalikes existed, but did so on other labels. In essence, Miller's approach was methodical in spending time on long-term artist development – a seemingly lost tenet of

A&R. "It was a function of several things," he says. "One of those is that while I'm a music fan, obviously, I have a very small collection at home. There's very little that I love. Even as a kid, there were only ever a few things that I liked. I think that was a lucky stroke. It was partly that, it was partly because I was very hands-on in the development of Depeche especially in the early days, in terms of recording and every other aspect. I wasn't handing it off to anyone else. It felt like it was something I wanted to do. It wasn't really a pro-active decision, I just simply didn't have the time or energy to do it and there wasn't stuff that I loved enough that I heard. I'm sure there was stuff out there, but I was at the studio and didn't have a chance to hear it."

That single-minded, life in a bubble existence is one that Ivo Watts-Russell at 4AD can sympathise with. "There had to be an element of 'everything else is shite', he reflects. "You *had* to have that. There were certain people you really liked, and if they had some success you were happy for them. Daniel didn't need the likes of me being happy for him, he had huge commercial success. There's been less music on Mute that I personally enjoy than many of the considered 'key' independent labels, and yet I have more respect for Daniel and therefore Mute than I do for probably any of them – because of Daniel as a man and what he believed in."

"I did see other labels who had early success do the opposite of what we did, and there's kind of a logic to say that isn't a good idea," Miller reflects. "Because you do get the feeling, 'Oh, we've had a hit, now we know how to do it, we can have lots of hits.' And even I felt like that at one stage. So you feel you know how to do it – but it doesn't work like that." Nevertheless, Mute proved that an independent record label could enjoy sustained success in the charts. Partially, one suspects, as a product of Miller's own stubborn response to being told such a scenario was impossible. That Mute was able to have those hits while being simultaneously responsible for some of the most ambitious, challenging and commercially repellent art was the neatest trick of all.

ROUGH
TRADE
RECORDS

PARIS

© · ℗
METAL URBAIN
1977

RT 001

MAQU

(Luger, Sch

Debris, Par

## METAL
### urbain

produced by METAL URBAIN &
Ross Crighton for ROUGH TRADE

16
33
45 78

## Chapter Eight

## The Graveyard & The Ballroom

## Rabid, Factory & Zoo

"The area is so neglected, so economically deprived and full of massive housing complexes, that the mood of the place was right and ready for a new movement in music with a markedly different criteria of success. What has developed is peculiar to Manchester and I can only hope that instead of going to London for future deals, the agents and record companies will come here."

*(Tosh Ryan, writing for Melody Maker on 14 May 1977, in an article entitled "New Wave Devolution: Manchester Waits For The World To Listen")*

Manchester music and 'independence' have come to be synonymous with the illustrious tragi-comic adventures of Factory Records. But after New Hormones' 'Spiral Scratch', the next Mancunian label to establish itself in the punk era was Tosh Ryan's Rabid Records, later unflatteringly referenced as "the Stiff-styled funny farm of the north" in the music inkies. As Vinni Faal, manager of the label's second act Ed Banger And The Nosebleeds would recall: "[Rabid] taught Factory everything they ever knew. They managed the top five single, the marketing scams, the situationist enigma, the unplayable records, they even managed the ignominious bankruptcy!"

Rabid announced itself in May 1977 with Slaughter And The Dogs' 'Cranked Up Really High'. This was base camp for a number of personalities who would become closely associated with the city's later artistic triumphs – notably the photographer Kevin Cummins and producer Martin 'Zero' Hannett. "It was a wonderful time for Slaughter," remembers Mick Rossi. "Rabid were truly the first independent label in the north of England. It gave us the platform in which to release our first single. I liked Tosh Ryan a lot, he's a colourful character, the only issue we had as a band was that we didn't receive a single penny from the sales of our live album or any of our releases on Rabid. We were young and naive. You live and learn, eh?"

Ryan himself is far from happy with the way recent histories have recorded the period. "I'm fed up of seeing Malcolm McLaren wheeled out and talking about how he invented this so called phenomenon. In my experience, this thing's happening everywhere. It was a kind of gestalt thing, happening across the country. There was a similar condition. People were organising their own gigs in back rooms of pubs, because there weren't any venues to play at. And universities weren't booking local bands. It really annoys me when Malcolm McLaren stands up and says I invented this. His attitude was very much that middle-class attitude. It's happened to the arts over the centuries. Interesting things happen, and he was interesting and he did use interesting reference points in the way he plagiarised things – he might call it homage, I don't know. But it doesn't pay a lot of respect to what was happening right across the country. There were a lot of people who came from a boom in the 1960s, just in Manchester alone if you think about what happened with Kennedy Street Enterprises, Herman's Hermits, Freddie & the Dreamers, hundreds of bands that were filling the top 10 worldwide in the late 50s and early 60s. All of those people were consigned to the rubbish bin when the collapse happened at the start of the 70s. It was those people who kept something going for another generation."

Essentially, Rabid Records was borne out of Music Force, an organisation Ryan, a then performing musician, was a part of. "In a loose political sense, it was a co-operative for musicians. It didn't have hard-line co-operative rules, so it was more like a collective." I asked him if there were similarities to the local Manchester Musicians Collective. "Not at all," he sneers. "This was run by musicians, not half-wits! The Manchester Music Collective was very much a middle class organisation which was more concerned with the ethics of the arts rather than what we were trying to do. Music Force was convened initially as a political organisation. It had the intention of breaking monopolies. It was there to promote self-management and self-interests, and cut back on the monopoly of the major music industries and also music promoters. It ran as an agency and a self-managing organisation and supplied PA systems and transport and set up gigs. It functioned at every level on what was essentially needed at that time."

"At the risk of getting papered into a cavity in Tosh Ryan's house," points out *City Fun* editor Cath Carroll, "I have to disagree that the Musicians' Collective was run by half-wits – they just had a different philosophy to Rabid." The MMC, a kind of musical outreach project for the North West Arts Association, had been convened by Dick Witts, later of the Passage, and Trevor Wishart. Further assistance came from Tony Friel (The Fall; whose first gig came at the MMC's behest), Frank Ewart (The Manchester Mekon) and 'press officer' Louise Alderman (also a Mekon and member of Property Of... alongside Carroll). "Despite all the new 'new wave' kids who got on board," Carroll continues, "the Collective was still a bit jazz-hippyish. They were certainly not as businesslike as the Rabid crew and perhaps their openness to any expression of a creative idea was a little generous. But they opened doors for a lot of young musicians who may not have been booked in a more traditional setting. You didn't have to be on [associated label] Object Music to be part of the MMC. And in putting out Grow Up's *The Best Thing*, Object was responsible for one of the best records to come out of Manchester, ever. Frank Ewart and the Manchester Mekon were very generous with their flat and their gear; they allowed so many bands to rehearse there, and set up the gigs, week after week. Of course, they didn't make any cash out of this. The half-wits!" In the liners to his MMC retrospective [Messthetics #106], Chuck Warner would note another connection between these founding fathers of the Manchester independent/post-punk scene and Factory's later success. Ian Curtis had adapted the bass melody from The Manchester Mekon's song 'The Cake Shop Device' for 'Love Will Tear Us Apart (with the Mekon's full blessing). Frank Ewart would also produce demos for The Stockholm Monsters and James

Object was extant from 1978 to 1981 and run by Hulme-based musician and DJ Steve Solamar (aka Steve Scrivener), originally as an outlet for his band the Spherical Objects, whose "existentialist psychedelia" was celebrated in print by early advocate Paul Morley. Object Music premiered with the Spherical Objects' debut album, followed a couple of months later with their two non-LP 45s, a Steve Miro single and an EP by the Passage. After the compilation *A Manchester Collection* came further records by the Passage, Grow Up, IQ Zero, Contact and others. All were drawn from the MMC's membership except for several Steve Miro projects (who had worked with Solamar since the mid-70s) and an LP by New York no wave band Tirez Tirez. Object maintained a strong commitment to the LP format despite prevailing expectations, releasing 16 full-length albums and a dozen singles and EPs.

Spherical Objects' *Past and Parcel* debut had been recorded at Arrow, the same studio used for 'Spiral Scratch', with £800 invested on the recording and a run of 1,000 copies (a second issue was remastered to correct problems on the original pressing). These would then be driven by Solamar down to London in a hired van, a scenario repeated several times over the next few years (Object would release records in batches so as to minimise time spent away from his day job as a computer analyst). Taking the decision to use Object as a conduit for other artists (though the Spherical Objects, very much a solo Solamar project, remained central), the label was profiled in the *NME* in September 1979 as one of the nine leading independent labels. "What I plan is for there to be quite a lot of releases on Object this year," Solamar commented. "We're planning releases by three Manchester bands, who'll get 50 per cent of profits after costs have been deducted. What will probably happen is that after a lot of activity on Object this year it will either be wound down to a large degree next year, or we'll stop production to concentrate on wherever Spherical Objects have reached at that time. It may be possibly kept over to release things I find interesting."

The label closed in 1981 when Solamar committed himself to the gender reassignment hinted at in earlier releases. The cover of *Past And Parcel* had featured male and female dolls with their hands nailed together while the lyric to its opening track, 'Born To Pay', noted "Sometimes I think I should have been a woman/Sometimes it'd be a lot easier that way". The label's final release was the Spherical Objects' *No Man's Land*. The message 'Special thanks to everyone who has supported us' appeared on the sleeve. Unable to hand over the reigns to a successor, Solamar closed the imprint, though she did help Steve Miro to transfer to Glass Records and financed the second Grow Up album before returning to a life in computer programming.

"Music Force grew out of the 60s," Ryan continues, "but was far removed from hippy idealism. The majority of those involved weren't remotely involved in hippy ethics. A lot of them were avid drug takers, but there was no sentimentality in terms of spirituality with the people who were involved. They were fairly strong socialists and interested in democratic politics. You're talking about a bunch of musicians who knew nothing else apart from playing in pop groups and beat bands from leaving school. This was a generation of people who went into the music business in the late 50s and did nothing else apart from play music until the early 70s when that whole touring thing had finished, it kind of collapsed because of the economics. Promoters were more interested in promoting discotheques. One DJ at £30 a night was far less hassle than promoting a rock 'n' roll band at twice or even three times that much. It was economics that forced us to create a self-management scheme, to run our own venues and promote our own music and bands. It was in a time of fairly high unemployment and you're talking about guys with families who'd done nothing other than play in rock 'n' roll bands."

Rabid was an obvious extension of those activities. "Music Force had a loose manifesto or constitution, which was to at all times break the unfair monopoly of the capitalist music industry, and also to establish its own channels of output. It also had a commitment to promoting new ideas in music. There was a lot of people involved in Music Force that were rock 'n' roll players who'd come to rock 'n' roll because there wasn't a jazz market as such. So there was good musicianship, and a lot of that musicianship was interested in promoting new ideas, and that was part of the manifesto. And part of that was to actually put product out as records. And we couldn't trust the likes of Decca and EMI and Columbia and CBS – any of those people weren't to be trusted."

An innate suspicion of the major labels was commonplace amongst independents, but in Rabid's case, geographical resentment also played a role. "Part of what Music Force was about was a kind of anti-capital, anti-London attitude anyway," Ryan continues. "We thought the business was concentrated far too much in the London area, and the press was as well. It did seem to us a total conspiracy to promote the south east and London activity and to not look elsewhere. When, to be quite honest, a lot of new ideas and creativity and talent was coming out of other parts of the country. It happened that a number of organisations around the country did spring up on a similar level, musicians' collectives and co-operatives. That was a reflection of the political times and the period. There was quite an interest in anti-racist politics, right to work politics, fighting for more fair opportunity. A lot of us were involved in supporting organisations like the Workers Revolutionary Party. It was very much an anti-fascist kind of organisation." But then he reflects. "When I say that, I personally feel that the majority of musicians involved in it hadn't a fucking clue about what we were doing."

"There was a hardcore at the head of Music Force that were dedicated and interested in politics," Ryan continues. "That included myself, Victor Brocks, a guy called Bruce Mitchell – a number of people who had all played in the same bands for years and years, and quite a lot of them had grown up together as well. One of the things that Music Force had in its manifesto was to have its best endeavours to produce material, or records. One of the people on the committee, that was co-opted on to the committee – someone I actually opposed being co-opted on cos he was a bit of a hippy! – was producer Martin Hannett." A chemical engineering graduate and former bass player in Mancunian hippy band Greasy Bear, Hannett would come to be regarded as the finest producer of the post-punk era. Not that it looked likely at this stage. "Martin's interest was in soundcraft and sound engineering and recording., he was avidly interested in new technology. He was co-opted on to the committee and it turned out to be really worthwhile. It ended up with myself and Martin and Bruce and a few other people more or less running Music Force, because the musicians involved were losing interest. It wasn't pandering to their egos enough. Musicians are an egotistical bunch. We were trying to create a fair industry where all bands got a crack at playing and got some recognition. There were cults of personality developing, and some bands thought they were far superior to other bands. There wasn't the same kind of democratic attitude we tried to establish in the first place. So a lot of musicians drifted off and went in search of their own promotion and fame, which had nothing to do with what we were trying to establish. Music Force had a few activities that were carved up between the people involved when it eventually collapsed. One of them was flyposting. Bruce and myself took over, I did most of that, and it became a very lucrative business, flyposting throughout the country."

Indeed, several musicians would become involved in the business as a sideline, such as Ed Garrity, then of Wild Ram, later Ed Banger of the Nosebleeds. "I used to work for Tosh's flyposting company. And we already had the band, so recording on Rabid Records was a natural progression. I can't actually remember whether or not we had the connection with the band first through Music Force or we started doing the flyposting, but it was all inter-connected. It was very lucrative – cos we had practically the whole of England – we would travel down as far as Coventry, Nottingham, Birmingham, up to Newcastle. It was very good money then."

"Another thing was trucking," notes Ryan. "We had a fleet of vehicles that we could call on that would rescue people for transport for gigs. The other thing was this side of things which wanted us to be able to allow bands to find out, and demystify, the whole process of getting a record out. And Martin kind of carved that off. All this activity went through my house and happened at my house. So we had flyposting going on from the house, we had bands coming through wanting to put records out. The whole thing was centred in my kitchen." Garrity: "Yeah, we'd go there for breakfast before we went out to work – but sometimes we'd never get to work. We'd have a joint and it could just turn into one long session."

Rick Goldstraw, member of the Ferrets and John Cooper Clarke's manager cum co-conspirator, was another of Ryan's flyposters. "The whole thing was tax deductible for the record companies, you see, cos it was advertising, so they did as many as they could. But they'd send far too many. Cos Ryan was a working class kid and insecure – any middle class kid would have just gone, 'fuck 'em'! – but Ryan's a grammar school boy, so he goes, 'You've got to put *this* many up.' So we get the posters, and say he's got 2,000, he'd give you 1,000, he'd put 20 in his poster collection, and he'd send the rest to be mashed up at the paper plant with his 'secret boy' and a transit van full of posters to be destroyed. And we'd put 50 up and go home. You couldn't do out else – where would you put 'em?"

Such was the bravado of the various crews, that this wasn't even an after hours job. "We were nine while five lads!" laughs Goldstraw. "But there were all these things of Ryan having fits about them being seen. What you'd have to do on the night of the gigs is get back from the motorway, and put loads of posters up around the gig, so the band's manager would see them. Then you'd cover 'em up the next day if there were any left – if a kid saw them wet they'd disappear to student flats. It was insane. The statistics were just crazy, and they just kept giving Tosh loads of money. And the more money they gave him, the guiltier he would get. I raised my children on that money. He made a fortune. You couldn't not make money. They would send up 10,000 double-quad Paul McCartney posters – you couldn't put 100 up! I know houses in Didsbury where the cavities are full of fucking posters! And Tosh was getting so much fucking money, he went, this is too much. And he got in touch with the tax people. Then it was, if you want paying, you've got to sign. We were like, fuck off, we're on the dole. So anyway Ryan had all this money so he said, right, I'm going legit, I'm opening a record company. But flyposting's an illegal profession! If the police come, you run. And he tried to put everyone on PAYE!"

In essence, Rabid Records wasn't a separate entity at all. "Yeah," admits Ryan, "apart from the fact that it forgot its political intentions and drifted into making money. That was acceptable to everyone because we'd been skint for so long, it was acceptable to earn some money, and we earned quite a lot. The flyposting business made a hell of a lot of money and employed a lot of people. A lot of musicians out of work ended up flyposting all over the country. And we employed a lot of session musicians on some of the recordings we did." The whole Rabid operation was staffed by "pissheads and junkies," Garrity recalls. "Wonderful! You could walk into the Rabid office completely sober and walk out stoned within no time at all. All you had to do was inhale the atmosphere of the reception room."

"Ryan brought in these two people, Lawrence Beadle and Martin Hannett," Goldstraw explains. "A couple of nastier bastards you couldn't find. Lawrence screwed my mate's girl. And my mate was a drinker. He was a young lad, and he went round every Friday night when he was pissed and threw a stone through Lawrence's window. It went on for months. The first thing that they did after they made [John Cooper Clarke's debut EP] 'Innocents' was to sign Clarkey to CBS. As soon as he'd signed the contract, what they did was bootleg him [the infamous *Ou Est La Maison De Fromage* album]. There were boxes of them in the office stacked six foot high. And John would never have thought to have said, 'What's that record with me looking like a cunt on the front of it, asleep on a train with my mouth open?' They never said owt. And they sold 20,000 mail order. £60,000. Clarkey could have bought the fucking avenue he lived in with that. And of course, this was meant to be going into the joint account. But Ryan was in the bank one day, stood behind Lawrence, watching him – and he saw Lawrence put the money in his own account. Ha ha!"

Goldstraw had a relationship with Ryan that went back many years. "I was always staying round there [Ryan's house]. I was kind of abandoned at a very early age – from ten I kind of brought myself up. I had the family house, but not the family! I was so scared of the dark, I'd go out on the road and get strangers – any fucker – to come back to our house, and stay until dawn. I'd tell anyone, come back for a brew. I hated the dark as a kid and I still do. So when I met Ryan, their house was like a hippy gaffe. Well, it wasn't hippy – they were anti-hippy, anti all of that, even though we dropped acid all the time, because we thought hippy was too soppy. Tosh was like my dream dad – sax-playing, dope-smoking liberal. But then he had a nervous breakdown on account of his wife. And I moved in properly then, to be with him during his bad times. In a way, I think he kind of resented the fact that I'd seen him in such a bad way. And he never trusted me musically. Me and him, we used to go and get jobs in the country in the summer, spud-picking, market gardening, any crap. And I'd take my guitar, electric with a tiny radio amp, and he'd take his sax, and we'd just jam all dinnertime. And if we'd been having a good time we'd just carry on playing in the afternoon and tell 'em to fuck off. He wasn't a good sax player in a technical sense, but he was like a Beefheart type player, and I wasn't a guitar player but I was a crackpot. But then he turned against me and he didn't trust me. So when we made Clarke's record, 'Innocents', there was another kid waiting there in the studio."

That kid was John Scott, and the record was Rabid's third release. The resentment still crackles down the years. "Clarkey was in these folk clubs. And you know Clarkey, he'd probably still be there! I carried a reel to reel tape machine two miles on my back to record him, and took the tape over to Ryan's to play him it. And he was like, 'Oh, yeah, I'm interested.' Then I took John over and I said, 'I trust this guy Tosh, more than anybody. If he wants to manage you, he's honest. He's got principles. He'll be straight with you. But John's very secretive. And the first thing they did was they sacked me! They didn't want any of John's deadweight mates! Not just me, but Stevie McGuire who did the drawings [on the cover]. Stevie was a great kid, but John was all for getting rid of him! And he chinned Ryan! Ryan said, 'How much do you want for the cover?' Stevie says £200. Ryan says, 'I've got a guy up the road who'll do one for £17.' So Stevie went and punched him. John was all for leaving everyone behind – he didn't want us mixing with his new friends, whoever they might be."

Steve McGuire should not be confused with cartoonist and illustrator Steve McGarry, responsible for much of the artwork on Rabid and Absurd releases. "I worked on JCC's *Fromage* album, but that was a year or so later," he confirms. "I think I did five or maybe six of the ten or twelve singles that Rabid released, two of the album sleeves and a lot of stuff for Absurd. I don't recall that they ever had particularly big budgets! I only really made decent fees when the acts signed to majors (Jilted John to EMI, Slaughter to Decca) and I got to create bigger budget sleeves. In fact, on most of the Rabid releases I'd be surprised if the recording costs were £200. Mind you, having read what Rick says, I now realise that I was using entirely the wrong negotiating tactic with Tosh!" In a further demonstration of continuity between Rabid and Factory, McGarry would design the 12-inch 'scaffold' cover for Joy Division's 'An Ideal For Living' in September 1978 at Rob Gretton's suggestion.

That wasn't Goldstraw's final run-in with Rabid. "My elder brother. He was a very, very tough fella. They didn't pay me at Rabid, no royalties, and they tried to credit the EP to themselves. They changed the first cover and put their names on it – charming. So my mum died, and there were four children, and they went, right, we'll do a three-way split on the headstone. And I went, I want to pay my share. So they run me to this fucking record company, and I said, 'Tosh, give me my royalties, my mum's died, and I want to buy a headstone.' And fucking Hannett and Beadle were like – you're not getting any fucking money. And I thought that was rather bad form. So my brother came in and he said, 'Hiya Tosh. What's happening?' And Tosh said, immediately, 'I'm just sorting your kid's money out!' Then Martin Hannett said, 'You're not getting any money'. So our kid said to him, 'Hello Curly, are you partial to fucking hospital food?' So Tosh says, 'Shut up Martin, here's your money, Rick.' And he handed over £200."

The Cooper Clarke albums offer a classic case study of majors pushing money into what remained essentially an independent enterprise. In an interview with Jon Savage in the sleevenotes to *And Here Is The Young Man*, Hannett stated that the CBS link came about via his relationship with CBS stringer Jeremy Ensor [formerly of Principal Edwards Magic Theatre]. It led to a meeting in Manchester with Maurice Oberstein, where he agreed to licence a Cooper Clarke album over "a cheap kebab". The deal was signed, he claimed, on the understanding that Hannett (and Steve Hopkins) would be in charge of the tracks.

"If you look at the John Cooper Clarke albums we produced for CBS," says Ryan, "you'll see such a number of musicians on there. Including people like Bill Nelson from Be Bop Deluxe, Pete Shelley – known musicians we used as session players. The production on those is remarkable. At the time they were being produced, I was really opposed to what Martin was doing. He was spending fortunes in the studio. By today's standards it was a very small amount of money, but at that time it was a lot of money. We were spending between 15 and 30 grand on an album, which was a lot of money in 1979 or whenever. John Cooper Clarke never recouped. We never got any more money out of CBS, because we were still paying back the advances. A lot of the advances Martin spent on new technology, like digital delay lines and harmonisers, and the very first CD player that I ever saw. I was amazed. He bought a CD player and it cost us £800 – what the hell are we doing spending £800 on a weird piece of technology? It didn't even record, it was only a player. I thought it was very interesting the way Martin produced those albums. He was a genius at producing, an amazing producer. He was without doubt way ahead of a lot of producers at that time. But he was also a pain in the arse."

Rabid's roster was always fairly lopsided. After the bootboy punk of Slaughter And The Dogs and Ed Banger & The Nosebleeds, it encompassed a punk poet in Cooper Clarke, a punk parody in Jilted John (later John Shuttleworth) and the baby-steps of underachieving pop evergreen Chris Sievey, later of the Freshies and Frank Sidebottom fame. Many were linked to majors. Slaughter were licensed to Decca, Cooper Clarke to CBS. Jilted John to EMI, and indeed, Sievey himself was taken up by MCA. Famously, Ryan once offered to 'punch out' an employee at the latter major for wearing flared Wranglers. "I think Chris is extremely talented," Tosh concludes. "I managed Chris's band for a long time. I lost a lot of money on the Freshies – a *lot*."

"I was probably instrumental in that [getting the Nosebleeds' single released by Ryan]," recalls Vini Reilly, "because I could actually play, which Tosh could relate to. I don't think he really related to the other members of the band because they weren't virtuoso musicians – not that I was. At least I could string some chords together. I think it was all sheer force of personality and commitment. We were all insane, really. We were all out of order. We were arrested about four times for various things and held overnight. Got up to all sorts of misadventures. But we were quite a formidable team from

Wythenshawe. So I think it was more being impressed with that, combined with the fact that I could play, that led to him giving it a shot. Tosh is great, a fantastic guy, still an amazing guy, and he's from Wythenshawe originally. He's very forthright! I'm still friends with all those lads. They haven't quietened down a lot!"

Other releases include a forgotten outing by Gyro, whose existence is again testament to Rabid's home-grown *esprit de corps*. "It was a guy called Chris Gill," remembers Ryan. "He was an exceptional musician, a really good guitar player, a good writer. And very much part of that kind of Manchester attitude – didn't give a fuck, would rather have a fight than a hit. That's what attracted us to a lot of people; their ability musically and the fact that they weren't people who would toe the line. They didn't want to pander. Some people wanted to pander to the whole stupidity of the music industry. I used to hate the idea that journalists, people like Nick Kent, they would come and cee us and piss me off with their stupid London attitudes. It just used to really get on my nerves." Still, you did send us Paul Morley.

Rabid's biggest seller was the fluke/flake punk hit by the aforementioned Jilted John, aka Graham Fellows, in April 1978. A Yorkshireman studying drama at Manchester Polytechnic, as Fellows recalled in the sleevenotes to the reissue of *True Love Stories*, "I'd written a couple of songs and I wanted to record them. So I went into a local record shop and asked if they knew any indie or punk labels. They said they knew of two; Stiff in London and Rabid just down the road. So I phoned Rabid up and they told me to send in a demo." The song, an update on John Otway's 'Cor Baby, That's Really Free', was submitted in demo form and re-recorded, under the auspices of Martin Hannett, at Pennine Studios.

'Going Steady' was originally intended as the a-side of the resultant single, until John Peel started playing 'Jilted John', which also became Fellows' new sobriquet. "John Peel must take credit for being the one who played 'Jilted John' repeatedly," notes Fellows. "And 'Jilted John Thomas' was a half-serious contender as a name for a while." With Piccadilly Radio also playing the song heavily, and Barry Lazell, Tony Parsons and Paul Morley singing its praises in the music weeklies, Rabid had a hit they were evidently unprepared for. EMI stepped in with a licensing deal – Tony Wilson in a *Granada Reports* feature on independent labels decried that action as a betrayal of the independent ethos; Ryan accused him of living in the past. But Wilson's research for that programme would, ultimately, trigger the subsequent formation of Factory.

No-one had expected the freak hit, not least Fellows' new peer group, including local musician Eddie Mooney, then of the Accidents. "I was walking down near the university, and there was an office," he recalls. "And then there was the John Cooper Clarke single called 'Innocents', and I looked on the back of it and the address was actually on the university campus. So I thought, what have I got to lose? I'll walk in and see if they'll sign up my little band. I went there and it was chaos, absolutely chaos in this room. At the time I was so naive, I just thought they were strange people – but of course I found out later they were all doped up to their eyeballs. But they were dead friendly, and the guy I spoke to was a guy called Mark. What he said was, get us a tape and bring it down to Anthony Ryan's house in Withington. So I said, OK, I will do. At the time, still being naive, we did a tape off the mixing desk and I turned up at this guy's house, Tosh, and there was another chap there who was a student at the Polytechnic, called Graham Fellows. He had this tape and I had my tape, and Tosh said I've only got enough money for one single at the moment – they were always skint. And he said, I'm interested in the Accidents, cos you're such a strange band, but I'm also interested in this other song Graham had. So we played our tape, which technically wasn't great. And he said, 'I like that, but let me hear the other one.' And of course the other one was 'Jilted John'. I said, that's dreadful, you'll never get anywhere with that!"

"I remember Jilted John coming in with his demo tape, I was there that morning," confirms Ed Garrity. "Tosh said, have a listen to this. He played it and I said, 'that's just rubbish'. He couldn't play the guitar, so he'd tuned the guitar to one chord and he was playing it with one finger, and he'd recorded it in his bedroom. But Tosh said, 'Do you want to record that with him?' Cos I had my band, and he offered it to me, and I turned it down – like a prat! And so it was my backing band on *Top Of The Pops* – the bass player, drummer and guitarist, they all agreed to do it."

The single eventually reached the top five. "It actually reached number four," Mooney grimaces, "I plotted chart history in green envy at the time." Although Ryan did hook Mooney up with Martin Hannett, in the end his single never did come out on the label. "When Jilted John charted, EMI were sniffing around and people like myself who had been part of that chaotic scene were nudged out a little bit as they smelt the big bucks," Mooney continues. "The next thing was they were trying to market [follow-up single] 'Gordon The Moron' and all that sort of stuff. I was walking down this road and Graham Fellows was on a moped, dressed in his Parker coat – we'd kept in touch cos he's a nice lad – but he was going, 'Eddie, you won't believe it, that song I did is in the charts!' And I *didn't* believe him." Garrity: "Eventually, he wouldn't do gigs, Jilted John, cos he wanted to be an actor, and there are all these calls coming in the office offering him thousands of pounds to do gigs. I said I'd do it with a backing band – nobody will know! Tosh was half coming round to the idea but then he said, 'Nah, we'll get sued.' I said, it'll be too late then!"

There was a further near miss link with the majors in the shape of The Out's remarkable 'Who Is Innocent' single. "Martin Hannett wanted to produce it at one stage," recalls guitarist George Borowski (oft falsely cited as 'Guitar George' of 'Sultans Of Swing' fame). "Then it wasn't going to be released because the other two members of Rabid, Hannett and Beadle, were resistant to us as a band. Tosh was convinced it was going to be a hit. And he forced it through. Off it went, and it was on radio and everything. It's kind of a lost classic. Tosh never forgave himself that it wasn't a hit. He said to me much later that that's the one he regrets most not doing as well as it could have done." It was later re-released on Virgin. "Chas Banks, the manager, and Tosh went to meet Virgin, and themselves and Chrysalis were interested in putting the single out. Because Rabid was celebrating a big hit single with 'Jilted John', they dug their heels in and said if you want the single, take the album, and Virgin said no."

Evidently, then, though Ryan's rhetorical suspicions of the majors were cast in stone at the outset, when opportunities arose, as they did with at least four of the label's artists, they were grasped. This contrasts starkly with Factory's more puritanical approach. Rabid was always a more pragmatic beast – staying true in that sense to Music Force's original mission statement about offering the local music community exposure and support. Some still see Ryan as an opportunist. Others might conclude that lofty idealism is OK for those who can afford it.

The Rabid story had a diverting endnote in the shape of Absurd Records, a spin-off label involving Lawrence Beadle, as well as Ryan. "There were a lot of divisions in Rabid between myself, Lawrence Beadle and Martin Hannett," Ryan admits. "We were on one side of the fence and Martin was going in another direction altogether. Martin wanted big money to produce BIG music. He was one of those people that helped push the music business into the stratosphere financially. He wanted to spend money on tricks in the studio. Consequently, he needed to get those deals to get the money to do it. I wasn't that interested at all. I wasn't even interested in the stuff we were putting out. I was more interested in a label we had called Absurd. Which was, at it sounds, ridiculous. Initially I thought Rabid Records was about that, producing unusual material that was pointing two fingers at the record industry."

Absurd's roster featured releases by Eddie Fiction (Garrity under a pseudonym), Cairo (Chris Gill of Gyro), 48 Chairs (John Scott), the Mothmen (members of John Cooper Clarke's band, various Durutti Column alumni), Bet Lynch's Legs (CP Lee of the Albertos and Scott again). The latter pair were also involved in the label's most famous release, Gerry & The Holograms' 'The Emperor's New Music' single. The record came glued into the sleeve, some of which arrived with a Rough Trade sticker warning unwary punters not to play the disc. The ruse was based on the fact that there were lots of unsold Slaughter And The Dogs singles and other Rabid over-presses they had access to, and it was as good a way as any to disperse them to the populace. Ryan clearly enjoyed the esoteric nature of these releases, but others were less convinced. "Chris Sievey was on it, everyone," says Garrity, "Gordon the Moron, Gyro, pretty much anyone who was on Rabid did a daft song for that. Tosh just said, if I give you £500, just do a song. So people would just go in and do any old rubbish. Everyone just took the money and did it all under different names. And I think that's what took the company down."

Unsurprisingly enough, Rick Goldstraw has an alternative theory about Rabid/Absurd's demise, which goes back to the real money-spinner behind both, the flyposting business. "A friend of mine, Gwyn Roberts, came in. He was called the Pieman, cos he had a finger in every pie. I brought Gwyn in to the Russell Club to take over from Alan Wise. He tried to sack me! He said that if he couldn't stay on the door taking the money, he couldn't keep track of what was happening in the club. He wanted to stay on the door and stuff his pockets with loads of fivers! So he ended up at Rabid as a sort of junior accountant. And what Gwyn did was sit and watch, to see where the weaknesses were. And he saw the flyposting making all that money, and the kids from Wythenshawe were really, really tough – Vinni and Mike Faal. Vinni was the Nosebleeds' manager. They ran Birmingham's flyposting, just like Terry The Pill ran it in London. But Gwyn recognised them as vicious operators. So he went to them and said – all this arguing with Tosh about PAYE and the price of posters, it's not necessary. It's not a legal business. If someone was to say to him, 'Fuck off or I'll punch you' – he couldn't phone the police. So that's what they did. The Faal brothers took over – 'We're taking the business, Tosh. Now fuck off.'"

The other 'underdog' Manchester independent was TJM Records, run by Tony Davidson, proprietor of rehearsal studios on Little Peter Street. The common perception was that Davidson was a rich boy and the label a plaything in comparison to his family's jewellery and scrap businesses. Their first signing, V2, would top the alternative charts in November 1978 with 'Man In A Box', selling 8,000 copies (a figure the label claimed to have shifted on 'pre-sale'). Further releases came from Slaughter & The Dogs, Skrewdriver, the Pathetix, Eddie Mooney, Victim and most notably, the Frantic Elevators, featuring a young Mick Hucknall. But TJM suffered an image problem. To all intents and purposes it was considered an even cornier label than Rabid. While the latter had conceptual ideas and political aspirations, the flyers which announced TJM's arrival ("The label for the discerning record buyer" and "The sound of tomorrow made for today") were laughably anachronistic, the nomenclature a leftover not even of the sixties but the fifties.

"I can always remember Mick Hucknall, this little ginger-haired guy, scrounging beer," recalls Eddie Mooney. "He was always hanging around, completely skint. You'd go see Tony Davidson to pester him to get some money, or find out when the record was coming out. He was hardly ever in, but there would be the forlorn figure of Mick Hucknall, with his short-cropped ginger hair and tank top. And he'd always say, 'one day we're going to be famous'. I used to laugh at him – I thought, no chance. We did a lot of gigs with the Frantic Elevators, and we did one at the Russell Club, which became The Factory, with V2. I remember me and Mark Standley [of V2] killing ourselves laughing at this ginger bloke doing these tracks where he'd just shout his head off in a Hawaiian t-shirt, and we thought he was hilarious. But after the punk era I met Mick again, and I said, 'What are you going to do, now punk's over? Are you going to get a job?' He said no, I'm going to do some soul music. I said, Mick, *no way* do you have a voice for soul!"

Of all the bands on TJM, few had as much right to complain as Victim, the Anglo-Irish band who managed to live up to their name spectacularly. After being enticed from Northern Ireland by a modest contract, they had their equipment stolen during their first week in Manchester, and immediately fell out over the format of their first release for the label, with Davidson trying to strong-arm them into putting out a four-track EP of previous demos. Forced to sleep in a derelict shop in Oldham Street while decrying the fact that their label owner was spending all his time in casinos, they came to hate Davidson with a passion. The song they finally gave him for release, 'Why Are Fire Engines Red', they'd agreed was the worst in their repertoire. And while they dithered over the use of a cover designed by Linder, TJM put it out anyway in a very unflattering sleeve featuring... a fire engine. In a final humiliation visited on them after they decamped to Illuminated Records, the proposed release of their next single (as part of the deal behind their package tour) was delayed when TJM mislaid the master tapes. They had to rely on the return of a copy they'd sent to John Peel.

Mooney, meanwhile, had become the label's next and final artist. "After Rabid, somebody mentioned this other label called TJM," he remembers. "I found this phone number, and I thought if Graham Fellows can do a daft record, I can do one. And I recruited a couple of young local lads, a drummer and a guitar player who'd hardly ever played, and I thought – what's the most ridiculous song I could possibly write? Hence 'I Bought Three Eggs'. We did it for a laugh really, and we recorded a rough demo of it in the cellar of the house I lived in. So I rang TJM from the phone box while I played a cassette on their answering machine. Mark Standley heard this and said to Tony Davidson he should put it out. At the time Tony had a Kevin Keegan hairstyle – he wasn't an alternative character. He's like someone you'd see on *The Apprentice* today – open-necked shirt, flares, and a mullet – *Billy the Fish* hairstyle and medallions, Mark Standley heard the message and said to Tony, 'This is bizarre, you've got to listen to this.' So I got a phone call back. They said, come down to the record company, which turned out to be a room in a warehouse. It was on Little Peter Street. It's all posh flats now, but at the time it was an old warehouse. When we went in there, it was a shock. I imagined someone with spiky hair or something, but he was a bit older than us, about 30. And he said, 'I like this, let's do a record!' We've never even done a proper gig or rehearsal. So I said OK, and within a week he had us in this studio in Manchester called Smile, where a lot of the TJM stuff was recorded. And the initial demo was kinda punky, but we got this so-called producer, Steve, a lovely bloke, but he didn't have a clue – we sounded more like Gerry & The Pacemakers. I was horrified when I heard the mix!"

'I Bought Three Eggs', TJM16, was the last record to be released on the label. "The label was starting to do OK," says Mooney, "but he was awful with money – he didn't pay any of his staff, and I never got a penny out of those records. A couple of the acts got lump sums, like Slaughter & The Dogs – but they were the Rossi brothers and you didn't mess with them. But he tried a couple of tours, which weren't properly organised, and I think he lost interest. I don't think it went under because of money, I think he just couldn't be bothered. He just stopped turning up. The label was very chaotic. Even the rubber plant in his office was never watered from the day he bought it. And as the rubber plant dwindled, so did his business. It was like a measuring stick. And in the end all that was left of the rubber plant was a lot of dry earth and a stick – which is when the label collapsed."

Davidson started another record label in the 80s, specialising in oldies, but this too was doomed. Afterwards, it's thought he returned to the family business. "He was pretending to be a svengali," says Mooney, "'You should go into showbusiness, my boy!' But as a person he was very charming, comical, funny, witty. But he wasn't the most intelligent – you just thought, this guy would be great selling double-glazing. He wasn't even remotely artistic – he was clueless on that level. It was bizarre he should be involved in this."

In fact, it's quite hard to find anyone with a kind word to say about TJM or Davidson – with the exception of Mick Rossi of Slaughter & The Dogs – perhaps because, as Mooney points out, their single was paid for in advance. "Like Rabid, I think we were the first band on Tony's label. I remember meeting him for the first time and he was always very smartly dressed, and he wore good shoes. He was a genuine soul and his word was his bond." Good shoes or no, others would contest his probity – Andrew Nicholson of The Pathetix, among them. He calls their decision to sign with the label as "without doubt the worst thing we ever did. We thought it was going to change everything and sure enough it did – we never really recovered from the experience. We'd have been better looking after ourselves, what momentum we'd built up was lost over a period where Tony [Davidson] played at being Richard Branson with his dad's money."

Stuart Murray of Fast Cars can afford Mr Davidson few kind words either. "We met Tony through his 'practice studios' (an old dingy warehouse in the dilapidated part of Manchester City Centre). He saw us a few times and decided he would like to sign us. We had recorded a demo at Cargo Studios in Rochdale, which had four tracks on it. We let the Manchester Collective, which we were members of, have two for their forthcoming album *A Manchester Collection*; the deal being we would get a percentage of the profits but our music would not be tied up in the future should we get another deal. We verbally agreed with Tony that he could have the other tracks for his *Identity Parade* album, thinking it would be a similar arrangement. Tony went to test pressing with the album and then produced a contract for us to sign. When we read it he wanted the rights to our songs forever! We still thought we might get a major deal at the time and didn't want to let him have, what we considered to be, two of our best songs, 'Tameside Girls' and 'Images Of You'. We decided not to sign it, which resulted in him not being a 'happy teddy' and having to have the album re-pressed. He did send a letter to *Sounds* at the time about it!"

"It's true the TJM label identity was disastrously unhip," admits Cath Carroll, "but they put out a few fabulous records. The first Distractions EP, 'You're Not Going Out Dressed Like That.' And that V2 record. You know with V2, in Manchester, we never really knew what we had. They played the Mayflower near Belle Vue a lot and were a rather hysterical pose, we thought, [Guitarist Ian] Nance especially. They had this super serious early 70s glam thing, just without the flares, it was pretty preposterous. TJM put them out without any irony, while we just couldn't make enough Jobriath jokes. But the last laugh is on us; they were quite brazen and truly just put the rock and roll out there – very heroic. We always thought they had an attitude but I think they wore so much make up, it just made it hard to see their face muscles move."

It's not hard to see Rabid especially, not least for its inverted snobbery towards London, as a precursor to Factory, the label that would come to define Manchester music for a decade to come. That's despite the fact that substantial antipathy continues to exist between various factions – witness the fallout to Michael Winterbottom's impish cinematic re-imagining of events that was *24-Hour Party People*. Similarities extend beyond intense regional pride and the city's indefatigable swagger to include a specific political motivation at least at the outset – both labels were 'socialist', albeit Rabid's was a singularly hedonistic, druggy strand of socialism and Factory's mingled love of the common people with naked elitism. There was also a fast and loose embrace of conventional business models. Factory became famous for its avoidance of paper contracts, but that was always the case with Rabid anyway; which is why ultimately the artists were able to cut deals with later rights vultures like Colin Newman's Receiver.

Most importantly, though, the nucleus of the creative milieu that formed around Factory and saw their apotheosis in Joy Division's success (Cummins, Hannett, *et al*) undertook their apprenticeship with Rabid – Hannett long maintaining a foot in both camps. Tony Wilson himself was unequivocal about Rabid being key to the idea of forming his own label. Factory's very first record (the 'Ideal For Living' EP) would be distributed by their then more established cousins. But as the 80s dawned, Factory would quickly overtake its ancestors as Manchester's premier record label, providing a back beat to the city that some have, not wholly hysterically, described as 'spiritual'.

Of course, the other important precedent was New Hormones, which had been revived in 1979 when, with Buzzcocks established as chart regulars, Richard Boon found himself with a little more time on his hands. It reactivated with releases by the Tiller Boys (an *ad hoc* ensemble sometimes featuring Pete Shelley, but pivoting around Eric Random and Francis Cookson) and Linder's Ludus, released simultaneously in March 1980. Boon was joined at various points in the enterprise by Peter Wight, the manager of Dislocation Dance, and Liz Naylor and Cath Carroll, who ran *City Fun*, fanzine, after Boon offered them free rent and phone use. Promoters Alan Wise and Nigel Baguely, of Wise Moves, ran a promotion agency next door and shared the rent, at least occasionally.

"At *City Fun*, we used to promote gigs, variously at the Mayflower, Band on The Wall and The Gallery," recalls Carroll, "and produced our own posters." That saw them join the precarious milieu of flyposters who remained the underbelly of Manchester's rock 'n' roll tradition. "We always dreaded flyposting, not because of the police, but because we'd heard about this flyposting mafia. We understood Salford and possibly Wythenshawe were involved, which is another way of saying broken legs. So we'd walk to New Cross at two in the morning. Liz would have the glue bucket in a Marks & Sparks plastic bag, and I would wear my GPO uniform and hide the posters in my postbag. We'd spend ages looking for a spot that wasn't in active use, but yet was in an acceptable place. Obviously you don't want to be papering over the front of Lewis's. We just dreaded being spotted so I'd pretend to be checking an address, while Liz threw up the poster. Like the Royal Mail delivers to abandoned shops in Shudehill at three in the morning! We had never knowingly seen Vinni Faal and were never really sure what he did, but we were always very clear on never wanting to meet him. Alan Wise and Nigel Baguely brought up his name a lot; there was much lugubriously dark hinting and we'd ask Alan what he meant and he'd go, 'never you mind, darlings,' in his best theatrical uncle voice."

There were many other semi-regulars at their 50 Newton Road headquarters, on the top floor of an old merchant's warehouse bang in the city centre, including many of the roster enjoying the 'open house' conviviality. Frequent guests included Nico and a star-struck (with Linder) Stephen Patrick Morrissey. "As you know," Morrissey would later tease Boon when the latter interviewed him for *The Catalogue* and asked him about his prior knowledge of independent labels, "I was not an unfamiliar face on the stairs of the New Hormones offices as a limbless teenager. It was then, very much, real independent art versus real major money and independent people were just much more my type. They watched BBC 2, for instance. They knew Emma Cannon." When funds allowed it, the office was stocked with cheap alcohol and speed. All visitors, however, would have to negotiate the short-tempered, one-armed ex-Irish soldier Tommy who manned the dilapidated lift. But at this stage New Hormones was very much considered the equal of Factory.

"Richard Boon took me to see the New Hormones office once," confirms Kevin Hewick. "I was impressed that it actually *looked* like an office. Everything Factory was, was on the floor in Alan Erasmus's flat or (after his break up with Lindsay Reade) in boxes in Tony's vast, empty, minimalist house he lived alone in, on Old Broadway. Truth be told, I got to develop a hankering to defect to Boon and New Hormones; it seemed more like a 'record company' should be." The rivalry between New Hormones and Factory was keen, but not without a shared spirit. "There was rivalry everywhere then," admits Linder, "between the north and south, between Factory and New Hormones, between every band. Like trying to put your finger on mercury, the post-punk period endlessly divides and sub divides, escaping easy classification and display. Even whilst singing, I still made mono prints, took photographs and was being photographed. Those were unique years within culture and arguably, we were participating in the last of the days of a British underground before the late eighties malaise."

While Factory became synonymous with Martin Hannett's production, New Hormones would use Stuart James, who had previously worked with OMD, Joy Division and an earlier incarnation of Ludus. Money was much tighter at New Hormones than at Factory (whom the label would eventually come to refer to as 'Fat Tory Records' in mocking tribute to Wilson's grandiose scheming). James didn't have the resources (nor Hannett's famously demanding nature) to indulge bands in the studio, yet still produced occasionally spectacular results. Similarly, though there was some cogent design in terms of the label's artwork, they didn't have the defining unanimity Peter Saville brought to Factory. They simply never had the budget.

But they did build a roster studded with literate art-pop. The Biting Tongues, originally formed to accompany leader Howard Walmsley's film of the same title, were eventually taken up by Peter Kent at Beggars' Situation 2 label. Dislocation Dance were formed out of the Manchester Musician's Collective and released their first single as a joint venture with New Hormones and their own imprint, Delicate Issues, but thereafter became the label's great white hopes. The Diagram Brothers had the kind of principled political viewpoints – critics would argue dogma – typical of a certain cadre of Manchester musicians. Divertingly, they tailored their lyrics to unarguable statements of fact. Hence tracks like 'Bricks' ('very useful objects, not expensive at all'), their first single for New Hormones. Other mavericks included the irascible God's Gift (whose belligerent 'Discipline' is a lost lo-fi classic), Eric Random and a single produced by Martin Rushent for The Decorators.

But despite some European success for Ludus and Dislocation Dance and the omnipresent support of John Peel, the label was feeling the pinch by 1982. Wright took up the offer of regular paid employment while on tour with Dislocation Dance in America, and shortly thereafter the Diagram Brothers broke up just as they began to make headway. The label closed with an attempted fund-raiser for CND organised by CP Lee of Albert y Lost Trios Paranoias, 'Cruisin' For Santa'.

New Hormones has historically been dwarfed by the success of Factory. The difference in their fortunes has been ascribed by some to the unprecedented access to the media Wilson enjoyed, as well as financial resources beyond New Hormones' reach. Despite the occasional sniping in *City Fun*, or attempts to wind up Factory's head honcho by Linder and others, relations between New Hormones and Wilson were cordial, almost fraternal. Wilson would repeatedly take the time to point out the importance of Boon in shaping the Manchester music scene, while Boon considered Wilson both a close friend and ally.

"I knew Richard much better than I ever knew Tony," says Carroll. "Richard had a very dry, campy sense of humour, and always seemed to be in a state of private amusement, though he could still express disapproval quite clearly, if so inclined. He was always respectfully circumspect when talking about Tony, as if trying to describe the indescribable with as much precision as possible. I think it was perhaps his affection for the man he was trying to describe. He never said anything negative about him. With Tony, if he told you to get to the next level, it was because he thought you'd achieved something important, so he was always making comments about what Richard should do next. Tony's advice was always something like, get Eric Random to take it to Vegas, launch Linder from a rocket from the top of Kendal Milne, get out of Didsbury. They had some complex drama in common such as Morrissey, the whole who did and did not sign him, and why – who wants to untangle that one? It was Richard who eventually took him to Rough Trade. Then there was the Linder connection; they had both worked with her. Liz and I never really pried too much into Linder's feelings about Factory. Richard just thought she was marvellous – as did we – and whatever she needed to do, she got to do it. He never pushed her to Vegas."

## Independence Days

Some New Hormones alumni argue, to this day, that Boon was the true innovator, but Wilson the man 'who could make things work'. That is perhaps true. But listening to New Hormones' output afresh, Dislocation Dance aside, it is difficult to locate a track with the potential to light up the charts or seize the zeitgeist as Joy Division/New Order or Happy Mondays would. "There were always great financial constraints," admits Boon. "I'm sure that did stymie things." Does he feel there are any records that could, perhaps, have done better? "Yes, I think Linder's could have done a lot more. And Dislocation Dance probably." In fact, in the event, Dislocation Dance's album *Midnight Shift* would emerge on Rough Trade where, in the absence of better prospects, and stony-broke, Boon had found a bolthole.

Factory had been founded in January 1978 by Granada TV reporter Tony Wilson and unemployed actor and band manager Alan 'Razzer' Erasmus. Formerly a member of the *Coronation Street* cast, and according to Wilson 'the only black kid in Wythenshawe', Erasmus's clients included The Durutti Column (featuring former Nosebleeds guitarist Vini Reilly). Wilson was a Cambridge graduate, making his way as a news reporter, often to comical effect (notably on 'Kamikaze' segments of the regional news stream, *Granada Reports*, which included water-skiing and, most famously, a misguided attempt at hang-gliding). Alongside a creeping fear of imminent death from his next stunt, Wilson not only nursed injuries, but also the idea of an ITV franchise show to rival the BBC's *Top Of The Pops*, only with typically loftier ambitions.

*So It Goes* ran for two seasons, comprising 19 separate editions, though it was never shown nationally. Wilson's own immersion in the new music was partly driven by its audience – one of whom, Stephen Morrissey, had sent in the cover of a New York Dolls album. A further parcel contained a tape of The Sex Pistols from Buzzcocks' singer Howard Devoto, then still Howard Trafford, along with an invitation to see them play support to the Pistols at a forthcoming Lesser Free Trade Hall show. Although Buzzcocks pulled out of the Lesser Free Trade Hall gig, unable to find a bass player, Wilson, and Erasmus, did keep the engagement – at one of the most mythologised gigs ever. The sheer number of attendees who would subsequently form their own bands, or claim membership of that select audience of 42 would be the subject of David Nolan's book *I Swear I Was There*. But, in brief, they would include Hook and Sumner of New Order, Devoto and Buzzcocks, Mick Hucknall, Morrissey and Martin Hannett. Wilson spent the next day at Granada Studios convincing them to allow him to put the Pistols on TV. There is some conjecture as to whether Wilson was confusing two separate

Pistols shows at the venue, and if he really took his demands all the way to the top – Granada chairman Lord Bernstein. Confusion caused, not least, to Wilson's winning habit of obfuscation – naturally related in the third person – in his 'autobiography' *24 Hour Party People*. Not a dissimilar figure to Wilson in that he saw no contradiction in conflating showmanship with socialist principles, Bernstein – or at least one of the Granada hierarchy, gave him his head.

The first season thus closed with the debut TV appearance by The Sex Pistols (who predictably horrified Wilson's superiors). Yet it was principally with the opening of the second series, running from October 1977, that Wilson was allowed, or able, to explore the new tide of punk and related music (the opening show featured John Cooper Clarke, Buzzcocks and Elvis Costello). But it all ran aground when Iggy Pop appeared on the second run of *So It Goes* in October 1977, during which an expletive was inadvertently broadcast, despite it being a pre-record, Wilson carried the can and the strand was culled at season's close. Erasmus, meanwhile, had been looking after bands and after a few false starts, encouraged Wilson to get involved with what would become Durutti Column. Wilson – a soft, if willing touch – immediately paid for rehearsal space in a scout hut in the south of the city, and gave them their impossibly pretentious name after the comic strip panel erected during a student takeover of Strasbourg University.

The name Factory (Wilson would deny any suggestion of Andy Warhol's New York milieu being an influence, stating instead that he'd taken it from a 'Factory Closing' sign) was invoked initially as the billing for a club night they organised. The Russell Club in Hulme hosted Durutti Column, Sheffield's Cabaret Voltaire and Joy Division in May 1978. Manchester Polytechnic typography student Peter Saville designed the posters after introducing himself to Wilson at a Patti Smith show. Not that he got them finished in time to put any up, because he couldn't find the correct yellow pigment, in a mildly unsettling portent of deadline-aversion to come.

And yet it is highly indicative of the ethos emerging around Factory that there was no outcry from the artists at Saville's somewhat surreal sense of proportion and priority.

"It seems funny to me even now," reckons the Durutti Column's Vini Reilly. "At the time it felt right. I'd met Peter a few times and he's a highly intelligent and sophisticated man. I have enormous respect for him, always have had. But he's an artist – the real thing. And to me, if the things were late, it didn't matter, because when it arrived it would be something special. So to me to rush a piece of art to meet a deadline, it runs against my ideals anyway."

By September Wilson, Erasmus and Saville had decided to record an EP as a vinyl document of the club, after initial discussions with Roger Eagle of Eric's over a collaborative Liverpool/Manchester venture fizzled out. The label proper was formed as a partnership between Wilson, Erasmus, Saville and producer Martin Hannett, with offices in Erasmus's home in Palatine Road. While Rabid was an acknowledged influence, instead of following the template of pushing out singles and then licensing their artists to majors, their intention was to concentrate on albums. Wilson had certainly learned the lessons of the immediate punk era. "The thing I remember specifically about starting Factory," he would tell *Q*, "is that independents are set up to get bands signed to majors. Everyone thinks that punk was all about some anti-capitalist response to the majors, but the Pistols signed to anyone; the Clash's first single came out on CBS, and Buzzcocks signed to United Artists the night Elvis Presley died. It was all major label stuff until this wonderful distribution network called Rough Trade started, and also Pinnacle, who used to supply dust bags."

The label's 'debut' release announced the conceptually mischievous nature of their catalogue – FAC1 was actually a yellow and black Saville poster for gigs at the Factory venue through May and June 1978. FAC2, 'A Factory Sampler' EP, the label's first release proper, featured acts who had appeared at the club (the aforementioned Durutti Column, Cabaret Voltaire and Joy Division, joined by John Dowie). Released in December 1978, but not widely distributed or reviewed until the following March, it sold out of its 5,000 pressing within just a few months, funded by the £12,000 Wilson had inherited in 1975 following his mother's death.

The bulk of the songs (with the exception of Cabaret Voltaire's, whose demo had been passed to Wilson by Richard Boon during New Hormones' hiatus) were cut at Cargo Studios – in a link forged via Wilson's television career. "Tony and I would talk superficially about TV shows and recordings but I'm afraid he left me standing when the conversation got any deeper," remembers Cargo's John Brierley, a former Granada cameraman. "He was a very eloquent and intelligent man and was good to listen to; he had almost boundless enthusiasm for TV and bands. Unfortunately we didn't speak about Factory or Joy Division until after I had set up the studio. In actual fact we really had little time to talk; invariably he would arrive in the news studio only minutes before transmission for frantic rehearsals – not the best time to talk about bands. I think I was converted though, and hence my enthusiasm grew when I set the studio up."

Saville's artwork, thematically inspired by Kraftwerk's *Autobahn*, utilised the industrial warning sign he had employed for the earlier poster. Stolen from a college door, it was both utilitarian and somehow foreboding in its functionality, and a deliberate break from punk's tradition of exclamation-mark design. Two further Saville concert posters followed before the first single artist release on the label, A Certain Ratio's 'All Night Party'. Released in May 1979, it was a notable early Hannett production, extensively using drum machines, with artwork featuring the corpse of comedian Lenny Bruce and Norman 'Psycho' Bates on the reverse of the sleeve. Merseysiders Orchestral Manouevres In The Dark came and went, but would retain Saville's services. As OMD's Paul Humphreys told Sean O'Neal, "When we first joined up with Factory, Tony Wilson said to us, 'Look, you just use me as a vehicle to go on somewhere else. I think you're going to be a successful pop band, and I don't think you can be that at the moment on Factory. So when we generate enough interest, I think you should move on.' And of course we said, 'No, no! We want to stay on Factory,' but when Virgin offered a lot of money to have us, Tony was happy to get rid of us, and we were happy to go."

Similarly, there were no objections to Cabaret Voltaire moving off to Rough Trade. "At that time, we would have quite happily gone and recorded more stuff for Factory," Richard H Kirk would recall to Denzil Watson, "because they were northerners and we had a bit more in common with them than Rough Trade. But Rough trade actually came up with the money to buy a four-track EP; so we went with them. It was almost mercenary... I think the only problem that would have arisen was that Factory had their own in-house art director, Peter Saville, whose work I love but I don't think it would have worked with Cabaret Voltaire."

Some of the further 'odd' additions to the catalogue, meanwhile, included headed notepaper, industrial earplugs as per the FAC 1 design, and most legendarily of all, Linder's 'menstrual egg timer'. Linder had been asked to record for Factory, but turned them down due to an earlier commitment to New Hormones. However, she did offer them the egg timer, FAC 8, as compensation: "I made sketches and small bloody beads that would be used to show menstruation – I have them still; ironically they look like medieval relics. I showed my designs to Tony Wilson who loved the whole idea. I have a sketch of the original, it's interesting – on one side of the paper are Tony's budgets for the next Factory single and then on the other is a drawing of the egg timer, except that that title is crossed out and Tony has written 'The Factory Egg Timer'. It was never made."

At this stage, however, there was no real indication that Factory would shoot to pre-eminence. "As I remember it," says Marc Riley, then a member of The Fall, "we didn't really see Factory Records as anything but 'another Manchester label' – particularly at the beginning. It was an extension of the Factory promotions set-up. At that time, the Warsaw/Joy Division stock wasn't particularly high. They played a lot of gigs around the town and Dave McCullough had started to champion them. But in Manchester (and beyond) they were definitely one rung below The Fall in the credibility/profile stakes (not for long – obviously). They also signed A Certain Ratio and The Durutti Column, who had supported us on several occasions, so at the beginning it didn't look like Factory Records was going to be a serious player in the music industry. It appeared to be sweeping up the better Manchester bands apart from The Fall."

"The key difference between New Hormones and Factory," ponders Cath Carroll, "was most of all about 'Identity in Location'. Richard was about art; that was central for New Hormones. But Factory began as a place to go. The Factory nights at the PSV were sold in a very iconic way by Tony. The club was commonly referred to as the West Indian Busmen's Association back then and you had to cross the footbridge into bleakest Hulme to get there, to this lonely little brick box by the Mancunian Way, just outside the Crescents. 'This is real Manchester' was the selling point – and it was. It wasn't a sometime disco like Rafters, on Oxford Road, traditional nightlife that could have been anywhere. Factory's records were an extension of this theme of place. The product was very high end and substantial, the physical presence mattered, it was as much a part of the bricks and industry of the city as it was entertainment. In releasing its first record, Factory was really announcing its entry into the history of the city. While everyone still fixates on Tony as the key to the label, he was always turning the attention back to the city, away from himself. You had to move a lot of hot air to shift the centre of the universe from London to Manchester in those days."

By the end of 1979 Rob Gretton, Joy Division's manager, had become the fifth member of the core Factory team, as the club closed (to re-open briefly the following year). He, like Wilson, had first encountered Joy Division playing at the Stiff/Chiswick Challenge in April 1978, though he'd made the acquaintance of Wilson much earlier, through DJ-ing at hip pre-punk bar Rafters. A former insurance clerk and baggage handler, his first loves were Manchester City (in contrast to Wilson's Old Trafford allegiances) and music – he was an early roadie for Slaughter & The Dogs and published their fanzine, *Manchester Rains*. Liking what he saw at that performance, Gretton approached Bernard Sumner at a phone box outside Manchester's central post office and asked them if he could manage the band. Various stories, meanwhile, have been put forward about the nature of the band's 'contract' with Factory. Bass player Barney Sumner maintains it was a single sheet promising the return of the band's masters after six months if all didn't work out. The more tickling legend has it that the deal was signed in Wilson's blood and contained only the following wording: "The musicians own everything, the company owns nothing. All our bands have the freedom to fuck off."

It was Gretton's masterstroke that the band's debut album, *Unknown Pleasures*, released in June 1979, should be housed by Factory rather than handing the masters to a major (or just as acutely, southern) record label. After abortive attempts at recording a debut album funded by RCA (the tapes eventually handed back and the label reimbursed its £1,500 investment), Joy Division had briefly hooked up with Martin Rushent's WEA/Radar-backed subsidiary Genetic to record demos. But ultimately Gretton persuaded them that it would be better to stick with Factory, on the basis that they were local and approachable, and had backed the band from the outset.

Reflecting on his maverick approach in an interview with Sean O'Hagan in 2002, Wilson, with the benefit of hindsight, acknowledged how unconventional the situation was. "It was the greatest deal any band ever had. Everyone says we were idiots, and in a way, I guess, we were. We had a heroic attitude to artistic freedom, and we thought normal contracts were a bit vulgar – somehow not punk. But that was the whole point – we weren't a regular record label."

"I loved that facet of Factory," concurs Vini Reilly, "that it was so, if you like, unprofessional. You could call it incompetent. It was run in such a way that gave space for human beings to be themselves, and not geared up to some corporate idea or scheduled. By then there was a bigger picture for me with Factory. I'd realised it was special. I didn't feel Factory was a record company. It didn't feel like a record company. I'd had talks with record companies, and found they were bloody awful and I hated them. So Factory wasn't a record company, it was just a group of people with some mad ideas, the imagination to have the mad ideas, and the balls to commit themselves to the things they'd dreamt up."

The sessions for *Unknown Pleasures* began at Hannett's Strawberry Studios in April 1979. Their producer delighted in behaviour that tested both the band's patience (insisting, for example, that Stephen Morris take apart and reassemble his entire drum kit because of a 'rattle' he had detected) and Wilson's wallet. But in insisting on calibrating each and every aspect of the music to his own personal satisfaction, and the introduction of digital delay through his binary echo invention, Hannett gave the recordings their unique, sterile beauty. Yet for all the press plaudits the lack of adequate independent distribution meant that half the 10,000 pressings were still being stored in a garage by year's end.

Joy Division, forever to be cast in the public mind as the broody, doomed romantics framed by Kevin Cummins' stark photography (the choice of black and white media at least partially a function of economics), were rapidly becoming a music press *cause célèbre*. With their debut Peel session booked, they graced the cover of the *NME* in January 1979; a placing writer and camp confidante Paul Morley had tried and failed to secure earlier. He'd previously posited the question 'How much longer before an aware label will commit themselves to this group?' in his review of 'A Factory Sample'. On the surface it seemed the upsurge in his band's fortunes was irreversible. But it's worth noting that for all the press fanfare, November 1979 single 'Transmission' had sold only 3,000 copies. With his girlfriend Deborah pregnant and recently diagnosed with epilepsy while still trying to hold down employment with the Job Centre, Ian Curtis was beginning to live life at a pace that would ultimately see his demise at his own hand.

The legend of Joy Division, though, had a legitimate musical rationale too, and it was Hannett that produced the spark. "His ability to translate their thoughts and needs into a co-ordinated work of art was the catalyst Joy Division needed," Deborah Curtis would later recall. Leaving Pete Hook's knee-slung bass to provide not just bottom end but melody, Hannett's laborious energetic was both claustrophobic and spare; as chill and spectral as a Mervyn Peake charcoal. The band, Curtis apart, hated the finished production, feeling Hannett had wrung the life out of their live sound. And both Deborah Curtis and the press, were startled at the maudlin, downcast lyrics, not least the revelation contained in 'Insight' that, at the age of just 23, Curtis was already feeling old and nostalgic for his youth. She sought confirmation from her father's GP about his prognosis; the doctor was ambivalent, then shot himself a few weeks later. That sense of fatality and resignation that always shrouded Joy Division was reflected in the obtuse, impersonal packaging – featuring an 'Outside' and 'Inside' rather than side one or two, with the track listing and credits absent entirely from the outer sleeve.

The impact of *Unknown Pleasures* was huge. Though it didn't chart, it did prove to others that an independently recorded and released album could be successful without taking London's shilling. And the dynamics of the sound that the band and Hannett had fashioned suddenly became ubiquitous, as would-be copyists formed by angst-ridden young men tapped into Curtis's somehow legitimising desolation as fuel for their own vinyl exorcisms. For two years, John Peel once recalled, all he ever seemed to receive in the post were JD-soundalike demos.

The label's second album, *The Return Of The Durutti Column*, effectively a collaboration between Vini Reilly and Hannett, further cemented Factory's reputation. While a variety of avenues had been explored under the guise of post-punk, *The Return* was arguably the most free-spirited record of its time, featuring styles ranging from jazz to classical, while Hannett's studio wizardry included everything up to and including the addition of bird song. In fact, the ever flappable Reilly had been absent for two of the three days of recording. The record, built around his bewitching guitar arpeggios and Hannett's synthesizer, was devoid of vocals. "I'd seen the Sex Pistols and Buzzcocks," Reilly recalls, "and I thought – this is really exciting. I hated progressive rock and the way jazz had gone. It seemed to me that punk was saying you can do absolutely anything at all musically. You can break all the barriers. I thought that would be an avenue for experimental music, which is what I wanted to do."

"I didn't really believe it was going to be an album!" he continues. "I'd done the Nosebleeds single and nothing really came of that. I just did it because I loved music. I didn't know if it was going to be an album or not, it was just the case of jumping at the chance of being in the studio. I actually didn't get up in time, Martin had to physically get me out of bed to get me to the studio – that's how little I believed it would happen. I was still doing late night petrol station shifts. But we had two days in the studio, and Martin spent a day with these old black sequencers and synthesizers and strange pieces of equipment in big cardboard boxes. I didn't know what on earth they were – but he was getting these noises from them and fiddling about. I didn't really appreciate what he was doing. I shouted at him and had a bit of a rant – 'I want to play my guitar!' I was very vociferous about venting my frustration about sitting around. It didn't phase him at all, he just looked at me over his funny glasses and said (quietly) 'Don't worry about it, Vini.'"

And naturally, that's when the 'magic' happened. "Then he made what sounded like bird noises, just after that outburst," continues Reilly. "And I started to play along. He said, wait a minute. And he made a beat on his mega-synthesizer things. And I just played a tune that came out of my head, 'Sketch For Summer'. It just wrote itself. Martin turned a few things on and told me to stop and then start again and he recorded it. Then he recorded an overdubbed guitar and it was finished. And the whole album was like that. I had maybe 30 little guitar pieces, sketches really. I didn't think they would be accepted as full, finished pieces of music. I was even more amazed when Tony presented me with a white label. I was completely baffled. 'What, this is really going to be an album? You must be insane! No-one's going to buy this!' Tony asked me who my favourite artist was And my favourite artist was, and to an extent still is, Raoul Dufy. So I just picked three prints from one of the books I had about Dufy and that became the sleeve."

Initial copies, however, also featured a sandpaper sleeve, inspired by Guy Debord's *The Society Of The Spectacle*, whose cover, made of similar materials, was intended to wear against its neighbours on a book shelf. "Tony got the idea from the situationists about the sandpaper sleeve. It was Joy Division that stuck the sandpaper onto the card. I was mortified. I didn't really know them. I went to the Factory office, which was one room in Alan Erasmus's house, but I had to walk out. I couldn't bear to join in. When it was presented to me as a finished album, I couldn't relate to it. I didn't know what to think – it was beyond my experience. I was really shocked. And about six weeks later Tony told me I could quit my day jobs [he was working both at the late-night petrol station and as a council gardener], and I was earning enough money to just do music, which was incredible. And the next thing is, what kind of guitar would you like – you can afford a decent guitar now. Yeah, I want one like Jimmy Page! A Gibson Les Paul!"

The other major cornerstone of early Factory would be A Certain Ratio, whose agit-funk slant on the post-punk dialectic betrayed similarities to Bristol's Pop Group (whom Wilson admired and had booked for a show at the Russell Club previously). But their early fervour was eventually lost to a smoothed-out soul-jazz pop that saw Wilson's interest wane, though he would, at their insistence, buy them the 'Sixth Army' shorts they wore at their prestigious London Lyceum show. All of which encouraged further accusations of Nazi fixations that afflicted Joy Division and Factory by proxy. Joy Division's name had been taken from Yehiel De-Nur's 1955 novella *House Of Dolls*, which (partially) fictionalised the brothels run in Nazi extermination camps for guards and to reward good behaviour by inmates. The name A Certain Ratio was taken from the lyrics to Brian Eno's song 'The True Wheel', but the ultimate source was a quote by Hitler concerning the classification of 'Jews' based on blood ethnicity. When reported in the *NME*, John Peel made an on-air announcement that he would not play their records any more. Years later, Wilson was still displeased. "Dear John," he would write as a sidebar on the event of the DJ's 50th birthday, "something in the sweet, wonderful charm of the man that on occasions descends into gullibility... 'I read it in *NME*' and 'Anfield is Heaven'."

A Certain Ratio themselves withdrew from the media and announced no further interviews after Paul Morley's cover story for the *NME*; a feature that, it has to be said, Wilson did a good job of hogging. "When a journalist writes a piece on a Factory group he is inevitably met at Manchester's Piccadilly Station by Factory's wizard Tony Wilson (to Hannett's mad professor, Gretton's hooligan, Erasmus' tramp and Saville's executive). And sure enough as we burst through the ticket barrier of platform nine there's the grinning Wilson, pushing loose hair out of his face, striding towards us in pathetic khaki balloons, happily sockless. He's skiving off more time from Granada Television." Indeed, Wilson did temporarily have more time on his hands, having been jettisoned from a promising anchor role on *World In Action* after turning up hours late, and stoned, for an interview with Conservative minister Keith Joseph after his car broke down. In the *NME* piece, ACR laid the blame for the khaki shorts (and fake suntan to hide their pale chicken legs) at Wilson's door. 'Factory' was referenced on no less than 30 occasions in the article – a 'breakthrough' band spending so much time discussing themselves in relation to their record label said everything about the intimidating stature of Factory already. A label whose roster had now expanded to include Section 25 from Blackpool, the immensely talented but ill-fated Distractions, Crawling Chaos from the north-east and Crispy Ambulance.

Another recruit was Kevin Hewick, albeit one more rooted in a traditional singer-songwriter vein. "How I got in on it all amazes me," reflects Hewick. "If the wind had blown a different way, I'd have been one of the hundreds of never to be heard tapes in the pile of bin bags Alan Erasmus kept in the corner of the lounge at Palatine Road. But I did stumble into their extraordinary scene, clueless and totally unprepared. I never did quite work out quite what the hell was going on but I guess that's how the great innovations and genius failures happened, they were born out of that chaos. Not being a Manc I was a real outsider for much of it, though Tony Wilson constantly kept me up to speed with the city's scene and its happenings and gossip – as according to him! Whereas Alan Erasmus seemed laid back about the madness; he was chilled before people called it chilled. With Tony it was a bit like a love affair with acts. For a time he was clearly very excited about me, filling my head with stuff like I was 'the best British songwriter since Elvis Costello'. But as it became painfully clear that I wasn't, he cooled, and the regular lengthy phone calls – him calling me – went down to a trickle. In the end they turned to me calling him and getting a piss-taking [future Happy Mondays manager] Nathan McGough on the other end."

Everything, however, was overshadowed by the death of Curtis in May 1980, a mere day before a planned tour of the US. The prophecy, which many would see his brief life leading to, was complete. The 'weight on their shoulders' proving too much, just as Joy Division looked set to break through with both second album *Closer* and devastatingly beautiful single 'Love Will Tear Us Apart' in the can. That the latter became a Top 20 hit in the hysteria following Curtis's death was of no consolation whatsoever. Indeed, it deepened the wound to know that, at the time the troubled singer had reached a plateau of poignant expression, he was hoisting a rope around an overhead clothes hanger in his Macclesfield kitchen. "I'd been warned on a train to London two weeks earlier by Annik [Honoré, Curtis's lover]," Tony Wilson would later tell the 2007 Factory documentary. "I asked her, 'What do you think of the new album.' She goes, 'I'm terrified.' I said, 'What are you terrified of?' She replies, 'Don't you understand? He means it.' And I go, 'No, he doesn't mean it – it's art.' And guess what? He fucking meant it."

In a low point for the British music press, eulogies saw writers abandon prose for poetics, as if to ghoulishly corner some of the myth for themselves. Dave McCullough's *Sounds* piece, which feverishly proclaimed "That man cared for you, that man died for you, that man saw the madness in your area," was undoubtedly the nadir. Meanwhile, Wilson switched between despair and flippancy – though a later *Face* story by Nick Kent, where he was quoted as saying "La Curtis dying on me was the greatest thing that's happened in my life – death sells", he vehemently denied. Further, he claimed he'd had it confirmed by that magazine's editor that no such quote existed on tape or transcription. Talking to Len Brown of the *NME* in 1980, in addition to profound sadness at what had occurred, there was also resignation. "It was an altruistic suicide – a very emotional and stressed,

Romantic thing, meant to help people." We should credit Wilson here with not trying to imbue Curtis with superhuman powers to heal the universal psyche as some clearly had. Earlier in the same article he'd discussed the way in which Curtis had felt himself becoming a burden on both his friends and family. "How he thought it was helping is perhaps a moot point, but somewhere in that very wild romanticism you'll find the seeds of why he fucked off."

For the rest of the band, it was business as usual, albeit in strained and dramatically altered circumstances. "We all knew quite early that we wanted to carry on," Peter Hook would later tell Jon Savage. "The first meeting we all had, which was the Sunday night, we all agreed that." Joy Division transmuted into New Order thereafter, with the addition of drummer Stephen Morris's girlfriend Gillian Gilbert on keyboards. Escaping the shadow of Curtis and Joy Division's legacy would prove problematic but not insurmountable. Wilson claimed the name came from Rob Gretton, inspired by a TV documentary on the Khmer Rouge and 'The New Order Of Kampuchean Liberation'. Perhaps a joke at Wilson's expense, the chances of Gretton and the members of the band not knowing of its less obscure connotation as one of Hitler's whims on the subject of the expansion of the Motherland are exactly zero.

Prior to the reluctant investiture of Bernard Sumner as vocalist, there was some discussion with regard to replacing Curtis with someone from the Factory ranks. "Wilson apparently suggested they consider me on vocals," remembers Kevin Hewick, "but nothing came of it, other than the one recording session that produced 'Haystack'." The latter, New Order's first studio recording following Curtis's death, was recorded by Hannett in June 1980. "Alan Hempsall of Crispy Ambulance was also apparently mentioned as a possible," Hewick continues, "having stood in for them when Ian was ill – nothing like the way depicted in *Control* [the subsequent Ian Curtis biopic by Anton Corbijn]. Nobody ever told me at the time that I was in the frame for vocals with what was to be New Order, I still don't even know if it's true or not. I'd imagine it would have been a nightmare if Alan or I had done it. It would have been seen as an affront to the sacred memory of Ian Curtis, [not least to] those of the Dave McCullough mindset. [They] made Ian their substitute indie Christ, and the strange perspective of history, which has turned him into a precious icon rather than the flesh and blood real man with the profoundly original talent that does deserve posterity. Ian's death did change everything, did touch many lives, from those close to him to those who never knew him but related to this lyrics and loved the band's music. People felt genuine grief and sorrow over it, but McCullough's absurd nonsense sowed the seeds of the Curtis cult."

In the summer of 1980 Factory launched a joint initiative with Les Disques du Crépuscule. Factory Benelux was headed by Michel Duval, a partner in the Plan K club in Brussels with Annik Honoré, alongside famed illustrator Benoît Hennebert. Another outlet, Factory US, provided distribution for the label's releases in America. Of more tangible historical consequence was the decision to launch the Haçienda night club in 1981, at Gretton's suggestion. A former Victorian textile factory was selected on the corner of Whitworth Street West and Albion Street in Manchester's city centre, which had most recently been used as a motor boat showroom, and Ben Kelly commissioned to provide the interior design on Saville's recommendation. The idea was sold to Wilson on the basis of 'giving something back' to Manchester, which he, rather grandly, would analogise as 'paying royalties' to the city that created the music in the first place.

The decision outraged Hannett, in his own way master of the conceited sweeping gesture. He's wanted to invest in a state of the art studio facility. He left the label and would sue for unpaid royalties (the case was settled for £35,000 before going to court in 1984). Wilson's reporting of Hannett's succinct astonishment at finding out £700,000 had been invested in the club – 'I'm a genius, you're all wankers'. Wilson would later elaborate on this in an interview with Craig Johnson. "Were it not for the utter stupidity of Alan Erasmus, Rob Gretton and Tony Wilson, he [Hannett] would have created the next music because he was desperate to get a Fairlight. It was a synthesiser computer keyboard, and basically what Martin, Stephen [Morris] and Bernard [Sumner] were doing with soldering irons in 1980, suddenly by 1983 there was a machine that did it called a Fairlight. We had no idea what one was, what we knew was that it cost thirty fuckin' grand and we were running the Haçienda and you could fuck off. So we used to row about this all the time. 'I want a Fairlight.' 'You can't have a Fairlight.' 'What's this piece of shit you're building? Where's my Fairlight?' He never got a Fairlight, Trevor Horn got a Fairlight and the rest is Frankie Goes To Hollywood and the rest is history. I've very recently begun to claim that we created Trevor Horn, by stopping Martin getting a fucking Fairlight. And then the big fight and they go and fall out with each other and it's the lawsuit and stuff." For his part, Hannett would tell Martin Aston in 1989 that "If you're a masonry drill, you eventually became slightly blunted. I found it necessary to go away, after my fight with Factory. I went back to my eight-track in my bedroom for a year."

Some of the artists were similarly unimpressed. "By late 1982," Hewick recalls, "there seemed to be no plan or place for me on Factory. Erasmus seemed to be less involved and Wilson was totally immersed in the Haçienda, which I'd been so against because I knew the lesser acts like me would be totally forgotten once this fantastical folly got underway. Un-with it as I was, I then had no grasp of how this was the way history was to be made again. At the time I thought – a night club where there once was Joy Division? I didn't get it. Disco rhymed with Frisco as far as I was concerned." Hewick would move on to Cherry Red after Wilson vetoed recordings he'd made with Adrian Borland and The Sound. "Tony's retort was that Factory would never release anything with 'a London band' on it." With Hannett's defection and that of Saville, also over money issues (though he would continue to provide artwork for the label), Wilson, Erasmus and Gretton formed Factory Communications Ltd.

The Haçienda's name came from a Situationist slogan, specifically *Formulary for a New Urbanism* by Ivan Chtcheglov, 'The Haçienda Must Be Built'. The cedilla (not used in Spanish, where a hacienda denotes an estate or ranch) was added to match the catalogue number ascribed to the venue, FAC 51. Situated upstairs was a stage, dance floor, cafeteria and balcony, while the ground floor housed a cocktail bar, The Gay Traitor (named in spy Anthony Blunt's honour). The other two bars were named after his colleagues – The Kim Philby and (after Guy Burgess's cryptonym) Hicks. Later, 'The 5th Man' was opened as a secondary venue after the lower cellars were converted. A planned games room was fitted out only for them to remember two weeks before opening that they'd need something more prosaic like a cloakroom. Such details were lost in the purchasing orgy that saw designer stools brought in from Finland, granite bar tops and a mahogany balcony. On the opening night Saville handed over the objets d'art that were the tickets on the actual day of the proceedings and Bernard Manning, the surprise compere, was booed off stage after a spirited 'fuck you' exchange with the new clientele. A temple of civic pride or the ultimate narcissistic folly? The Haçienda was both.

"It would have been alright it would have been the little cottage industry thing, if the Haçienda had just been a little dingy club that didn't cost much," drummer Stephen Morris would recall to Ian Harrison in the sleevenotes to the reissue of *Brotherhood*. "It was the scale of it all. Compare it to something like Alan Erasmus' Factory boat, for example, which was half-submerged – fine! Or the Factory car he drove into the Haçienda. He lost the keys and couldn't move it so they bricked it up. There was a fucking car in it when they knocked it down. The Factory Zimbabwe label – another great idea!"

Almost from the outset the Haçienda haemorrhaged money – not helped by the fact that, despite lofty design standards, the policy was to keep both door and bar prices low. Although the tariff would be raised later, it had little consequence when the venue became the pulsing heart of Manchester's dance music revolution – garnering a clientele who would far rather buy Ecstasy tablets than pints. The money came from Factory, and as joint directors, New Order themselves – reportedly more than £10,000 a month at one time. It didn't matter too much while New Order were riding high [although Messrs Hook and Sumner might dispute that], which they were doing via the spectacular success of 'Blue Monday'. The group's initial post-Curtis releases were laudable and, arguably, far more artistically engaging than anyone might have anticipated in the circumstances. But by 1983 they had found their own voice; emerging from their former singer's shadow and seamlessly absorbing New York club rhythms into a warm, beguiling electronica which maintained the bludgeoning melodic undertow of Hook's bass runs. At that time the best-selling 12-inch release in history, 'Blue Monday', in splendidly iconoclastic fashion, reportedly cost Factory money (3 pence) on each copy sold due to Saville's elaborate cover design. Though the original die-cut sleeve was withdrawn to minimise any financial shortfall, that was less aggressively reported.

The Factory roster up until 1985 had featured a cluster of acts who were lumped together in the press as generic 'Factory bands'. Some certainly were derivative of the sound Hannett and Joy Division had established – such as The Stockholm Monsters (though Wilson would opine that they were "The Mondays five years too early"), Section 25 and The Wake. But the other cornerstones of the roster were always more variegated. A Certain Ratio continued to mine a hybrid of post-punk funk that channelled aggressively polemical lyrics. The Durutti Column were never less than fascinating, though Reilly's inventiveness as a guitarist and musician seemed to exist in inverse proportion to his commercial viability. And Quando Quango, led by Factory A&R man and Haçienda DJ Mike Pickering, began to break down the barriers between rock audiences and dance fans that would build an audience that would eventually embrace Factory's *heirs apparent* to New Order, The Happy Mondays.

Pickering was an old acquaintance of Gretton's (they'd met while hiding from marauding Nottingham Forest fans) who had been a face on the early

Manchester punk scene. "I used to hang around with Joy Division and Rob," he would tell Robin Murray, "but then I went to live in Holland and people that I squatted with in an old waterworks had an old hall and they said "if you want to use the hall, you can do, I did my first real DJing there, in Rotterdam. I was playing Chic and so on, which was weird in those days. Also, we put loads of bands on. Amongst other things I put on New Order's second ever gig after Ian died, and when Rob came over he said "we want to open a club in Manchester, you've got to come back, you can stay at my house." So I actually went home almost immediately – I wanted to come back anyway. They had just bought the building that became the Haçienda at that point."

And yet the most important band in the independent world of the 80s, The Smiths, never did release a record on Factory. "The Smiths version about not signing to Factory is that Wilson was a cunt," Wilson told Andy Fyfe. "Blah blah blah. But my version of the story is that Factory was two and a half years old and a dinosaur. I was extremely depressed about Factory at the time. The first New Order album had sold poorly, and I felt that I couldn't sell the first James single or the first Stockholm Monsters single, and thought my company had lost something. I didn't know what but I thought it had gone stale and I wasn't going to saddle Steven [Morrissey] with a shit record company. And Steven was a nightmare to work with." He would also tag The Smiths, without actually naming them, for being 'the one Manc band' who 'fucked off to London and failed miserably to invest in their own town' in *24-Hour Party People*. In a documentary sequence broadcast in 1985 on *Granada Reports*, in which Wilson held the *NME*'s Smiths' cover aloft, he rides his hobby horses into the ground. First, he quizzes Messrs Rourke and Joyce on that decision to move to London, manages to talk about Mozart with Marr, then crosses swords with a surprisingly inarticulate Morrissey – addressed as Steven, which Wilson knew well he hated. He concludes by asking him why he wants to be a pop star – although surely Morrissey was to the manor born – going back to his theory that he always envisaged the singer as being 'our James Joyce'.

Instead, at the height of the Smiths' popularity in 1985, Wilson released the first record by The Happy Mondays, ring-led by barrelhouse poet Shaun Ryder – a man with a Dr Seuss-like delight in juggling nonsense words and metaphor. Alongside the Stone Roses, and to a lesser extent, Oldham's Inspiral Carpets, the Mondays would become key contributors to the faintly ridiculous 'Madchester' phenomenon (though the term was not coined for another four years). "Someone had to take Black American music," Wilson would later tell *Manchester After Dark*, "add irony and English rock. They did it and everyone fucking copied them. Three months later you get 'Loaded' by Primal Scream and 'Fools Gold' by Stone Roses and everyone is like, 'Oh my God, the world has changed.' It was the Mondays that did it."

The whole movement could have been autocue'd on Wilson rhetoric – namely an unapologetic assault on any kind of deference to the nation's capital. "Rock 'n' roll is a history of small cities," Wilson would tell Andrew Smith of the *Guardian*, retrospectively, and debatably. "Usually, those cities have two and a half years of ascendancy, then they're gone. But this place had virtually 20 years as the centre of everything – that was the miracle of Manchester."

Factory was itself changing. *The Festival Of The Tenth Summer*, culminating in an all-day show at the G-Mex in July 1986 commemorated a decade passing since the Pistols' Lesser Free Trade Hall show. Designated with catalogue number FAC151, it also offered a handy moment for reflection. "The fact that the Haçienda started to work and started to make money," Wilson told *Recoil* fanzine, "I think was in part due to a surge of energy provided by G-Mex. There was a change, and our 'perestroike' began to take effect. But it wasn't because we saw ourselves being at a low ebb or anything like that. It was occasioned by Gretton saying at the beginning of that year that he wanted to take New Order to CBS. He said New Order would sell more records there. And I knew he was right, because CBS would make the singer sing on the videos, would employ pluggers and strike forces and so on... I thought, well, why are we still staying with the old ways? It was time to change, time to adapt. So in the spring of 1986 we employed a strike force for the first time and got [Cath Carroll's] Miaow and The Railway Children into the Top 150. For about two years a whole lot of changes began to take place... We had [by 1989] fifteen or sixteen acts on the label, but it became necessary to carry on with just those that had the will and the talent. Those that can sell records and want to sell records all around the world. And of our new acts we had two that could do that; Cath Carroll and Happy Mondays."

Later, quizzed by Danny Kelly in the *NME* in 1992, Wilson reflected on the way the whole concept of independent music had changed in the mid-80s. "This whole thing – 'what is indie?' – is tying people in knots, causing them to lose sleep. All it ever meant historically was independent distribution, following the example of the American indies. Yet we've spent months now agonising over the question, wrestling with it. What is 'indie'? What does it mean? I'm sure lots of people will tell me what it means in the next few months but I really have no idea. In the mid-80s and at its worst, 'indie' meant a ghetto for bands who weren't going anywhere. At its best, 'indie' is this strange industry that flourished, and is still flourishing, in the aftermath of punk, and has made a half or two-thirds of all the most interesting music in the world... mountains of good music. For four years now, I've avoided the word and called them 'small British labels' instead. It's like guys in Blackburn, those tiny techno labels, they're pure indie."

The upturn in the Haçienda's fortunes grew from its axiomatic role in importing the American house music boom, thanks to the Detroit-Chicago crate-digging of Pickering, whose Friday night 'Nude' sessions began to attract capacity crowds from 1986 onwards. The later 'Hot' nights, hosted by Pickering alongside John Dasilva, provided hair of the dog refreshment to clubbers desperate to recreate the euphoria of the Ibiza club scene. Otherwise, however, Factory itself didn't benefit much from the house boom; Wilson admitting that one of his great errors was 'not to appreciate' Pickering sufficiently. "You never recognise a prophet in your own country," he would state of the DJ, who went on to A&R DeConstruction Records. "Rob and me had seen what was happening at the Haçienda," Pickering would confirm, "and wanted a dance label. But Tony – God rest his soul – said, 'Darling, dance music will never happen.' When he was alive he openly admitted that, so I'm not slagging him off or anything. So with my management at the time we set up DeConstruction from a little office in Islington. I'd be getting white labels in a flat box on a Friday night and we had it signed by Monday afternoon. We were selling millions of records, and if Tony had let us do the dance label, it would have saved Factory."

The Mondays, meanwhile, whom Pickering had first brought to Wilson's attention after seeing them play Salford Youth Club, had 'Wrote For Luck' remixed by Martin Hannett at the suggestion of Erasmus and manager Nathan McGough – Wilson would only find out second-hand during the filming of the accompanying video. Presumably because, at their second last encounter, Hannett had pointed a gun at his head (at one point Gretton had a restraining order placed on him). But the single only picked up substantial sales following its 'Think About The Future' remix by Paul Oakenfold and Steve Osbourne (after an attempt to resuscitate it by Vince Clarke of Erasure had failed). The same duo would helm production of Factory's last great album, *Pills 'n' Thrills 'n' Bellyaches*.

While the Haçienda had begun to establish itself as the hub of the new dance music paradigm, it also attracted a deal of negative publicity around its drugs culture. In July 1989 Claire Leighton collapsed on the dancefloor and became Britain's first ecstasy fatality after being rushed to hospital. Though she actually purchased the drugs in Stockport, the long queues routinely snaking round the Haçienda's entrance were known both as a peripatetic party locus prior to the evening's main event and a dispensary for 'E' users. "We had the usual crisis meeting," Wilson told *The Big Issue*. "There was a feeling of, 'Why us, why our dancefloor?' First of all there was revulsion and tragedy and sadness. That kind of death is pretty awful. None of us knew about Ecstasy deaths then, the idea that someone's body boils. And also we didn't understand the repercussions. Complete underestimation." That brought unwanted scrutiny from the police, exacerbated when rival gangs began to invest in state of the art automated weapons and moved in on the scene. A closure order was only averted after the hiring, at great expense, of George Carmen QC, and a three-month shutdown to calm the situation.

Factory's decadence, meanwhile, continued unabated. Having opened both a bar (The Dry Bar, FAC 201) and retail outlet (The Area, FAC 281) in Manchester, they moved offices to a new headquarters on Charles Street, close to the BBC's Oxford Road building, in September 1990. Although it was the Haçienda that would continue to be the principal drain on resources, the extravagance of the build quality and furnishings at Charles Street are the trappings with which most associate Wilson's naivete. With design again by Ben Kelly, the Arne Jacobson chairs and boardroom table ("the most brilliant table in history") hung by wires from the ceiling, at a cost of £30,000, have passed into Manchester folklore. So too Gretton's exasperated attempts to chase Wilson round said table to throttle him on learning of the price tag. And that's not even to mention the zinc roof, only visible, so Wilson claimed, by helicopter.

In April 1991, Factory's totemic production genius, Martin Hannett died. Having rejoined the label following the legal disputes, he was behind Happy Mondays' second album *Bummed*, but most testimony suggested he was now becoming so erratic artists, even those desperate to be touched by his 'genius', were finding him increasingly difficult to work with. He remained possibly most haunted of all the Factory personnel by Curtis's death, and had put on a huge amount of weight due to his heroin addiction – so much so that, it was said, he was too big for his designated coffin.

But Factory's problems really accelerated through 1992. In terms of sales, New Order and The Happy Mondays dwarfed the rest of their catalogue, and there were problems with both. After having taken time out with various solo projects (Electronic, Revenge and The Other Two), New Order put great store – and finance – by their comeback album; £400,000 was expended on *Republic*, recorded in Ibiza. The Happy Mondays, meanwhile, were living the high-life at Eddy Grant's studio in Barbados. Ostensibly recording a new album, *Yes Please*, they were in reality attempting to ingest their own body weights in drugs on a daily basis. Manager Nathan McGough had sold the idea to Wilson on the basis that the island was heroin free and that might get Ryder 'off the brown'. It may have been heroin free, but Barbados was also, it turned out, home to a vibrant crack cocaine culture. Cue high jinx on an island in the sun at Factory's expense, with numerous hire car write-offs, broken bones and general thievery. The zenith of the madness came when, according to legend, Ryder attempted to sell Grant's studio sofas to local dealers. The bills were soaring and even Wilson became alarmed.

London Records, under the auspices of Roger Ames, started circling the increasingly debt-laden label, but that deal fell through when it emerged that Joy Division/New Order's prestigious back catalogue was not in actuality owned by Factory, due to their early non-contract relationship. "It was always presumed by London Records that we had no contracts," Wilson would explain to Paulo Sedazzari of *G Spot* magazine in 1994. "But there *was* a contract drawn up in '79 to say there was *no* contract, which I signed in blood. It was just a page and a half and I'd forgotten it existed. It turned up in the tax investigation. We faxed it to the solicitor, he got very upset and said to us, 'Don't you realise – if you don't have a contract, you don't own the group's future, right?' 'Right.' 'But you do own the back catalogue which you paid for the production of. Unless... you have a piece of paper like this that specifically says you don't.' And we went, 'Oh, sorry'. But another major reason, that people don't realise, was the property collapse . Peter Saville now says he told me the collapse was coming but I can hardly remember it, it must have been late in the day." Indeed, as the recession gripped at the start of the 90s, as well as escalating costs at the Haçienda and confounded expectations of new product from their two major artists, Factory was attempting to grapple with a massive write-down of property assets. At one time with an estate valued in the region of £2.5m, they were now worth only a fraction of that amount, and that, more than anything else, was the hole Factory had dug.

Bankruptcy was declared in 1992. London – the indignity of that label's name not lost for one minute on Wilson – was able to pick up the cream of the artists they wanted without having to bail out the stricken label. At the time Factory's head of A&R Phil Saxe was desperately trying to sign two bands –

Pulp and Oasis. The Haçienda struggled on until 1997, but was seriously damaged by both drug scares and violence. Driving the story ever onward to high farce, a £10,000 metal detector installed to deter knife and gun carriers failed due to the metal floors underpinning the venue. By 2003 it had become a luxury apartment block, and a huge part of Manchester's musical history was entombed in its foundations.

Gretton quickly set up his own Rob's Records imprint in 1993, and enjoyed a Top 3 hit almost immediately with Sub Sub's 'Ain't No Love (Ain't No Use)'. He continued to work with New Order, persuading them to reform in 1998 after a five-year hiatus, but would die, aged 46, from a heart attack in May of the following year. Erasmus kept clear of the limelight. "Alan doesn't want the attention," suggests Vini Reilly, "he refuses to have anything to do with any public stuff, he's very private. That's the way he likes it. It's a bit frustrating for me, because he deserves a lot of praise for everything he did."

An attempt to revive the label – Factory Too aka Factory 2 – was made in 1994, in collaboration with London Records. The first release came from the Durutti Column. "I thought it would be a lovely way to start," stated Wilson, "Vini Reilly of Durutti Column has been loyal and stayed with me." Yes, Tony. But no-one else would have him, would they? But none of Wilson's new signings would scale the heights he was expectant of (though he helped caretake a reissue programme under the billing Factory Once). But finding the economic imperatives of London unsurprisingly divergent from his own, he severed ties and formed first the short-lived Factory Records LTD then, in 2006, F4 Records. The latter was put on hold when Wilson discovered he had cancer. Several friends gathered round to raise funds when, by dint of the NHS postal code lottery, it was revealed he was denied stocks of the Pfizer drug Sutent, which he believed was prolonging his life.

When Wilson died of a heart attack, at the age of 57, in August 2007, there was an outpouring of public emotion that revealed both the affection in which he was held and the enemies he had made. In an implausibly mean-spirited obituary, *The Telegraph* noted that he had a "monstrous ego", was surrounded by cronies, and variously described him as "arrogant", "smug", "preening" a "pretentious loudmouth" and possessed of "overweening vanity" and "total self-obsession". It also, naturally, prefigured mention of 'Manchester' with 'windswept' as all good metropolitan journalists must do. It's illustrative of the degree to which Wilson alienated some. But most Mancunians were happy to line up behind his unremitting advocacy of their city. While he was undergoing cancer treatment, there was vague talk about organising a benefit festival. The title "Tony Wilson's a cunt" was mooted. And would have been an appropriate and affectionate choice.

Some tried to intervene directly. "Thank you for your email dated 1st August 2007 regarding our medicine SUTENT® (sunitinib) and funding for you friend Tony Wilson," came the reply from Pfizer's Hannah Roberts. "I am sorry to hear that Mr Wilson's local primary care trust (PCT) has denied him funding for Sutent therapy. Pfizer takes very seriously its shared ethical responsibility with the NHS to make its medicines available to patients who need them. Unfortunately Pfizer is unable to sponsor Mr Wilson's continued treatment by offering compassionate supplies of Sutent... As you will appreciate, decisions by the NHS to deny patients funding to treatment places us in an ethically very difficult position, and as a company we are fighting for a better system of evaluation for new cancer drugs within the NHS. I hope this letter explains the steps Pfizer UK has already taken to play our part in making this treatment available. On a personal note, I would like to offer my sympathy for Mr Wilson's current situation."

On an ever more personal note, Tony Wilson died 10 August 2007.

As Steve Shy remembers, speaking before his death, slating Wilson was a favoured Mancunian pastime – though woe betide anyone from outside the city who tried it. "Tony, as everyone will tell you – everyone loves him to death, but no-one will tell him to his face. Everyone tells him how much they hate him. He's done so much for Manchester, but you must never, ever let him know. I can remember once, they were filming for *So It Goes*, either a Clash or Magazine show, and he said, 'Do you want a drink?' 'Yeah.' There were about three of us. He went to the bar and went straight to the front. The woman said, 'I don't give a shit who you are, you get to the back of the queue'. So he went to the back of the queue. By the time he got to the front, I think he was buying a round for about 30 people. Nobody says thank you to Tony, everyone just takes." Or, as Rick Goldstraw remembers; "When Tony was working at Granada, all us junkies would wait outside. And he'd let us into the green room so we could have something to eat and drink, before we got chased away." Fittingly, Tony Wilson's coffin was emblazoned with its own catalogue number – FAC 501.

"Tony would say ridiculously inflated things," remembers Carroll, "but he never stuck me as an egotist; a lot of the time he appeared to be parodying himself. He took criticism very seriously and he was surprisingly vulnerable. Tony had a lot of stuff to sell and had a keen sense of responsibility towards the label and the town of Manchester; it was like the family he had to support. He was a showman and appeared successful, so having set himself up as the font from whence much of value and importance flowed, he had to say 'no' a lot, That's difficult and we don't like hearing it. People would be persistent; it had to be quite wearing."

"Just how lucky I am that I knew him," adds Vini Reilly. "He was quite something. He taught me an awful lot; he was a very educated guy. I had a lot of guidance from people – I didn't have a good education, I was expelled. So a lot of my education, if I've got any, came from other people. Tony was one of those people. He was very good at communicating information and ideas and concepts and stimulating your imagination. He was just a very, very close friend. I used to baby-sit his little son, and change his nappy. It was very family-orientated. We talked about anything, there were no no-go areas. You always got the truth and a bit of wisdom and a bit of philosophy thrown in with Tony. It was just an unspoken friendship. We got on from the moment we saw each other. Tony and Bruce [Mitchell; Durutti Column percussionist] have always been my mentors. My own father died when I was 16, at exactly the time when you need a dad to look up to, I didn't have one. So Tony and Bruce have both given me focus and got me away from... unhealthy people? Just great friends."

Some commentators, like writer Mick Middles, have stated that they are not "particularly comfortable with the Tony Wilson industry that has sprung forth... because they are transforming him into some kind of saint which, with respect, is something he most definitely wasn't." Others, like Tosh Ryan, speaking to me prior to Wilson's death, though his comments are still applicable, are suspicious of the way the label's whole iconography has been constructed. "It's that whole thing about rehashing a past that really wasn't that valuable. I find that quite odd. I'm going out at the moment with a woman who used to be involved in Factory Records, and she's involved in writing a book about Ian Curtis – how many more FUCKING BOOKS DO WE NEED ABOUT IAN CURTIS! I just find it's really sad that a lot of people are living in the past when there are some really interesting things going on and some interesting things to do. There's a planet to save! Instead, we're concerned about rehashing idiotic music from the 70s and 80s."

But Wilson's legacy endures. He may have blanched at the indulgent nature of 2008's Tony Wilson Experience – a 24-hour talk-a-thon on the subject of his, and Factory's, legacy. More likely he would have warmed to the preposterous ambition of the enterprise, just as he eventually came round to his non-spiteful but acute portrayal by Steve Coogan in *24 Hour Party People* (his ruminations on the 'additional commentary' DVD are as amusing as the main feature). Speaking to the BBC in 2001 he said, "In a sense Factory's two great bands were Joy Division/New Order and the Mondays. Although I think a lot of people actually, unlike me, like Factory for the really weird, really interesting bands, I'm an elitist. I'm proud of the fact that two of the greatest bands in history... they both changed music. Joy Division/New Order changed music twice, and the Mondays changed music to create acid house. They're my kind of bands. It would have been wonderful to have Oasis or in the previous generation The Smiths. Except they weren't bands that changed music; they were brilliant, but they didn't change things . . ."

Eric's, Liverpool's first punk era label, grew out of Roger Eagle's eponymous club in Matthew Street, formerly home of The Cavern. Opened in October 1976, it became a haven for the city's punk community; most of whom, seemingly, were members of the Big In Japan clique that appeared on Eric's first release. Absorbed as much by fashion and style as music, the roots of Liverpool's most mythical band stretch back to connections made at local hairdressers A Cut Above The Rest. Jayne Casey, shortly to become Liverpool punk's 'It Girl', caused a stir when she decided to shave off all her hair – which added to the salon's mystique and magnetised it for similarly wayward youngsters. She was soon joined by both Pete Burns – sacked within weeks for being abrupt and rude to customers, then re-hired – as well as his future wife Lynne Cortlett and eventually Holly Johnson.

Casey would subsequently set up a market stall, Aunt Twacky's, also in Matthew Street, taking on Paul Rutherford as her assistant. It was while serving there that she came into the orbit of Eagle, a revered Northern Soul DJ at Manchester's Twisted Wheel and promoter at The Liverpool Stadium, a pre-war indoor boxing ring that hosted some of the north-west's most notable 70s rock gigs. Eric's was started in partnership with Liverpool University graduate Pete Fulwell and Deaf School road manager Ken Testi. Eagle considered Casey and her bizarre coterie of associates natural allies. They were invited, *en masse*, to the opening round of gigs in October 1976 and quickly made the club their own. Eric's downtown New York vibe is remembered as akin to CBGB's in terms of the affected cool of its clientele and the squalor of its toilets. There was also a slight whiff of Paris Left Bank radicalism in the air; partially due to the art school clientele but also augmented by the leftover leftist detritus of its previous incarnation as The Revolution, which ran to *papier-mâché* busts of Castro and Guevara.

It was, also, notoriously snobby. The Accelerators were one of the local bands who never got to play there. "Roger came across as a hard-nosed business type who refused to help us out," remembers Accelerators guitarist, Kathy Freeman. "Yet I remember once he invited me to his flat – no ulterior motive – and played me all his favourite fifties obscurities and gave me a cassette, I think it was called Basement at Eric's or something. It included some wild instrumentals." Many others attest to Eagle's paternalistic Music 101 lectures. "Roger was always teaching you," Casey would tell Paul Du Noyer in *Liverpool. Wondrous Place*, "but in a way that was not oppressive to a young person." The imposing scale of his record collection and zealotry in distributing compilation tapes drawn from its contents remain key to the subsequent development of popular music in the north west. "Towering and glowering," Bill Drummond would record in his book, *45*, "the third-greatest visionary in rock 'n' roll. Anyone from my generation out of Liverpool who ever made a record is eternally in his debt – or can blame him for the mess we have made of our lives."

Formed in May 1977, Big In Japan started life as a trio of Bill Drummond, Phil Allen and Kevin Ward, playing their first show two days after seeing The Clash gig at Eric's. Drummond, born in South Africa to a Church Of Scotland preacher but a native of Galloway since childhood, had arrived in Liverpool to take a job designing for the Everyman Theatre, He'd fallen under Eagle's spell after attending one of his final Liverpool Stadium promotions, Dr Feelgood. Soon he was helping out as a handyman at Eric's. "Yeah, that's what I did," Drummond confirms. "If a wall needed putting up, I'd put up a wall. If the bar needed moving, I'd move the bar. I'd do the get-ins for bands as well, and stage security." A secondary catalyst came after Ken Campbell staged his 24-hour 'happening', *Illuminati*, at The Liverpool School Of Music, Dream, Art And Pun, based in an arts complex in Matthew Street. "That was the Armadillo Tea Rooms," Drummond explains. "It used to be O'Hanagan's tea rooms. That was the hang out. All the rival gangs in terms of what was going on musically or creatively in Liverpool had their own tables in the tea rooms. It was like a triangle between Eric's and Probe [Records] and The Armadillo." Campbell had persuaded Jayne Casey to join the *Illuminati* cast while Drummond busied himself on the set. She insisted Holly Johnson should be enrolled in the fledgling group before she'd continue. The expansion eventually led to Ian Broudie, drummer Peter 'Budgie' Clark and Dave Balfe swelling the ranks. Initially they had a three-song repertoire, one of which featured Casey reading out that week's Top 20.

Eric's the club begat Eric's the label, essentially A&R'd by Eagle. Its first release was, naturally enough, Big In Japan's debut single, a split a-side with the Chuddy Nuddies (The Yachts under a pseudonym). Eagle christened it 'Brutality, Religion And A Dance Beat'. When Drummond dared to ask why, he was regaled with a list of artists who had embodied those traditions and appraised of the fact that incorporation of same was 'rock 'n' roll rule number one'. Eric's would also house the first releases by Casey's subsequent band, Pink Military, two pre-Frankie Goes To Hollywood Holly Johnson singles and the debut by The Frantic Elevators. The latter's singer, Mick Hucknall, was another taken under Eagle's wing.

Fulwell, meanwhile, released the debut single by Pete Wylie's Wah! Heat when Eagle rejected it on a second Eric's related imprint, Inevitable Records, in the early 80s. Inevitable would also unveil Wylie's one-time partner in Eric's one-night-standers The Mystery Girls, Pete Burns, under the name Nightmares In Wax, as well as the first single by his more famous subsequent band, Dead Or Alive. The label's fourth release, Wah! Heat's 'Seven Minutes To Midnight', garnered reams of press, including an *NME* front cover story by Paul Du Noyer. Other releases would include the first vinyl by Modern Eon, It's Immaterial and China Crisis. Fulwell would go on to manage a clutch of Liverpool pop bands, including Wah!, It's Immaterial and Black.

It was Big In Japan alumni Balfe and Drummond who would be responsible for Liverpool's most distinctive punk era label, however. "Were we downhearted when Big In Japan didn't go further?" ponders Drummond. "Not at all, really. We had meetings with a couple of record companies, and they weren't interested in us. And it didn't take much hindsight to realise *why* they wouldn't be interested in us. Although at the time we were a little disappointed." Zoo Records initially had no fixed abode. "The office was basically the phone box down the end of the road – I lived off Penny Lane, and there was a phone box at the end of Penny Lane. Ian McCulloch, Gary Dwyer and Pete Wylie had a flat about 100 yards from me, above a chippy on Penny Lane. I used to go down there, sit at the kitchen table and go through things. We didn't really think of it as an office. It was just wherever we were."

Zoo was chosen as the title of this new enterprise after Balfe decided to throw his hand in with him – meaning original moniker Bill's Records was jettisoned. The inspiration was twofold; punk provided the impetus, but Drummond's favoured listening at the time was black American music. "For most of the first half of the 70s, what I was into was black American music. We didn't call it R&B at that point – R&B meant 50s music. The music that was coming out of small labels all over the States, especially the southern states, that's what I was into and that's what I collected. I loved the visual look of the labels. I loved TK out of Miami; they had crossover hits with Betty Wright and KC & The Sunshine Band. Before I was in Liverpool I spent two years at art school in Northampton, and there was a specialist shop there for DJs. Hardly any of this music existed on albums, it was all imported 7-inch singles. So when I started Zoo, that was as much of an inspiration as the punk thing, to have a label like that, though I knew nothing about these artists, I would just go into import shops and buy them on impulse, based on the names or how the labels looked. The punk thing, we didn't even call it that in 1977 – that was something the newspapers called it. But that 'just go out there and do it' thing, yes."

The first release was a posthumous EP of Big In Japan recordings, which materialised in November 1978. Subsequently Zoo housed the earliest recordings by a new breed of Merseyside post-punk pop bands that were finally able to spring the city from its 60s nostalgia trap. The most notable were the obtusely named Echo & The Bunnymen and The Teardrop Explodes – comprising two-thirds of Liverpool's legendary Crucial Three, who never went further than rehearsals, but featured the baby steps of Messrs Cope, McCulloch and Wylie.

Drummond had fallen in love with the Bunnymen after watching their first show, supporting The Teardrop Explodes in November 1978. After releasing the mature, uber-cool psych-pop 45 'Pictures On My Wall' for Zoo, they would be ghosted away to Warners subsidiary Korova via Rob Dickins. Drummond remained their manager, charting a course of wilful perversity typically culminating in the grand gesture performance – be it in the Royal Albert Hall, the Isle Of Skye or the home-spun 'Crystal Days' day-long activity break. The Bunnymen at their peak, as Drummond once recalled in a sleevenote, were "a glory beyond all glories". The Teardrop Explodes, who also made their debut on Zoo and recorded two further singles, were, for a short time, almost the Bunnymen's equal. Both Balfe and Drummond served as managers, and in Balfe's case, keyboard player.

Cope and McCulloch started out first as band and then label mates, but would take turns in knocking spots off each other in the press; each unflinchingly begrudging of the other's success as they battled for the status of Merseyside's authentic post-punk icon. McCulloch would take particular delight in attacking Cope's 'woolyback' credentials as a middle-class former teacher training student from Tamworth. Cope gave as good as he got and is still doing so (notably in his *Head On* autobiography). At their height, it added a delicious frisson to Liverpool's music scene. And yet, "on the whole, they got on with each other," Drummond states. "It was only once success started happening that it became more obvious. That was more the rivalry between Ian McCulloch and Julian Cope [than the bands]. And what had gone down politically when they were in The Crucial Three. There was more rivalry at that time between Pete Wylie and the Bunnymen/Teardrops. The Bunnymen and Teardrops would gang up together against Wylie, and vice versa, because Wylie was the most charismatic and vociferous. And still is."

The Teardrops recorded first. "The Teardrops were further down the line," says Drummond, "they were more musically accomplished. The Bunnymen were more an idea at that point". Cope has publicly credited Drummond with his transformation from 'farm punk' to pop star. "I was goaded into becoming a rock star by Bill Drummond," he would tell *The Guardian* in 2008, "and the pseudo-intellectual side of me thought it would be quite charming." By the turn of the decade, spearheaded by the Teardrops, Bunnymen and Wylie's various Wah! incarnations, Liverpool was the foremost principality of pop for the first time since the Beatles' heyday. And none of them were giving an inch in acknowledgement of their peers. "There were only about five good things in the 80s," McCulloch would tell this writer in the 90s. "Us, New Order, R.E.M. I can't think of the other two."

Zoo's distribution was rudimentary. "Dave Balfe and I would drive down to London in his dad's car," Drummond recalls, "pick up boxes of records from the pressing plant we used down there, sleeve them in the back of the car, then cart them round the independent shops and small distributors. Geoff Travis at Rough Trade was a phenomenal inspiration. We went in, and we weren't thinking what we were doing with the Teardrops and Echo and the Bunnymen was the future of *anything*. It was just us doing stuff as best we could, with our mates, or our rivals, but Geoff was a real inspiration. As were the other people who worked at Rough Trade at the time, like Richard Scott and Mayo Thompson. You couldn't leave their set-up without feeling – it's worthwhile, whatever we're doing."

Later, in 1979, Zoo moved to Chicago Buildings, close to Brian Epstein's NEMS. "The walls were turquoise," reminisces Drummond. "We had a carpet, a dark, dusty green, must have had the ash of a million cigarettes ground into it, not that either me nor Balfe smoked. We had my carpentry work bench, with cupboards underneath it where we kept stock. We had one chair, a desk, and a telephone. We didn't even have a filing cabinet. And we had an old sofa someone had given us. Nothing on the walls. We didn't have a record player or cassette player. All we had was an answaphone, which used cassettes in those days. If a band brought a cassette back from the studio, we would listen to it through the answaphone speakers. Nothing more than that. If it passed that, it was good." In the city of a thousand jealousies, Zoo actually kept a low profile. "We didn't get many demos sent, because nobody knew where to send them. Some bands in Liverpool would try to attract our attention, but generally their attitude was more, 'fuck them, we can do that ourselves.' There was so much rivalry in Liverpool, they wouldn't want to come to us, they'd want to do it themselves."

The label also showcased the emergence of Drummond and Balfe as artists in their own right. The plan was to record something with the charm of 60s girl group offerings by such as the Shangri-Las pinned to a disco backbeat. Art student Lori Lartey was recruited as vocalist because she "looked weird and pretty and vulnerable with big sad eyes" after they saw her in the street. 'Touch', credited to Lori And The Chameleons, was cut with the assistance of former Deaf School drummer Tim Whittaker and Gary Dwyer of the Teardrop Explodes. Issued in July 1979, it immediately picked up strong reviews ("genius" frothed Dave McCullough in *Sounds*, "an impossibly sexy record" eulogised *NME*'s Paul Rambali) and was subsequently licensed by Sire. But despite daily exposure on the Dave Lee Travis show, 'Touch' would stall at number 70 in the charts. Follow-up effort 'The Lonely Spy', which used a KGB narrative in place of its forerunner's oriental theme, bankrolled by Sire, failed to do the expected business. The £4,000 advance they'd received for it was useful, however, and was pumped into The Teardrop Explodes to help them record their debut album. "Nobody was interested in signing them," Drummond recalls, "so we thought we'd see if we could record an album ourselves, and then we got a deal with PolyGram for it."

Eventually, however, Drummond's loyalty to his two major bands was tested. "That did happen, in that I stopped managing the Teardrops, or rather sold the management of the Teardrops, a long time before I stopped managing the Bunnymen. I did see the bands in different ways. I always saw The Teardrops as Julian Cope – it wasn't to begin with, but it became that way. The Bunnymen were very much *a band*. The sum was greater than the parts, and that was not the case with the Teardrop Explodes. It was easier to have loyalty to the Bunnymen, because it wasn't a loyalty to any one individual.

With the Teardrops, as soon as [keyboard player] Paul Simpson left, right near the beginning, it was very much Julian's thing."

Zoo managed to earn itself a place on the fabled Factory catalogue (FAC 15; 'Factory Meets Zoo Half-Way') when Drummond and Tony Wilson combined to organise a festival in a disused coal-field near Leigh on the August bank holiday of 1979. The line-up featured the stars of both camps; Joy Division, A Certain Ratio and The Distractions from Factory, the Bunnymen, Teardrops and Drummond's Lori & The Chameleons from Zoo. The idea was mooted by Wilson, whose label shared a friendly local rivalry with Zoo, reflecting a municipal pride rooted in musical as well as civic allegiances. But his enthusiasm for the project was spectacularly misplaced; it took months to organise, and the local promoter, Joan Miller, was bankrupted. "The difference between the Manchester groups and the ones from Liverpool," Wilson shit-stirred to the press, "is that in Manchester the groups steal their equipment and in Liverpool their parents buy it for them." Intriguing to note that, nearly 25 years prior to subsequent London mayor (horror of all horrors had Wilson lived to see it) denouncing Merseyside for its 'victim culture', the bragging rights Wilson half-mockingly evoked were crime statistics. Yet it's equally true that the fact that *Unknown Pleasures* emerged on a home-grown independent and *Crocodiles* on a London-based major reflected something about the group's cities of origin.

But then Drummond argues it was largely practicalities. "We folded because of finances. Tony Wilson told me, 'Bill, don't do that', when I was about to sign the Bunnymen to a record label in London. I had this conversation. 'Look, you've got a well-paid job at Granada TV, you can do this financially.' We couldn't. We didn't have the finances he had, or the confidence and media savvy. He was already a major figure in the media in the north-west. We were still on the dole. To get off the dole, we had to sign to a major record company." Or, as he would deliberate in his book, *45*. "Up until then none of the rash of indie record labels that had sprung up around the UK in the wake of the punk DIY ethic had produced anything but seven-inch singles. As far as I was concerned, this was part and parcel of some vague ideology. I assumed that most other people out there running small independent labels must think the same way. That they too were going for the eternal glory of pop and the seven-inch single. The Alan Hornes, the Bob Lasts. So when Tony Wilson implied I was selling out and buckling to the power and money of London, I didn't get what he meant. As far as I was concerned he was the one compromising, by giving in to the indulgent muso tendencies of Joy Division and letting them record an album for Factory." Zoo had lasted for nine singles, plus a Scott Walker reissue and the elegantly packaged *From The Shores Of Lake Placid* compilation album.

Drummond took a post with Warners that was inevitably never going to fulfil him. "I don't know if it was inevitable, perhaps it was with hindsight," he says. "The reason why I took a job with Warners, or WEA as it was then, was because I was financially fucked. I'd borrowed £12,000 to set up a PA company with the guy who used to do the sound for the Teardrops and Bunnymen, and that all went wrong. So I owed the bank £12,000, and I needed to get myself out of that situation, so I took a consultancy job. They gave me an office, all my phones free, all that kind of stuff. But once I was in that situation, I was completely seduced by it. I became *the record company arsehole*. It just didn't work. I couldn't function, basically, creatively, in that situation. I couldn't do anything that was worthwhile." There was chart success for one of his signings, Strawberry Switchblade, but Drummond learned that "having a couple of hit records doesn't mean success on a major. In record company terms, you've got to have two very successful albums to pay for everything." His enthusiastic backing and patronage of Brilliant, in particular, would have been ruinous for a smaller company. In July 1986, on the advent of his 33 and a third birthday, he resigned from the corporate music industry, issuing a grandiloquent press release to that effect. "Well, I had a three-year contract, and I don't think they'd have renewed the contract with me anyway. But I'd made a decision before my time was up that I'd resign and handed in my resignation."

He had already cut himself adrift from managing the Bunnymen a couple of years previously, and subsequently recorded a solo album in Galloway, backed by The Triffids. *The Man* included 'Ballad Of A Sex God', his tribute to recently deceased Bunnymen drummer Pete De Freitas, as well as the infamous 'Julian Cope Is Dead'. The latter, a fantasy about assassinating his former charge to avoid him soiling his legacy, had been inspired by the Cope track 'Bill Drummond Said', and, doubtless, Cope's complaints to the press about Drummond's lack of fiscal transparency. Dave Balfe also moved on to work with the majors, folding his Food imprint – originally an independent distributed by Rough Trade – into the Parlophone empire. He would retire to the 'Country House' made famous in Blur's number one single on the proceeds, return with Sony in the late 90s, before completing a scriptwriting course.

By 1987 Drummond had formed Justified Ancients Of Mu Mu with Jimmy Cauty of Brilliant, enjoying a number one record with 'Doctorin' The Tardis' (under the guise of The Timelords). The duo subsequently formed The KLF, who turned into an unlikely hit machine, the proceeds of their considerable chart success facilitating such stunts as the depositing of a dead sheep at the door of an after-show party following the 1992 Brit Awards. And, most famously, the ritual combustion of £1 million sterling on the Isle Of Jura in 1992. The fact that their accountant couldn't write off the loss as an 'artistic statement' would facilitate a tax bill of £330,000 as a kicker. Otherwise the exercise was undoubtedly a high watermark in the art over commerce debate.

## Chapter Nine

## The Sound Of Young Scotland, Northern Ireland and Wales

## Fast, Postcard, Good Vibrations and Z Block

In 1977 Lenny Love, encouraged by his friend Bruce Findlay (of Bruce's Records), founded Sensible Records in Edinburgh, with the specific intention of releasing the first record by The Rezillos, the estimable but offbeat group formed around Edinburgh's art school campus. Love, moonlighting for Island while working in an *ad hoc* capacity as the band's manager, named the imprint in honour of Captain Sensible of the Damned. 'I Can't Stand My Baby' was released in July 1977, making it Scotland's first punk record, followed in short order by Dundee's The Drive (who released 'Jerkin' for NRG in August) and fellow Edinburgh natives The Valves ('For Adolfs Only'; Zoom, September).

Findlay, as well as being the enabling link behind The Rezillos' debut single, was also Zoom's founder. He had started his record shop in Falkirk in 1967, building it up to a chain of 13 stores before selling the equity to Guinness Holdings. He'd long thought of starting a label after time serving as an A&R advisor for, again, Island Records, of whom he was a large customer. However, a series of rejections of his recommendations, some of whom would achieve significant success, hardened his resolve. "The next thing is, the Humblebums, come up, with Gerry Rafferty, Billy Connolly," Findlay recalls. "The Vikings move to London and Alan Gorrie formed Average White Band, things like that happened. They'd say, 'Quite a lot of the artists you've mentioned do go on to success, Bruce, have you ever thought of starting your own record label?' 'Aw come on, it takes millions to start a record label. I can't afford to do that.' They said, 'We'll help fund you. We've helped Virgin, Chrysalis, Charisma.' And it's true, they'd distributed a lot of labels and helped them. So I went out and looked for a band, with a view to signing them to my new record label that Island were going to fund, a band called Cafe Jacques. I fell in love with them, flirted with them and wooed them for a month or two, then got in touch with Island." Of course, Island, almost inevitably, passed. Findlay was incensed. "You NEVER like the bands I've mentioned! I'm not going to be an A&R scout for you [any more]."

In the end, the group moved to Epic. "It took ages to make a record. During which time, punk happened. Chiswick happened, Stiff happened. Records could be made, singles, for a few hundred pounds. The industry was so slow, a bit like they were when Napster and downloads happened – it was the same thing then, they were caught on the hop, the majors. And that inspired me. That's why I started Zoom. I was buying the records, driving down to London. I met with Jake Riviera, bought the Damned single – great. Lenny Love and I were pals, and Lenny was talking about starting a record label. He said, 'I'm thinking of signing The Rezillos.' I said, 'Great, Lenny, The Rezillos are fantastic.' 'But,' he said, 'I don't have the money. I want to sign them and make the record.' I said, 'for fuck's sake Lenny, I'll guarantee to buy 500 copies of the single even before you've cut it – cos they're so hot, they're cold! That way you'll have the money.' I called a meeting at my house – which Lenny didn't turn up at to begin with! The Rezillos said, 'Who's going to pay for this, if we make a record with Lenny?' I said, 'Well, Lenny will pay for it, but if he doesn't have the money, I'll put the money up.' They said, 'What's in it for you?' I said, 'I'll sell your record! I'll make profits. I know you're going to sell records.' So I helped Lenny get that off the ground, and at the same time went for my own signings and found a band called Sale – which was a dreadful name. They changed it to The Valves. I signed them and produced it myself, effectively, with an engineer. I'm not a musician, but I just sat there encouraging them. Go for it, guys! And it was brilliant. We sold thousands and thousands of the first single."

Findlay was also partially behind one further landmark Scottish independent single. "The week after I released The Valves, The Skids came in to see me – Ricky Jobson and Stuart Adamson, in my shop in Edinburgh. They had a brilliant demo of 'Charles'. It was fucking great. 'What about you doing it with Zoom?' I said, 'I've just released my first single, give me a chance!' I wanted to get up and running. But my philosophy is every single town in the country should have a record label. 'You're from Dunfermline – I know the guy in the local record shop Sandy Muir. Why don't you go in and see if he'll make it with you?' 'Do you think that's an idea?' 'It's a GREAT idea – do it! Get him to phone me if he has any doubts.' Funnily enough, he did. Sandy phoned and asked why I wouldn't do it. I said, because I've just done it, I'm new to the game, I don't know what I'm doing yet. I'm not ready to do my second record!'"

Muir liked The Skids well enough, but didn't have a clue as to how to make a record. "I said, it's easy, the record is made, they've done it – they don't need to go into fancy studios. I gave him some contacts. I said, if you have any doubts about this, Sandy, I'll order 500 in advance, I'll give you a written order. I'll pay you when I get the records, but I guarantee it. 'Why would you do that? What's in it for you?' I said, 'Sandy, I'll make tuppence profit off every record, or whatever it was in those days, when records sold for about 50p or 60p, I'll make my profit. Also, I want to be part of this. I want my

shops to be part of it. Sandy, that's why I've never owned a record shop in
Dunfermline, cos you're there, and you've got a good record shop. I'm not
that kind of capitalist, like Richard Branson.' So he did, and started a record
label called No Bad Records. And The Skids came out with that single and
then signed to Virgin!"

Neither No Bad nor Sensible went any further, however. Sire jumped in to
sign The Rezillos and that was, effectively, job done for Love (the label's only
other release was Neon's 'Bottles'). Rezillos singer Eugene Reynolds did try
desperately hard to convince Love to sign The Cramps after he'd seen them
playing in New York, but without success. For Reynolds, 'moving on' meant
moving from an independent to a major – almost more so, given their
geographical location and the lack of resources any of the Scottish
independents could muster. "Everybody at that time was putting out their
independent single," he recalls, "and we certainly wanted to do that. And our
second single, which came out on Sire, '(My Baby Does) Good Sculptures',
was meant to be a Sensible release anyway. That got taken over by Sire
Records after we'd recorded it. Even while we were in the studio, it changed
from being a Sensible record to being a Sire release. So we did go very quickly
from an independent to a major. I think as much as everyone was singing
the praises of independents, nearly every band went over to a major – it's
just the way it was."

Zoom stuck around for slightly longer, following The Valves with PVC2's 'Put
You In The Picture', in reality a halfway house for the former members of
chart act Slik, featuring Midge Ure. "Having made my own record, you had to
discover proper distribution," says Findlay. "I phoned a couple of people that
did distribution, but effectively I did my own. I jumped in my car, drove to
London, went to Rough Trade Records, who didn't have a record label at the
time. I talked to Geoff Travis and played the record to him. 'Great, I'll take 100
copies', or something. 'I'm thinking of starting a record label too.' You should,
I told him. Everywhere I went, places like King's Lynn, Manchester, Liverpool,
Birmingham, Newcastle – I found independent shops everywhere. They took
my records. When I went round a second time, people were starting their
own labels. They'd say, 'I've got a record as well.' Everyone had that attitude.
All the indies had little picture sleeves, and they were brilliant. There was an
attitude to do them that the majors just couldn't manage, that they were
slow to latch on to. There was a movement, albeit a loose movement. There
was no formal association of independent music shops or anything – fuck
that – there was a loose friendship between the shops up and down the
country. And we all knew we were part of a revolution."

## Independence Days

When PVC2 faltered and re-emerged as The Zones, minus Ure, Findlay hooked his label up to a marketing deal with Arista to access finances. Releases from Mike Heron, The Questions and Simple Minds followed, but from 1978 onwards he would concentrate on managing the latter band and would close Zoom in 1980. Simple Minds' evolution lay in the 'Stiff/Chiswick challenge' auditions hosted at Edinburgh's Clouds venue. Johnny And The Self-Abusers (featuring a young Jim Kerr) and The Subs (with future Simple Minds member Derek Forbes) would end up with deals with Chiswick and Stiff respectively (on the latter's presciently titled One-Off subsidiary). In the fall-out from the Self-Abusers' split, one half of the band, led by John Milarky, became the Cuban Heels, recording for their own Housewife's Choice imprint. The other, Simple Minds, led by Kerr, were signed to Findlay's Zoom-Arista tie-up in December 1978. "I finally took on Simple Minds' management and gave up Zoom Records a few years later, so it closed again," says Findlay. "I had to become business-like. The record label was going to become a struggle for me. Simple Minds were signed to Zoom under a separate licence through Arista. Arista were crap, and we couldn't wait to get off." Arista's 'crapness' manifested itself in wholesale panic at the lack of success Simple Minds' first two albums achieved, and an attempt to convince them to become a 2-Tone band.

With The Skids signing to Virgin, The Rezillos to Sire and Wishaw's The Jolt moving to Polydor, the cream of Scotland's initial punk crop had been co-opted by major labels in a manner that reflected the nation-wide picture. All three would have cause to regret those decisions. "We should have stopped making records, or at least should never have signed to a major label," Skids' singer Richard Jobson later recalled to Brain Hogg. "We had a ridiculous contract – eight albums cross-collateralised with a publishing deal and a £5,000 advance." The Rezillos soon run aground with Sire, Fay Fife famously pushing cake into the face of Seymour Stein's wife at a record label reception. The Jolt ended up deeply resenting Polydor's attempts to remould them as a "Tartan Jam", despite the huge £90,000 advance they were offered. "It was only when we signed to Polydor, and in particular with The Jam's producer Chris Parry, that we were talked into the whole Mod thing," maintains the band's Iain Shedden. "Considering the label already had a three-piece Mod outfit on the books, it was an incredibly dumb move. But we were young and, of course, in the music business, you learn by your mistakes."

"It's easy in retrospect to look at the punk era and say it was all about ideals and independence and revolution and breaking down barriers," Shedden continues. "For some it was about all of those things. For others it was a fashion, but for many of the aspiring musicians opportunity and escape were just as important as belonging to any so-called punk movement. After supporting the likes of The Jam, XTC and The Saints in Glasgow every major label and a similar number of independents were after our signatures. There was a growing belief back then that bands who came from outside of London no longer had to move there in order to have a career. This was deemed another breakthrough in the do-it-yourself atmosphere of the era. Where the idealism started to blur, however, was in the melding of business to art. Any art form is open to commercial exploitation and I'm not using the word in a derogatory sense. Punk had many bands pressing up 500 singles and sending them off to *NME* and *Sounds*. A review could add significant numbers to your next gig. This was another good example of punk being able to survive without the help, initially at least, of fat-arsed record company executives. Such idealism was only suited to the short-term, however. You could still be independent, it's true, but if you were any good as a band you still had to get your work out there. Stuck in the heart of Lanarkshire's bleak industrial landscape (our first Polydor press release used that term) it wasn't so attractive to continue doing it all by ourselves, for ourselves, or to stay in that part of the world. Like Scottish footballers, boxers and soldiers before us, part of the attraction of suddenly being accepted was the prospect of getting the hell out of there. Not because Scotland isn't beautiful, because it is, or because we didn't love our families and friends, which we did, but because we had sniffed adventure on the end of Polydor's oily rag and we wanted more of it. Bruce Findlay had vision and he talked a very good case for the independent route and for staying in Scotland while travelling it. We decided against it. That may have been a mistake on our part, but we'll never know for sure."

There were other notable Scottish one-shot independents. Edward Bell's New Pleasures housed Another Pretty Face's 'All The Boys Love Carrie' single (featuring a young Mike Scott) before Virgin came in for the band, whose demos had been financed by Findlay. And while the Associates founded their own label, Double Hip, they were similarly indebted to Bruce's Records for making the next step possible. "I was working in Bruce's Records when Billy Mackenzie and Alan Rankine came in with their 'Boys Keep Swinging' 7-inch," recalls Sandy McLean. "We bought twenty-five, but they asked if we could keep the other 300 copies in the shop and come back and get them. No problem. About two weeks later the phone rang, and it was this American guy called Hal Shaper, from Sparta Florida Music. 'I understand there's a Scottish band who does one of our songs – we publish David Bowie.' I said, 'Yessss.' 'Do you know them?' 'I know *of* them.' 'Look, they haven't done anything wrong, I really love the record, I'd like to contact them.' So I got Alan and Billy to ring the guy up. They went to London and recorded demos and the rest is history."

But the first independent Scottish record label of real stature – one in which McLean would also play a role – was Fast Product, run by Bob Last, an Englishman who had dropped out of university in Edinburgh. Fast would become synonymous with three groundbreaking post-punk acts – The Mekons, Gang Of Four and Human League – as well as a sophisticated, and often playful, grasp of graphic design and presentation.

Last met Jo Callis of The Rezillos while working as tour manager for Edinburgh's Traverse Theatre. Soon he and colleague Tim Pearce had jumped ship to assist the band, eventually becoming their manager. "I dropped out of an architecture course at university, and was working at the Traverse," recalls Last, "and designed a few shows there. I got to know Jo, and got involved building the Dalek for their stage show. I was kind of roadying for them. We were going round the country and it was a very small scene, and you very rapidly got to encounter all sorts of people. That led to a lot of things."

Fast's identity was immediately and defiantly intellectual, implicitly challenging theories of consumption. In fact, it wasn't a label *per se* – merely an outlet for whatever ideas Last hatched. "It was actually started in 1976, as a 'brand'," he states, "which I suppose was an act of provocation at that time. I hadn't decided what I was going to do with it though. I was a fan of movies and interested in the visual side of things, but I was looking for the right thing. I was looking for some kind of communication. My partner at the time, Hillary [Morrison], bought me a copy of 'Spiral Scratch', and that was absolutely what crystallised it. OK, this is what we are going to do. It was very specifically that. You were already hearing The Clash and so on, but it was very much 'Spiral Scratch'."

The Mekons, though not native to Leeds, were domiciled there on arts courses. "We opened for The Rezillos at the Ace Of Clubs on Woodhouse Street in October 1977," Jon Langford recalls, "just a few days after my 20th birthday. We had no intention of making a record. Bob saw us play and asked us to make a single – I don't think he had a label at the time. I don't think we knew much about his background, but it was pretty obvious that we were all a bunch of wanky art students." 'Never Been In A Riot' was the result. "Tim [Pearce] found a cottage in the Borders," says Last. "I can't even remember who owned it. He borrowed some microphones and a Revox and it was recorded in the living room. It wasn't a studio at all."

'Never Been In A Riot' sounded so dramatically amateurish that when Hillary Morrison took a consignment down to Rough Trade Records, Geoff Travis turned them away. "That's true," says Last. "He refused to stock it, because it was so badly put together!" The a-side's commentary on the punk explosion, in common with so many other totemic independent releases, signalled a rejection of the posturing of its originators. "I really liked The Clash," Jon Langford would tell *Crawdaddy*, "but it was a bit... they were already on a major label and playing big shows and it was all a lot of bravado. Half of our songs were really about being in Leeds, not being in a riot. The Clash had the song called 'White Riot', which made perfect sense if you were kind of, you know, the cool, white, London punk who wanted to show solidarity with the black kids who were in the Notting Hill Riots, which is what the song is about. It became a 'Born In The USA' kind of situation, where it's a good song, but by the time it made it up the M1 to Leeds, the kids in Leeds were thinking, 'White riot?' It sounded like some kind of fascist anthem. Which we thought was kind of a clumsy thing to do perhaps, with the best intentions. After that, we came up with a song called 'Never Been In A Riot', which was about us being art students."

One of the b-side tracks, '32 Weeks', documented the exact labour hours required as exchange for consumer items. The Mekons internal dialogues (demystification, separation) mirrored their label's concerns; deftly flagged by the archness of its moniker. Product was a functional, non-descript, utilitarian term, especially when given a prefix 'Fast' that suggested the throwaway and worthless. Ironic self-reference and absurdity were tenets of post-modernism and Last, well versed in art theory, could hardly have chosen a more aptly duplicitous name for his franchise. Stiff had already shown that a good motto goes a long way in establishing a label's culture and agenda. Fast opted for "difficult fun" and "mutant pop".

"Half the pleasure of a record was buying the marketing; the package," Last told Brian Hogg, "but because entrepreneurs looked upon this as a necessary evil, all areas of the media were becoming bland. I saw no reason to do that. It was a part of the product, therefore we would get as excited and as interested in the presentation, and make sure that the whole thing relates and makes sense." Conceptually, The Mekons' output boasted obvious synergies with Last's own convictions. "All the songs on the first single were performed at the Ace Of Clubs, I think," notes Langford. "We didn't have much material and John Keenan, who ran the club, insisted we couldn't play any slow songs (which was our original plan). I'm sure Bob saw something in us that fitted in with his own plot for Fast Product – parallel thinking methinks."

"Obviously there was something smart behind what they were doing," notes Last, "an uninhibited seizing of the tools of the trade to get their point across, without worrying about acquiring some conventional set of skills. I've always been interested in skills, and have respect for skills, but I'm not interested in cultural products that are defined by those skills. I'm only interested in the skill in the service of something interesting. I suppose The Mekons were the absolute extreme example of that, in that they were very smart, had interesting things to say, and almost zero skills (laughs). They were appealing from that point of view. Because we did have this brand, and even before we put anything out there was an image and attitude; we used it to reinforce certain things that I liked that other people were doing."

The second artists featured on the label were Sheffield's 2.3, led by Paul Bower, who'd previously played in Musical Vomit, formed in the mid-70s as an outcrop of the local Meatwhistle youth drama project. Bower established the city's first punk fanzine, *Gun Rubber*, co-edited with Adi Newton (later Clock DVA) while working on the bacon counter at Lipton's. Bower's attempts at putting 2.3 together were quaint, though somehow fitting for a Fast project – for a while he walked round with a t-shirt advertising 'drummer wanted'. As well as 'Fuck The Front', which got them into hot water with the then resurgent National Front, unrecorded staples from their early sets included 'I'm So Bored Being Bored About London'. The latter, like 'Never Been In A Riot' very much a play on the Clash's repertoire (in this case 'London's Burning' and 'I'm So Bored With The USA'), featured the lyric "London's Burning they all shout/But I wouldn't even piss on it to put the fire out".

The Fast connection came after Bower met Last when 2,3 supported The Rezillos at a Doncaster Outlook show (Bower would also recommend The Human League to Last, having organised their first show). Although 2.3 were already falling apart internally by the time their single was recorded in Edinburgh, they were rewarded with the *NME*'s Single of the Week accolade. 'Where To Now?' was, like the label's debut release, notable for its scrutiny of punk's development. As Jon Savage pointed out, "like Joy Division's contemporaneous 'Novelty', [it] acutely captured the sense of post-punk disappointment."

The third Fast release was not a record, but a combined press release cum manifesto, 'The Quality Of Life No. 1' (FAST 3). The plastic bag contained a nine xeroxed collages, a slice of orange peel and a note stating "… information can only be disseminated via packaging… the initial idea has to be moulded into a package." It sold for 75p at selected outlets. As Last elaborates, "We were always deadly serious and also making jokes at the same time. '32 Weeks' was like that, too. Part of the whole point was to keep people unsure, to tread that line – it was up to you if you wanted to take it seriously, and if you did you'd find things in there, and if you wanted to take it as a joke, you could do. Part of that joke was – you had to be in the know to get it. And that was part of the whole branding thing. There was a whole visual thing I was always interested in, coming from graphics and architecture, so part of that was using the opportunity of that aesthetic. I was familiar with people like John Heartfield, who did the propaganda posters just before the Second World War. I was interested in that. So on one level it was a serious arty project, but we did it behind that jokey element. Notoriously, every one of those bags had something organic in it to make it rot, and so therefore become unique." It was a wheeze that worked on several levels – surprisingly enough, even financial. "Bob Last is selling bags of old rubbish for 70 (sic) pence," Jon King of Gang Of Four would later state to Mary Harron of the *Melody Maker*. "Now, what major record label wouldn't love to get away with that?"

FAST 4, The Human League's 'Being Boiled'/'Circus Of Death', was an enthralling, hypnotic example of early UK electronica recorded on primitive home-assembled equipment. Far from the model of the band that would achieve enormous success in the mid-80s, the initial incarnation of the group combined wry/macabre lyrical concerns with a sound spectrum drawn from Sheffield's industrial base and increasingly affordable synthesizer technology. Fast was building a winning hand of acts intent on salvaging the initial punk ideal from retrenchment and rancorous conservatism.

That was certainly the case when the roster was augmented by the aforementioned Gang Of Four, a group who boast legitimate claims to being the most inspirational architects of the post-punk aesthetic – insofar as they could without entirely divorcing themselves from rock 'n' roll dynamics. What they did eschew were rock 'n' roll *platitudes* – in an almost Stalinist manner; the derision one of their number faced when he placed his foot on a monitor in a suspected 'rockist' pose serves as an appealing illustration. Having recorded their first demos (including 'Love Not Lust', which would evolve into 'Damaged Goods') at the end of 1977, they despatched a tape to Fast. The connection came through The Mekons, who chivalrously told Last that Gang Of Four were by far the better band. The 'Damaged Goods' EP emerged in October 1978, but it was to their only release for Fast after an approach was made by – of all companies – EMI. As the band's Andy Gill later explained to Jon Savage, "It was like a production deal. They gave us the money, we gave them the tapes. We had total control over the packaging and the production of the records. From the beginning, we picked EMI as being a perfect label for us to be on; one of the biggest industrial conglomerates in the UK – a huge multinational, trading in everything from arms to entertainment. If we'd been on Rough Trade, it would have been a far less potent juxtaposition." If only The Clash had made swiping the swag sound so damned *compelling*.

Fast's next release came from The Scars, its first 'domestic' signing, in March 1979; Adult/ery', backed by 'Horrorshow'. Another band who had made an impressive showing at the Stiff/Chiswick Challenge at Clouds, as well as being the first Scottish act on the label, the Scars also represented a break from the art school milieu that had dominated the label's output previously. "The initial artists, they did have that background," admits Last, "the art school dance goes on forever in informing popular music. But then we saw a second generation of kids who were inspired by what we were doing, people like The Scars or Fire Engines. These guys had left school or were labouring on building sites. They had a torrent of ideas in their heads that suddenly they thought they could do something with."

Partially as an attempt to satisfy that demand, Fast showcased The Prats, The Flowers (Hillary Morrison's band), DAF and others, including the first officially released recording by Joy Division, across a series of 'ear comics'; three EPs; two of them 12-inches, the third a double 7-inch. Famously, Earcom 3 featured a track by The Stupid Babies – children (one of whom was actually a young Adamski) complaining, somewhat uharmonically, about their babysitter. "We were making a series of singles that, while rough, were a perfect set of 'moments'," Last recounts, "and we were getting massive amounts of feedback and mail from all over the world, and people turning up on our doorstep – all this stuff we seemed to be inspiring. And we did this to create an environment to take the pressure off. And also an environment where it was a bit like a collage thing – four or five things that might not have worked on their own, suddenly had some kind of different property when put alongside each other. I still really like some of the stuff on the Earcoms."

Fast's final release was the debut single by San Francisco's Dead Kennedys, 'California Uber Alles', licensed from the band's own imprint, Alternative Tentacles. "Bob Last of Fast Product saved the band," says singer Jello Biafra. "We'd done an east coast tour, and gone to New York as total unknowns. It might have been too soon. I went through culture shock. Some of the other guys... you start to learn a little bit more about everybody that way, and I wasn't liking what I was seeing. The guys who'd played in bar bands were acting like that again. I was like, well, maybe we're done, but I'll wait and see if the single goes anywhere. Then it did! Here we'd had this random stroke of luck that had eluded The Avengers, Dils, X, Weirdos on down. I've always tried to look at that and keep reminding myself that it wasn't necessarily because we were the best band at the time, it was just pure, dumb luck. That meant that the horrible east coast tour had not been a complete waste after all. Jim Fouratt of a club called Hurrah's had hosted Bob in New York and played him a whole bunch of records. The ones that Bob Last liked the most were 'California Uber Alles', Middle Class's debut EP and another San Francisco duo Noh Mercy, some of which wound up on Earcom 3. And 'California Uber Alles' already existed as a kick-ass single so he had something to release without having to record or pay for it. I was pretty blown away, because I grasped how important Fast Product was at that time. People were waiting with baited breath for the next Fast single after he'd sprung The Gang of Four, The Mekons, Human League, Scars and others."

Last isn't quite sure that's how it worked out. "Jim Fouratt was a good friend at the time. I went over to New York and stayed with him, that's true, but actually, Dead Kennedys was completely coincidental to that. Noh Mercy and Middle Class were both things that Jon Savage brought to my attention, as I recall. I loved both of them. But separately to that, I'm not sure if Dead Kennedys didn't come about through John Peel. At that time we were very close with Peel, and I think I phoned him up during the show. 'Who the fuck are these people? What's their number?' That's my recollection."

'California' was immediately successful, which might have been enough to cement Fast's future. But Last was not interested. "It was the perfect single to end that series of singles," he says. "You couldn't have a higher note to go out on. We did have some discussion or interaction with Jello and Dead Kennedys, or Hillary did, about an album. But I wasn't interested enough in albums at that time. It wasn't what the label was about – the label was about special moments." Last's rationale for Fast's briefest of tenures was that the label was outgrowing its original concept. The alarming strike rate of his A&R choices had seen to that. He states now that 'California', 'Where Were

You?' and 'Damaged Goods' were all doing brisk business. "We were on the map at that point, but partly why I think we have become iconic as a label is because we did stop."

In a break with independent label tradition both past and present, Last actively encouraged his (predominantly English) bands to leave the label if better offers came around. Which is exactly what transpired with The Mekons, Human League (both Virgin) and Gang Of Four (EMI). But he also maintained links with the bands. "Bob was well into us climbing into bed with Virgin," recalls Langford. "He produced the single 'Work All Week' and the first album up at [Virgin studio] The Manor. I had breakfast with him and [Richard] Branson one morning – very weird. I thought he was the gardener."

Last did set up a second label, pop:aural, inaugurated in December 1979 with the release of The Flowers' 'Confessions'. Boots For Dancing, Restricted Code and Drinking Electricity all recorded for the label, though with less impact than the Fast generation of artists. "We never quite got it right," admits Last, "though I think some interesting things came out of it. The Flowers was almost right, same with Restricted Code. It just never quite clicked." However, for David Rome of Drinking Electricity, at least the release gave him the opportunity to quit the legal profession. "We sent out our cassette to all and sundry," he recalls, "and got a reply from Bob Last. He rang up and said he'd like to release it. Bob was great – but we didn't meet him until the day we went into the studio. We signed the contract and then drove up to Spaceward Studios in Cambridge. I arrived early and started to record the b-side, having never been in the studio or done anything like this in my life before. Then Bob turned up a couple of hours later. And we did the vocal on the track in a couple of days. He produced the tracks and designed the artwork. The artwork was great; he had a really good visual sense. It was his chance to be the producer as well, I think." Last concurs. "That's true. I became very interested in the studio and the sonic elements, from a technical point of view." Rome thereafter decided to form his own record label, Survival, announcing the fact to Lord Denning's surprise on the receipt of his practitioner's certificate at the Law Society.

Probably the band with the greatest potential on pop:aural, however, was the Fire Engines – much admired by the likes of botany student Alan Horne, who would subsequently form Postcard Records. But the breakthrough never came. "The record we put out, 'Candy Skin', did fantastically well, and it still holds up," says Last. "But then we tried to get more serious about Fire Engines in terms of poppiness, and we did 'Big Gold Dream', which some people like, but I still can't listen to. It frustrates me enormously, because we were just on the cusp of getting them to do something else, but it just didn't work. By then, also, the whole management thing was really taking off, because we took The Human League to Virgin. Rather than trying to continue to put Human League records out, I became their manager because we were really ambitious for them. So they were on a big label and I had to make a decision whether I was going to go with that." Last would continue in management until moving into film projects in the late 80s. "The last band I managed was Scritti Politti, and I resigned some time after their third album. Then I started working on music with film – I'd always been a fan of film, and now I had some music skills to bring in, in terms of sound. I was able to use that as a platform to get into producing."

When Ian Ballard started his Leytonstone record label, later to unearth Manic Street Preachers and become the long-term partner of Wild Billy Childish, he entitled it Damaged Goods in tribute to the record Last released as FAST 5. "I loved Fast Product," he confirms, "it was short lived, but every record Bob Last put out was fantastic. The first Mekons and Human League singles are to die for. I just fell in love with the style of it, too." Fast's influence is, indeed, widely acknowledged. Tony Wilson was candid about its (self-evident) impact on Factory. In fact, had circumstances been different, Joy Division might have stayed with Fast. "We decided not to sign them," Last says, "because we were worried about their playing around with certain political imagery. We were uncomfortable about that. Warsaw had supported Rezillos a few times and we knew them, and they came up to meet us, and we knew Rob (Gretton). We decided not to go ahead. We talked to Tony [Wilson] a few times about how to run a record label – not that we really knew anything about it!" It's diverting to ponder how different history might have been, but even without Joy Division, the Fast catalogue remains a model of, as one commentator put it, 'how to do things right'. "To my mind," reflects former *Zig Zag Small Labels Catalogue* editor David Marlow, "Fast, as an enterprise, although it was all slightly art school, was the spiritual foundation of the whole independent movement."

Yet Last is well aware of the pitfalls of mythologising the independent label boom, or any suggestion that such enterprises were inherently superior. "It's much more nuanced and complicated than that. We always stated that we never claimed to be an independent label – we were more dependent, because we didn't have any money. The idea that independent is better – it's a much more complex picture. There was a certain moment where a gap opened up in the media world where you could get attention for things you were doing. For a while, the major companies lost the plot and lost control. There's a modern day parallel now where the multinationals don't have things locked down. But one of the reasons we finished the label was because we didn't see any point, in and of itself, of building it as an independent business. It was about the products we made, not about the label structure. That was almost coincidental. Independents just become bigger independents. If you're working within a capitalist economic system, they're all on a continuum in the same sort of process. And the less capitalised you are, it's perfectly arguable, the less independent you are. Part of the jokeyness we got involved in was because we didn't want to claim ethical superiority. Yes, we really believed in things that we were saying, we thought it mattered, and we were excited and energised about it. We hoped that people listened to the records and bought them and saw the bands. We wanted to change people's lives, but we never, ever claimed any ethical superiority over anyone on EMI or whatever."

One of Britain's finest contemporary songwriters and soon to be the short-trousered, fringe-shrouded doyen of the fey indie crowd, Edwyn Collins, from Bearsden, started out in the aftermath of punk. The son of an art lecturer father, he formed the Young Beats, alongside Alan Duncan, in 1976, aged 17. The Nu-Sonics, their title taken from the make of Burns' guitar that Collins had purchased second-hand, came into being with the addition of civil servant cum drummer Steven Daly and guitarist James Kirk, formerly of the Machetes. As Daly recalled to Alan Horne in the sleevenotes to *The Heather's On Fire*, "'I can't imagine that we did more than six gigs as the Nu-Sonics. At one point we had such problems finding a drummer that I took up the drums and Edwyn graciously agreed to sing. Which was fine because they were his songs anyway." They were formed prior to attending the Clash's White Riot gig at the Edinburgh Playhouse on 7 May 1977, but seeing that band up close helped cement their resolve. The other key moment, as Collins revealed to Mike Cimicata, was the release of 'Spiral Scratch'. "In the immediate post-punk period it was very much a feeling of DIY, and the pivotal single was 'Spiral Scratch' by Buzzcocks. It had a breakdown of the recording costs on the sleeve, and it was on their own label New Hormones. And that made us realise, well, that kind of thing was possible."

The Nu-Sonics' half dozen appearances included one at the Silver Thread in Paisley as well as a support to the Backstabbers at Maryhill Borough Hall in Christmas 1978. Simon Goddard recalled the gig for *Uncut*, with the Nu-Sonics set abridged after two numbers when a member of the infamous Maryhill Fleet grabbed the microphone from Collins and demanded the band 'Gi' us some fuckin' Showaddywaddy'. "We just had to run to the dressing room," Collins told Goddard, "lock ourselves in and call the police." The imagery is pure World War II submarine drama, a distressed captain flooding the torpedo room and its crew to save the ship. "There was this one guy who didn't make it in time. We were too scared to open the door and help. I still remember his screams as they kicked the fuck out of him."

The Nu-Sonics set eventually embraced covers of the Velvet Underground's 'We're Gonna Have A Real Good Time Together' (rescued from a 1969 live album) and, more perversely, the 'Mary Tyler Moore' theme and Chic's 'Dance Dance Dance'. The latter consisted of an improvised jam on stage while guest vocalist Andy Shoes shouted 'Yowsa' repeatedly into the microphone. Aloof and camp, Collins took to the stage wearing a sling, which most thought was arty affectation, but actually resulted from having cut his hand with a Stanley knife. A disbelieving audience repeatedly chanted "You fucking poofs" at the ensuing spectacle.

Amid this bear-baiting stood Alan Horne, shortly to set up Postcard Records, who was probably unique in detecting Collins' star quality at this early juncture. The band reminded him of the detached cool of the Velvet Underground, and he quite fancied himself as the Warhol-esque lynchpin that could stitch a Factory scene together. But by the time he'd arranged to release the Nu-Sonics' debut single, they'd transformed themselves into Orange Juice in May 1979. The switch came in order to distance themselves from punk's increasingly macho rhetoric: "Calling ourselves Orange Juice," Collins later recalled to Brian Hogg, "was part of the sense of mischief which, in essence, describes our career. It sounded absurd in the context of punk."

Horne, a fanatical musical archivist and avowed snob, was one of the true mavericks of the early independent movement. The blithely sarcastic leader of a cadre of self-confessed elitists, he offered a ready clash with Geoff Travis's urbane, communal hippie ethos. Horne, conversely, was stubborn, caustic and dismissive as part of a convincing act of studied misanthropy. According to Dave Cavanagh's *My Magpie Eyes Are Hungry For The Prize*, he had overcome his original shyness by reinventing his persona while touring Europe, returning to Glasgow as a combative figure, turning self-doubt outwards and projecting immeasurable piety, assurance and disdain. For example, he published his own fanzine, *Swankers*, which featured a cartoon strip, *Carnage At Auschwitz*, with the singular intention of upsetting his flatmate Brian Taylor, then also a member of proto-punks Oscar Wild. Horne invested one of his student grants in the latter's career, which lasted but one gig. But just when it seemed he would never find substance for his arrogance, he chanced across Collins.

Weaving in and out of the same narrative were Josef K. An extension of guitarist Malcolm Ross, singer Paul Haig and drummer Ron Torrance's former band TV Art, they'd changed names when original bass player Gary McCormack left to join The Exploited (to be replaced by former roadie Davie Weddell). After Ross met Orange Juice's Steven Daly at a gig, they began co-ordinating joint performances; Josef K hosting Orange Juice in Edinburgh with a reciprocal arrangement in Glasgow. In July 1979 A ten-song demo was recorded at Mike's studio in Edinburgh, and mailed to the likes of Radar, Rough Trade and Arista. Eventually Daly, who had walked out of Orange Juice due to personality conflicts with Horne, offered them the chance to record their debut single, 'Chance Meeting'. Released on Daly's new label Absolute, it was again recorded at Mike's, and produced by Nobby Clark, original singer of the Bay City Rollers. "Absolute was set up to release 'Chance Meeting'," notes Haig. "It had nothing to do with rejection from other companies [as has been reported]. In fact, I seem to remember that we had extended interest from Arista, but we decided not to follow it up." Absolute would also release the sole single by The Fun Four, Daly's new band.

Horne was both surprised and impressed, surmising that if Daly could achieve all this, there was no reason why he couldn't. So he made efforts to build bridges, offering to drive Daly to the pressing plant while coercing him into rejoining Orange Juice. Daly eventually acquiesced, after The Fun Four's single, 'Singing In The Showers', did nothing. Horne, alongside Collins and Orange Juice bass player Dave McClymont, founded Postcard as a means of pressing Orange Juice's debut EP, 'Falling And Laughing', in February 1980.

Horne undertook absolutely no due diligence in establishing the label, nor did he feel much like venerating his elders, be they major labels or the new breed of independents. Yet Fast was such a pivotal influence, even he couldn't deny it. And it showed. The label ident; a kitten beating on a drum, was taken from a 18th century Louis Wain picture, symbolic of the kind of tooth-achey sentimentality and Tartan kitsch that accompanied boxes of shortbread foisted on tourists. The label was actually set up as a co-operative. £500 was raised for the purpose, with Collins and McClymont providing half of that sum. The 'Falling And Laughing' EP was cut at John McLarty's studio, beneath a tailor's shop in Paisley (recording expenses less than £100). Lovesick, gauche, naïve and thrilling, 963 copies were pressed, 800 including a bonus flexidisc of 'Felicity' (originally intended to accompany a fanzine called Strawberry Switchblade which they'd abandoned "because it was shit").

They were placed in the boot of Horne's dad's Austin Maxi as Collins and he undertook the long drive to London. They made their way directly to the Rough Trade counter, who took 300 copies. Small Wonder in Walthamstow took another 100. A week later they would return, banging on the doors of every record label they could think of, and introducing themselves personally to John Peel. "Alan marched into the foyer in Broadcasting House and just demanded to see him," Collins would tell Julian Henry. "Alan is a bit arrogant, and when Peel appeared he just said to him, 'All these Liverpool groups you're playing are shit. Glasgow is the next place where it's going to happen.' Then we heard Peel on the air saying how he'd just been confronted by a truculent youth who said that the Liverpool thing was over, and then he proceeded to play Echo And The Bunnymen. Peel didn't like our record, he only played it once."

Travis recommended that Horne press up another 1,000 copies of 'Falling And Laughing', but Horne spurned his advice. Instead, he put Orange Juice back to recording, using Castle Sound studios in Edinburgh on the advice of Bob Last. He also booked in Josef K, whom he'd now enticed to the label. Adapting the old Motown slogan 'The Young Sound Of America' to 'The Sound Of Young Scotland' was a deliberately disingenuous gambit rather than any attempt to foster a regional identity – though Horne's reverence for Motown was genuine. His vision was a label combining the gravitas of Motown, Atlantic or Stax (revered singles from those labels were kept in a fetishised 'box' at his flat), with the elevated cultural pomposity of Andy Warhol's Factory. There were even discussions about whether or not they should record in mono for added period charm. He was, with just one single under his belt, unapologetically shooting for the stars. "Music should always aim for the widest possible market," Horne would inform Paul Morley in October 1980 for an *NME* article that characterised him as 'an insolent whizzkid equivalent to Wilson, Last and Travis'. "The charts are there. That's where you need to be." Morley had a job stemming the tide of self-idolatry. "I consider that we're the only punk independent because we're the only ones doing it who are young. Everybody else has come from the back of a record shop or are businessmen."

Horne made the return journey to London clutching the tapes for 'Blue Boy', Orange Juice's second single, utilising a Vox organ borrowed from Alan McGee's band Newspeak, and Josef K's debut 'Radio Drill Time'. Travis had agreed to a licensing and distribution deal, on the provision that 'Blue Boy' measured up to 'Falling And Laughing'. Travis wasn't immediately impressed, which outraged Horne, firm in his conviction that 'Blue Boy', which he and the band had laboured over intensively, was conclusively the finest single of the year. There never had been any love lost between the two parties, and with this rejection, Horne exploded. Later, sat in a café with Collins, he ran into the road in open invitation for cars to run him over. "We left the offices very downhearted and Alan seemed to go into a crazed depression and started wandering about in the middle of the road, saying 'Let them run me over, let them kill me,'" Collins later told Julian Henry. "I said, 'Look, Alan, give me the masters, I'll phone around some of the major record companies and see if I can get us a deal that way.' So Alan said, 'Take the masters. Betray me. But that'll cost you £25,000.' He was insane."

Horne skulked back to Scotland to release the singles himself, using money borrowed from his parents for the pressing and a dual-purpose, reversible sleeve. Each was coloured in with fluorescent crayons to keep costs down. Luckily, Horne had found a further ally in Dave McCullough of *Sounds*, who travelled north and wrote a two-page feature on Postcard. But Travis now changed his mind. He resurrected the original 50-50 pressing and distribution deal. Horne, sensing blood, negotiated him all the way down to a 85/15 split. There was a further tariff in that he'd have to overcome his personal objections to Horne's demeanour. But 'Blue Boy' *was* extraordinary. As Brian Hogg would write: "It was 'Blue Boy' which emancipated Scotland's pop, providing undreamed of directions and hope to new, aspiring musicians. After it nothing could be the same again."

The focus on Orange Juice over Josef K was deliberate. "Josef K were pawns," Horne would later tell Hogg. "There to make the label seem more solid and bring Orange Juice more attention. I felt I could build excitement by creating this package around them." The label's third signing, meanwhile, was a one-off release by Australians the Go-Betweens, after their 'Lee Remick' single impressed Collins and Horne. The latter claimed the discovery came when he was browsing the 'G' rack in Rough Trade, looking for Vic Godard singles. Go-Between Robert Forster revised the myth slightly in an interview with Alastair McKay of *The Scotsman* in 2003. "[Horne is] an inventive person in terms of his memories. I'm happy he was in the Rough Trade shop, but I'm pretty sure he was there with Edwyn, and Edwyn steered him away from Vic Godard towards the Go-Betweens." Forster would become well-versed in Horne's McLarenesque/Warholian antics. "I remember there was an article done on us while we were in Glasgow, for the afternoon paper. All of us were on Alan's front steps in order to have a photograph taken. I was standing there with Orange Juice, and him, and a few other people. The photographer was just about to take the photo and Alan, from nowhere, whipped out a tambourine and put it right in front of his face, exactly like Warhol on the cover of the first Velvet Underground album. It was amazing, I had never seen that tambourine before, and there it was, bang in front of his face."

An international signing at this juncture seemed a reflection of the stature Postcard had suddenly acquired. Horne's tiny second floor tenement flat at 185 West Princes Street had become the hub of the Glasgow music scene. And Horne – an outsider by nature – felt both valediction and disgust. But mainly valediction. "Horne just loved being this kind of Andy Warhol figure," recalled journalist Billy Sloan, "with his retinue of beautiful people hanging around him, sneering at everybody and just being totally dismissive of every other band, not just in Scotland, but across the world." It was quite something indeed. Glasgow, mythologised (with some degree of accuracy) as the 'hardest city' in the UK had suddenly bequeathed the arts a record label that was setting an agenda which was not only coy but self-consciously camp. The credo of punk was that vocalists should sing in authentic regional accents. Collins' use of an English upper class vernacular ('Simply Thrilled Honey', 'Felicity') with a nod to the phrasing of his beloved Al Green, allied to the foppish haircuts and outlandish dress sense, were more of an invitation to violence than any assemblage of grunts, leathers or denim ever could be. Meanwhile, the label's sound – trebly, almost bereft of bass – conveyed a sense of shimmering, brittle artifice. Justin Currie of Del Amitri encapsulated the obliteration of machismo Postcard stood for perfectly in the documentary *Caledonia Dreamin'*. After spotting Edwyn Collins from the top deck of a bus, "I wrote 'I love Edwyn' on my schoolbag in fourth year and got called a poof."

In 1981 Rough Trade organised a two-night showcase for Postcard at the Venue in Victoria. The impetus behind the label and its bands was staggering. Prompted by McCullough's piece, in what would become a customary cavalry charge by the London print media once it was decided an area was 'hot', the long neglected Scottish music scene was now the subject of feverish journalistic and A&R interest. Bidding wars broke out as a clutch of Scottish bands broke through in the wake of Postcard (The Bluebells among the beneficiaries), with Edwyn Collins and Orange Juice cited as the figureheads. Only that brave new world was about to fall apart for Alan Horne.

As per Horne's designs, Orange Juice were Postcard's leading lights, but Josef K were also a critical success. Yet their debut album, *Sorry For Laughing*, was shelved. Twelve tracks were recorded, again at Castle Sound, and scheduled for a January 1981 release before Horne told the press he'd decided it was 'too clean and well-produced'. "That was *our* verdict," contends Haig. "We decided the finished mastered tracks were lacking a raw/brittle cutting edge. This had also happened on the single version of 'It's Kinda Funny'." The claim was made that 2,000 or 3,000 copies were pressed but were to be destroyed. It was bunkum; only 20 test pressings exist, along with proof sleeves. Mystery continues to surround events, however. "It's possible there was a conscious effort made," says Haig, "without our knowledge, during the mastering process of the record, to 'bland out' the tracks a little, in order to make them more commercially acceptable."

Michel Duval's Les Disques du Crépuscule then released Josef K's finest moment, 'Sorry For Laughing', the reworked title-track from their debut, in April. Horne reconsidered his strategy. Their second attempt at recording a debut album, *The Only Fun In Town*, was released in the summer of 1981. "'Sorry For Laughing' was more of an attempt to produce something approaching a pop record," admits Haig. "*The Only Fun In Town* was a return to the fragmented, angular sound that was the essence of Josef K live." But it didn't sell as well as anticipated. And expectations were indeed high, with Josef K touted in some quarters as heirs apparent to Joy Division. In the event, former supporter Paul Morley complained of a "bungled" production, while others carped at the 30-minute running time, with much of the material already available. The band's original claim in interviews that they would split up after releasing their debut album had come back to haunt them, albeit after they'd recorded it twice.

The fourth and final act to appear on Postcard Records was Aztec Camera, whose leader Roddy Frame had never quite outgrown his schoolboy crush on David Bowie. "I made a demo tape and sent it to everyone," Frame would recall to Steve Jelbert of *The Quietus*, "Rough Trade, Factory – they all turned us down. But not to Postcard, because we read an interview with Alan Horne and he was a horrible man... Then I met Edwyn. Him and Horne came down to see us at the Bungalow Bar in Paisley. The rest is history." Their debut single, 'Just Like Gold', was recorded the night before Frame's 17th birthday. The sound of young Scotland indeed.

By the advent of Orange Juice's fourth single, 'Poor Old Soul', tensions between the band and Horne became vicious, prompted, at least in part, by the temptations of major label record offers. Not that there was any kind of unanimity in the band itself over what to do. When Polydor sent scouts to an Orange Juice gig in Leeds, James Kirk wore an undertaker's coat and refused to plug in his guitar. But Orange Juice did, indeed, finally sign with Polydor, in September 1981, thereby ripping the heart out of Postcard, especially after Horne was frustrated in his attempts to entice Dave Henderson's Fire Engines, who elected to move to Bob Last's pop:aural label instead. What could have been the perfect Postcard band in terms of conceptual continuity – Altered Images – decided they were better suited to a major. "As soon as we realised EMI and Columbia were interested in us," Clare Grogan noted in *Caledonia Dreamin'*, "there was no way we were going to go to Postcard. We were going to sell out, we were going to sell our souls and be on *Top Of The Pops* in a year, and that's what happened."

Horne himself took London Records' shilling and, backed by Roger Ames, founded Swamplands in the mid-80s. But it was an ill-fated venture – arguably because of its reliance on existing rather than new talent – including records by Paul Quinn, Davey Henderson's new band Win and James King. Or perhaps because Horne ran riot with unsupervised budgets and spent rather too much of his time at lunches and equipping his office with such essentials as a dentist's chair and stuffed mongoose. Given the money that was squandered on art budgets, missed deadlines, and outrageous expense claims, it's not hard to see Swamplands as a mini, faux-indie Casablanca.

Postcard only ever had four acts, their output comprising just over a dozen singles. But there was a level of innovation, and cheek, that distinguishes the label, alongside a dichotomy – for while the artists would sing of their vulnerability and self-doubt, the label itself displayed arrogance on an unprecedented scale. For example, Horne would promote each of his acts by suggesting they were the 'contemporaneous reincarnation of '69 Velvet Underground', simply alternating the date for different acts, while actually sending cut-out pictures of the Warholian legends to Rough Trade after they asked for promotional pictures. "I'm still nostalgic for those times," Roddy Frame would relate to Mike Pattenden in 1990. "We made some beautiful records. It had the best bands around; Aztec Camera, Orange Juice, Josef K – but our problem was that we alienated everyone. I'm sure everyone thought we were poofs – Edwyn with his fringe and Alan going on the radio and saying 'I don't like rock music, the only good music with a beat is Tamla Motown!' I don't think there was a *real man* on Postcard, that's what attracted me to it."

Postcard did revive in 1992 to re-release archive Orange Juice material, plus work by Paul Quinn, the Nectarine No. 9 (which saw Horne finally 'get his man', in terms of Davey Henderson of the Fire Engines), plus Vic Godard, but then disappeared again. Yet Postcard's influence was more lasting than its brief sub-two year existence and handful of releases might suggest. It is not difficult to locate where the acorns fell. The condition of being lovelorn was no longer uncool, but once again a natural state of being for teenagers. Those half-dozen records embraced their fumbling efforts in romance, dwelling seemingly eternally in the intensity of the moment. The *C86* bands and even The Smiths betrayed a clear debt (not only in sound, but Morrissey's mocking effeminacy). Josef K and Orange Juice are searingly obvious influences on the likes of Franz Ferdinand, whose Alex Kapranos bought his Postcard singles from the back of Glasgow's Paddy's Market. Stuart Murdoch even referred to his Belle & Sebastian as aspirant "sons of Postcard". "If you were around in Glasgow back in the day," Shirley Manson of Garbage would tell *Word* in 2005, "you'd know where that sound originates from, specially Josef K, but it's all for a new audience and they're young men with their own unique spin." Others have been less generous. Horne, meanwhile, lives quietly in Glasgow, refusing to entertain any involvement with the 'nostalgia industry'.

Horne's one-time flatmate Brian Superstar (aka Brian Taylor), meanwhile, had joined The Pastels, formed by Stephen McRobbie, who cultivated an image that amplified Orange Juice's slightly doe-eyed, wistful, schoolboy demeanour, albeit without Collins' trademark smirk. Horne, reputedly, loathed them with a passion. McRobbie played a prominent role in the development of Scotland's independent scene, establishing the 53$^{rd}$ & 3$^{rd}$ imprint, titled after the eponymous Ramones' song, from 1985 onwards, alongside Sandy McLean of Fast Product. "Stephen had the A&R input," McLean recalls, "and because the Shop Assistants were about to put Safety Net' out, he got [guitarist] David Keegan on board, because he knew it would do well. I basically put up the money for all the recording, manufacture and distribution, and that was great fun. Stephen had really good ears, and he brought us the BMX Bandits, Jowe Head & The Househunters, Talulah Gosh and the Vaselines."

53$^{rd}$ & 3$^{rd}$ effectively documented the first wave of 'twee' indie-pop (aka anorak, shambling, or whatever the *NME*'s sub-editor dreamt up on a given Monday morning). A sound/aesthetic that saw its zenith in the Sarah Records roster and (elements of) the NME's *C86* compilation. Taluluh Gosh's name had been taken from a Clare Grogan quote, while the band itself formed after Amelia Fletcher and Elizabeth Price bonded over the fact that both were wearing Pastels badges at an Oxford club night. They'd recorded their debut single for Sha-La-La, the imprint Matt Haynes ran as a prequel to his involvement with Sarah Records. And for whom Fletcher's subsequent band Heavenly would record prolifically.

"When The Legend! [Jerry Thackray; Alan McGee's close friend] worked for *NME*," McLean continues, "he was a big supporter of our stuff. He had Talulah Gosh on page three before they even put a record out. So we went down to London to see them in a crappy pub, and asked them to do a record. And they already had written the song, 'The Day I Lost My Pastels Badge', so they were quite keen to be on Stephen Pastel's label! They came up to Edinburgh and recorded four songs. We listened to those and didn't know what to release as a single, so we ended up putting them out on two singles ['Beatnik Boy' and 'Steaming Train'] on the same day in November 1986 – and they ended up both being number three hits on the indie charts."

The label also released some notable American recordings, including Ben Vaughn, discovered by *Next Big Thing* fanzine editor (and Cramps' fan club founder) Lindsay Hutton, Beat Happening and the Screaming Trees. They almost signed My Blood Valentine too. "When they left Lazy Records," McLean recalls, "me and Graeme Roberts, also ex-Fast Product, wanted to sign them. The band were up for it too, as they knew Graeme from touring with the Soup Dragons (he was their road manager and taught them how to drink – they were very young). Stephen wasn't so keen on them at the time, so it wasn't followed up quickly. One day the phone rang at the Fast Forward office and it was Colm Ó Cíosóig from the band who was very apologetic, but said they were signing to Creation Records. Here in the 21st century, Stephen admits he was wrong and didn't get it at the time, but they are now one of his favourite ever bands. And I'll bet Alan McGee wishes they had signed to 53rd & 3rd, saving him a lot of money and grief."

The Pastels themselves had debuted in 1982 with a release on Whaam! Records – tellingly set up by Dan Treacy and The Television Personalities; very much their spiritual ancestors. Indeed, long-standing TVPs bass player Jowe Head would record extensively alongside The Pastels, as well as leading The Househunters as staples of the 53rd & 3rd roster. "The Pastels very much benefited from having records out on Whaam! and Rough Trade," McRobbie would later tell Heather McDonald, "as those labels had very strong identities which helped consolidate our audience's sense of where we belonged and what we were about. Rough Trade was my favourite label and Whaam! was the Television Personalities' label; their listed address was the Kings Road, I couldn't think of anything more glamorous." As he would add to Jon Dale in 2002, "53rd & 3rd was flawed in so many ways and my involvement was often quite marginal. I was just happy to help some of my friends get their records out." While the twee pop phenomenon saw its rebirth in Bristol with Sarah and London with the early Creation (and a relocated Alan McGee), the architects of that aesthetic were, with apologies to Dan Treacy, very much the Postcard generation.

The pre-eminent independent label in Wales was Cardiff's Z Block collective, though its roots lay in the Ebbw Valley. The name was taken from an annex in Crosskeys Sixth Form College, a mining town a few miles north-west of Newport, where Phil John, Simon Smith, Andrew Tucker and Spike Williams, among others, would congregate – often just to play table tennis while skiving lectures. Z Block's first release was the 'Don't Give The Lifeguard A Second Chance'/'(WTB) White Tiger Burning' single of May 1979, credited to Reptile Ranch. In fact, that name hadn't been settled on until after the record had been pressed, with the band still to play a gig. Both songs appeared on either side of the vinyl, as both a cost-cutting measure and homage to The Desperate Bicycles. In an almost surreal twist, they'd also met Scritti Politti in a motorway service station on their return to Wales after picking up the singles, a confluence of events that led to Ian Penman reviewing their single in the *NME* ("A more serious than usual DIY... Shaky but unselfish").

Thereafter the Z Block enterprise was relocated to Cardiff in April 1979, barracked at Walker Road above the lodgings of one of the city's prominent Hell's Angels. "Determined to spread the gospel of independent record production to local bands," Tucker would write for the *Cardiffians* website, "an evaluation of the local talent and live venues available was undertaken. Expecting to sweep all before us, it was something of a shock when the first band we went to see was Young Marble Giants. Even playing to an almost empty Grass Roots Coffee Bar, with an indifferent audience of wannabe punks and local layabouts, they were obviously something very special." The Grass Roots would quickly become a haven for the local music community, and within a couple of months hosted a poster inviting local bands to contribute songs to a compilation album.

*Is The War Over?* eventually followed in October, featuring contributions from eight local bands, most notably Young Marble Giants. "There was little quality control involved in the selection of bands," Tucker noted, "if you turned up to the meetings and brought a cheque, you were in." Recorded live at the Grass Roots, the exercise was funded by the bands themselves –£120 securing eight minutes of needle time. The album's indebtedness to the prevailing DIY ethos was hammered home again via the appropriation of the Desperate Bicycles' 'It was easy, it was cheap, your turn next' mantra on the rear sleeve. There was also the by now customary faithful breakdown of production costs for the release. These were quickly recouped – pressed in an edition of 2,500, the 1,000 advance sales booked by Rough Trade alone meant that all costs were immediately covered.

Stuart Moxham of the Young Marble Giants was not initially similarly beholden to the same stockpile of early independent releases as Z Block and Reptile Ranch. "No, not at all," he recalls. "I was more or less completely oblivious to all that. I had a very parochial attitude. I remember watching the Rough Trade documentary on *The South Bank Show* and thinking – pah, bunch of lefties! I just thought [of] Decca, EMI, Philips, Chrysalis – all the trendy labels. But it was magical, really, that you could make a physical record. It never occurred to me. So meeting Reptile Ranch and the whole Z Block thing was a revelation. You didn't have to go through the hierarchy, you didn't have to fight the fact that you were in Cardiff and no one gave a flying one – you could actually do it yourself. It was just a question of technology and a little bit of money. By splitting it through all the groups on that particular scene we made *Is The War Over?*"

"Personally I didn't like punk rock," he continues. "Musically it was rock 'n' roll over again, just a bit faster, with puerile spitting and swearing. A very limited London thing that the music press were blowing up. It was only in retrospect that you realise it was a huge catalyst and essential. You have to bear in mind I was 25 at this time. I'd grown up listening to all the rock giants, Motown, progressive rock. Looking back we were on the cusp of a massive technological change in music. The cassette was new. It was like, wow, you can do your own recording on a tiny machine that you can take anywhere as an alternative to vinyl. Before it reel to reel was expensive and bulky and the microphones were no good. I'd been buying five quid reel to reel Grundigs and things from junk shops in Cardiff since I'd been a kid, to mess about with. But then synthesizers and Fairlights were coming in, and samplers and sequencers were on the horizon. It was a really interesting time technologically. We were into Eno and Can and Kraftwerk. There was a lot of sexiness in getting away from conventional instruments."

Moxham viewed their prospects as akin to being on 'a hiding to nothing'. "We were in Cardiff; we had no money, we were all unemployed. But that gave us the time to work out what we were trying to do. But nobody we knew had ever been successful through music. So what we had to do was be as noticeable as possible. And in the era of punk and noise and aggression, the obvious thing to do was go the opposite way. So the whole minimalist, 'quiet' thing was a sort of conscious choice. And getting away from the wall of sound, getting away from production, getting away from musical complexity. And basically using our Cardiffian blues roots. That's how we came up with what we did."

As a direct consequence of *Is The War Over?* Young Marble Giants – who had momentarily split up before the album's release – would be signed to Rough Trade. Geoff Travis dutifully rang the number on the reverse of the sleeve only to find out it was the nearest public call box. Z Block's output, meanwhile, amounted to a further single by Reptile Ranch and a four-track compilation EP, both drawing on financial assistance from Rough Trade. But the loss of Young Marble Giants had a dispiriting effect. "There was no big bust up of the band or label," notes Tucker. "It just kind of dissolved away in a combination of non-activity, lethargy and indifference into ultimate non-existence."

Wales had other independent labels, among them Pwdwr Records – home of the first Welsh language punk single, in the form of Llanelli's Llygod Ffyrnig, whose guitarist Gary Beard recalls: "It got a very positive reaction. It got a lot of airplay, a lot of Welsh language coverage, but also John Peel was very supportive." Again, however, the influences were clear. "The Desperate Bicycles were *definitely* the spur for us." Other Welsh labels of note included Ralph & The Ponytails' Ponytunes, Caenarfon's Sain, founded as far back as 1969 by Oxbridge languages student Huw Jones and architect graduate Dafydd Iwan and still going strong with a staff of more than 30. Among the graduates of the label were Cardigan-based mod-punk hybrid Ail Symudiad, who in turn started their own Fflach label in 1981. Another early punk venture was Steve Mitchell's Sonic International Records. Mitchell would later be behind the briefly successful/notorious 80s/90s label, Fierce Recordings.

In Northern Ireland, one independent label dwarfed all others. Belfast's Good Vibrations was founded by Terri Hooley from his record shop in Great Victoria Street. As Guy Trelford, co-author of the exemplary account of the province's punk years, *It Makes You Want To Spit*, notes, it wasn't the only label, or even the first. Just undeniably the most important. "Cliff Moore's It Records label based in Portadown was inspired by a visit to Rock On and

Chiswick Records in London, taking its name from the small chain of record shops he owned. It released the first *bona fide* Northern Irish 'new wave' 7-inch single in 1977 – 'Big City'/'All Day And All Of The Night' by Speed. It should also be remembered that The Outcasts made their vinyl debut on the same label. However, It Records and other Northern Irish labels such as Shock Rock and Rip-Off were completely overshadowed by the success of Good Vibrations."

A former Kodak processing worker, Hooley had started out with music as a sideline, selling mail order records from his home, which eventually turned into a stall at St George's Market. When his friend Dave Hyndman obtained a lease on a derelict building in Great Victoria Street, in order to set up a community printing press, he invited Hooley to help out with the rent. Hooley promptly occupied the first floor, above a health food store at ground level. With a full-colour wooden cut-out of Elvis Presley pointing the way upstairs to passers-by, Good Vibrations soon became a focal point for the local music scene. "That came from friends of mine at art college, John Carson and Leo McCann," Hooley confirms. "Because we were on the first floor, I wanted to put something on the street to attract attention, and I wanted it to be something that everyone in the world would know. So we were going to use Jesus Christ, but we chose Elvis instead." It would become so well known that after it was 'borrowed' by Queen's university students during their rag week, its disappearance made the local TV headlines. Hooley found himself, to a large degree by accident, right at the centre of the punk movement. "It was a chance for me to relive my youth – and I haven't stopped. It was all good fun at the time. Nothing had happened in Belfast since the 60s with Them. There was no recording industry here as such. It just seemed, from everything I'd learned before, that I was waiting for this moment in my life."

Not that it was the only record shop in town to serve that community, as Brian Young of Rudi notes. "Before Good Vibes opened the main record shop where people in Belfast would meet and hang out was Caroline Music in Ann Street in the city centre. It had both a knowledgeable and friendly staff – Kyle Leitch from the shop actually helped a lot of locals bands, including Stiff Little Fingers. He 'managed' Rudi for a short time and it was Kyle that arranged the cheap rates we got in Solomon Peres studio in Templepatrick to record [Rudi's Good Vibrations debut] 'Big Time'. Caroline was also bang up to date on all the new punk records. Later, when Good Vibes opened it was quite a bit outside the city centre – then inside the infamous 'ring of steel' security gates/checkpoints where everyone had to be searched when you went into the city centre. These were locked at night apart from a couple of the main gates which stayed open – but as no-one went into the city centre much at night back then that hardly mattered. Terri's shop was located on Great Victoria Street, which was pretty nondescript back then – in later years that street became the 'golden mile ' of restaurants/night-clubs etc. Back then it was close enough (and safe enough) to walk to – just a few hundred yards from the main city centre and also far enough outside the 'ring of steel' that the rates were much lower."

Its entrance stairway bedecked with posters advertising local shows, frequently liberated by enthusiastic visitors, a growing community of local punks would congregate and converse. Eventually one of those upstart punks, Wee Gordy Owens, asked Hooley to attend a show at The Pound, with The Outcasts and Rudi playing. It's worth acknowledging Owen's broader role as an activist/agitator on this early scene. "Gordy was a few years younger than us," says Young, "but we'd hooked up as he was nuts about music. Gordy lived in Sandy Row, only about 100 yards from Terri's shop and just never bothered going to school. Gordy soon became legendary cos of his phone exploits – not everyone had phones at home back then. But Gordy had a red public call box near his house and he used to ring up Tony Parsons and other journalists with a pile of 2ps and ask them all about the 'happening' punk acts. Tony used to slip him all sorts of people's phone numbers and many well known rock stars were doubtless unamused to have Wee Gordy ring them up and start asking them all sorts of personal questions or slagging them off in a broad Belfast accent. Typically, if we ever went to (or more often gatecrashed) a house party, Gordy would invariably make straight for the phone if there was one and ring up the likes of Joan Jett in Los Angeles. As soon as Good Vibes opened, as it was close to his house, Gordy basically haunted the shop."

At the Pound show, Hooley was enthused both by the music (especially Rudi's) but also the youthful spirit of rebellion that occasioned the audience reaction to the arrival of the police and UDR. As a direct result, Hooley looked into the possibility of helping finance a flexidisc, to be given away free with *Alternative Ulster* – one of the earliest punk fanzines from the province. Written by Gavin Martin, Dave McCullough and later Roger Pearson, its debut issue had come out in September 1977. The connection was straightforward – by the second issue it was being printed by Just Books Print Workshop, which shared the same Victoria Street premises. But when Hooley looked at the costs, a flexi was only marginally cheaper than real vinyl. Hence the release of the first Good Vibrations single, 'Big Time'/'No.1' in April 1978. An indignant tribute to the DIY ethos and a rejection of the star circuit, it became Belfast punk's defining anthem.

"Just Books involvement in the Good Vibes story is often unfairly overlooked," notes Young. "Dave and Marilyn printed most all of the local zines very cheaply and provided any advice that was needed on how to set em out etc, and printed most all the band posters. They were very much from an anarchist background and I think imagined that a lot of the bands here might share their politics. They had an artists workspace in Lombard Street which they let bands rehearse in and hire vans for us and provide folks who would drive us to gigs outside Belfast. Dave also printed all the early Good Vibes sleeves – the dreaded fold-over A3 sheets which we all spent hours folding. The flexidisc idea was mooted I think after *Sniffin' Glue* gave away 'Love Lies Limp' by ATV. But when Terri priced it, it would been silly not to spend the extra 2p or whatever. Cliff Moore [It Records] had already proved it could be done locally and so we played a heap of gigs to raise the money to pay the recording/pressing costs. There were no contracts and we agreed a 50/50 split. It was the first time any of us had been in studio and as we didn't know any better we simply played and recorded the entire backing track as we played it live. George Docherty produced the session and did a great job. At the time I remember we thought it was kinda 'clean' sounding but in hindsight he did us proud and I only wish he had produced our other Good Vibes recordings."

A demonstration of the naivete of the exercise can still be seen on the label credits. Young: "I remember when we were designing the label we simply copied what was on other 45s and so put 'permissive songs' as a publishing credit – which didn't ever exist. In fact none of us (including Terri) even knew then that there was such a thing as publishing. We only discovered that a few years later when Pete Waterman signed us to a publishing contact with Leeds Music. He was horrified and assumed we'd been ripped off by Good Vibes. We had to reassure him none of us had a clue what we were doing at the time."

Hooley relished being at the hub of the phenomenon. He immersed himself in the local music scene, DJing between bands, joining the Harp Bar committee as well as distributing a regular leaflet with gig and release news and, later, helping to found a Punk Workshop. The latter helped to get mainland bands such as The Nips and The Fall to visit, but later flagged when it became a committee-based exercise. "The Punk Workshop was just a name I wanted to use for the Harp bar," he recalls. "I didn't want to do just gigs, but do other things at the time, running reggae discos and so on. I wanted to call it something strange. I talked to friends and people involved in Good Vibes that were helping me. We didn't have a clue what we were doing half the time, and there was no point talking to bands, because they had no sense. They were only interested in talking about their band, none of the wider things – and that's still the case with some of them!"

He also had significant obstacles to overcome. So stagnant had Northern Ireland's showband dominated music scene become, that no pressing plant was available in Ulster, meaning pressings had to be shipped from either Dublin or London. Fold-out poster sleeves – which looked cheap even in the current climate – were usually hand-assembled by the bands. No contracts were signed by any of the acts, and the majority of the singles were recorded at the cheap Wizard Studios facility run out of a converted disused clothing factory in Belfast. Eventually the underdog's constant ally, John Peel, played 'Big Time' when everyone else on the mainland ignored it (Hooley had sent copies to record labels in a wholly benevolent attempt to secure them a 'proper' recording contract). Without doubt it would be the release that put Good Vibrations on the map.

The label documented all the early local bands; Rudi, Victim and The Outcasts, before the release that would ensure Good Vibrations' place in posterity. It came not from Belfast, though, but from Derry's Undertones. Recorded on 16th June 1978, the 'Teenage Kicks' EP resulted roughly from two parts accident to one part design. In truth, the band had been on the brink of breaking up prior to its release. They'd also only persuaded their errant vocalist to rejoin so they'd leave behind something to remind everyone that Derry really did have a punk band back in the day. 'Teenage Kicks' wasn't even intended to be the lead track, either.

The connection came through Hooley's friend, Bernie McAnaly. "His brother Sammy worked for a TV company called Radio Rentals," remembers 'Teenage Kicks' author John O'Neill. "That's who my brother Vincent and Feargal [Sharkey] worked for at the time. Bernie's brother heard that we were looking to try to make a record. So he told his brother, Bernie, if he could help out."

Bass player Michael Bradley takes up the story. "Sammy had the Radio Rentals van when Feargal wasn't using it, so Sammy would have given us lifts with the gear up to the Casbah. So we made the demo tape that was rejected by Stiff, Chiswick and Radar – it must have been Feargal who gave it to Bernie via Sammy. We knew Good Vibrations was happening because we'd heard [Rudi's] 'Big Time' on John Peel, and read a little bit about it. So we felt a wee bit left out. Bernie gave the cassette to Terri Hooley. Terri has said on more than one occasion that he never actually listened to it. But he was asked so many times about it by Bernie that he says he remembers walking across a zebra crossing in Belfast and going 'Aye, OK, tell them OK'. News came back down to us via Bernie, and Bernie drove us up there. That's how Terri got the tape. Terri wasn't an A&R man, really. He did see a couple of bands. But he just decided – this band should make a record. He may have thought, because we were from Derry, it would be good to do a band from outside Belfast. But he gave us the go ahead, and it was all organised for June, and he put up the money for it."

"Up until then," O'Neill continues, "all the Good Vibrations bands were from Belfast. I remember when we went up to Belfast the day before recording it, we were playing at a concert with all the other Belfast bands. I remember thinking that night, I'm not sure how good we are, but we're at least as good or better than the other Belfast bands. That made us confident going in to record the record the next day." The single was intended as a memorial more than a launching pad for a pop career. "We obviously didn't expect anything like the reaction the record got. We had been playing for maybe a year, and a year may not sound like a long time, but at that age, a year is like a lifetime almost. And we had got to the stage where we thought we were just banging our heads against a brick wall. We thought well, at least we'll put a record out to prove there was a punk band that existed in Derry at the time, some kind of document to prove we did exist."

"The Undertones always had a bit of chip on their shoulder about the Belfast bands," notes Young. "Quite understandably too, as they had been playing for at least as long as any of the Belfast bands yet been relatively overlooked by most all of the local zines which were Belfast based and raved mostly about local Belfast talent. Historically too, there has always been a rivalry between people from Belfast/Derry and some folks here definitely saw them as 'hicks from the sticks'. In hindsight, it gave them a real sense of purpose. When they played the Battle Of The Bands, where the rest of the line-up was all the smug Belfast bands who hung around Good Vibes (including Rudi) I guess they saw this as a chance to show everyone who was boss. I remember them setting up that afternoon and sound-checking and we were all laughing at this geeky roadie they had who was wearing crappy plastic sunglasses and PVC strides. Then they started playing and the geeky roadie started singing and we all realised immediately that they were good, very good."

Independence Days

The Undertones had agreed that their best song was 'True Confessions', but then relented on the title. "We called it the 'Teenage Kicks' EP because obviously we were teenagers," explains O'Neill, "and it just had a good ring about it – the 'True Confessions' EP wouldn't have been as good. I still don't think, even when we played the song live then, it stood out any more than any other song. We obviously thought it was one of our best songs to put it on the EP. But we thought 'True Confessions' was the best song on the record. It just made sense, after calling it the 'Teenage Kicks' EP, to put it first on the record. That's the only reason I think it was chosen. Our blueprint was the 'Spiral Scratch' EP by Buzzcocks. That's why we chose to do an EP. There were four songs on that, so that was all we were thinking of – the four songs to be taken together as an example of what we were like, not one particular song." In fact, there are also similarities in cover design between the two records. "We probably stole that idea as well," laughs O'Neill.

In order to get to that point, they had to persuade Feargal to return to the band. "Aye," recalls Bradley. "I remember phoning him from the O'Neills house, which was the centre of operations. I definitely remember saying, listen, just make the record. And he said all right. I still can't remember what the argument was about. God, we had so many fights and leavings. To-ings and Fro-ings." And they never did find out who wrote the derogatory local graffiti immortalised on the cover: 'The Undertones are shit pish counts wankers.' "It could have been anyone, to be honest," notes John O'Neill. "At the time, punk wasn't that well known in Derry. We had a core following of 50 people or so, and friends, but apart from that we were treated with a lot of suspicion. And there was nobody really playing any music the way we were. So there was a lot of antipathy against us too." "Usually in Derry," Bradley points out, "about 30 people would come forward and claim that. But no-one has. I think it's because they can't spell cunts right. Who would own up to that?"

John Peel, meanwhile, was utterly entranced. But he wasn't the only one. Seymour Stein had a similar moment of revelation when he heard the DJ play it on his show. "I was going down to see the Searchers play. Something came up a couple of times where I couldn't. I had the most horrific headache that day. I said, 'Oh my God, I can't get out of it a third time.' We're on the road down to wherever they were playing, a south coast seaside town. Paul McNally was working for me at the time, and we're listening to John Peel. All of a sudden this record comes on. And I screamed, 'Pull over, pull over, stop the car!' He thought it was something to do with my headache. 'Are you all right? Do you want to go to the hospital?'" He turned white as a ghost. I said

'No, it's this record, it's fantastic!' God bless him, John Peel played it over and over that night. And he gave out all the details. And I said, 'I've got to sign this band, they are fucking amazing!' I said to Paul, 'Look, my name is Stein, yours is McNally. Don't you think it's better that *you* go to Northern Ireland?' He did. And he was so impressed when he went to Feargal's house. In Feargal's front room there were all these awards that Feargal had got in Catholic school for winning singing contests."

It became apparent that The Undertones would not be Good Vibrations recording artists for very much longer. Hooley made no attempt to stand in their way. "At the time," notes Bradley, "he would have been perfectly within his rights to say, listen, I own the copyright to 'Teenage Kicks', so any deal you do with Sire, I should have a percentage of that. He would have been 100% entitled. And he didn't. 'Away you go, good luck to you!' He still jokes with me, I see him quite regularly. He says he's discovered a legal document, which shows that he owns the copyright to 'True Confessions'! And we're going to be hearing from his solicitor! But he doesn't mean it."

The deal negotiated with Sire saw a delegation – Bradley and Sharkey – despatched to London, with the rest of the band waiting by the telephone at O'Neill central. Why those two? " I was the smartest!" laughs Bradley. "In terms of O-Levels! But I would be completely and utterly financially incompetent. Feargal because he would have been seen as being the hardest-headed. He wouldn't have been afraid to put the case of the band forward. Whereas the others would have been too self-effacing. That's interesting – why me and Feargal? Maybe to keep an eye on Feargal (LAUGHS). I always make comparisons with 1920 and Michael Collins, when they went over to London to negotiate. It reminds me of that. Because John and Damian and Billy were back home. They had the veto to a certain extent. I remember being on the phone in this flat in London. And it was like those Michael Collins treaty negotiations. I would be the representative, in hostile territory. Billy [Doherty] and John from the safety of the O'Neill's house – 'The Rich Kids got more!' And I had to cup my hand over the phone and say to Seymour, 'We'd like more money!' And that kind of wee New York Jewish voice went – ahhhhhhhhh! I think he did give us more money, but he was probably going from a very low base anyway. He knew he wasn't dealing with Alan Klein here. These are boys who would have taken a couple of planks of wood and a mirror."

Good Vibrations went on to issue several more singles, including notable ones by Ruefrex, Protex and The Outcasts (who also released the label's first album), and an entirely ridiculous artefact featuring Hooley himself on vocals. The musical vocabulary of the label's output was distinctive, too. These releases were effectively pop-punk affairs, rich on hooks and melody, without the self-referencing that labels such as Fast, Postcard, Factory or Rough Trade embraced.

Brian Young still bemoans the conditions of production, however. "The fastest selling Good Vibes 45 post 'Teenage Kicks' was 'I Spy' by Rudi. It should have done much better than it did but was crippled by a truly tragic production by Davy at Wizard studios. After 'Big Time', Terri arranged most of the Good Vibes recordings via Wizard studios. That was fine for the Undertones who were tight and knew what they were at, but not so fine for everybody else. What Good Vibes sorely lacked was a competent producer with vision and imagination who would both encourage and motivate the local acts into making the best goddamn records they could and which they could be proud of – a local Martin Hannett/Martin Rushent/Nick Lowe/Vic Maile if you will? Instead, we had to make do with a guy who owned a string of hippy shops selling platforms and satin flares who mostly used the studio to record demos for his own showband circuit combos. The bands most certainly had the material – but Wizard's lamentable production jobs steered far too many potentially great records straight into the dumper. But they were the only studio in the centre of Belfast who would let Terri run up a tab."

After signing Leamington Spa's Shapes, Hooley also opened up a Good Vibrations International franchise. "That was a piss take," he acknowledges. "In the 60s, you had Pye International, but it was just a piss-take. At that time we were getting demos from people all over the world, with no money to put anything out. I remember years later, clearing out Good Vibrations, and finding this tape of a band from Dublin that Sinead O'Connor was fronting at the time, In Tua Nua. One time we almost put out a record with Glen Matlock. He'd put it out in England and it hadn't sold, but it did well in Good Vibes, so we talked about putting it out as a green vinyl release. But in the end I didn't get on with his manager."

Hooley also did his best to help the Good Vibes bands get on. "One apocryphal tale that is true from later on," adds Young, "was when Terri was over trying to get a deal for some of the bands with Polydor. They offered him the grand total of, I think, £6,000 for Rudi, Protex and Xdreamysts – but insisted Rudi would have to sack our drummer, who was a 'madman'. We refused and the other two bands were signed up. We reckoned we had a lucky escape after what we saw them do to both bands.

However, cash flow problems – specifically late or non-payment by distributors – would lead to Good Vibrations' bankruptcy in 1983. Within a year Hooley had managed to square the debts and resurrect both the shop, which eventually relocated across the street, and label. But effectively, the moment had been lost. Hooley would continue to trade in records at various premises. The label stumbled on too, reviving in the early 90s and releasing one of Hooley's favourite singles, 'Time Flies' by Tiberius Minnows, with whom he is still currently working, plus records by PBR Streetgang and Four Idle Hands.

The beauty of Good Vibrations and the Ulster punk scene was that sectarian politics, which dominated the province's outward image, were set aside. Hence the roster accommodated both the Undertones, a band from a strong republican background who, initially at least, refused to be drawn into any discussion of the Troubles, and outspoken Shankhill Road Protestants Ruefrex. In many ways, Northern Ireland caught punk in its purest sense, and its participants' unwillingness to compromise that ideal can be seen as a small part of the building of consensus that has restored peace to Northern Ireland. "Good Vibrations was like a ray of sunshine," notes Guy Trelford, "cutting through the dark grey that shrouded the moribund city of Belfast in much troubled times. It offered hope, gave inspiration and a sense of optimism to the nation's morose youth. But above all else it gave us Rudi, Undertones, Outcasts, Ruefrex, Victim, Protex, Moondogs."

"Belfast was a ghost town at night," Hooley recalls of the pre-punk city. "It was the only city in Europe where people didn't use the city centre." But he's wary of overstating how much those relationships helped bring peace to the province. "I don't know about that. Jesus Christ, I was set upon so many times. It's nine years since anyone tried to kill me." A not insubstantial peace dividend, you might have thought. "I suppose. I was practically beaten to death nine years ago, I couldn't walk for two weeks. There was a band here way back called Offensive Weapon, a National Front band, and Johnny Adair (i.e. loyalist Mad Dog Adair) was in the band. I got them banned from every gig here, and I think it was because of that, and Johnny Adair was back on the streets again and took a dislike to me." He has no hesitation about putting that in print. "No, I'm bringing out a book next year, and it'll be in that!" There's also a movie about to be made about his life. "People always ask about the film, and I say, yeah, it'll last three and a half minutes too." Ah, just like all those breezy Good Vibrations singles. Who would he like to play him? "I don't give a shit, as long as they're tall, dark, handsome, and hung like a donkey."

Ruefrex's drummer Paul Burgess would face attacks from both sides due to his outspoken lyrics. He's also a good source for pricking any over-inflated claims about the role punk played in the peace process. "Ruefrex never enjoyed the kind of cosy relationship other Northern Irish bands had with Terri Hooley and Good Vibrations," he reflects. "The camaraderie often cited by Rudi, The Outcasts and a variety of Harp Bar flotsam and jetsam who hung around the place was relatively unknown to us. And to my mind, the claims that Good Vibes set out to be some engine of reconciliation and an oasis of non-sectarian fraternity is little short of revisionist nonsense. If Good Vibes came close to providing any of these things, it was because a loose affiliation of non-conformists and agitators adopted the shop as the focal point for Belfast punk – not the other way around. For some, there was definitely an alternative 'Youth Club' vibe to the place, where kids could hang out all day, posing in their leathers and pins, flicking through record sleeves, and listening to the latest cuts. And in that regard, the place certainly served a purpose. But for anyone in a Belfast band at the time, the primary function of 'this 'ol hippy' and his beloved shop was his willingness and aptitude for releasing the records of local bands and getting them airplay. This big, camp, one-eyed space cadet made all that possible, God bless him! And if any legacy be required, surely that's enough."

"It wasn't always sweetness and light," Burgess continues. "I do recall at a latterly infamous gig in Omagh how Terry – on being bugged one too many times by me for a release date for 'One by One' – let go a strangled yelp and brandished a stool above his head. In fairness, this was unusual and somewhat out of character. Ruefrex seemed to have that effect on people. Anyhow, a semi-ape-like creature and muscle-friend to the band known as Mahaffey ensured that Terri would in fact not strike down the one true voice of Ulster agit-politico-pop and he left somewhat chastened. Hardly good artist-label relations, but we were all making it up as we went along."

*It Makes You Want To Spit* co-author Sean O'Neill concurs. "No-one went to punk gigs here thinking that they were anti–sectarian. Nobody even thought about it. It just happened naturally through the music without anyone having to make a big point about it. Perspectives change with the passing of time and when hindsight kicks in. I can recall reading at the time that The Outcasts 'You're A Disease' was not about VD, as I'd thought, but about scorning religion – surely the most lethal disease in Northern Ireland at the time." But then, as he rationalises, "Yeah, punk really *did* mean something more than a fashion trend in Northern Ireland. It brought kids together from both sides of the religious divide (unheard of at the time).

It also straddled class backgrounds too. There were two very polarised communities in Northern Ireland back then. I can remember in the early 80s when all the Mod revivalists were wearing those red, white and blue Union Jack shoes. In Belfast, they actually sold green, white and orange pairs, too!"

"I'd certainly agree that to suggest that punk deliberately brought any huge changes in the way people thought or behaved here would be revisionist and hopelessly naive too," notes Brian Young. "But it's also undeniable that punk, by its very nature, did make you question things and look at things differently. I know many people who did ditch at least some of the usual tired Northern Ireland attitudes – and many who didn't. What I would say though is that, definitely more by default than design, punk in Northern Ireland had a generally constructive/positive impact. I'm sure it was the same in many other places – but that certainly was a sharp contrast to the public face of UK London-centric punk which was so deliberately, studiously nihilistic and negative, at least on the surface."

Hooley and Good Vibrations have latterly been honoured, and given a financial shot in the arm, by the local music community in two significant benefit shows. The first, featuring The Undertones, Shame Academy (ex-Rudi/Outcasts) and Ruefrex, helped him to re-open as Phoenix Records in the city's Haymarket after his North Street Arcade premises burned down. A second, with a similar line-up (minus Ruefrex), on the 30th anniversary of the release of 'Big Time', took place at the Mandela Hall in Belfast. Immediately prior to which Hooley, via his friend Arthur Magee, was the recipient of a glowing eulogy from former US president Bill Clinton. "By supporting young musicians in Northern Ireland and introducing them to audiences in England and elsewhere, Good Vibrations not only helped individual musicians to realise their dreams, but also offered listeners the opportunity to better understand and appreciate each other through the common language of music." According to Magee, when he passed the note to Hooley, he was, for the first time in his life, "speechless".

Not for long, mind. "Aye, that was embarrassing. When I heard, I said, 'fascist bastard'. 'You can't say that, you're going on radio tonight and television tomorrow morning.' 'What? We're not telling anyone!' But they'd informed the press, the bastards. And I went on television and I said, 'well, he *is* a musician.' But so is Tony Blair, and if I'd have got a letter from that Tory bastard I'd have killed him." Maybe Clinton is a closet Protex fan? "You never know! One time someone wrote from the House of Commons asking for a copy of one of our records. So we sent him one and asked for a cheque, but he never paid!"

"I still think Terri deserves a lot more in terms of recognition from the city of Belfast for what he did," adds Bradley, "and what he continues to do. The great thing about Terri is that he never made any money from it. Even if that was his intention, he was financially incompetent! But I think his intentions were just to get the music out there, and the old Communist ideas he used to have, old socialist ideas, were quite heartfelt. It was about making records and not any personal gain." A point also conceded by Brian Young. "Though I've fallen out bitterly with Terri more times down the years than either of us would care to remember, he's still, underneath all the bravado and bluster, one of the eternal good guys and the world would be a much duller place without him."

Hooley's still a people's man. "Five years ago," he recalls, "they started planting these trees here after an article in the [Belfast] *Telegraph*; Elton John, Bono, Cliff Richard, and a few locals like George Best and Alex Higgins. A few people wrote in and said, never mind that, where's the tree outside Good Vibrations? Within a couple of weeks there was a tree there, and we planted it! There were some of my friends there, some ex-paramilitaries who'd done 16 years in jail were invited along. People said, you shouldn't invite these people along. I said, but these people are changed people and they're out in the community talking about peace and that's what we want."

And Hooley's still up to his eyes in music ("shouldn't that be *eye*?" volunteers a waggish Sean O'Neill). Having relocated Good Vibrations – the name restored – into new premises in July 2008, the label released its first recordings for 17 years in September, in the form of *Leonard Cohen's Happy Compared To Me* by the Minnows. And it all came about with a little help from his friends. "After the benefit for me in May this year for the 30th anniversary, we got new premises that belong to friends of mine. The guy who did the cut-out of Elvis was born in this house! It's a three-floor terrace house in the Belfast centre, Winetavern Street. I met Sean McCann whose family owned it, and they said, 'We're going to do it all up for you.'"

"Then I did this bus tour," he continues, half-enraptured, half-astonished. "It was 'Terri Hooley's Alternative Belfast'! That was me riding about telling stories, reading poems, with a guitarist. But there's nowhere left! The Harp bar and the punk venues and everywhere else from the 60s has all gone. So we went to Stormont, and went down Cypress Avenue, because of Van

Morrison. And [Ian] Paisley lives there. And I was stood outside his house going 'Never! Never! Never!' I was legless. When we opened up the shop we had tons of publicity and everyone was glad we were back. When we got burned out four years ago (in the aforementioned April 2004 North Street Arcade fire) we lost everything, and we lost most of the history of Good Vibes." But again, friends are helping out. Brian Young of Rudi, Good Vibes' first signings, is among those to have donated memorabilia. "Brian always says I would never let the truth stand in the way of a good story... but then, neither would Brian! We're setting up a bit of a museum. I'm trying to get a complete collection of singles and albums back, and posters." Did any of the kids who nicked posters from the wall back in the old days return them? "Believe it or not, we had a 12-inch copper plaque that was stolen from the original building, and we got that back. Someone had a guilty conscience and returned it."

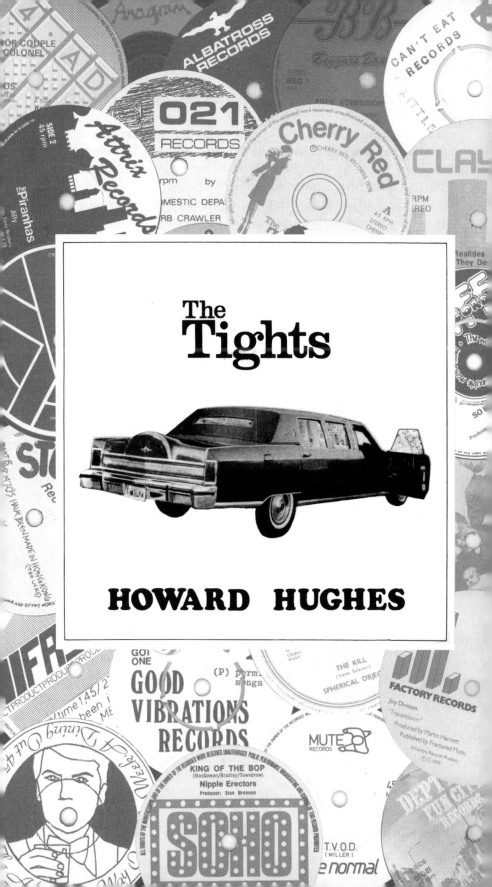

# Chapter Ten

## Ever Present

## Cherry Red Records

Cherry Red was founded not by a music industry ingenue, but a former financial controller with Bell and general manager at Magnet, two established middleweight record labels. Iain McNay's experiences there had soured him to the politics of the mainstream record business, but new developments would afford him the 'window of opportunity' to start something on his own terms. Cherry Red grew from a promotion company he'd jointly founded in 1971 alongside Will Atkinson and Richard Jones, taking its name from a favoured Groundhogs song. Its initial business was promoting concerts at the Malvern Winter Gardens and other local venues.

McNay was living in Thornton Heath, Surrey, working as an accountant for an American film company. "Richard was into seeing bands at the Croydon Greyhound," McNay recalls. "I was into music but not overly so at that time Richard said he and his mate Will were thinking of promoting gigs at Malvern Winter Gardens a 1,200-capacity venue, and he wanted someone to help look after the financial side. It sounded interesting as a hobby that fitted in with my day job. I went to Malvern, met Will etc, and thought this is great – I can do the promoting and, as I like walking, then go off up the Malvern Hills at the weekend. I didn't know what type of bands we'd have, but Richard and Will were confident it would work. So we started on 3rd July 1971, the day after my birthday, with Hawkwind and Skin Alley. We really didn't know how it would work out. We had the expense of paying the band something, pay the cost of the hall, promotion etc, but in the end we had about 600 people and just about broke even, so that was a positive step."

The operation evolved to become, in McNay's words, "almost a community service". Finances were watched closely. "A lot depended on us finding out what did or didn't work and we didn't make too many mistakes to begin with. It was also a question of having the bands available that would pull sufficient people. I remember we booked The Strawbs three or four months in advance. When we had them, 'Part Of The Union' was near the top of the charts that week, and we'd booked them on a fixed fee – £1,000 guaranteed. I have to confess we sneaked a few over the capacity that night and it was a very successful evening." All of this continued in parallel to McNay's career in the music industry. "In the summer of 1972, a year after starting the promoting, I worked for De Lane Lea Studios. They had three film studios in Soho but also had a studio called The Music Centre just by Wembley

Stadium. They had bands there like Wishbone Ash and Vinegar Joe, and I do remember saying directly to at least one band that they should come down to Malvern."

By the time that punk came along in 1976, they were immediately receptive; but cautiously so, as Jones remembers. "We had the Sex Pistols booked as the SPOTS [their 'secret' name to allow them to tour following the Bill Grundy farrago]. I recall Iain saying to me, 'We're going to have to tell the Winter Gardens the real deal over this, they can't just turn up, because they would blow it.' He spoke to Glen Kilday, the venue manager, and he said, 'There's *no way* I can allow that, I'll lose my job,' and we had to pull out." Some of the punk bands who did come to Malvern included The Stranglers, Damned, Adverts, etc. "Looking back over the punk period," notes Jones, "the only major band we didn't book apart from the Pistols was the Clash the Winter Gardens was too small a venue for them."

McNay rented the flat above Jones's parents in Wells Road as a base of operations when he visited, where Jones could also produce artwork for posters and tickets, and began selling records he'd taken back to Malvern. "The interesting punk stuff wasn't really available in the local record shops," McNay recalls, "so we got a buzz going with the punk scene in Malvern and that was the beginning of us promoting punk gigs, which led to Richard finding The Tights. They were Malvern's answer to the Sex Pistols, young 15- and 16-year-old kids in a punk band. Richard had been to see them and liked them, and suggested starting the Cherry Red label to put their records out."

It was at Malvern Wine Bar on New Year's Eve 1977 that Jones finally persuaded Iain McNay to start a record label. "We got a 15-minute set together and started to play parties and pubs," recalls Tights bass player Barry Island. "We soon attracted the attention of Cherry Red and a meeting was arranged with Iain McNay. Iain was really excited by the new punk scene and said Cherry Red would be interested in putting up the money for us to record a debut single. A demo was recorded in a local builder's warehouse comprising three songs; 'Bad Hearts', 'It' and 'I Can't Sing'. Iain loved the demo and promptly booked Millstream Studios in Cheltenham to record our first EP." McNay was able to utilise the contacts he'd built up in the industry. "John Acock was an engineer at De Lane Lea Studios, who also came from Malvern, and had started to produce records, like Steve Hackett albums. I got friendly with John and played him a demo of The Tights. He really like them and agreed to produce our first release."

Cherry Red thus became a record label on 2<sup>nd</sup> June 1978 with the release of 'Bad Hearts'. It was single of the week in *Record Mirror* and, endorsed by plays on John Peel a week later, swiftly sold out of its first pressing of 2,000 copies. It would ultimately sell double that amount. McNay arranged for Rough Trade to take 300 copies initially, with the sleeves and records manually repatriated on their return from suppliers. Again, though, he could sense a better way to do things, and utilised another business contact, David Thomas of Magnet, who had started Spartan Records. "We were their first clients," says McNay. "They had a warehouse at the back of Wembley station, and The Tights singles were the only ones sitting in the warehouse to begin with. They didn't know about Rough Trade and Rough Trade didn't know about them, so we introduced them to each other. In the early days, Rough Trade couldn't get into the mainstream shops. Because Dave and Tom [McDonald; David Thomas's business partner] came out of the more establishment side of the record business, they knew how to get into Woolworth's and the other chains. Rough Trade were part of an alternative network, so that was an important relationship, and it was the start of the comprehensive distribution network that had eluded the whole independent system before that."

A second single by The Tights, 'Howard Hughes', followed, though not without some difficulty in finalising the artwork. "I was going to do the cover," remembers Jones. "The obvious connection was to have the big limo he drove round in with the windows blocked out with newspaper. Because there was no internet, we had to come up with the limousine. At that time Will was working for a funeral director, so he arranged one weekend to borrow a sleek modern hearse, a Ford, and we got it in a car park and put newspaper all over with windows and photographed it. It looked absolutely brilliant but the photos didn't work at all. So we used the picture of the car, got newsprint and substituted that over the newspaper-ed windows."

The success of a second single persuaded McNay to make a full-time commitment to Cherry Red. "I'd left De Lane Lea in '74, joined Bell Records, then left to join Magnet Records in May '77. I'd joined Bell Records when a job came up as their accountant. Bell was so successful at the time; Showaddywadday, Gary Glitter, David Cassidy, Bay City Rollers – lots of really big acts. I saw it as an opportunity to get into the record business in an exciting, successful company. Bell was owned by Columbia Pictures in the States. I was there for three years. After it became Arista Records I had the chance to join Magnet Records as general manager, working for the man who is now Lord Levy, which I saw as a step up in terms of my experience."

## Independence Days

It was his experiences with Bell that began to convince McNay that his future should be self-determined; that he was no ladder-climber. "When Bell became Arista it started to become more corporate. Previously I'd just been reporting to the UK managing director, and now I was reporting to the financial vice-president in New York. It was a whole corporate thing creeping in. I was never a very good corporate animal, to be honest. I was very much my own man, going off with projects I felt strongly about. When I was at Bell, although I was officially the financial controller, I was adding things under my wing the whole time. I took over the business affairs because no-one was doing it, then the licensing out, because no-one was doing it. I just took on jobs because I wanted to learn. So it was a fusion of having an understanding of how money works, which you need to run a label, but also having an openness and an interest in real creativity – you get good creative people to do what you can't. And that's the foundation of a good business."

By the time the second Tights was released in the autumn of '78, McNay had committed himself full time to Cherry Red, working out of his flat at 199 Kingston Road in Wimbledon. "I was getting to the end of the line with working for other people. I just felt that there was an opportunity. In that first wave of punk, there was a whole change, not only in the music, but in the structure of the music business. There were record companies springing up all over the place, there were new distribution companies, and promotion companies and marketing companies; all kinds of freelance services to back it up. So it was just a very exciting, productive and fast-moving period. At the time I must have been about 31 or 32, and I just decided that this was my chance to have a go at running my own business. And if I'd left it too long, maybe that window of opportunity would have gone."

The third release on Cherry Red was the first of a number of records licensed externally. McNay had been reading about Destroy All Monsters in the pages of *Sounds*. "They had a picture of Niagara, the [female] singer. And because of the credentials of the band – there was Mike Davis who'd been in the MC5, and Ron Asheton from the Stooges, and Niagara looked great – I just thought, and I hadn't even heard the record, that I can see this working. I wrote to the record company, IDBI (I Don't Believe It). They were a Detroit label, run by a journalist called David Keeps. He managed Destroy All Monsters. We licensed it for $500 or something. And we put it out in the UK on red vinyl, to make it different from the American one. It got great reviews, and I got loads of pictures of Niagara from David, mostly scantily clad, and I gave them to *Sounds*, and they'd turn up in their letters page. For the next few weeks, everyone who come round to my flat, I would ask them to write a letter to *Sounds* demanding another picture of Niagara. So we had a little letter-writing campaign going."

Cherry 4, meanwhile, was a one-off single by Staa Marx, winners of the annual *Melody Maker* Rock Contest. The pre-eminent artist on the label's early roster, however, was former Mott The Hoople keyboard player and industry veteran Morgan Fisher. "I knew we would never survive financially from just selling 4,000 singles as we did with The Tights," recalls McNay. "It wouldn't pay any wages. You might just pay your costs and get your money back, but you're not going to make money out of it. So at the back of my mind I had ideas for albums. I came across the Morgan Fisher album that became ARED 1, our first, through a guy I became friendly with called Maurice Bacon, who was the drummer in John Otway's band. He was living in the same house as Oliver Mills, who was helping me with A&R a little bit. Oliver was involved with The Photos, whom we came very close to signing before they went to Epic."

Fisher had recorded a prog rock album (under the simple billing 'Morgan') for a major label in 1972, which had ultimately been shelved. Six years later, "a cheerful chap called Iain McNay strolls up and says, 'I've just started an independent label and I'd like *The Sleeper Wakes* to be our first album release,' referring to said dust-covered LP. 'So you want to release my prog album at the height of the punk era? Go ahead – be my guest!'" McNay's unlikely enthusiasm was enough for Fisher to "throw in my lot with them".

McNay hit upon the idea of a compilation of independent singles for the label's second album release. "There were all these labels putting out singles, obviously us, Rough Trade, Industrial, etc. So we did a compilation. It was fairly easy to put together – kind of like K-Tel or Ronco, who put out mainly TV advertised compilations with all the big hits. So, I thought, these are *not* hits from '77, '78 and '79, but they had sold pretty well, and it seemed a good idea to do a collection of them. I remember sitting in a cafe in Oxford Street waiting to collect a tape from Genesis P.Orridge. Throbbing Gristle were on the compilation, and I'd spoken to Genesis on the phone and said I needed a title, and it was his idea to call it *Business Unusual*. That record did really well, selling several thousand very quickly."

Meanwhile, Morgan Fisher was busying himself setting up his own in-house studio, or perhaps in-bedroom studio might be a more appropriate description. "Iain magnanimously gave me carte blanche," he continues, "meaning he would release anything I recorded at zero expense in my newly created four-track home studio. And thus, following my first Cherry Red single, a corny ballad-piano version of my chum John Otway's 'Geneva' (backed with three excerpts from my solo prog album *Ivories*), the Hybrid Kid was born. Pipe Studios was a tiny bedsit in Linden Gardens, Notting Hill, London W8 (fifth floor, no lift), with a bed that folded up into the wall. I could just squeeze in a four-track tape deck and a tiny mixer, and managed to produce the first Hybrid Kids LP at a total cost of 25 quid."

The concept of the Hybrid Kids was to take a familiar song and re-record it in a totally different arrangement. "Iain loved the idea and we succeeded in perpetrating the hoax on BBC Radio, until I finally blew the gaff because I wanted to announce, 'This is me, folks – all me own work!' But it was fun coming up with all those names. The Burtons came from the high-street tailors where I had my first mod suit made in 1966. Jah Wurzel came from Jah Wobble. I tried to do a serious rap/dub version of 'Wuthering Heights' the way the illustrious bassist might have done. I was completely inept at this and, in complete nutter ignorance of the fact that 'Wuthering Heights' is based in Yorkshire, descended into a scrumpy-ish Cornwall accent. 'Owt on the woild and windy mooooors . . "

While Morgan Fisher's mischievous ego (and alter egos) provided the cornerstone of the label's early output, the reissue of the Hollywood Brats (Cherry 6) 'Then He Kissed Me' was a further example of McNay's jackdaw A&R mentality. In fact, he'd nearly worked with the band during his time at Bell until Clive Davis took the label over as it became Arista. "Clive Davis said something like, 'Don't be stupid, this isn't what we want to do on Bell Records,' so it never got released," McNay, for whom opportunities are frequently delayed rather than lost, recalls. "So I knew of the band from then. I'd seen them play a couple of times at a club in Piccadilly. That was kind of the coincidence. I was nervous about putting the album out as I didn't know how it would sell. And that was my first deal with Caroline Exports, the export company owned by Richard Branson. Dave Loader was the managing director, Richard Bishop the buyer and Brian Leafe looked after production. They were all later involved in Armageddon Records. I was very friendly with Richard Bishop and he said, 'Why don't we do a deal on the Hollywood Brats?' He thought it would export quite well. He said, 'You give us an exclusive three-month export period at a decent price and we'll guarantee to buy 1,000 albums.' I thought, that's great. That will cover the cost of doing the album. I knew I couldn't lose money on it."

The Runaways were the label's second American artists, signed after McNay had seen them support The Stranglers at the Roundhouse. Once again, it was a demonstration of his willingness to look at something that others had deemed past its sell by date. "I was quite a fan and someone told me they were having trouble getting their latest album released in the UK. *And Now The Runaways* was their last album before they broke up – they were managed by Toby Mamis and Peter Leeds, who also managed Blondie. This was after they'd broken up with [famed svengali] Kim Fowley. So I rang up and got hold of Toby, and said I'd really like to do it. He was great. We paid $5,000 advance for the UK rights, and when it came out, we did different coloured vinyl on the album, and again it did really well on export. But pretty much the band was all falling apart by that point."

Their willingness to sign with Cherry Red arose partially from recognition of McNay's work with Bell. "I was a big fan, as was Joan, of the whole glam and glitter scene," says Mamis. "And Bell Records had so many of those bands. There was reassurance from us that he knew what he was doing because he came from Bell, oddly enough. I was in London with Joan, recording three songs with Steve Jones and Paul Cook of The Sex Pistols. And I think I invited Iain to the studio to talk about the Runaways album that had never been released in England. And he had a lot of energy and it was a no-brainer to say sure, let's get it out there." Released in September 1978, *And Now...* failed to reach the charts in Europe or America, but it did prove to be the label's first consistent seller.

Assiduous scouting for low-risk investments was one plank of Cherry Red's foundations. Another was that it was the first independent label to cotton on to the benefits of developing a publishing arm. A number of deals were struck across the independent spectrum, often with artists who were completely oblivious to the potential income stream. "A painless publishing deal can be yours!!!!!" trilled the advert which appeared in *Zig Zag*'s small labels catalogue. "Don't sign away YOUR publishing until you've talked to the boys at... Cherry Red!" Interested parties were directed to Theo Chalmers at the company's Kensington Gardens Square address.

"I knew nothing about publishing," McNay reflects. "At my last day at Magnet, I spent a couple of hours with a guy called Grant Goodchild who ran Magnet Music, their publishing arm, and he explained the principles. But when I started all I had were basic contracts. I knew what MCPS was, PRS was, but that was it, I had to learn it all. The funny thing is, the fact that I knew hardly anything, but I knew *something*, got me off to a great start.

Because none of the independents had publishing. I think Mute's publishing
was a guy called Rob Buckle, who had a company called Sonic Music. He was
quite smart and he got involved with Daniel Miller right at the beginning
and signed Daniel's publishing and administration and looked after
Depeche Mode's publishing and everything else. But there was no-one else.
Rough Trade Publishing came along a few years later. So we got all kinds of
publishing deals in the early days because there was no competition. And I
wasn't necessarily pushing that hard because I was still a one-man company,
but I was picking up publishing when I could."

Also, in December 1979, McNay hit on the idea of an independent music
chart. There had been numerous informal attempts to document the growth
of independent music previously, including *Sounds* ad-hoc (and not always
regular) New Wave chart that began in 1977. But these tended to take their
findings from a single shop or outlet, as well as punk or new wave records
issued on major labels. McNay had contacts at *Record Business* magazine,
and the first independent chart was printed there in January 1980, compiled
by Barry Lazell. The premise was simple; that the records had to be
independently manufactured, distributed and marketed without recourse to
the machinery of the majors. That distinction ruled out the larger
independents, like A&M, Chrysalis, Island and Virgin, who by that time had
all accepted distribution support or more. The result was an oasis of
recognition for the likes of Rough Trade and Cherry Red, but also Factory,
Mute, Small Wonder, Postcard, Crass, and the innumerable one-off cottage
industry labels. There were advantages in providing a clear picture of success
at a lower-rung in the music industry. Labels were able to compare their
fortunes, while it also served as a useful publicity tool and serviced the
labels themselves by allowing foreign licensees to see what was hot in the
market. It also allowed record shops who might lack expertise an idea of
which records to stock.

Another of McNay's innovations was the licensing deal he signed with
Bristol's Heartbeat Records, run by Simon Edwards, in 1979. "That was
simply a practical thing. Simon had put the first single out by The
Europeans, and I financed the second one, by the Glaxo Babies, which he
didn't really have the money for." Indeed, this was one of the first P&D –
production and distribution deals – that would later become a feature of the
independent sector. "Iain McNay at that time seemed not too different to
me," reflects Edwards, "in that he was running the business from his home,
though his obvious pedigree from previous jobs within the industry put
him way ahead of anywhere I was. He certainly showed an interest in what

I was trying to create down in Bristol, and was suitably impressed by The Glaxo Babies and others as I waded through my pile of demos and ideas. What I needed was the financial backing to set the label up, to be able to take bands into the studio to record demos and singles, and to commission a graphics wizard for artwork for sleeves and promotional material, while I did all the co-ordination and general leaping about. Iain seemed sympathetic to my cause and offered me a production deal, whereby Cherry Red would finance my recording costs and manufacturing, then pay me a percentage on sales once the costs had been recouped. Manna from heaven for me at the time, as it gave me my freedom to pick and choose which bands I thought would work well within the label."

Cherry Red's own breakthrough success was another American signing, Dead Kennedys. 'California Uber Alles' was released in June 1979 on the band's own Alternative Tentacles label, and a tour of America's east coast was booked, but proved a disaster. "We lost our shirt on the flights," recalls guitarist East Bay Ray. "When I got back, Bob Last called me and said he wanted to put 'California' out on Fast Product in Edinburgh." The record was released to widespread acclaim among what was rapidly becoming a moribund UK punk scene.

"I was obviously aware of the band because they had 'California Uber Alles' out through Fast," recalls McNay, "and I really liked it. I hadn't thought beyond that. One day I got a call from a guy called Chris Gilbert. I'd had some dealings with him because he managed Andrew Matheson of the Hollywood Brats. 'My partner Bill Gilliam has just taken on the management of a band called Dead Kennedys. They're looking for someone to do an album, would you be interested?' I said I would. Chris invited me up for a meeting and introduced me to Bill. We got on fine, and he explained the band wanted $10,000 to do the album. I said I'm definitely interested and went off to think about it. I didn't have the $10,000 at that stage, because Cherry Red was in a formative period. We'd put out the Runaways album and that had done well for us, and a fair amount of singles and other albums. But we'd had nothing that had sold more than a few thousand. So I was wondering how I was going to get this $10,000, but I didn't tell Bill that. My only other reservation; I liked the name Dead Kennedys, because it was controversial, but I wondered whether that was going to block me too much for radio play or anything else. So I mused and then decided I was fine with the name and I'd get beyond that OK. I was having lunch one day with the Caroline buyer Richard Bishop, and chatting about my dilemma, that I had an opportunity with Dead Kennedys, but I didn't have the money to pay them what they wanted. Richard said, 'Maybe there's a deal where we give you the money, and you give us a good price on export, and a three-month exclusive, which means during that time you wouldn't sell to any other exporter.' I thought, that's not a bad idea. So we ended up doing the deal and Caroline gave me the $10,000 and I gave them this special price on export for three months, exclusive."

Not only was the album an immediate success, but the next single, 'Holiday In Cambodia', became one of the best-loved punk singles of all time. "I remember Iain saying that he had the opportunity to release the Dead Kennedys album," recalls Richard Jones, "and what did I think about that? And I hadn't heard 'Holiday In Cambodia' but I was familiar with 'California Uber Alles' on Fast. And without even hearing 'Holiday In Cambodia', I said, you *have* to do that, it's a no-brainer. Buying the album was a master stroke."

It was McNay's intention to have Dead Kennedys' cover of 'Viva Las Vegas' released as the follow-up. "I thought we could get daytime Radio 1 on that. Obviously, Peel had played 'Cambodia' and I think Mike Read played it as well. I thought it wouldn't be too difficult to extend it – we wouldn't have got the breakfast show, but we would have got late afternoon shows for 'Viva Las Vegas'. I was very keen on this and even scheduled it. Then Biafra said no, he didn't want to release it. I said fair enough, but we'd got partly down the line on that, and even organised a plugger to work on it. I thought we could have had a Top 40 hit with that track and broken the band to a whole different audience, but it wasn't to be."

Instead a remixed version of 'Kill The Poor' was released. "'Kill The Poor' was just yanked off the album and a different mix thrown on the single," Biafra affirms, "to derail Iain McNay's scheme to release 'Viva Las Vegas' as a novelty single, confine us to that and move on to another project. We said no, it's going to be 'Kill The Poor', and you're not putting 'In-Sight' out as a flexidisc, or yanking 'Viva Last Vegas' and putting it on as the b-side, whether you like it or not." Despite that, one of McNay's other ideas did work perfectly. "What we did for 'Kill The Poor' was a series of adverts in the music papers," says McNay. "Shortly before the single came out, there had been the annual Conservative Party conference. Thatcher was elected leader. I took a picture of their platform at the Conservative Party conference. I got our art director to change 'Conservative Party' to 'Kill The Poor'. So I ran a series of ads which had the Conservative Party shadow cabinet with 'Kill The Poor' above it, advertising the new single. I thought if the magazines and newspapers see the advert in advance, they won't let me run it. So I found out what their deadlines were and delivered it a few minutes before, so it would be hard to pull. We got it in all the magazines and weeklies. We did get taken to an advertising complaints tribunal. But all they said, three months later, was 'don't run that advert again', which of course we had no intention of doing."

It wasn't McNay's only Tory-baiting gesture. The release of 'The Compassion And Humanity Of Margaret Thatcher' is illustrative here. "What inspired us was that Stiff Records put out an album called *The Wit and Wisdom of Ronald Reagan* which was a blank album," McNay recalls. "And I thought it was a good idea but a waste of vinyl, because you couldn't do anything with it. So I had this idea of doing 'The Compassion and Humanity of Margaret Thatcher'. And what we did at the time was release a cassette and a videotape, and they were both blank, obviously. Because she didn't have any compassion or humanity, that was my feeling at the time. And in those days, a blank cassette or videotape was of some use, because obviously you could re-use them. And they both sold several hundred copies when they came out." The concept represents the essence of McNay to a tee. The idea may not have been wholly original, but it had legs, and it also underlines his stolid aversion to any kind of wasteful excess.

'Too Drunk To Fuck', the final single Dead Kennedys recorded for Cherry Red, was, of course, even more controversial. Bearers of the t-shirt with accompanying slogan were legendarily arrested in three continents. In fact, it's become something of an urban myth – scour any town in the UK and you will inevitably find some middle-aged punk claiming the honour. "It was the first Top 40 single with the word 'fuck' in it," says McNay. "The day it charted, they used to have the countdown on Radio 1 of the Top 40. I rang up the producer and said, 'why don't you play the b-side – that has no swear words?' I knew they wouldn't play the a-side. In the end all that happened, they said, 'at number 36 there's a record by a band calling themselves Dead Kennedys' – predictable but disappointing."

When McNay declined to further investigate the American (pre-hardcore) punk scene for fear of stereotyping the label, Biafra was vocal in his disappointment. He believes Cherry Red could have helped a clutch of truly great bands, whom he would eventually release through Alternative Tentacles, get records out. Asked about this now, McNay is philosophical. "Biafra is possibly completely correct. It's very hard to say." But his reasons for not taking that route – that he didn't want the label to become genre-specific – betray another motif that remains to this day. The label is in love with branding itself 'eclectic', often misapplying the adjective. Punk, for Biafra, was a way of life and intrinsic to his philosophy and worldview. McNay was a fan of punk, and grateful for the opportunities it afforded him, but not locked into its discourse to the same degree.

Dead Kennedys' immediate success masked some less notable endeavours. Neither Emotion Pictures nor Alan Burnham's records sold in any quantity, though the latter was interesting for being Daniel Miller's first non-Mute production. "I went for a meeting with Alan and Iain McNay and it was somewhere in West London," Miller recalls, "and my car broke down, and Iain had to come and pick me up. That was a pre-production meeting. It was either the first or second thing I'd produced that wasn't on Mute, and even then, I hadn't produced very much. I wasn't a record producer by any stretch of the imagination. I guess it was Iain's idea to bring me in. It was definitely an approach. It was before Depeche Mode, and I'd done some of my own stuff and started working with Fad Gadget, but I was extremely inexperienced as a producer, because that's really not what I was. Anyway, I remember doing it at Blackwing Studios, I'd been working there quite a lot at that time, with an engineer called Eric Radcliffe, who owned the studio, who I got on very well with and he ended up producing Yazoo and many other things. I can see the session quite clearly in my mind – I can see Alan crouched over his mellotron, trying to get it to work. I was trying to push it to be a bit more electro and less prog, but we got on fine and we agreed to differ. But as I said, I wasn't really a producer, so it was an interesting experience."

*Fresh Fruit*'s success meant the label now had a reasonable level of stability. Sitting in his apartment in Kingston Road, Wimbledon, McNay considered his options. "I had the opportunity, if I wanted, to expand the company. But to do so I would need more people, and to have more people, I needed to keep the income coming in. Theo Chalmers had been running the publishing one day a week without getting paid. I took him on as a full-time employee to carry on with the publishing, and partly to help me on the label side. Because we were selling more records there was a lot more work to do. I also wanted to get a proper A&R man in, as Richard Jones had long since stopped doing that. I was never going to be a proper A&R man. I didn't have the aptitude. Theo and I had a short list of people we'd both met, and we thought of Michael Alway at that point." McNay had been taking regular calls from the young promoter from West London, involved with a band called Scissor Fits. He would present them to McNay as the next Beatles; though it's doubtful that the Beatles would ever have recorded a song called 'I Don't Want To Work For British Airways No More'. McNay didn't share his enthusiasm for the band, but he did take on Alway. "He had the drive and enthusiasm. He ran a venue called Snoopy's in Richmond, which was in the basement of a hotel there. He knew the scene well and people seemed to like it, so we offered him the A&R job which he was happy to accept." Alway took a £50 a week commission and all but moved into the Cherry Red offices in Bayswater – he was between girlfriends, whose houses he generally made his residence, and set about reshaping the label's future.

The Cherry Red roster at that point did not look auspicious. Despite successful licensed American releases (Runaways, Destroy All Monsters), Dead Kennedys apart, their 'new' artists had failed to deliver. Alway had a vision in mind. But while he set about establishing it, he would work with what was available. The first example being 'Hungry, So Angry' by Medium Medium. Occupying similar territory to the Pop Group, Gang Of Four, etc, operating out of Nottingham meant Medium Medium never quite registered on the post-punk radar to the same extent as those peers. Yet their 'extreme dance music' shared similar roots and produced one *bona fide* era classic, 'Hungry, So Angry'. They made their debut in 1979 with 'Them Or Me' on the London independent Apt Records, a song which later transferred to the hip (not least with John Peel) regional compilation *Hicks From The Sticks*.

"I still don't understand why Mike Alway wanted to sign us," says the band's Andy Ryder. "But at that point, I think Cherry Red were still looking to find out which direction they were going in." That's probably true. For McNay's part, he believes Alway sees Medium Medium as "something he wouldn't have signed if things had been different. Having said that, Medium Medium has had definite legs over the years, and when it came out, I thought it was good, and the single did OK." Alway concurs. "The Medium Medium thing was a different type of contractual situation. I did not discourage the situation, but I did not bring Medium Medium to the label. Chris Garland [then the band's manager] approached Iain, and Iain may have asked my opinion, and I wasn't in any way against it. It seemed to me that they were worthwhile – it was something we could do immediately and it seemed the right thing to do in order to be a bit of an antidote to some of what had preceded it. But I didn't have anything like the emotional investment in Medium Medium that I did in Eyeless In Gaza or Five Or Six. Medium Medium was not my initiative, but they had my support."

The 'Mike Alway era' started in earnest with CHERRY 19, Five Or Six's debut release, 'Another Reason' c/w 'The Trial'. "They were the outstanding character group of the scene that I was running in Richmond," Alway says, "which in those days involved a great many local groups of a considerable standard. It's unthinkable now, but then we were running clubs and putting on shows five nights a week, three bands a night, and Five Or Six were one of those groups. I was always aware that they had a certain amount of local bias. I think if Five Or Six had been a demo tape that arrived in the post from somewhere else, I don't know if I'd have carried the flag in that way."

It wasn't just about the music with Five Or Six, but also "the type of people" they were. "They were very much on my wavelength," Alway continues. "They were very enquiring and very interested, very positive people. They had a great attitude – they were a little bit Wire, a bit Vic Godard, a bit Monochrome Set at their strangest. I think their role was to be obtuse. I think Five Or Six were our This Heat. They used to bash about – they weren't good enough musicians at that time, in a way, to make the type of records that Ben and Tracey were about to make, or certainly that the Monochrome Set could make. But they had a good attitude and a role to play in the machine of it all. They were very much an inspiration, very good people to work with. I was able to bounce some of the things I was doing on the label off them, and I knew I would always get critical and honest reactions. They weren't in any way fawning. After Five Or Six they all went on to do something within the entertainment industry. One of them managed Goldfrapp, one of them is the international manager of 4AD Records. One, John Yorke, became head of drama at the BBC. They had a much more eclectic spread of sensibilities than any normal group would have, that's what set them apart for me. As with so many things, they were moving a little bit fast for the public possibly. It was as much as they could possibly do with the very limited resources that a very young Cherry Red could provide. They had very little to work with, as did all the groups at that time."

The liaison with 2nd Layer – essentially Adrian Borland and Graham Bailey of The Sound – grew out of the label's friendship with Borland. "I first met Adrian probably around 1979, when the first Outsiders album [his original band] came out," recalls McNay. "He'd formed his own label with his father, and they were, in a way, also trying to make it as an independent label in the early days. I loved The Sound, and was very happy to put out 2nd Layer on Cherry Red. Adrian and I both supported Wimbledon FC. I used to see him now and again on the terraces there." "We considered The Sound was work, and 2nd Layer was fun," remembers Graham Bailey. "That sounds ridiculous, because The Sound was fun too, but it was something where we could really let ourselves go. It didn't matter what anyone thought or what was said or anything else, it was a censorship-free us." Alway remembers that "The

Sound at the time were looking to get a contract with a much bigger label and ended up with Warners, We had become friends with Adrian, and he was someone that we all liked. And he liked us as well. But because he knew Cherry Red was the wrong context for The Sound, he signed with Warners/Korova. So he created 2nd Layer as a side project, as something for us to have."

Another release, this time a retrospective one, came from a referral by Richard Jones, in the form of 60s psychedelic mavericks The Misunderstood. "I'd heard them on the John Peel show [Peel managed the band for a time and was a fierce advocate] and he used to play both 'Children Of The Sun', and in particular 'I Can Take You To The Sun'," Jones remembers. "It was obviously something he really liked – you could just tell when he was introducing it. It felt special at the time and even now I think both songs stand up well, and that caught my attention. Many years after that, I was talking to Iain, and he was saying, there must be some older things worth releasing. I said, you ought to seriously consider this. And all I did was give him the name and title of the record – out of which he managed to find it and negotiate its re-release. He brought out [Misunderstood compilation] *Before The Dream Faded*, which had those two tracks on it, and also released it as a single."

Other oddities of this nature included a Marc Bolan album. "Michael was trying to trace the rights to the John's Children records we later put out," McNay recalls. "He tracked down Simon Napier-Bell, whom he got on well with. Simon offered us the Marc Bolan album, which was basically old tracks that had been re-done with contemporary musicians. The album charted in the Top 100, the single went in the Top 75 and we sold quite a few albums." The tracks had been recorded by Napier-Bell on the first evening he'd met Bolan. "Later, when he died, I decided to dig them out and re-record them as I thought he might have recorded them at that time," Napier-Bell recalls. "It was very difficult because they were just him and an acoustic and the tempos were wildly out. But I edited the tapes as far into tempo as I could, then got Clem Cattini – for me, always the very best session drummer – to come in and play to them. He was brilliant at upping and downing the tempo with Marc's original guitar and vocal. I then dubbed on a bass guitar and the other instruments, instrument by instrument, until we had what was the finished album I gave to Iain."

The meeting with Simon Napier-Bell was 'fascinating', Alway recalls. "Simon attempted at that meeting to sell me a record called 'I Like Boys' by Quentin

Crisp, which I foolishly didn't licence from him. So I came back with the Bolan album, and there was definitely a sense of cobbling together some sort of album from bits and pieces and giving them to us, but what the hell. Iain seemed happy to accept that and plough on. I think Iain's position was, 'Mike, I know this is not ideally what you would want to do at the label at this point, but we've got to pay the wages.' That was certainly his mantra when we did [hugely successful punk compilation] *Burning Ambitions*. And he even came in to me and apologised and said, 'look, I know you'll think it's shit, but we've got to do it, and I said, 'all right'."

The deal was done. "We were both at Kensington Garden Square at the time." Alway adds. "Memorably, there was a studio downstairs run by the guy who worked with Abba, Marcus Osterdahl. We were upstairs at the top of the building in the Cherry Red office. I remember Simon Napier-Bell threw a party in Marcus Studios one winter afternoon. They phoned Iain and said, 'look, we've got a party going on down here, get your arse down here.' And Iain told him to go fuck himself – we were all upstairs working hard on his behalf, and we weren't going to make an appearance at the party. It was a mid-air collision between the old ideas and the new wave ideas. Iain will probably remember that. But Iain did get on pretty well with Simon; there was a recognition that they were fundamentally different people, but there were ways in which they could help each other."

There was also a deal with Adrian Sherwood's Creation Rebel that Alway had misgivings about. "I don't know anything about that type of music," he says, "it's not my field. I don't understand it. I liked Adrian and we could get on, but we had no real common ground there. He brought Mark Stewart [ex-Pop Group] into the office and I was pleased to meet him, and I could have worked with Mark Stewart, but Adrian was the definitive producer – it was all Adrian. We ended up at the studio at somewhere like Basing Street. It was very late at night, and he had a room full of Rastas, and they were all smoking, and the volume of the music was – a runway at Heathrow. The music was incredible, and he was a fantastic technician – a remarkable individual, a real one-off was Adrian, but I just had no empathy with his music whatsoever."

The Sherwood connection came about via an unlikely source. At the time, Alway was trying to court The Fall. "Mark E Smith was a friend of Adrian's," McNay recalls. "I remember spending a couple of evenings in Adrian's flat off the Finchley Road with Mark and Adrian. I understood that Adrian's work wasn't necessarily something that Mike was personally enamoured of, but I thought what Adrian was doing was very interesting, and I'd really liked the first New Age Steppers album that came out. We worked out a deal whereby I pretty much left the creative side entirely up to Adrian, and he delivered finished albums and artwork." Like *Burning Ambitions*, it was hardly Alway's cup of tea. "Not at all. But I had to accept it because we were building the company up, and Iain was entitled to do these things. I completely accepted that situation – especially because Iain was honest and aware of it. He would say, really, this doesn't fit with what we're doing, but... But it didn't work. It's not without artistic merit, it's just a different world. But I didn't find it an impediment. I didn't think like that at the time. Mainly because Iain wasn't heavy with me about it, and because Adrian Sherwood was so likeable."

These releases aside, Alway began to shape the roster by bringing aboard a series of artists – Ben Watt and Tracey Thorn, Eyeless In Gaza, Felt, The Passage and ultimately his adored Monochrome Set – that would establish the label's marque. Not, however, that he wanted a heavily stylised 'sound'. One of Alway's inspirations was Verve Records. "Not in the Jazz period, but in the mid-60s, when they had the Righteous Brothers, the Mothers Of Invention, the Velvet Underground, Astrid Gilberto and Ella Fitzgerald. It seemed to me that if a record label can have all of that disparate artistry, and make it work classily, they have something going for them. That's what I wanted Cherry Red to be, I wanted Cherry Red to be the Verve of that generation. Although I knew there was a sound by which Cherry was likely to make it, which is the one most closely connected to the sound we all know and love, I wasn't certain of that at the time. I have to say that I was also feeling that I wanted the label to be eclectic in the truest sense. Labels at the time always had the same sound. By and large Factory had the same sound, Durutti Column apart, 4AD, etc."

A handful of contemporary post-punk records that reflected Alway's tastes are also pivotal. "The records that had the influence on me to go in a 'light' music direction that ran contrary to the way things were going? They were 'Ambition' by Vic Godard, the first Durutti Column album on Factory and the Young Marble Giants album on Rough Trade. All those things said to me that 'light' music has a place in this revolution." The roster was built on this predisposition to aesthetic beauty, in an almost neo–classicist vein. "Very much so," Alway admits. "I saw a role, a place for Cherry Red. What I liked about the fact that it was 'light' music was that I knew it would have an international market. Whatever the blasting impact of punk rock, it was never going to translate in terms of overseas and the mainstream. One always realised that punk rock would be the immediate impact, then a couple of aftershocks, but it wouldn't last forever. It would always be replaced by more sophisticated music."

Among his first recruits to that end were synthesizer duo Eyeless In Gaza. "Their tape – it wasn't a demo, it was a cassette of a master tape – was in the post on the first morning that I worked at Cherry Red," Alway recalls. "I'm grateful to them because I was able to work my way into Iain's back room of his house in Wimbledon in those days, and offer him something well worth getting involved in, almost from the minute I walked in his door. Eyeless In Gaza was more connected to the idea of the Scott Walker thing, of a very highly distinctive vocal sound. You could argue that Martyn Bates certainly had a very 'love it or hate it' type of vocal. That type of thing is usually a major plus when you're looking for groups with what I would call character. Eyeless In Gaza were completely in your face, and a really challenging sound – very fresh, and very vital and very bold. I didn't know how long this privilege was going to last and I had to get some quality on to the label quickly. It had to be something that would stand out – and they certainly offered that."

"We sent out tapes of our first album," recalls Eyeless In Gaza's Martyn Bates, "and from the first batch of, I think, five tapes sent out, we had two offers for deals – with 4AD and with Cherry Red. For us, there was absolutely no point in our choosing music as a means of expression if we were being 'advised' by anyone. Back then, Cherry Red were entirely happy for us to do exactly what we wanted to do. So, after an initial meeting, we chose to work with them." It was initially a successful relationship, though some of the mutual enthusiasm petered out. "My feeling back then was that Cherry Red were trying to 'run' too quickly, to move faster than they were actually able," Bates recalls. "From nowhere, it seemed to me then, a sudden pressure was on us to 'break through'; make short pop singles; to 'up' production values and re-record stuff, etc. This at a time when people would continually tell us that they couldn't get our records in the shops. In Europe we'd be playing packed clubs and halls where often there would be another 200 to 300 souls outside who couldn't get in. Then people would still tell us – guess what? – we can't find your records in the shops. Admittedly, it was a turbulent time of exponential growth and change for everyone involved with the job of selling independent music. I just remember resenting the 'outside interference' – after all, we signed with Cherry Red and NOT to 4AD precisely because we'd have the total artistic freedom and control that we wanted and required. The feeling from us was, if we are going to be told what to do, then we might as well pack it in and make baked beans instead, not art."

"I think Eyeless should have stayed closer to the pop side and got the balance a bit better," Alway suggests, with hindsight. "I was not guilty of allowing Eyeless In Gaza to indulge themselves. On the contrary, my attitude to them became more professional. I would say to them, you've got to do 'that' to qualify 'this'. Martyn is a very good person, somebody that brought a tremendous amount of knowledge to the label – he really knew a lot about modern music, he was ahead of most people in that respect. And he had tremendous enthusiasm for different things. You would think to yourself, this person can only go on to do good things, really."

Ben Watt was, like Five Or Six, signed on the basis of local knowledge. "He was also to do with the clubs we were running in Richmond," says Alway. "He knew Five Or Six. He was a friend who was making music that had something of Vinni Reilly [Durutti Column], and a bit of Nick Drake, certainly. I played him things like Can and Quicksilver Messenger Service, and he seemed to appreciate those sorts of things. He just fitted into where we were going, really. I remember Iain did not want to sign him at the beginning, and he was quite right, because he saw a folk singer, basically. There was nobody like that in the scene at all at the time. But somehow the initial single 'Cant' got made. There was no great reaction, though it was a nicely crafted record. But we were able to resolve all the problems by pairing him with Tracey [Thorn], really."

"Ben came from a jazz background," recalls Alway. "His father was a bandleader and very successful. His mother was a writer; a very middle-class background. Ben was better equipped to deal with everything. He'd been to St Paul's, a private school. He was very smart and very determined. I don't know how far he could have gone as a solo artist. I think he could have made artistically significant records, and possibly even sold well, but we were always thinking about John Martyn at that time. That's what I saw in him in the beginning – more John Martyn than Nick Drake. I didn't really see a folk person, I saw something modern, with that element of 'strangeness' that John Martyn had, and, to some extent, that Robert Wyatt had."

Indeed, for his second single, the 'Summer Into Winter' EP, Watt worked with Soft Machine legend Wyatt. "Robert lived here in Twickenham," Alway continues. "We attempted to contact him, just before the Tracey thing had started really – somebody for Ben to collaborate with on the second single. Ben picked up the phone one day, called him and went round there. They got to a studio in Kensington, and Robert contributed to the record. It gives it a certain richness; the voices work very well together. It was part of the learning curve, to use a hideous phrase, so it was useful for Ben at that time. For us, it was one step at a time as far as Iain was concerned, but at least we were making records now with Ben, and moving forward." "Of course I remember working with Ben," Wyatt told me in 2007. "'Walter And John' was my first gay love song! It was sweet. I was really honoured to be trusted to do that properly, I really liked it. I think Ben Watt just got in touch with me and phoned me up, sent me a cassette or something."

As Alway suggests, the label would eventually get the best out of Watt by pairing him with Tracey Thorn, at that time signed to the label as part of The Marine Girls. John Acock, Cherry Red's first producer, recalls an evening spent in Iain McNay's company. "If we could turn the clock back! I came back to Iain's place and he said he had some tapes sent in, just before Mike Alway joined. One of them was The Marine Girls and Tracey Thorn. Iain said, 'Listen to this, see what you think'. And her voice then wasn't bad and The Marine Girls had something, but I didn't recognise she was going to be the voice of the 80s, so I passed on it!"

The Marine Girls were formed in 1980 in Hatfield, Hertfordshire, by school-friends Thorn and Gina Hartman; eventually joined by sisters Jane and Alice Fox. "Like lots of bands made up of school friends, in The Marine Girls we had somewhat diverse tastes," Thorn recalls. "Jane was always quite interested in jazz, while Alice used to traipse around after Spear of Destiny. But we all converged with the Young Marble Giants, and they were something of a touchstone for us. It would take another 20 years or so for the Kings of Convenience to spell it out, but it was that 'quiet is the new loud' kind of belief. Then, when I met Ben, we had two records in common – the Vic Godard album *What's The Matter Boy* and *Return of the Durutti Column*. Our motto became that line taken from the b-side of [Subway Sect's] 'Ambition', which goes: 'We oppose all rock n roll'. Mike Alway, I think, really understood that stance, and that it was coming from somewhere progressive, not reactionary."

"I don't remember The Marine Girls being all that central," Alway recalls. "It was something we were just cultivating. That's not to say we didn't have the attention on it, but it was moving at its own pace. And then Tracey's [solo] album came along and suddenly that changed everything. I thought The Marine Girls was OK, it certainly had its moments of originality and poetry and beauty, but I think to some extent we did see what was there with Tracey, and we were beginning to think in that direction. The Marine Girls was always a question of catching it, really. Live, they were incredibly charming. That was where they were really good, if they were live and jangling around and bashing about on charming songs, it was fantastic. They didn't know what they were doing and they didn't care, it was all very artless and natural. That's a very precious thing. You have a lot of responsibility, you're doing something that is very gentle, and I wasn't about to destroy it, but Tracey ended it herself by going to Hull University. That dictated the way the things were going to be."

"Our gigs were certainly fairly shambolic," Thorn confirms. "We *were* totally artless, but not without attitude. It took a certain amount of guts to get up at gigs and be quiet and un-show-offy. Alice was fantastically confrontational though, and would invite anyone out for a fight if she thought they were being disrespectful. It's not quite true that it ended when I went up to Hull. I went there in 1981, and the second Marine Girls album *Lazy Ways* was made in 1983. The trouble really was that by then I had met Ben, and formed Everything But The Girl, and also made a solo record. I was being torn in different directions. And realising I wanted to be the lead singer, which I just wasn't in The Marine Girls."

"At some point they all came to the office," Alway recalls. "I remember saying to Tracey, you should meet Ben Watt. I don't know why I said that, I think it was because I was aware I had played him her voice, and it appealed to him strongly. And she said, 'I'm not going to... blah blah blah'. She was just a kid, and it was all said in good humour. But it was just a complete coincidence that there were these parallel careers, both on Cherry Red Records. The remarkable coincidence was that they both ended up, quite separately, attending Hull University. They didn't know each other at the time. And Ben became aware of the fact that she was there, and put a message out for the two of them to meet." "I think Mike played me Ben's first single, 'Cant'," Thorn confirms, "but I didn't get it at all – it's a bit avant-garde-folky. I would surely love it now, but in those days I was narrow-minded in the way of most 19-year-olds. It *was* a coincidence us both going to Hull, I wanted to go to East Anglia but failed my interview."

"They took the name Everything But The Girl from a furniture shop in Hull," Alway continues. "And the first single was done as a sideline. It was still The Marine Girls, or, by then, Tracey Thorn's solo album, and Ben's solo album. It just ran in parallel really. Tracey's solo album wasn't meant to bring an end to The Marine Girls by any means. It was there to complement The Marine Girls. We couldn't make The Marine Girls into something other than what they were. What they were was fabulous, but they were at a certain technical level. Tracey, we could see, without it being rocket science, could go somewhere else. Because of the voice, but also because of the *willingness* to go somewhere else. She may have come from Hatfield and been very young, but she wanted to go forward. So when that was set up it wasn't to replace The Marine Girls in any shape or form. But she was in Hull with Ben, she could more easily work with Ben than with The Marine Girls back in Hatfield. So anyway, they made 'Night And Day' as a bit of fun on the side, and we were doing it to see what would happen. But I did think the two voices together might create something special."

The satisfying 'fit' between the two voices was just as much of a revelation to Thorn. "It was a complete surprise. I had Ben pegged as a bit of an oddball. I think it was true, and still is to a degree, that he was more naturally experimental than me, very forward-looking always. But at the same time, he has always respected my more poppy sensibility. That was what made the collaboration interesting for both of us."

Another cornerstone act of the house that Alway built were Birmingham art mavericks Felt, led by the inimitable Lawrence [Hayward]. "Felt I knew about because I'd read about them," Alway says. "I made a call, and Lawrence sent me some music to listen to. I'd read about them in the music press. It was very early on. It was probably the review of [debut single] 'Index', which likened them to Manuel from Fawlty Towers. I thought, I've got to hear this. And it [a review written by Alway's later collaborator Dave McCullough] seriously did liken Lawrence's guitar sound to Manuel and it was single of the week. It was great really, because you could procure that record and hear the madness of that record, and see the potential in it for you, in full knowledge that no other label would touch it with a barge pole. It's interesting that what Felt actually played me was quite different to 'Index'. 'Index' is a barrage of de-tuned and atonal guitars. What they eventually gave me was much more musical. It related, but it was quite different. Lawrence had quite cleverly built around Maurice Deebank's melodic ability as a guitarist. He was almost a Spanish guitarist, Maurice. Felt we also saw live a couple of times, and they were *hopeless*. They just couldn't sing, they couldn't start, they were embarrassed, they had red faces."

Alway had invited McNay along to one gig, and instantly regretted it. "I'll tell you the honest truth. We went to see them at the King's Head in Acton. And they started their set, and I think I got two numbers in and thought, they are just *so weak*. Iain is going to get me in the morning and say, 'what the fuck do you think you're doing?' Funnily enough, he knew –

intelligently – that the live context wasn't really their world. And what magic needed to occur, was going to occur in the studio. And that's all that really mattered. A lot of people have made great records and been hopeless live. I felt for Lawrence, because he was such a perfectionist even then, and he didn't have the technical ability or the equipment, all those frustrations really. They were charming kids, they turned up all dressed in the right shirts, straight off the train from Birmingham. They were very, very young at the time, and Lawrence was an idealist from a provincial background who was intelligent, definitely a poet, and a vulnerable person. He didn't have any business sophistication. I think what's undone Lawrence through the years is the fact that he's never been prepared to entrust someone with those responsibilities. That's your death warrant, really. It's quite a tough world, there are lots of wounds in it, and you need the right representation, you can't live in a vacuum."

It is significant that Felt, like so many artists on the label, had been picked up after they'd self-released their debut record. The fact that Cherry Red nurtured or schooled talent more often than making the initial discovery reflects two things. First, it was indicative of Alway's ambition to get 'quality' on the label as soon as possible to gain and preserve momentum. But it was also, in part, a result of McNay's cautious business approach. Unlike other heads of independent labels, he was never one to bet the farm on a favoured son or daughter, preferring to spread liabilities and mitigate potential losses. Another artist who had demonstrated the ambition and capacity to release his own record was Thomas Leer, one of the architects of the electronic revolution of the late 70s, when a cluster of artists on independent labels augmented the DIY rhetoric of punk with newly affordable synthesizers.

Leer's association with Cherry Red produced a rich, but ultimately brief catalogue; 1981's '4 Movements' 12-inch EP, 1982's double 12-inch 'album' *Contradictions*, and the 1982 single 'All About You' (which later graced Cherry Red's state of the nation address *Pillows & Prayers*). It's a body of work that traces Leer's love not only of Krautrock and the avant garde, but also soul music and Frank Zappa. The results were critically acclaimed – both '4 Movements' and 'All About You' were, like debut single 'Private Plane' before them, accorded single of the week status. Yet Leer's objectives were defiantly non-commercial and less exhibitionist. "After my first single, I wanted to free myself up from the actual mechanical process of putting a record out," says Leer, "so the obvious thing was to look for a label I could work with. Cherry Red just happened to be the friendliest bunch I came across with a real enthusiasm for the music. A good mix of people, too. Sort of eccentric and level headed at the same time."

"When The Passage and Thomas Leer were signed," Alway states, "I was at the stage of wanting to see what would happen with a lot of different sounds. I didn't think Thomas Leer owed anything to any particular label. I wanted there to be a different type of connection and a spread of things. I always say that Dick Witts [The Passage] and Thomas Leer would say that they felt outside of the discourse of the label's evolution. But that was partly geographical. Thomas only lived in South London, but we were never quite able to establish the same empathy. I went over to see him pretty often and he was always very friendly. [But] I think Thomas wanted to be on a major record label being very successful, and he certainly had the ability to do it. There were people like Paul Morley writing very positive things about Thomas in the press, giving him itchy feet. He was entitled to those comments, he deserved them, and the inevitable happened when he joined ZTT. You get that stuff in the press, and you suddenly find people saying 'We haven't got enough money to record with'. Then it starts to become a different sort of relationship, less of a pleasure."

The aforementioned Passage formed out the Manchester Musician's Collective in March 1978, led by Dick Witts, a presenter on Granada TV and former percussionist with the Hallée Orchestra. With numerous line-up changes but retaining Witts as the key artistic contributor, they recorded two EPs and a debut album, *Pindrop*, for Object Music, but disputes with the label led to its deletion shortly after release. From there they hooked up with Virgin/DinDisc to distribute their own label Night & Day. By the time they came to Cherry Red they were reduced to a duo of Witts and guitarist Andy Wilson.

"I remember we had a show at Raymond's Revue Bar with The Passage before we signed them," says Alway. "I remember Iain coming out of there absolutely thrilled. It was only about half full, but they were absolutely on stonking form." Yet the problems in their association mounted quickly. "I was unable to get the press to react to them quite as willingly as I was with The Monochrome Set. I don't know why. It was partly, I think, because they were a Manchester band. I think Dick would have been disappointed at the amount of press reaction. I can't say exactly why it happened, but it was just cooler. The Passage had already had a hit with *Pindrop*. They were not to be *discovered* again. If the record we'd made with The Passage had been their first album, I think we'd have had a better reaction. The history; the fact that they were from Manchester, that they had an attitude – things were already logged long before Cherry Red came on the scene. It may have counted against them to some degree. But I still think they were an outstanding band – musically, very good. And Dick was a much better vocalist than people would give him credit for. It just didn't quite fit in – lots of things were right about it, but it only took one thing to be wrong for it not to work. It was just a shame. They were just probably on the wrong label. I think Dick really felt that he wanted more prominence; he was probably entitled to it. Dick had a very good album and wanted to get it out on an enthusiastic label. They came to us because we were enthusiastic. We were, and we did make progress for them, there's no doubt, but they couldn't kick on to the next stage."

"I think it was more the case that we came to them because we wanted to record more work and Cherry Red allowed us to do so after we left Virgin," maintains Witts. "In fact, Cherry Red had a rather sexist image then, which we didn't hold with – the very name, the logo at that time of the woman, and so forth. I do remember, though, that Iain McNay did take notice of criticisms and made changes. That would have impressed us more than the age of the people there. We were politically driven, and our failure, perhaps, mirrors the failure at that time of the left. I recall we were touring the USA and the promoter had fucked up on dates and our manager wired to Cherry Red for support money, which was declined. That kind of thing rankled."

The Nightingales were another staple of the Mike Alway era, and represented the most obvious link to contemporaneous post-punk; they have often been called the Black Country Fall and Alway admits that, had circumstances permitted, he would certainly have signed Mark E Smith to the label. They were abrasive and corrosive in comparison to many of the other bands Alway would champion, but no less literate. "It was Mike who originally approached us about the possibility of signing The Nightingales," recalls singer and lyricist, Rob Lloyd, "and we met up. He came to Brum to watch us play, and we just talked about the whole thing. I really liked him. He was good to work with. I can't pretend that I particularly enjoyed all the other acts on Cherry Red – my musical taste is a little different to the things that he just loved, like The Monochrome Set. He *loved* them. I just don't get them at all. But when I was dealing with him, it didn't bother me that we had different musical tastes, I just liked the idea that he thought about things. He was one of the better people I've come across in my years making records. He really knew his stuff."

Indeed, the one band to fit Alway's template for Cherry Red most snugly were The Monochrome Set, whose early singles for Rough Trade had led to an unhappy berth at Virgin. "Those initial records [on Rough Trade] are so startlingly original in their vernacular, the use of language, and the sensuousness and the quality of the phrasing of the vocal, is so magnificent," eulogises Alway. "I thought, this guy Bid, this is pop's Mel Tormé; almost Sinatra, in a curious way. The Monochrome Set were going to be enormous. I thought Bid was in a different class completely. He had absolutely everything – the intelligence, the looks, the attitude, the humour, he had the right background. He was tough and able to be charming. He had everything going for him completely. And he produced those absolutely astonishing records. What I did become aware of was that the two albums they made for Virgin, The Monochrome Set may have had a problem with their attitude. It was to do with their humour, it wasn't because they had a poor attitude. They're very nice and decent people. But you could see how people *might* be intimidated by them. A record company executive at Virgin would be intimidated at how clever – in a whimsical way – Bid and Andy Warren were. Andy Warren has a very, very particular sense of humour that it's easy to get pissed off with. He tried winding Iain up on no end of occasions. He would get up to all sorts. But they were, for me, a composite of everything that my musical history amounted to. They were twangy, poppy, film soundtracks and psychedelia – it was a bit of everything in just about the right proportions."

When Virgin dropped the band, The Monochrome Set were without a deal, and minus a drummer, as JD Haney moved to America to become an academic. Lexington Crane was recruited in his stead. "'Jet Set Junta' was a demo we did for Do-It Records [the Ants' original label], and we used that demo to get the Cherry Red deal," states Bid. "I don't know really why Do-It didn't take it up. The story that you may have read is that Andy and I sat down with an A-Z of independent record labels, and by the time we got to C-H we got a deal. That's actually true. We skipped out a few people, obviously. And yes, the next page was Cunt Records. It just so happened that Mike was already a fan." He certainly was. "One day I got a phone call from Andy Warren out of the blue," he recalls. "He said, 'I'm Andy Warren from The Monochrome Set, would you be interested in hearing this demo?' I said, 'Bring it in. If it's anything like as good as what you've done, we'll work with you.'"

Alway has gone so far as to say that he modelled the whole ethic of [his subsequent label] él Records on the band. "It's not *completely* true," Bid affirms. "He sort of modelled the Monochrome Set slightly too. The Monochrome Set were the closest to what he thought his ideal band was. It wasn't that he thought his ideal band *was* The Monochrome Set. [We] weren't exactly like that. I think the Monochrome Set fulfilled one of his ideals. We certainly influenced each other. Mike influenced us as well. But it wasn't quite as definite as that."

The Monochrome Set's association with Cherry Red was announced with the release of the hilarious 'The Mating Game'. While the subject matter pulled no punches on the joys of animal mechanics, it was conveyed with Bid's own brand of spectacularly detached nonchalance. "What a bizarre thing to release as a single!" Bid acknowledges. "It got reviewed in *Smash Hits*, which I still have, with a picture of this 13-year-old grinning at the camera having done a review – which is just, 'Well, I like it, but it's *dirty*'." But it was also wonderfully clever; as filthy as a rugby song, but *politely* so. That said, it was never going to get any airplay. Did anyone ever question its release? Bid can't remember. "They left us to it because that was the way it was run. We didn't take singles seriously at all. We never thought any of our singles were going to sell or get airplay. So we always felt it was a real irritation that a record company would ask us – 'What will you put on the b-side?' We'd say, 'B-side of what?' That was our attitude. It was only [later] with Warners that changed, and even when we did the album with Cherry Red, we didn't think there was any point in putting out any of those singles at all. We're not like that, we're not a singles band."

Alway's notoriety, meanwhile, had spread. Urbane and articulate, he had a charisma that drew many into his circle. One of those was future Creation Records head Alan McGee, who spotted him at an Eyeless In Gaza show at the Moonlight in 1981 and immediately realised that he was the 'most likely to' figure in the nascent independent music story. Combining both the label's A&R and press functions, Alway pushed as well as stuffed envelopes, often spurred on by Andy Warren and Bid. Press releases became less items of advertorial as exercises in the surreal. One priceless example included the assertion that Bid had been approached by Indian cricket hero Sunil Gavaskar – for advice on preparing a wicket in Bangalore.

Alway's tenure at the label reached its apotheosis with the budget compilation album, *Pillows & Prayers*. "Mike was usually an early starter, and was always full of bright new ideas on Monday mornings," McNay recalls. "'Iain, I've got to talk to you,' he insisted as I walked into the office one beautiful autumn day in 1982. 'I've got a great idea. I think we should put out a compilation album of all the acts we are currently working on. That's Ben, Tracey, The Monochrome Set, Eyeless, Felt and all the others. It'll be a really good album. But Iain, it MUST sell for less than £1. I'd like to make it 99p.' Mike had a habit of doing this first thing in the morning. The following morning Mike had a title, and an image for the sleeve. *Pillows & Prayers* was born and the young girl blowing the bubble was to become quite famous. Mike had found the picture in an old encyclopaedia that had been given to him by his grandparents, so she was almost certainly not around to enjoy her fame. The name *Pillows & Prayers* had come from an old Victorian children's book he had found in a junk shop." The album was released a few weeks later, on 25 December 1982. McNay: "What better day to release it than Christmas Day? We pressed up 10,000 to start with, little knowing that within a year it would sell 120,000 copies. It entered the independent album chart at number one, and stayed in the independent Top 30 chart for nearly a year. We had great reviews everywhere, and the compilation really did help to make people much more aware of the other acts on the label. In particular, Everything But The Girl, Felt and The Monochrome Set received a big boost to their profiles."

But Cherry Red's moment in the sun at the vanguard of the independent movement was not to last. And *Pillows & Prayers* was partly to blame. Relationships changed, as artists queried why their new press profile had not resulted in greater promotional support and increased recording budgets. There were also money issues. McNay paid Alway's rent and bills as well as providing an expense account. But there was frustration at the limited recompense he was otherwise receiving. Arguments became more frequent as Alway increasingly found himself the buttress between artist and label. McNay, for his part, considered *himself* a buffer between Alway and the financial responsibilities and logistics of running a business. "Mike had set things up that way," he says. "He wanted to deal directly with the artists, and be the front person for the creative side of Cherry Red. That was fine. Where something needs support, I'm there – and that was the case at the time. But he was the buttress because he chose to be."

Alway began to envisage a second label, a feeder mechanism between Cherry Red and the majors, licensed by the latter, where acts who had achieved a certain degree of prominence could be, effectively, promoted; thus to enjoy all the concomitant delights of major label backing and distribution. Cherry Red's independence, meanwhile, would be safeguarded – at least as far as Alway was concerned. It was an idea that fell on stony ground. "I think he may actually have said 'over my dead body,'" Alway recalls. McNay's insistence on independence had become a defining mantra. While he relished the role of 'outsider', he had also become one of the fiercest advocates of the benefits of collaboration within the emerging independent sector. In both 1982 and 1983 he stood for election to the British Phonographic Industry on a platform of widescale reform. On the second occasion he was successful, encouraging other independents to join the board of the BPI as part of his campaign. It was the first of a series of commitments to the independent ideal he has maintained to this day, helping to develop trade organisations that deliver a level playing field. At the time Alway approached him about the possibility of linking with a major, he was intractably welded to the ethos of independence.

So Alway was greeted with an emphatic refusal, and the chain of events that would lead to the end of his A&R watch at Cherry Red was set in motion. There were other factors at play. McNay had long since developed an interest in meditation and spirituality, to the extent that they'd become passions equivalent to Alway's devotional immersion in music. Prompted by the interest shown by old friend Morgan Fisher in the teachings of Bhagwan Shree Rajneesh, in the summer of 1983 he visited the Oregon ranch the guru had made his base. "I was away for a couple of weeks at the New Music Seminar," McNay recalls. "I was meant to go to San Francisco, but I thought I'd visit Morgan in Oregon to see how he was getting on. So I changed my flight and went to Oregon, spent ten days there, and then came back as planned." Later he would eventually convert to the cause, becoming a *sannyasin* and taking the new name Aukash.

In the interim, however, he would have to deal with Alway's resignation, who had decided to set up his 'second tier' label, Blanco y Negro, with Geoff Travis, under the supervision of Rob Dickins at Warners. And he was taking Everything But The Girl, The Monochrome Set and Felt with him – the jewels in Cherry Red's crown. "When he wrote his letter of resignation," McNay says, "he put it on my desk and told the girls in the office. One of them called me to say he'd resigned. Another thing happened on that day too. I'd flown overnight from New York, had a quick shower and come into the office. And there was Mike's resignation letter, which I'd been mentally prepared for. But I also had to deal with another situation. Phil Langham, who ran Anagram Records, had been using drugs in the office. So I had to fire him that day. I always liked Phil, but I couldn't have that in the office. Someone had complained about this going on in my absence. The Mike thing got to me a bit. I rang Geoff Travis, and demanded he came round to see me. To give Geoff his due, he came round that evening. I told him what I thought. I think we both felt better afterwards. He didn't apologise and he stood his ground, but at least we had that face to face meeting. And I was disappointed I never got that face to face with Mike until much later."

The hurt was keen, and to an extent, justified. McNay had imagined that great things lay ahead of the pair, believing their relationship capable of withstanding the fractious outbursts that had characterised it of late. While Alway had become "a dab hand at repairing telephone handsets" that would occasionally be bounced off the office furniture by his employer, he had now reached the end of his fuse. Had McNay not been absent from the office, things may have been different. Almost certainly, one surmises, in person McNay and Alway might have reconciled their differences. "I only ever remember breaking one telephone," McNay protests. "I had my moments of volatility, but so did Mike. And actually, I think I coped with the adversity reasonably well. I'm good at regrouping and moving forward. Mike's resignation was a shock and surprise. I just wished I'd had the chance to talk to him. The whole thing could have collapsed, but it didn't."

"At the time, things were running for us," he continues. "I'd agreed a budget of £10,000 for the Everything But The Girl album that became *Eden*. We'd already agreed to get Robin Millar as producer. I felt we could do it on our own, in a similar way to how Beggars Banquet and Graduate had. I wanted to see if we could do it without involving a major record company. If the first Everything But The Girl album had come out on Cherry Red and not charted, which we expected it to do, I would possibly have looked again at Mike's suggestion. Around that time as well, we had the Fantastic Something single out. We'd got some nice airplay on Capital, and there was a lot of interest. Seymour Stein and a couple of people from Warners in America came round to hang out with us for a day. And Mike felt that, because we weren't a bigger company, we weren't building on the Capital airplay. But we did have a decent plugger, we got Capital on board, and the sales response simply wasn't there. I got Pinnacle to monitor it in the London area, because of the Capital plays, and there wasn't the response despite the airplay. I didn't feel we'd lost out simply because we were a smaller company. So I disputed Mike's analysis on that."

The artists' sympathies lay squarely with Alway, and that was especially true of Everything But The Girl. Despite a statement to the press that he would not allow the duo to leave under any circumstances, eventually McNay retracted, and Watt and Thorn moved to WEA in exchange for a one-point percentage on the profits of their first eight albums, plus ownership of their

Japanese masters. "I took a firm line originally, but they hadn't told me 100% they wanted to leave," McNay says. "Ben called me one day and said, 'Iain, we really want to talk to you about this. We're not happy.' We met at a McDonald's in Queensway – I was a vegetarian then! I remember vividly, on my walk there, there was a torrential hailstorm. And I got absolutely drenched. The three of us sat down, and they basically said they wanted to leave Cherry Red and go to Blanco. I was very disappointed and sad, but I accepted it. I never get into fights with artists like that. It would have been futile. They'd made their mind up, and I decided I was going to make it as easy for them to leave as I could. So I spoke to Rob Dickins and I let them go without an advance. I could have asked for one. I just got the 1% override and the Japanese masters, because Ben and Tracey's solo albums had come out in Japan and I thought there was something there of value. But I actually made it easy for them to get out of the deal. I liked them, I liked their music, and I didn't want to end up with a big legal tussle." "We ONLY went cos Mike did," Thorn states. "And don't forget, we never felt we were 'going to Warners' – we were going to Blanco y Negro, with Mike Alway and Geoff Travis. Somewhat foolishly we paid no mind to the major label behind it all – we just thought they were a chequebook, and that we'd have a fabulous time being indie and imaginative and they'd just pay. It didn't quite turn out like that of course, and I think there were losses as well as gains. But we couldn't have stayed at Cherry Red without Mike, it was as simple as that."

Other deals were cut as McNay, in the final analysis always the pragmatist, rescued what he could from the embers of Cherry Red's first incarnation. Felt didn't make the jump. Both Alway and Lawrence were keen, but Rob Dickins wasn't convinced of their viability. McNay did, however, take a compensatory sum for terminating his contractual claim on The Monochrome Set. And they, like Everything But The Girl, would soon discover the greener grass at Blanco wasn't all they'd supposed. "Cherry Red was a fantastic label at the time," Bid laments. "And probably the happiest time I've ever had. In early 1983, in music, it was the happiest time; the atmosphere at Cherry Red's old office was fantastic. Mike was not mad yet. Everyone was still hopeful, and then it kind of all went sour. Everything was working up to the point where everyone left for Blanco y Negro and Warners. And I was certainly partly to blame. When you get loads of money waved at you, and you're not used to it... We should have stayed at Cherry Red. We were right to move from Rough Trade to DinDisc at the time – well, probably not DinDisc, but we were right to move from Rough Trade. But we weren't right to move from Cherry Red, we shouldn't have done it. But pretty much as soon as Mike had gone, Cherry Red started to collapse. I think Iain became

– although he hid it – extremely bitter for a few years about all that. I think in retrospect what should have happened was everyone should have said, listen, they're offering us loads of money, let's go do it for a year. I mean, Iain made some money out of it. He got a cut of the deal. We should have just said to Iain, can we come back here after they drop us? So it would have been a mutual money-making exercise. Had we all said that, half of the bands would have come back to Cherry Red, because they all got dropped! There was no maturity at the time. We were in a situation none of us really knew anything about. We didn't know how to handle it."

"The fact that Blanco didn't work out, I take full responsibility for," says Alway now. "In truth, I'm far from the only person to blame but I made a few ill-considered choices. When the records by Sudden Sway and Monochrome Set came out on Warners, the nature of their failure disturbed me. When a record fails independently it remains its charm. But when a record fails on Warner Brothers, it somehow loses its mystique. The worst thing about the days with Blanco was everyone ringing all the time, saying, 'What's going on?' 'When are we getting our cheque?' And I had to deal with this machine that had the turning circle of the bloody Spanish Armada."

Alway sensed the gravity of his mistake with sickening haste. "It was an ill-fated and ill-planned thing. Had Cherry Red done what I'd hoped was going to happen – if Iain had done another label, a two-tiered label with a major – who knows? But philosophically, that was not possible for Iain at the time. Back then he couldn't do it. But we would have been able to have the best of both worlds. He would have been able to have spent other people's money making the Monochrome Set enormous, and being able to maximise all that potential, without having to risk anything of his own. The Monochrome Set would have got what they wanted, and Iain would have got what he wanted. That was all it was, really. My theory about Blanco y Negro and what I wanted it to be was right in principle, but we did it in the wrong way. I don't know if there's a record to be put straight. My behaviour before and during might seem strange to people, and I'm always willing to set down why that was. Because it doesn't come out of any evil intent." McNay wasn't interested in spending other people's money. "I wanted to make it work, simply, on our own terms. Remember, I'd been around the music business for some time now, and I knew what would happen. If you take someone else's money, you lose control, both creatively and on the business side – those providing the money get the say."

Geoff Travis saw the Blanco 'mistakes' at first hand, but maintains that the label was an incredibly successful venture – just not, perhaps, for Mike Alway. "We signed Everything But The Girl, and that was the jewel in the crown, and Mike had Ben doing a solo thing and Tracey doing a solo thing. He knew them. I went up to visit them at university in Hull and talked about our new grand venture and talked them into signing to us. So that was a great beginning. *Eden* – you couldn't start the label with a better record. It was a big success. It wasn't like, 'Mike, you can't do that. What do you want to do? We'll do it.' But of course Mike wanted to do The Monochrome Set and Subway Sect, all these things that I'd done and I thought their best was past. But I didn't say a murmur, I didn't say you can't do it. But he spent a huge amount of money doing those things, in the scheme of things. I don't think I ever berated him and said, 'No, you can't do this, Mike'. Because it was his idea. I knew that we had to have some success pretty quickly, otherwise we weren't going to have this label much longer. I don't know if that occurred to him or not. When I signed Dream Academy, I don't think he liked that. Fair enough. But we had a number four hit in America and a big hit in the UK. And I love that record, 'Life In A Northern Town'. Otherwise I wouldn't do it. I don't think he was particularly interested in Jesus & Mary Chain. Fair enough. But Mike is a very odd, eccentric character. He would say, 'I can't go out.' 'Why Mike?' 'Because there are these people . . .' Strange things like that. I don't know what he meant by that – I don't know if he meant he had agoraphobia."

Certainly, Alway has never been a fan of crowds, and increasingly shunned gigs. "The environment was not appealing to me; darkness, strange people and unrelenting noise. I chose instead to stay home and plan a label based on Steed and Mrs Peel with a dash of Keith Floyd." "I didn't really understand," reflects Travis. "I thought it was some strange paranoia, or some strange adding to the legend. I always *really* liked Mike, but it became obvious we weren't on the same wavelength, and I think he just stopped. I accepted Mike's eccentricities. I wouldn't have expected him to have been in the office from nine to seven. But I did find it strange that he wouldn't go to gigs. I do kind of regret it didn't work out. I saw it as Mike's thing, really. It would have been great to have signed The Pet Shop Boys, that would have been a good artist for Blanco. I think Bid was very disappointed when it didn't happen. I don't know what Mike had promised him. There were moments when it nearly happened. Mike had a fantasy that The Monochrome Set were the greatest band in the world. But unfortunately there's a huge difference between believing a band's the greatest band in the world and them selling lots of records. Sometimes it happens, not always. I suppose Mike was at the top of his game, and he had signed lots of very good bands, you can see why that might make you think you can make anything happen."

Alway maintains a slightly different theory in regard to Blanco. "I'm sitting there with Geoff Travis, and I finally realised at some point, the dismal truth – which is that these people are talking to us because of The Smiths. They're not talking to us because of anything I've done. Even Everything But The Girl – it's about The Smiths. They're just not interested. They'd take these other things on, and they might even get hits with them, but I began to see there was no empathy there. It just struck me that all the pleasures involved in, if you like, the cottage industry side of it, were being denied by the corporate structure. They're just different people. It's not that the people at Cherry Red were better people than the ones at Warners, they're just different people, as they are today. It's like trying to compare yourself with a bank manager." Travis doesn't buy the Smiths theory. "They bought the Smiths catalogue separately – we sold millions of records with Everything But The Girl. Blanco was a very successful label for Warners."

Bid, meanwhile, saw The Monochrome Set dissipate through bodged promotion on their 'sure-fire' hit single, 'Jacob's Ladder'. He, too, realised that the Blanco set-up was not for him. "Mike blew a whole load of money on a really class recording, have you heard Anthony Adverse? That was a cover version done with a band called Working Week, and it was for Kenneth Williams! And after we recorded it, Mike told me 'I'll ring Kenneth Williams now.' (LAUGHS) He'd just blown five or six thousand on one recording, and then he asked George Melly to do it. Eventually he got this nice but bland singer to do it. It lost loads of money and that was it. For our part, we'd just been to America and lost loads of money on the tour. And for us there was no question now we were offered loads of money to go with it. And then of course Warners completely screwed up 'Jacob's Ladder'. For about two or three weeks it had massive airplay, but that was before it was released. By the time it came out, the DJs were saying, I don't think this will get anywhere. It was so badly fucked up! Then four weeks after it was released, they started recording the video for it!"

"How Bid could not have 'made it' in some way is extremely unfortunate," opines Alway. Bid isn't convinced for a moment. "But we could *never* have been big! It's blindingly obvious, to me, personally, we could never have been a Top Ten band. It's just not possible. We were never commercial entertainers." Despite that, Alway's enduring love of The Monochrome Set helped to form the ethos behind a new label – where his aforementioned love of Messrs Steel, Peel and Floyd could come into play. It was started at Warners before the end of his tenure there. "The original inspiration for él Records was Rough Trade-era Monochrome Set," he says. "They had the attitude of Elizabeth Taylor and Richard Burton – the way you want stars to be. It was superior and it was better. I suddenly thought, Christ, everything's possible here. Richard Ingrams described Peter Cook as a conservative anarchist and that is what I saw él as, as a manifestation of conservative anarchy. People that inspired me were people like Richard Briers. I had this conversation with Alan McGee who said Malcolm McLaren inspired him, and I said, for me, it was Richard Briers. He thought I was off my head. And there are other sitcoms like *Reggie Perrin* – I really loved that slightly bonkers, straight Englishman in the suburbs idea. Those fragments all added up to a greater force of motivation and ambition." For él to proceed, however, he needed a backer. Which is when he made a painful return to the Cherry Red fold. "Going back to the bosom of Cherry Red seemed to me inexplicable when Theo Chalmers advanced the idea to me. And, to Iain's credit, he accepted my return – though there were some very hard things said."

For a certain cadre of observers, although sadly one extremely limited in size, él would become the most artistically vital independent label of them all. Certainly it released a number of quite extraordinary records, and Alway takes deep pride in the depth of its original roster. "There were all those people who really should have been on Warners itself but for one reason or another weren't. I had writers like Nick Currie (Momus), Vic Godard, Bid (Monochrome Set) and Karl Blake (Shock-Headed Peters). But there were other people on the periphery of él, such as Phillipe Auclair (aka Louis Phillipe). The start of the label was to do with taking things that already existed by their own virtue, and then there was a change in approach That came with 'Valleri' [by the King Of Luxembourg, aka Simon Morgan]."

Alway saw él, to a much greater extent than he did with Cherry Red, as an opportunity to carve something in his own image. "The new way was to idealise popular music on a conceptual and physical level. It depends on all the parts harmonising together; the artist, the producer and myself. I wanted to take off on an adventure that had a uniqueness and unity to it. I didn't want to spend all my time arguing with artists about artwork, basically being a part of the service industry. It was about putting out records that had their own fabulous character as an antidote to the utter crap around, which was ruining British pop music for me. I wanted to make records that had no apparent market. I thought the groups I want to work with don't exist, so I'm going to make them exist. Then we're going to go to the top of the charts and then the world will change." Or, as Rob Fitzpatrick would eulogise in his 2008 *Guardian* retrospective, "él revelled in its thrillingly sly upper-class style. His artists weren't knuckle-dragging gangs from rough backstreets: they were presented as languorous Vogue models, archbishops' daughters, royalty. There were songs about the British Empire, soufflés, choirboys and stately homes, but there was never the merest whiff of snobbery, just the crisp, lemony cologne of a delicious privilege shared." From the titular lower-case, accented opening vowel and beyond, él petitioned for otherness and grandeur and scale and majesty in an increasingly narrowing and dour pop world.

The worldwide chart domination didn't quite happen, though él did achieve a cult following and impressive sales in Japan, where the label proved a big influence on the J-Pop phenomenon. Eventually Alway lost control of the label as Cherry Red's Martin Costello attempted to turn it into a commercial proposition – which, of course, was beyond impossible. Alway, once again, felt "utterly helpless", but simply couldn't win an argument on the basis of sales alone. He feels the under-cooked albums released against his wishes in this period, by Anthony Adverse, Felt and The James Dean Driving Experience, are blots on his discographical landscape, carbuncles that he would never have tolerated had the situation been different. él's adventure ended in 1988.

Yet él would rise again with Alway at the helm in 2005. It continues under the Cherry Red umbrella as one of several specialist reissue labels. "This is not me giving up on my ideal of él Records to go straight as a back catalogue dustman," Always states. "I'm releasing records that mean something to me. As with él being different to Mute, Factory, 4AD etc, I'm trying to make the new él different from any other reissue label. The way I try to do that is bringing people like Edgar Varèse into this world, and people from the jazz field. I want to take months conceptually, so this will be a month of Brazilian music, next month Indian music, then a month of guitar music, etc. Or vocal music or soundtracks. I'm listening to people like William Byrd and thinking about how to do choral music from the 16th century on él – and I think I'm going to get away with it. It all draws on an audience that's interested in learning and enquiring. I'm ready to feed that audience. That's what I enjoy doing."

Cherry Red, meanwhile, never really replaced Alway. "Mike's assistant in A&R and press was John Hollingsworth," McNay recalls, "and he took over. And then we worked with bands like Red Box and Laibach. But around '86, my interest was drifting off somewhere else, to my spiritual adventures. I pretty much left Cherry Red from 1987 to 1991, for four years I had nothing to do with it, really. And I travelled. Martin Costello, who ran the publishing, ended up also running the label."

McNay would become active with the label again in 1991, repositioning Cherry Red as a catalogue specialist, placing it in good stead to benefit from the CD boom of the early 90s. Initially he bolstered the catalogue by careful acquisitions, often buying bombed out independents. "That was when I started coming into the office more, and I saw that if I was going to get more involved in Cherry Red, which I quite fancied doing, that the whole picture with new bands was very difficult. We had Prolapse and Tse Tse Fly and other bands, and we were still making records with Alien Sex Fiend. We'd got the records into the independent charts OK, but it didn't generate very much in terms of sales. That's when I realised that the only way get it back on a firm business footing was to go down the catalogue route. So I bought Flicknife Records, I bought No Future, which had been started by my original A&R guy Richard Jones. We bought Red Rhino and Midnight Music. The old formula wasn't working. If you wanted to break a new band, you had to get success and that cost a lot of money. It was a risky business. I'm never one not to take a risk, but it could have bankrupted the company if you'd got it wrong and backed two or three bands that didn't happen. We still did some new recordings, but the basis of it was catalogue. And we were well ahead of the game there. Other independent companies that are around have done that and made a good business out of it, but we were probably the first. And we started a series of collectors' labels, for Punk, Psychobilly and Goth, which was Mark Brennan's idea. We also started almost a whole new genre, by releasing football related compact discs, which we compiled."

Cherry Red, in what was effectively its third phase from the 90s onwards, developed into an umbrella network for a number of labels run by enthusiasts with particular fields of expertise. The most prominent among these are Joe Foster's Rev-Ola (the former Creation subsidiary), Mark Stratford's RPM label, Mark Brennan's 7T's, Mark Powell's Esoteric and, of course, él. Each of these are quality-focused entities with fairly exact niches. On an average month, Cherry Red releases up to 40 compact discs on up to two dozen discrete imprints. There is also a burgeoning video archive, a book publishing arm and a dedicated internet TV channel.

McNay is fond of saying that he doesn't mind being disliked, as long as he is respected. "I prefer to be liked – but you can't always have that." The taciturn demeanour is a highly individual mix of zen philosophy and hard-nosed businessman, and a deeply ingrained but similarly idiosyncratic morality. For example, he liked Tony Wilson, but distrusted his more cavalier approach to business, which led to him not paying his artists, suppliers and employees properly. There are few more heinous crimes in McNay's book.

McNay remains a very astute deal-cutter. He knows that value exists in the unfashionable – or will do in the future. Witness the decision, in particular, to snap up the publishing of former United Artists bands like The Stranglers and Buzzcocks at a time in the late 80s when 'punk was over' at a bargain price. In 2006 they were part of a catalogue sold to BMG/Universal for a substantial sum of money. Though McNay credits Martin Costello with putting together those deals, he approved them, and managed to ringfence a large kernel of songs from the label's heritage acts – The Monochrome Set, Felt, Eyeless In Gaza and others. "It didn't affect the purchase price, they wanted the bigger stuff," he says. "We kept about half the copyrights. There were two good reasons. One, they were acts that I felt close to personally. Secondly, I didn't want those songs getting lost in a huge corporate environment. A lot of the artists were grateful to stay on Cherry Red, because they can always pick up the phone and talk to us, where they could never do that with Universal." Yet McNay considers the publishing side of his business merely 'another asset'. He is implacable in discussion of the above coup – in fact, he disputes his actions were anything more than good sense – yet remains most nostalgic for that moment in the early 80s when Cherry Red was at its zenith as an upstart record label. "There's a good reason for that. I'm a do-er. What I really like doing is putting out records, and most publishers just collect money."

Alway, meanwhile, remains contrite to the point of being heartbroken about the now distant events of 1983. He is unworried, he says, about the friction discussing such matters might cause in his ongoing relationship with McNay, but argues that it is painful in terms of dealing "with my own conscience". McNay will express in person that Alway remains one of his favourite people in the world, and that "we both made mistakes". Beyond that, it is difficult to say truly whether he has taken on board the role his rigid personal outlook played in an exquisitely sad finale. McNay disagrees with that analysis. "It's what happened at the time. You can't change things, but I really believe in the flow of life – and what I've always tried to do is not fight life, but accept the flow. And that's what I did. I don't believe in staying in situations where there's conflict and a lot of uphill struggle. I don't think there's anything wrong with the decisions I made all those years ago."

Whilst it is true that Cherry Red remains a successful independent institution, Alway will maintain that, for a brief period, with his hand on the A&R rudder, allied to McNay's business savvy and drive, the potential was there for something much greater. He still feels the loss of that moment acutely. "It was the *chemistry* at Cherry Red that was unique. In 1983 Cherry Red was my life. I had ambition in the best, purest sense, and though sometimes turbulent, the relationship with Iain was the perfect balance. The Blanco y Negro idea was a good concept that I felt certain would have augmented Cherry Red perfectly. But I should have had the sense to wait until Iain felt ready. Had he and I continued to work together, we'd have consolidated our position amongst the leading independent labels, and the history of independent music might have been very different. I will always have that on my conscience."

But perhaps the fact that such a successful businessman (which McNay definitively is; his decisions having kept Cherry Red ahead of the game at crucial points) could ever co-exist with a man given so wholeheartedly to a singular aesthetic vision is the miracle. And even then, their dynamic was, and is, more complicated than such a surface reading would suggest. "Some people think it's all about money with Iain," Alway says. "It really isn't. It never has been." That's doubtless what led David Cavanagh to describe McNay as "perhaps the most *sui generis* record company owner to have emerged from the punk rock upsurge" in *My Magpie Eyes Are Hungry For The Prize*. One of a kind would be the appropriate, though more prosaic, translation.

# Chapter Eleven

## Do They Owe Us A Living?

### Crass, Southern, The Anarcho Punk Labels and Punk in the 80s

One of the most divisive statements made regarding the early days of punk was that the movement died the day the Clash signed to CBS, courtesy of Mark Perry of *Sniffin' Glue*. The Sex Pistols had been enticed by EMI four months previously, but it was the polemic of the Clash and their ideological cleavage that turned heads – and inspired misplaced hopes. The Clash camp, via manager Bernie Rhodes, were reluctant to divulge their signing-on fee, but £100,000 was later admitted to. With punk exploding everywhere in the light of the Grundy affair, this had escalated quickly from an initial £25,000 proposed by Chris Parry at Polydor. Despite grabbing the biggest offer on the table, having negotiated the famously parsimonious Maurice Oberstein into a substantial advance, Strummer remained cynical. "I think they see us as a threat to their fantastic rivers of money, you know?" he told John Tobler in a Radio One interview. "They see us as something to block it up, right?" But as Clash biographer Marcus Gray points out, "Maurice Oberstein did not sign the Clash because he saw punk as a threat to CBS and its established artists, but because he saw no difference between the band and any other potential money-making proposition."

The Clash were immediately defensive about their decision. In conversation with Kris Needs in March 1977, Mick Jones claimed: "You've got to make records. You can do your own label, and not many people will hear it. This way more people will hear our record." He also claimed that the band had extracted full creative control as part of the deal. That assumption, which was self-evidently not based on a close inspection of the fine print of their contracts, would unravel with unseemly haste.

That dialogue about signing to a major would haunt The Clash down the years. Speaking to Paul Morley in 1979, Strummer stated that Rhodes and McLaren's machinations in bringing the Pistols and Clash to majors stopped the punk movement dying on its feet, as its American CBGB's equivalent had before it. "CBGBs on the Bowery was how it stayed for five years. It never came out of there. Our stuff and the Pistols' stuff was great. I don't want to brag, but it didn't deserve to stay in a hole in Covent Garden [The Roxy] for five years." It's a dubious proposition. The early punk movement certainly provided a gateway for dross, but a large number of fine minds and artists would also slip through. And often continued to produce vital music long after The Clash ceased doing so.

Typically, Rhodes himself would paint the decision as ideological, invoking Marxist terminology. "An independent?" he queried when tackled by Paul Rambali in 1980. "You mean a small business. If you don't have access to gain the means of production, whatever you do is peripheral." It's a typical Rhodes folly. The Clash *never* had access to the means of production. Neither, it could be argued, did artists who recorded for independents unless they were pure self-starters. If there was justification for The Clash's decision to sign with CBS, it was on grounds of pragmatism and ambition. In ideological terms, it never did have a leg to stand on.

In June 1977 Perry had handed over control of *Sniffin' Glue* to Danny Baker, whose editorial redressed the previously condemnatory tone. "There's no point screamin' to the converted on privately owned/distributed labels that could sell about two hundred, is there? We wanna be heard, fuck being a cult." Perry, however, wasn't changing his opinion. As he explained at length to Gray *in Last Gang In Town*. "I was insisting it was up to bands like The Clash – that were very popular and were courting a lot of record company interest – to say, 'No! We're not going to become part of the establishment, we're gonna do it ourselves.' I knew it could be done. The Buzzcocks did their first EP themselves. We did the *Glue* without being part of a big publisher like IPC. I think the last *Glue* sold about 20,000 copies. Even if we take The Clash's arguments about wanting a bigger audience, distribution problems, and whatever, it's still possible. The Pistols had stirred this thing up. They'd made this thing interesting to a big audience, they'd made everyone look at us to see what was going to happen next. There was a massive audience for something you could have done on your own. I mean, UB40 proved that later with their own label. And yet The Clash go and sign to CBS. If you talk about just music, it doesn't matter – I've got loads of CBS albums – but if you talk about what The Clash talked about in their songs, then they completely sold out... CBS were one of the biggest weapons and communications systems manufacturers in the world, this massive conglomerate! Basically, it's why the world's dying, because of industries like that. If you look at it in those terms – and I'm no longer that serious that I want to, but if you do follow my argument – they completely sold out."

The wisdom of signing to CBS, ultimately, revealed itself quickly. The headline advance figure was enticing enough. But absolutely everything; equipment, producers, tour support and promotion – would come out of the band's pocket. For all Rhodes' rhetoric and sabre-rattling (though he was wise enough to secure himself 20% gross on the deal) he'd signed The Clash to the classic 'stupid record company contract'. Taking a big advance that would soon be exhausted left them at the whim of their 'employer'. In later years you didn't have to tell a wizened Joe Strummer of the impact of their decision. "If it's Monday, the record company must be pissing on me," he told Jack Rabid of *The Big Takeover*. "If it's Tuesday..." The group's problems with CBS plagued even their most successful years, and ultimately led to Strummer dropping out of view after the band's break-up for almost a decade, so frustrated did he become with contracts he had ill-advisedly signed in 1976.

One celebrated acknowledgement of the band's undue haste in signing to CBS arrived with 'Complete Control' (a retort to CBS's decision to release 'Remote Control' as a single against the band's wishes), Yet one of the standout songs on their triple-album suite *Sandinista!* is arguably much more revealing. 'Hitsville UK', inspired by a trip to Detroit to see the Motown studios where 'The Sound Of Young America' had been hand-crafted, reminded Strummer of those labels back in the UK who had carried the torch for a similar aesthetic. "They say true talent will always emerge in time," ran the lyric. "When Lightning hits Small Wonder/It's Fast Rough Factory Trade/No expense accounts or lunch discounts". The doffing of the cap seemed clear-cut enough – though it's worth noting all the mentioned labels – with the exception of Lightning, if that citation were indeed intended – were ones who existed *after* the group had signed on the dotted line with CBS.

If Strummer was temporarily lost in appreciation for a generation of UK independents, his decision to sign that CBS contract spurred on several of the labels invoked in 'Hitsville UK'. "We were disappointed when The Clash signed to CBS," Geoff Travis of Rough Trade notes. "We saw that as a sell out, I guess, but that just renewed our endeavours to do what we did." Which rather prompts the question, did Travis ever query Mick Jones about the CBS call when they were working together, finally, with The Libertines? "No!" he laughs. "You have to give an old rocker a break!" The great Clash/CBS debate (and it remains, indeed, an almost inexhaustibly fascinating and axiomatic moment) informed some of the independent movement's key records. 'Never Been In A Riot' by The Mekons satirised the group's clumsiest early statement of intent, 'White Riot'. More obliquely, Scritti Politti's 'Skank Bloc Bologna' attacked the band's then current 'Magnificent Seven' schtick. But it would be the extended family of activists living in a communal house in Essex that took the argument to its logical conclusion. That conclusion being, beyond any shadow of doubt, that you could sell millions of records and truly inform, influence and occasionally inflame a worldwide audience without recourse to traditional record industry mechanics. You simply required the will.

The thrust of independent music is, at one level, to provide an outlet for artists at the margins of commerce. If we accept that premise, independence stands as a philosophical corrective to the brutal Darwinist logic of the mainstream music market, rather than simply an alternative business model (and the frustrations in grasping that are key to the perception of other labels, and individuals, discussed in this book). One of the key influences on that discourse came from the Small Wonder stable directly referenced in 'Hitsville UK'. Small Wonder's greatest legacy, however, was serving as midwife to the anarchist punk generation spearheaded by Crass. There were other groups who would explicitly and repeatedly rail against The Clash's fateful decision to 'take the money'. Crass, drawing on a far more extensive back-story and knowledge base than others who *instinctively* felt the 'betrayal', started out almost as a crusade. Ultimately, however, that crusade quickly developed into something much less one-dimensional and ultimately transgressive.

Crass was more than a band; rather, it was a co-operative anarchist commune whose values and philosophies drew on the beatniks, the sixties counter-culture and French literature. They were interested in radical ideas about feminism, pacifism and activism. Those interests predated punk, but they were alive to the possibilities when it took hold. "When, in 1976, punk first spewed itself across the nation's headlines with the message 'do it yourself'," the group would recall in the notes to *Best Before*, "we, who in various ways and for many years had been doing just that, naively believed that Messrs Rotten, Strummer etc, etc, meant it. At last we weren't alone."

Crass came into being in North Weald, Essex, at the behest of Penny Rimbaud (Jeremy Ratter) and Steve Ignorant (Steve Williams). Rimbaud first moved into Dial House in 1967, while still working as a part-time teacher, and embarked on establishing an open house community partially inspired by the film *The Inn Of The Sixth Happiness*. However, the death at what he believed to be the hands of state apparatus of close friend Phil Russell, aka Wally Hope, convinced him that such a passive alternative lifestyle was insufficient. He began to write songs with Ignorant, who had become a regular visitor. Initially, and for some time thereafter, this comprised "just fucking about" more than any serious musical venture.

## Do They Owe Us A Living?

As the band grew the line-up remained flexible in terms of both their role and their level of participation, bass player Pete Wright the only 'musician' involved at the outset. It depended to a large extent as to who was sharing living space at Dial House, which became the engine room of a whole counter-culture task force. The Pistols and Clash initially inspired the key participants, but they were always at least as interested in talking up literary influences (the beat poets, French existentialists) and folk protest singers from Woody Guthrie to Bob Dylan. By the summer of 1977 they'd amassed enough equipment to play occasional benefit shows and, famously, got themselves banned from punk's most famous fleapit. An event they dutifully recounted on 'Banned From The Roxy', from their debut release *Feeding Of The 5,000*, which used the pretext of their expulsion from punk's most iconic venue to rip into the British government's arms policy. Another of the lyrics on *Feeding*, 'Punk Is Dead', directly sniped at the Clash's marriage to a major ("Schoolboy sedition backed by big-time promoters, CBS promote the Clash, But it ain't for revolution, it's just for cash"). "Obviously there was a lineage between that group of punk bands," notes Rimbaud, talking on a bitterly cold morning in Dial House in January 2009, "but they were a clique. In a way they were quite elitist as well, quite chauvinistic. These were the things that became very obvious to us. When Strummer said do it yourself, he didn't really mean it."

"Throughout the long, lonely winter of '77/'78," Crass later stated in their sleevenotes, joint statements being preferred policy, "we played regular gigs at The White Lion, Putney, with the UK Subs. The audience consisted mostly of us, when the Subs played, and the Subs, when we played. Sometimes it was disheartening, but usually it was fun. Charlie Harper's indefatigable enthusiasm was always an inspiration when times got bleak, his absolute belief in punk as a peoples' music had more to do with revolution than McLaren and his cronies could ever have dreamt of. Through sheer tenacity we were exposing the punk charlatans for what they really were, a music-biz hype." Thereafter they realised that their then drunken ramblings needed to be more focused. So they binned the booze, started printing their agenda on pamphlets and published the magazine *International Anthem*, plotting the course of a non-career which, they decided, would end when the calendar turned round to 1984.

In the meantime Jimmy Pursey of Sham 69 offered to help them "market the revolution". They declined. See 'It's The Greatest Working Class Rip-Off' on *Christ The Album* (1982) for further exposition of the group's attitude to the class divide and what they saw as the commodification of proletariat rebellion. In figureheads Rimbaud and Steve Ignorant, Crass had a near-perfect antidote to the class apartheid that existed so perniciously then and still dogs commentary on the period. It remains a monstrous fib (and a peculiarly Anglicised one at that) that the punk movement can legitimately be retrospectively colonised by either class faction. The insurmountable truth is that any creative and artistic gains – and achievements of a wholly more pragmatic nature – were fuelled by cross-party initiative and plurality. That Rimbaud and Ignorant's unification of a punk ideal would be tested by the 'reunion' shows of recent vintage, in which trace elements of class ideology re-emerge and separate, does not detract from what was, for the entirety of the period they collaborated, a supremely successful accommodation.

"I never suffered any illusions about the Pistols," Rimbaud reflects now, "except they were a great band. Undeniably a great band. But I don't think they ever made any statements that they intended to be anything more than a hedonistic outfit. And they were great at that. Within the tradition of rock 'n' roll, they were supreme. My argument has always been that if it hadn't been for Crass, those early punks would simply now belong within the canon of rock 'n' roll, as a natural extension – New York Dolls, Pistols, whatever happened next. It wouldn't have come out of the framework of what rock 'n' roll is perceived as being. But the serious political ambitions we brought into it actually created a movement, which is traceable in all sorts of areas. Initially we didn't have political ambitions, but we very quickly landed ourselves with them. Initially, Steve and myself were just fucking about, literally. No ambition whatsoever. Certainly no ambition to become a rock 'n' roll band, and no interest in becoming a rock 'n' roll band. As other people started to take us seriously, so we were forced to take ourselves seriously. But it wasn't within the framework of rock 'n' roll, it was within the framework of what we were saying. Certainly if I talk about my own lyrical content, I was just talking about what I've always talked about, which was ideas, which inevitably are political. I remember at one time Strummer saying he intended to set up a radio station – wow, that's a great idea. But the promises were never fulfilled, although I do think he tried to make up for it in later days."

"It's one of those things where you think you're in the same game," he continues, "and I suppose that's what I did think, initially. I was taken in, if you like. I only saw The Clash once, in Chelmsford, and I really liked them. I liked the style, I liked the attitude. I sort of 'believed' it. So it *was* a huge disappointment. The Clash were shipping themselves off to the US, making an extreme and unacceptable contradiction. So we felt we were on our own, whereas we thought we were part of this game, almost like kids in a playground. We suddenly felt on our own. We'd gone along with some of the conceits of early punk, 'Anarchy In The UK', and all that sort of stuff. But with the Sex Pistols, it was an archetypal nihilistic agenda, which fitted very well into the entire rock 'n' roll tradition, no different to The Who, and probably as powerful and as good a band as that. The rock 'n' roll theatre was just continuing in its own way, And that's just the rock 'n' roll circus. The Pistols belonged firmly within that. I'm not critical of that. That's what rock 'n' roll always has been – schoolboy revolution, a lot of fun, a great Saturday night out – but it's no more than that. The Clash had certain political pretensions, but not the age or experience to see them through. Strummer showed later in his life that he had some genuine political ideology, which he tried to practice. Somewhat misguidedly, but then that's *my* political view. So they moved slightly to the right or left of the rock 'n' roll lineage, and that's where they collided with us. We took the baton. They fell back very quickly into that lineage, and we were out on our own – and that's where the punk movement started, in my view, rather than rock 'n' roll history, which is where that lot belong, and rightly so, because they were good rock 'n' rollers. We weren't. What we did was far more within the framework of the avant garde than rock 'n' roll. We made of rock 'n' roll a sort of avant garde art statement, much closer to Dada, if you like, than anything else I can think of, in terms of the breadth of our statement and the diversity of it."

Crass were also politicised, to a large extent, by the first of many concerted attempts to co-opt what they were doing. "There was a sense of promise about early punk, and I'd include the American crew in that. We thought we were joining a club, by going out and playing. We used to go and play with the UK Subs at the Red Lion. This is fun, everyone's getting along. And then Rock Against Racism turned up and said, will you do a benefit for us? The Subs and ourselves did it, with some reggae band. That's when I thought, something's happening here." RAR were, famously, closely linked to hard left politicos like the Socialist Workers Party. "Hard left, and also hard left within the framework of hard *white*," thinks Rimbaud. "I thought it was very white, middle class, Trotskyist, university based thinking. I had no time for it. There was capitalist business, and on the other hand leftist politics, and both were keen to buy us out in one form or another. 'Get us on board'. I had an equal distaste for both. In fact, probably a greater distaste for RAR, who were less honest. We got a lot of stick for that, for our attitude to that. Interestingly, RAR were the first people to offer us money for playing. We did the gig for them. At the end of the gig, some bloke came up with a wad of notes. 'I thought it was meant to be for a cause?' Yes, it is. Here's the money.' That was the first time we'd ever been paid for a gig. And that was the last gig we ever did for them. We became very critical of them after that. That money should have gone to whatever cause they were doing."

Crass would, conversely, become synonymous with the 'benefit' show, raising funds, or awareness, for issues ranging from rape crisis centres to animal rights. 'We actually helped to organise the Astrid Proll benefit [for the England-based former Baader-Meinhof member] because she was a friend," recalls Richard Williams of The Passions. "We knew her as Anna and she worked as a mechanic teaching young people at a youth project in North London. I also remember Crass phoning up and desperately wanting to play at the gig (being anarchists I suppose they would), but there wasn't space on the bill for them. They were very disappointed." "Yes, we did have contact with Astrid Proll," Rimbaud remembers, though it actually went further than that. "We were visited by a woman with a young kid, and she was actually doing bank jobs, with her kid, to finance what remained of the Red Army Faction." He doesn't mean *clerical* bank jobs, either. "No, with a shotgun! Or whatever she was using, in mainland Europe. We had a policy of never, ever allying ourselves to anyone, even if we believed in what they were doing. From extreme radical groups to less extreme, most of them, at one time or another, did get in touch."

Escaping pigeonholes, they nevertheless became most closely associated, almost by default, with anarchism. The act of refusing demarcation seemed to force it upon them. "Just as the rock 'n' roll thing started exposing its lies, we felt we had to expose our truths," says Rimbaud. "The anarchist thing wasn't because we wanted to be seen as anarchists, it was because we were trying to say, to both right and left, fuck off, we don't want to be identified with you. We're not part of any Trotyskyite scheme or some capitalist heist. We're individuals doing what we want to do. Actually, we then had to learn classical anarchism very quickly. We'd always lived as anarchist individuals, but we didn't have any history – it was a crash course. We hoisted ourselves on our own petard in that sense."

Crass had aligned themselves with Small Wonder Records in Walthamstow after a visitor overheard what they were doing and took a copy of a tape to Pete Stennet. He offered them the chance to release a single, but unable to decide on which tracks to select, Crass instead recorded everything they'd written to this point, releasing the results as the 12-inch mini-album, *The Feeding Of The Five Thousand*'. Or they would have done, had not staff at the pressing plant deemed opening track 'Asylum' (aka 'Reality Asylum') offensive ("I am no feeble Christ, not me" it began, "He hangs in glib delight upon his cross"). It should be pointed out, however, that in this case it was not a knee-jerk response from the authorities but shop floor workers in Ireland who objected to the lyrics. Their response to this censorship was to release the record with a blank space where the opening track should have been, entitled 'The Sound Of The Speech' (aka 'Freedom Of Speech'), though subsequent reissues, in a rather more forgiving climate, have restored 'Reality Asylum'. Charges of 'criminal blasphemy' were eventually dropped, though notification of this was accompanied by a grave warning not to release any further records. "That was like a red rag to a bull," notes Rimbaud.

Stennet wearied of the police intimidation that engulfed the band (including a raid by the vice squad) and was increasingly involving him, so Crass set up their own label as an interim measure, establishing an ethos of cottage-industry independence that would set the mould for third wave 'anarcho-punk'. 'Reality Asylum' was initially re-released as a 7-inch single in June 1979 backed by 'Shaved Women'. "We started the label purely to release a single that we couldn't release any other way," Rimbaud recalls. "Partly because Small Wonder didn't want to touch it, because of the legal problems. That was 'Asylum'. We were able to find a pressing plant and a printer who were prepared to do the job, as long as they remained incognito. One was a printer in Essex, Basildon. He'd never done anything of that sort before. The pressing plant was related to Saga, who did the huge classical range [and had links both to Joe Meek and later, reggae independent Trojan]."

Retailing at just 45p, and funded by an inheritance left to rhythm guitarist Andy Palmer by his grandmother, it lost them money on every copy sold (they'd forgotten about VAT). The 'pay no more than' drill they maintained across the label evolved thereafter; records would be individually priced on assumptions about what they would sell to reach a break-even point, and therefore fund subsequent releases. Despite the Director of Public Prosecutions having dropped the Criminal Blasphemy case, intimidation continued. "We just put out the one single as Crass Records," says Rimbaud, "but were still with Small Wonder. It was solely because we didn't want to put Small Wonder under threat after we'd been warned by the DPP that they'd 'have us'. But that didn't stop the authorities' interest in Small Wonder or in us. We thought it was a bit unfair on Pete to do this. At that time, we were doing our second album for Small Wonder. We said, 'Look, Pete, why don't we pull out? You go on distributing it, but we'll take responsibility for it.' There was no pressure from him to say let's call it a day, he was a really good guy. That was completely amicable, but I'm sure he was quite relieved."

The group's second album, the double LP *Stations Of The Crass* (September 1979), therefore transferred to Crass's own imprint. "We didn't have any money to pay for that album, so we borrowed it from Poison Girls. We did a pressing of 5,000. That sold out in the first few days and we re-ordered 20,000. And they sold, too. We were suddenly making lots of money, even though it was marketed at a very low price. We'd budgeted it on selling 5,000, so after it went on selling and selling, we very quickly had a load of problems. At that point, we said to John Loder at Southern, we can't really cope with what's happening." Loder first met Penny Rimbaud in 1968, bonding over a shared affection for Hendrix, Zappa and Stockhausen. By 1970 they had formed their own experimental, avant-garde band, EXIT, using Loder's love of DIY electronics (he studied electrical engineering at City University). He would eventually assemble enough equipment to build a studio in the garage of his north London home, principally financed by mini-cab driving.

"We asked him, will you take over as our financial manager?" continues Rimbaud. "Which he did, but not in the traditional sense, he actually became a member of the band. That's where Southern started – prior to that, John was doing advertising jingles. When we got the money, we weren't really happy about that – we hadn't set out to make any money. We were a bit bemused at what to do with it. So the immediate idea was, we'll put it back into trying to expand our ideas through allowing other people access to our studio and financing. Never with an idea of making more money, really just to expand the ideas. We then adopted this policy of doing one single, and generally speaking, a band would come in on the Saturday, record it, and on Sunday we'd mix it, and that was that. We started using Rough Trade for distribution. Our ears were to the ground, we'd hear of a band, we'd get in touch with them. They'd come in. Everyone wanted to be on the label, because they knew it would be good marketing for them."

Crass Records thereafter offered a home to left field punk activists and misfits, almost as an extension of the 'open house' ethos that prevailed at Dial House, starting with Honey Bane, whom they knew through The Poison Girls' connection, then Poison Girls themselves. Both, of course, had also worked with Small Wonder (Bane as part of Fatal Microbes). Though they shared some stylistic similarities and political reference points with the likes of Crass, Conflict and Flux Of Pink Indians, there were a number of important

438

differences between Poison Girls and their peers. Not least the fact that they were led by a former *NME* secretary and middle-aged mother of two – the wonderful Vi Subversa. And she had a lot of pent up anger to disperse. "On occasions the message has come from the audience to us that we're too old," she would tell Phil Sutcliffe. "Well, it took me 40 years to find my voice and I'm not going to let a bunch of narrow-minded 15-year-old bigots take it away from me now!"

Originally formed in Brighton in 1976, as an extension of a cabaret project, Poison Girls relocated to Burleigh House in Essex to become near neighbours of Dial House. They would play many gigs together and later collaborated on the 'Persons Unknown'/'Bloody Revolutions' split single in aid of the short-lived Wapping Autonomy Centre. Songs like 'Bully Boys', whose specific target was ambivalent beyond mocking machismo attitudes, managed to unite both the Socialist Workers Party and the National Front in condemning them. Significantly, they were among the first of the Crass roster to open their own spin-off label, Xntrix, with the release of the live *Total Exposure* album in 1981 (although Flux's Spiderleg offshoot issued a retrospective Epileptics single that same month). The label would also house releases by Conflict and Rubella Ballet, two of the latter (Gem Stone and Pete Fender) being Subversa's children.

Later Crass releases featured Zounds, Flux Of Pink Indians, Conflict, Rudimentary Peni, The Mob *et al.* Each got one shot – the abiding logic being that Crass weren't a record company out to exploit the careers of their 'roster'. And they sold in their tens of thousands, though the pricing policy ensured that everyone was happy if the break-even point was reached. Each beneficiary would, seemingly, form their own label on similar principles: Spiderleg (Flux), Mortarhate (Conflict), Outer Himalayan (Rudimentary Peni), All The Madmen (The Mob) etc, though Zounds switched to Rough Trade and, to some consternation, Honey Bane would sign a contract with EMI. It was in exactly this viral manner that anarcho-punk unfolded like one of Crass's famous nine-panel wraparound sleeves. "We hope we're the last of the big punk bands," Crass told Mike Stand of *The Face* in 1981." The very fact that we are big is a sign of the failure of what punk was all about. But we do feel it's building up behind us now, hundreds of bands and fanzines."

The pricing policy came about "because we were living very cheaply," says Rimbaud. "We grow our own vegetables and didn't have any costs, so why should we get involved in profit? We didn't need profit to live. I remember when we printed all the 'Asylum' stuff ourselves, probably the first 10,000 covers we printed here, on grey paper. I was at school with a guy who married the daughter of a wealthy mill owner in Edinburgh. They had this warehouse full of paper they wanted to get rid of, so we brought tons of it down here. It gave us years and years and years of paper. Some of it we've still got! It's going a bit yellow now. So stuff was just there. People gave us things. I still live that way. If you don't have anything, stuff turns up. The way of preventing things turning up is having stuff in the first place. Nature abhors a vacuum, space fills. That's always been my philosophy, McCawberism, something will always turn up. Sometimes it doesn't, money notably. But then I don't care about that particularly. The whole operation was run on that level."

Even so, not everyone was in a position, either in terms of having the discipline or financial wherewithal, to cut the apron strings. "Eventually people would say, 'what do we do next?' recalls Rimbaud. "But the idea was really to show people *how* to do it. I got involved in production, but it wasn't until way towards the end that I got involved in production for other bands in a real sense. I was initially there to provide access, to show people how to do things, what was possible, and to help them get what I thought, or what they thought, they wanted. That worked very well. It was done on a 50-50 deal, generally. With the Poison Girls we did much more generous deals – on *Chappaquidick Bridge* [their 1980 album] they got 100%. We made absolutely nothing. Most of the records hardly ever paid for themselves, so there was very little money in it for anyone, including ourselves. It was making use of the money we were creating [through Crass the recording artists, whose releases typically averaged between 50,000 and 75,000 sales]." Although income generated by each release was recycled for the next one, they were fortunate in not having to wait until costs were covered. "We were always financing it from our takings, which were massive, because we were selling so many thousands of records, we had the capital to do that. We financed the label, basically, and put out lots of stuff that cost us a lot of money, in real terms. But that didn't really matter. What interested us, quite simply, was to get stuff that we thought was making a valid point out into the market."

The criteria were aesthetic and political, never commercial. "That was how the decisions were made. There had to be some sort of broad agreement, ranging from the somewhat aggressive anarchism of someone like Conflict, to the completely surreal nature of [Icelandic group fronted by a young Björk] K.U.K.L.; two extremes of anarchistic behaviour or thought. But broadly there had to be common agreement – people weren't 'run through it', it [selection] was done on listening to the bands and the things they

wanted to say. And you'd have funny things like when Captain Sensible
wanted to 'say something', he got in touch with us. 'Can we do a single? I
want to say something.' We agreed. We wouldn't have done 'Happy Talk'.
Probably! He's a lovely man, Captain. And a fine artist."

The first *Bullshit Detector* volume was released in 1980. As *Last Hours*
magazine would note, compilations "actually defined the anarcho-punk
movement both culturally and politically". The reasons for this were multi-
fold, but essentially related primarily to economics. A 'comp' could offer a
snapshot of a musical scene and community, with costs divided by the
contributors. However, the logic behind the first and most famous anarcho-
punk compilation series was slightly different. Borrowing a phrase
employed by The Clash (again) on their song 'Garageland', the series title
was loaded with significance. 'Garageland' had been written in direct
response to Charles Shaar Murray's barbed comments about the Clash's
'coming out' gig at the Screen On The Green in 1976, in which he suggested
they were the sort of garage band who should return there with the engine
left running.

The fragmentation of punk occurring at the time of the record's release was
stark. A street youth movement – Oi! – almost single-handedly punted by
*Sounds* journalist Garry Bushell, was one faction, fast, aggressive hardcore
punk from the likes of GBH and the Exploited another. There were also the
first sightings of the Ants/Banshee-inspired positive punk/early Goth scene.
To these could now be added a fourth front, the anarcho or peace punks, who
had grown up around Crass, whose entire *raison d'être* seemed to be
principled and sustained opposition to the state.

Though Crass had existed as a force since 1977, the real impact on that
demographic of bands was most visibly felt with the arrival of the *Bullshit
Detector* series, arguably pushing the logic of Crass beyond anything else
they did. Despite the rhetoric, not everyone had the whys, wiles or
wherefores to make records happen, but the *Bullshit Detector* series lowered
the barrier to entry further than even the Desperate Bicycles could have
imagined. A tape recorder, cassette and a postage stamp was now sufficient.
A biscuit tin could serve purpose as well as a guitar. And everyone can sing.
Well, perhaps not. "But," notes Rimbaud, "the biscuit tin and the bedroom
have produced some very profound art."

There was a downside to this – many of the bands on the *Bullshit Detector*
volumes were awful. To the casual listener, quality control was seemingly

non-existent. At least in a conventional sense. But quality control there indeed was, albeit with more complex parameters. "We had hundreds and hundreds of tapes," Rimbaud remembers, "and out of that we made three *Bullshit Detectors*. And we could probably have done another two or three. We *were* very selective – we listened to absolutely everything that arrived, and most of it was dross. But other things stood out. Why? Because someone had something to say, something had a quality. How do you judge art? And we'd have quite a team of us listening. But I believe then and now, that if punk had an ethos, then it was represented in its purest sense more by *Bullshit Detector* than anything we did. And that's why we did it. That said more about what punk was really about than any known band could do, because you become removed from it. However hard you tried, and we tried harder than any other band to maintain that ethos, never to buy into the rock 'n' roll pantomime bit. But however much we tried, we inevitably were perceived within that. You couldn't do that with *Bullshit Detector*. *Bullshit Detector* was where we started – which is why we're on the first one, Steve and myself doing 'Do They Owe Us A Living' on the first one, because that's what we were."

Some notable acts did emerge from each of the volumes; The Sinyx, Amebix and Alternative from Volume 1; Omega Tribe, Anthrax, Toxic Ephex and Chumbawamba from Volume 2; and Napalm Death from Volume 3. To find those relative treasures though, there was an enormous amount of gristle and bone to sift through. The tone, equally, was somewhat hectoring and a little reductive (especially the *ad nauseum* anti-war diatribes). But the effect was unarguably astonishing, coming closest to delivering on punk's democratising rhetoric than anything comparable – and truly offering a route from the bedroom to the top of the (indie) charts in double time. Toxic Ephex's 'Police Brutality' appeared on the 40-track second volume, and, as they noted, "it climbed the dizzy heights to top the punk indie charts on October 8 1982, and to fourth place in the national indie charts, selling around 15,000 copies. The band got £135 in royalties... [they were] major recording artists of inter-galactic mega-status (well, their ma's and da's were faintly pleased, and the wifey down the chipper asked 'Kin ye get me Rod Stewart's autograph?')"

As the sleevenotes would (somewhat piously) attest, "Don't expect music when the melody is anger, when the message sings defiance, three chords are frustration when the words are from the heart". Again, this was a knowing twist on punk lore – whose early history those mythical 'three chords' had long loomed large in. *Sniffin' Glue* had produced a (misprinted) diagram with the slogan "Here's one chord, here's another, and there's a third. Now go out and form a band". And there was the similarly infamous "The Damned can now play three chords, The Adverts can play one, here all four at..." tour billing. Now, even that entry-level stipulation – knowledge of a barre chord or two – was ripped away.

"*Bullshit Detector* was more than another unimaginative compilation series," notes Brian Sheklian, of Californian record label Grand Theft Audio. "It was a small but well deployed battering ram against the industry imposed barrier that separated the audience from the performer, and the performer from releasing a record without major backing. The graphics, the recordings, screamed anyone can do it, anyone can have a say. How many of the bands on it had a manager, a lawyer, a booking agent, or even enough money for a trip to a proper recording studio? Sure there were a few ropy recordings on there, but those bands inspired others who thought they could do better, to put those words into action and actually do something."

*Bullshit Detector* also provided something of a template for punk compilations; similarly politicised DIY labels springing up in France (New Wave Records), Brazil (the Ataque Sonoro compilations) etc, alongside thousands of cassette releases. Labels such as Xcentric Noise in Cottingham, run by Andy 'Shesk' Thompson, actually predated *BSD*. Thompson had sent Crass a copy of his *Beat The Meat* C-60 compilation, the first in a series of cassette releases documenting worldwide punk, sometime in late 1979. "I definitely remember getting *Bullshit Detector* in stock in 1980 at the record shop I worked in, the late great Sydney Scarborough's in Hull, and thinking 'they've copied me, the bastards!' No, I didn't think bastards to be honest, because Crass were just something so special, sincere and intense. I definitely recall that 'Cancer' by Icon [who later became Icon AD] was on there from the *Beat The Meat* tape, and I got a letter from Penny. But the scene was all about that, anyone creating-inputting-outputting and having things to say was a great thing and it was worthy word and tuneage to be spread." The releases also featured some of the earliest drawings by hardcore/metal legend Pushead (aka Brian Schroeder). "I was never a businessman," confesses Thompson. "Things just got bigger than I could handle on about £35 a week at the record shop. Red Rhino were brilliant and helped me out loads. I started trying to help some local bands but just didn't sell enough." These days a photographer, Thompson recalls with huge affection the days when "it was just me in my bedroom, knocking out cut 'n' paste, excited every morning in case another Brazilian or European gem of a C-60 might pop through the door."

443

That excitement was transmitted readily. This was a new global village whose principal currency was self-addressed envelopes – usually with postage stamps 'soaped' for repeat use – and tape-trading, with money rarely changing hands. "Xcentric Noise R.A.T.S (Records And Tapes) was the first UK label to my knowledge to actively promote international punk from outside the UK and USA," remembers Charlie Mason, whose group Atrox contributed to the label. "Andy's cassettes turned me and a host of other people onto the worldwide explosion of punk and hardcore that we'd spend the next few years immersing ourselves in. Along with BCT Tapes in the US, he produced compilations of bands from around the world, opening up a lot of minds to foreign language punk." The better known protagonists included Finland's Rattus, Brazil's Olho Seco and Canada's Neos. It was a gateway not only for the curious, but also a restorative boost to isolated punk communities everywhere from Poland to apartheid South Africa; territories still under the yoke of state censorship and repression. "It gave them the exposure outside their countries they deserved," Mason continues, "at a time when only a tiny number of pioneering 'zines or mail order outlets would give them a mention."

Certainly, *Bullshit Detector* and its offspring served as a reaffirmation of core values in stark contrast to the inexorable slide of some of the original punks in seeking acknowledgement for their musical chops – coded by plaintive cries that they were just good, old-fashioned rock 'n' roll bands at heart. Key offenders? That'd be The Clash. "I think that our ethos hasn't altered," Rimbaud observes, "which is why we're still broke and didn't 'make' anything, in that sense of the word, out of that era of our lives. It's because we're still *playing*. When I say playing, I mean in the way that kids do. Our interest has always been to turn things upside down, to make things available, to say, yeah, this is possible. And part of the way we live here is a statement of that possibility; that you can live with nothing, and that's how we survive. I got very disillusioned with punk because to me it very quickly became rock 'n' roll. And I'm not interested in rock 'n' roll. I never have been really. Jazz, to me, carries the ethos of punk far more purely than all of this retro stuff."

Of course, one of the big problems was that Crass inspired a wave of copyists. It prompted a stylised makeover that ran from the visual presentation of records to the 'barking' Estuary English vocals. But parrot-like plagiarists aside, looking at the sequence of singles that Crass released, there is extraordinary variety there, from the Dada-inspired lunacy of The Cravats to the apocalyptic lullabies of The Mob to the playful insurrection of Zounds, etc. The Cravats' 'Rub Me Out' is arguably the finest of that initial run of singles; stewed in off-kilter saxophone, with The Shend playing the hunted paranoiac to thrilling effect. "I think Pete Stennet at Small Wonder gave Penny one of our singles," he says. "He just got in touch and said he'd really like to produce the next single. We did that with him and [engineer] John Loder. It was more like being part of a family rather than a business. Just sitting round in someone's lounge talking about going on holiday and making records, rather than how many units you could shift."

When asked which are his favourites among those Crass singles, Rimbaud struggles. "It's difficult to say, really. One of the most important things to me was that I liked who I was working with. I can honestly say that all of the people I worked with, I got on with and enjoyed. There's some tracks I did with other bands that I absolutely adored – *Chappaquidick Bridge* for the Poison Girls, which was a massive production job. Or 'No Doves Fly Here' by The Mob, or the K.U.K.L. album, where I put in a huge production load, was involved in the arrangements, etc. Those are the ones that jump to mind. But whatever I got involved in, I got completely involved in, or I don't do it. So everyone I worked with, I put the same degree of effort and enthusiasm in. I can't do things unless I'm 100% involved with them. Otherwise I get so bored I can't be there. If I become divorced from it, I just lose all interest, and go to bed and sleep. Because there's nothing better to do. I feel that with everything that I do, so it's a difficult question for me, because I was 100% into it.

"I was really trying to act as simply a go between with most of the bands," he explains further. "When I felt that what they were trying to say could be said in a more dramatic way – then I'd do that. And that's what happened with 'No Doves'. I thought, this is potentially a really *great* song, but what they're doing is really not that interesting. It was like a canvas that hadn't been properly completed. I said to Mark, look, I think we could make this 'big', we could really do something with it, because you've got a strong song. And Hit Parade was another record where I put in a huge amount of my own personal creativity, on top of their own, to enlarge on their ideas; because their ideas were so good. And there tended to be other people – Conflict or Dirt, the more archetypal punk bands, that I didn't really do a lot with, because there wasn't an awful lot there to do. It was raunchy punk or whatever, and that's how it came out. That's why Poison Girls were so lovely to work with, because they were so rich in ideas, and sometimes not able to push them through to the conclusions that they wanted. And they were the only people, initially, we did albums with, because they were our particular mates, and they'd helped us finance the label, etc."

All the Crass singles' covers featured a distinctive brand logo; a black circle with the artist name and record title stencilled in white. "Both Gee [Vaucher] and myself trained as graphic artists," explains Rimbaud. "Both of us prior to Crass had brought money into the house by doing book design and that sort of stuff. And part of training as a graphic artist wasn't just learning type[setting], it was also thinking in terms of marketing; a lot of the projects at college were – this is the product, how do you design and market it? How do you create a corporate idea?" In fact, Naomi Klein credited Crass as being one of the first innovators of brand identity in her book, *No Logo*. "And it was," agrees Rimbaud. "It was very much the idea of creating a corporate identity."

"There were only two bands who released singles through Crass who somehow persuaded us to alter in some way the corporate logo," he continues. "On the Poison Girls 'Promenade', we only used half a circle. And The Cravats wanted to do it black lettering on white, rather than white on black." The Cravats were happy with the concession, but otherwise fit snugly into Crass's brand vision. "We really liked it, actually," The Shend admits, "because a lot of the graphics were based on Dada, which was the art we employed with all our releases anyway. Utilising surrealism and Dada and the childlike qualities of music, to make music ridiculous and funny to get a point across. All the Crass symbols and stuff like that, that stuff was invented in 1918 or whatever – so we felt aligned with them on that. We basically didn't sound like any other Crass bands. Not straight down the line punk, we were jazzy wierdos. I think people were surprised they released Cravats stuff. How does this fit in? But we didn't really care."

"It's interesting," Rimbaud notes of those two releases, "that because they weren't instantly recognisable as being part of the corporate identity, it did affect the sales – no question of that. Minute variations, but sufficient variations to make them not recognisable. It was a very distinct policy that things should have an instantly recognisable image. So we developed a format into which anything could slip; in most cases the bands were left to do the artwork, BUT the artwork had to fit into the circle that went on the front."

In fact, it's largely only in retrospect that the artwork that emerged from Dial House has come to be acknowledged for both its conceptual integrity and its aesthetic richness. "Gee [Vaucher] is an extraordinary artist," says Rimbaud. "If Gee were to paint a corpse, for example, it would be hand-painted with extraordinary care and incredible beauty. So though the art might have been a vile subject, the care and love that went into the creation of it was of itself the energetic. Whereas just cutting out a picture of a corpse and sticking it on a piece of paper has a rather negative energetic. And I think that was the hidden power of Gee's work; the fact that so much obvious love went into its creation. However ghastly the image was, one was at the same time being made to look at it and think – my goodness, this is extraordinary. Peter Kennard, the political artist who teaches at Royal College, had been showing Gee's paintings, thinking they were photographic. He'd been showing students examples of her work for years, projected in lectures, as photo montage. It wasn't until he met Gee that he learned they were paintings, and he then understood the true meaning of her work."

Some of those designs ended up becoming almost universal symbols, though their cultural cache may not have been taken in exactly the way intended. "It's strange," nods Rimbaud, "particularly when it's people like [David] Beckham. He was wearing stuff with Crass written in diamante for quite a while [as did Angelina Jolie]. I think it's even stranger when it's your own handwriting. On one of our early things, I did an 'a' with a circle around it, and I've got a very distinctive line in my handwriting, which was actually a copy of Bernard Buffet, his way of writing. It was a way of pissing off my dad, who could write in perfect copperplate. I didn't want to write like my dad, even though he was always trying to make me. I'd seen a Bernard Buffet picture with his signature – oh, that looks good. So I developed this rather cranky way of writing, which I still employ, I can't write any other way now. And that 'a' became THE 'a' (i.e. the circled 'A' denoting anarchism), with the ends sticking outside the circle, because I don't stop my line. That's strange, because it's a very personal thing that becomes a very public thing. When I travel and see people wearing Crass stuff on their flesh, never mind their jacket. I don't think I like it very much."

It's fascinating to examine Crass's A&R policy, in so much as it was totally divorced from its conventional function; to identify music that will sell. And it becomes even more complicated when you add in the benevolent paternalism that was at work. Because, whether he liked it or coveted it at all, and you suspect he did not, Rimbaud was wise enough to realise that 'power' exists within all situations and relationships. It cannot be extinguished by good intentions. "I suppose I have to admit to a degree," says Rimbaud, "there was some cynicism. Someone like Conflict – I really, really liked Colin [Jerwood; vocalist]. He's a very complex personality, but I liked him. They used to be followers of the band, and Steve [Ignorant] got on with them particularly well. I can't say I was particularly enamoured of their public face. To a degree, it was a case where it was better to have them on board than not. To what degree there was an element of control going on – cynically, there probably was. I don't know how much of that is retrospective thinking. There was a very deep belief that we could manage if we could stick together."

In effect, the approach was analogous to 'broadening the church'. "I think so, to bring on board stuff that maybe I felt was a little bit dodgy, within my own political framework. I'm being very self-critical – maybe I saw them as a slight threat. The only people who got away with that was [anarchist group] Class War, because they weren't containable within a rock 'n' roll framework. So they were actually able to set up an alternative to the trajectory that we were on, and it actually became quite a powerful alternative. I like Ian [Bone; Class War founder] a lot, and get on very well with him – just as he thought our politics were crap, I thought his politics were crap. It didn't mean we couldn't have a bloody good laugh if we were on a demo together. I always got on very well with him. But they were a threat. I regarded the sort of empowerment that they created as very dangerous for kids who didn't have some sort of political awareness. And I saw that happen time and time again. So in that sense I thought they were a threat to our 'power', our power being one that I think was deeply considerate of the dangers we might be creating for other people which we didn't carry ourselves. I think we had a deep sense of social responsibility. My criticism of Class War is that it was deeply socially irresponsible in a lot of senses."

One of the drawbacks of the one-off singles deal approach was that some artists needed more than just an initial investment of time and money. "We began to realise that some bands couldn't cope. They'd put out a single, get the exposure – and generally speaking, if they did put out a single with us, they'd get a lot of media attention by the standards of the day. And they couldn't cope. Either they didn't have the financing or the suss to do so. So we then created a second label, Corpus Christi, which we effectively gave to John Loder. Because we'd recorded at Southern, John was our sound engineer as well. With Corpus Christi, he was running two commercially viable outfits. One was the studio itself, the other was his own label. So he started expanding into what is now Southern Records, and also set up the distribution thing and joined the Cartel."

"We still had the broad control over Corpus Christi," Rimbaud continues, "in the sense that he always would say – 'I'd like to record such and such.' We were more casual with that label about content. If something cropped up that was, say, vilely sexist, we wouldn't have allowed it to happen. But we were much freer about allowing opinions and views that maybe we wouldn't have wanted to support directly through Crass Records. That was also a way of allowing John a financial situation where he could set up deals with bands, etc. I'm not even sure what some of the deals were. It also enabled him to expand from Corpus Christi into allowing people like Conflict or Flux of Pink Indians to create their own labels, within Southern, and then sometimes move out of Southern. Which is what happened with One Little Indian. All the time what we were trying to look for was to give people access to setting up their own thing. Initially we thought people would just do it, but that was expecting too much, and they didn't have the financing. So Corpus Christi was invented as a stepping stone. That policy was taken through everything we did. Our gigging principle was that whatever money we made from gigs, that money would be put back into the community where we made it. Say we went to Clayton-le-Moors in the Lake District, the money would be put back into that community. We'd find out maybe there was a rape crisis centre, or a CND group, or a local band needed a drum kit. The whole policy was to expand the DIY ethos, which was very dear to us. How can we make the most of any situation for the situation itself? The way we dealt with recording was similar. We didn't want to own anything or anyone. There were no contracts. Nothing was ever signed, it was all on trust. Inevitably within that situation, occasionally things went wrong. They do. And they're more likely to go wrong if people take 'a straight course'. Maybe someone would get a manager, or someone would sign with [publishing collection agency] MCPS, whatever. That would create problems for people trying to operate outside the system. Someone like John, basically speaking, the moment he got a phone call from a manager, that would be the end of his relationship with the band. Because he couldn't and wouldn't deal with that. His attitude was, if that's the way you want to go, go with it. That's how he survived."

Yet are not managers and agents the legitimate advocates of a band's interests? "I think that's true," says Rimbaud, "but then, if those were their interests, they weren't ours, in our defence. We weren't in the least bit interested in anything commercial." In recent years, Southern has not been without its detractors. "When we worked with Southern," notes Chumbawamba's Boff Whalley, "most of the people there were lovely, lovely folk who worked their arses off for the bands. But we learnt to our dismay that the publishing deal we signed with Southern was about three times as bad as any publishing deal anywhere else; a total con. Took us ages to get out of it, made no money on it, and regretted not getting advice about it beforehand. In the cold light of experience, I find it incredibly sad that the members of Crass have sold untold hundreds of thousands of albums and CDs but aren't getting money from it. Despite the low cover price, they should be getting publishing money, enough to allow them to do what they want to do creatively and artistically and politically. But that's my personal gripe about Southern, it was a part of it that we found rotten."

Rimbaud counters that "John was good at playing with money, and created an empire out of Southern, which I never resented. While we were floundering and trying to survive after the band, John was running a very successful business. But that was fair enough, because it was part of the deal. He remained very honest throughout. How he did that and be such a successful businessman is anyone's guess. He was just brilliant with money. He didn't use any of it – that was the funny thing. He still drove around in a rotten old van, lived in a crappy place in Wood Green, and never thought of making the studio nicer – it just didn't occur to him, any of that. So it was the game of money he liked, I don't think he cared a fuck about *having* money. And he was always hugely generous with projects that he knew would make no money whatsoever. Either with us or anyone else. He was always willing to put his oar into anything. I used to see people getting annoyed with him if something wasn't happening as fast as it might, whatever, and sometimes John might have appeared to be devious. But he was juggling so much, particularly with money, that everything was on a see-saw. I could see that, and some people couldn't, and they were a bit badmouthed towards him."

"John was so totally at ease yet in control of any situation," remembers Dick Lucas of The Subhumans, "never got flustered, never forgot who people were, and had the knack of convincing through his conviction. He really liked Subhumans to a degree that he apparently reserved for Crass and Rudimentary Peni. He didn't like either [Lucas's subsequent bands] Culture Shock or Citizen Fish half as much – just to show I'm not wearing rosy glasses! He was younger than our parents, but old enough to seem semi-parental, something that would explain the degree of loss felt when he died. He was definitely a one-off, and we were lucky to know him."

Among the bands Loder picked up, that Crass had passed on, were UK Decay, who had featured on the first volume of *Bullshit Detector*. "I didn't really like them," admits Rimbaud. "I didn't dislike them as people, they were a really nice bunch of guys. He liked what they were doing, and that was fine. Or someone like Fugazi, that John picked up on." The latter band had grown out of Minor Threat and Washington DC's Dischord Records stable, whose DIY approach, hard-headed rejection of commercial compromise, commitment to all-ages shows and community action, mirrors the early goals of Crass Records. "Because he was seen as Mr Crass," Rimbaud continues, "people tended to gravitate towards John, and in America he picked up a lot of contacts through his reputation as a member of the band – and that was good, a really comfortable set up. In retrospect, I regret we weren't a little bit more sensible with the capital that was floating about. The studio would have been here [Dial House], but in those days, there was a big radio station on this land, so we couldn't set up a studio here. If it had have been, we would have now owned it. We, effectively, having had thousands, possibly up to a million pounds, floating around at one point, never bought or invested in anything. In retrospect it was bloody stupid. We are still hopelessly in debt over this house, almost bust. I don't resent it, but I regret not having been a little bit more sensible with the capital that we had, because we could have paid for this instead of having the constant headache."

That was effectively the story of the Crass label until the early 90s. "Then I was talking to John," Rimbaud recalls, "and saying, this is probably a bit daft, we're not actually producing anything any more. You're working for us at far below what you could be or should be making in manufacture and distribution. So we then, effectively, realigned it all. Although the label exists still, and we own it and have complete artistic control, the financial administration is all through Southern, and we simply get royalties. It's no longer a share-out, and we pay them just as any other band would pay their manufacturer and distributor. The label itself is sacrosanct, in the sense that nothing can go in or out. I've been remastering it recently, trying to make the final statement on it, making sure the artwork is properly done and writing little essays to accompany each album. It's not very nice having that sort of heritage to carry – especially if it's grubby. And it was beginning to get grubby. So we're trying to make it into something beautiful, something that will have the value and hold it."

Crass the band ceased to exist in 1984; just as they had promised. "We became seen as po-faced, hardened anarchists, but there was deep humour," insists Rimbaud. "The irony to us was never far from the surface, the fact that we could laugh absurdly at it, while people were taking it so seriously. The one time the shell actually cracked was a gig down in Exeter. We suddenly realised how fucking stupid it was. It was the only rock 'n' roll performance we ever did, and everyone was into posing like Pete Townshend and fucking about. And of course, it went down really, really well! And it was a complete self piss-take. We were barely able to play because we were laughing so much at ourselves."

As well as Loder personally engineering records for Björk, Fugazi, the Jesus and Mary Chain and others, he started a network of labels operating out of Southern, in partnership with his wife and artist, Sue. As Crass Records closed with the dissolution of the band in 1984, Southern took up the slack, offering a home for maverick bands and artists, while retaining the original ideals with which they were founded. There were no concessions to bigger businesses when they expressed an interest (which they did on several occasions). Loder remained a reclusive figure, declining requests for interviews, until his death in August 2005, at which time Rimbaud composed the following obituary for *The Guardian*. "He displayed a reticence which extended even to his closest friends. For that reason, very few people were aware that during the last 18 months he had been battling with a brain tumour, which finally killed him. But just as John's studio has become legendary, so has his insistence that quality of product should come before quantity: his angle, small is beautiful, was the big idea."

You can make a good case for Crass being the most influential punk band of them all. Certainly they probably had a more profound impact on the way people live their lives – from the protest movement, through a new consciousness about environmental impact to vegetarianism, than anything that is, as Rimbaud suggests, as transitory as 'rock 'n' roll. He thinks that's due, in large part, to the 'real nature' of what they accomplished. "I do believe that it was only through our actions – and I don't mean in choosing to be a rock 'n' roll band – but the way in which we act within whichever theatre we choose to live our lives. It's the authenticity of the experience that we bring to something that generates that effect. I think we were absolutely extraordinary as a group of people. There was anything up to a dozen of us on the road together. We had absolute commitment to each other, firstly, and then to the situation, and absolute honesty within that. Which isn't to say there weren't big problems outside of that – but within the theatre we'd chosen to enact, we were absolutely 100% – unfailingly. At our own cost. When we came out of that, we realised the cost in terms of our relationships, with ourselves and with each other. But as a human experiment of absolute belief, it worked. Everywhere I go I'll meet people in every walk of life who have been deeply affected by what we did. And that's because we were genuine. I'm not saying we were genuine people, but we were genuine *within that situation*. Having to put aside doubt, which is always corruptive. We couldn't operate

If we were going to doubt it. These were common agreements that created a force. I'm quite sure that was the power of the Nazi regime. I'm not advocating that, obviously, but the power of it came through the cadre of people who had no doubt. Or look at Thatcher's fucking outfit. Blair failed against Thatcher, because Thatcher had no doubt. Blair did, and that made him weak. And detestable. One has to, somehow or another, admire Thatcher for that, although I loathed what she did."

That does not mean, however, that Rimbaud has any great sentimental attachment for some of the 'anarcho punk' groups who followed; particularly those who merely xeroxed (often literally) Crass's arguments, and followed their lead uncritically. That early sequence of Crass releases still comprises an exceptional body of work, but thereafter there was a good deal of the unthinkingly repetitious – as if a new orthodoxy had been established. Several of these releases aped the surface monochromatic artwork of Crass without ever equalling their aesthetic dynamism, or contesting the assumptions behind them. "The anarcho punk movement was an anathema to me," Rimbaud concludes. "I wasn't interested in it. I didn't like it. I think it was very divisive in any case. It was a very convenient way for the business to put us outside the business – us and everything we were related to. I don't think we isolated ourselves, we were isolated by the industry, who couldn't contain us. It was only very late on that we realised we were completely separate, and that wasn't a separateness that we sought. We refused to do commercial gigs etc, but that wasn't to make ourselves separate, it was to ensure punters got a decent, fair deal." There was a pragmatism to some of those aspects of 'not playing the game', too, rather than necessarily ideology. For example, the reason songs were credited to the group as a whole arose directly as a means of preventing individuals from being picked off by the DPP or other agents of the law.

"All of those things were directed towards the people who wanted to buy our records or come to the gigs," Rimbaud insists, "to give them the fairest deal. We weren't trying to put ourselves out of the framework; we wanted to be *in* the framework. [Garry] Bushell criticised us for not being in the belly of the beast. That's actually where we wanted to be, and in fact, we were. Even now, most punk history books don't really incorporate us – they just harp on about the rock 'n' roll aspect. Fair enough. But it's not honest. Something else happened that was one of the most powerful youth movements that existed in the 20th century, and it has parallels to the Dada movements and existential movements in its cultural effect."

# Independence Days

By the time the band had ended, they'd done their best to disrupt assumptions about what they represented, especially musically. "We went into almost auto destruct mode to circumvent all of that," Rimbaud acknowledges. "Which is what our last output was, from the extreme jazz of *Yes Sir I Will* (1983) to the European avant garde of *Ten Notes On A Summer's Day* (1986). They were both attempts to completely smash the mirror. And it sort of worked, it did break the mirror. Which is why I really resented Steve's thing at the Shepherds Bush Empire [vocalist Steve Ignorant would perform *Feeding Of The 5,000* in its entirety featuring guest musicians in 2008]. To my mind, whatever the intention was, that was an attempt to put back the pieces of the mirror. You can't do that. We had very effectively smashed the mirror. In a way there's a freedom in that. It's quite possible, I hadn't thought about it before, but maybe it's Steve doing that gig that inspired me to go back and do what I've been doing recently, which is remastering everything and redesigning [the back catalogue]. Basically because that just seems dirty. So, in a way, I want to recreate something that's honest and good and has something of the energetic of what we did 30 years ago. I just get a profound tiredness from something like that Shepherds Bush thing, the faux quality of it, the ersatz experience, which I so hate. It's so the direct opposite of authenticity."

"A little while after the band had folded," Rimbaud remembers, "I was in Battersea Park, and there was the Jesus Army, with a bloody big tent there, trying to convert people. I was with Eve [Libertine], and we strolled in and we were immediately accosted. They had a team at the entrance, and they had different sorts of people within the team – some slightly tweedy, some slightly alternative. They knew how to target – so we got the slightly grunge Jesus Army member come and talk to us. What I found appalling about it was that they were using all the same things that you could have accused us of using as tactics – the free hand-outs, the warmth, the generosity. Exactly the same things, exactly the same sort of audience. Mostly younger, disillusioned kids, who are always on the lookout for some meaning in their life. They were exploiting all the same obvious needs that I'd like to think we *weren't* exploiting. One shouldn't really assume that the Jesus Army weren't being equally altruistic. The Jesus Army believed in what they were doing. I don't happen to believe in it, but that isn't to discredit their systems of belief. But I found that quite disturbing, really. However honest and genuine or whatever – you can't destroy the myth-making within situations, however hard one tries. I tried like the devil within Crass with *Yes Sir* and *Ten Notes*, both of which were almost exclusively my creative input. Other people did it, but they did it with resistance in both cases. I was trying to subvert the whole thing, to break the myth. But you can't do it. It's impossible. Once you've been mythologised, the myth simply continues. It's like a kangaroo pocket, everything will fall into it."

Among the least conditioned and musically stereotyped bands to emerge from *Bullshit Detector* (they contributed 'Three Years Later' to the second volume) were Chumbawamba, who started out with something akin to anarchist vaudeville. "We'd been making tapes of stuff for a while," notes band member Boff Whalley, "odd, Frank Zappa-inspired things. It never seemed like it was in the 'Crass' vein. But we were identifying ourselves as anarchists, while being wary of the 'mohican' end of things. We weren't being snotty or snobbish, just aware that we didn't want to get sucked into some cult thing. We were still really into pop stuff like the Monochrome Set and Wire; still really into belligerent northern stuff like The Fall; and all the while reading Malatesta and *Black Flag* and all that. We sent a cassette of stuff to Crass – it was a Zappa-inspired 20-minute 'concept' piece, lots of different things linked up musically – without ever having heard of the *Bullshit Detector* thing. The first we knew about *Bullshit Detector* was when we got a letter from Crass months and months later saying they'd decided to use part of what we sent. They snipped a bit from the 20-minute piece and stuck it on there."

"We didn't know Penny then, or later, or now," Boff continues. "I love Penny, he's a big part of my growing up – even now, I love to read and hear what he says. I think I've maybe had thirty seconds conversation with him. He's such a clever bloke. Always has been. But I've had such disagreements with what he's said, too. We also did a fanzine, which we called *The Obligatory Crass Interview*, the joke being that there wasn't a Crass interview in it [at a time when nearly ever fanzine seemed to carry such a feature as a pre-condition of its existence]. Basically, our connection to the Crass people/band/label was because we loved *Feeding Of The 5,000*, loved them live and partly, through them, started to learn about anarchism/radicalism/revolutionary politics etc. We loved that whole DIY scene – thought it was something huge and exciting and important. They were the bee's knees – but we certainly weren't going to try to play like them, or sound like them. We still loved Orange Juice and the Marine Girls, and we had this idea that Crass were a southern thing, that it somehow didn't quite translate into the football-loving heartlands."

And yet, Boff concedes, Crass were 'instrumental' in 'us becoming what we were'. "They kept us eager and questioning and interested. They were a part of the music scene that nobody had encountered before. We fed off their ideas so much. Our problem was that we took them at face value and believed that biting the hand that fed us was part of the process. The two most influential people in my political/cultural education were Penny Rimbaud and Johnny Rotten. Neither of these would be happy to hear that, I think. We were definitely privileged to have been part of that, early on. When we got the track on *Bullshit Detector 2*, we sat around and made a definite plan of action. How to take this further. Crass had made a statement about wanting to encourage bands to do things on their own, so we took it as a nudge in the right direction."

Several bands similarly took that option. The origins of Flux Of Pink Indians' Spiderleg imprint originate in The Epileptics, a previous incarnation of the band, based in nearby Bishops Stortford. "What the hell Crass ever saw in The Epileptics, at first, we have absolutely no idea!" recalls Kevin Hunter. "The Epileptics were doing songs like 'I Wanna Give You A '69'. Crass obviously couldn't have heard the lyrics, but maybe they liked the attitude." Nevertheless the alliance served the band well, as Flux of Pink Indians became part of the wider Crass movement and discourse.

Conflict would establish Mortarhate, under whose flag sailed several unremarkable anarcho groups, the best of which were Icons Of Filth, The Lost Cherrees, Hagar The Womb and Potential Threat. Chumbawamba themselves set up Agit Prop and, after releasing debut single 'Revolution', set about planning a full album, *Pictures Of Starving Children Sell Records* was unarguably among the most persuasive records to emerge from the anarcho punk movement. "We had definite studio days booked in to record an album," recalls Boff, "and we had a set of songs to record. And then the *Live Aid* thing began to creep into popular culture. This big thing that was going to happen, and why, and what it meant, etc. Of course, we had concrete objections to the whole charade. With about two weeks to go before we had our first day in the studio (and that was a big day in those times, proper studio days and proper studio costs), we had a meeting. It was suggested that we scrap all the lyrics we had and re-write the whole thing so it was about *Live Aid*. Everyone agreed, some reluctantly. We had frantic rehearsals and writing sessions and came up with a whole new album, written to the tunes of the proposed album."

"I still have the pile of books we speed-read to get ourselves acquainted with the Africa/charity situation," he continues. "All we knew originally was that we didn't trust Bob Geldof and Freddie Mercury to know what was happening, and to come up with the best solution. We wanted to be provocative but at the same time informed. The second thing about *Pictures* is that we wanted to make an 'anarcho-punk' record that didn't sound like one. We wanted it to be clever and weird and up and down and not to everyone's taste. We wanted it to embrace pop, alongside the distortion pedals. We talked to Red Rhino, the distributors, and made it clear that this was a strange record. We went into overdrive for the ten days recording and tried to piece together something strange and interesting. Then we concocted the sleeve, making all the song titles look like titles of chapters in a book. We spent ages with the sleeve, mimicking the then-current Habitat colours, making it all cool and fashionable, except that we had the tiny picture of the starving child obscured by the price tag."

It would be the first album released on Agit Prop. "We were careful about how much everything cost, etc. We did our own press releases and promo, cynical as possible, sent it to people we vaguely knew at radio stations and music press. And that was it. There was no big PR offensive or anything. We just sent about thirty or forty copies out to the press. And it picked up from there. At this point we were still in control of everything, but Red Rhino were paying for studio time and pressing costs. We had a relationship with Red Rhino, which was based partly on our vision of their set-up, as we saw it. The boss of this 'independent' company drove a BMW. The workers caught the bus. The company were indebted to the success of The Wedding Present's *George Best* album (a lovely record) to keep them afloat. So really, we kept ourselves at a distance from their general day-to-day workings. Agit Prop started as a vehicle for us releasing our own stuff and branched out into helping other people put out records. It was so shoddily run! We weren't very good at being a record label. We didn't have definite roles within Agit Prop – other than some people being better at promo, others at artwork, others at finances etc. But we knew all that with the band, anyway. We'd always shared out the various tasks."

The parallel to Crass and 'speed-reading' subject matter (Crass; anarchism, Chumbawamba; a specific, and grotesque, incidence of record industry hypocrisy) is illuminating. Their inclination to disrupt expectations rather than riff on the accepted musical discourse also approximates Rimbaud's instincts in the latter days of Crass. Chumbawamba's second album, *English Rebel Songs*, was "a direct challenge to what we seemed to be steeped in at the time – the DIY punk movement," Boff confirms. "We loved it, but knew we needed to somehow do it differently. Of course punk is about change, challenge, ideas, etc. But that could apply to *a capella* singing, if you so wish.

We didn't really have any intention of singing the *a capella* songs live; but it was important that we set up the idea that punk/anarcho-punk/DIY etc wasn't just four blokes with loud guitars and fast drums. As it happens *English Rebel Songs* didn't come out for ages after we'd recorded it, 'cos Red Rhino went bust. We had two albums recorded and pressed when they went bust – *English Rebel Songs* and *Sportchestra*, a double album of songs about sport. We had to wrangle and wrangle and negotiate and discuss with receivers and lawyers etc to eventually get that stock from them. Because Red Rhino had gone bankrupt we were left with the studio costs for both albums, which we didn't legally have to pay, but which we did anyway, cos we thought it unfair that the studio should get shafted cos Red Rhino messed up."

If Chumbawamba were in any doubt about the rigour with which 'DIY punk' branding was policed, and the stylistic limits set on it, they found out when *Maximum Rock 'n' Roll* refused to review *English Rebel Songs. MRR*, for well over two decades, has become the pre-eminent arbiter of international punk, initially under the late Tim Yohannon's stewardship. "We stayed at the *MRR* house in San Francisco for a couple of days, with Tim Yohannon etc," Boff recalls. "They were lovely people, very friendly and helpful. But we couldn't get over the barrier of them refusing to acknowledge *English Rebel Songs. MRR* was reviewing hardcore South American bands singing racist songs, (cos they were loud and guitar-based) but wouldn't review ours 'cos it was 'folky'. It made us dig in our heels even more about music, politics, ideas, perceptions, etc. And of course the Americans really didn't have any inkling of the political implications [as explored on their subsequent album *Slap!*] of 'dance music' – rave, warehouse parties, criminalisation, cops, etc."

Chumbawamba's records would sell in the region of 10,000 copies each. "In the early days especially, we made bugger all from record sales," admits Boff. "We were always happy to break even. Agit Prop's releases by other bands all failed to break even, except for Credit to the Nation – and their best-selling single we just gave away to One Little Indian, because they could sell it properly. The pricing of every record we ever made has been discussed in meetings. Costs, recording, publishing, distribution, promo, equipment, studios, advertising, all that stuff. It always comes up. Long discussions between us all about whether or not to put an advert in the *Guardian Guide*, or whatever. We never have had anyone booking studios for us and that sort of thing."

Thereafter, Chumbawamba would famously join the despised EMI. It may not have been counter-revolutionary, but it was at least counter-intuitive. And having a number two hit on the back of that, 'Tubthumper', threw everyone a googly. The reaction from some in the 'movement' was as dismissive as might be imagined. As one anarcho distribution service noted recently while advertising "First and Second Demos and the *Individual Possession* LP – all studio tracks from a bunch of sell out cunts. £2.50." It's alarming that someone would be so hysterical about a band whose material they are continuing to sell (illegally). Of course, given Chumbawamba had previously taken to throwing red paint over Joe Strummer's post-Mick Jones Clash when Bernie Rhodes sent them off on a busking tour, they now found themselves having to repeat some of that band's mantras about access and the need to get the message out.

The most successful label to emerge out of the anarcho punk movement was undoubtedly One Little Indian, formed by former Epileptics and Flux Of Pink Indians bass player Derek Birkett. It built on the lessons learned in an earlier venture, Spiderleg. Flux had released the 'Neu Smell' EP for Crass before Spiderleg was inaugurated with two EPs of archive Epileptics material. The first was a re-recording of the '1970s Have Been Made In Hong Kong' EP, originally issued on local Hertfordshire label Stortbeat before disputes over alleged non-payment of royalties strained relations. The re-recording featured Rimbaud himself on percussion, stepping in at short notice when The Epileptics' own drummer refused to record. The second, 'Last Bus To Debden', was a posthumous live recording from September 1979. It featured 'Tube Disaster', one of anarcho-punk's most celebrated songs (probably because in the midst of so much austerity and seriousness, it betrayed a wonderfully macabre sense of humour), which the remoulded Flux had re-recorded for 'Neu Smell'.

But it was with the release of the Subhumans 'Demolition Wars' that the label really established itself as arguably a second-tier Crass. The latter band, though endorsing many of the anti-capitalist sentiments of the anarcho-punks, had both a superior musical foundation and an impish sense of humour. They quickly became the third-ranking anarcho band beneath Crass and Conflict via a series of EPs for Spiderleg and their 1983 LP *The Day The Country Died*. The latter reached number three in the independent charts (and would later provide the title to Ian Glasper's encyclopaedic chronicle of the entire anarcho-punk movement).

"We were more excited at the idea of being on Spiderleg than we would have been had Crass asked us to be on their label," recalls singer Dick Lucas, "as we'd already met Flux. We thought the continuation of the cheap price tags on sleeves and black and white artwork, which both Crass and Flux [and Conflict etc] had done was a good idea for its visual statement of intent and where we were 'coming from'. It also made economic sense – colour sleeves? Decorating the twisted truth with fairy lights to sell the product? And not cheap!"

Asked if he saw the anarcho scene as belonging within the greater discourse of independent music, Lucas notes that "The Cravats were on Crass Records, as were Hit Parade, and neither were musically punk rock at all. So we are talking about attitudes, really, as to what makes a scene. If we go by the dress sense then all the black clothing was a visual disregard and disdain for what was laughingly called 'independent' music and all its bouffant trappings. If we go by the music, the boundaries are too blurred to instantly know an anarcho band by their notes alone: so it's the message, in the lyrics and on the sleeves, that defines to the point of applying a label of 'anarcho' to a subset of punk rock. As for the contextual state of indie music at the time, well, anarcho-punk was happy to be left beyond the peripheries of fame, celebrity gloss and fancy dress, and wouldn't play the game. The game was the spectacle and there's the rub – the system functions on the back of our diversions."

There were other approaches to the band prior to the release of their second EP, 'Reason For Existence'. One came from Small Wonder, the second from Sus Records, best known for the Case EP 'Wheat From The Chaff', and would-be entrants to the Oi! fold. "They were from South London and we turned them down after we'd met the chaps in charge, one of whom stood before a fireplace like someone else's uncle on acid telling us all about the music industry for half an hour. In the same room stood an art table holding the preliminary layout for a porn magazine."

Thereafter The Subhumans, in keeping with the best traditions of anarcho baton-passing, established their own record label Bluurg (which in addition to vinyl released more than 100 cheap cassettes, and was actually extant during the Subhumans' time at Spiderleg). "Before I was even in a band," remembers Lucas, "I was swapping bootleg tapes of the Pistols, Banshees etc, and numerous Peel sessions, with similar 'killing the music industry' types advertising in the back of *NME* and *Sounds*. My tapes list was the first Bluurg list. After I recorded a Members gig in July 1979 I got into recording any gig I went to, or played [his first band, The Mental, were operational by then]. And as interest died in what were becoming increasingly shite quality bootlegs of now disbanded groups, I made the Bluurg list exclusive to local bands [from the Melksham-Trowbridge-Warminster punk rock triangle in Wiltshire]. After seeing the Instigators being awesome live, I decided to expand it to anyone I liked/who had something to say. From dodgy Pistols tapes for £2.50 to local/unheard music for a 'blank tape and 20p'."

It was a huge undertaking, but one Lucas found immediately rewarding. "Excitement cancels out mental effort as a concept, and I generally get excited by making/creating things. Releasing tapes was easy, and it took the experience of recording a record or three and finding out the details of who does what like pressing and distribution to make the next step of doing it myself more realistic. Even with that, and the 'Wessex '82' EP [a vinyl compilation of the best local punk bands] all recorded, I didn't have the money to make the records. Which is where I accepted John Loder's offer of paying for it to get made and doing the distribution through Southern. It did make me think, 'This is how DIY, exactly?' But on the other hand this was the set-up that resulted in both Crass and Spiderleg Records coming into existence, so this was John being very DIY indeed and helping labels and bands out, because he could. When I was cycling 14 miles a day to a crap job and then coming home to 20-30 letters a day, the peak busy time just after *The Day The Country Died* came out, it wasn't the letters I resented, it was the job! I quit soon after."

Flux's own *Strive To Survive Causing Least Suffering Possible* topped the independent charts, featuring a gatefold sleeve recalling the police intimidation the band had been subjected to. They then did much to alienate their audience, and more particularly the authorities, with *The Fucking Cunts Treat Us Like Pricks*. A Dada-inspired exercise originally intended to be an EP, it had the rare distinction of being as musically abrasive as its title suggested; the wretched, agonised vocals recorded in the toilets of Southern Studios. Themed on the experiences of a band member who had been sexually assaulted, copies were seized from retailers, one of whom, Manchester's Eastern Bloc store, was charged with displaying 'Obscene Articles for Publication for Gain'.

Spiderleg also housed the first recordings by Amebix – largely credited with being the inspiration behind 'crust' punk (an amalgam of anarcho and 'black' metal influences). Another band to emerge through the *Bullshit Detector* route, they were well versed with the Crass/anarcho dialectic. But as the band's Baron Von Aphid would state, "The sound [on their Southern Studios' recorded 'No Sanctuary' EP] was really dominated by the

Crass/Spiderleg agenda, which was to thin the guitars out, so the mix was really not what we were looking for." Again, the job lot package of Crass values – political, philosophical, aesthetic – that accompanied releases on the interwoven labels can be argued to have restricted the artistic liberty of some of its artists. Flux's elaborately packaged 'Taking A Liberty' single proved to be the label's last stand, as Birkett decided to move on to One Little Indian Records, founded with fellow travellers from the anarcho scene in South London in 1985.

Despite being something of a holdover from Birkett's anarcho roots – initially One Little Indian functioned on co-operative principles with assistance from Birkett's wife Sue and ex-Flux guitarist Tom Kelly – the repertoire reflected diverse musical interests. "The intention was to make records for fun," Birkett later conceded to *Music Week*. "I didn't want a record company. [When Spiderleg finished] I decided to start another label and just make records for the love of music. The anarchic punk scene had got too violent." One Little Indian was inaugurated with the October 1985 release of the abbreviated Flux's *Uncarved Block*, a record, produced by dubmeister Adrian Sherwood, employing industrial and ambient textures. There was a clear break, sonically, with its anarcho-punk heritage, as AR Kane and They Might Be Giants joined the roster.

However, their earliest breakthrough signing, Iceland's Sugarcubes, came directly from that activist punk scene (members were formerly in K.U.K.L., including Einar Örn, who was studying at Central London Polytechnic and thus wired into the Crass/Flux circuit). If critics had pointed out that singer Björk Guðmundsdóttir, a former child recording artist self-tutored on Discharge and Ella Fitzgerald records, was a rare talent during her time with K.U.K.L., several more noticed now. Indeed, the media attention on her would somewhat overshadow and undermine the group's success.

Fellow travellers with Crass philosophically, the Sugarcubes grew out of Bad Taste Inc, an organisation formed in 1986 to establish a base for Reykjavik's Bohemian arts community, with cafes, poetry bookshops and a record label. The Sugarcubes were, effectively, the 'pop music arm' of the operation. "We had all played before," Örn would explain to Mat Snow, "but with the Sugarcubes we decided to play pop music and totally disgust ourselves. We looked at each other and said, can we play this – it's such a cliche? And we said, fuck it, we can, because we're the Sugarcubes. We're a pop band, a living cliche." Just as Rimbaud attests that the establishment and maintenance of the Dial House open house ethic was ultimately more important than anything he achieved with Crass, Bad Taste's legacy, and continuing operations, have been responsible for Iceland punching several divisions above its weight in terms of contemporary music and art. And to suggest that they are in any way responsible for any minor international banking collapses might be gilding the Paris quadrifolia (member of the lily family found in lava crevasses, to save you a google).

The Sugarcubes produced a run of exhilarating, Peel-adored singles and a terrific debut album, *Life's Too Good*, in 1988. However, as Birkett would tell Phil Sutcliffe, the partnership nearly didn't get that far. "We wouldn't have existed but for Rough Trade. When we wanted to record The Sugarcubes album in 1988 and we didn't have any money, RTD (Rough Trade Distribution) fronted us £100,000. Then, when the record suddenly started selling, we had a cash flow crisis; we didn't have enough to press up extra copies quick. It could have badly affected the band, their moment could have passed, but Rough Trade and Daniel Miller pulled me out of it with another loan. They did it to allow us to exist outside the major label system." In fact, it was not the original intention that *Life's Too Good* should come out on One Little Indian at all. Birkett had arranged for its release via a major, but the band resisted when the A&R contact tried to shape the way it was to be recorded and presented, Shortly after its release, Jay Barbour joined as One Little Indian's business affairs manager. They are the only label discussed in this chapter, we can surely say, to have ever had one of those. One Little Indian was becoming a 'grown-up' label, with all that entailed.

But it was those harbingers of rave culture The Shamen, previously purveyors of a psychedelic/political pop hybrid who had recorded for several labels before joining One Little Indian, that provided the next big push. They appealed to Birkett specifically because they reminded him of his political activism in the late 70s, though he was somewhat taken aback when they abandoned what he perceived to be their psychedelic leanings for a pure dance groove. In his *Melody Maker* essay on the band, Paul Lester noted that only Scritti Politti, Joy Division/New Order and Primal Scream had successfully undergone a similar journey – key contributors all to what we now understand as an independent ethic. The band themselves were initially frustrated when critical acclaim wasn't consolidated, especially after 'Pro-Gen' proved a hit with DJs. It all fell into place when a remix of that same song, retitled 'Move Any Mountain', reached number four in the charts in July 1991. Unfortunately, its success was overshadowed by the death of Will Sin in a swimming accident in the Canaries while filming the accompanying video. The Shamen's chart success, which peaked when

'Ebeneezer Goode' topped the UK charts in August 1992, proved fleeting, and was effectively over by the end of 1993.

That year Chumbawamba joined One Little Indian. They had atypical Crass pedigrees, mixing theatrical elements with a diffuse take on music that eschewed the abrasive three-chord logarithms favoured by most of those influenced by Crass. Yet that connection certainly played a part in persuading Chumbawamba to throw their hand in with the label, as Boff recalls. "Yes, it was because of Derek Birkett, ex-Flux. He was (and is) a lovely bloke. He still wanted to do radical stuff despite being in a successful business. Yes, we liked his success outside 'punk' – with Björk etc – but really we just trusted his integrity. I think the problem with Derek was, he was an idealist who found himself in a world full of realists. His financial advisors constantly were telling him, no, don't do that, you'll go bankrupt, etc. But basically he had this successful independent label which was exciting and interesting and which we felt proud to be part of, for a while. And we thought it connected us, umbilically, to that Crass/Flux anarcho-punk world, but without the grime and cider and punks pissing in their own pants while they lay on the floor at gigs. We thought, this is where the anarchist music thing can go – it can spread and diversify. We'd toured with Björk and Sugarcubes (as K.U.K.L.) and saw where they were taking their musical ideas. We loved dance music. And we thought, let's get involved with Derek and One Little Indian and see what happens."

Other signings during the 90s included Skunk Anansie, led by shaven headed lead singer Skin (Deborah Dyer), who initially scared Birkett half to death, Kitchens Of Distinction, the Sneaker Pimps, Alabama 3 and Rocket From The Crypt. However, it is Björk who remains the label's crown jewel, channelling Icelandic traditional music, dance rhythms and effervescent pop through one of the late 20th century's most distinctive vocal prisms. *Debut*, released in 1993, sold five million copies worldwide (its original break-even budget had been estimated at 25,000 sales). "The extraordinary thing about Björk," Birkett would confirm to *Music Week*, "is that she does everything herself. She deals with people directly and she puts 150% of what she has into what she does. And people give a lot more back." Björk can legitimately be seen as representing the commercial high watermark of the anarcho-punk generation – yet she is an artist of such raw promise, she would doubtless have outgrown whatever musical and social framework originally sustained her. Either way several of her values; notably an ambivalent view of fame and a distrust of music business interlopers, link directly to her past. "When The Sugarcubes insanity took off," she would tell Valur Gunnarrsson,

## Do They Owe Us A Living?

"I had a one-year-old boy. I decided that if he didn't like riding on buses, I would abandon music and head for the fish factory. He liked riding on buses." One Little Indian, similarly, retained much of the original vision of anarcho punk despite scoring enormous chart success. Exactly how much of that vision has been retained has been a subject long debated in puritanical anarcho circles. Though distributed by Virgin/EMI from 1998 (following an earlier deal with London, and a subsequent placing with Pinnacle until its 2008 collapse), One Little Indian has otherwise maintained its independence.

Away from the anarcho sector, a series of labels of late 70s/early 80s vintage kept an unapologetic flag flying for punk, despite being told at every turn that the zeitgeist had long since decamped and their rosters were artistically meaningless, if not actually remedial. In some cases these oft-overlooked catalogues were guilty as charged; propagating a moribund, intellectually shrivelled version of the punk promise. But the snobbery around the period overlooks both great individual records and also historically important ones.

One of the many independents to grow out of the retail/collecting fraternity was Alex Howe and Alan Hauser's Fresh. Hauser was a keen record collector, former mobile DJ and promoter, as well as sometime hippie activist. "One of the things coming out of that scene was that we all tried to become self-sufficient," he remembers. "So I left my boring accounts clerk job in around 1970. I saved up and travelled. We then tried baking candles and selling joss sticks and electric yo-yo's and collector's records and magazines at festivals. I ended up doing mail order records, scraping a living out of that for a few years." Hauser, still long-haired but indignant at the way hippy culture had sold out its counter-cultural credentials, had the classic Road to Damascus moment when he saw the Sex Pistols play live. "And a few weeks later my hair had been cut off. I met some young guys performing in a punk band, and they were quite alienated from society, as I thought I was, and I thought they were a suitable band to foist on the public. I first heard them rehearsing on a bus. They took great pleasure in being obnoxious, and they went under the name Raped. Incredible characters."

After getting them a few gigs as *ad hoc* manager he eventually formed his own imprint, Parole, with which to promote his discoveries, who caused a deal of controversy beyond their name after releasing an EP indelicately titled 'Pretty Paedophiles'. "Sean [Purcell; vocalist] and I had been jokily throwing around silly band names," Hauser says. "One I came out with was Peter And The Paedophiles. A couple of weeks later, Sean on his own decided on the name. I grimaced and tried to say no, but he very, very much insisted on it, and he had all the band backing him up. So I might inadvertently have suggested it to him, but no, the EP title wasn't my idea." Hauser put a good deal of his own money into Raped and Parole, which also released singles by The Four Kings and Disturbed, but struggled both with the financial insecurity and the workload. He tried to pitch The Cuddly Toys, as Raped had more prosaically become, to the majors, with little success. With an album in the can, he approached Iain McNay about the possibility of releasing it on Cherry Red, but eventually decided the more natural collaboration was with old friend Alex Howe.

Howe had been running a stall opposite Ted Carroll's Rock On in Soho Market since 1978, and had announced he was starting a proper record store, or a glorified pre-fab shed as others disparagingly referred to it. Under the name Wretched, inspired by exactly such derogatory descriptions of the premises, he also started a distribution business with assistance from Rough Trade. "I knew Alex through dealing in 'collector's records'," says Hauser, euphemistically. "He started distribution in early 1979, and we were very aware of Marc Zermati's Skydog as one of the first indie labels – things like the Flamin' Groovies' *Grease* in 1973, Iggy's *Metallic KO* in 1976, even Jimi Hendrix's *Sky High* in '72. Wretched bought a bunch of records from Bizarre Distribution, co-owned by Marc Zermati of Skydog, including imports and hard to find stuff. When 'Spiral Scratch' was reissued in '79, it was all over the papers, but many shops couldn't get it. I remember going to Alex's uncle's, and he had thousands of copies of 'Spiral Scratch' in his front room." Howe, for his part, had been fielding a number of enquiries from aspirant musicians about the possibility of releasing their material through Wretched. As a consequence the two parties talked about starting a label jointly, Hauser folding his Parole roster (which by now included Family Fodder and The Wall) into a new project, to be titled Fresh.

Fresh was an umbrella for several roles; that of distribution agent, retail outlet, mail order supplier and eventually a record label, which began in June 1979 with Family Fodder's 'Playing Golf (With My Flesh Crawling)', like many of the first dozen releases, jointly credited to Fresh and Parole. Subsequent releases featured The Dark, The Art Attacks, Second Layer, Bernie Tormé, Cuddly Toys, Wasted Youth and UK Decay. The latter was arguably the most momentous release – helping bridge-build between punk and what would subsequently be termed Goth, via the brief, media-christened 'positive punk' movement (they would eventually affiliate with John Loder's Corpus Christi label). Chron Gen, meanwhile, were at the forefront, alongside the Exploited and Anti-Pasti, of the UK's third wave of punk – critically derided but collectively a massive seller in the early 80s. It helped the label become an established presence in the independent charts. "It was a time when singles would sell and people weren't interested in albums," notes Hauser, "and the industry was in shock because people only wanted to buy one or two tracks. We didn't have a team of marketing people, or take out huge adverts. Our expenses were low."

Hauser headed the label's A&R as label manager, with Howe, who owned the company, also putting forward suggestions (among them Manufactured Romance). Day to day operations were conducted in an atmosphere that was "completely chaotic and often hilarious", with many of the musicians on the roster doubling up as staff. Thus Menace bass player Charlie Casey, Howe's right-hand man since Soho Market days, oversaw distribution, while Phil Langham of The Dark did telephone sales. "The Dark modelled themselves on Menace," Hauser recalls, "and Charlie got Phil the job at Fresh [he would later run Anagram Records for Cherry Red]." Graham Combi would join the hub too, responsible for the physical distribution of product to shops. There was a similar level of excitement to that experienced across the board among the independent community at this time. "Suddenly bands were able to make a record and have an outlet," Hauser acknowledges. "And they were grateful for that. A lot of the artists we've dealt with have been interesting characters. Very few have been careerist. We've always steered clear of that type of personality. We didn't have a sound for the label, but we had an attitude."

Towards the end of Fresh's reign, having had to pass on Southern Death Cult because of lack of finances, Hauser was keen to sign Johnny Thunders. "I'd vaguely known [Thunders' manager] Leee Black Childers, because the Cuddly Toys would gatecrash Jane County's parties a few years earlier, before he came into Fresh with a Levi Dexter single. Johnny hadn't been heard of for a couple of years by then, he'd gone back to Detroit and done nothing since *So Alone*. Punk was history, and the New York Dolls was even further back in history. So it was, 'I've got some tapes, don't know if anyone's interested?' He was talking to Marc Zermati who'd known him since the early days. But Bizarre had gone bust and Skydog was dormant. So we did the deal with Leee in December 1981, but didn't get to release anything immediately because Marc had the tapes."

Meanwhile, Fresh was in its death throes. "Alex had succumbed to all the pressure and excitement and fun that was happening with the label and distribution. There was a bit of a recession on around '81 and '82, and a few businesses had gone bust and the sales weren't what they were. Alex took some time out and came back, and realised he didn't want to continue any more. It was too stressful and there wasn't any money there. It was going bust and he didn't see a way out. That was a difficult time, obviously. John Knight, my school friend old mobile disco partner, had come to stay in my kitchen after his marriage had broken up. He then met Alex, who hired him to run his distribution for a while till they fell out. So when Alex said he was going to give up, myself, John Knight, Graham Combi and Steve Brown [of Red Records and Fresh's export manager] got together and said, we have to do something with what we've got and what we know. And we formed Jungle Records, starting with buying the label off Alex, and talking to various distribution customers."

After releasing the Thunders tapes, which initiated both Jungle's single and album catalogue, the roster rebuilt itself around a clutch of former Fresh artists, such as Play Dead and Family Fodder. Noting the sales potential of the 'new punk' phenomenon, now in full flow, bands such as The Adicts, Action Pact and The Enemy were housed on a specialist subsidiary, Fall Out, co-A&R'd by Steve Brown. "It seemed to be a self-defining genre," says Hauser, "and very much people saying 'punk's alive'. We did a great Urban Dogs album too, featuring Knox of The Vibrators and Charlie Harper of the UK Subs [the latter band would also enjoy a long spell with Fall Out]. We were releasing a lot of stuff on Jungle too, but there was a bit of a rush on Fall Out because of the demand. And there were some punk bands on Jungle as well, like Rubella Ballet and Newtown Neurotics and Peter And The Test Tube Babies."

Some of the staples of the main Jungle roster included the barely quantifiable Creaming Jesus and A Popular History Of Signs. It was also home to releases by Goth drama junkies Fields Of The Nephilim and American darkwave exponents Christian Death. "I remember Phil Langham dragging me down to see Alien Sex Fiend at the first night of the Bat Cave," remembers Hauser. "We spent half an hour in the queue, because there was a lift, and it would only take two or three people at a time, and the place was half empty. But gradually it filled up. It grew and grew and was a fantastic club. Many a night I spent there. And the whole Goth scene grew out of that. One of the partners, Steve [Brown], ended up managing Fields Of The Nephilim after we did their first record."

Hauser and Combi would also work with artists' own boutique labels. "Part of the Cartel thing was the evolution of 'pressing and distribution' deals," says Hauser. "Bands would go, 'Great!' And so we'd have to do the same for our bands. It was never a very satisfactory arrangement. Things would sell in good quantities back then, so it sometimes worked, but bands really needed the backing of a label." Vanity publishing? "Oh, yes, it's a bit of that. It was partly because we came out of being a distributor, because sometimes people brought us records and we'd distribute them." Industrial conceptualists Test Department had their own dedicated imprint, Ministry Of Power, alongside Conflict's Mortarhate.

Later, Mint Records (originally Mint Sauce, while confusingly, a different Mint suffix accompanied each subsequent release) would emerge as Jungle's most distinctive subsidiary, via its initial brace of signings, Mercury Rev and Mutton Gun. Most of the Mint roster were loosely affiliated to the two core bands. A&R'd by Combi, in the early 90s it saw Jungle, once famously denigrated as a label specialising in 'the fag end of punk', come perilously close to being fashionable; Jungle has, to its credit, never been a label particularly troubled by image anxiety. Success on Mint came early with Mercury Rev's *Yerself Is Steam* in 1991, which somehow dovetailed with the prevailing effects driven Thames Valley shoegazing culture but added enough combustible derangement, both personal and sonic, to stand apart. Mutton Gun member David Boyd, formerly of Rough Trade, would go on to found Hut Records at Virgin (one of the most successful 'faux-indies' of the period), but first introduced the label to Galaxie 500's Dean Wareham, who was involved in various projects. Mercury Rev's Jonathan Donohue, meanwhile, helped bring Radial Spangle to the imprint (issued in collaboration with Beggars Banquet), and also appeared with Cellophane, another band from upstate New York, which for a brief period seemed to be the most musically fertile territory on the continent. Later, Spacemen 3's Sterling Roswell was a further addition to the imprint.

Still active in the new millennium, Jungle releases thereafter became more sporadic, with a greater concentration on back catalogue; a reflection of both the mounting problems of launching new bands and the effects of a lengthy investment in a Fields Of The Nephilim comeback album. Hauser and Combi are still there, working out of an old school record label office in Chalk Farm, now with a buoyant new label Goldtop (together with the studio now resident in their old vinyl warehouse). New releases include Geraint Watkins as well as Nephilim offshoots NFD and The Eden House. And to bring things almost full circle, they have acquired rights to release the Skydog catalogue.

## Independence Days

There were a number of independent labels that, like Jungle, kept faith with punk, as it became more provincial and less self-referential, and definitively more working class. The first wave of punk bands had signed to CBS, to Virgin, to EMI. But the third wave of the early 80s, with the occasional exception, made such noises as they were capable of on their own labels or distinct independents. The most successful included No Future, Clay, Riot City, Criminal Damage, Razor, ID Records and the reissue specialist, Link.

No Future was founded in 1981 by Chris Berry and Richard Jones, the latter having served time as Cherry Red's first A&R scout. Berry, who lived in Malvern, was working for the Ministry of Defence where he met Jones, who initiated him to the punk phenomenon, and the idea of No Future was hatched over a lunchtime chat. An advert was placed in *Sounds* asking for punk and skinhead demos. "Unfortunately, I gave them my home telephone number," recalls Berry. "So my mother would be fielding calls all day from weird groups before I got home from my day job." In the first week the advert ran, they were in receipt of 300 cassettes. They found premises in Malvern following their debut with Blitz's 'All Out Attack'; which arrived in the post as a finished master. Initially they pressed 1,000 copies, and a local printer made the gatefold sleeve, with rubber-stamped labels. These were piled in the back of Berry's car, and driven down to Rough Trade. They took the lot. "Simon Edwards rung me up a week later and said, I think you'd better press another 5,000," recalls Berry. "A week later he said, we need 10,000. It went to number one in the independent charts. Also, at that time, *Sounds* would print Top 20 sales charts from different shops, so I made one up called Punky Norman's in Worcester" Blitz topped that chart too, alongside another Malvern punk band No Future had signed, The Samples. The Partisans' 'Police Story' was their second release; the band was so young, Berry and Jones had to arrange a chaperone for bass player Louise Wright at the insistence of her parents before they could commit to any gigs. Their next offering was a sampler drawn from the cassette influx, *A Country Fit For Heroes*. The cover photo was pinched without permission, based loosely on the *Pillows & Prayers* model of a cheap compilation and suggested by Jones, his rationale being that lots of the bands that had contacted them had at least one good song. The first pressing of 25,000 sold out almost immediately.

Most of No Future's roster was drawn from working class industrial heartlands; Blitz and the inter-related Attak came from New Mills in Derbyshire, the Partisans from Bridgend, Red Alert from Sunderland, Blitzkrieg from Southport. Blitz's debut album almost made the top 30 of the national charts. They invested heavily in a full colour sleeve and lyric insert, and such was the demand they had to use two separate pressing plants. They also picked up *punk pathetique* exponents Peter And The Test Tube Babies, who'd had some exposure on John Peel. Vocalist Pete Bywaters said they'd be interested in signing and Berry met them while he was on a union conference in Brighton, though eventually the arrangement would sour due to disagreements with their manager Nick McGerr. Channel 3 was licensed in from Robbie Fields' Posh Boy label in America in the expectation of a similar reaction that Cherry Red had enjoyed with Dead Kennedys – although the first band itself knew anything about the arrangement was when they received fan mail from the UK. The Partisans album, mixed by John Loder at Southern Studios, was also successful.

The label continued from premises in Malvern, with no A&R department, just the occasional journey down to Rough Trade and chats with Daniel Miller. "Everything we put out sold," recalls Berry. "I would think nothing of loading up a van at three in the morning and taking records down to London." Impressed by Miller's ability to run a label without contracts, Berry and Jones adopted the same model; 50-50 deals, royalties only, with no advance. Initially each release sold comfortably more than the 2,000 copies required for break-even, with press virtually guaranteed from Garry Bushell in *Sounds* (Bushell also introduced them to the label's most controversial act, The Blood). There was an attempt to sign both GBH and Discharge, who opted to stay with a more local label, Clay, but otherwise, with the exception of Channel 3, all the No Future bands approached the label rather than *vice versa*. Initially selections were predominantly handled by Jones; Berry taking a more active role as the label developed. Eventually Berry would leave work to go full time, persuading his father it was a good idea on the basis of what were now impressive sales figures. Some of the material to be released on No Future might have been a little difficult to justify within the confines of the MoD, in any case. Especially The Violators' 'Summer Of '81', probably the most vehement anti-police statement ever recorded by a UK band ("There's blood on the street, and the smell is so sweet, cos another blue bastard has just gone down")

However, after the initial wave of success, Berry and Jones "over-reached". The graph comparing record sales with production costs began to narrow and then cross. "Also, some of the bands started to believe their own publicity," Berry concludes. Whereas before they'd been happy with a local 16-track, now they wanted to come to London and use state of the art studios. The downturn forced them to sell the label. "The formula had slowed down, it got harder to find new bands, the bands themselves got more tricky and wanted advances, and the music scene was changing again. We had a go at a label called Future." The latter was invoked with Blitz's 'Telecommunication', a sharp left turn into electronica from the group's original four-square punk. "It sold OK, was radio friendly, but didn't do nearly as well as their early releases. They were accused of selling out by the press, and I got tired of it all. I'd always wanted to move to London, Richard wasn't so keen, perhaps that would have killed us off earlier, or perhaps we'd have survived."

Berry continued with Future Records, which ran for a dozen releases, as well as working with And Also The Trees, its mainstay act alongside Blitz. "The final straw was an offshoot of Blitz doing a cover version of 'Suffragette City'," he recalls, "and that was probably the end. I was in the Stockport studios, and the sound engineer had a good voice, so he sung the song. [Guitarist] Nidge was a good bloke, but he wasn't Mick Ronson. It was very sad. It had been a fantastic 18 months or two years, and I had to go and get a proper job, and went into retail."

Founded by former Beggars Banquet employee Mike Stone after moving back to Stoke-On-Trent to marry his girlfriend Kim, Clay is best remembered for the flourishing of GBH and, in particular, Discharge. Convening a second-hand retail outlet under his own name, Stone's experiences of working with The Lurkers and Merton Parkas in London left him itching to get back in the game. "Though I came away with nothing from Beggars," he recalls, "I had the knowledge, and the fire and inspiration to want to do something." The shop also instilled in him the belief that the public appetite for punk, far from being dead as declared by the print media, was voracious. "Nobody's servicing these kids, I thought. They clearly want it, but they can't get it anymore. That's what I picked up on. The Pistols and Clash were art school boys, a different thing altogether. All the people I saw come into the shop were working class punks." Clay was incorporated as a label in 1979. "I was naive about finances, but my brother-in-law at the time had a transport company, Spencer Transport. He started us off with two £500 shares and became a silent partner." After 18 months, Stone was able to buy back the shares.

"I didn't know much about the music scene in Stoke," he concedes, "but people knew I'd worked at Beggars. One day a girl, Tanya Rich, came in. She said she managed this band called Discharge. 'Why don't you come and see them?' They were playing at Northwood Parish Hall, near where I lived. It was unbelievable. It was sweaty, packed, leather jackets and spiky hair. I walked through the door and a big piece of raw meat came flying through the air. I was knocking on at the time, I wasn't exactly a teenager. I thought, 'God almighty'. This band kicked in. 'Fuck me!' What *is* this?' But they were great. I got talking to these lads, and I could barely get a sentence out of them. They didn't talk. Communication was out of the window. 'Why don't we do a record?' They agreed."

Discharge's 'Realities Of War' EP was Clay's first release in April 1980. Though under-produced, it was remarkable for the savagery of its disposition, a kind of pneumatic drill minimalism that sounded like aural trepanning. Music, or at least punk, hadn't passed this way before, or been quite so reductive and intense. Nobody suspected it, but Discharge would become one of the most influential groups in the history of late 20th century rock. "We went up to this little studio in Market Drayton just outside Stoke, Red Ball Studios," recalls Stone. "I went in there with them, and I did the stupidest thing I said to [vocalist] Calvin, 'Let's track your vocal on here. Me in my naivete! We tracked it, and when I look back at it now, we shouldn't have done. We did it all in four hours. But when you listen to that first record, it's *totally* ridiculous. I pressed it up, sent a few copies to John Peel, started going round the wholesalers and independent distributors. We did a good sleeve, and the record was totally different to anything that was out. I could feel the distributors sniggering. 'We'll have a few copies off you, Mike.' I had this old BMW at the time, driving round with these records. I palmed a few off. Rough Trade, Fresh, went all round the country. It started trickling steadily. One day I was at home decorating. And John Peel played it on the radio. I nearly fell off the stepladder. That was it, a week later it went ballistic. All the dealers were ringing me up." It would eventually sell around 40,000 copies, while Discharge would cement their legacy with 1982's starkly packaged *Hear Nothing, See Nothing, Say Nothing* album. A milestone in the development of a 'thrash' aesthetic within punk, though its influence was more acutely felt within the hard rock/metal firmament, its hectoring infatuation with the agonies of war mirrored the output of Crass. Indeed, at the time Discharge, by dint of their pacifist pre-occupations and stark, monochromatic artwork, were viewed to have a foot in the anarcho camp. Garry Bushell, the isolated advocate of new punk in the mainstream press, was so indignant at Discharge's lack of concession to tune or melody, meanwhile, he almost expired in one memorable editorial. "Umpteen versions of the same pneumatic drill solo... awful... no tunes, no talent, no fun... dull, boring and monotonous... the musical equivalent of glue-sniffing."

Stone would go on to have similar success with GBH, though their influence was less noteworthy. In a less than crowded field, the Birmingham quartet proved among the more photogenic of the street punk brigade (though, notoriously, their debut Clay 12-inch would be titled 'Leather, Bristles, Studs and Acne' because that's all that could be made out after a trip to a photo booth). "They were playing the Victoria Hall in Hanley," remembers Stone. "And I was thinking, I need some more bands. The bass player didn't turn up. They played half the set without him. I was quite impressed by that! They were getting spat at left, right and centre, and Colin [Abrahall; vocals] just spat back. Most people were, 'Don't spit at us, we don't want that.' They just did the business. I went round the back and said, 'fancy doing some records?' They knew about Discharge. That helped me, and gave me a bit of standing. I found this place in Rochdale called Cargo, I took GBH up there. When we were mixing 'Leather', a local taxi rank was coming through on the monitors. I said to the engineer John Brierley, that sounds great, we'll leave it! Yet that was a step up in quality."

Clay had several other acts that were effectively one-off signings. The Killjoys (not Kevin Rowland's group) and Plastic Idols were local Stoke outfits (the latter signed before Discharge). White Door were an offshoot of prog rockers Grace, and there was a one-off album from The Climax Blues Band. But then Clay's lack of adherence to punk orthodoxy was hardly unexpected, given that Stone had first seen Pink Floyd play in 1966 and remained primarily a rock fan. Play Dead were at the forefront of the burgeoning Gothic movement, while more conventional punk fare came from Abrasive Wheels, The English Dogs and, to turn the story full circle, The Lurkers. "The Lurkers had a different singer," remembers Stone, "but that came about because of our friendship. I liked one of the singles, but I don't think it quite worked, to be honest. I always had a lot of hope for [guitarist] Pete Stride, always thought he was pretty talented. Play Dead were a fantastic band. This really saddened me. As a label I was moving on. I did try to go for people who had a bit of substance, and it was around the period when Clay went bust, and it really pissed me off. But they suffered from a lack of press and image, which plays such a part in English music. In fact, nearly all the Clay bands, apart from Discharge, suffered from that."

Stone remains fondest of Demon, the hard rock band he manages to this day. Associated with the New Wave Of British Heavy Metal by default rather than intent, they were the fourth release on Clay, and went on to record two albums, *Night Of The Demon* and *Unexpected Guest*, that were licensed to Carrere Records. The latter went top 50. "When it came to the third album *The*

*Plague*," Stone recalls. "Freddie Cannon, who managed Carrere, turned it down. Atlantic thought it was the best thing since sliced bread. But it took six months to sort the contract out; it was like the *Magna Carta*. I was up to sixty-page contracts! Different ball game. I went to the New York Music Seminar, and the Atlantic boys were there to see me. They literally frog-marched me down to their office. I thought to myself, I'm going to make a story up here. I said, 'I've got an appointment with CBS, by the way.' James Wylie, who later managed The Eurythmics, worked for Martin Mills at Beggars Banquet. Martin had taken me over there and said, 'You can use my solicitor if you like.' I had no idea what to say, so James said, 'Ask for £40,000 or £50,000.' 'You what?' I couldn't believe it. We did an eight-album deal, with me bluffing my way through. And we got it. When they put it out, they changed the sleeve, threw it against the wall and it didn't stick." Stone found the high finance posturing both bewildering and highly amusing. "And now," he laughs, "the singer, Dave Hill, is working at Alton Towers, and I'm driving a van!"

That change in circumstances was brought about by distributor Pinnacle's collapse in 1984. "I was on the phone one day with someone down there, saying Pinnacle's gone bust, you won't be getting your money," Stone recalls. "I was stunned. I was owed about £23,000. When you run a record label, you run it on what's coming in, and I already owed a similar amount of money, on studios and advertising. I wasn't worried about my own finances. As long as I could eat and run my car, I was quite happy. But I'd spent this money. I actually cried, to be honest. I broke down round the back. I was by myself, I ran the entire label by myself, and I went round the back and just cracked up. 'What am I going to do?' I knew it was the end. I didn't have any money. Others could cast aside a loss, but they had money in reserve. I actually lost about £40,000 in the end."

He had no inkling. And it wasn't the first time it had happened, either. "It wasn't just Pinnacle. Fresh had gone bust on me and they owed me £6,000. An accountant here in Stoke I employed, unbeknownst to me, had got hold of Alex (Howe) and done some kind of settlement on a monthly basis, where Alex was paying this accountant back. And I didn't know about it! This guy was pocketing the money. We found out, and he came in and said, 'Oh, I was going to save it for you for a rainy day.' Lying bastard. So poor old Alex, who I thought was the devil's son, was doing his best to pay me back, and I didn't know anything about it!"

Stone did try to keep the company afloat, but found things spiralling out of his control. "One day I got a phone call from a guy called Frank who worked for Colin Newman at Trojan. 'Look, we'll give you x amount of money for the catalogue.' And it was enough money to cover most of my debts to the bands and other companies. I ended up about £6,000 in front. Which I spent on classic cars, cos that market was booming. And the next week someone pulled the plug on that! Stoney makes another blunder! I moved to Wolverhampton and started Sonic Records, and kept working with Demon. I'd sold everything to Trojan except Demon. That was the thing I most loved, that I thought would one day make some money. I believed in them as writers and musicians. I still believe that. He came up to the shop with a box transit van, and took *everything* to do with those bands, including the artwork. Really, I should have hidden it! But everything was on the premises, and Colin Newman was a very shrewd man. The biggest mistake I made in this whole deal is that I chucked in the publishing! What I should have done was said, 'OK, but I want so many points.' And I didn't. And I paid the penalty when six or seven years later, Metallica did two Discharge cover versions on *Garage Inc.* That was a knife-twister, to lose the record label and then find out that one of the biggest bands on the planet had covered one of the least coverable bands I could ever imagine. No disrespect to Discharge, but I never, ever saw that coming."

Had he retained the publishing, Stone would now be a rich man. "When Clay went bust, I became a very weak person. I was punched in the guts. When I sold all that, I was at my weakest point. I was a little bit naive, a little bit ignorant, but weak. I took the money and run. Only I didn't, I took the money and paid all my creditors back! I'm quite embarrassed about it all, and I beat myself up about it. I'm older now and I could really use the money and I regret what happened. But I'm still very proud of what we did and the records we released."

Flicknife's catalogue, meanwhile, comprised a bizarre mixture of Hawkwind and their innumerable spin-offs such as Inner City Unit and Robert Calvert solo recordings, plus new punk bands like Erazerhead, Major Accident and Instant Agony. There was also classic pop from the Barracudas, and proto-Goth from Zero Le Creche, Alien Sex Fiend and The Marionettes. Run by ex-biker Mark 'Frenchie' Gloder and his wife Gina Nares, Flicknife was inaugurated in 1979.

Hawkwind's decision to throw in their lot with Flicknife after breaking from RCA was explained by Dave Brock to Alan Moore of *Sounds* in 1982. "[RCA] is a great big company, bringing out 20 albums a week and anything a bit unusual tends to get pushed to one side. Now on the other hand you've got

## Do They Owe Us A Living?

Flicknife, who brought out the 'Urban Guerrilla' single, and they're a small independent label... I think we're happy with the personal touch that you get with Flicknife. I mean, you can get on the phone and get straight through to Frenchie and Gina... with RCA there's no contact with people. Or, you'll have a guy on the case for a couple of weeks and then it'll just evaporate."

That was the attraction for others on the roster, too. "We got involved with Flicknife records through Pete McCarthy, who approached us after our second gig," Zero Le Creche bass player Terry Miles remembers. "He said he was a manager involved with a group from Yorkshire called Southern Death Cult. Frenchie was erratic, but he was fun to work with". Or, as drummer Richard Olley recalls, "Flicknife's offer meant that we got a single released. Frenchie was a really cool bloke. Had vision and wasn't too stressed about stuff. Seem to remember he had this cool little Morris Minor van." Hawkwind weren't the only group to defect from a major. "After EMI had ditched us we were rather chastened and also desperate to establish our survival and commitment to pursuing the direction we set with songs like 'Violent Times'," Jeremy Gluck of The Barracudas told NKVD. "[Frenchie] loved The Barracudas and wanted to record our second album with us." Flicknife ran to some eighty or more releases before retiring hurt, its catalogue sold, like so many other 80s punk labels, to Cherry Red. Gina went on to manage a coffee and flower shop in West London, while Frenchie has retired from view.

Razor Records wasn't a pure punk play like No Future, its catalogue, like that of Flicknife, split between new punk and more quixotic releases. Its proprietor, Robin Greatrex, boasted a long apprenticeship in the music industry, having taken his first job in Southwark's Tunnel rehearsal studios, working with Island and Chrysalis artists, including Bryan Ferry and Bad Company. Later he started a management company and press agency with Camilla Hellman. Their most notable clients included Tyla Gang and Straight Eight, who were signed to Pete Townshend's Eel Pie, as well as Gary Holton of Heavy Metal Kids, whom he'd managed while at The Tunnel. "The press agency paid better than the management," confirms Greatrex, "We worked with Showaddywaddy and the Only Ones. The management side petered out because we found it increasingly hard to get recording contracts." One of the last acts they signed for management, however, was Chron Gen, who had just left Miles Copeland's Step Forward. Greatrex helped them put an album together for Secret Records, which promptly hit the Top 40. "I thought, that's incredible." It convinced him to start Razor, which was ostensibly modelled on Secret.

Razor's seed money came from Geoff Hannington of Logo Records, with whom Greatrex had a separate management company. Hannington had just started his own distribution network in East London, I.D.S., which employed Peter Misson, who would become Greatrex's right-hand man. Misson looked after Razor's royalties and invoicing and "kept everything on an even keel". Initially, finances were impossibly tight, as Greatrex notes, "Peter and I never took a farthing from the label in the early days. All our money went on producing records and licensing." With their I.D.S. advance they signed Max Splodge, who had enjoyed some unlikely novelty punk chart success but fallen out of favour at London Records, as well as Suffolk's *Clockwork Orange*-inspired punk band The Adicts. The latter had graduated from Dining Out, arriving at Razor following a brief stay with Jungle subsidiary Fall Out. Contrary to expectations, "The Adicts did really well," recalls Greatrex, "but Max's single did really badly."

"Essentially it was a punk rock label," Greatrex reflects on Razor's development. He was far from being a punk himself, of course, but found himself well disposed to the urchins his label sheltered, "especially after being a manager for a long time, dealing with aspiring artists, the punks were just a breath of fresh air. They were great fun." The Adicts took off almost immediately. They were, after all, nothing if not photogenic, in a genre where the defining visual characteristic seemed to be unyielding conformity. "They got the front cover of *Sounds* and *Melody Maker*," Greatrex remembers. "Carol Clerk was walking on ice doing that at the *Maker*, she really went out on a limb." The Adicts also built up a following in America, where they were signed by Seymour Stein at Warners subsidiary Sire after touring the west coast. "But it didn't work, and in the end we got the album back from that. It just didn't really take off. And the Warners thing, you need success before they throw all the marketing behind it."

There were great hopes for another punk band distanced from the leather jacket and mohican image *de jour*. "We loved The Newtown Neurotics, they were like a rawer version of The Jam," says Greatrex. "I just wanted street bands with guitar based music. The Adicts were great live. I came from a background of live work – you had to see something before it made sense." Cock Sparrer came with a reputation – enhanced but arguably misappropriated due to the emergence of Oi! – as London's premier street punk band and most riotous live attraction. They too sold well. Things were destabilised to an extent when I.D.S. went bankrupt. "But then we joined the reformed Pinnacle. And we did lots of exports ourselves, packing the records and shipping them. Peter had been in Island Record in sales, and knew loads of little tricks to get by."

Beyond punk, Razor engaged naturally with other youth cults. They licensed a Lambrettas record from Elton John's Rocket Records, and released both a studio album and a live set recorded at the 100 Club by The Purple Hearts, as their contribution to the Mod Revival. Greatrex loved both acts. "It was great, being an old scooter boy myself! I couldn't afford the sharp suits to be a proper Mod, though." There was a rockabilly band, The Long Tall Texans and a Saints album licensed from EMI, while old stagers The Angelic Upstarts were signed to a subsidiary, Picasso. They also had a tilt at the New Wave Of British Heavy Metal market with Samson, featuring future Iron Maiden singer Bruce Dickinson.

Stranger still was the liaison with punk's sworn enemies and voodoo dolls of preference, Genesis. If Razor was never truly tied down to its caricature as a punk label, Greatrex severed any delusions of insularity by re-releasing their first album. Yet it was an astute move financially. "It was Peter Misson that spotted it," he confirms. "We'd buy back copies of *Record Collector* and go through them. I found a shop in Notting Hill that had the Genesis first album for £40. That was a lot of money in those days. Jonathan King owned the rights. We contacted Jonathan's representative, Carole Broughton, and did a deal. And that did really well, and we also acquired the Zombies catalogue from Carole." Razor also mopped up the soundtrack to *Spinal Tap*. "We were in hysterics laughing at an early showing in Chelsea, but there were only about six people there, and they were mystified. They thought it was a real documentary. I had a press officer girl, Kate Harper, and she was very switched on. We put an application into what was then PolyGram, and as we were broke, we offered them just £1,200. And they took it. We were flabbergasted. We got massive press on it, the front cover of *Kerrang!* It did really well. We had a two-year non-exclusive licence, and after a year PolyGram put it out as well in a fit of pique."

Gradually, however, Razor began to wind down. "I started doing some other things," Greatrex admits. "Peter started his own royalty business. We were doing more and more reissues. We'd done punk, rockabilly, Mod, and the new wave of heavy metal, but we kind of ran out of things. We were doing four albums a month and the sales were slowing down. I tried to sign some more acts and they didn't work out. Overheads were going up and we hit the end of the Thatcher era and it was very tough times. The reissuing thing, everyone got into it, but when we started there was nobody doing it, and we couldn't keep up with it. And the majors got nervous about giving away the family silver."

Razor's primary acknowledged influence was Secret Records, run by Martin Hooker. Secret didn't actually start out as a punk label; its first release being Martin Atkins' Brian Brain project (which had so nearly been taken up by Ivo Watts-Russell as the putative 4AD's first release). Gem Howard-Kemp served as Hooker's right-hand man. "I joined up with Martin just after The Exploited's *Punk's Not Dead* came out, which was the label's first album," he recalls. "But for the first singles, they were more of an indie label. Martin was based in Luton, but then picked up the Exploited singles and went in that direction." Secret subsequently enjoyed huge sales and an astonishing run of chart returns, with a roster featuring Infa Riot, 4-Skins, The Business and Chron Gen. The latter's debut album arrived in a cover bedecked with a distorted photograph of Howard-Kemp. "I think I was the ugliest person they could find!" he says. "There was a guy called Mez who did our artwork and photography. People were taking whatever images they could get, particularly in the punk era, and we just used whatever was around. It just so happened that I'd had some photos taken by Mez, and they were stretched and the rest of it; the band liked it, and we went with it."

Secret lasted for three years, and almost every album they released, which included a number of Oi! compilations, charted. However, in sales terms, The Exploited's runaway success dwarfed all else. "That was the one that really took off," Howard-Kemp acknowledges. "It was really UK hardcore rather than punk – the difference between the Exploited and the Pistols was *enormous*. The whole movement just took off." He remembers being part of the entourage that rolled up for the Exploited's *Top Of The Pops* debut with 'Dead Cities'. "Surreal! The funniest thing was Big John [Duncan; the group's burly guitarist] trying to dance to 'The Birdie Song' with Legs & Co!" The fact that this was the dancing troupe's final credited appearance on the programme may be more than coincidence.

There was also some diversity at Secret, though – if you wish to acknowledge a record featuring not only Keith Chegwin but also his twin brother, as well as releases by Lovely Previn (André Previn's daughter). "These things come along," recalls Howard-Kemp. "Every so often you get offered things. And you think, actually, if we did that, we could make some money and it would fund something else. It opens doors. You suddenly get into different places. You can be as true as you want to your roots, but at the end of the day, you have to fund them."

Hooker would betray his love of metal by signing Twisted Sister, at that time bereft of a contract, but then found himself out of a job. "The financial backers behind Secret decided to roll out the people who ran it," remembers Howard-Kemp, "so Martin was gone. Then after that they did some ridiculous stuff. I stayed on for about a year, and we did things like The Dossers and Dinah Rod And The Drains – a song about Dennis Nilsen hiding bodies in his drains. Sold about six copies. Then there was another band that was the son of the guy who ran the tyre company opposite – it was an A&R department gone mad. They didn't bring in any new people, they just got rid of the person who had made them successful."

Secret went into administration in 1983. Hooker, in the meantime, had founded metal imprint Music For Nations through Zomba. Howard-Kemp joined him there after Secret collapsed, "We had Rough Justice, with Agnostic Front, Crumbsuckers, GBH, a lot of American hardcore, and the thrash label Under One Flag. After Secret, we were better funded in order to give the labels an identity. You knew what you were buying – if it was on Music For Nations, you knew it would be some form of hard rock, Rough Justice was punk and hardcore, and Under One Flag was extreme thrash metal." The duo also worked together at Dreamcatcher, purchased by the omnipresent Colin Newman of Receiver/Trojan fame in 2006 when Hooker retired. "It brings everything full circle," says Howard-Kemp. "The company that Colin Newman owns that bought Dreamcatcher is actually Secret Records. Over the years, the Secret name has moved through different hands, so it still exists. And now Dreamcatcher is owned by Secret."

Riot City grew out of Simon Edwards' Heartbeat Records in Bristol. Its second single by The Glaxo Babies had been funded by Cherry Red in one of the first production and distribution deals in which both benefactor and frontline label were both independents, and its success encouraged a long-term collaboration. Ultimately, Heartbeat's most lasting contribution was arguably the finest of the local band compilations that thrived in the early 80s, *Avon Calling*. Featuring artists such as The Europeans, Glaxo Babies, Private Dicks, Apartment etc, all of whom released singles for the label, it led John Peel to pronounce it the regional compilation by which all others should be measured. Although the tone was decidedly post-punk, angular and experimental, one of the bands featured on it were unreconstructed punkers Vice Squad, fronted by Rebecca Bond, aka Beki Bondage.

By 1980, Vice Squad were in the dumps. They only played six gigs in the entire year, after being banned from just about every venue in the Bristol area, due to violence. A planned Rock Against Racism tour fizzled out due to bad organisation. Then, at the final scheduled show at Trinity Church Hall, Simon Edwards turned up. He liked the band – and indeed, had fought for their inclusion on *Avon Calling* much to the disgust of some of the other acts. He took a deal to Cherry Red, but this time the answer was a firm 'no'. "Bottom line was that I loved it," Edwards recalls, "and Iain [McNay] didn't. It was the first time he had ever waned from my choice of releases. That prompted the parting of ways for Heartbeat and Cherry Red, not because of any great falling out, but more due to the general sales of recent releases, probably not having been as good as Iain had hoped. There was still the joint publishing deal that would remain, and hell, we had become friends and have remained such ever since. Irony of irony would be that in years to come, Vice Squad would eventually sign to Cherry Red's Anagram label after leaving EMI!"

As a result of McNay's rebuttal, Edwards offered Vice Squad a singles deal, providing finance for the pressing if the band could cover studio expenses. The new label would be a joint partnership. A friend of the band, Bill White, put up the money to vouchsafe their end of the deal. Guitarist Dave Bateman coined the (intentionally topical given the social climate) name Riot City, which was launched with the release of 'Last Rockers' in January 1981. John Peel played the track several times, and drummer Shane Baldwin had the initiative to track down journalist Garry Bushell to The While Lion, the *Sounds* staffers' favoured watering hole, in order to get some coverage. The ruse worked well, and the single would go on to sell more than 22,000 copies, reaching number seven in the independent charts.

The band remained involved in the day to day running of the label until their touring schedule and recording commitments, which eventually led to Vice Squad signing to EMI, began to take precedence, at which time Riot City was effectively run by Edwards alone. In the meantime, however, the label had attracted a roster of bands which the founding group either introduced to the label or approved of – the Insane, Court Martial, Abrasive Wheels, the Expelled and Chaotic Dischord. Edwards certainly had his critics – Garry Bushell, a seemingly natural ally, would refer to Riot City as 'the dustbin of punk' (though in releasing Emergency's 'Points Of View' it housed one of the finest examples of third generation UK punk). Crass criticised the label for being a 'back door' to EMI, given that they retained the Riot City logo on releases – even though Edwards was against Vice Squad's migration.

## Do They Owe Us A Living?

In fact, the provenance of that 'back door to EMI' story is rooted in the paranoia over authenticity, integrity and independence that always attended the anarcho-punk scene. It actually had no basis in reality whatsoever. "I was partly to blame," notes Charlie Mason. "Having read a piece by the Chumbas, in, I think, *Maximum Rock 'n' Roll*, I wrote an embarrassingly sympathetic article in the zine I co-edited urging people to boycott Riot City. It was lurid and *Sun*-like. Truly atrocious 16-year-old snotty boy half-baked politics – no fact checking, 'believe the hype' drivel. Which might have been OK had we not had some articles in the same issue by another co-editor about Riot City bands. Simon received a copy of the finished zine from this other guy and not surprisingly, he hit the roof. He called my mate and extracted my phone number. That evening I had a barely restrained though just polite phone call from an apoplectic Mr Edwards who told me he had considered driving down to Dorset to have it out with me face to face! That I was 16 and very apologetic as he explained how wildly wrong the whole ridiculous farce was, was enough to dissuade him. Though he rightly made me agree to paste an apology over the offending article in all remaining copies – which I did. I did however think 'I'll just check this though,' shutting the door after the horse had bolted. I wrote a letter with a stamped addressed envelope to EMI and asked if Riot City was a subsidiary of theirs. I'd intended to print their reply either way and apologise in the next issue of the zine. Bizarrely, rather than replying to my letter, EMI forwarded my letter and SAE to Simon to reply to! Shortly after, I got a sarcastic note from Simon on the EMI compliment slip he'd been sent by them. It took me an hour or so to realise exactly what had happened there, and that I'd probably added insult to injury, though ironically this was a bit of penance on my part for the first error of judgement. Shortly after that I got a photocopy of a letter Simon drew up and sent round to the whole zine network wherein he decried the misinformation foisted by "Crass, Chumbawamba, Chaz, and others....." That Chaz, sadly, was me. He urged us to 'get back to our copies of *The Sun*'. It stung, but he was right."

Although Edwards was initially upset by Vice Squad's decision to move to EMI, the two parties remained friends, and members of Vice Squad would continue to appear on the label under pseudonyms. The most entertaining example being Chaotic Dischord, who gloried in taking punk profanity and sonic excess as far as they possibly could. This was actually a hoax band, started by Baldwin and Bateman of Vice Squad with roadies Igor and Bambi. The name, a corruption of Riot City signings Chaos UK and Disorder, was an attempt to ridicule Edwards' tastes in 'hardcore' punk. In the event, Edwards discovered the ruse, but by then, incredibly, the joke, rather than wearing thin, had resulted in sales of 10,000 copies of 1983 album *Fuck Religion, Fuck Politics, Fuck The Lot Of You*. Eventually though, the label would close as the boom in third wave punk ground to a halt, Edwards concentrating on his full-time job as a route planner for the AA.

Other third generation punk labels included Inferno, overseen by Keith Thornton and Brian Harris out of Birmingham's Tempest record store, which began life with The Varukers 'Protest To Survive' EP in March 1982, after the latter band simply announced themselves one day in the shop. They also released material by Dead Wretched and Criminal Class. Sheffield's Pax was one of many labels set up by Marcus Featherby. Having started out as a budget domicile for the Sheffield post-industrial set, including releases from The Stunt Kites, UV Pop and Danse Society, Pax briefly signed The Exploited after their split from Secret. They were firm friends until the latter's Wattie took umbrage over perceived financial skulduggery and made threats leading to its owner going into hiding. From which he's never returned.

Both WXYZ and ID were run by famed London promoter John Curd, of Straight Music fame, whose life in music saw him collaborate with everyone from James Brown to Talking Heads to Eminem. Between them his labels housed material by Anti-Nowhere League and a slew of psychobilly institutions including The Meteors and Guana Batz. The Damned also recorded for the label, as did the pre-Godfathers Sid Presley Experience. Eventually bought out by Link Records, the catalogue was subsequently passed on to Cherry Red. "Am I getting paid for this?" Curd queries down the telephone, on my tentative approach, before deciding, given the negative response, he'll take his secrets to the grave.

Duncan 'Dunk' Mason founded Rot Records in 1981 to house the output of his band, Riot Squad, after watching John Peel eulogise the Desperate Bicycles on a TV documentary. Riot Squad would subsequently move on to local Mansfield label Rondelet, after owner Mike Commaford heard their first demo. Already home to Anti-Pasti and Special Duties, Rondelet initially couldn't seem to make up its mind whether it was a punk or metal label, having been put together for the purpose of releasing Witchfynde's 'Give 'em Hell' single. Other NWOBHM artists included Gaskin and Heritage, while there was also, bizarrely, a contribution from 'Britain's first million pound black footballer', Justin Fashanu, 'Do It Coz You Like It'. Commaford and Witchfynde would soon come to blows, but the label also entertained The Membranes, whose John Robb remembers his handlers only as "inept" (though some of its bands, such as Dead Man's Shadow, would follow one of the Rondelet staff to London imprint Expulsion). Robb himself had one of his innumerable tentacles in Vinyl Drip, forged as a sideline to his *Blackpool Rox!* fanzine exploits, which served as an outpost not only for The Membranes, but also Bogshed (Robb's former Membranes collaborator Nick Brown, incidentally, would start Clawfist in 1990, originally a singles club based on the premise of Sub Pop).

Mason eventually revived Rot after the split from Rondelet and his own band, expanding the roster with The Varukers, English Dogs etc (the punk labels of the early 80s swapped 'assets' frequently). Rot continued until its distributor Red Rhino folded, Mason going on to sell second-hand cars, though he would also oversee the bootleg LP series *Punk Lives Let's Slam* and faced a court action from Picture Frame Seduction over the return of master tapes.

Mark Brennan, bass player with The Business, and Lol Pryor, previously owner of Syndicate and Wonderful World Records, were behind Link Records. Their first project was the compilation album *Oi! The Resurrection*, alongside releases by Section 5 and Vicious Rumours. Combining this output with material by more venerable/name-recognisable groups such as The Business and 4-Skins to get themselves into the racks of record stores, they concurrently established Dojo in their capacity as consultants to reissue specialist Castle Records. With Pryor's focus increasingly leading him in that direction, Brennan took a breather before setting up Captain Oi!, a punk reissue independent which gave a welcome lick of paint to reissue projects in a genre previously notable for the short shrift afforded it by the majors.

Never fashionable with the media, beyond partisan support from Garry Bushell at *Sounds* and to a lesser extent Carol Clerk at *Melody Maker*, this rump of independent labels, if it did reflect a retrenchment from the original punk vision, also sold in huge quantities. As one Bristolian musician told me, reflecting on the adventures of Riot City, "We were all sitting around The Moon Club one day, All of us had been in arty bands on the local scene. All of whom got a lot of press. And there was Shane there from Vice Squad, who always used to get the piss taken out of them a bit. They weren't arty or whatever. But then someone said, 'Yeah, but Shane's the only one who ever sold any records.' And that shut everyone up."

## Chapter Twelve

## Get Rid Of These Things

## The Cartel, its labels, and the building of an independent infrastructure

If 1979 was boom time for UK independents, that was in stark contrast to the fortunes of the record industry generally. It was a terrible year for the majors. American sales slumped 11% to $3.7 billion, which was the first decline since World War II, and the fallout spread to the UK. "Until 1979, the business was judged recession-proof," wrote Fredric Dannen in *Hit Men*. "You couldn't make too many bad mistakes, because sales growth covered them up. So it seemed, anyway, to an industry drunk on the disco craze." In fact, while independents such as Rough Trade blossomed, savage cutbacks were the order of the day across corporate boardrooms. The majors claimed that video games such as *Space Invaders* were robbing them of teenage coinage. Just as with the downloading scares of the new millennium, there is always, seemingly, a good reason unrelated to their own deficiencies, for revenue woes.

The US independent sector's response to the new paradigm of music was both slower and more piecemeal. Independent distribution in the US declined steadily through the 1970s and quite precipitously after 1980. And although independent R&B labels continued to launch American chart hits right through the birth of hip-hop, not one of the punk or new wave imprints (or bands) left a lasting impression on the industry. For example, Dead Kennedys, the pre-eminent American punk band, were forced to release their debut album through a small British independent (Cherry Red), leaving groups such as The Avengers frustrated in their wake. Indeed, it could be argued, and Biafra concedes elsewhere, Dead Kennedys *became* America's pre-eminent punk band because of the exposure a European profile gave them. There were specific reasons for this: Stateside geography in particular. On the one hand this made it all but impossible for a new band to tour profitably. Yet on the other it allowed innumerable smaller acts to claim local chart honours, especially during the breakout phases of the R&B, doo-wop, soul and garage band scenes.

There were a handful of established indie labels such as Greg Shaw's Bomp!, the Titan and Power Play labels for power-pop, the Bay Area's Beserkley and Ralph, and LA's punk label nonpareil, Dangerhouse – each of whom might sell a thousand copies of most releases. Yet not one of them ever 'graduated' an artist to national chart status or, indeed, served as a stepping stone to a successful major label contract, with the possible exception of X (Dangerhouse then Slash to Elektra). Hundreds of smaller labels and one-off indie 45s were distributed with at least modest success by Bomp! in Los Angeles, Pig Productions in Ontario and Disques du Monde in New York. Local 'one-stops' and the dominant import distributor, Jem, carried some indie LPs, although their markets were limited and hits, if any, happened on a strictly local level.

Malcolm McLaren's lack of success with the New York Dolls and the cooler reception afforded acts such as Patti Smith, Pere Ubu, and The Ramones in their own backyards further reinforced the general consensus that, by the late 1970s, any form of innovative American music was commercial poison. Seymour Stein's visionary signings to Sire excited minimal sales in the States, but did much better in the UK. But the most sustained investment in American indie bands may have come from Miles Copeland's Faulty Products sub-label (for IRS acts who failed to get distribution via A&M). Even as Copeland's British signings went on to multiple hits, however, the Faulty label and distribution network folded after two years.

"The main culprits in America's 'indie failure', if you're looking for them," notes Hyped2Death's Chuck Warner, "were the lack of a monolithic national music press, and the geographical isolation of its major musical scenes. *Rolling Stone* was useless, *Creem* couldn't fix on a coherent identity, and the rest were just fanzines. Meanwhile, the UK music papers' constant anxiety and haste to beat each other to the next best thing [who were almost by definition unsigned or on an indie label] gave everyone a fair blast of free publicity. And where in the UK a new band could sign on to an established act's tour and play every night for two weeks across the country, the logistics for travel and available venues in the US were prohibitive. Bands with aspirations to something bigger could emigrate to San Francisco or LA or New York, where they might at least eke out a living, but major label stardom remained pure fantasy. That's another reason the mainstream music press was so reluctant to take chances on new trends or scenes, and why everyone from *Bomp* to *Trouser Press* to *New York Rocker* to *Maximum Rock 'n' Roll* organised themselves by 'scene reports'."

"When we did 'Spiral Scratch'," recalls Richard Boon, "the independent distribution infrastructure really wasn't in place. And it was probably a spur to it being put in place or developing. Gradually, Rough Trade expanded from mail order to actually contacting similarly minded regional shops, supplying them directly, which of course led to the Cartel. There were lots of conversations. One thing that opened up was the beginning of an informal network of activists, if you like. There were lots of ideas being tossed around all the time, but they were in a position to develop it. Richard Scott played the fundamental role."

"I'd started with the mail-order," Scott confirms, "and everything just grew out of everything else. There were people coming into the shop and asking to buy for *their* shops. You got mail orders that turned out to be from overseas shops, from Amsterdam and so on, who wanted to buy in bulk. It grew from day one. Spotting the exact moment when it turned from mail order to wholesale would be very difficult. Everything was done on the fly. We talked about it a lot, but there was never a plan." Those discussions were held among "whoever was there". At the end of each day, "we'd just sit at the table in the rear and talk about it. Initially it was Geoff and I taking orders and pulling them, then we got in a couple of people to help out. There wasn't all that much room at Kensington Park Road, so we built a shed in the yard – I got a builder friend of mine to do that. He came and built that, and that became our main wholesale base. And the fire escape from the synagogue next door opened straight into it."

Initially the principle of the 50-50 contract that Scott had first advocated for the Rough Trade label continued to be the operating premise for distribution. But that soon shifted. "We ended up doing more generous deals. The 50-50 thing fell apart fairly early on. It was maintained in spirit, but my original two-sentence contract was quickly expanded to cover all sorts of other criteria."

Established in 1982, its arch name suggested by Geoff Travis, The Cartel was a natural extension of Scott's activities organising Rough Trade's distribution. It resulted in Rough Trade co-ordinating the efforts of five outlying branches in addition to its own home turf, London; Fast Forward in Edinburgh, Revolver in Bristol, Red Rhino in York, Backs in Norwich and Probe in Liverpool. "The Cartel started because there wasn't sufficient room in the back room of Rough Trade to service everyone," explains Scott. "The only way to deal with it was to box up stuff to send out to the good regional shops so they could deal with the other shops in their area. It was a spatial problem. I also thought it was important to try to set up centres where labels and shops could focus regionally rather than be in London – that was politically important. I saw London as being over-important." The Cartel was formally inaugurated at a meeting convened at a hotel overlooking the Clifton Suspension Bridge near Bristol, though discussions about the enterprise were well advanced by the time it was rubber-stamped. An associated chain of retailers with sympathetic principles and synergistic ambitions, given the title The Chain With No Name, also grew out of these meetings.

The strength of the original Cartel was its regional diversity. It brought into alliance retail-focused personnel who had grasped the breakthrough of the late 70s and were committed to establishing an alternative to major label distribution systems, arguably the final stumbling block denying independents a level playing field. Scott's intention was to provide a new backbone to the system that was sustainable, cohesive and accountable. "I was central to that," says Scott. "I chose the shops, but it was a fairly straightforward choice. We were selling more to those shops than any others, and they knew the material and they knew their market, and they were selling a lot. Anything that was half-decent in those days could sell 10,000. But there were never any contracts between Cartel members. We just met every quarter."

Scott's first lieutenant – though at this stage there was still no demarcation in either salary or hierarchy between Rough Trade personnel, was Simon Edwards. "I brought him in because he worked at Inferno Records in Birmingham, whom we dealt with a lot," says Scott. "They were the biggest importers of Jamaican music at the time. When their Inferno van came by, we'd buy five or ten thousand pounds' worth of vinyl off them. And we could turn that round straight away – it would sell. He wasn't my deputy – he was just a very important part of the team, not least because of his A&R overview." He too would liase with constituent Cartel members. "When I was still doing New Hormones in Manchester," recalls Richard Boon, "I'd had a meeting with Simon and he'd said, 'This is what we're trying to do. Rather than coming to Rough Trade directly, you should be dealing with Geoff Davies at Probe, the north-west member. And use him to ship things around.'"

Although there were initially six full members of The Cartel, there were also unofficial second and third tiers. For example, Jungle Distribution, recently co-founded by Alan Hauser with other former Fresh Distribution personnel, helped independent records reach mainstream outlets. "Fresh had just started an account with a small chain that turned into Our Price," Hauser recalls. "Rough Trade had started distribution by then, but they didn't want to deal with Our Price because they were too 'corporate'. So when we started Jungle, they were happy for us to supply that chain. Rough Trade were the boring social worker-type bureaucrats, and we were the rock 'n' roll revolutionaries – well, that's simplifying things a bit, but we had more fun than they did! Our Price went quickly from fifty shops to two hundred. Then

## Get Rid Of These Things

Rough Trade made arrangements with regional distributors in each area as The Cartel. We were unofficial members. We couldn't be official members, because we were in London, and that was Rough Trade's patch. So when Our Price got to two hundred shops, we were out-selling most of the other Cartel members; getting Depeche Mode sometimes direct from Mute and New Order and The Smiths from Rough Trade and putting these into the chain. Then we got squeezed. Our Price, as chains do, wanted a returns facility, and insisted that all their suppliers gave them that. Rough Trade refused to let us have a returns facility with them, because now the Our Price contract was so big, they wanted it. And so we were buying from them and our returns pile was building up. We managed it for a while, trying to turn a blind eye to it. We were actually going to form a new wholesaler fifty-fifty with Rough Trade; there were legal agreements drawn up, but John Knight, who ran our distribution, back-pedalled on it, he didn't want to do it. So we sat on it for a year. Eventually Rough Trade got their way and the Our Price account and, of course, gave them their returns facility. John left the company and then met up with John Loder from Southern and started SRD (Southern Record Distribution)."

Like Fresh/Jungle, each of the constituent Cartel members had their own back-story. Geoff Davies' Probe Plus would become the most significant Liverpool label of the 80s, while the Probe shop from whence it grew had its own distinguished history. Davies was another shopkeeper who had strong links to the hippy era, having personally met the Dala Llama – though he can't remember much about it. Indeed, the first incarnation of Probe was as a 'head' shop that was once busted for stocking *Oz*. "I started Probe in January 1971," he remembers. "It was a weird, specialised, cut-price record shop – we used the expression 'head shop'. I was a bit of a hippy-ish type. It was the first shop of its type in the sense of its attitude, which all came from me, and it was completely unlike any normal record shop. And the stock reflected my taste, which was rock 'n' roll, and reggae, world music, folk, country, jazz and blues. Anything I liked, really. It was a weird looking shop. I never used to even have a till, just a box. We'd do second-hand and cut the price of new records. That was a novelty. Virgin mail order had started up then, but it was completely unheard of to cut the recommended retail price. The first goal had been to do a good second-hand shop, but as the plan formulated, it was obvious I wasn't going to be able to get enough stock."

Davies set about creating his own personal ideal of what a record shop should be. "It was run by people with similar tastes and attitudes," he continues. "It was very carefree. People could sit on stools in front of the counter. A couple of regular tramps would come in – though sometimes they'd be there for too long. And that shop was near Liverpool University. That was a success. We then opened a place in a hippy emporium horribly called Silly Billy's, with our records in the basement. That was successful too, and by October 1976, we opened up in town, just round the corner from the Cavern Club, Button Street, which turns into Matthew Street." Davies had seen The Beatles play the Cavern several times, and the location was within a stone's throw of Roger Eagle's Eric's club. "We got in on the punk thing, even though I was a bit old for it," Davies admits, "I was in my mid-30s. But we were the first shop in the north-west selling independent punk singles. All the Stiff stuff, imports, the first Television single, etc. I loved the punk attitude – not too keen on the stuff that came later. But that period of punk, '76 to '79, was just great."

The shop's outer steps would host every local vinyl nut, musician and scene wannabe. More often than not the true apostles and architects of Liverpool's punk revolution could be found inside, serving, in the very loosest terms, behind the counter. Probe became synonymous in the punk era for the acerbic staff members, with Pete Burns and wife Lynne as tormentors in chief. As one-time customer Mick Mada recalled: "This queen was a bitch. If they didn't like you or your choice of record, neither Geoff nor Pete would serve you unless you had a letter from God. Tactics ranged from the ever popular 'Fuck off, you blurt, buy that shit at WH Smiths,' to the fantastic 'Yes, son, I'll get that from the back.' They'd then hide in the back, have a cup of tea, go the pub... No way would they come out until you left the shop."

Davies, however, maintains that the shop actually had a strong spirit of camaraderie. "Some people would come in every day. And they'd say sorry when you were locking up, but they'd be late tomorrow, cos they had to sign on first." Davies had left school at 14 and worked in 'conventional' retail, developing something of a hard shell as a result. "So it was quite likely that if someone was obnoxious, you'd be sarcastic or give them some lip back. I know Julian Cope says something in his book [Head On] that is actually not quite true – that someone asked for a Rush record and I wouldn't sell it to them. We did have borderline records by the likes of Rush or Deep Purple that I didn't like, but some of our customers did. I would sell those records. I wouldn't lose a sale! But I'd just make some sarcastic remark. Being in the centre of town you'd get a mix of people; punks, rockabillies, skinheads – they were a fucking nuisance – all the black people cos we had so much good reggae and we were the only place in the north-west for Jamaican imports. Occasionally I'd have to ask people to leave sometimes. I employed Gary

Dwyer of Teardrop Explodes at one point, unsuccessfully, to move people out of the shop when it got crowded. Gary was a big lad, but a terrible doorman. He looked the part, but he was useless, so I ended up doing the job myself."

"Pete Burns was actually mostly polite to people," continues Davies. "But he had this great mouth – I remember thinking he was like Joan Rivers, just so funny. I once had to intervene with someone trying to fight Pete Burns once – the nearest I got to a fight in 30 years – but people would sometimes come in and want to jeer at him or attack him, just because of how he looked. But Probe was friendly – it had a stool in there, and we'd make people a couple of tea. I think this thing about being nasty to people has been overplayed." This writer's own experience of Probe doesn't match the off-putting reputation. Dawn Wrench, a student and a feisty bargain hunter, once purchased a terrible album by Middle Of The Road – so terrible it didn't even feature 'Chirpy Chirpy Cheep Cheep' on it – which had been marked down to one pence. The shop's staff cheered as she went up to the counter and applauded her exit from the shop. 'Thank fuck for that, someone's bought it.' But, as Wrench pointed out, "it was worth it for the bag". Probe's distinctive monochrome 'Bedlam crowd scene' carrier was very much the item to be seen walking around town with.

In a broad sense, Probe was the retail outlet for the Eric's generation. "Me and [Eric's co-founder] Roger Eagle went to see the building where Probe stood before we moved there," remembers Davies, "he was interested in having an office space in there, after winding up doing the Liverpool Stadium concerts. We became good friends. I used to put him up many a time, cos he was still travelling up from Manchester. He took a little area of the shop where he was planning things, selling posters and tickets for Eric's shows. He moved out after about nine months of the shop opening."

In May 1981 Davies began to run Probe Plus Distribution from his famously tatty, disorganised upstairs office. "Richard Scott knew about Probe, and said it had been one of the inspirations for the original Rough Trade shop," Davies says. "That's true," admits Scott. "Geoff was a wonderful man – he started off as a runner for the Liverpool stock exchange. But Probe, apart from maybe Sam The Record Man in Toronto, was probably the best record shop I've ever been in, in its heyday. I remember he had a hundred different Elvis albums in boxes on the counter – an absolutely extraordinary record shop."

"We were among Rough Trade Distribution's biggest customers," Davies continues. "Richard asked if we wanted to join this Cartel thing, and wholesale independent records in the north-west of England. I was very reticent about it, because I was just about to start up the label and I was always over-committed. But he quietly convinced me to do it."

Unfortunately, Probe would be the first of the founding fathers to leave that network. "By October 1984, I was almost forced to pull out, because I was in so much debt to the other Cartel members," Davies says. "The idea was that we'd buy from each other. I was dealing with, say, a market stall in Holyhead or a shop in Burnley. I would go up in an estate car two or three days a week to these people. They didn't have accounts with major labels, and you had to prove to them that these punk records would sell. I used to leave them on sale and return. Then you'd go back and most of them would have sold, so you'd convince them to pay up front for stock. But a lot didn't seem to want to settle their debts. They'd disappear and you could never find them. I was in a right hole. Richard Scott offered me a get-out, really. We'd spoken about the state I was in financially, and he suggested he could get most of the Cartel debts wiped, and in return, I'd pass my customers on – I had built up a network of over 90 shops, from North Wales up through Lancashire and most of Cheshire. I must say, I was quite relieved. I felt I'd sort of failed and messed up, but the burden was lifted. I was getting a bit tired of going to these Cartel meetings too. There was less and less talk about music, it was targets and things like that. And I was beginning to feel the odd one out. The others were a bit more business-like than I was."

Davies had launched the Probe Plus label at roughly the same time he was cajoled into joining the Cartel. Yet neither of the predecessor Liverpool punk era labels, Eric's and Zoo, were a major influence. "We used to stock records direct from Zoo, but there was no great friendship with Bill Drummond. I used to know all the bands because Julian [Cope] and [Ian] McCulloch were always hanging round the shop, and we'd go for a drink in the Grapes up the road. But I was never dead crazy about them – Julian's music was OK at first, but I didn't like the first album, with all the brass. The Bunnymen I got tired of. For me, McCulloch has always been a big-headed, tight, pain in the arse. So it taints the music. The reason why I first did Probe Plus was coming across some bands that I knew were having trouble getting records out. It was almost an extension of the Cartel thing – I'll have a go at seeing if I can get this out. I wasn't taking it dead seriously."

The label was inaugurated in November 1981 with Ex Post Facto's debut single. However, the Probe Plus name only appeared for the first time on its second release by Cook Da Books, as initially Davies didn't want to attract attention to his involvement. "I wanted to just put a toe in the water and keep it fairly anonymous. The band had actually packed in and fallen out with each other in '84. But my first album was by a Somali Scouser, Mr Amir, which was reggae, really." Throughout, the label remained pretty much a sideline. "I wasn't giving it my all, and some of the stuff I'd released wasn't really me. I'd pay bands to go into the studio and sometimes they wouldn't even turn up. The bands disappointed me in that way, so I took a more active interest in the recordings. So by '85 I was actively co-producing the records I was doing. The period from '84 onwards is the period I'm happiest about. Most of them were flops, but what made all the money was Half Man Half Biscuit."

Nigel Blackwell's Birkenhead group had amused most everyone with their initial releases, scandalising children's TV programmes, pondering the allure of European football kits and fetishising unlikely television icons like snooker referee Len Ganley. Or lambasting *Liver Birds* actress Nerys Hughes – loathed by many on Merseyside for her fake Scouse accent. John Peel loved them, but they were refreshingly hopeless at climbing any greasy poles. Most famously they refused to make a scheduled TV appearance on *The Tube* because Tranmere FC were playing at home that evening, despite Channel Four offering to fly them by helicopter to the game.

Perhaps, given such an innate lack of careerism, it should have been no surprise when Blackwell decided to derail the momentum by breaking the band up, but it was still a blow to Davies. "The last gig was October 3rd '1986, at the Chelsea College, London," he recalls. "We had another gig booked in Birmingham, and I phoned Nigel to make arrangements. He said, 'I'm not doing it.' 'Why? Are you not well?' 'Nah. I'm fed up with the lot of it. I can't be bothered.' I went along to see him, went over the water, but that was that. He'd had enough. We'd had nearly a year of lots of activity, they were the darlings of the press. Although it came out at the end of '85, *Back In The DHSS* was the biggest selling independent record of '86. 'Trumpton Riots' was the co-biggest selling single. By the time 'Dickie Davies' Eyes' came out, it had just got to number one in the indie charts when Nigel dropped this bombshell on me. I just accepted it. We didn't fall out, though it cost me a few bob. I had to get a fake doctor's note for him! It was fairly inconvenient, but I kept on paying him on sales of the records. And he sold his guitar, and a few years later he said he'd written some new songs. And that's how it's been since. I've never had a recording contract with them. And when they were ready, we'd do some recording."

Other bands on the label included Gone To Earth, the closest the region came to an approximation of the punk-folk hybrid of The Pogues. "I co-produced their first single," remembers Davies. "I brought in Sam Davis, who I knew from years ago as a member of Deaf School. And we called ourselves the Bald Brothers, cos we were both prematurely bald." Psychotic stoner freak-punks The Mel-O-Tones would evolve into The Walking Seeds. "Their first album is a really powerful record – the best version of 'Iron Man' I've ever heard, it's terrifying! That was my idea, 'let's make this really horrible and nasty sounding.'" The Walking Seeds included in their ranks both Bob Parker, omnipresent behind the Probe counter at the time, and later La's guitarist Barry Sutton (though half of Liverpool, seemingly, played with the La's at some point). Davies also introduced the world to Wirral poet and later author Jegsy Dodd, whose *Winebars and Werewolves* album sold well in 1986. Dodd's backing band, The Bastard Sons Of Harry Cross, were named after the feisty pensioner played in the local *Brookside* soap opera franchise by fellow Wirral native Bill Dean. Some wit on the set consequently couldn't resist the temptation of displaying one of the band's flyers in the same character's bungalow. Davies has released records on Probe Plus intermittently since its 80s heyday, but eventually sold the shop and retired. He remains involved with various musical projects, however, and can still talk about music for hours, and with undiminished enthusiasm.

Unlike Liverpool, Norwich has never been celebrated as a hotbed of popular music – the siting of Alan Partridge's hapless, exiled DJ there serving as some kind of barometer of its distance, both geographical and aspirational, from the larger urban arts centres. Backs, the East Anglian arm of the Cartel distribution chain, predictably started as a shop, titled after a pub of the same name in Norwich's city centre. From there it moved naturally into wholesale, at which time Rough Trade approached them to organise its distribution network in the region as a founding member of the Cartel. "Johnny [Appel] set it up," notes current Backs employee Derek Chapman. "It started as a record shop back in 1979. And then Rough Trade, also a shop at that point, were starting their distribution of all the independent labels. What they did, in effect, was to find the best independent shop in each area, and go to them and say, 'Would you like to distribute these labels for your area?' It was based on the fact that they were best record shops in the different regions."

Cartel meetings were hosted in the different regional centres on a round robin principle. "So everyone would troop off to York or Bristol or whatever," remembers Chapman. Were the meetings fun? "They were! They got a little political after a while, with strategies and things. There were some pretty punchy characters, and to be fair, a lot of them are still working in the independent music industry. There's still a lot of them around. Or sometimes they went on to record labels, of course. It's an obvious point for us to make, but the distribution side is one of those things that did tend to get forgotten. But a lot of those mavericks running independent record labels needed the support of a distribution network – we're also funding them in terms of manufacturing costs and so on, which some people, no names mentioned, sometimes forget. It was a fertile time. Because the record shops were in the front line, people were coming into the shop asking us for records that weren't on the EMI listings – so it was a natural extension to hunt out these records because people wanted them. Where the hell do you get the Desperate Bicycles, or Stiff Little Fingers, or the Normal, whatever these records they were asking for, from? So it developed from that period. We didn't create the demand, we supplied it."

"It then developed over the next few years," Chapman continues, "each member of the Cartel began to find its own distribution and labels, obviously reflecting what was going on locally and nationally. And then we started to sell them all amongst ourselves. We would pick up on a label and sell it to Red Rhino, Fast, Rough Trade or whatever, and they would equivalently give us their stuff to sell in our area. If Red Rhino had a new release, we would take a hundred copies or something, and sell however many we could, and pay Red Rhino for what we'd sold. And they'd probably take a hundred copies of one of ours, and sell what they could and pay us."

The move to helping local bands distribute their records was as obvious to Backs as it was to their fellow Cartel members. Among the first examples were the Romans In Britain sampler *Welcome To Norwich: A Fine City* and the Disrupters' first EP, 'Young Offender'. The latter was released under the auspices of anarcho-punk label Radical Change, while the former subsequently housed the debut single by one of the compilation album's leading lights, The Higsons ('I Don't Want To Live With Monkeys'). It sold 15,000 records before the band moved on to another Backs' affiliate, Waap! and thence a series of unsuccessful relationships with a variety of suitors. Having demonstrated that they could successfully finance and distribute subsidiary imprints, the shop staff decided they'd have a crack themselves. Backs Records was an immediate success, with The Farmers Boys, like The Higsons before them, a huge hit with John Peel, though they too would jump ship to a major.

Even without the two bands whose lustrously melodious pop had single-handedly invented a 'Norwich sound', Backs continued to enjoy qualified success. Gee Mr Tracy and the Bible both did well for them after a run of misfires (Testcard F, Happy Few, Gothic Girls, Mad About Sunday). The Bible subsequently found themselves restored to a major (singer Boo Hewerdine having previously recorded for Phonogram with The Great Divide), as they were first licensed to, and then signed by, Chrysalis. "We had to be realistic," notes Johnny Appel. "If the band has released a couple of singles and done really well and you have people sniffing around offering all sorts of things, the next stage is an album. If we wanted that LP to be successful enough, you're talking vast sums of money. If you haven't got it, why be stupid? We hadn't got the money. We could do with some as we had fledgling bands coming along that needed investment. It was a way for the band to get what they wanted – to sign to a major label with unlimited resources and an opportunity for us to glean back a few pounds to invest in new bands."

Moreover the Backs' team routinely referred to their label as 'comic relief', and very much a diversion from the day to day business of stocking, distributing and promoting records. "Distribution was the main business, that's where all the efforts went," confirms Chapman. "The label was how we *lost* the money we made. The Backs label almost came to a halt in the early 90s. I think the last release was Venus In Furs. We called it a day on that and started a different label. It was briefly resurrected five or so years back for a Farmers Boy release, the BBC sessions album, and just for old times' sake, we put it on the Backs label." Their commitment to the Cartel was ongoing, however, at least until the collapse of Rough Trade Distribution in 1991.

Chapman maintains that the independent ethos remains strong in terms of Backs' activities. "Yeah, and it's always going to be driven by the music, really. For new music to come along it needs ways of being disseminated and distributed. So it tends to come out through the independent network rather than a major, because we're fleeter of foot and faster to react. Whereas once the machine of Universal Music Inc or whatever they're called tries to move, it can take a while."

South-west Cartel member Revolver grew out of the independent record shop run in Bristol by Chris Parker, with Lloyd Harris originally looking after distribution. Sited in the 'Triangle' at the top of Park Street, Revolver was a focal point for the city's post-punk arts community and musicians, with shop floor graduates including Grant Marshall of Massive Attack. In a familiar pattern, Parker also set up Recreational Records, whose releases

included the first singles by local reggae act Talisman and Bristolian punks
the X-Certs. Jamie Hill, who would go on to be Revolver distribution's
warehouse manager, was a member of two bands who recorded for its in-
house label; Mouth (who featured Nellee Hooper of The Wild Bunch and
Rob Merrill, later of Roni Size's Reprazent) and Animal Magic. "Richard
Grassby-Lewis of the Startled Insects produced most of the records in Bath,"
Hill recalls. "But Chris Parker was definitely the main guy. With Mouth we'd
just done a bedroom demo, so we turned up at the shop on the Triangle,
played them the tape, and got a yes. We'd only played two gigs and had
about five songs."

Revolver was an exemplar of a Cartel staple; that of record shop turned hang
out turned epicentre of the local music community. "We used to knock off
school when we were about fourteen, fifteen," Mark Stewart of the Pop
Group would recall in *Straight Outa Bristol*, "go for a smoke over a mate's
house and every Friday we'd go to Revolver to listen to the new reggae pre-
releases, right? We used to talk about this van from Zion that every Friday
would bring the pre's. Revolver would only stock so many records, but I was
heavily into the dub stuff so as the two lads in the shop were playing
through the pre's to see which ones to stock, we'd check the dubs [dub plates
or reggae acetates] to try and find which ones we wanted. And then [it
turned out] that it was Adrian [Sherwood] delivering on the van to Revolver;
it was his first driving job and he was bringing the dubs down to Bristol
when he was eighteen or nineteen."

Present in the shop from 1975, Mike Chadwick, alongside Harris, would take
control of distribution from 1983, offloading the retail side to Roger
Doughty, former owner of Cheltenham's Drifting Records and a member of
the pre-Pigbag group Hardware. But unlike other Cartel members, from that
point Revolver's retail/distribution disciplines were entirely separate. "I
started working weekends at Revolver around 1983," recalls Sean Mayo.
"Then Roger [Doughty] moved to Bristol and bought the shop. The
distribution moved to the Old Malt House, just off the M32. I moved to that
side of it, and went into telesales and packing orders. It was a four-man
operation with me, Pete Theelke and the two directors, Mike Chadwick and
Lloyd Harris. The way it worked with the Cartel was you had a loose but
very loyal group of companies that represented things regionally. Each
company would be acquiring labels to distribute through The Cartel, then
trading records between them for wholesale. Each company would then
tele-sale to their area. We were selling to the whole of the south-west, South
Wales, the whole of Cornwall, Devon, down to Dorset. You had call cycles

with the shops. Back then the business was so strong, you were dealing with these people on a weekly basis, pre-selling releases, four to six weeks in advance, and also taking stock orders. We also did our own exports. It was friendly. We were all into it for the same reasons. It was about the music. But not just the music – it was independent, and all that represented. It was doing it for all the right reasons."

Jamie Hill remembers the Revolver warehouse, despite the turbulence that it would endure during his time there in the late 80s, as a convivial place to work. "We had a lot of fun working alongside the Cartel boys who had an office next to us, and we were always arguing about what went on the stereo. I remember once I had a massive order to get out of the way, so I got in there really early, about six o'clock. Mike Chadwick was a massive hi-fi buff. He'd just buy the latest stuff. He'd bought this amp and it was like a concrete box. I'd never had it above about two, but that morning, I cranked it up to nine. And within minutes I had the police knocking on the warehouse door."

The Revolver shop, meanwhile, would become one of the many victims of the redevelopment of Bristol's city centre in the new millennium, joining a glut of independent retailers to bite the dust as real estate was leased to chains and franchises. It is still widely mourned within the Avon music community, though, as Doughty points out, it wasn't just creeping mono but also micro-capitalism that did for Revolver. "One of the final nails in my coffin was when one of the Revolver distribution guys bought Tony's Records [run by Tony Dodd, who initially helped start Heartbeat Records with Simon Edwards]. He'd tried to buy my shop, but went for Tony's instead and renamed it Imperial. He did OK but it stole the fire from my business. Prior to that Ralph Cumbers [aka electronica artist Bass Clef] had come down from London and set up Replay [the last Bristol independent record shop to close in 2006]. One of my ex-guys went to work for him. Although Bristol's a big city, it's only got a limited number of record buyers. I was at the top of a steep hill with no window space. When there was no competition it was fine, when other shops opened, it fell off. I clung on and put more and more money into it, ignoring advice from my accountant, and lost a lot of money. In the end it was the landlord who put the boot in, under the illusion he could re-let easily. About eight years on, it's still empty! I left behind Banksy's artwork on the door as well – which I'll forever regret!" [The Bristolian graffiti artist's stencil and screen-print work has sold for upwards of £100,000 per item at auction]. I also had John Peel and Cure signatures in the shop from when they visited, but you can't keep everything."

# Get Rid Of These Things

Based in the shop founded in York, Red Rhino Records provided the base for The Cartel's north-east network, and like most of the other constituent members, was a successful label in its own right. Formed by Tony Kostrzewa and Adrian Collins, the label's first release, under original title Double R Records, was an unremarkable power pop effort by The Odds. The second, by the Akrylykz, featured later Fine Young Cannibals singer Roland Gift. Thereafter the roster varied between experimental post-punk (Mekons, Zoviet France, Hula), punk (Xpozez) and Goth (Red Lorry Yellow Lorry, Skeletal Family, 1919). These were predominantly bands drawn from the label's immediate Yorkshire vicinity, partially explaining the predisposition towards the latter genre, whose undisputed heartland was Leeds. Red Rhino later issued Pulp's first recordings while subsidiary imprints included Ediesta and Red Rhino Europe (based in Belgium and distributed by Play It Again Sam Records), which saw releases by Front 242 and The Butthole Surfers.

Kostrzewa, an ex-Mod, was twenty seven when he started the shop, having spent time in London in shipping and accounts, concurrently helping later Throbbing Gristle member Chris Carter run the Orpheus Lites psychedelic light show. He moved to Norwich in 1973, where girlfriend and later wife Gerri had embarked on studies at the University of East Anglia. While there he befriended Robin Watson, proprietor of local independent record shop Robin's Records. That in turn inspired the idea of Red Rhino, established in York's Gillygate in June 1977.

Robert Worby became involved with Red Rhino via his band, The Distributors. "We'd released our first single on our own label," he recalls, "and we needed to get it distributed. Red Rhino had just started their distribution system, and it was Adrian Collins who did that. He had the idea of buying a van, putting shelves in it, and driving around the north east, as far as Durham, Newcastle, Hull, Selby etc, distributing DIY punk singles. We took in a box of our single and Red Rhino sold a few for us. They were interested in us, and we were having some success; Peel sessions, lots of gigs etc. We recorded our second single at Easy Street Studios, in East London, 'Lean On Me' (RED 5). I had the idea that instead of pressing it ourselves, we'd try to get a record deal. I took the tape into Red Rhino and Adrian and Tony Kostrzewa listened to it and ended up releasing it."

Worby had an interest in production, having worked with local Wakefield act Strangeways. "They were signed to Real Records, which was Dave Hill, who was managing The Pretenders. I produced some demos and they liked what I did, so I ended up working with [Strangeways singer] Ada Wilson. I'd composed electronic music before; I knew about *musique concrète*, where to put microphones, editing, how compressors and EQ worked. I had ideas about modifying instruments. I made a single with Ada, 'In The Quiet Of My Room'. I put drawing pins in the piano hammers on that. I'd taken 25 copies of Ada's single to Rough Trade and met Geoff Travis – it had been single of the week in *Sounds* and the records were all in a box under Ada's bed in Wakefield! Rough Trade didn't know where to get them. So I took down twenty-five and they said, 'We want two hundred!' We didn't know how you did things. We were just making it up." Because of his production skills, Kostrzewa invited Worby into the Red Rhino fold. "Tony asked me to help out at Red Rhino. I became the in-house producer, working with all kinds of bands. I spent weeks in a studio in a village called Pity Me, near Durham, where 'Nellie The Elephant' was recorded [which became Red Rhino Distribution's biggest success when it sold half a million copies in 1984]. I became interested in how the label worked too – and I thought, they're not selling enough records. But while all this was going on, Tony and Adrian had a big bust up and fell out. Adrian left Rhino, but I stayed, because there were opportunities there."

Worby saw Kostrzewa at close quarters. "He trained as an accountant. He was a second generation Polish immigrant [his father was Polish, his mother from Yorkshire], and his parents put a lot of pressure on him to do well; to be a doctor or a solicitor or an accountant. And he *hated* the name Kostrzewa; he hated that Polish connection. He always called himself Tony K. His name is actually Julian Anthony Kostrzewa. In those days, if you were a sole trader, it was a legal requirement that you needed your name on your headed notepaper. So it would say, 'Red Rhino Records', then at the bottom, 'Sole Proprietor JA Kostrzewa', in the smallest font you've ever seen. He hated having to do that."

"Tony was basically a shopkeeper," Worby continues, "he had a shopkeeper mentality. Adrian didn't come from that background and was much more adventurous. But the label was funded by the distribution business, and that was doing extraordinarily well. And the retail business was doing well too; it was a very good record shop. People would travel from places like Leeds to go there. The so-called warehouse was in the back room, racked out with loads of records. It was tiny. I used to do promotion and plug their records – they didn't know how to do that. 'You simply go down to Radio One and give one to John Peel.' Tony just expected things to sell by word of mouth. He was: 'Sell the record, get the money.' Give records away? He wasn't keen on that, or PR work at all. I gradually built that up. I knew we had to get the records played in Europe. Bands like Hula were touring in Holland and Germany, and we had to find distribution companies abroad. So we hooked up with [exporters] Cargo."

Working from home, due to the lack of space at the shop, Worby would check in each Monday. "After close of business I'd go upstairs to their flat, talk to Tony and his wife Gerri, and we'd make plans. They'd cook a meal then we'd go down the boozer. And bands would come over, like Hula or Red Lorry Yellow Lorry. The other thing I did was say to Tony, 'You need a publishing company. There's money to be made on publishing.' He came up with the name Screaming Red Music." In the immediate aftermath of Collins' departure, Kostrzewa's A&R skills were shaky. "Tony signed a load of really crap bands," says Worby. "He signed a Newcastle poet called Nod who made a record called 'Dad' – *awful*. There was another guy called Steve Dixon, a journalist for *ID* magazine who lived in York; a bit of a ducker and diver. And he persuaded Tony to put a record out ['Candy Blues']. Tony was easily persuaded – he was a nice guy. Steve said, 'I work at *ID*, I know everyone at *NME*, blah blah.' Tony said, 'You've got to work with Robert, he'll produce it.' Steve couldn't play, couldn't sing, nothing!"

After his departure from Red Rhino Adrian Collins became a rep for a major record company. "Then Adrian wanted to start a record label; he'd got some money from somewhere," remembers Worby. "He asked me if I'd join him and become a partner. But he'd had this huge bust up with Tony Kostrzewa, so I knew if I went with Adrian, Tony would throw me out. Adrian also wanted to get Jon Langford involved, because The Mekons had taken their second album, *Devils, Rats and Piggies* to Red Rhino, after they'd been kicked off Virgin."

That new label, CNT, also based in York and run by Collins, Worby and Langford from November 1981 onwards, took its name from the Confederación Nacional del Trabajo (an umbrella organisation of Spanish anarcho-syndicalist labour unions). It would release records by The Three Johns and Mekons, both featuring Langford, as well as The Sisters Of Mercy's second single and the first recordings by The Redskins (originally formed as No Swastikas in York), whose unique hybrid of Motown and punk was filtered through a strident Socialist perspective. Singer Chris Dean employed the vernacular of class struggle and solidarity ('Unionize', 'Lean On Me') and the phrasing of a soul singer in an attempt to reconcile Lev Bronstein (birth name of Leon Trotsky and title of their debut single) with Levi Stubbs. Dean would later assume the identity of writer X. Moore, becoming, as characterised by Langford, "The *NME*'s SWP bogey man".

Langford had already enjoyed a crash course in the music industry. The Mekons had made their debut on Bob Last's Fast Product then, perplexingly, signed a contract with Virgin Records, recording an album at The Manor, with all the expense that entailed. It wasn't ever going to be a lasting relationship, as Langford confirms. "I think it was a big low point for The Mekons. We floundered and flopped about uselessly on Virgin. The only thing that was any good was the 'Teeth' EP, which we recorded and produced ourselves up north. Then they dropped us." Red Rhino was Langford's next port of call. "They did the second album, mainly cos Adrian Collins worked there, and had really great ears, taste, vision, etc. Adrian introduced me to Robert [Worby] while he was still living in Wakefield. We formed CNT when Tony K fired Adrian from Red Rhino. I really loved working with both of them on CNT, and if it wasn't for the hostile intentions of Red Rhino, CNT would have done a lot better."

Harlow's Newtown Neurotics were also politically minded, mining a deft punk-pop derivative in opposition to the prevailing glue-sniffing blues ethos of the third wave of punk. "It was 1981," remembers vocalist Steve Drewett, "three years after Margaret Thatcher came to power and I had written 'Kick Out The Tories' very quickly to play on an imminent Right to Work march. Afterwards, I decided to demo it and the recording was later included on a cassette compilation. One day, Adrian at CNT asked me to send him a copy after reading a rave review of the track in the music press. CNT had an eclectic roster of acts but records by The Three Johns, The Redskins and ourselves seemed less like single releases in the traditional sense, and more like pieces of broken pavement levered up from the floor and hurled at the government. When I signed with them for 'Kick Out The Tories', the contract impressed me. This legally bound document had a banner design at the top depicting Spanish anarchist anti-fascists manning barricades. I realised that with Jon Langford's fantastic graphic design and the attitude of the label this was exactly where I wanted our music to be, with CNT. I wear those three letters with pride, still emblazoned on my guitar to this day. CNT Hujos Del Pueblo A Las Barricadas en discos!"

Elsewhere on the label, Dutch squat anarchists The Ex were analogous to a lowlands Crass. Carlton B, Morgan, a civil servant who wrote for Leeds fanzine *Attack On Bzag*, edited by future *NME* editor and *Loaded*/laddism inventor in chief James Brown, was a strange hybrid of dub and Beefheart.

## Get Rid Of These Things

His 'Shave The Ayatollah' was, however, outshone for pure weirdness by Vicky Talbot's 'Don't Get Fooled Again', which featured a young girl singing The Who standard, badly, to Stylophone accompaniment.

The comparisons between Fast and CNT are obvious; they both managed a similar amount of 'catalogue', were highly critically regarded and capable of wilful commercial sabotage (in the Vicky Talbot release there are distinct echoes of The Stupid Babies' 'Baby Sitters' *Earcom* appearance). "I don't think we thought about the Fast Product model much," suggests Langford. "We just wanted to get good bands out on vinyl and Adrian really had his ears to the ground – great, long, dangling ears. Adrian was the leader and rightly so – I am useless at any form of label management and brought a lot of stuff that sold zero, although the Three Johns and Mekons did some of their best stuff for CNT, I think. I helped mix stuff, did artwork, worked with the bands, even joined the Sisters Of Mercy for a month or so in 1981."

While many of the bands on CNT were avowedly socialist, they had to appeal to at least one of the partners musically. "We were all big lefties," admits Langford, "and while Adrian was disillusioned SWP [Socialist Workers Party], I was fairly unaligned and Rob was a big old post-structuralist commie. Those were the bands we came across. The Sisters were pals and fairly non-political on most levels, Carlton B. Morgan was a Satanist." Even so, he admits the gang of three "used to like going to the corner cafe in Chapeltown to plot the overthrow of the government and major labels and bitch about Tony K at Red Rhino." For Worby, music and politics were related factors. "It was both." Commercial considerations, however, weren't that high on anyone's agenda. "Adrian was really exceptional," says Langford, "and me and Worby helped to foil many of his better ideas by refusing Prefab Sprout, New Model Army and others in favour of non-commercial projects that tickled us." Worby well remembers Adrian Collins' enthusiasm for Prefab Sprout being dashed. "Jon and I said, 'Nah, it's crap, sounds like the Beatles.'"

Worby's engagement in the enterprise, however, had to be conducted under a cloak of secrecy. "It was, 'I'll work with you guys, but Tony must never find out!' So I had the pseudonym Colin Stewart, who's still a fictional character in the Mekons! I began to work with Adrian, and one of the first things I did was the Sisters of Mercy single, 'Body Electric', which we recorded at KGM Studios, an eight-track in Bridlington, round the back of the Conservative Club. It was immediately single of the week in *Melody Maker*. Andy [Andrew Eldridge] wasn't pleased with the production, even though it was successful, and I didn't work with them again. I did actually tell Tony that I'd produced that single, and he said 'I don't want to talk about it'. He was pissed off that it was single of the week. I think Tony suspected I was involved with Adrian, but he never really said anything. Then I formed Low Noise Music, the CNT publishing company. So I had a dual career, working with Tony and with Adrian. I also did the sound for the Mekons, and played with them."

While Worby continued his association with Red Rhino, there were frustrations. "In 1984, a friend of mine moved to New York. I went to see him for the whole of that September. I realised my English accent opened doors. I went to see Ruth Polsky at Danceteria. She had booked the Mekons and Gang of Four for their new year's party the previous year. And they'd got so drunk, they were basically sent home – they lost their passports, guitars, everything. But Ruth was interested in booking British bands, and she'd heard about Red Lorry Yellow Lorry, Mekons, Three Johns and Sisters of Mercy. She told me about a guy called Peter Wright who worked at Dutch East India. I went to his apartment and persuaded him to start plugging Red Rhino artists, with a view to touring them there. 'What do you need to sell records to a small record shop in Indiana?' I wrote it all down on a notebook – I've still got my notes. I went to see Tony one Monday night, and I talked him through what they needed. Tony was keen, but he was going to have to give away hundreds of records and he would have to pay Peter Wright to plug them. He came round to the idea eventually, So I'd send Peter the records, and he'd send them out to college radio stations. I even wrote little one-liners for the telephone sales people. I think Tony thought immediately we would sell 10,000 records rather than 3,000 – but those things take time. And he went very cool about it all. I found it frustrating, I'd done all this work, running up a huge transatlantic phone bill setting it up, but he was always holding back."

Nevertheless, Red Rhino's American invasion was at least a partial success. "The first band Ruth Polsky booked was the Sisters of Mercy," Worby recalls. "They were very successful. We'd got the first CNT single out, which Andy used as PR material to sign a deal with Warners for Merciful Release. He'd insisted that, although the record was on CNT, it was also a 'Merciful Release' single. I said to Tony, 'That's how you do it!' So in 1985, the following year, we went to New York's New Music Seminar. I persuaded Ruth to book Red Lorry Yellow Lorry for two gigs, one in Boston, one in New York. I said to Tony, 'We need to do massive PR on this, 500 records given away.' Tony wasn't going to do that. Red Lorry Yellow Lorry did a really good gig at the Seminar. Tony paid for me to go, and he had a stall there – that shopkeeper mentality again!

But he wasn't really doing what was necessary. What was really big in those days was mailing lists. I'd go to people like Scott Piering [famed Rough Trade plugger]. Scott very generously gave me a mailing list – they were like gold dust. Peter Wright made me a mailing list in America. And I copied those, and sent records out to radio shows all over the US and Australia. Tony would say, 'Why are you sending records to Australia? We don't sell any there.' Well, you won't if it's not on the radio!"

Meanwhile Kostrzewa was growing "extremely envious" of the success of CNT. "He was very angry with The Mekons," says Worby, "very angry with Jon because of the breakdown of the relationship with Adrian Collins. I never actually found out what the argument was between Tony and Adrian; even Adrian never told me. But it went very deep." CNT was effectively ended by Kostrzewa's retaliatory actions. "Tony basically put the boot into CNT. CNT was distributed by Rough Trade, and the Cartel was forming – Tony said to them, if you distribute CNT, I'm out of here. Tony wanted to destroy the label, basically. It was a vicious, malicious, spiteful act by Tony, and that scuppered CNT."

Collins elected to stick with The Redskins, managing them and signing them to Decca. Eventually Worby too would make his exit from Red Rhino. "I was doing more and more with The Mekons, I went on tour with them in 1986 in America, and Tony was getting really pissed off with this. He said, unless you can turn up once a week, forget it. I couldn't guarantee that. Gradually I crept away from Red Rhino. I'd gone by the time they collapsed. Tony's A&R skills were not very good. Kelvin [Knight; shop assistant and drummer for Delta 5] tried to become the A&R department with Tony. We had a tea chest heaped with demo tapes, and he'd listen to some of them. Tony would do that initial filtering, then play me some stuff. I would say yea or nay, or say if I thought I could do something. Kelvin was also doing some production with Red Rhino, trying to get more involved in that. I'd moved from the production side into trying to sell records, which was extremely difficult. Before I left, the label was in decline, because Tony was managing things extremely badly. He was moving money around, trying to keep things going. He began lying about things. He would lie to me, lie to the bands, lie to his wife. Gerri was keeping an eye on the money, she worked in an insurance company as a computer programmer or something, and she was worried the money was going down the drain. Tony had a brick in the wall behind his bed where he kept cash. He'd made a load of money selling bootleg records at record fairs – he had one of the biggest collections of bootlegs I've ever seen. Friends of his sold them rather than him. And those were the people who became Nine Mile.

That's where they got their money from originally, bootleg record fairs, funded by Tony with the cash behind the brick."

Simon Morgan was there when Red Rhino spread its wings to help bankroll Nine Mile, initially titled Red Rhino Midlands. "I first hooked up with Robin Hurley, Graham Samuels and Simon Holland in the early 80s," he recalls. "They seemed to have a farming background." Hurley admits there's a grain of truth in that. "I went to Welsh Agricultural College in September 1975 to do a qualification in agriculture. Probably like a lot of young men at that time, I didn't really know what I wanted to do in life. And due to my parents living near to a farm, I ended up working on one. On the very first night I got to college, we went down to the pub and I bumped into Graham Samuels. We hit it off and became friends, mainly through a passion for music – which even then superseded our interest in agriculture. Neither of us had any thought of getting into the music industry. My course involved a year away from college, so from July 1976 to August 1977 I went up to a farm just north of York, as part of the course. During that time Tony opened the Red Rhino shop. And me being a young guy there with a love of music, every Saturday I would make the pilgrimage into York and buy records from Tony. It was the era when punk really started breaking and it was an exciting time."

The customer-vendor relationship flowered into a social alliance, but stayed as such while Hurley completed his studies. "I finished my course, and I started working for ICI and Ciba-Geigy in agricultural chemicals. I kept in touch with Tony and Gerri and would go visit them and see concerts in York or Leeds. At one point I said, 'Tony, I really admire what you've done, you've built a great record shop. It's got a fantastic reputation, I'd love to do something similar.' He told me how he'd done it, and the money he'd needed. So I started looking round in the Midlands – we'd identified a slight gap in terms of strong independent record stores in certain cities. I looked at vacant shops and went to apply and found the landlords wouldn't let to a young guy with no retail experience. The Cartel was gradually gaining strength, and I went to Tony and we talked about starting a distribution business – he may have suggested it. 'Why don't we go into partnership and do Red Rhino Midlands?' So it was in effect a mirror image of what he was doing in the north."

To this point the region lacked a specialist distribution point. "The Midlands was serviced from the south by Rough Trade, from the south-west by Revolver, from the north-west by Probe and from the east by Backs. But given the number of people from the Black Country, there wasn't really a proper

Cartel member. So we started Red Rhino Midlands in 1983. At that point, the partners were me and Tony, and possibly Gerri too. It took me about four years to save up enough money. I put up the start-up capital and Tony put in the stock. I think it was about £15,000 I'd saved." And yes, some of that money did come from behind the brick, and from bootlegs, but only a fraction of it. "I *would* go to record fairs to make money for this long-term goal," Hurley states. "I'd buy bootlegs off Tony, but collectibles too, Siouxsie and the Banshees picture sleeves and things like this. But the majority of that money came from me saving up from working for agrochemical companies. I had a wife then who was very supportive, and we saved up. And at a certain point we took the plunge and went to find a warehouse in Leamington Spa. We identified that as an area where you could feed the Midlands of England, and also, quite frankly, it was a pleasant place to live. And getting a lease on an empty warehouse was easier than getting a shopfront. I needed a number two, and I'd kept in touch with Graham Samuels. I met him at a pub in Camden and persuaded him to move up to the Midlands to join me. Then we hired Simon Holland [a former member of The Great Outdoors], then Simon Morgan [also a former band member, of Domestic Bliss and The Hop], as a general helper, as we needed."

While still known as Red Rhino Midlands, Morgan got a tantalising look at their warehouse. "I was blown away. It had previously been a carpet joint, but was now filled with records. Every record I'd ever wanted to own, but had never been able to afford. There was a small office area at the far end, and a desk and three phones just outside that for taking orders. I was so excited when Robin asked me to work for them; I could hardly contain myself. One of the first things they gave me was a white label of *Spy vs Spy* by Billy Bragg. I loved it. Of course, it was all Sisters Of Mercy and March Violets on the national scene then. One of the first jobs they gave me to do was to drive up to York to collect some stock from Red Rhino North."

They were admitted to the Cartel shortly thereafter. "Richard Scott once told me that Tony didn't tell anyone in the Cartel that he was starting Red Rhino Midlands," Hurley recalls. "Suddenly, at one Cartel meeting, he promptly announced he was starting this company in the Midlands – a very typical Tony K move. I think there was a little bit of controversy, as you can imagine, because all the other companies had some income coming out of the Midlands. It may not have been their lion's share, but it was part of their income. But we were welcomed in as fully-fledged members, so we had a seat at the table at subsequent Cartel meetings. We had an equal voice in the sense of voting, but obviously it took a while for me to get my equal voice in that – in terms of speaking up at meetings when you're dealing with strong characters like Tony. At that point, Tony was one of my closest friends and I very much deferred to him. I guess there was a sense that we were junior partners in the early days, but that's to be understood. But the other Cartel members welcomed us very quickly and very willingly. That's one thing I always liked about the Cartel; they were always really nice people to work with."

From Morgan's viewpoint, the pecking order at Nine Mile ran Robin, Graham, Simon. "And then me! I made most of the tea! My official job was Order Puller. Simon would take the orders over the phone, hand me a piece of paper with records and quantities on it, and I would 'pull' the order, pack the boxes, label them for postage, and plonk them by the double doors for collection by the daily courier van. Robin and Graham sat in the back office drinking tea, talking to important people, and playing the kind of music I regarded at the time as 'adult'." That's a scenario Hurley somewhat disputes. "I didn't just sit in the back room drinking tea! *Everyone* was packing records and pulling orders and that was a really enjoyable part of the business."

"We were always busy," Morgan continues. "I often didn't have time to put me fag out! Shed loads of Goth fare, like the aforementioned Sisters, Violets, Alien Sex Fiend, Sex Gang Children, Danse Society, Play Dead... though the biggest 'seller' we ever shifted obscene units on was 'Nellie The Elephant'. Bands would roll up looking for deals. Pop Will Eat Itself, The Wonderstuff, and Balaam & The Angel were all given deals of some kind, and Chapter 22 Records were bank-rolled." Red Rhino Midlands was fairly typical of the broader Cartel in that its employees were essentially music enthusiasts; but many, like Morgan, were also politicised by the independent ethos. "I'd plaster the boxes with 'Coal Not Dole' stickers, pad the order out with miner's strike literature, bung in stacks of free 'Enemy Within' badges, stickers and flyers, and conduct my own one-man war against Thatcher from deep within the bunkerage of Nine Mile Fantasy Island." Morgan retained his job for 18 months, until Tim Niblett was taken on. "Sadly he was killed in a car crash one morning on the Banbury/Warwick road, and things were never the same after that."

Hurley and Kostrzewa would ultimately drift apart. "Red Rhino Midlands had made a bit of profit," Hurley recalls. "Not a huge amount. Graham had put a lot of 'sweat equity' into it, so I wanted to reward him and give him a minority share in the company. And I wanted to give some profit-share and bonuses to the other people who worked for me in return for a good year.

## Get Rid Of These Things

That was the first divisive conversation between me and Tony. He wasn't keen on either of those proposals. I suggested I'd like to buy him out of the company and with Rough Trade's help we bought out Tony and Gerri's shares in about '85 or early '86. With that loan from Rough Trade, which was repaid, it brought me closer to Rough Trade both emotionally and philosophically. I started going down to London more often, and for a short period became the National Sales Manager for the Cartel, when we had things like New Order and Depeche Mode and Dead Kennedys and The Smiths, all these things becoming chart successes for the Cartel. That meant WH Smiths and John Menzies, people who hadn't previously stocked Cartel releases, having to take notice. I would go the head buyers at Virgin and HMV and spent two days a week in London while Graham was running Red Rhino Midlands." The operation was retitled Nine Mile on conclusion of the buyout. "The name Nine Mile came from my love of reggae," says Hurley. "It's the town in Jamaica where Bob Marley was born and is buried, a little hamlet."

Kostrzewa, meanwhile, had spread himself thinly, both in terms of finances and commitments. "One of Tony's character flaws," says Worby, "is that he was desperate to be liked. So he would promise bands all kinds of stuff he could never deliver. I remember a dreadful time when Ron Wright of Hula went to see Tony to get a cheque to pay for some studio time they had booked. 'Tony, we need to get a cheque off you.' 'Sure, the cheque's in the post.' That was his famous line. And of course, it never arrived. So Ron went over to York, and Tony said, don't worry about it, we'll go to the bank now and get the money out, so you've got the cash to pay the studio tomorrow. On the way to the bank, it's getting late, three o'clock. The bank closes at half past three. So Tony says, let's have a chat. He sat Ron down and told him about how everything was going to be great, the new record was going to be fantastic, etc. He kept him talking till the bank had closed! Ron was livid. Basically Tony was robbing Peter to pay Paul."

Red Rhino Distribution, which had taken warehouse space in Eldon Street, collapsed in December 1988. It did so at exactly the same time as *The Catalogue* [the in-house Cartel publication whose 'business manager' was Kostrzewa] appeared with an editorial note stating that "rumours of [Red Rhino's] demise are, as the saying has it, greatly exaggerated". The label was also shut down, and bankrupt stock snapped up by Brighton shop Vinyl Demand, who sold it off cheaply via adverts in *Record Collector*. Three years later, the much-loved Red Rhino shop, having relocated to larger premises in Goodramgate, closed its doors for the final time.

Kostrzewa became a manager at a *Laser Quest* centre before starting
promotion and management companies. Worby remained on cordial terms
with him post-Red Rhino, but events would see that relationship sour. "I was
working with The Mekons but I was still in touch with Tony, and when he
moved to Leeds he came round my flat a couple of times. One day [in 1994]
we found out that Cherry Red had put out the second Mekons album, *Devils,
Rats & Piggies*. Hmm. That's funny – cos either Jon or me still had the tapes in
our flats! And we hadn't done a deal with Cherry Red. How come Cherry Red
have put a CD out, without us knowing? Of course, Tony said he had the
copyright on the record. There was no contract. All I had was a letter of
agreement for The Distributors – we agree to release this record and share
the profits 50-50. Of course, we never got any money because 'profit' was
never defined. But The Mekons? They never signed a contract."

Eventually the matter was resolved after a cease and desist order was issued.
"What happened was that Tony had persuaded Iain McNay that he'd got the
rights on the Mekons second record," Worby continues, "and they cut it off a
vinyl LP. And Tony just took the money – that's how he operated. He
presumed he had the rights, but he never did. Tony was never keen on
contracts. He didn't like the idea. He worried that he could be sued. Tony left
a message on my answering machine [about this] that I kept, and it's on a
Mekons record. The message was, 'I'm really, really sorry. I just wanted to get
the record out.' I just thought, you're a pathological liar. You're lying so
much, you're beginning to *believe* the lies you're telling *yourself*. 'I'm sorry
Tony, but I don't want to be involved.' When he died, I wrote a letter to Gerri
saying all of that – I said that Tony was doing deals that I could not be any
part of. She wrote me a letter back saying, funny enough, if Tony was alive
today, he'd agree with you."

For all that, Kostrzewa deserves credit for many things. For example, he
sponsored the efforts of Dave Henderson's *Offbeat* magazine [itself a
successor to the similarly short-lived *Underground*] in the late 80s, and
helped several labels get a start, as Henderson attests. "I know Tony made
quite a few enemies over the years, but he also did propel the careers of quite
a few people, too. Sadly he died last year [in May 2008] which was really sad.
I ended up getting emails about his slow demise and eventually sorting
tickets for his kids for Glastonbury and meeting his wife again. He was very
outspoken; well, he spoke so fast you could never get a word in. And, as you
know, dealing with bands, there are a lot of wayward egos and invariably
there were a lot of people who didn't make it in bands with similarly
reactionary personalities. I kept out of it thankfully and to be honest don't

know exactly what happened. It was obvious there was a lot of friction and when people lose their jobs and money, as they did, it's always going to kick off." Richard Scott, too, credits Kostrzewa with being probably the most forceful presence in regional independent distribution. "Tony was the backbone of that regional structure, and I found him extremely good to deal with." Despite misgivings Worby, like so many customers of the original Red Rhino shop, has fond memories too, not least of Kostrzewa's legendary enthusiasm. "Tony could be such a great guy. We had some great times. It was extremely exciting selling Red Lorry Yellow Lorry into the States. We felt we were conquering America."

"One of the sad things about my relationship with Tony was how it crumbled," says Hurley. "Rob's comments about Tony becoming a pathological liar – sadly, I have to agree 100%. It became very disturbing not to know what to believe when he would talk to you about things. With me moving to America it naturally put some distance between us, and there was no need to keep a dialogue. I always regretted it, but he was the sort of person who lived life his own way and no-one was going to change that. I did bump into him at the Cannes musical festival around 2001. It was very cordial, and we went for a drink and a chat. Later, Gerri reached out to me and said, 'I don't know if you've heard, but Tony's got sick.' She said he'd really been getting back into listening to music. I work at Warners, so I sent him a big box of things like Neil Young, Warren Zevon, Jackson Browne, Fleetwood Mac, The Grateful Dead; things I knew he'd loved from the first time I got to know him. So I had an email dialogue with him and Gerri. But I never got to speak to him. I was due to speak to him the day he died, actually. I rang at the allotted time and Gerri told me the bad news. But what really affected me was going to the funeral. Quite honestly, I expected this huge Cartel reunion, a huge turnout. It was quite sad how few of the people I'd expected were there. Unfortunately, that was a reflection of Tony's *modus operandi*, which was to fall out with people. It's the saddest memory I have of the man. He was so great in a lot of ways. When I told people I was going to the funeral, they asked why. But frankly, I wouldn't be here if it wasn't for this man, I wouldn't be in the music industry. So while we had our major differences, I was glad we made up at the end. He was a pivotal person in my life, even though he was a royal pain in the arse for parts of it. It's a shame that a lot of people whose lives he touched weren't at the funeral. It's a shame people couldn't put it behind them."

Prior to Red Rhino's collapse, Nine Mile had been annexed into the central Rough Trade operation, as Hurley took up the offer of an expeditionary role in America. "Rough Trade Germany was doing well at the time, and they were doing quite well in Benelux," he recalls. "They had this outpost in San Francisco and they wanted to grow Rough Trade in America, so that when Geoff Travis had a band, they didn't necessarily have to license it to a major label in the US. They asked me if I would like to work in America for a year and assess the growth potential for Rough Trade. I jumped at the chance, it was a dream come true. I decided to merge Nine Mile into Rough Trade so that it would become more like a sales outpost. I was optimistic and naive and very idealistic at the time, as were a lot of the people working in the Cartel, thinking this could be a new model, and an industry that would thrive for a lifetime. In hindsight it didn't, obviously. Graham Samuels went on to run Rough Trade Benelux in Amsterdam. People like Simon Holland stayed in Leamington and ran that division, with a few other people. But I moved to America in July 1987 and shortly after Graham went to Holland." Samuels would eventually oversee BBC Music (where he was partially responsible for the success of 'Bob The Builder') before joining Sony, while Hurley heads Warners' Rhino (no relation) imprint.

Fast Forward, which grew out of Bob Last's Fast Product label and was based in Alva Street, Edinburgh, offered a slight diversion from the norm in that it was a standalone distribution point. Most of the other Cartel members were shops who'd taken gladly to a wider role in distributing the products of their peers. "By the time it was Fast Forward, it was nothing to do with me," states Last. "We did continue for a while looking to be part of that whole distribution system, but I couldn't make it work. So we shut down and some people who worked for me took it over, using the Fast Forward name for some continuity."

"The Cartel discussions had started in 1982," notes Fast Forward's subsequent manager Sandy McLean. "We agreed on a name, and Lloyd Bradley from Revolver did a few designs and the company bosses voted on them. We met every couple of months, with Richard Scott and Tony K from Red Rhino being the most active. Fast Product was seen as an equal partner, as Bob was making big waves with his acts. Fast Forward basically ended when we did a quarterly stock check in early 1984, I think, and the results were a £3,500 loss for the quarter. It wasn't even our main year-end stock check, but rather than trade on or try to turn things around, Bob declared we were insolvent and immediately pulled the plug on the operation. Overnight he laid off everybody except Nick Haines and myself, and we were given a week to return stock to the suppliers. Nick was guitarist in The Flowers alongside Hillary Morrison [Bob Last's partner]. He was at Fast when I arrived. And

## Get Rid Of These Things

Simon Best was the drummer. Simon was running Fast Product for Bob.
Simon went off to go to university and he head-hunted me from Virgin – I'd
joined them after Bruce's Records went bust."

"Bob had wanted to have a one-stop wholesaler operation," McLean
continues, "like EUK, rather than the purely indie model of Rough Trade and
Red Rhino. So we had been buying stock from Virgin and Island Records
(where he had contacts via the Human League and Heaven 17) on a
ridiculously low margin of 5%. That was probably the main reason for the
collapse of our profits. With a 5% profit margin (at best) you have to sell
every copy of every release to make any money, whereas with the Cartel
product it was exclusive to us and the margin was tripled. As the general
manager of the company, I have to take responsibility for taking it down, but
if it was my company I would have ditched the major label stuff and traded
on longer, as turnover was good and we had The Smiths just kicking off."

"It turned out to be a very good break for me that Bob withdrew from
distribution," McLean continues. "I got to start my own company and my
own label, and get paid a wage by someone else while doing it. My first call
was to Tony K. He arranged a three-way meeting in York with himself and
Richard Scott, where I showed them Fast Product's turnover figures and
accounts. They were puzzled with the decision to close so abruptly, but
thought there was good turnover there and wanted to keep the Cartel flag
flying in Scotland. Tony came up with the model we later adopted, and the
money to get an office and pay wages for Nick Haines and myself. He
encouraged me to start my own distribution company, while wholesaling
Cartel product to the Scottish record shops and sending the orders to York for
despatch by Red Rhino. Tony was incredibly encouraging and generous with
both his time and money, and I owe him a lot."

Tony K's investment allowed McLean to adopt a dual role. "In the mornings
I would phone the shops and work for the Cartel doing the wholesale side.
And we'd drive to Glasgow once a week with a car full of records. Gordon
Montgomery, who started Fopp (later the UK's largest chain of independent
record shops), was my best account. The freedom I was given in the
afternoons was to do my own thing for Fast Forward distribution. I did the
53rd and 3rd label with Stephen Pastel [see chapter nine]. Also I had a label
called DDT, which had bands like The Cateran, who later became the
Joyriders. We put out the McCluskey Brothers, and James King and the Lone
Wolves – tough Glasgow guitar player, really into Johnny Thunders. Charles
Bukowski mixed with the Heartbreakers! And We Free Kings, who were

Mike Scott's favourite band at the time – he eventually nicked their fiddle player for the Waterboys – and Swamptrash, who were led by illustrator Harry Horse."

"The first few years," he continues, "when Red Rhino paid my wages, Tony K basically encouraged me to do that – he just said go out there and create product, promote good local music by Scottish bands. It was a great time. I used some of my contacts from the Fast Product days – like Rob [King] from The Scars, I put out a couple of singles by his funk band Lip Machine. Rob went off on a tangent and got into George Clinton stuff. Jo Callis [ex-Rezillos] was in the Human League at that time, and did a project called S.W.A.L.K. Jo gave me a master tape and the artwork for that, it didn't do that well, but again, it was a really fun record. I also did a generic rockabilly label called Mental Records. Because I was doing the wholesale for the Cartel, I knew what sold to the shops. And I put out a heavy metal label too for my sins, picking up local bands like The Crows."

The Alva Street office was both incestuous and "a real hub of activity" at that time. "Many times I would look up and there was John Robb typing a piece for *Sounds*," McLean recalls, "or The Legend! labouring over something for the *NME*. When they were in Edinburgh they would hang out at the office. I hired a local musician to work on the phones, Chris Connolly from Finitribe. After a few months of working there, for little or no money, Chris called up Alison at Southern and told her how much he liked their records, which we were selling to the shops. He went down to London to Southern and ended up in the back room, where Al Jourgensen of Ministry was recording. Al gave him a big line of speed and got him to do some spontaneous vocals, which later ended up on a Ministry and Pailhead single. He lives in Chicago now, and Alison still distributes his records twenty odd years later. When he moved to Chicago I gave his job to Davie Miller, who became Finitribe's singer."

The Cartel members' efforts were supported by an in-house magazine published by Rough Trade Distribution, *Masterbag*, which would subsequently evolve into *The Catalogue*. Edited first by Ian Cranna (in its *Masterbag* incarnation) then Brenda Kelly, Richard Boon took over after a five-year spell in production for Rough Trade when Kelly left to start *Snub TV*. "It was a very uneasy publication," Boon recalls, "because it fell between two stools. One being the trade magazine for the independent sector, and also needing to have a consumerist element to survive. It was funny mixing between being the propaganda wing of the Cartel, and actually getting people to read it." It's easy to imagine the horse-trading for editorial space among its benefactors being a headache. "Different Cartel members would have different priorities at different times," Boon says, employing what is doubtless a well-grooved diplomatic take on the subject. "It wasn't quite as specific as you're suggesting. But, yes, it was there in the background."

The tone of *The Catalogue* was, in retrospect, often gnawingly self-analytical rather than indulgent. As early as *Masterbag*'s fourth issue, an editorial fretted that "the use of the word '*Masterbag*' is helping to reinforce sexual stereotypes through the use of language." A later issue of the rebranded magazine (May 1986) saw writer Ian Johnson criticise Mute (who two pages later, paid for the rear page advert) for being "the worst example" [of the big three; alongside Factory and 4AD]. Daniel Miller's transgression? Letting Spartan handle Mute's product "as well as the Cartel... This means that the shops can hold out for a deal because both distributors are fighting for it." Four years later, in 1990, the same magazine was still sniping at Miller for his intransigence. "The dual distribution was a major argument," concedes Boon, "as Rough Trade and the Cartel expanded, there was a strategy to get labels exclusively through Rough Trade and the Cartel. It was a very polemical argument. Daniel only made his mind up in the latter days of Rough Trade, unfortunately. When Factory opted to go exclusively through Pinnacle, at the same time 4AD wanted to be exclusively through Rough Trade. The immediate thing that happened was 4AD had a number one with M/A/R/R/S and Factory had a number one with the New Order album. Because you'd have the reps from each distributor going into retailers offering them different deals, or discounts, it weakens everybody's position."

Yet despite such insular argumentative undercurrents, almost akin to family bickering, *The Catalogue*, leafing through its back issues, had an enviable cast of writers (Martin Aston, Ian Gittins and Boon himself) and was a fine shop window. Umbrella, an association of independent labels arising out of a series of open discussions held at the ICA, was another initiative. The immediate issue was to campaign against the intrusion of major label subsidiaries into the 'Independent Chart' hosted by trade publication *Music Week*. Formally launched in March 1985, these first tentative steps at collective advocacy are key to the development of the now powerful AIM organisation chaired by Martin Mills of Beggars Banquet.

"I think Umbrella was significant," recalls Iain McNay of Cherry Red, "because it was the forerunner of AIM, and AIM is a big player now. Brenda Kelly called this meeting in central London of independent labels. I thought, here's an opportunity, why don't we start something a little bit, not formal, but organised? So we started Umbrella. I remember that one of the people who was very supportive was Richard Boon." Other key staff included Brian Leafe, formerly of Caroline Exports, who counselled labels on such matters as changes in copyright law and dealing with collection agencies.

"It was Iain McNay who instigated a whole series of open meetings between labels and distributors," Boon remembers. "Rough Trade had hired London Records' sales force to work on The Smiths, which was controversial. Geoff had talked to some of his peers about this decision, and there was a meeting discussing that. Was it controversial, if the distribution was still independent? Was it OK to contract out services even if they were owned by majors? And at the meeting about that, Ted Carroll and Iain McNay came up as well. They said, we need some kind of discussion group or forum where all these things can be thrashed out. That's how Umbrella came about. I think Ted came up with the name. People like Ted and Roger [Armstrong] and Jumbo Van Renen from Earthworks and Charlie Gillett from Oval had got together in a similar way earlier to put world music branding into retailers, and do rack cards that said world music. There were bits of co-operation and market strategies emerging out of what were very informal discussions."

By the end of its first year, Umbrella was drawing 60 or more representatives at its meetings. "For two or three years, when I went on my travels, it staggered a bit," recalls McNay. "But it was a regular forum for independent labels to meet and share experiences and views. And we did do a bit of lobbying, and discussed things like independent charts. And we organised a day school in London which was really successful – several hundred people came."

"Iain put a lot of energy into organising a weekend conference, with panels and workshops, inviting as many people as he could," explains Boon. "It was like an indie trade conference. It needed some people to co-ordinate it, and I became one of them. There was a sort of vague election, but actually, it was really people who had a bit of time and energy." McNay was amazed at the response. "We had panels on helpful things for independent labels, such as international, A&R, etc. It served a valuable purpose and when AIM started many years later, I like to think, to some extent, they took some inspiration from Umbrella."

According to Boon's contemporaneous notes in *The Catalogue*, "The Seminar could have marked the death throes of The Umbrella's young life, but turned out to be its salvation... the Seminar was a qualified success.... While some aspects of certain panels were blatantly advertorial, the willing participation of people more normally associated with the interests of majors and professionals from the industry's ancillary workers (such as MCPS, PRS and PPL) was still to be welcomed. Providing, of course, that our callow youth remembers all those warnings about taking sweets from strangers." New members were encouraged to join for the peppercorn rent of £10 per annum.

All the time Rough Trade Distribution had continued to grow. "People have a perception of Rough Trade as a record label," states Richard Scott, "but that was only about one tenth of what went on in terms of turnover and personnel. The sales structure, in building an access system for DIY, was far more important than the label. At Rough Trade Distribution and Wholesale we had over 40 people working for us – which is more than the regional distributors put together – and looked after something like 200 labels." His day to day memories of working in that environment revolve principally around the graft. "It was just *dense*, from about ten to seven, just fielding orders, talking to people and packing. It was one huge blur, in a way – just a phenomenal amount of very complicated activity. All we could do was respond as best we could to the demand, which was extraordinary. We didn't really have much time to stop and think about it. People just drifted in, almost fell in off the street, and they always seemed to end up doing something different to what they were taken on to do. And they just gravitated to the bits that they did best. We didn't advertise – only once, to bring in middle management, Mark Swallow, who was extremely good. It was all done by word of mouth. Later on we had interviews, but not in the early days. We just said, come and help us, please, and they settled in to what they did best."

Between 1986 and 1990 the turnover had quadrupled to £40 million. Overall Administrator Richard Powell oversaw much of that, but would have to navigate a company whose agenda was never clear. "When Richard Powell was brought in," notes Boon, "the drive was to be outwardly as professional as possible, but internally to be as radical as possible. They were quite different ambitions! I think Rough Trade Distribution and The Cartel were possibly over analytical internally, in constantly assessing the mechanism of what was going on. In hindsight, that was slightly blinkering."

"The things that Richard Powell found that were wrong with the structure," says Richard Scott," "like duplicated transport costs, were unarguable. But as soon as you accepted that argument, you accepted that the regionally based structure had to change. It was the end of the cosy social structure. But those were the times. The nature of the overall record business was changing very fast."

Powell was immediately a divisive figure. "We were shafted by Rough Trade," states Sandy McLean of Fast Forward. "We were getting 7.5% at the top. We were charging a 30% distribution fee, but we had to give Rough Trade 22.5% of that. And the initial deal was, 'You'll get that back. The terms will change once we get the warehouse in King's Cross.' But the buggers never did change that. Our bank manager just said, this doesn't add up. When it all got centralised, Richard Powell came along. He said I couldn't do both – continue to work for the Cartel doing wholesale and having a 'conflict of interest' by having my own distribution company. He made me choose. Only through some clever ducking and diving did I manage to continue doing both. I could be very, very brutal about the way it ended."

It's often stated that Fast Forward followed Red Rhino into receivership in 1989; but that's not technically true. "We didn't go bust," says McLean, "we just ceased trading. Rough Trade had been really decent about Probe when it went under. But Fast Forward was closed by Mayking pressing plant. I owed Mayking £26,000 and [Mayking founder] Brian Bonnar said, 'If you can't pay me, that's it. You're insolvent.' I could have kept going, but Simon Edwards at Rough Trade – someone I hope I never meet again – just decided, no, that's it. One of my friends called from London one Monday saying, you're on the front cover of *Music Week* saying you've gone under. 'What? What are you talking about?' He read me the article. Rough Trade had sent a press release to *Music Week* without telling me, saying I'd shut the company. They said I was going into administration. 'What the fuck are you talking about?' Simon just said, 'I've heard from Mayking that you're closing down. We're not going to return your stock or give you a penny. We're not helping you out at all.' They basically just shafted me, left me swinging. I struggled on for a few more months, doing a bit of export. I did a deal with Mayking. Brian Bonnar was actually reasonable. He said if I could get together half the debt, he would get a county court judgement against me to cover his insurance policy, and he'd get the rest of it from that."

"When Rough Trade said that was it," McLean continues, "I had to see my accountant. He said I had to do 'an orderly realisation of assets on a pro-rata basis' – that phrase is ingrained on my brain. It basically means paying off creditors on a proportional basis. It meant playing with a straight bat with the funds that came in. Most people got paid off, but a few labels got bumped here and there. But I was able to keep my house, and that was the main thing."

Nightshift, a Scottish record label cum distributor founded by Brian Guthrie [brother of Robin Guthrie of the Cocteau Twins] to release the first Lowlife record in 1985, tried to pick up some of the slack, but faced a hangover of suspicion. Guthrie acknowledged as much in an interview with Lindsay Hutton. "We do handle a small number of the labels, but the majority [of ex-Fast Forward clients] are not dealing with us. Some because they're not carrying on due to financial constraints and others who, simply, in the wake of Fast and Red Rhino going down the tubes, don't trust the Cartel set-up." Those suspicions would ultimately prove well-founded.

"Brian Guthrie was working in the office for Fast Forward," says McLean. "He worked there for two years before we closed the office. He also had the freedom to put out his own stuff. He had this band, Lowlife, that his brother Robin produced. They sold really well, to the continent, and they probably did 10,000 copies of every album; decent money coming in. Brian kept in touch with Rough Trade, because he'd been going to the meetings. I couldn't, I couldn't be seen to be doing any distribution work at all, so I was just concentrating on wholesale to the shops."

The Cartel's problems were exacerbated by what was becoming a top-heavy hierarchy that wasn't necessarily any more efficient at decision making. "It had become unsustainable," says Boon. "There was a whole shift in attitudes to labels. I remember when Clive Selwood came to Rough Trade with the idea for Strange Fruit [a label dedicated to reissuing classic John Peel sessions]. Basically he wanted an advance. And there was a point where advances were things people didn't get. And he went to Pinnacle with Strange Fruit because Steve Mason [who had bought the ailing distributor in 1984 after its second crash] offered him money. And Simon Edwards and I spent a lot of time with Clive Selwood, and we had to go to the main board with details of all the meetings we'd had, and all the things we'd discussed. Basically what went wrong was that they wanted money, and Rough Trade wasn't offering any. A similar thing happened with Creation."

An acceleration in senior staff turnover hardly helped. Powell had gone by April 1989. Ex-Pinnacle general manager Dave Whitehead, who had headed up distribution since 1986, gradually taking over Richard Scott's role, lasted till December. By that time Simon Edwards was also out the door. A new MD was found in George Kimpton-Howe, previously right-hand man to Mason at

Pinnacle, who arrived in June 1990 as Sales & Product Director. His opening gambit, proclaimed in the pages of *The Catalogue*, was that he intended "to stabilise the company by creating a broader and firmer base catalogue sale, and in so doing introduce new and exciting styles of music – not to mention video – and break down some rather antiquated attitudes which have surrounded Rough Trade as a company." It was an impressively pompous start. Not entirely coincidentally, an unspoken turf war broke out between RTD and Pinnacle, his former employers, for top dog status as the country's foremost independent distributor.

It's widely perceived that the collapse of Rough Trade Distribution in 1991 'did for' the independent community as then was, and that's largely true. But the end of The Cartel had already destroyed much of the original camaraderie and spirit. Despite rude health in terms of sales in the independent sector, here were clearly underlying problems, the biggest being 'centralisation'.

"We were all just called to Birmingham," recalls Sandy McLean, "after George Kimpton-Howe had taken over. That was pretty controversial on its own – Pinnacle had always been the enemy since day one. There was a whole business style that everyone found abhorrent. The Pinnacle style wasn't ours, and this guy was running the show – it just got more gruesome. It wasn't a huge surprise when we got called to the meeting in Birmingham – oh God, everyone knows what happens in Birmingham. Everyone knew – don't take the company car keys! We got statutory redundancy. So yes, everyone was pretty pissed off at that point."

The *Music Week* headline in its 7 July 1990 edition was "Cartel folds, Rough Trade takes control". Boon, in his August editorial for *The Catalogue*, did his best to dampen the anxiety. "This 'Cartel' thing was and always has been a marketing exercise, a profile-building hype for a bunch of UK regional (if not at the time – 1982 – when they decided to operate in concert – marginal) independent distributors, sharing a common sales structure. And it was the sales structure which, if anything, was The Cartel. Those guys 'n' gals on the phone or in the dealer's face hustling the new Go-Go Frogs album on Hope In Hell Records. The real ol' mechanics. And all that's happening... in real terms, is that the regional telesales people that constituted (formally and formerly) 'Cartel Wholesale' are coming under one centralised roof... Rough Trade Distribution's, who owned 'Cartel Wholesale' anyway, and the Cartel name is consigned to history and the record sleeves of back catalogue from labels who can't afford the plate and artwork changes..." However, Boon's following statement would prove to be unduly optimistic. "So we can all rest easy. No-one's going out of business – not for the foreseeable future and fingers crossed, the incomprehensible spanking new computer system and building Rough Trade have now established will prevent that – and labels large and small will continue to be serviced successfully, it not better."

Of course, there was a lot more to it than that, but then Boon, while far too conscientious to play Lord Haw Haw for the new regime, was duty bound to look at his glass as half full. "Well, that was the PR spin," says Sean Mayo of Revolver. "For quite a while all the telesales operations working out of regional offices were reporting directly to sales management in London at Rough Trade, to a guy called Jeremy Boyce. It all came to a head when George Kimpton-Howe came along. He was a completely different beast to anyone in the company at that point. He was ruthlessly conservative and commercial. He didn't seem at all music orientated. Within months there was an ultimatum. They wanted to close all the regional telesales operations and relocate them all to London. Everybody was offered redundancy or relocation, and I took redundancy. That was the end of an era. A number of people will tell you now that once that happened, the heart of the whole thing was ripped out of it. A lot of really good people were lost from the industry at that point."

"Sean Mayo and I, when we got paid off in Birmingham," recalls McLean, "went on the tear together. We drank all the champagne in all the mini-bars; we were bad boys that night. He lost his contact lens cleaning equipment and went mental at the desk clerk, who wouldn't come up and let us in his room after he lost the key. We threatened to break the door down, and to call 999, and eventually he came up and let us in. We then drank the fizz in HIS room's mini-bar."

In retrospect, it seems hard to quantify just how bad a decision the centralisation of the sales force was. Telesales is a job that comes loaded with negative connotations, but the vast majority of the Cartel's team were primarily music fans who knew their markets, could spot trends and had developed strong bonds with local retailers. Where once The Cartel could claim to have its ear to the ground throughout the UK, now the whole operation was becoming as remote and centralised and *London* as the major labels.

That rush for centralisation wasn't confined to the sales team. "It had all worked very well for a long time," says Derek Chapman of Backs.

"Previously, each member of the Cartel had to have a warehouse in their own area, servicing the shops in the area. In the late 80s, it all went to a centralised warehouse in London, at which point the balance shifted, and it all started to go pear-shaped, as the costs involved changed. The releases were still coming in from all over the country, it was just the practical matter of running a very large, cumbersome warehouse in London, really. And the costs involved in all that. The way the Cartel worked throughout the 80s was six or seven companies working together to form a network of distribution. For various reasons, bit by bit, an arm of the Cartel changed, moved, or collapsed and broke."

One of the few personnel to virulently oppose the 'centralisation' had been John Loder at Southern – never a Cartel member but a sympathetic partner on many levels. "John said, I don't trust centralisation," recalls Penny Rimbaud. "He was the only one who said no. And that ultimately made Southern a very powerful distribution outfit. It was an incredibly wise decision. I remember talking to him about it, and I said, it seems to make sense to centralise. But he was absolutely resolute, and came under a hell of a lot of criticism for that." Richard Scott concurs. "John was always an outsider – but I personally liked him. We tried very hard to sell stuff for him, but he had such a complicated way of dealing with things that it wasn't easy. He was a loner. He came to see me in Hastings before he died, and he was very proud of the fact that he'd sold his millionth Crass record. He was awkward, but I always enjoyed dealing with him."

Others, however, could see the benefits of centralisation. "The central distribution model was very contentious," admits Robin Hurley. "My view was that it was emotionally a difficult thing to grasp. But if you think about shipping a Billy Bragg album from London to the Midlands, and from the Midlands to HMV Birmingham, it clearly would be a more economic move to go from London straight to Birmingham, with Nine Mile just being the selling company."

Revolver, too, decided to break away from The Cartel. Within months of taking redundancy rather than relocate to London, Sean Mayo found himself back manning the phones in Bristol. "I was doing exactly the same job. And it felt like doing it for the right reasons again. Then Revolver and APT, which was the remainder of Red Rhino, merged. Several of their people relocated to Bristol." Revolver's push for independence (in relative, but contextually rather loaded terms) proved astute. Mike Chadwick eventually formed Vital Distribution in 1993, which would become the largest independent music distributor in the UK by the turn of the century.

Meanwhile, the prophecy that Rough Trade Distribution could seamlessly fill the hole left by the Cartel's collapse proved flawed. "Distribution made some terrible, terrible mistakes," says a rueful Geoff Travis. "The ones I always talk about – the purchase of a computer system that didn't work for a few months, having a lease on King's Cross and then getting a new lease on a new building – like having two flats without being able to afford it. Then credit control failed to spot big debts from other companies that maybe they should have picked up earlier. Those were the three things that crippled us. Those three things were what brought the company down."

It's worth putting some flesh on those bare bones. In July 1989 vast new premises of 31,000 square foot were secured off Seven Sisters Road in Finsbury Park. A new computer system was installed to look after the increased inventory and invoicing (another 15 labels were to be added to the existing 55). It would cost more than half a million pounds, and was chosen despite advice from other distributors about their own arrangements (there were suggestions RTD were trying to install untested but potentially more efficient technology to try to get the jump on Pinnacle). It simply didn't work for several months, fraught attempts at its installation spanning the attempted move from King's Cross to Finsbury Park, a costly location secured in haste. To the extent that RTD had overlooked the fact that, in addition to saddling themselves with a new £350,000 pa warehousing commitment, the lease on the King's Cross property had yet to expire and they would have to continue to shell out more that £50,000 pa on that. Meanwhile, eyes strayed from credit control. One client in particular, Parkway Video, owed the company a figure in excess of £500,000. There were knock-on problems with VAT not being paid. And that all added up to a cash flow crisis.

With the enormity of these problems, Travis attests that any attention focused on his activities, and the apparent largesse he was expending on running Rough Trade the label and its American arm (an investment estimated to be £100,000 per month) were entirely spurious, or possibly diversionary. He remains adamant that they should have had no impact whatsoever on the sister company's operations and it was simply bad business discipline that created problems. "Some of the distribution people would argue that the cash strain of investing in America was a liability," he says. "I would argue that the American business plan was totally on point and we were working very steadily towards break even. I thought we had a really good company in that period in America, we had Lucinda [Williams], we had Mazzy Star, we had Galaxie 500. Some really good records. We were selling records and doing well, so I don't accept that argument. So it was really down to the personalities. It's a flaw in my character in that I wasn't really interested in fighting for control of the board, and all that kind of stuff. I'm not interested in having a battle for power."

Robin Hurley, who oversaw the American enterprise, backs Travis's analysis, though he does admit that the commitment stretched Rough Trade. "I think what most pleased Geoff is that we were slowly beginning to have an A&R base out of America." He proffers the same three artists as evidence; Williams, Mazzy Star and Galaxie 500. "We were starting to have an impact. But there was a huge investment in the States, which definitely drained the reserves of the UK mothership." In addition to the three crucial factors Travis points to (computer problems, a double lease and credit control), Hurley also identifies a fourth. "At the time we had huge growth in Germany. The German government reviewed the tax the company paid over the growth period, and levied Rough Trade Germany with a big retroactive tax bill. Those things hit just about all at once. I think Geoff's right, it may not have been overnight, but we were definitely making the right strides in America. I'd be the first to say though, when I came over here, I should have gone to work for SST for a year or something; observe from the inside the pitfalls and problems the American market would present to us. Rather than the sort of arrogance – we've done so well in England and so well in Germany – we can do it here. The size of this country means there's nothing that's comparable."

One by one, dismayed at the bottleneck, independent labels closed their accounts with RTD. There were 40 lay-offs and redundancies announced just before Christmas; the house of cards tumbling fast. As if the group didn't have software problems aplenty, disgusted and soon to be jobless staff further sabotaged the computers. Kimpton-Howe received a human faeces in a record box as a festive thank you. Elements of the warehouse team affiliated to Class War took to vandalism and writing graffiti on the walls. By the start of 1991 One Little Indian (who had not long since borrowed funds from Travis to finance The Sugarcubes album) had transferred its accounts to Pinnacle. Creation had made the same switch just a few months before due to Alan McGee's growing disenchantment with Rough Trade. A board meeting was held, and the larger creditors informed of the urgency of the problems (not that many hadn't already guessed) and a corporate recovery team, led by David Murrell of KPMG accountants, appointed.

## Get Rid Of These Things

What happened next, though, was extraordinary, if ultimately futile. It says as much about the best aspects of the UK independent music community as any 'winning runs' any of them might have achieved in their heyday. In February 1991 an emergency meeting was called. The assembled throng of concerned creditors and affiliates and staff were informed that the company owed £3.6 million. Mute, 4AD, Situation 2/Beggars Banquet and Big Life were among the companies owed six-figure sums – Mute alone accounting for £800,000, while the Rough Trade label itself was owed more than a million. The aforementioned bigger players, rather than pushing for an immediate liquidation petition, which would have been the norm, elected to put forward an action plan. They formed a negotiating committee. The settlement they worked out – which relied on nobody breaking rank and pushing for receivership – meant that any prior debts to this point would be classed as historic. They would be paid off through income generated from the sale of the Rough Trade label itself, the Smiths catalogue and the US and German branches of the company. Other contingencies included a 'fire-fighting' fund for the smaller, more vulnerable labels, and an escrow account to pay out incoming monies and receipts more quickly, to help restore faith.

It didn't work out like that. Asset sales are tricky things at the best of times; when the world and his wife knows you need the money quickly, you are at a distinct disadvantage. The Smiths catalogue, for example, would eventually go to Warners, but only after protracted discussions with the band and a sequential lowering of the headline fee expected. Rhythm King signed a new deal with Sony (at least for their most commercial acts) and Big Life moved to PolyGram. They had their own artists to pay and mouths to feed and suddenly the law of the jungle overtook the spirit of camaraderie.

A second meeting was scheduled for 14 May 1991. The negotiating committee was able to report back that 26% of historic debt had been repaid. But the asset dispersal would require further time. The committee offered two ways forward. One allowed RTD to continue trading with debts written off, in the hope that it could eventually recoup monies owed. It was a leap of faith and there were complications over the percentage of money that would go to the labels and separate creditors such as pressing plants. They rejected the offer on that basis. The alternative was to create a new company, RTM (Rough Trade Marketing), that would liase with established distributors to get their records out, securing advances in the process that would be significant enough to take a healthy bite out of the debt mountain. Two offers were investigated and considered. The first was for £2 million from PolyGram, the second of £1 million from Steve Mason at Pinnacle.

The negotiating committee voted to accept Pinnacle's offer. It was a principled stand in the circumstances, meaning less guaranteed money in the pot, but one that had pragmatic elements – the new company would remain independent, and its output would not lose priority, as many suspected would happen, to PolyGram's core releases. Also, Mason, though widely derided for his open advocacy of Thatcherism, had established a reputation for paying invoices on the nail. That was something everyone in the independent sector would welcome. The fact that Pinnacle had helped make Pete Waterman's PWL the most successful UK independent label of them all via the chart fluff of Kylie and Jason and other monstrosities was less roundly applauded.

On 31 May 1991 Rough Trade Distribution ceased trading, and RTM took the reins the following week. But it was to be a false dawn, any salvage operation becoming a non-starter once Rough Trade America collapsed. "We stayed afloat while we tried to find buyers for the company," recalls Hurley. "We were very close to Warners in America, through Seymour Stein, but they wanted 51% of the company. Rather stupidly at that point we dug our heels in and offered them 49%. That was the deal-breaker. With the benefit of hindsight, it was a crazy point of principle given what we ended up with."

By September Pinnacle had acquired Rough Trade's German operation and had, definitively, triumphed over its one-time distribution adversary. The publishing arm was purchased by Iain McNay's Complete Music after an abortive attempt by Cathi Gibson and Pete Walmsley to retain it. Some of the vernacular of business foreclosure was adapted, almost inevitably given the nature of the suffering parties, into the title of an album to raise funds, released by Beechwood. *A Historical Debt* featured royalty-free contributions from Erasure and Depeche Mode (Mute), The Shamen (One Little Indian), Charlatans (Beggars), M/A/R/R/S (4AD) in addition to Rough Trade staples such as Scritti Politti, Television Personalities and Robert Wyatt.

One of the medium-sized labels to bear the brunt of the RTD collapse wished only to speak off record. He remembers the day when Kimpton-Howe first took office. "He reckoned he saw the Grim Reaper walk past the window as soon as he sat behind the desk." The same source later met, completely by chance, a member of KPMG at an unrelated party during the negotiations. He doesn't retain a favourable impression after said accountant drunkenly boasted that he 'controlled the future of independent music in the UK' as if it were some prize truffle. As he further concludes, for all the good intentions behind the negotiating committee, the commitment to historical debt and sundry well-intentioned efforts such as compilation albums, "the whole 'you get such and such per cent of what's left over' is *crap*. You've got to pay lawyers, jump through hoops and do a ton of paperwork before you get anywhere near it. In the end, there's sod all left and it's just not worth bothering with." The effect on independent music's infrastructure was calamitous. Many labels disappeared. Some, like Cooking Vinyl, just about survived, though it took Martin Goldschmidt five years to regain the label's equilibrium, and in the process he lost his partner Pete Lawrence and for a short time the label was a 'paper' bankrupt.

One of those labels in a particularly invidious position was Bill Drummond's KLF Foundation. "Jimmy Cauty and myself were down £300,000," he says. "Because the label was owned by us, and we were the only act on the label, we had nothing else. We'd just had a major hit single, and we'd no idea if we'd have another. Bang. And we'd incurred a ton of costs. All the recording costs, having PR, all of that. And they've gone down and we're owed £300,000. If that single hadn't taken off in other territories we'd have been completely and utterly fucked. Everybody was anxious, but we had nothing else in the pipeline. Daniel Miller could go off and knows he's still got Depeche Mode and Erasure or whatever. At the end of the day, there was nothing to be had back. Even now, when I hear the name KPMG on the news representing huge clients, a shiver goes up my spine. If a company goes down a company goes down. They'd be smooth-talking but, actually, there was nothing left."

Richard Scott fiercely counters claims that it was distribution that pulled the company down. "It's a total misconception. I remember meeting the auditor a few years after Rough Trade had gone down, and he said what KPMG found was that Rough Trade Group needed about £2 million to survive. And that was, incidentally, KPMG's bill! (LAUGHS). What broke down was the fact that there was no management. As I've said, Richard Powell is a seriously misunderstood character in this story, but he'd gone. Simon Edwards had gone and so forth. And Geoff and Will Keene just didn't get on. It was just too big. It had been overtaken by the marketplace; CDs started to come in and the writing was on the wall. Rough Trade Distribution did not cause the collapse. I have the accounts here. It's just untrue. Even at the end, the distribution side had enough labels and enough business to be wholly healthy."

For Scott, the demise is related to the decision to take the label in what he views as a mainstream, chart-focused direction. "For me, it peaked in terms of interest and excitement in the early 80s. Rough Trade was at its height from 1978 to 1983 or 1984. It sold more and more from that point, but it moved more into the mainstream. Therefore its status as a DIY access structure had changed, but then the music industry had changed. It lost its aspiration. Geoff became too involved in trying to emulate others in terms of chart success. If you think of all the early Rough Trade bands, they didn't sell in the quantities that someone like Joy Division or Depeche Mode or Cocteau Twins did. But we were excitingly varied. When the Smiths came along that was it. I never liked the Smiths. I didn't find them musically interesting."

"I can't say I was standing there rubbing my hands with glee when [the collapse] happened," reflects former Cartel employee Sean Mayo, "but equally, I can't say I was surprised. A lot of people *were* rubbing their hands with glee. No-one wants to see people lose their job, but what had happened was the antithesis of what Rough Trade and the Cartel started out as and what we wanted it to be."

And if the knock-on effect on artists, labels, manufacturers and everyone else involved in the micro-economy of independent music was chilling, the pain was shared closer to home. "I didn't have a job any more!" notes Boon. "There were some people who wanted to try to keep *The Catalogue* going. Bill Gilliam from Alternative Tentacles tried financing something called *The Independent Catalogue*, which was edited by Jenny Lewis, which didn't last very long. It didn't get very much support from labels or distributors, because it was all reeling."

It might be a stretch, but it's hard not to parallel the Cartel revolution and collapse with the failure of the left in the 80s. "Yes, the end of Old Labour!" laughs Richard Scott. "That would be an interesting thesis! And one I would personally subscribe to. But I can hear a lot of people laughing at it, too In the end it was all a bit more complex than a left-right thing. There were huge changes going on in society, and in the music industry and media. The Cartel sales structure – if you add in all the labels and all the people in the regions and all the bands, it touched thousands and thousands of people."

But did it feel like the end of the dream? "Yes," admits Richard Boon, "I think it did."

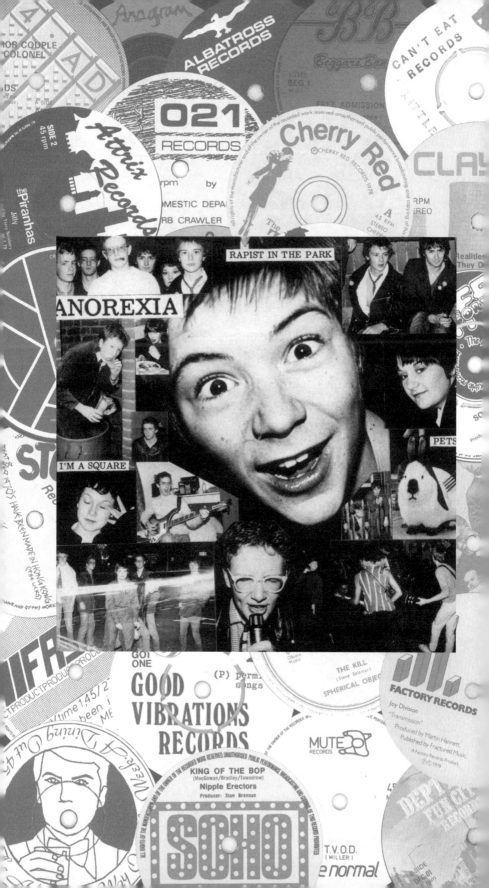

# Chapter Thirteen

## For How Much Longer?

## They Also Served

Birmingham's foremost independent label of the era was Dave Virr's Graduate Records, almost singularly notable for the monumental chart success it achieved with local reggae act UB40. Graduate started in 1969 as a record shop in Dudley, with Virr expanding the franchise around the Midlands until it eventually encompassed six outlets. He would also work as a manager and disc jockey, under which guise he first encountered UB40. Yet another retailer to decide, on listening to the outpouring of new records on John Peel, that there was no reason why he shouldn't start a sideline to his principal business, he did so in 1979. His initial five releases – including such forgotten names as Eazie Ryder, Venigmas, Last Gang, Circles and Mean Street Dealers – flopped miserably. But in January 1980 he signed UB40 and released their debut double a-side single, 'King' c/w 'Food For Thought', which peaked at number four in the national charts. Two further Top Ten hits followed, while the attendant album, *Signing Off*, which followed in August, would achieve platinum sales.

This was unprecedented success for an independent label of the time. However, to an extent, Graduate was isolated from the 'indie' discourse due to the nature of UB40's music, and the (mostly stupid) accusations that it amounted to a watering down of Jamaican reggae and was therefore 'inauthentic'. UB40 would quickly move on to Virgin (via their DEP International subsidiary), but Virr had made his money back, and then some. More importantly, the realisation that an independent record could be such a consistent seller (*Signing Off* stayed in the charts for a year) was an important psychological boost acknowledged by several 'cooler' independents.

Nothing else on the Graduate imprint would come close to emulating that level of success (The Sussed's 'I've Got My Parka', the immediate follow-up to UB40's debut single, being a particular embarrassment). Their next best bet was Brighton's Chefs, whom they courted in two separate incarnations. "We signed to Graduate for a ridiculously small advance," remembers singer Helen McCookerybook, "and they didn't know what to do with us. At one stage one of their guys helpfully suggested that I should wear make-up all the time." Virr had come to see them play in a church hall in his new BMW to conclude the deal (nearly accidentally totalled by the group's van), which resulted in the wonderful '24 Hours', licensed from The Chefs' original Brighton label Attrix. Renamed Skat ("a stupid idea") the band also released a version of 'Femme Fatale', which wasn't quite so good. An entire album remains unreleased after the group ran out of steam. Virr would have some success, however, with a subsidiary imprint. The Maisonettes' 'Heartache Avenue' emerged on Ready, Steady, Go!, providing Virr with one further Top Ten hit. Thereafter he worked as a consultant to the music industry, as well as artist manager (clients including original Beatles drummer, Pete Best). He passed away in December 2006, with the business continuing under the stewardship of wife Tina.

Newcastle's indie lynchpins were Kitchenware Records, though their various entanglements with majors disqualify them from being viewed as a 'true' independent. The label was established in 1982 as the 'recording wing' of The Soul Kitchen, a club night that had successfully booked gigs by The Fire Engines, Aztec Camera and New Order – with film shows or photo exhibitions in place of a conventional support act. Founded by Keith Armstrong, manager of the city's HMV store, alongside Paul Ludford and Phil Mitchell, Kitchenware's first release was the compilation video cassette, *A One Way Ticket To Palookaville*. More conventional vinyl offerings followed in 1983 from Hurrah! and the Daintees, before they reissued Prefab Sprout's 'Lions In My Own Garden, Exit Someone' in April, originally released on the band's own Candle label a year previously.

Announcing the talents of songwriter Paddy McAloon, Prefab Sprout dominated the subsequent release schedule as Kitchenware licensed the recordings to CBS, alongside records by the Daintees (this time with Martin Stephenson given lead billing), Kane Gang (licensed to London) and Hurrah! By 1988 the roster had swelled to encompass Cathal Coughlan's Fatima Mansions. "Kitchenware worked with many majors then, and also with what was then Red Rhino as an indie distributor," Coughlan recalls. "Their formal affiliation with Sony is a much more recent thing. They literally tried all angles from when they took me on in '88. The best period was when the Mansions records were just coming out through the indie network, and we were playing to people with a persistence which [his former band] Microdisney never quite managed." More recently, the label has secured great success with The Editors.

Pre-eminent in Brighton were Attrix Records, formed out of Rick Blair's shop of the same name in Sydney Street. Its first release, 'Hard Times' c/w 'Lost Lenore', boasted a possibly unique brand synergy (Attrix the shop, the label, the group). As well as introducing the aforementioned Chefs and Piranhas (latterly the most successful band on the Brighton scene) and the sadly overlooked Birds With Ears and Dodgems, Attrix would add an inch or two to the growing pile of inspiring regional compilations in circulation around the turn of the decade. In this case it ran to a series of three volumes, documenting a fertile local punk scene based around The Vault rehearsal rooms and Alhambra pub in the form of *Vaultage '78, '79 and '80*. At least two of which were wonderful. Blair passed away in May 1999.

Y Records was founded in Bristol in 1980 by former Stranglers and then current Slits and Pop Group manager Dick O'Dell. The label's name was retrieved from the latter's debut album for Andrew Lauder and Jake Riviera's Radar, with whom they'd severed ties by the end of 1979 after learning of parent company Warners' links with arms manufacturer Kinney Corporation. In terms of eating capitalism from the inside, they did manage to leave Radar £40,000 in the red on their investment, according to some accounts effectively killing the enterprise. Y was established with backing from Rough Trade, its releases jointly catalogued. The 'Where There's A Will There's A Way'/ 'In The Beginning There Was Rhythm' split-single, shared between The Pop Group and The Slits, announced its investiture. Thereafter it remained squarely focused on spin-offs from the same musical gene pool, including Pigbag, Rip Rig And Panic, Maximum Joy, Glaxo Babies and Scream And Dance. As Phil Johnson noted in his book *Straight Outta Bristol*, these all "tended to call on the same revolving troupe of personnel. Where Pigbag were into Afro-funk and James Brown horn riffs, Rip Rig and Panic were named after a Roland Kirk album and flirted with free jazz and avant-garde sloganeering. Rip Rig and Panic also featured the young Neneh Cherry (and at one point her step-dad Don Cherry, the former Ornette Coleman Quartet trumpeter), who had also recorded with Mark Stewart and Ari Up of the Slits as the New Age Steppers on Adrian Sherwood's On-U Sound label."

In May 1981 Y enjoyed one of the biggest independent hits of the era with the release of Pigbag's 'Papa's Got A Brand New Bag', an infectious tribute to James Brown's similarly titled rump-shaker. It would stay in the independent charts for some 70 weeks. Us Corporation, as Pigbag were originally titled, had landed their first gig supporting The Slits at Romeo And Juliet's in Bristol, playing a 20-minute version of the song, written by Simon Underwood, whom the band had persuaded to join after his exit from The Pop Group. The following day O'Dell had them record it for Y, prompting them to adopt the name Pigbag as a tribute to clarinettist and percussionist Chris Hamlin's dog-eared cloth bag, which featured a silk-screened warthog. The breakthrough led to a licensing deal with Stiff America and hectic touring. However, the group would decline an initial offer of a *Top Of The*

*Pops* appearance due to the BBC's proviso that the song be edited down (they did relent on their stance when it was re-released in April 1982 and sped to number three in the national charts). Hamlin left the group immediately after the song's initial success, however, citing 'too many egos' in the band, leading to legal disputes over authorship and royalties. Even in principled independent circles, where there's a hit, there's a writ.

O'Dell would use the breakthrough to sponsor several new and ostensibly left field acts, notably Greek-born opera singer/"scat valkyrie" Diamanda Galas's extraordinary debut *Litanies Of Satan*. It comprised just two tracks; the title-song and the impressively titled 'Wild Women With Steak Knives (The Homicidal Love Song For Solo Scream)'. "'Wild Women With Steak Knives' is the nightmare of the killer who has murdered her husband and is escaping from the police," Galas explains, "running through red lights on crystal meth, hearing the cop cars chase her into the brick wall which looms unseen, but assuredly, ahead."

Neither this, however, nor other releases by acts including The Promenaders (featuring avant garde musicians such as David Toop and Steve Beresford), the all-female, nine-member Pulsallama, nor the hip hop of Fearless Four and a rightfully revered Sun Ra 12-inch, managed to secure the label's future. Shriekback probably came the closest to repeating Pigbag's success, though they would leave Y for Arista in 1984 after disagreements with O'Dell. The label eventually collapsed, its catalogue acquired by Kaz Records (part of Castle Communications). Later O'Dell would found the progressive house label Guerilla in the 90s, home to artists including Leftfield and Spooky. He currently manages Bat For Lashes.

Two other Bristol labels of the period deserve mention; Fried Egg and Wavelength. The former may be unique among British independent labels of the era in that its origins were essentially theatrical. Andy Leighton, music publisher of *The Rocky Horror Show* and formerly guitarist and administrator of the Crystal Theatre, founded the imprint in 1979. The label initially served as an outlet for Shoes For Industry, who featured four Crystal Theatre musicians (one of whom, Tim Norfolk, would subsequently form Startled Insects; whose production credits span Goldfrapp, Massive Attack and Madonna, as well as numerous BBC soundtracks). Vocalist and saxophonist Paul Bassett Davies, meanwhile, writes regularly for TV and radio, and in 2005, with Leighton as his co-producer, scripted the animated feature film revival of *The Magic Roundabout*.

## For How Much Longer?

The Fried Egg roster included several gems but defied ready classification; resembling a smaller scale, and more vaudeville Stiff. They even organised a *Be Limp* tour (a fairly obvious play on that label's branding). "Stiff were a huge influence," admits Leighton. "Once McLaren had exposed the major record companies for the perennial ignorant buffoons they are most of the time, Riviera and Robinson wrote the book for aspiring indie labels. A good friend of mine at the time, Joly [MacFie] of Better Badges, purveyor of fine badges and fanzines, was always close to the epicentre of the Stiff/Rough Trade axis, so I had a fairly good insight into the workings of the indie scene at the time. The *Be Limp* tour came out of the Bristol University Students Union's president and social secretary's initiative involving mainly Fried Egg and Wavelength Records-signed Bristol bands. Ex-president Martin Elbourne is now booker for Glastonbury Festival and the ex-secretary Dave Cohen writes for *Have I Got News For You*." Others on the roster included The Stingrays, who had graduated from Heartbeat and whose drummer Sean McLusky would later become an infamous London music promoter Various Artists scored a cult hit with 'Original Mixed Up Kid' while Southampton art students The Exploding Seagulls became Peel favourites. The Art Objects (who effectively became The Blue Aeroplanes), meanwhile, billed themselves as 'the world's only poetry dance band'. Fried Egg's 'most likely to' candidates, Electric Guitars, would, ironically, transfer to Stiff. The 1981 compilation album *Egg-Clectic* amply highlighted the bizarre nature of the label's wares.

So why did Fried Egg close? "Crystal Theatre broke up in 1981 and I went off to work with The Penguin Cafe Orchestra management team in London for a few years," says Leighton. "And it wasn't making any money, the hope being that a Madness or a Costello would break through and become the cash cow. Without Mike Oldfield cash-flowing Virgin, they would never have made it to the major league. Various Artists could have made it; Trevor Horn came calling for them, but they turned him down! If the Electric Guitars had been one of the first signings rather than the last, we might have had a chance with them. You could just about break even if you got the pressing numbers right but by 1981 the indie distribution scene was getting slightly tougher and perhaps that particular golden indie era was in decline already and the buffoons were on their way back to gaining control again." Wavelength, meanwhile, in addition to singles by The Spics (ex-Cortinas), Gardez Darkz, Joe Public and Colourtapes, issued three compilation albums designed specifically to promote local bands; The *Bristol Recorder* series. The idea, which came from Elbourne, Jonathan Arthur and Thos Brooman (who now runs WOMAD) was to incorporate a magazine filled by advertising to help with costs.

After leaving Y, The Slits found a temporary berth with London independent Human Records. As early as 1977 Steve Melhuish had used the turnover from his Bonaparte Records shops to launch an eponymous record label [see chapter four]. By the early 80s he was ready to try again. "Human Records was far more commercially successful," he recalls, "I had separate finance for that. We had the Slits and Dangerous Girls, and when I signed the Au Pairs, they hit the front page of the *NME* a week later, which was fantastic. Initially it was a 50-50 venture, going through a distribution company called Stage One Records. They were interested in distributing a label so they could get more independent labels to join. I knew the sales manager, then got to know the guy who owned it. He put the hard cash up and we ran it from our shop in King's Cross, which was Bonaparte's London office." On the staff at Human were Saul Galpern and Chris Youle, who in a previous life has been MD at RSO Records, home of the Bee Gees and Eric Clapton. "Chris added the 'professional' experience to enable me to sign a higher calibre of artist", notes Melhuish.

"They were talking about putting out records, and I wanted to be part of that side of things," Galpern recalls. "I remember there was a couple of rooms upstairs from the shop, and they turned them into a room where myself and Chris did the label, and they brought in a girl to do press, Versa Manos. She's worked for the Pistols, which I thought was really cool. The first thing we came across was the Au Pairs from Birmingham. And the first album did very well – *Playing With A Different Sex* was a cool record; very well received, good press. I think they could have been a bigger band, but they were a bit destructive – credit for their politics, but they were *very* uncompromising."

At one stage, Human was successful enough to open international outlets. "I've got a picture of Gang Of Four doing a gig in our New York shop, which my brother Guy ran," recalls Melhuish, "the only independent English record store there at the time. I've also got a copy of the independent charts from 20 December 1980 for that particular week. We released four singles and three of them got into the charts; The Au Pairs, with 'Diet', The Slits with 'Animal Space' and then The Dangerous Girls 'Man In The Glass'. Which is not bad when you start up a new label."

However, the Slits deal (their management shared the building in Bonaparte's King's Cross branch) proved a one-off. "Obviously I did think about doing lots more with them," concedes Melhuish, "but we didn't have that opportunity. They were betwixt deals, and their Island album had always sold really well for us. I remember speaking to the Associates and

## For How Much Longer?

Billy MacKenzie in a lot of depth. I was a huge Billy MacKenzie fan, and I remember him coming into the shop at King's Cross with Alan Rankine. I was that near to signing The Associates and Beggars pipped me to the post, cos Martin Mills had some money coming in from Warners. I had a beer with Martin Mills about three weeks ago at an AIM meeting. He's worth millions and I'm worth about half a crown, but that's neither here nor there!"

Human ended when Melhuish's 50 per cent partner "decided to pass on the company to a person who shall remain nameless, and that person I couldn't deal with, so I moved out of it." He was tempted to start a third label, but in the end, declined. "I had, at the time, nearly 100 people working for me. I had an office in New York and a shop, a warehouse in Los Angeles, a warehouse in Montreal and six shops. I spent a lot of my time on planes and I found sex and drugs and rock 'n' roll was beginning to get to me by the mid-80s. It wasn't to be." But old habits die hard. "The irony now is that I've set up a record label at Christchurch, Greenwich and Westminster University where I now lecture. I'm still working with bands."

"All I remember," says Galpern, "is that one minute we were doing Human, and the next we were being told to go to a new office in Victoria to start a new label." That label would be Kamera Records, whose roster included The Dancing Did, Charge and Blood And Roses. There were also two albums by The Fall sandwiched between their spells with Rough Trade and the second Au Pairs long player. "Kamera was Chris Youle," states Galpern. "One of the bands that was interesting was Aerial FX – that was Chris Hufford and Bryce Edge, later managers of Radiohead." Galpern can't remember, however, how it all came to an end. "I think it was financial stuff. There was something strange there, but I just remember having to focus on getting a proper job. So I went to a major label and then started Nude (which would enjoy huge mainstream success with Suede throughout the 90s). Human and Kamera had given me a good grounding in how things work."

Bill Gilliam's adventures in music are extensive, but he is probably best known as commissar of the UK branch of Alternative Tentacles and the man who brought parent group Dead Kennedys to international notoriety. "I used to be a booking agent for people like Sham 69," he recalled, speaking to me in 1996. "And while I was doing Sham 69 and stuff, I was sniffing round this band from the States with this silly name. I just thought it would be fun to get them over here. Eventually I got them the deal with Cherry Red. Before that I got thrown out of just about ever record company without them even hearing the tapes." Although Alternative Tentacles was inaugurated in

America, it had its original base in London. "We set up in England first before the States. At the end of the first [DKs] tour, we worked out that there were plenty more groups in the American underground scene, like Dead Kennedys, that would be received well over here. And they were never, ever going to get record deals and record releases. So we decided to start the label in order to do this compilation, *Let Them Eat Jellybeans*; seventeen tracks from the US underground scene. We had some good names on there. Quite a few who did go on to do well. But we started that here. All that got going in the States was the mail order first of all, because it was a lot easier to start a label over here in those days. The distribution problems in America were, and still are, a nightmare." When AT did get a footing in America in 1983, it's significant that it was through Mordam, set up by ex-Rough Trade US employee (and *Maximum Rock 'n' Roll* co-founder) Ruth Schwarz.

Early AT releases included classic North American punk/hardcore from DOA, Fipper, Black Flag *et al*. But Gilliam passed on a proposed 7 Seconds release. "Only because of the cover," he recalled. "The US 7-inch had this guy with what is now an extremely fashionable haircut, but in those days would have been interpreted as a skinhead. And he had this aggressive thing with his fist up to the camera – this striking image on the cover. You've got to get past that and get people to read the lyrics. When you're in Central Europe and you're talking to kids that have dropped out of school early, expecting to read American slang? It wasn't always successful. I remember when we were in Stockholm and this big guy came up with a swastika on his shirt and said, 'Yeah, we're Nazis too! So come out to our house...' It was just the cover, what with the Oi! thing still going." 1981's *Strength Thru Oi!* compilation, apart from corrupting a Nazi slogan for its title, also featured Nicky Crane, a particularly violent member of various far right denominations, in a similarly aggressive pose. "The whole notion of Oi! and skinheads," Gilliam continues, "having spent a couple of years with Sham 69, I knew about skinheads. I just figured it was something that Alternative Tentacles didn't need to do."

As the label evolved, activities were split between the transatlantic bases, with the London operation starting out in Kensington Square Gardens before moving to King's Cross and finally Finsbury Park. There, visitors were greeted with a sober notice on the door featuring Winston Smith's famous bat logo demanding 'No junk mail, no religious weirdos'. Throughout, Dead Kennedys singer Jello Biafra called the A&R shots. "Biafra has always had this thing about needing to see a band before we did anything with them," Gilliam confirmed. "And he needed to know he got on all right with them as people. We could certainly have had a more busy release schedule if Biafra didn't have those rules of engagement." And yet, surveying undisturbed stacks of albums by Hungarian primeval hardcore group Galloping Coroners, or the much talked about but less frequently purchased schizophrenic-savant recordings of Wesley Willis, Gilliam would admit to a touch of bemusement at how me might be expected to retail some of Biafra's more esoteric tastes.

Prior to formalising Alternative Tentacles in 1982, Gilliam had formed Upright Artists the year previously as a booking and management agency, working with the Meteors among others. This, too, eventually became a label. Upright's first release was by The Meteors in all but name – the Clapham South Escalators' 'Get Me To The World On Time' came about when Island A&R director Andrew Lauder refused to release a single to promote their album, leading manager Nick Garrard to smuggle the masters to Gilliam. From there Gilliam would build a roster around Serious Drinking, The Higsons, Yeah Jazz, Benjamin Zephaniah and the Bluberry Hellbellies.

There was further crossover between Gilliam's interests. For example, the Beatnigs, featuring Michael Franti and Rono Tse, made their debut on Alternative Tentacles before transferring to Gilliam's next label, Workers Playtime, by which time they had evolved into Disposable Heroes Of Hiphoprisy. Worker's Playtime also released material by Welsh language punks Anhrefn, Brit hardcore deconstructionalists Snuff as well as former Upright staples Serious Drinking and The Higsons. All took place while he continued to run Alternative Tentacles' London base. Eventually, however, Gilliam's relationship with Biafra would sour, and he has latterly retired from the music industry.

One of the 'progressive' forces that grew out of punk, if you accept the pejorative, was founded on the oft-brittle entrepreneurial instincts of Dan Treacy of the Television Personalities. '14th Floor' had appeared on Teen 78 Records in 1978, followed by the 'Where's Bill Grundy' EP on another custom label, King's Road. Thereafter Treacy took a sabbatical, before being coaxed out of retirement by Geoff Travis to cut a handful of records for Rough Trade. His long-term collaborator Ed Ball, meanwhile, had established Clockwork Records. It only released two singles, The Teenage Film Stars' (There's A) 'Cloud Over Liverpool', which was the first record to feature Treacy and Ball with future long-term collaborator Joe Foster, and Dry Rib's 'Alaska'. However, it did offer something of a continuation of the original King's Road/TVPs/'O' Level aesthetic, a blend of art pop and stylised, peculiarly

English psychedelia. The Teenage Film Stars' second single, 'I Helped Patrick McGoohan Escape', would reaffirm those whimsical sixties reference points, though it emerged on yet another Ball imprint, Fab Listening.

Treacy and Ball subsequently formed Whaam! in 1981, its title taken from a Roy Lichtenstein painting. "We had problems at Rough Trade over the Dutch tour," Treacy would explain to *Slow Dazzle* fanzine. "They put it together at the last minute just to keep us happy, and it was an absolute disaster. They didn't book hotels or anything and I got ill and came home and they took £600 out of my royalties for gigs that we didn't do which was totally wrong, so I just went, 'Oh, I've had enough'. So me and Edward set up Whaam!" The label lasted for three years, its catalogue spanning 15 singles and ten albums (though some never reached the pressing plant). Many were TVPs-related releases. "The launching of Whaam! was mainly about The Times," notes Ball, "who were my band with Dan playing with me. We played live as The Times before Dan reverted back to the TVPs name for our first album releases."

"We didn't have any money, we just went and recorded a single each," Treacy would say of Whaam!, which was distributed through Rough Trade. "We didn't make anything on those first two records, then the Marine Girls record that we put out (their *Beach Party* LP) sold so many and made so much money it funded the label." Treacy would intermittently record for both Rough Trade and Illuminated during this period, the latter releasing the TVPs' *The Painted Word* after Treacy failed to settle his bills at the pressing plant. But then Illuminated went under itself just after its release. Whaam! too would eventually close after an out of court settlement made by George Michael's pop group, who had unknowingly appropriated the name. As Ball adds, The Times' debut album *Pop Goes Art!* (and Whaam! itself) furnished Alan McGee's Creation "with an immediate vision" – a fact McGee has acknowledged openly. And a vision that Ball, as a key contributor to that label (he became Creation's label spokesman in 1988 as well as a recording artist), would help bring to fruition.

Dreamworld was founded as Whaam!'s successor in 1985 by Treacy and Emelee Brown, Ball having left Whaam! to concentrate on The Times and his new Rough Trade imprint, Artpop! The original intention was for Dreamworld to reissue deleted TVPs repertoire, but it gradually drew into its release schedule the likes of Hangman's Beautiful Daughters, 1,000 Violins and Mighty Lemon Drops. Anything that Treacy turned his hand to was, however, unlikely to be founded on sound financial principles. Dave Newton of the Lemon Drops found that out to his cost. "No, we never got paid a penny, and that was despite recording our single, 'Like An Angel', for about £96 and it doing very well (selling an estimated 15,000 copies). Sometimes we'd stay at Dan's flat, and we'd all be flaked out after a night on the town. Then Dan would disappear behind a curtain and suddenly be ready to go again..." Ed Ball concurs. "It's true – by the time I'd moved on Dan's working methods were, shall we say, far more cavalier. I'm tempted to suggest that our working partnership instilled disciplines in both of us, and that perhaps Dan was influenced by the wrong people after parting." Dreamtime collapsed in 1988 after which, doubtless wisely, the remainder of Treacy's troubled but always fascinating pop career was accommodated via a variety of third party labels.

Glass Records was a one-man effort initially run from an office in Kilburn by Essex-born Dave Barker, a product controller for PolyGram from 1979 to 1983 who had previously been a typesetter and paste-up artist. His decision to set up Glass grew out of admiration for Rough Trade and Cherry Red, though Pat Fish [aka Glass mainstay The Jazz Butcher] would teasingly assert that Barker only started a record label to give himself more album covers to design. "Not true," Barker responds. "But funny." In fact, Glass was originally started to document Barker's band of the same name. Glass-1, their June 1980 single 'New Colours', had its b-side produced by old college friend John McGeoch of Magazine, while the second release was a solo effort by Glass songwriter Ciaran Harte. The record label grew from there under Barker's auspices, with distribution support via Illuminated and subsequently Pinnacle and Nine Mile. The P&D deal with Nine Mile allowed Barker freedom to release pretty much what he wanted thereafter. With minimal resources, he talked himself into the good books of the London print media, to the extent that he was able to organise American tours for his artists and even sign US acts for European distribution. Though it was widely held that he was financially 'clueless', he tempers that as "financially naive, maybe. I did run a label for eight fucking years after all! But no, I was not remotely interested in the financial side of the 'business'. Definitely."

Barker was able to preside over a catalogue of close on a hundred releases on Glass, including Where's Lisse?, Religious Overdose, In Embrace, The Servants and inevitably The Membranes, boosted by sympathetic fanzine coverage. *Blam!*, one of the finest examples of early 80s xerox culture, seemed an in-house Glass publication at one point. Robert Hampson subsequently joined Barker as assistant, until his band Loop began to take off, convincing Barker to sign The Pastels, who became the label's best selling act alongside The

Jazz Butcher. But like so many others Glass would be knee-capped by the end of Red Rhino, to whom Barker had signed following Nine Mile's merger with Rough Trade. Six months later Red Rhino collapsed. By that time Glass had notched up arguably its most enduring releases; Spacemen 3's *Sound Of Confusion* (1986) and *The Perfect Prescription* (1987), though Barker maintains they hardly caused a sensation at the time. "The best record I ever released on Glass," Barker adds, "was *Upwind of Disaster, Downwind of Atonement* by The Walking Seeds in 1989." He cites *Robespierre's Velvet Basement*, by Nikki Sudden and Dave Kusworth's Jacobites, as his next proudest offering. The 1986 compilation *50,000 Glass Fans Can't Be Wrong* retains enormous appeal as a sampler, too.

Barker regrouped with the Paperhouse label, a subsidiary of Fire Records, and an early home for Teenage Fanclub. Later he would be headhunted by Creation, to whom that band had gravitated alongside The Jazz Butcher. Alan McGee promptly branded Barker a 'genius' and promised to make him a millionaire, furnishing him with his own imprint, August, which released records by Shonen Knife, Eugenius (formerly Captain America who recorded for Paperhouse), Ween, Boyfriend and 18 Wheeler. The millions were not forthcoming. None of the acts were particularly successful, though Japanese cartoon-noiseniks Shonen Knife certainly earned acres of newsprint, and the label was closed in 1994 after substantial losses. However, McGee's decision to drop in to see 18 Wheeler play live at King Tut's Wah Wah Hut in Glasgow on 31 May 1993 on Barker's recommendation introduced him, and thereafter the world, to Oasis. Barker returned to Fire for three years thereafter, notably signing the Telstar Ponies, who included former members of both Teenage Fanclub and 18 Wheeler, before starting God Bless Records. Spanning nearly a dozen albums, God Bless was probably best known for Laptop's epic 'End Credits' single (famously using extracts from a girlfriend's answering machine), which secured creator Jesse Hartman a deal with Island. Thereafter Barker returned to graphic design.

Glass was one of several similarly inclined labels; Red Flame & Ink, Illuminated, Midnight and In Tape, who mined a seam of experimental post-punk pop that pre-dated the Creation-inspired labels of the late-80s and their overwhelming adherence to 60s pop sensibilities. Dave Kitson's Red Flame and Ink labels, based in London, grew out of his activities promoting at the Moonlight Club in Hampstead, and between 1983 and 1985 were tied to Virgin's 'indie' subsidiary, 10 Records. The roster featured The Room (whom Kitson also managed), The Moodists, C-Cat Trance (ex-Medium Medium), Anne Clarke, Severed Heads, Phillip Boa & The Voodoo Club and

Artery. Alongside Cherry Red, it was one of the few independents to grasp the importance of publishing, building a substantial catalogue. Kitson was earlier tangentially involved in Armageddon Records (set up by Dave Loader and Richard Bishop, graduates of Caroline, Richard Branson's export company). Kitson executive produced the 1981 various artists compilation *Moonlight Radio* that showcased some of his favourite bands from his Moonlight vigil, including both Artery and The Room, Red Flame's two 'most likely to' groups.

Illuminated was run by Keith Bagley, shifting its focus from punk-orientated leftovers (Poison Girls, Destructors) to a slew of groups on the cutting edge of the marriage of industrial and dance music (400 Blows, Portion Control, 23 Skidoo). Among its core contributors was later soundtrack composer Simon Boswell (ex-Advertising), who produced several releases for the label (notably 23 Skidoo's 'Coup', whose cover featured the artwork of Neville Brody, while its content was later sampled by the Chemical Brothers for 'Block Rockin' Beats'). "After producing Sex Gang Children's 'Dieche'," remembers Boswell, "I got Andi Sex Gang [one of the label's most prolific signings] involved in my first film soundtrack, with Italian horror director Dario Argento."

Former Dining Out founder Dave Henderson also joined as in-house designer. "Anything but get a job," he recalls. "I also did a couple of [compilation] albums called *The Elephant Table Album* and *Three Minute Symphonies* with the likes of Nurse With Wound, Nocturnal Emissions, Chris And Cosey and the like that went through Illuminated [via Xtract Records]. I worked at Illuminated from the early days when Keith also co-ran IKF Distribution. Then Keith brought in a guy called Angus Robertson from Island and his brother, Nigel Bagley. Keith lived in Hackney and his wife Caroline seemed to fund what he was doing from her day job in computing. I remember taking Last Few Days and 23 Skidoo around to his house and we were knocked out by his record collection. He was a huge music fan. I met Youth [Killing Joke etc] at a gig a couple of years ago and we were talking about him as Youth did an album as The Empty Quarter for Illuminated. He was saying how Keith was a true music man who spent everything he had to release music – proper indie. No idea what happened to him though, although I do remember after they released the *Illuminati* album by Robert Anton Wilson he reckoned that Wilson was furious and had threatened that he was going to put a curse on him. Stranger things have happened."

Nick Ralph and Steve Burgess, veterans of *Dark Star* magazine, launched Midnight Music in 1982. "At the time we had a record shop in Crouch End," recalls Ralph. "After a couple of years, Steve and I parted ways. He kept the shop, which was always his baby. I had only seen it as a stepping stone towards a label, and I took the label and kept the name." His first signings were Sad Lovers & Giants, picked up from their own Last Movement imprint (Midnight's roster later incorporated guitarist Tristan Garel-Funk's subsequent band Snake Corps). The second artist to be signed to the label proved to their most consistent seller, however; Robyn Hitchcock had previously been a regular shop customer. "We released Robyn's solo recordings after he left Armageddon and Albion," Ralph confirms. "We coaxed him out of 'retirement' – he had got fed up with the record business." After issuing some extant but unreleased 'home' recordings, they got him back in the studio and re-released much of the Soft Boys' back catalogue, beginning with an outtakes album and EP. "Later Robyn had his own labels for solo and Soft Boys releases," Ralph continues, "which were administered by us as if they were our own releases. We also administered Genesis P.Orridge's Temple Records, including Psychic TV, towards the end."

Midnight's sister companies included a publishing arm and recording studios. "The studio was the greater part of our indebtedness to the bank," Ralph confirms, "but we liked to 'indulge' our artists and we couldn't afford to do that paying third-party recording costs. We were one of the first mixing to digital masters." Perhaps uniquely among UK independents of its size, Midnight had a strong mainland European bias, its acts touring regularly, and proving most popular, in France, Spain and the Lowlands. In addition to signing The Essence from Rotterdam, Midnight opened an office in Paris, licensing albums by Billy Bragg, the Wedding Present and others for French distribution, and giving Chameleon Mark Burgess an outlet for his Sun And The Moon project. Initially intended for France only, it was also issued in the UK and became the label's fastest selling release. Mark Burgess subsequently signed to the label and recorded tracks at Midnight's 'second' studio in Rotterdam.

Later A&R decisions, borne out of circumstance, saw Midnight move away from its initial focus on cultured, cosmopolitan art-rock. Both The Wolfhounds and McCarthy joined the label when September Records ran aground. A similar exercise rescued Medium Cool's roster of The Waltones, Corn Dollies and Popguns. "We took over the September and Medium Cool labels in their entirety, saving both from oblivion," confirms Ralph. "Paul Sutton continued to manage the Wolfhounds and Andy Wake worked for

Midnight for a while on promotion after we took over his label." There was also folk-rock from Blyth Power and Hackney 5-0, former Monochrome Set member Lester Square's The Invisible project and well received releases from Cindytalk, This Mortal Coil contributor Gordon Sharp's ongoing solo project. But the label sundered in the early 90s. "The men in suits wanted it to make money," complained Ralph, "which it didn't. But all we wanted to make was music. Which we did, lots of it."

Asked to spell out the gory details, Ralph acknowledges that the recession hit Midnight hard. "The bank had loaned us a lot of money with little financial input from ourselves. Then, as the recession took hold and we weren't repaying any of it, they decided to cut their losses and get whatever they could out of it, the main assets being the recording studios and equipment. I think they were worried we would asset-strip it ourselves so moved in to prevent it. I suppose the reality was that we over-stretched ourselves, and were far too ambitious for our resources. We failed mainly due to insufficient sales and had built up a lot of unsold stock. We lost out through some distributor debts, but we also benefited from help from them as well. Red Rhino had helped us with licensing for France and Pinnacle (under Steve Mason) had helped us out of trouble nearer the end.

The last six to twelve months were very hard. We were hoping to trade out of it and might have done if the bank had been more patient, but we couldn't get our new releases out at the right times. Some never came out at all, including a finished album by The Waltones – we had released just a single under their new name Candlestick Park. And on top of everything else, we had committed to large advance payments for Temple Records. Plus the idea of having our own studios didn't work out as well as it might. We still ended up using other studios as well and that might have made a difference, but I wasn't strict enough!"

In Tape, founded in 1983, dutifully exposed staple 'indie' journeymen of the period alongside some plainly more esoteric brands before floundering at the turn of the decade. Based in Sale, Manchester, it was set up by Marc Riley following his defection/ejection from The Fall, alongside Jim Khambatta, who also worked as a record plugger for Factory and later, 4AD.

The initial releases were two Marc Riley & The Creepers' singles; 'Favourite Sister' and 'Jumper Clown', both of which drew on Riley's Fall legacy. The latter was a self-evident dig at former employer Mark E Smith. Beyond the (justifiably cruel) titular reference to Smith's sartorial inelegance, the impetus was Riley's desire to set the record straight. "'Jumper Clown' is self-explanatory," Riley points out, before quoting the lyrics. "'Dare to dance on an Aussie floor – bloody nose – bloody bore'. It was the tale of my exit from The Fall. The fight is well documented, except in Mark's 'autobiography', which paints a completely different picture to what actually happened. Mark likes to portray himself as a hard man, not to be messed with on one hand, and a victim on the other. He made out I attacked him for no good reason, giving him a right beating, apparently. Ha. As Steve [Hanley], Paul [Hanley] and Craig [Scanlon] will tell you, Mark took umbrage at our dancing at a Sydney night-club after the first gig of the '82 tour. He came on to the dancefloor, slapped the band one by one, till he got to me. I was the last to be approached so, unlike the other fellas, I knew what was coming. I stopped him and pushed him away. A couple of minutes later I confronted him and he hit me. And I hit him back; one punch each, both in the face. How can I put it? He came out of the trade-off much worse. We were both then thrown out of the club. A couple of months later, I was out."

"I always say the second best thing that ever happened to me was being asked by Mark to join The Fall," Riley continues, "the first best thing was getting the sack. I saw what it did to my best mates, Steve and Craig. The first In Tape single, 'Favourite Sister', was actually a song rejected by Mark that I recorded with Steve and Paul. Mark wasn't best pleased. When I got shown the door, Steve offered to come with me – which was fantastically brave and loyal of him. We'd been best mates for 15 years at that point. I thanked him but told him he'd be mad to leave The Fall. I can't imagine them having grown as they did without Steve in there. I think Mark owes me a drink for that. He owes Steve an awful lot more."

In Tape thus became the bolthole for Riley and his Creepers, though he still doesn't quite understand the provenance of the name, chosen by Khambatta. "It seemed to make sense to Jim, though. I remember getting a call from Alan McGee just after 'Favourite Sister' came out, asking me if I wanted to sign to his new label, Creation. As I had my 'own' label, I turned him down. We picked up a few bands; Yeah Yeah Noh!, The Janitors, Gaye Bykers on Acid, Membranes, Asphalt Ribbons (pre-Tindersticks), Frank Sidebottom, talk about eclectic! I think that was the main problem. The label had no 'identity'. There was no such thing as an 'In Tape Sound'. It was all over the place. Just as the title of the In Tape compilation points out, *It's A Mish-Mash*. It certainly was."

## For How Much Longer?

That's something Derek Hammond of Yeah Yeah Noh! can attest to. "I'd seen the little news item in the *NME* which put In Tape forward as a whole new kind of label: they didn't sign you, you signed them. Not sure how that was supposed to work! In the meantime I'd got together with my old barman chum John Grayland – head of entertainment at Leicester Poly and another Fall fan – and formed Yeah Yeah Noh! proper, having been using the name for bedroom tapes for long enough. By the time we came to making demos, it was just us and a crap little drum machine. The sound was incredibly tinny and fragile – pathetic clanks and bonks, John's play-in-a-day twangy guitar and my gruff talk-overs. I remember the letter we got back from In Tape, saying we probably weren't expecting anyone to get back to us on the strength of such a shite demo, but they wanted to sign us and do a single. I remember going to Manchester and meeting Marc, who wasn't nearly as scary as I thought someone out of The Fall might be. As we all now know, of course, he's a lovely eccentric with a very gentle sense of humour. He lived with Jim Khambatta in a big student-ish house with ceilings 12-feet high. We were blown away seeing our crap little demo by the cassette player, and being told Craig Scanlon liked it, too." "Generally speaking," interjects Riley, "I'm not a complete arsehole. Perhaps that should be written on my tombstone? *Here lies Marc Riley – He wasn't a* Complete *Arsehole*."

"Those In Tape 'mansion' days from 1983 to 1987 were great," he continues. "We lived in a big house in Sale. Me and [his wife] Trace in one room. Jim ran the label and lived in another. Eddie [Fenn; Creepers drummer] lived in one room. Craig Scanlon lived upstairs. We all played a lot of football, drank lots of ale and went to a lot of gigs. Most of my memories of that time are happy ones."

Many of the subsequent additions to In Tape's roster led directly from Yeah Yeah Noh! "John [Grayland] was a natural 'player manager'," Hammond recalls. "He was a natural politician, a contact builder, talking to the bands, a fanzine graduate, arranging swap gigs and helping to build a network; The Membranes. Three Johns, Redskins, etc. Incredibly friendly, generous people. I chipped in with my Brum connections, cos now I was at university there; Hippo Hippo. Ted Chippington. Terry and Gerry, Mighty Mighty, etc. We felt like we were part of something at the time, though it was never given a name by the inky press – provincial indie? And it didn't last too long; just 1984 to 1986. The miners' strike gave us all something in common, as there were hundreds of benefit gigs going at the time. A sense of right and wrong and purpose, maybe – though of course it was nothing to do with the music in most cases."

Some examples of the link-up included the "sarky skiffle" of Terry & Gerry, which followed a discussion with Hammond at the Barrel Organ in Birmingham. The Janitors' guitarist had guested on Yeah Yeah Noh!'s second John Peel session, while another Leicester group, Gaye Bykers On Acid, like The June Brides, were friends from gigs. "In retrospect," notes Hammond, "we were responsible for quite a few early signings. Even though Marc had been on the scene for ages, The Fall connection was a bit of a hindrance when it came to meeting new bands, as most would assume he'd be a bit of a terror! The only band signed before us was local Mancunians, Implied Consent."

"Jim's philosophy was that he wanted to run it like a major label," notes Riley, "release all kinds of different music, run expensive fly-poster campaigns, etc. And in the end I had very little to do with the label. So I left Jim to it, taking The Creepers' back-catalogue with me and leaving Jim the rest. We were selling something like 8-9,000 records [each release] by the time we quit. I think the Gaye Bykers were our biggest sellers at around 20,000. I never really took much notice and I don't think some of the bands got the money they were owed. Not because Jim was taking it – he was as poor as a church mouse. Jim was really hard working and determined, but the whole label was 'cross collateralised' – which meant that a band that lost money would be propped up by a band that made a profit. That was the deal we had with our distributors Red Rhino. Not good." Red Rhino's collapse would prove a dagger to In Tape's heart as with so many other labels.

Abstract Sounds was one of the early 80s independent labels founded by an industry insider. Proprietor Edward Christie had enjoyed quite an apprenticeship. "I was very interested in trying to write songs, but it was hard to get anything into the big publishers or major record companies," he recalls. "Looking back, they were all rubbish, so I can understand. Through a girl I met I got into a music management company, GTO, looking after David Bowie, Gary Glitter and the New Seekers. I could drive a Rolls-Royce and the management company wanted a driver. One of the first jobs I did was take paperwork round to David Bowie's management, the first time I'd ever seen men in make-up and weirdly designed clothes. Through Laurence Myers, who was one of the first managers to lease masters to record labels, there was a connection to Bell Records. He put a production company together, paid for the recording and subsequently licensed them to a label. Afterwards I did regional promotion at GTO, working with the Walker Brothers, Billy Ocean and Heatwave. When they were sold to CBS I went to CBS's promotion department, working with Abba and Bruce Springsteen. Then Laurence decided to form another record company, Gem, which was one of the first 'independent' labels financed by a major, RCA. He asked me to come over, start the publishing and do a little A&R. We signed the UK Subs and VIPs, and we had a number one hit with Patrick Hernandez. But it was a bit of a doomed venture. That closed, and I decided to start my own indie label, because that was the thing that was happening; the market was there, singles were selling well. And that's how Abstract came about."

Christie's defection from a major to a scratch independent, starting in 1981, offered a degree of culture shock. "You come down with a thump. The first thing you realise is that you're financing everything. Every £100 is a lot of money when you're trying to put a record together. The first record was a band from Edinburgh, FK9 ['Our Condition']. We sold about 200 copies and I lost about £1,500. That was my savings, redundancy money and bits and pieces. Expense counts when you're doing it on your own. If it doesn't work, you're in trouble. Suddenly I was having to talk to people at *Sounds* and *Melody Maker* and *NME*, and trying to get hold of John Peel, who was never in my orbit before. It was a total re-education and quite terrifying. Later, when John Peel gave us some support, my wife would say, 'Why have you got the radio on at midnight in the bedroom?' 'I'm listening to see if John Peel is going to play The Three Johns.' With a major company, I wasn't that bothered – Abba was going to get played [regardless]. But with your own record, every little thing counts. You're excited at getting a review or even a press release published. It was absolutely personal. At times you'd get angry when people slagged off the record or the label."

A "big saviour" came when Christie packaged *Punk And Disorderly*, a 16-track 1981 compilation of emerging new punk bands, which reached number three in the independent charts. But Abstract's catalogue never really settled on a specific genre, its earliest realistic hopes for a breakthrough revolving around all-female punk trio The Gymslips. "The Gymslips I have bittersweet memories of," reflects Christie. "We put a lot of effort into them, and they were just starting to break through when they got a new manager. The new manager put ideas into their heads, and they wouldn't do the next album with me. I decided to back off. I was going to put everything into doing it." Instead, Christie continued on his course, releasing material by The UK Subs (whom he'd first signed to Gem after catching them at The Roxy) and 1919 before alighting on the two bands that, more than any others, would define the label's image, New Model Army and The Three Johns. The former were belligerent, antediluvian moralists, the latter just as politicised but wont to throw in a cover of Madonna's 'Like A Virgin' for diversion. It led to the perception that Abstract was a northern label, when in reality, it was based in Kempe Road in north west London.

"There are some A&R people on some labels where they've just loved music and they've had a whole style and a way of doing it – things like Mute and 4AD," Christie surmises. "My musical interest was quite varied. I put all sorts of things out; heavy rock, indie-rock, dancey stuff. There's no question when you sign something, you're looking at potential sales. It wasn't a hobby or luxury where you could put out something that you loved but it flopped. I needed to sell records, to get promotion, to get some success at some level so I could do the next record. Every record counted. The Three Johns was one of my proudest moments. Three fantastic blokes, and they delivered fantastic records. We had some bad luck when one of the singles, 'Death Of A European', got a lot of daytime airplay. And then of course, we had the Heysel football disaster. I think they wrote some brilliant stuff and it *was* commercial; we should have been able to cross that over."

The Three Johns also brought Christie into the orbit of Alan McGee. "I remember Alan ringing me up, asking me to bring the Three Johns to play at the Three Johns pub in Islington. It was kind of a joke. We'd go down, and Jesus and Mary Chain were supporting them. Alan said, do you want to do anything together? Probably one of the biggest mistakes I made was to turn him down, but his costings were completely out of my league."

The label's biggest selling album was New Model Army's *Vengeance*. "There were a number of punk poets around, and I'd heard about Joolz [singer Justin Sullivan's romantic partner, who painted New Model Army's artwork and would also record for Abstract]. I found out Joolz was managed by a guy called Nigel Morton, who'd managed the VIPs, whom we'd had a hit with on Gem. I rang Nigel and asked if he had a contract. And he was also co-managing New Model Army. He said, 'I've got this other band, do you want to come see them?' I saw them in Brixton with Nico and signed them. They were very successful and a great bunch of guys. OK, Justin was quite strong-willed and the rest of it, but I like that in an artist. We put the album out and it went to number 48 in the national chart. It was number one in the indie chart, and stayed in the indie charts for 70 weeks. I was very proud of doing that."

That the band moved to a larger label seemed inevitable, though Christie remains philosophical. "Hugh Stanley-Clarke, who worked for me at Gem Records as a junior scout, was at EMI and wanted to sign New Model Army. It just made sense. I got some money from it when they bought out the rest of my contract. In many ways it was beneficial. EMI, to give them their due, put a lot of money into them. If they had an album out, you knew about it, there were posters and flyers everywhere. It just kept *Vengeance* selling all the time. So rather than having a hit and going away, I had a steady trickle of business and income, and so did the band. There was disappointment, but also there was benefit from it."

Other bands on the label included the jangly indie-pop of The Janitors and 1,000 Mexicans, a one-off LP by the Moodists, and an album by former Swell Map Nikki Sudden. Christie then came across a band that took him away from preconceptions about an indie label. "I signed a little pop-reggae band called The Cool Notes. They came to me with this track, 'You're Never Too Young', and I thought it was fantastic. Loose Ends and Jaki Graham were happening in the soul market. We tried to hawk the record around, but no-one would do it, so I said I would. We paid £300 and went into a studio, recorded it, and it was hammered on the pirate stations." Unfortunately, the rewards were not immediately forthcoming. "We were distributed by the first incarnation of Pinnacle. We were doing good business with them. In those days, singles really sold. We did about 40,000 of 'Never Too Young', which stalled just outside the top 40. The following week, Pinnacle went into liquidation. I'd paid for all the pressing and promotion, and there was going to be no money coming back. COPS were manufacturing most independent records at that time. And they were the people you owed most money to. All the labels sat down and agreed a long-term repayment of the debts. The meeting was very amicable. Everyone looked at each other and said, if we don't do this, we'll all lose. It was a very worrying time, but only for a short period. Then Steve Mason bought Pinnacle, and we all re-signed to Steve because we'd had dealings with [his former company] Windsong, and they were brilliant payers. That's what we needed to be reassured about. I knew that I'd be able to pay COPS back because of the New Model Army and Three Johns catalogue. The other big saviour was that compact discs came in. Suddenly we could re-sell our catalogue again. It completely re-opened the market again. Not just for the indies but the majors. It was dark, but didn't last too long, so we just got on with it."

With that resolved, Christie tried to engineer a deal for The Cool Notes. "But like today with hip hop, British soul was not really wanted by the major record companies. So we ended up doing the second record, 'Spend The Night'." His faith was rewarded when it became the band, and label's, biggest hit, reaching number eleven in the national charts. In a similar vein, after enjoying significant success marketing extreme metal acts, Abstract is currently in the process of trying to break a roster of new UK hip hop artists, including Blak Twang and Klashnekoff. "You take that gamble," reflects Christie, "you have to move on."

As post-punk uncoiled into various stylistic satellites, like-minded independent labels evolved to service them. So it was with the emergent Goth culture. Prior to a one-off single with CNT, the pre-eminent group to emerge from the dry ice, The Sisters Of Mercy, formed their own record label, Merciful Release, to issue debut single 'The Damage Done'. "The story which has passed into Sisters folklore," Gary Marx recalls, "that I stole a sizeable sum of money from my employer of the time to finance the recordings which became the 'Damage Done' single, is pretty much the truth (if you view creative accounting as theft). It's fair to say that more thought went into the non-musical aspects than anything contained within the grooves. That should be immediately obvious to anyone who's actually heard it. The songs didn't really go on to feature much in the live sets. We only ever played 'Damage Done' live once to my knowledge. The single, really, was just a wild, hurried scribble on a map we hadn't even fully unfolded, rather than a direction for the band – which was only me and Andrew [Eldritch] at the time. The music lacks many of the hallmarks of later releases, not least because Andrew only sings on one of the songs, but the sleeve set the template for pretty much everything that's followed for the band in its various incarnations. The head and star logo, which was conceived firstly as the label for the 7-inch vinyl (because we enjoyed the mild nausea induced by watching the head rotate on the turntable) has long outlived the tunes. For those who believe in self-fulfilling prophecies, the first thing we did to promote the single, before it was ever released, was to place ads in the 'records wanted' section of the music press, offering £25 for a copy. Clearly it's gone on to outstrip that figure several times over." The March Violets, Salvation and James Ray & The Performance were among the other acts to call Merciful Release home, which, by 1984, was distributed by Warner Brothers.

Reception Records, another artist-owned imprint from Leeds, was founded by David Gedge primarily as a vehicle for The Wedding Present, who made their debut in 1985 with 'Go Out And Get 'Em Boy'. Later it would house releases by This Poison and Cud. An archetypal story of a start-up overcoming initially limited resources, each band member chipped in £5 a week from their dole to fund that first release. Gedge, who legendarily subsisted on a diet of mashed potato, travelled to London on a coach to pick up the pressings in a further effort to economise on transport costs. In the event the single was picked up for distribution by Peter Thompson at Red Rhino, who had nevertheless declined a request to fund the recording. As soon as John Peel started championing it, however, Red Rhino provided them with £400 for a follow-up single, 'Once More'. By the advent of *George Best*, the group's debut album, Red Rhino were prepared to commit £30,000 to recording and £20,000 for promotion. It sold 18,000 copies within a fortnight, knocking The Smiths' *Strangeways Here We Come* from the top of the independent charts. Yet Red Rhino was rapidly running into financial problems (see Chapter 12). Unlike some others, The Wedding Present remained on excellent terms with their distributor up to the point of its collapse, by which time they'd already accepted an offer to join RCA while Reception was mothballed.

Chapter 22, founded in 1984 by Balaam & The Angel manager Craig Jennings in Warwickshire, was originally intended merely to be a showcase for his charges' first two singles, with the specific intent of landing a major label contract. But, with the assistance of Nine Mile, it gradually evolved to include a roster featuring The Wild Flowers, Mighty Mighty and, for a brief time, The Mission. But the reputation it acquired as a Goth label was somewhat misleading. Signing American no wave heroes Suicide was a significant coup, and the label had claim to fostering their nearest contemporary UK equivalent in the form of Loop's insistent, narcotic psychedelia. Pop Will Eat Itself, meanwhile, will forever be associated with the much maligned 'grebo' movement that shot to popularity in the Midlands, though their principal success came with RCA.

Nearby in Nottingham, Digby Pearson had been writing for *Maximum Rock 'n' Roll*, American's punk bible. He started Earache Records in his bedroom on the back of a Enterprise Allowance grant to indulge his passion for extreme American hardcore bands like DRI. His first release was a joint effort with Tim Bennett of Children Of The Revolution, licensing an album from Seattle's Accused, before a split LP featuring Concrete Sox and Heresy. But it was the merciless, synapse-snapping hardcore shooters of Napalm Death that entranced John Peel, drawing on anarcho-punk spirit, Discharge and the primal extreme metal work of bands like Celtic Frost. Soon Pearson had a roster of gore/horror/speed merchants on his books including Morbid Angel, Godflesh, Carcass and Bolt Thrower. Earache continues to this day and has reinvented itself as a musical genre as much as a label.

One of the most lovably idiosyncratic independents of the mid-80s also had roots in Nottinghamshire. Ron Johnson Records became synonymous with a cadre of bands who were as politicised as they were off kilter; Big Flame, Stump, Shrubs, Mackenzies, Jackdaw With Crowbar, A Witness. Several were in thrall to The Fall to varying degrees, though Big Flame's inspiration was resolutely the Gang Of Four. Characterised by the fine art of the sonic squall, and deviance from 4/4 rhythms (whether desired or unintentional), Peel seemed to love just about everything on the roster. Ron Johnson would be saluted as label of the year by *The Catalogue*'s readers in 1986, its annus spectaculus, with The Ex's elaborately packaged '1936' double single voted best single. But it was a 'Blue Monday' moment. Snatching defeat from the jaws of victory, it emerged that the packaging of '1936' was so elaborate it lost Ron Johnson money on every copy, meaning a net deficit of £15,000.

Established by Dave Parsons away from his shifts as a biscuit packer, Ron Johnson was never the most business-savvy of propositions. Its final release was 1988's 'Who Works The Weather' by The Great Leap Forward (the band formed in the wake of Big Flame's collapse), Peel mourning its loss on air. But its output is still recalled with great fondness, and for good reason; Big Flame's 'Why Popstars Can't Dance', much touted as an influence by the likes of the Manic Street Preachers, being one of the all-time great independent singles. And, in a narrative where exploitation of bands by record labels was routine, it demonstrated that the reverse could also hold true. Parsons would be bankrupted and lose his house as reward for his seven-year commitment to the project.

"For me," says Parsons, "Ron Johnson was a great label for the first twelve releases or so. Big Flame were pretty much perfect. Personally I don't think they ever surpassed the first thing they did for us, 'Man Of Few Syllables'. Even though 'Two Kan Guru' and 'The Cubist Pop Manifesto' 12-inch were straying from the three-track EP path, I was proud that we never buckled to pressure to put out a Big Flame LP. I think that would have been absurd and close to unlistenable. I think Big Flame were a great band – and probably my favourite on Ron Johnson. A Witness too, performed pretty much consistently. Generally speaking, I liked most of their stuff and their lyrics were good. I found Vince from the band a little hard to get on with. It seemed like he always thought I was out to exploit them somehow, or was favouring others above them. Truth was I was just doing my best to put out some records, with the minimum of business advice from the distributors who funded the pressings."

"If I knew then what I knew now," a rueful Parsons continues, "maybe Ron Johnson would have become a Creation or a Factory. Unfortunately I wasn't pushy enough, or knew enough, and was certainly far too naive and easily swayed. I made plenty of awful business decisions and wasted money – no doubt about that. But, especially in the early days, I think my A&R ear was as good as anyone's. What Stump did for us I thought was excellent, musically: they weren't happy with the recording, and I didn't have the money to remaster it when the drummer (a pain in the arse) complained his cymbals were hissing. The MacKenzies I liked but I always felt they were Big Flame impersonators."

He's more rueful still on the subject of The Shrubs. "I wished I'd never signed them. Nick Hobbs had too much experience of the music business to pressure me with. I had none. To be perfectly frank, he railroaded me into making decisions that I knew were wrong at the time, and agreeing to them spending preposterous amounts of money. They spent, I think, £5,000 recording four tracks direct to master that were nothing special (whereas the whole A Witness LP cost £500). I was expected to pick up the tab. Nick had 'professional' ideas about his basically amateur band that was on a basically amateur label. I should have told him what was what, but he was God knows how many years older than me (remember, I was 23 years old at the time) and one of the most manic people I'd ever met. I know his heart was in the right place, but I never found him at all easy to get along with. On top of that, I didn't really like most of their stuff: again, a couple of corkers, but a lot of filler. And that was the beginning of the end really. All the others had some decent songs, but not anything worth shouting about. And at the end of the day, the ONLY band that made ANY money at all was A Witness: so they are the only ones who can have a beef about the business side of things with any real justification. Even then, I know Vince and Nick were 100% committed to their personal causes. The problem with small-scale labels is like having a large family, where everyone demands that they're the centre of attention (at least in their own minds) and assumes that the 'father figure' has all the answers and all of the resources. Successes are never questioned, and, if not expected, hailed as just rewards; whereas failures are remembered as personal let-downs and breaches of trust somehow. Dealing with twelve bands, all of whom think, naturally enough, that they are the best, was a parental role that I was probably too immature to bear. Yes, the business was a shambles: but so were most of the bands!"

There was also the dizzying array of artist-generated one-off imprints. Paul Rosen, aka Paul Platypus, formed Irrelevant Wombat Records with his colleagues in Exhibit A in 1980. "We released two self-released singles, with help from Swell Maps, then set up Namedrop Records with Philip Johnson to release our experimental collaborative 10-inch under the name Doof. That was followed by a 10-inch by my next band, Twelve Cubic Feet, and then Philip's first solo LP (Johnson was a prolific 'cassette' artist)." After a final single emerged, Rosen formed Cold War, also contributing to Mark Perry's Reflections project, released on Cherry Red. "I used to pester [Cherry Red A&R head] Mike Alway about whatever I was doing at frequent intervals. I had ambitions for further entrepreneurship, too, at the same time as hanging around with the stars of the future – I was at Cherry Red's offices with the Marine Girls when Mike showed Tracey Thorn the first Ben Watt single and told her to meet up with him in Hull."

Irrelevant Wombat is a great name for a label, but not quite as good as Mole Embalming Records, a Leicester independent initially founded by Graham Summers, Mick Bunnage, Sherree Lawrence and Alan Jenkins of The Deep Freeze Mice to facilitate their first four albums. The name was changed to Cordelia ("after my cat," Jenkins admits) in 1984, and has since released material by American maverick R. Stevie Moore, Dolly Mixture and Jody & The Creams. It is still active as part of a shop cum studio enterprise more than two decades later, the label principally serving as an outlet for Jenkins' own projects and "whatever else comes along". Other candidates for best label names include The Tufty Club (Crosstalk A/V), Thin Sliced (King Kurt, Helen & The Horns), Snotty Snail (Notsensibles) and Groucho Marxist (Defiant Pose).

Another artist-founded label was agit-folker Robb Johnson's Irregular Records. At the start of the 80s he'd been a member of Grubstreet on the London pub circuit. "That was sometimes a bit dispiriting, but not nearly as depressing or insulting as having some latest-haircut A&R desk-Johnny sniff dismissively at your work. A friend called Lynne Mitchell decided I needed to make appointments with record companies. It was a haircut called Wally Brill at A&M Records who was a wally too far as far as I was concerned." His sound engineer friend, Bruce 'Moose' Thompson, persuaded Johnson to go it alone. "I thought up the name Irregular because I didn't expect we'd be doing anything on a regular basis. The first album came out in 1985 and it was all very DIY and punk rock in ethos, if not in sound, funded by donations from friends and family, completely oblivious to any zeitgeist, and selling fuck all. It wasn't till a good few years later we thought about attempting to get distribution." From there the label would eventually provide a home to The Astronauts, Maggie Holland, Barb Jungr, Carol Grimes and others, and it remains active – kind of. "I patiently explain to artists that actually being on Irrregular, a one-person fabrication with not a lot of enthusiasm and absolutely no budget whatsoever, is not in itself a guarantee of huge sales and cult status. But people tend to hear what they want to hear and substitute a lot of wishful thinking for what they don't. Irregular has an interesting song-orientated catalogue; it doesn't really fit pigeonholes or suit zeitgeists or the latest haircuts. People find their way onto Irregular by accident or by recommendation, usually."

The overlord of the artist-label sub-genre (with an acknowledgement to Cleaners From Venus/Martin Newell's Man At The Off Licence imprint, its wares memorably traded in exchange for vegetables and other produce) was indisputably Razz. It documented the footfalls of indomitable Mancunian Beatles' devotee Chris Sievey and his band The Freshies across a bewildering array of cassette and vinyl. As far back as 1971 Sievey had plagued record labels, staging a sit-in at Apple which led to him recording (an unreleased) session. So persistent was he that at one stage he was able to publish a book of record company rejection slips. A sequel consisted entirely of rejections from Virgin Records alone. There is limited mileage in extolling the virtues of an 'independent' artist quite so desperate for a major to come knocking on his door. But Sievey's resilience and love of the unrepentant, usually convoluted expression of affection was a winning formula. 'I'm In Love With A Girl On The Manchester Virgin Megastore Checkout Desk' provided a long overdue, but ultimately fleeting, brush with fame and fortune. "In the biz, you get to meet all the top people," the opening lines can. "Trouble is, they never seem to be the sort we pull". What could have been a slightly creepy stalker anthem was rendered an utterly sincere missive of love unrequited. Billy Bragg, one can surmise, might well have been listening.

Licensed to MCA from Razz, 'Megastore' was the closest Sievey came to stardom (and what a fantastic celebrity he would have made) until he was swallowed whole by *papier-mâché* homunculus Frank Sidebottom. The MCA-Freshies tie-up led to the only anti-nuke anthem ever to parody ELO ('Wrap Up The Rockets') and the ultimate record collector's song '(I Can't Get) Bouncing Babies By The Teardrop Explodes'. It is not unknown for audience members at Sidebottom's shows to demand encores of 'The Men And Women From Banana Island Whose Stupid Ideas Never Caught On In The Western World As We Know It' to general bemusement. Oh, and The Freshies' 'No Money' may well be the most painfully accurate song ever written about the independent music industry.

It wasn't just post-punk and experimental labels who benefited from the independent surge. Other youth 'cults' got a look in, too. Though obviously not the focus of this book, the New Wave Of British Heavy Metal was driven to an extent by the rejuvenating energy of punk, but its adherents were not ready to ditch, or mask, their affection for rock 'n' roll. And the NWOBHM (that fantastically cumbersome acronym) was driven, at least initially, by indies. Primary among these, by some margin, was Neat Records, founded by David Wood of Impulse Studios in Newcastle in 1979 (though its ownership would later transfer to Tygers Of Pan Tang vocalist Jess Cox). The subsequent development of the 'black metal' and to a slightly lesser extent 'thrash metal' aesthetics can be squarely laid at the feet of Neat's leading lights, local stars Venom – routinely cited as an influence on Metallica, Anthrax, Megadeth *et al*. Other staple Neat acts included Jaguar, Blitzkrieg, White Spirit and Raven. The label's main competitors at the turn of the decade included Heavy Metal Records and Ebony. The former had been founded by Paul Birch with the singular intention of providing an outlet for The Handsome Beasts, but it became best known for Witchfinder General and its compilation series, *Heavy Metal Heroes*. Ebony, under the stewardship of Darryl Johnston, began with a series of compilations of unsigned artists (its better remembered graduates including Mercyful Fate) while their biggest success came with Grim Reaper, who would eventually transfer to RCA. Later the indie-metal baton passed to Martin Hooker's Music For Nations/Under One Flag [see chapter eleven].

The Mod Revival was largely the province of major labels. The Lambrettas signed to Elton John's Rocket, Secret Affair's I-Spy imprint went through Arista, while The Chords, like reluctant scene-leaders The Jam, were on Polydor. However, the movement did throw up a handful of independents. Hi-Lo started out in 1980 to accommodate the output of Squire. But any attempt to build the brand was handicapped by the necessity to bunny-hopping distributors. "We were distributed first by Stage One, then I.D.S., then Backs and the Cartel, then EMI," remembers owner Anthony Meynell. He recently revived the label after it was 'mothballed' in 1987 (it re-emerged briefly as Antenna Records in the late 90s). The Killermeters' first single was released on pressing plant imprint Psycho (a lesser known variant of the Ellie Jay model; used frequently by impoverished bands as an 'off the peg' alternative to the logistics of manufacturing a record oneself). It's also worth pointing out that the 60s-loving Whaam!/Artpop! imprints were also considered by many to be allied to traditional Mod values, not least through The Direct Hits, while songs such as 'I Helped Patrick McGoohan Escape' (Teenage Filmstars *and* The Times) and 'Biff Bang Pow' (The Times) are frequently to be found on genre compilations.

## For How Much Longer?

One other label of note associated with the Mod Revival was Tortch Records, based in Hinchley Wood, Surrey. Inspired by what proprietor Steve Budd had seen Rough Trade and Mute achieve, it was set up initially to support The Directions, whom he managed (and would subsequently evolve into Big Sound Authority). "The label had no musical ethos," he would tell *Bored Teenagers*, "other than to release records that I liked and its main purpose was for me to have a method of enticing bands to work with me as their manager." The 'Three Bands Tonite' EP was pressed in a denomination of 2,000 copies at a cost of £129.50 and sold through Rough Trade. But other releases, unaligned to the Mod Revival, were probably more noteworthy. Tortch would issue the first EPs by both The Sound ('Physical World') and The Cardiacs (as Cardiac Arrest; 'A Bus For A Bus On A Bus' EP), the leaders of both, Adrian Borland and Tim Smith, graduating from '77 Surrey band Gazunda. Tortch also released the second Scissor Fits EP (featuring later Cherry Red A&R head Mike Alway) and the 'Flesh As Property' EP, which contained the original version of 'Courts Or Wars' (scheduled to be reissued as Cherry Red's 21st single but pulled) by Sound side project Second Layer. Budd would go on to a management career representing The Sound as well as Lloyd Cole, Heaven 17 and producers such as Tony Visconti and Arthur Baker.

While Ace's Big Beat subsidiary kick-started the garage/rockabilly revival movement, other independents such as Roy Williams' Nervous Records, Alligator (whom Nervous eventually acquired) and Soho provided significant background noise and impetus. Soho issued the first recordings by The Passions, Shane MacGowan's Nips/Nipple Erectors, The Jets and The Inmates. Inevitably there was a strong link back to Ted Carroll and Roger Armstrong at Ace. Stan Brennan and Phil Gaston had, like Armstrong, completed their studies in Belfast, and wound up inheriting their Soho market stall (re-titled *Rocks Off*, rather than *Rock On*, to provide thematic continuity). Later, they would establish the Vinyl Solution chain with the assistance of Yves Guillemot. "Unfortunately," recalls Brennan, "personality differences meant Phil and I left Yves in West London and we relocated to Hanway Street." Said cramped premises, off Tottenham Court Road, were affectionately dubbed 'The Microstore' in deference to the vastly more spacious Virgin Megastore nearby.

Soho Records ran for just over two years, the highlight of its catalogue The Nips' 'Gabrielle' (in its death throes it also released their *Only The End Of The Beginning* album). Brennan kept the shop and Gaston the label after they parted company. The latter put together the Nips compilation *Babes, Bops And Bovver* through Ace, and recorded 'Champion The Wonder Horse' under the sobriquet The Mighty Clouds of Dust (Dead On Records). He also wrote and recorded 'Tommy's Blue Valentine' with Cait O'Riordan and Pride Of The Cross (through Big Beat) and penned 'Navigator' for The Pogues' *Rum, Sodomy and the Lash*.

Brennan stayed in retail until 1991. In that time he started the Media Burn, Absolutely Free! and PM labels, whose output encompassed albums and 12-inch releases by the Stingrays, Prisoners, Mighty Caesars, Surfadelics, X-Men, Milkshakes, Nigel Lewis, Golden Horde and the Locomotives, "before sadly going down in the Red Rhino bankruptcy". Absolutely Free! also housed Buzzcocks' *Live At the Roxy* (one of the few legitimate 'Roxy' LPs) and The Purple Things (Gary Bonniface's band post the Vibes) while Pogue Mahone released 'Dark Streets of London', their Brennan-produced 1984 debut single, for PM. Brennan subsequently acted as the group's manager and produced debut album *Red Roses for Me*. Thereafter he returned to professional psychology – the subject he'd previously studied at Queen's.

And, of course, there was 2-Tone, which spearheaded Britain's indigenous ska craze of the early 80s – though following its first release, credited to The Special A.K.A. Vs The Selecter, it would be signed up by Chrysalis (The Beat's Go Feet label also linking with a major; Arista). That single alone is noteworthy, however. It came out on 2-Tone after the band faced a series of rejections, and was recorded for £700 using a loan from a businessman known only as 'Jimbo'. The b-side was an instrumental Noel Davis had recorded a couple of years previously, originally under the title 'The Kingston Affair', but both his contribution and the track were eventually credited as 'The Selecter'. Rough Trade asked them to double the print run from its original 2,500 copies. Thereafter pressing of the single, which eventually graced the Top Ten, transferred to Chrysalis, at which time it also attained its distinctive, chequered sleeve. 2-Tone quickly became a definition of a style, its own radiant if compact genre. The history of UK accommodation of Jamaican art had a precedent for that. Melodisc subsidiary Blue Beat, the UK label which had imported the original rocksteady and ska sounds (Prince Buster among them) into Britain in the 60s, likewise lent its name to the music. And in one of those wonderful twists, Blue Beat's name and rights were later acquired by Buster Bloodvessel of Bad Manners, one of the groups who came out of the 2-Tone boom but never signed to the flagship imprint.

In attempting to crystallise the fundamental importance of the etymology of the term 'independence' as opposed to 'indie', it's perhaps worthwhile looking at an example far away from world of Parka, leather jacket or trenchcoat. The term 'independent' remains a far clearer-cut concept in other forms of music. For example, to attempt to apply the 'indie' maxim to a classical recording artist would appear nonsensical. And yet, 'indie classical labels' have thrived for a substantial period in the UK and their development echoes several principles of the labels discussed in this book.

"The main movers in the classical world are the independents," states Martin Anderson of Toccata Classics. "The biggest of them, Naxos, releases far more CDs a year (and at budget price, too) than all the majors combined. Come further down the scale and you have a number of important independents like Hyperion, BIS and Chandos (all founded around the same time in the early 1980s, probably not by coincidence). Naxos has a catalogue that is close on 3,000 releases strong (built up over the twenty years since it was founded in 1987). BIS, Hyperion and Chandos probably have close on 2,000 issues each in their catalogues. There is also a huge range of small labels out there, each trying to carve out a distinctive niche. The interest in the independents is in the richness of the repertoire they are prepared to tackle. The majors almost never release any music that is not from the mainstream (the last major initiative of any scale was Decca's mid-1990s *Entartete Musik* series of music banned by the Nazis), whereas the independents are continually bringing out recordings of interesting material, much of it new to the catalogues. Another important difference between the majors and the independents, and this is a major factor in the contrasting repertoire, is that the majors tend to have a few star artists who go chasing the same mainstream repertoire, backed up by expensive publicity campaigns. The world has changed enormously since the majors would indulge every pianist on their books who wanted to lay down his readings of the central standards, but the choice of music is still fiendishly conservative. The independents may have a handful of musicians they like working with, but it's generally because they come with suggestions of interesting repertoire (or revisit familiar material with unusual playing styles, as the early-music did, and continues to do). The sales are then driven by reviews rather than advertising."

Beyond the established independents lay a vast hinterland of UK labels with ostensibly few pretensions towards growing any brand identity. Numbering thousands of releases, the DIY genre, save for a few select artists, had been largely forsaken until American Chuck Warner felt compelled to curate it. Just as *Nuggets* documented the psychedelic underground and the *Killed By Death* bootlegs made available worldwide buzz-saw punk obscurities, Warner's *Messthetics* series, which grew out of his Hyped2Death website, attempts to preserve a rich stream of creativity that flourished in the post-punk era. One whose value was only sporadically recognised as it carried so little in the way of commercial possibility.

A more lofty comparison would be the *Folkways* series, in so much as *Messthetics* is an effort to ensure that this seam of cultural capital is not lost, or tarnished further by some of the more vampiric catalogue farmers. In the process Warner has managed to bring the whole dissonant, disparate genre into some sort of focus. *Messthetics* takes its name from the onomatopoeic Scritti Politti track first announced to the world, fittingly, on a John Peel session. "I know what we're doing/We know how this sounds" 'sang' Green Gartside. A thousand UK bedrooms reverberated to reciprocal invocations. Johan Kugelberg, noted collector and enthusiast, is one of those who was charmed. "The godlike glory of DIY records," he fulminated in the introduction to his standard reading essay on DIY's 100 greatest records. "The shoddy xerox sleeve; the rubber-stamped label, the cheapest pressing imaginable; the inside jokes in the label copy; the hiss of the overloaded two-track; the hum of magnetic tape deteriorating; and the sounds!"

At number one with a bullet in said list was, unsurprisingly, the Desperate Bicycles, with whom a few informed music fans and critics might have had a passing acquaintance. But Sir Alick & The Phraser, Scrotum Poles, Horrible Nurds and I Jog & The Tracksuits? Or labels like Wreckord Records, Half Wombat and Dead Hippy? Warner found himself enticed by these tiny mysteries. "I started acquiring this stuff in the late 70s and early 80s because I was running a mail order business in rare 60s and 70s psychedelic records," he recalls, "and I would buy collections all the time. There would often be punk and post-punk stuff in there so I had an increasing quantity of stuff that no-one was asking for. I also bought one collection from a German guy who'd had a standing order for every independent single that was released at the time. I would try to interest people in the stuff we're now calling DIY and post-punk, but couldn't. Still, the more time I spent with it, the fonder I grew of it myself. Meanwhile, of the 15 people on the planet who were into it; all of us knew four or five of the others, but there was no ongoing scholarship."

"The seeds for *Messthetics* were probably laid for me when I heard the first British psych-pop compilation *Chocolate Soup For Diabetics* in 1981," Warner continues. "Here was an entire compilation of amazing music that I'd never heard before; I knew The Creation and all that, but the idea that there were these legions of no-name bands that all had this sound was mind-blowing.

## For How Much Longer?

With *Messthetics* I wanted people to hear this stuff – the DIY bands – and fall in love with it like I did."

The DIY bands that Warner collates existed within the broader framework of post-punk but outside of its conventional dialectics; a function of both aesthetics and economics. It can be hard work pinning down exactly why a record is delineated as DIY beyond the obvious act of self-creation, but Warner was able to identify certain aesthetic criteria. Spontaneity and primitivism, especially in the form of nasty keyboards and found sound, and ambivalence towards tuning and song convention were among the key signifiers of the 'correct' attitude. There were debts to Dada, to Brecht, to Situationism, to Vivian Stanshall and to both the music hall and art school traditions, in addition to conventional pop and punk's empowering thrust. "British juvenile fiction and TV science fiction also deserve a mention somewhere," adds Warner. "Punk was great and all, but no more formative for much of the DIY set than *Boy's Own*, *Fireball XL5* or *The Prisoner* or *Doctor Who*. 1977 also forced its year-long/year zero pall of silence over everything that anyone had loved and valued *prior* to 'New Rose', 'Anarchy' and 'Spiral Scratch'. DIY made it possible for everyone to reconnect to all that again in whatever way they pleased. To a certain extent glam, alone, survived as an identifiable dimension of punk."

Some of the more (relatively) prominent artists working in this territory include Steve Treatment, Danny & The Dressmakers, The Mud Hutters, Instant Automatons, Thin Yoghurts and The Homosexuals. Trends within trends can be detected. For example, the London squat bands had a more tangible connection to conventional punk dynamics than elsewhere. Those groups that worked around and within the Manchester Music Collective were besotted with the possibilities of electronic gadgetry, while the higher proportion of women reflected the city's traditions of political activism. There was a leaning towards minimalism in the early South Wales DIY scene and of grittier subject matter in the Midlands. Themes were indeed often colloquial (Grinder's 'Wickford's So Boring?'; Scissor Fits' 'I Don't Wanna Work For British Airways'; Six Minute War's 'Giles Hall', about the civic venue that excluded them in Camberwell), or self-referential (Funhouse's 'Teenage Bedrooms' talked about 'making your own groove grotto'). Some protagonists had hippy backgrounds, others were art school theorists, but more still were tortured adolescents. Indeed, in terms of psychology, "there are some remarkable things," Warner notes, "such as the fact that DIY attracted legions of gay teenagers, who could not foresee a career in the conventional music business. You had an artificial pool of over-talented musicians who couldn't face the treacheries and risks of entering the mainstream music business. So from 1978 until the Haçienda took over, DIY basically had the pick of the litter. Once the Haçienda takes off, and the record companies start to realise you can be gay and fashionable and be promoted, that's where the legal crap starts to erode too. The market embraced young gay men as a hot new commodity – both as exploitable 'product' and as energised consumers."

If punk had inverted common music business stereotypes, notably the concept of musical proficiency as virtue, DIY bands took that a step further, to the point where it almost became an abstract. All of the original punk bands, from the Pistols to The Damned to Buzzcocks to the Banshees, would eventually self-define themselves as 'great musicians', often with justifiable cause. The fascinating alternative was to have creative minds focus more purely on the 'idea', unburdened by concepts of musical *progression* or material reward. "The one consistent element to everything on *Messthetics* is that the music is unselfconscious," Warner asserts. "While they were making this music, they're not trying to make a hit or be artists, and that's so freeing."

The Desperate Bicycles, Scritti Politti's 'Skank Bloc Bologna' and 'Spiral Scratch' were "clearly the most important influences, initially," says Warner. "And the other one would be Throbbing Gristle's wittily-named debut *2nd Annual Report*, especially for the later cassette scene." But Warner also suggests that records by The Swell Maps, The Raincoats and Subway Sect – all on Rough Trade and widely aired on Peel – "helped make a rougher, more shambling approach to music-making more imaginable to would-be bands. They legitimised and made accessible the sound." In effect, they served as 'primers' to less hidebound aural expectation. In order for the circle to be complete, those records *tutored* would-be musicians as to what was possible, or perhaps more importantly, acceptable. "People heard those records and liked them, whereas if they'd heard the original DIY singles, they might not have liked them. That said, there's an entire generation of rock critics and people in the business who have *never* been able to get beyond the production side. They're culturally stuck and they need a sheen of studio confidence before they can subjectively enjoy something."

"The other real breakthrough," Warner continues, "was when people realised how simple it could be to put out (and *sell* out) their own single – despite the fact that it wasn't *that* cheap. Not all the bands who could or should have put out 7-inches did, but as soon as The Desperate Bicycles said 'go and do it', the floodgates opened. There was a breakthrough realisation, then a flood.

## For How Much Longer?

Something parallel happened on the cassette scene. Although the first cassettes were all referred to as 'albums', and indeed, they all contained album-ish quantities of songs, a new species of music expanded to fit the format. There was an appetite for environmental sound and tiny modulations of noise; the ambient thing had been brewing in the background and people were already spending £3.99 on *weightless* albums. But there was a cult of cool that went along with that, and then people realised they could do it themselves."

However, lest you imagine that such practices result in an audio experience that is unwelcoming, there is a warmth and uncontrived innocence to these bedroom communiqués. And, as Warner insists, "everything on *Messthetics* is at heart a pop record. Everything has a hook." He accepts that reflects his own tastes; further, that the series merely tracks certain themes across a much broader spectrum. "*Messthetics* represents a false centre, the idea that there's some convergence of a DIY sound; whereas most of the bands, if they were evolving at all, were evolving outwards. There were musical trajectories that spiralled *outwards* far more than they spiralled *in*, toward something, say, akin to the Desperate Bicycles."

Perhaps the ultimate expression of the DIY ethic, however, eschewed vinyl completely. The development of the compact cassette made low-tech re-recording of music far cheaper and more affordable than even the Desperate Bicycles had envisioned. "What happens with cassettes," Warner elaborates, "is the band becomes a completely optional arrangement; you don't need to have a going concern, it's more up to individuals, and you can record under 40 or 50 different names. The range is expanded by overdubs in addition to electronics and more recording home gadgets. And instead of the 7-inch, you have the yawning C90 format that encourages, or permits, extended experiment, at best, and at worst a tremendous amount of padding. Thus the way that DIY sounded different on cassette was driven more by the format and the number of people involved than by any particular divergence of agenda or interest. Now, unfortunately, it's entirely possible to pick up ten really interesting-looking tapes from back in the day and not hear anything I like. Overall, I guess I'm interested in reissuing not more than 5% of maybe 5% of releases, so a lot of what's on *Greatest Hiss* [The *Messthetics* 'cassette' sampler] needs to be understood as accidental pop. It might be the only three or four-minute song on the tape."

One of the first cassette bands were South Humberside's Instant Automatons, whose *Radio Silence – The Art of Human Error* album was yours if you sent them a C90 and stamped addressed envelope. A profusion of cassettes, and subsequently vinyl, followed on their Deleted label. Like so many other bands of their ilk, their musical foundation, alongside adolescent poetics, was fumbling electronics fashioned from physics lesson discoveries, home-made synthesizers and drum machines. And yet they were able to write songs that were hugely charming; like 'Peter Paints His Fence' (dub reggae from Scunthorpe?) or the punchy skiffle of 'Short Haired Man In A Long-Haired Town'.

Fuck Off Records, established by former Here And Now member and *International Times* writer Keith Dobson (aka Kif Kif Le Batteur) took the Automatons' example and established a chromium dioxide cottage industry. Run from his Street Level studio, which he'd inherited from Grant Showbiz, on Portobello Road, Fuck Off issued dozens of short-run cassette releases, made available to the world at large by Joly MacFie's Better Badges. Located in an office above the Street Level studio and then best known for fanzine distribution, Better Badges offered a unique twist on the 50-50 deal – the number of fanzine copies returned to the author or band was equivalent to those it retained to sell to cover costs. Fuck Off's first release was 012's *Back To Sing Again For Free* in 1979; which featured Dobson himself on guitar (he would later form World Domination Enterprises). Afterwards came a slew of compilations, with some of the most prolific artists including Danny & The Dressmakers (who featured future 808 State member Graham Massey and released more than 20 cassette albums), Wilful Damage, Missing Persons and Digital Dinosaurs. These and other releases were profiled in columns written in *Sounds* and *NME* by writers such as Mick Sinclair (himself a DIY recording artist under the guises of Milkshake Melon and Funboy Five).

The DIY boom period probably lasted from 1978 to 1982, after which some of the major players either stalled, went to college/work or moved on to more professional musical ventures. But in the blurred majesty of their xeroxed or hand-drawn 7-inch covers, scrappy musicianship and unbridled will to communicate *something*, the *Messthetics* cast, grasping for anonymity rather than posterity, can be seen as the quintessence of a truly independent spirit. 'There's no pictures, no pictures of us," Harlow's Sods sang back in September 1979, documenting their unwillingness to have their faces on the cover of their 7-inch single, "There's no pictures, it's too much fuss."

## Independence Days

## Post-Script

## Where Do We Go From Here?

What's in a word? Well, 'indie' music has become the stodgy staple of the charts, a generic for anodyne guitar-based music of middling pace with certain pre-defined characteristics; a flat-pack rhythm section, verse-chorus-verse mechanics, and an angsty vocal. In 2007 the *NME* conducted a poll on the *Greatest Indie Anthems Ever*. Only just over half of the selections were actually released on an independent label. Oasis were all over the shop. Buzzcocks, Scritti Politti and The Desperate Bicycles were predictably absent.

The concept of 'indie' has become almost meaningless beyond branding.

In the period under discussion, 'independent' meant The Cocteau Twins and Discharge, Big Flame and Yazoo, Annie Anxiety and The Durutti Column, The Marine Girls and The Birthday Party, Scraping Foetus Off The Wheel and Orange Juice, Test Department and Swell Maps. Pick your own exemplars.

Meanwhile, among the slurry of 'indie' comps released in 2005 (through BMG, natch) was one carrying the foreboding title *Revolutions: Alternative Bands, Radical Music*. Here comes the promo copy: "The 2CD *Revolutions* is an up-to-the-minute collection of the hottest cutting-edge sounds from the likes of the Kaiser Chiefs, the Bravery and Bloc Party. Join the revolution, or be first against the wall." See you over at the wall then, chaps, and I'm packing heat (OK, a thermos flask).

It would not be too much of a stretch, although arguably a convenience, to lay this retrenchment at the door of the early 90s when major labels started to incorporate their own 'indie' dependents (tautology noted) such as Hut, Nude and Dedicated. It's not the case that no two records from the original 'independent era' ever sounded alike. If all the Fall and Joy Division copyists had jumped up and down at once, tidal waves would doubtlessly have engulfed Japan. But there was also massive creative dissonance and variety; records not just influenced by the Pistols and Buzzcocks but by Zappa and girl groups and Stockhausen and the Bonzo Dog Doo-Dah Band. The fact that the 'indie' diminutive now expresses a musical template highlights both artistic retreat and the final rite of homogenisation of this particular cultural cycle.

Many of the *dramatis personae* of the original independent label boom were record store employers and employees. A few came from within the mainstream record industry, but were by nature greater risk-takers than that environment could tolerate. Some were artists themselves, or philanthropists helping friends. Many emerged from the 60s counter-culture and others still were long-standing bootleggers. In short, there is no over-arching rationale or single determining characteristic to the leading players – even a 'love' of music is not universal (though in the case of best practice, it certainly is).

And yet the demographic is quite defined. The characters in this story are predominantly, but not exclusively, middle class. With the exception of Alan Erasmus at Factory, they *are* exclusively white. Until Jeanette Lee joined Rough Trade, and overlooking the part played by Pete Stennet's wife Mari at Small Wonder and members of the Crass/Rough Trade co-ops, the independent boom was astonishingly *male*. Viewed kindly, that simply reflected an extension of the 'record collecting nerd' mentality. A more biting critique might be that it constituted one of the last dominant 'boy's clubs' to survive 70s feminism (perversely, the likes of Ivo Watts-Russell, Daniel Miller, Geoff Travis and Mike Alway are among the least 'blokey' sorts you could wish to meet). The debate over whether punk truly provided a new space for women to express themselves in art is seemingly endless (and I've decided that it did, so y'all can stop now). There are just as many texts devoted to its attendant psychological and societal ramifications; the subtext being 'punk changed everything'. Well, perhaps not everything after all.

Beyond that observation, the story here is of circumstances conspiring; what Watts-Russell equates as the 'stars being aligned' and Iain McNay characterises as a 'window of opportunity'. As extolled earlier, the geography of the UK played no small part. So too the shift in musical culture from a hippy to a punk ethos, with many participants shipping sizeable philosophical baggage across the divide and back again. As with punk era musicians, there were few label heads who jumped straight into the melee without some kind of back-story in music (in a further blow to the repeatedly debunked 'year zero' theory). But all felt empowered and energised by punk's DIY ethos. Others saw the potential for exploitation of same, and several had a foot in both camps. The subsequent giddy acceleration truly was an outstanding feature, however – like buses, you wait for one independent label to come along (let's say Ace, 1975-6) and then two hundred arrive at once.

In almost every case, the men behind independent record labels (now we have satisfied ourselves on the gender business) had a thorough grounding in music and usually fully-formed tastes. Others, whose roots were in administration or business affairs, brought to the table their knowledge of the workings of the record industry; be it from retail, from bootlegging or from inside the heart of the beast itself. Most were in their late 20s or significantly older. Good Vibrations' Terri Hooley's assertion, that he'd 'been 'waiting for this all my life', is not uncommon. The advent of cheaper technology and manufacturing capabilities, a ready audience primed by punk for almost anything released (particularly) on 7-inch vinyl by an independent record label and the majors' sloth in responding are all contributory factors. And, while it's always dangerous to talk about 'auteur' labels for want of dismissing the considerable labours undertaken backstage (this is a story with its fair share of credit-hoggers), to a certain extent the catalogue of those labels reflected the interests, personalities and tastes of a handful of individuals. Behind whom circle a thousand one-shot iconoclasts – which would have been Mute's destiny had it not been for wholly unforeseen commercial approbation. Pure chance and timing also plays its part.

The legacy of independent retail and record shops such as Rough Trade, Beggars Banquet and the various Cartel members hangs heavy throughout. With that sector of the industry currently decimated, it's hard to see how anything similar – in terms of the unifying, us against them *esprit de corps* of the independent heyday – could happen now.

In August 2006 it was announced that Beano's, sited across three floors on Croydon's Middle Street and probably the country's most famous collector's shop, was on the brink of extinction. There's been an incremental thinning in the number of record shops on London's former vinyl oasis Berwick Street, immortalised on the cover of Oasis's *What's The Story Morning Glory*. Sister Ray, which itself had taken over the ailing Selectadisc outlet, went into administration in the summer of 2008 (though original owner Phil Barton would buy it out). Cardiff's Spillers Records, the oldest independent record shop in Britain, established in 1894, is still around – but only after intervention from the Welsh Assembly opposing the move to 'clone cities'. Helical Bar, the property developers concerned, threatened rent hikes of up to 100% unless the store relocated. "If you walk down Oxford Street," wrote investment director Michael Brown, "you do not see niche record stores among the chains. We warned [Nick Todd: Spillers' owner for the last two decades] that he is standing in the way of progress."

If you take record shops out of the picture, a vital conduit in terms of the community that underpinned the 'golden years' of independent music disappears from the equation. The distribution of end product is the most telling and obvious feature, but record stores like Spillers also served as a hub for the culture of independence – flyers for gigs, distribution of local fanzines, musicians' wanted adverts – as well as a place where music fans congregated. That is not to suggest that music cannot thrive and prosper under altered conditions, but by its very nature it will be a different beast, not grounded in the spirit of mutual co-operation that governed the original independent ethos. MySpace is great 'n' all; in its own way democratising and empowering. And in many ways it's ripped apart the old indie/major conundrum, offering an alternative means to distribute and market music (though 'selling' seems somewhat more problematic), and destroying any need for an infrastructure like the Cartel. But digital transactions, paid for or *gratis*, lack the layer of discovery and adventure that the traditional record shop once nurtured and which in turn fed the artistic diversity of the independent boom. It's a remote process in contrast to the intimacy and community of old. It's also legitimised soul-sapping insincerity.

By the time independent music begins its slide into 'indie' (1988 or thereabouts), the compact disc was well on its way to becoming king – with the consequent back catalogue gold rush taking some of the emphasis away from 'new music' at both the majors and the independents. Regardless of arguments about sonic fidelity, vinyl artwork was a crucial part of the aesthetic thrill of buying a record. Whether your poison was 4AD's 23 Envelope designs, Saville's work on Factory or even a particular denomination of punk (from Crass to Oi!), these were partisan, tribal choices. And, yes, habit-forming for collectors, who to a large extent underpinned the economics.

"The word 'independent' means a lot to me," notes Gareth Main, who recently launched *Bearded* magazine, which goes so far as to exclude major label-affiliated acts from its pages. "To me it represents the underdog, the downtrodden and the under-appreciated. There is a lot of romanticism in the idea of somebody packaging 7-inch records in their bedroom despite the fact they know nobody will ever hear it. Of course the 'independent' record industry encompasses a lot more than that, but it is the very British idea of rooting for the underdog. Major labels have all the help they need to get noticed, it's rewarding to only focus on helping those who don't have the resources to get where they – arguably – deserve to be."

Contemporary independents continue to thrive, of course, not least Domino, Bella Union, Shifty Disco, Damaged Goods and Fierce Panda. AIM (Association Of Independent Music), tangential philosophical heirs to the

## Where Do We Go From Here?

Desperate Bicycles' less formalised 'up and at 'em' credo, offers a leg-up to any potential combatants. Long may they all flourish, or at least survive independent music's perennial distribution crises. All are doing something vital, even if it's just rejecting Coldplay's demos. Old-timers such as Beggars, Cherry Red and Rough Trade have faltered, prospered and evolved. But the likelihood of any return to the years of artistic glut and shared adventure that hallmark the period under discussion in this book seem remote, simply because the conditions of its creation have ceased.

## About The Author

Alex Ogg is a London-based freelance author and journalist. He lives in Leytonstone with his partner Dawn and children Hugh and Laurence. Contact details: www.alexogg.com

Previous books by the same author:

No More Heroes
The Hip Hop Years
Top Ten
The Men Behind Def Jam
Rap Lyrics From The Sugarhill Gang to Eminem
Radiohead: Standing At The Edge

# Other titles available from Cherry Red Book

No More Heroes: A Complete History of UK Punk 1976 - 1980 - Alex Ogg

Indie Hits 1980 – 1989 - Barry Lazell

Burning Britain: A History Of UK Punk 1980 - 1984 - Ian Glasper

The Day The Country Died: A History Of Anarcho Punk 1980 - 1984 - Ian Glasper

Trapped In A Scene: UK Hardcore 1985 - 89 - Ian Glasper

Death To Trad Rock: The Post-Punk fanzine scene 1982 - 87 - John Robb

Hells Bent On Rockin: A History Of Psychobilly - Craig Brackenbridge

Deathrow: The Chronicles Of Psychobilly - Alan Wilson

Goodnight Jim Bob: On The Road With Carter USM - Jim Bob

All The Young Dudes: Mott The Hoople & Ian Hunter - Campbell Devine

Johnny Thunders: In Cold Blood - Nina Antonia

Music To Die For: Guide To Goth, Goth Metal, Horror Punk, Psychobilly etc - Mick Mercer

Number One Songs In Heaven - A Sparks Biography: Dave Thompson

The Legendary Joe Meek: The Telstar Man - John Repsch

The Secret Life Of A Teenage Punk Rocker: The Andy Blade Chronicles - Andy Blade

You're Wondering Now: The Specials from Conception to Reunion - Paul Williams

Many artists and labels featured in this book can be found amongst our catalogue of
CD releases and reissues – please check www.cherryred.co.uk for details

You can also watch in depth interviews with many of the people included in this book on
www.cherryred.tv

We're always interested to hear of interesting titles looking for a publisher.
Whether it's a new manuscript or an out of print title, please feel free to
get in touch if you've written, or are aware of, a book you feel might be suitable

ideas@cherryred.co.uk

**www.cherryredbooks.co.uk**